THE GOSPEL
AND THE LAND

*Published in association with
the Catherine and Lady Grace James Foundation of Wales*

THE GOSPEL
AND THE LAND

Early Christianity and Jewish Territorial Doctrine

———————⟫✦⟪———————

BY

W. D. DAVIES

M.A., D.D.

Corresponding Fellow of the British Academy
George Washington Ivey Professor of Christian Origins,
Duke University

UNIVERSITY OF CALIFORNIA PRESS

BERKELEY, LOS ANGELES, LONDON

University of California Press
Berkeley and Los Angeles, California

University of California Press, Ltd.
London, England

Copyright © 1974, by
The Regents of the University of California

ISBN: 0-520-02278-5
Library of Congress Catalog Card Number: 72-82228
Printed in the United States of America

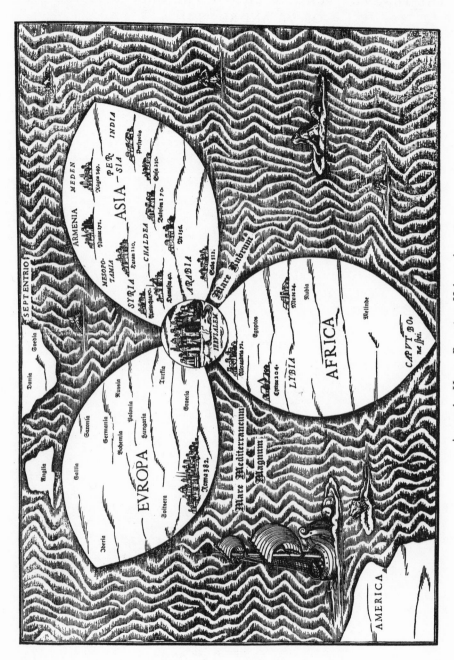

A map by Henry Buenting, Helmstedt, 1581

CONTENTS

CONTENTS

CONTENTS

PREFACE

This volume grew out of the D. J. James, Pantyfedwen Lectures on the Catherine and Lady Grace James Foundation for the year 1968, and is to honour the memory of a family of philanthropists. I recall with pleasure the courtesy of Mr. Tom Jones, Secretary to the Foundation, and the warm welcome given to us by Principal F. Llewelyn-Jones and the Registrar, Mr. A. Davies, on behalf of the University College of Wales, Swansea, and by our former teacher and life-long friend, Dr. Alun Oldfield-Davies, on behalf of the Trustees of the Foundation. The work was also communicated, in part, to the Divinity School, Yale University, as the Shaffer Lectures for the same year. I much appreciated the hospitality of the Dean, the discussion in the Graduate Colloquium under Dr. Paul Minear, and the written comments of two of its members, now Dean W. S. Towner, and Professor D. L. Bartlett. It is a peculiar pleasure for me, through this volume, however tenuously, to evoke again the connection between one of the great universities of the United States and the land of its founder.

I also delivered parts of the volume at The Jerusalem Colloquium on Religion, Peoplehood, Nation, and Land: The Truman Research Institute, Hebrew University, Jerusalem, 1970; the First Presbyterian Church, Richmond, Virginia, as the Dr. Walter Lapsley Carson Lectures, 1972; Carleton University, Ottawa, Canada, 1972; Queens College, Charlotte, North Carolina, as the Thomas F. Staley Lectures, 1973. At all these cities we received a warm hospitality which, expressed in their several different ways, is common to them all.

It is to be emphasized that this work is strictly a prolegomenon, its aim simply to present some of the data for the consideration of its much-neglected theme. As will emerge from the following pages, the term "the land" as used here is very fluid. It usually denotes especially the promised land of Israel, conceived as a totality, but, as in the sources, so here, that land is often subsumed under the city of Jerusalem and the Temple therein, which serve as its quintessence. I am acutely conscious that in traversing a long stretch of comparatively fresh ground, I have not merely missed many aspects of the landscape, but also failed to assess adequately those that I have seen. In particular, in concentrating on the presentation of the data, I have not been able to trace the complex ramifications of the various traditions concerning the land represented in the sources—a task requiring the labour of many students. But the work may serve to draw attention to the motif and problem of the land, and, indirectly, to the importance of other *realia* in Judaism for the understanding of the emergence of Christianity. I much regret that the work of G. W. Buchanan, *The Consequences of the Covenant*, Leiden, 1970, came into my hands too late for adequate use.

I have been fortunate in the help of many. The Research Council of Duke University and two Deans of the Divinity School, R. E. Cushman and T. A. Langford, were always supportive. My former assistant, Dr. Günter Stemberger, shared his thought and supplied a most necessary appendix. President Louis Finkelstein, Professors C. H. Dodd, David Daube, Abraham Heschel, Saul Lieberman, R. B. Y. Scott, and E. E. Urbach gave much insight; and, across the years, in stimulating friendship, Dr. J. W. Parkes and Rabbi Frank Tannenbaum have challenged me to critical response. I am especially grateful to Professors Roland Murphy, O.Carm., James A. Sanders, D. Moody Smith, and F. W. Young, who read the typescript and made valuable criticisms and suggestions, and also to Professors J. H. Charlesworth, E. M. Meyers, O. Wintermute, and to Professor L. H. Lesko, of the University of California at Berkeley. The work of our Librarian, Professor Don Michael Farris, has been beyond praise. My assistants, Father Benedict Viviano and especially Mr. Alan Culpepper, helped in many ways. The latter corrected the typescript, drew up the bibliography and indices, and, particularly by his thoroughness, spared me much. The enthusiasm of a former pupil, Mr. James Bullard, now of Stanford University, added fire to my initial concern with the theme. Mrs. Patricia Haugg cheerfully typed the manuscript and spared no pains to prepare the typescript as completely as possible. To all these, as to Mr. William McClung, Editor at the University of California Press at Berkeley, who took a special interest in this work, as well as to Mrs. Susan Welling, Reader, and to Professor Amos N. Wilder and D. Norman Hjelm, of the Fortress Press, for permission to quote from *Grace Confounding* (Philadelphia, 1972, p. 1), I tender my most appreciative acknowledgements. What I owe to my wife is beyond such.

W. D. D.

DUKE UNIVERSITY

February 3, 1972

ABBREVIATIONS

AA	*Alei Ayin.* The Salman Schocken Jubilee Volume, Jerusalem, 1948–52.
AARJ	*American Academy of Religion Journal.*
ADPB	American Jewish Daily Prayer Book.
AMJV	Alexander Marx Jubilee Volume, New York, 1950.
ARN	*'Aboth de Rabbi Nathan.*
ARNA	Version A of ARN.
ARNB	Version B of ARN.
ARNS	Solomon Schechter's ed. of ARN, Vienna, 1887.
BA	*Biblical Archaeologist.*
BASOR	*Bulletin of the American School of Oriental Research.*
BDB	Brown, Driver, Briggs, *Hebrew Lexicon.*
BJRL	*Bulletin of the John Rylands Library.*
CBQ	*Catholic Biblical Quarterly.*
ET	*The Expository Times.*
ETL	*Ephemerides Theologicae Lovanienses.*
HE	Eusebius, *Historia Ecclesiastica.*
HJP	Saul Lieberman, *Hellenism in Jewish Palestine*, New York, 1950.
HTR	*Harvard Theological Review.*
HUCA	*Hebrew Union College Annual.*
HZNT	*Handbuch zum Neuen Testament.*
IB	*Interpreter's Bible.*
IDB	*Interpreter's Dictionary of the Bible.*
ICC	*International Critical Commentary.*
JBC	Jerome Biblical Commentary.
JBL	*Journal of Biblical Literature.*
JE	*Jewish Encyclopedia.*
JQR	*Jewish Quarterly Review.*
JSS	*Journal of Semitic Studies.*
JTS	*Journal of Theological Studies.*
KJV	*King James Version of the Bible.*
MABO	Louis Finkelstein, *Mabo le Massektot Abot we Abot de Rabbi Natan*, New York, 1950.
MPG	Migne, *Patrologia Graeca.*

MT	Masoretic Text.
NTD	*Das Neue Testament Deutsch.*
NTS	*New Testament Studies.*
PA	*Pirqê Aboth.*
PEQ	*Palestine Exploration Quarterly.*
PRJ	Davies, W. D., *Paul and Rabbinic Judaism.*
PTP	Bernard J. Bamberger, *Proselytism in the Talmudic Period,* Cincinnati, 1939.
RA	*A Rabbinic Anthology,* edd. Montefiore and Loewe.
RB	*Revue Biblique.*
RGG	*Die Religion in Geschichte und Gegenwart.*
RHPR	*Revue d'Histoire et de Philosophie religieuses.*
SB	Strack, H. L. und Billerbeck, P., *Kommentar zum Neuen Testament aus Talmud und Midrasch.*
SG	C. G. J. Montefiore, *The Synoptic Gospels,* 2 vols., London, 1927.
SSM	Davies, W. D., *The Setting of the Sermon on the Mount.*
TDNT	*Theological Dictionary of the New Testament,* trans. of TWZNT.
TL	*Theologische Literaturzeitung.*
TS	*Texts and Studies.*
TWZNT	*Theologisches Wörterbuch zum Neuen Testament,* ed. G. Kittel, G. Friedrich.
USQR	*Union Seminary Quarterly Review,* New York.
VT	*Vetus Testamentum.*
ZATW	*Zeitschrift für die alttestamentliche Wissenschaft.*
ZDPV	*Zeitschrift des deutschen Palästina-Vereins.*
ZNW	*Zeitschrift für die neutestamentliche Wissenschaft.*
ZTK	*Zeitschrift für Theologie und Kirche.*

All the other abbreviations used will be familiar; certain common convential spellings have been retained in references to the Qumran writings and Rabbinic sources. Transliteration, though possibly not consistent throughout, will be readily understandable. For translations the following are used: the Soncino editions for the Midrashim and the Babylonian Talmud; Schwab for the Jerusalem Talmud; Danby for the Mishnah; Goldin for the *Aboth de Rabbi Nathan*; for Philo and Josephus, the Loeb translations. Where clarity demanded, the notations from these translations are included.

Area—no test of depth.

Emily Dickinson, *Letters*

Infinite riches in a little roome.

Marlowe, *Jew of Malta*

He came where he wasn't expected
as He always does,
though a few mages were tipped off.

He came where even the Apostles couldn't go along,
in Nazareth of all places, on the edge of nowhere;
they had to place it in David's home town.

He is always one step ahead of us;
the space-age calls for new maps
and its altars and holy places are not yet marked.

Amos N. Wilder, *Grace Confounding*

PART I

THE LAND IN ISRAELITE RELIGION AND JUDAISM

Whoever walks four cubits in the Land of Israel is assured of a place in the world to come.

T. B. Kethuboth 110b–111a.

Whoever goes up from Babylon to the Land of Israel transgresses a positive commandment, for it is said in Scripture, *They shall be carried to Babylon, and there they shall be, until the day that I remember them, saith the Lord.*

T. B. Kethuboth 110b–111a.

I. INTRODUCTORY

Christian origins have usually been approached in two ways which, paradoxically enough, have not been mutually exclusive. One approach, bearing the authority of a very long history and renewed with vigour in this century, has emphasized the radical newness of the Gospel as a supernatural phenomenon breaking into this world with startling discontinuity in a manner that defies rational analysis.[1] The other approach, more characteristic of the nineteenth and early twentieth centuries, has sought to understand the emergence of the Christian faith as a phenomenon within history, which, partly at least, can be interpreted within and over against the contemporary religions. This second approach has generally forked in two directions, one leading to the Graeco-Roman world and one to the Jewish; and the Christian faith has correspondingly been illumined in terms either of the Hellenistic syncretism or of the Judaism of the first century. Only within recent decades has the recognition grown that the Hellenistic and Judaic cultures and religions of the period cannot easily be sharply separated, but reveal deep interpenetration.[2]

But even when the attempt has been made to understand Christian origins in their setting in the Hellenistic and Jewish worlds, it is the concerns of Christian scholars that have usually determined how that setting has been exploited, and what aspects of it have been considered significant for the illumination of the Christian faith. This is especially true of the way in which Judaism has been examined as a background to Christianity. Long before the emergence of modern scholarship, the pagan faiths of the Graeco-Roman world that vied with Christianity for the allegiance of men in the first century had died. But Judaism has persisted as a living faith to the present, and because of this a peculiarly contemporaneous relevance and urgency has always remained in the discussion of the relationship between it and Christianity. In view of the actuality of Judaism in the Christian world, one might expect that Judaism would have helped to formulate the terms of the discussion between the two faiths. In fact, because of the overwhelming dominance of Christianity, the discussion of the interaction between Judaism and the

[1] C. F. D. Moule, *The Phenomenon of the New Testament*, Studies in Biblical Theology, Second Series, 1967, p. 77, writes: "whoever tries to account for the beginnings of Christianity by some purely historical, non-transcendental event, runs against the difficulty that there seems to be no such event of sufficient magnitude or of a kind such as to fulfil the need."

[2] See *PRJ* and n. 30, Ch. 5, p. 91 below.

Gospel has been governed almost entirely by those concerns that Christians themselves have deemed important. As a result, it is doctrines in which Christians have been particularly interested, such as those about God, Man, Sin, Creation, Revelation, Prophecy, Reward and Punishment, etc., that is, theological and metaphysical abstractions, that have been emphasized in attempts to understand how the Gospel emerged from and impinged upon Judaism. The Jewish faith came to be understood largely as a body of ideas with which Christian doctrines could be compared and contrasted: it came to be examined in terms of Christian categories but seldom in terms native, or peculiar, to itself. And once Judaism came to be interpreted as a body of ideas or doctrines, certain consequences followed. Ideas, to be true, must be valid for all persons at all times and places. Any local or geographic particularistic elements in Judaism could not but be regarded as insignificant or, at best, secondary, and could safely be overlooked.

This explains why the question of the land in primitive Christianity could be so neglected. Even Rabbinic Theology itself, in reaction to and imitation of Christian Theology, from which it borrowed its philosophical tools and methods and by which it was stimulated, concentrated on themes dictated to it by the need to defend itself against the specifically Christian challenges, and neglected such awkward, particular doctrines as that of the land. Rabbinic thinkers themselves, understanding Judaism in terms of or in reaction to Christianity, unconsciously and consciously, asked what significance a particular place, Palestine, could have in their Faith; and Christian scholars, naturally governed by their own doctrinal interests, easily neglected the *realia* of Judaism and, in particular, its traditional concentration on the land.[3] So it is that neither the *Interpreter's*

---

[3] I am indebted to G. Cohen in *Zion in Jewish Literature*, ed. A. S. Halkin, New York, 1961, pp. 38ff on "Zion in Rabbinic Literature." In modification of the position indicated it has to be recognized that Rabbinic thinkers were naturally often preoccupied with adapting the Torah to life in the Diaspora, and that they also often relegated the hope for the land to the End. But the dominance of Christianity in Europe did "intimidate" Jewish Theology. For an example of the way in which Jewish thought interacted with Christian, see "The Dissection of the Dead in Jewish Law," by Immanuel Jakobovits, *Tradition*, Vol. 1, No. 1, Fall 1958, pp. 77ff. The Jewish opposition to such dissection only sprang into life in 1737, the very year when the Christian debate issued in favour of it. The matter had to come to a head among Christians before the Jewish authorities declared themselves (p. 90). The point made above is further illustrated by the structure of *A Rabbinic Anthology*, ed. C. J. G. Montefiore and H. M. Loewe, London, 1938. While much of it is governed by typically Jewish concerns, e.g., chapters 2, 4, 5 on "God's Love for Israel"; "Israel's Love for God"; "The Law," etc., much is also dictated by an unconscious concern to make Judaism in some way doctrinally comparable with Christianity. A comparison of the division of materials in The Mishnah, the foundation document of Judaism, with that of the Anthology is revealing. The work of Montefiore generally illustrates the understanding of both Christianity and

Dictionary of the Bible, published in 1962, nor two recent French Biblical dictionaries[4] have any articles on the land. *The Peake Commentary*, 1962, gives two references to the theme in its index; *The Jerome Biblical Commentary*, 1968, virtually ignores it; and in the *Wörterbuch* of Kittel–Friedrich, 1933, just under four pages are allotted to it. And, although there are innumerable references to the land in the document of their concern, the neglect of this theme has been as marked among Old Testament scholars as among those of the New Testament.

But, despite its neglect until recently in formal Rabbinic Theology, to overlook the emphasis on the land in Judaism is to overlook one of the most persistent and passionately held doctrines with which the Early Church had to come to terms. The doctrine is traceable throughout the Old Testament, the Apocrypha and Pseudepigrapha, the Qumran Scrolls, and the Rabbinic and Hellenistic Jewish sources. Here we shall deal with it as it impinges on the New Testament. The hope for the land—sometimes called a "dogma of Judaism"—could not but have engaged the earliest Christians. In the life, death, and resurrection of Jesus, they had witnessed the inauguration of the End.[5] For them the hopes of Judaism had, incipiently at least, been fulfilled. How did they react to the hope that dealt with the land of Israel? Are traces of their discussion of this question discernible in the New Testament? Can the separation of Church and Synagogue be illumined by reference to the problem of the land? We offer some general suggestions, almost all exploratory rather than affirmative. We shall begin by setting forth the role of the land in the Old Testament and in Judaism, and crave the indulgence of experts in the Old Testament as we do so.

There are certain notions concerning the land in the Old Testament and Judaism that reflect or are parallel to primitive Semitic, other Near

---

Judaism as consisting of noble moral teaching. Equally illuminating is the structure of another anthology, *Everyman's Talmud*, ed. A. Cohen, London, 1932. In order to illustrate how natural it is for Christians to discuss Judaism without reference to its *realia*, I have decided to print in appendices two treatments of the relationships between Judaism and Christianity; one emphasizes the similarities and the other the differences between them in purely doctrinal and moral terms without reference to the land: they are typical. It is true that at the emergence of Reform Judaism in the nineteenth century there was much learned discussion of the land among the Reformed, but this was in order that its significance for faith might be denied.

[4] *A Companion to the Bible*, trans., ed. J. J. von Allmen, New York, 1958; and *The Dictionary of Biblical Theology*, trans., ed. Xavier Leon-Dufour, New York, 1967. But another French scholar, J. Bonsirven, does recognize the land, see *Le Judaïsme Palestinien*, Vol. I, 1934, pp. 97ff, and especially *Textes Rabbiniques des Deux Premiers Siècles Chretiens*, Pontificio Instituto Biblico, Roma, 1955, under Index on Israel: Terre Sainte, for references, p. 740. Contrast G. F. Moore.

[5] Mark 1: 15 and parallels; Gal. 4: 4; Heb. 1: 1, etc.

Eastern, and, indeed, widespread conceptions about the significance of their land to a particular people. They are mentioned here for the sake of completeness, not because they are of primary importance for our purpose.

First, the notion occurs that Israel is the centre of the earth. Mircea Eliade has connected this notion with that of sacred and profane space, which is common in human societies. Sacred space is that space which has manifested an irruption of the divine and which alone, therefore, is real or possesses being. The religious man desires to live as near to this sacred space as possible and comes to regard it—the place of his abode, his own land—as the centre of the world. To this belongs cosmos, order: outside it is chaos, where demons and alien spirits rule.[6]

The notion that the land of Israel is the centre of the earth occurs in

[6] Mircea Eliade, *The Sacred and the Profane—The Nature of Religion*, trans., New York, 1959, p. 20. For Eliade the distinctive characteristic of profane space is its homogeneity, the essential sameness which, to profane man, appears throughout the natural order. The sacred, as an irruption of the divine, is manifested as a break in this homogeneous condition. Thus Eliade distinguishes the hierophany, the manifestation of the divine power, as appearing at a particular point within the profane space, and reconstituting this point so that it is recognized as no longer participating in the homogeneity of the surrounding area. The particular land of a religious man is regarded as representing the cosmos, appearing as the *imago mundi*. The representation of the land as the centre of the world is not a geometrical concept, for there can be many "centres of the world,"—homes, temples, lands. Rather, centrality in this instance is a metaphysical category, describing a relational aspect between a particular land and its god (p. 43). According to Eliade, the concept of centrality implies the orientation of the mind of primitive man. Possession of a territory, ownership of a home, participation in a community, all enforce this idea of orientation. When the individual is in his land, he is "oriented" in an ordered cosmos, he feels "at home." Taken outside his land he is "disoriented" and has no ordered frame of reference. Expressed mythologically, when outside his own land, he is outside the cosmos in chaotic space, which can only evidence the rule of demonic, inimical powers (p. 22). Eliade's views concerning the general relationship between sacred and profane space are supported by the observations of Bronislaw Malinowski, *Magic, Science, and Religion, and Other Essays*, Boston, 1948, pp. 92–93. Malinowski in this section describes how, in the mythical history of one particular group which he investigated, the creation myth states that the ancestral leaders of the community came out of the centre of the earth through certain volcanic holes. The community is built around these points of origin, and its traditional hunting and farming areas are located in the surrounding countryside. Its mythic structure explains the geographical location of the community and its land in terms of the origins, or descent, and its relationship to this land as that pre-eminently chosen by the ancestral leaders. Again Emile Durkheim, *The Elementary Forms of Religious Life*, trans., New York, 1915, pp. 307–308, confirms and differs from much in Eliade's work. In defining what he means by the sacred, Durkheim states: "Religious force is only the sentiment inspired by the group in its members, but projected outside of the consciousnesses that experience them, and objectified. To be objectified, they are fixed upon some object which thus becomes sacred; but any object might fulfil this function. . . . Therefore, the sacred character assumed by an object is not implied in the intrinsic properties of this latter: *it is added to them* (p. 229)." Thus the element of stress in Durkheim's definition is power or force. However, for him, as an anthropologist, this force is described as a sociological bond of the community. The latter part of this definition especially seems to diverge from that of Eliade, since for Eliade sacrality is the intrinsic property of any object deemed sacred by primitive man. Lévi-Strauss, *The Savage Mind*, Chicago, 1966, should also be consulted in this connection, on "mythic societies."

6

Ezek. 38: 12. In the end of the days, when many peoples out of the nations will have been gathered upon the mountains of Israel to dwell in security, Gog, of the land of Magog, is to advance against them. The people of Israel are described as those:

who dwell at the centre of the earth.

This notion also emerges in Ezek. 5: 5: "Thus says the Lord God: This is Jerusalem; I have set her in the centre of the nations, with countries round about her." Here the emphasis is demographic, that is, on the visibility of the conduct of Jerusalem to all the nations of the world because of her centrality.[7] The notion persisted, as in the Ethiopic Enoch 26: 1, where Enoch's visit to Jerusalem is described as his going to "the middle of earth." In Jub. 8: 12 Noah assigns to Shem as his lot, "the centre of the earth." We learn what this is explicitly in Jub. 8: 19,

---

[7] The M.T. of Ezek. 38: 12 reads:

וְאֶל־עַם . . . יֹשְׁבֵי עַל־טַבּוּר הָאָרֶץ׃

טַבּוּר stands for the highest part, hence the centre. The LXX renders it by "navel":
κατοικοῦντας ἐπὶ τὸν ὀμφαλὸν τῆς γῆς.
For Ezek. 5: 5 the M.T. has:

כֹּה אָמַר אֲדֹנָי יֱהוִה זֹאת יְרוּשָׁלַם בְּתוֹךְ הַגּוֹיִם שַׂמְתִּיהָ וּסְבִיבוֹתֶיהָ אֲרָצוֹת׃

The LXX has: Τάδε λέγει Κύριος "Αυτη ἡ Ιερουσαλημ ἐν μέσῳ τῶν ἐθνῶν τέθεικα αὐτὴν καὶ τὰς κύκλῳ αὐτῆς χώρας. That the conduct of Jerusalem is *visible* to the nations is a common notion in the Old Testament. Especially in Ezekiel, what goes on in the city reflects upon Yahweh himself among the nations. See, for example, Ezek. 22: 4–5; 1 Kings 8: 41–43. Pertinent also is Zech. 8: 20–23; 14: 1ff.; Pss. Sol. 17: 23–51, especially 17: 32. The notion of Jerusalem as the cosmic centre may be pre-exilic. Martin Buber refers to Is. 2: 1–5 (which may be pre-exilic) and Is. 19: 24–25, a remarkable passage in which "Israel" is a blessing "in the centre of the earth (NEB)." The RSV here renders: "in the midst of the earth": so M. Buber, *Israel and Palestine*, 1952, p. 32. The Hebrew of 19: 24 is:

בַּיּוֹם הַהוּא יִהְיֶה יִשְׂרָאֵל שְׁלִישִׁיָּה לְמִצְרַיִם וּלְאַשּׁוּר בְּרָכָה בְּקֶרֶב הָאָרֶץ׃

The LXX has simply: τῇ ἡμέρᾳ ἐκείνῃ ἔσται Ισραηλ τρίτος ἐν τοῖς 'Ασσυρίοις καὶ ἐν τοῖς Αἰγυπτίοις εὐλογημένος ἐν τῇ γῇ ἣν εὐλόγησεν Κύριος Σαβαωθ. The Hexapla does not help. Is the NEB an over-translation here? Does it negate the purpose of the verses which express the remarkable, almost unparalleled idea (see G. B. Gray, *ICC, Isaiah*, p. 341) of the coordination of Egypt and Assyria with Israel—a point missed in the LXX also? See also Eric Burrows, *The Labyrinth*, ed. S. H. Hooke, 1935, pp. 45–70 on "Some Cosmological Patterns in Babylonian Religion," which provides rich materials on the theme. He shows the Middle Eastern background to the notion of cosmic centrality. He suggests that the emphasis in the Old Testament on the theocratic centrality of Israel is a counter-claim against Babylonian pretensions which knew a naive temple-centred universe (pp. 52ff). The Royal Temple of the Babylonian God Marduk was said to be built on "the bosom of the earth," and the *ziggurat* to the famous God of Nippur (Mesopotamia) bore the inscription "bond of heaven and earth." See further Friedrich Jeremias, "Das orientalisch Heiligtum," *Angelos*, 4, 1932, p. 63; A. J. Wensinck, "The Ideas of the Western Semites Concerning the Navel of the Earth," *Verhandelingen der Koninklijke Akademie van Wetenschappen te Amsterdam*, 1916.

where Mount Zion is described as "the centre of the navel of the earth."[8] The context of these verses is geographic, the division of the earth among the sons of Noah. But the centrality of Jerusalem is connected also with other holy places—the Garden of Eden as the Holy of Holies, and Mount Sinai as the centre of the desert, a combination that became important in later Christian speculation (Jub. 8: 19).[9] Josephus, *Jewish Wars*, III. 3. 5 refers to Jerusalem as lying at the very centre of Judaea, "for which reason the town has sometimes, not inaptly, been called 'the navel (*omphalos*)' of the country (*mesaitatê d'autês polis ta Hierosoluma ouk askopôs omphalon to astu tês chôras ekalesan*)." See also the Sibylline Oracles v: 248–250 which refer to "...the godlike heavenly race of the blessed Jews, who dwell around the city of God at the centre of the earth."

Israel, then, is the centre of the earth, Jerusalem the centre of Israel; Mt. Zion the centre of Jerusalem; and, further, according to T. B. Sanhedrin 37a, the meeting place of the Sanhedrin lies within Mt. Zion and, again, within the Temple on its summit. The passage from T. B. Sanhedrin 37a reads:

The Gemara on Mishnah Sanhedrin 4: 3, 4, is as follows:

Whence is this derived?—R. Aha b. Hananiah [3rd century Amora] said: Scripture states, *Thy navel is like a round goblet* ['aggân ha-Sahar] wherein no mingled wine is wanting [Cant. vii, 3]. *Thy navel*—that is the Sanhedrin. Why was it called "*navel*"? Because it sat at the navel-point [i.e., the centre] of the world [Compare Tanhuma, Wa Yikra, xviii, 23].

And, finally, at the very centre of all the earth, stands the '*eben shetiyyah*, the foundation stone, which in the Second Temple occupied the place of the Holy Ark.[10]

---

[8] The psychological reasons for the use of such a term as "navel" (ὀμφαλός) in connection with the centre of the earth and with holy places are explored by Richard L. Rubenstein, "The Cave, The Rock and The Tent," in *Continuum*, Vol. Six, Summer 1968, pp. 143ff. Sacred caves and tombs, he argues, suggest the security of the womb. For example, "the entire precinct of Jesus' nativity (has) been instinctively made womb like." R. Patai, *Man and Temple*, London, 1947, p. 85, refers to the legend that just as the body of the embryo is built up in the womb from its navel, so Yahweh built up the earth beginning with and around the foundation stone, or rock, the navel of the earth. The rock is not womblike, but it is the original fruit of the cosmic womb. The notion in Eph. 2: 21 that the Church "grows" around Christ as the cornerstone or foundation has been connected with this. It is precarious to emphasize the psychological motif of "womb-tomb" because other than psychological interpretations of the data concerned are also possible.

[9] For evidence, see J. Jeremias, "Golgotha und der heilige Felsen: Eine Untersuchung zur Symbolsprache des Neuen Testamentes," in *Angelos*, 2, 1926, pp. 74–128.

[10] The foundation stone (אֶבֶן שְׁתִיָּה) is mentioned in M. Yoma 5: 2. M. Yoma 5: 1 describes the awesome activity of the High Priest at the Ark and then 5: 2 reads:

After the Ark was taken away a stone remained there from the time of the early prophets

8

There were other places for which the claim of being the centre was made. In Jud. 9: 37f it is implied, perhaps, that Gerizim is the centre.[11] Elsewhere Bethel was such, as may be implied in Gen. 28: 11f.

Such ideas had much influence on later Christian speculation, but for our specific purposes they are not of primary significance. As already

[that is, the time of David and Solomon; Danby p. 167, n. 11], and it was called "Shetiyah". It was higher than the ground by three fingerbreadths....

The "place" where this was is clear from the following passage in 5: 3–4, where the term "the place whereon he had stood" is given prominence. שְׁתִיָּה comes from the root שָׁתָה, "to lay a foundation." The gemara in T. B. Yoma 54a–54b reads as follows.

AND IT WAS CALLED SHETHIYAH [foundation]: A Tanna taught: [It was so called] because from it the world was founded.[a] We were taught in accord with the view that the world was started [created] from Zion on. For it was taught: R. Eliezer says: The world was created from its centre, as it is said: *When the dust runneth into a mass, and the clods keep fast together.*[b] R. Joshua [80–120 A.D.] said: The world was created from its sides on, as it is said: *For He saith to the snow: "Fall thou on the earth"; likewise to the shower of rain, and to the showers of His mighty rain.*[c] R. Isaac the Smith said: The Holy One, blessed be He, cast a stone into the ocean, from which the world then was founded as it is said: *Whereupon were the foundations thereof fastened, or who laid the corner-stone thereof?*[d] But the Sages said: The world was [started] created from Zion, as it is said: *A Psalm of Asaph, God, God, the Lord [hath spoken],*[e] whereupon it reads on: *Out of Zion, the perfection of the world,*[f] that means from Zion was the beauty of the world perfected. It was taught: R. Eliezer the Great said: *These are the generations of the heavens and of the earth, in the day that the Lord God made earth and heaven.*[g] The generations [the creations] of heaven[h] were made from the heaven and the generations of the earth were made from the earth. But the Sages said: Both were created from Zion, as it is said: *"A Psalm of Asaph: God, God, the Lord, hath spoken, and called the earth from the rising of the sun to the going down thereof."* And Scripture further says: *"Out of Zion, the perfection of beauty, God hath shined forth,"* that means from it the beauty of the world was perfected.

a. The suggestion is that Zion was created first, and around it other clods, rocks, formations, continents were formed until the earth was completed.   b. Job 38: 38. c. *Ibid.* 37: 6. The picture here (Rashi) is that of a skeleton or frame, which filled in, gradually solidifying from all sides towards the centre, which is last in foundation. All Scriptural verses here are used as intimation not logically but illustratively. Here is an amazing anticipation of the modern theory that the world was founded by the solidification of vapours, the Talmudic account ascribing this gradual creation to the will of God. d. Job 38: 6.   e. Ps. 50: 1.   f. *Ibid.*, 5: 2.   g. Gen. 2: 4.   h. All things of heaven, the stars, sun, and moon.

At the present day the Dome of the Rock, the Moslem shrine, is claimed to rest on the foundation stone, אֶבֶן שְׁתִיָּה. For Delphi, see n. 12 below. Following J. Jeremias, see n. 9 above, Burrows, *The Labyrinth*, pp. 55ff connects the cornerstone of Is. 28: 16 with the Temple rock. He refers to a Targumic tradition that that rock closes "the mouth of the *tehom* (*Targum Pseudo-Jonathan* to Exod. 28: 30)." (*The Targum of Isaiah*, ed., and trans. by J. F. Stenning, Oxford, 1949, ignores the stone in its rendering and interprets it as a king.) The foundation stone was situated at the highest point on the earth (see p. 138 below) and connected with the underworld. Burrows, *The Labyrinth*, p. 56, discovers the notion of the cosmic centrality of the Rock also in Ps. 29: 3 "Yahweh sat on the Flood" and Ps. 74: 12. This is precarious. H. M. Lutz, *Yahwe, Jerusalem und die Völker; zur Vorgeschichte von Sach. 12: 1–8*, Neukirchener Verlag, 1968, p. 153, contrasts the foundation stone ideology with the notion of Yahweh's founding of Jerusalem, as in Is. 14: 29–32; 28: 14–18. Trust in Yahweh, not the Stone, is the important factor for Israel.

11 The mountain is near to Shechem which is mentioned in the context. Compare John 4: 5, 20. Sychar in John 4: 5 is sometimes identified with Shechem (see Gen. 33: 19; 48: 22; Jos. 24: 32).

indicated, they are widespread outside the Old Testament in many cultures. In no way do they belong to the peculiarity of the Biblical understanding of the land.[12] They belong mostly to the same category as

[12] The Greeks thought that they lived at the centre of the earth, the oracle at Delphi was called the navel (ὀμφαλός) of the earth. See *A Companion to Greek Studies*, 4th ed. L. Whibley, Cambridge, 1931, section 11, and pp. 421ff. How little the notion of centrality had to do with geographic realities is well illustrated in the introduction on *Geography* in the volume cited, section 1. Despite the claims of Israel, we read that: "The harbourless shore of Palestine precluded its inhabitants from holding communication by sea with other countries." And, despite the claims of Greece, "the eastern shores of the Adriatic are singularly destitute of good harbours," so that there was at first little intercourse between even Greece and Italy: so too Jerusalem and the Temple are not situated on the most impressive geographic spots. The same indifference to geographical actualities emerges at Delphi itself. There the temple of Apollo is not on the site that naturally and geographically suggests itself for worship (see H. W. Parke and D. E. W. Wormell, *The Delphic Oracle*, Vol. 1, Blackwell, Oxford, 1956, p. 5). The evidence for regarding Delphi as the centre of the earth is presented by Parke and Wormell, pp. 3ff. They refer to The Homeric Hymn to Apollo 214ff: "far-darting Apollo, first went through the earth seeking an oracle-centre for men." In Euripides, *Iphigenia in Tauris*, 1247ff, Apollo's mother, Leto, after his birth on Delos, carried him to Parnassus where "a serpent, a huge monster of Earth, ministered the oracle of the earth Goddess. 'Him, while still a babe, still leaping in your mother's arms, you slew, O Phoebus, and mounted on the godlike oracle, and now sit on the golden tripod, on an undeceiving throne, assigning to mortals the oracles from beneath your prophetic shrine, as neighbour to the Castalian streams and holding the hall *midmost of the earth* (our italics).'" There is evidence (Parke and Wormell, *The Delphic Oracle*, pp. 6ff) that Delphi was earlier associated with Gê, the earth goddess; the worship of Gê was displaced by the introduction of Apollo. Associated with Gê was an egg-shaped stone, called ὀμφαλός (navel), situated in historic times in the innermost sanctuary of the temple. This marked the "*navel*" of the Earth—a spot determined by Zeus. It was probably the oldest cultic object preserved at Delphi and originally a sacred stone, with its own "power" or "holiness" or "manna." According to Parke and Wormell, "similar baetyls are regularly found in association with the Mother goddess of Minoan art" (*The Delphic Oracle*, p. 7). How reminiscent the ὀμφαλός at Delphi is of the אֶבֶן שְׁתִיָּה is clear: both were associated with the Earth. It is sometimes forgotten that there is also a cave associated with the foundation stone in Jerusalem: even pictures of the stone make this clear. Note again that the sanctity of Jerusalem, like that of Delphi, was in despite of its geographic location (see N. Porteous, following A. Alt, in *Verbannung und Heimkehr: Festschrift für Wilhelm Rudolph*, ed. A. Kuschke, Tübingen, 1961, on "Jerusalem—Zion: The Growth of a Symbol," p. 236). This agrees with the view that "the sacred" is "given" "not made" (see M. Eliade, *Patterns in Comparative Religion*, New York, 1958, p. 369), and explains why there is such a continuity in the history of sacred places from one culture to another. For example, the Cathedral at Chartres was erected on an ancient Druidic religious centre. The example from Chartres might suggest that the sacred is to be equated with the beautiful. This is not so. The Church of the Nativity in Bethlehem is not a beautiful place, but it is extremely sacred. Note that the use of unhewn stones for the altar is part of the "givenness" of the sacred. (The words of Maurice Barrès in *La Colline Inspirée*, deserve quotation. "Il est des lieux qui tirent l'âme, de sa léthargie, des lieux enveloppés, baignés de mystère, élus de toute l'éternite pour être le siège de l'émotion religieuse. . . ils nous communiquent une interprétation religieuse de notre destinée. . ." I owe this reference to Professor Wallace Fowlie.) See J. Pedersen, *Israel: Its Life and Culture*, Vol. III, London, 1926, pp. 201, 205. On the navel of the earth see the exhaustively documented article by S. Terrien, "The Omphalos Myth and Hebrew Religion," *VT*, Vol. 20, 1970, pp. 315–338. In Buddhism, creation begins at the centre of the earth; in Islam, the ka'aba, the city of Mecca, is the centre. See Eliade, *The Sacred and the Profane*, pp. 377ff. In view of all this, we need not follow R. de Vaux in finding the concept of the centrality of Jerusalem a late climax to the love of the city: it was probably very early.

the arrangement of the maps of the world which I knew as a boy. In these the earth was not only largely coloured British red, but invariably had its centre in the British Isles, and, on closer inspection, in England, and, on still closer inspection, in London, until finally one detected Greenwich, by which the world sets it clocks but on which not even the sun itself would ever set. Nor are such ideas peculiarly British in the modern world. Readers of the very first page of Charles de Gaulle's *Memoirs of Hope*, trans., 1971, will recall his understanding of his beloved France as "this human amalgam, on this territory, at the heart of this world."

We now come to another emphasis on the land which, though important in its own right, also does not belong to the peculiarity of the Old Testament and Judaism. It is the emphasis on the land of Israel as the place where Yahweh abundantly gave material gifts of all kinds to his people; it is the emphasis that makes so many Old Testament passages useful in Harvest Thanksgiving services. We encounter here that element in Israel's thought on the land which it probably owed primarily to Canaanite culture, but which it may have met before it settled in Canaan. There was a time when the patriarchs were understood in terms of animism and the like. The picture which W. Robertson Smith[13] drew of the development of a relationship between a god and his land in the primitive mind is familiar: it is a picture of animism and similar ideas. Because primitive man was primarily concerned with the satisfaction of immediate physical needs, any area that offered such satisfaction became marked. On the ground of its fertility, usually because of the presence of a stream, or spring, or some other source of water, a certain spot would gain the reputation of being unique. Or, again, a peculiar conformation of rocks might create the belief that a place was in some way different.

Certainly such a notion is ubiquitous. See R. de Vaux in H. M. Orlinsky, *Interpreting the Prophetic Tradition*, Cincinnati, O., 1969, p. 298. On Jerusalem as centre, see further Pedersen, *Israel*, Vol. III–IV, pp. 262ff. What we have written above on the relationship between the beautiful and the sacred is not to be pressed. Jerusalem's beauty was praised (Ps. 48: 2; contrast LXX 47: 2; Lam. 2: 15; T. B. Sukkah 51b; Kiddushin 49b; Jos. *Ant.* IV).

13 W. R. Smith, *Lectures on the Religion of the Semites*, New York, 1969, pp. 115–119. Smith points out that "the feeling of a real and intimate connection with the land...makes for cohesion, for local patriotism, for a feeling of union and kinship within the community (p. 92)." Smith refers to 2 Kings 17: 24ff, which concerns the Babylonians who were brought into Samaria after the deportation under the King of Assyria, and were attacked by lions and beasts of the land because "they do not know the law of its god." This passage shows that the relations of a god to his land were not merely political or dependent on his relations with its inhabitants. The power of the god is intrinsic to the land itself. Contrast Durkheim's view of the dependency of the god on his worshippers, *Elementary Forms of Religious Life*, p. 38. Pedersen, *Israel*, Vol. III, 1926, pp. 201, 205, stresses the importance of sacred stones and pillars in primitive sanctuaries; the use of unhewn stones for altars, as we saw, being especially significant in this connection.

For whatever reason, a place would become associated with an irruption of the divine and a gateway to a god. But because primitive man was a nomadic tribesman or huntsman, he could not conceive of the god as limited to one spot. The god surely moved within the area of man's seasonal migrations in search of water and grassland. And so the entire area which the god was considered to frequent became identified as his land, even though the first spot where he had manifested himself continued to be regarded as his home. As we have stated, it is against such a picture that the patriarchal period has often been understood. But few would now argue that the patriarch's religion is thus explicable.

In any case, it is the continued settlement in Canaan and the encounter with a static culture dominated by Baalim that made the relationship between a god, as the giver of good gifts such as we have referred to, and his land acute. For the Canaanites, the god who guaranteed the fertility of the soil and the abundance of the harvest was Baal, "the husband" or "lord" of the land. The sanctuaries of the Baalim were usually situated in secluded, isolated spots near a source of water. The temptation for Israel to adopt them—sanctuaries and Baalim—was almost irresistible. The battle waged by Israel against the Baalim in the interests of Yahweh need not be described here. It is sufficient to recognize that, despite this battle, the functions of the Baalim were transferred to Yahweh, and it has been held that the reiterated emphases on the blessings of the land came into Yahwehism through Canaanite Baalism. G. von Rad thinks that even the phrase, "the land flows with milk and honey" has come from this source. And he further notes as coming from the same source: "the descriptions of an almost paradisal blessing on human progeny, on the offspring of the cattle, on basket and kneeding-trough, the fruit of the fields, rain for the earth, peace, deliverance from wild animals and so on; these descriptions would surely seem to have been composed under the influence of Canaanite nature—religion (Lev. 26: 3–12; Num. 13: 23, 28; 14: 7f; 24: 3f; Deut. 28: 2–7)."[14] We may be allowed to question the exclusive ascription of such motifs to the influence of Canaanite religion without rejecting von Rad's main emphasis.

At this point it has to be recognized that the question of the relationship of Yahweh to the land of Israel is not to be treated in total isolation from the relationship of Yahweh to the whole universe. In the Old Testament the notion of creation as a totality is late: the term *bârâ'*, to create, is not

[14] Gerhard von Rad, *The Problem of the Hexateuch and Other Essays*, trans., E. W. T. Dicken, New York, 1966, p. 89. See n. 18, Ch. 2, p. 23 below.

used of Yahweh before the Exile. But certainly in the later strata of the Old Testament, Yahweh is always the creator so that it became wholly natural to regard him as the source of the gifts of the natural order entirely apart from his special relationship to Israel; the Canaanite heritage in this respect could easily be assimilated without any sense of incongruity.[15]

We have now dealt with two peripheral aspects of the understanding of the land in the Old Testament and Judaism; they do not, however, constitute its peculiarity. Before we pass on to that peculiarity, we might add another purely geographical factor which greatly impressed Israel in its thought of its land; that is, the difference between the land of Israel, which Yahweh cared for directly by the giving of rain, the proof of his constant concern, and the land of Egypt, which was at the mercy of the fluctuation of the Nile and, therefore, less directly the object of Yahweh's care. Israel was under Yahweh's immediate supervision in a way Egypt was not: the soil of Israel received water by the direct will and decision of Yahweh. Deut. 11: 10–12 makes this clear:

For the land which you are entering to take possession of it is not like the land of Egypt, from which you have come, where you sowed your seed and watered it with your feet, like a garden of vegetables; but the land which you are going over to possess is a land of hills and valleys, which drinks water by the rain from heaven, a land which the Lord your God cares for; the eyes of the Lord your God are always upon it from the beginning of the year to the end of the year.[16]

Such a sentiment, however, touching and beautiful as it is, does not constitute a peculiarity in the religion with which we are dealing. Few peoples have not discovered some geographic sign of grace in their lands.[17] Wherein, then, does the peculiarity about which we speak lie? In two places.

[15] W. H. Bennett, *The Post-Exilic Prophets*, Edinburgh, 1907, pp. 136, 164, on בְּרָא; *PRJ*, pp. 163ff. It is significant that the Divine immanence in creation and the Divine activity in redemption came to be expressed through the same instrument, the Wisdom of God. See James Barr, *Old and New in Interpretation*, London, 1966, pp. 18ff, and p. 23, n. 18 below; W. Zimmerli, *Man and his Hope in the Old Testament*, Studies in Biblical Theology, Second Series, Naperville, Ill., trans., 1968, pp. 60ff.

[16] Compare Buber, *Israel and Palestine*, pp. 24ff. "Of all lands," he writes, "this is the one which by its very nature is in a special way subject to and dependent on the providence and grace of God." Egypt and Canaan are deliberately compared: "the very nature of the land of Canaan bears witness to the unremitting providence of God. And it is its nature that qualifies it to be the pledge of the covenant (p. 25)."

[17] Herodotus, 2: 12f, reports that Egyptian priests had contrasted their land with Greece in the same way, and Buber thinks that this Egyptian point of view may be the background of Deut. 11: 10–12. But whereas the Egyptians considered dependence on the vicissitudes of climate a disadvantage, the Deuteronomist finds in this a sign of and means to divine grace. See Buber, *Israel and Palestine*, p. 26. That the discovery of grace in one's own land is

13

probably universal need not be argued. Readers of Dostoievsky's *The Possessed*, for example, will recall his references to Holy Russia. Some national anthems amount to a glorification of the land. It is tempting to suggest that well-established nations do not emphasize the land in their national anthems, whereas insecure and emerging or suppressed nations do. The English national anthem speaks of the monarchy particularly, the French of a historical event, "le jour de gloire"; contrast Germany's *Deutschland über Alles*. Doubtless political and constitutional factors enter into the emergence or creation of national anthems that make any single explanation of their peculiarities suspect. But consider the national anthems of smaller nations, for example, those of Wales, Israel, and Syria. That of the latter contains the words:

> Defenders of the Fatherland all hail . . .
> Not heaven's self is more sublimely grand
> Than where our forbears glorified our land.

(Cited by 'Abd Al-Tafahum, *Religion in the Middle East*, Vol. 2, ed. A. J. Arberry, Cambridge, 1969, p. 388, n. 1. He refers to A. J. Arberry, *Aspects of Islamic Civilization*, London, 1964, p. 394.)

II. THE LAND IN THE HEXATEUCH

1. The Land of Promise

First, the land is a promised land.[1] To disentangle the various currents
that have gone into the concept of the promise of the land is exceedingly

[1] Gerhard von Rad, *The Problem of the Hexateuch and Other Essays*, trans., E. W. T.
Dicken, 1966, p. 79, declares that: "in the whole of the Hexateuch there is probably no more
important idea than that expressed in terms of the land promised and later granted by Yahweh."
Buber finds the promise unique. "Among all the traditions of the world this is the only one
that tells of the promise of a land to a people (M. Buber, *Israel and Palestine*, London, 1952,
p. 19)." On p. 18, Buber defines the promise as follows: "The Promise means that within
history an absolute relationship between a people and a land has been taken into the covenant
between God and the people." Yahweh had brought other peoples to their various lands
(Amos 9: 7), but only in the land of Israel has the relationship between Yahweh and the
people concerned developed into a covenantal one: "The other peoples led by God which
have received a land from Him do not know His true name, His nature, His universality and
His claim; each of them knows only that their god, the tribal god, led them into this land and
presented it to them (Buber, p. 19)." The claim to uniqueness is always hard to prove.
Classical scholars might refer to the history of the Roman Empire as involving a not wholly
dissimilar concept. But this cannot be pursued here, nor the claim of 'Abd Al-Tafahum,
Religion in the Middle East, Cambridge, 1969, p. 366: "We do not rightly understand the
Old Testament's sense of place and people unless we know that it mirrors and educates the
self awareness of all lands and dwellers. The nationhood of Israel, the love of Zion, has its
counterparts in every continent. Its uniqueness lies, not in the emotional experience, but the
theological intensity." F. W. Walbank in his work *A Historical Commentary on Polybius*,
Vol. 1, Oxford, 1957, p. 16, on *Tyche*, where he recognizes that Polybius is not consistent,
nevertheless, writes: "To a large extent the personality with which Polybius invests *Tyche*
is a matter of verbal elaboration, helped by current Hellenistic usage, which habitually spoke
of *Tyche* as a goddess; and this helps to explain many of the inconsistencies, for consistency
is not essential to a rhetorical flourish. With regard to its main theme, however—the work of
Tyche in making Rome mistress of the world in fifty-three years—one must allow for at least
the possibility that as he looked back on this startling and unparalleled process, Polybius
jumped the step in logic between what had happened and what had had to happen, and so in a
somewhat muddled way invested the rise of Rome to world power with a teleological
character. . . ." We do not suggest that this teleology is parallel in *intensity* to what is found
in the Old Testament and Judaism. See *Pronoia* and *Tychê* in Jos., *Jewish Wars*, iii.

Two lexicographical points need to be made. The verbs translated in the KJV as "to
promise" are אָמַר and דָּבַר, which normally refer simply to utterance without the connotation
of promise. The verb most often connected with Yahweh's intention to give the land to
Israel is "to swear", שָׁבַע. "The sworn land" would be a more accurate rendering than "the
promised land." See the concordances and the list given by G. von Rad, *The Problem of the
Hexateuch*, pp. 79f, and especially p. 167, n. 12, below.

Again we must emphasize that we shall be concerned with the term: אֶרֶץ in this work. The
Old Testament uses two Hebrew words which can be translated by the term "land" in
English, that is, אֶרֶץ and אֲדָמָה. In Hebrew they are, in some cases, similar in meaning, but
they are not to be taken as identifiable. L. Rost in a study in *Das kleine Credo und andere Studien
zum Alten Testament*, Heidelberg, 1965, pp. 76–100, on "Die Bezeichnungen für Land und
Volk im Alten Testament," holds that the two words express different conceptions. אֲדָמָה

15

difficult. Let us begin with those texts where the promise emerges in the oldest strata of the Pentateuch, which, it is generally agreed, occur in Gen. 15 [EJ].[2] In Gen. 15: 1–6 we read as follows:

After these things the word of the Lord came to Abram in a vision, "Fear not, Abram, I am your shield; your reward shall be very great." But Abram said, "O Lord God, what wilt thou give me, for I continue childless, and the heir of my house is Eliezer of Damascus?" And Abram said, "Behold, thou hast given me no offspring; and a slave born in my house will be my heir." And behold, the word of the Lord came to him, "This man shall not be your heir." And he brought him outside and said, "Look toward heaven, and number the stars, if you are able to number them." Then he said to him, "So shall your descendants be." And he believed the Lord: and he reckoned it to him as righteousness.

Here Abraham is promised an heir. There is no explicit reference to land, but there is an implication in 15: 4 that the land which Abraham possessed at that time was to be handed on to his son.[3]

---

perhaps etymologically related to אָדַם ("to be red") (see L. H. Koehler and W. Baumgartner, *Lexicon in Veteris Testamenti Libros*, 1958, p. 13), suggests the reddish-brown colour of the arable soil. It designates primarily the land as habitable, cultivatable, the place of man's dwelling, without political or national connotation. Rost, p. 92, writes: "Aus der Betrachtung konnte אֲדָמָה als ein in allen Fällen unpolitischer Begriff ganz ausscheiden. Dagegen wurde אֶרֶץ als die territorial Grundlage eines Staatswesens herausgestellt, die es einen גּוֹי, einem Volk gesstattet durch seinen עַם die bevorrechtete Männerschicht der Vollbürger, zur staatlichen selbständigkeit zu gelangen."

[2] For the sake of clarity we recall that J and E date from a period stretching from the late eleventh century to the early eighth century B.C. and that they were fused into one complex after 722 B.C.—the fall of the northern kingdom: D is seventh century.

[3] According to G. von Rad, *Problems of the Hexateuch*, pp. 84f, the fact that the land is not mentioned in the promise to Abraham in Gen. 12 increases its significance. Only one item in the promise is given at a time: in Gen. 12 it is progeny. It is implied, though not stated, that Abraham is to have an heir. In the passages cited and throughout the Old Testament the boundaries of the land vary. Note the following passages.

(a) Exod. 23: 31ff: I will set your bounds from the Red Sea to the sea of the Philistines [that is, the Mediterranean], and from the wilderness to the Euphrates.... [Only in the era of David and Solomon did the Israelites control such an area, 1 Kings 4: 24.]

(b) Num. 34: 1–10: The Lord said to Moses, "Command the people of Israel, and say to them, When you enter the land of Canaan (this is the land that shall fall to you for an inheritance, the land of Canaan in its full extent), your south side shall be from the wilderness of Zin along the side of Edom, and your southern boundary shall be from the end of the Salt Sea on the east; and your boundary shall turn south of the ascent of Akrabbim, and cross to Zin, and its end shall be south of Kadeshbarnea; then it shall go on to Hazaraddar, and pass along to Azmon and the boundary shall turn from Azmon to the Brook of Egypt, and its termination shall be at the sea. For the western boundary, you shall have the Great Sea and its coast; this shall be your western boundary.

This shall be your northern boundary: From the Great Sea you shall mark out your line to Mount Hor; from Mount Hor you shall mark it out to the entrance of Hamath, and the end of the boundary shall be at Zedad; then the boundary shall extend to Ziphron, and its end shall be at Hazarenan; this shall be your northern boundary.

You shall mark out your eastern boundary from Hazarenan to Shepham..."

(c) Deut. 11: 24 defines the land more generally:

Later in the same chapter, in 15: 17ff [JE] we read:

When the sun had gone down and it was dark, behold, a smoking fire pot and a flaming torch passed between these pieces. On that day the Lord made a covenant with Abram, saying, "To your descendants I give this land (*'eretz*), from the river of Egypt to the great river, the river Euphrates, the land of the Kenites, the Kenizzites, the Kadmonites, the Hittites, the Perizzites, the Rephaim, the Amorites, the Canaanites, the Girgashites and the Jebusites."

The promise is referred to again in Gen. 12: 1–3 [J] in the following terms:

Now the Lord said to Abram, "Go from your country (*'eretz*) and your kindred and your father's house to the land that I will show you. And I will make of you a great nation, and I will bless you, and make your name great, so that you will be a blessing. I will bless those who bless you, and him who curses you I will curse; and by you all the families of the earth shall bless themselves."

What is common to all these passages is that a land is promised to Abraham's descendants: the land they are to possess is to be theirs by divine authority. In other respects the passages differ: in Gen. 15: 17–21 the land defined is clearly, by implication, less extensive than that contemplated in Gen. 12: 1–3, where Abraham's descendants are to become a great nation and to impinge upon all the families of the earth.

These passages have been variously assessed. First, according to some they are creations of a late period, the Exile, when Israel felt that its possession of the land was in jeopardy. She accordingly sought to bolster her claims to the land by recourse to a supposedly ancient divine promise to Abraham. The promise, in this view, is not grounded in early tradition, but is a late literary and theological construction. This view has not gained adherents.[4]

Every place on which the sole of your foot treads shall be yours; your territory (*g^ebûl^ekâm*) shall be from the wilderness and Lebanon and from the River, the river Euphrates, to the western sea.

(d) Joshua 1: 2–4 reads:

Moses my servant is dead; now therefore arise, go over this Jordan, you and all this people, into the land (*hâ-'âretz*) which I am giving to them, to the people of Israel. Every place that the sole of your foot will tread upon I have given to you, as I promised to Moses. From the wilderness and this Lebanon as far as the great river, the river Euphrates, all the land (*'eretz*) of the Hittites to the Great Sea toward the going down of the sun shall be your territory.

It is clear that "the land of Israel" was never defined with geographic precision: it is an idea as well as a territory. It seems always to have carried ideal overtones without geographical and political precision. For an examination of the various boundaries, see G. W. Buchanan, *The Consequences of The Covenant*, 1970, pp. 91–109. M. Gittin 1: 2 for legal limits.

4 See R. E. Clements, *Abraham and David*, London, 1967, p. 23. He refers to H. Gunkel, "Abraham," RGG, 2nd ed., 1, col. 66; J. Hoftijzer, *Die Verheissungen an die drei Erzväter*, Leiden, 1956, pp. 52ff.

Secondly, it has been urged that the promise is exceedingly ancient, going back to pre-Israelite and even pre-Canaanite times, when the god of Abraham, the god of a nomadic clan, promised to his devotees the two great needs of nomads—a land and numerous progeny. Later when the descendants of this clan were incorporated into Israel, their god, the god of Abraham, later known as the God of the Fathers, was identified with Yahweh who had brought Israel out of Egypt. In this view, the promise was given by the god of Abraham before Israel had entered Canaan: it envisaged not the gift of the whole land of Palestine, but simply the strict inheritance of Abraham.[5]

Recently, in the third place, the view has been forcefully presented that Abraham had already entered Canaan when the promise came to him. Of necessity, the god who gave the promise was not the god of a nomadic group, who had no land of his own to give, but the god of a settled community who owned the land which he gave in promise. The god concerned was, in fact, the El deity of Mamre at Hebron where Abraham dwelt. His name was possibly *El Shaddai*: the land he promised was the territory around Hebron referred to in 15: 19 as the land of the Kenites, Kenizzites, and Kadmonites etc. It is essential, in this view, to recognize that the patriarchs were not merely nomads but leaders of settlements in the agricultural land of Canaan. The emergence of the promise of the land is to be understood as the legitimization of the settlement of the patriarchs in Canaan.[6]

To discuss each of these views would prolong our work inordinately, and, fortunately, for our purposes, we need not assess the different theories of the historical origins of the promise to Abraham. In this sphere, as in the question of Canaanite influences on certain Old Testament passages noted above, interest in Israel in strictly historical origins, if it ever existed as such, was submerged as the tradition developed, and became insignificant and irrelevant. For the understanding of our proper task what is important is not the rediscovery of the origins of the promise to Abraham, but the recognition that that promise was so reinterpreted from age to age that it became a living power in the life of the people of Israel. Not the mode of its origin matters, but its operation as a formative, dynamic, seminal force in the history of Israel.[7] The legend of the

---

[5] A. Alt, "The God of the Fathers," *Essays on Old Testament History and Religion*, Oxford, 1966, pp. 48, 65f. For a critique of A. Alt, see Clements, *Abraham and David*, pp. 24ff, and H. H. Rowley, *Worship in Ancient Israel*, Philadelphia, 1967, p. 14.

[6] Clements, *Abraham and David*, presents this view with great clarity.

[7] Clements, *Abraham and David*.

promise entered so deeply into the experience of the Jews that it acquired its own reality. What Jews believe to have happened in the Middle East has been no less formative in world history than that which is known to have occurred.

The reinterpretation to which we have referred concerned two things: the identity of the author of the promise and the content of the promise. As for the author of the promise, historically, if we follow Exod. 6: 3, the god who gave the promise could not have been called Yahweh, because Yahweh was unknown by name to the patriarchs. Perhaps most scholars would agree that it is the Yahwist, that is, the formulator of what is known as the J tradition in the Pentateuch, who identified the original deity who had given the promise to Abraham with Yahweh.[8] In this way it could be claimed that the god who gave the promise to Abraham also led Israel out of Egypt and became the God of Israel.

The history of the content of the promise is far more complicated. If we follow Clements,[9] it was governed by the political vicissitudes of the people of Judah and Israel and largely formulated by the Yahwist. In the original promise to Abraham the content of the promise consists of progeny, blessing, and a land. In three passages a new relationship to God is also promised.[10] It is the promise of land alone that concerns us. The promise of the possession of the hereditary land of the clan or tribe, whether around Hebron or not, implied in Gen. 15: 1ff, was expanded to include the land from Egypt to the Euphrates (Gen. 15: 18). Further, Israel is to become a great nation, numerous as the stars of heaven in number (Gen. 15: 5). Thus the promise is made to foretell the rise of the Davidic empire and subserve the interests of that empire. According to Clements, the covenant of Yahweh with David at his installation at Hebron (2 Kings 5: 1ff) both reflects the Abrahamic covenant and influenced its interpretation and transmission.[11] The Yahwist saw a connection between Abraham and David: for him the Abrahamic covenant

---

[8] *Ibid.*

[9] *Ibid.*, pp. 47ff. The relationship of the promise to Israel in J is such that some scholars feel that the Yahwist can be identified as the High Priest under King David, that is, Abiathar. See Peter Ellis, *The Yahwist*, Notre Dame, 1968, pp. 308ff.

[10] See Exod. 6: 4–7; Gen. 17: 7, 8 (all in P); G. von Rad, *The Problem of the Hexateuch*, p. 84. On the significance of "food" for primitive man, see B. Malinowski, *Magic, Science and Religion*, Boston, 1948, p. 25. If the supply of food is scarce, primitive man regards its acquisition with an attitude approximating religious awe. The pertinent passages for the promise of land, progeny, blessing and a new relationship are listed by G. von Rad, *The Problem of the Hexateuch*, pp. 79f.

[11] E.g., Deut. 1: 8; 34: 4; 11: 8–9; 10: 11; 1: 35; 30: 5; 7: 13; God is the God of the Fathers (in the plural) 4: 1; 12: 1; 29: 22, 28.

found its fulfilment in the extension of the Davidic Kingdom; the promise to Abraham was of the rise and triumph of that Kingdom. The local dimension of the land in the promise originally made to Abraham was transcended. This means that the Abrahamic covenant became subsumed under the covenant with David, and this in turn explains according to Clements, why there are so few references to Abraham and his covenant in the pre-exilic prophets and in the pre-exilic cultus.

As long as the Davidic dynasty prevailed, the appeal to the promise to Abraham, now absorbed into the Davidic covenant, could be neglected. But in times of dire crises, as in the eighth century, when the threat of Assyria was real, and the self-identity of the people was shaken, the Abrahamic covenant again gained recognition and importance. In Deuteronomy, although the covenant at Horeb is given the pre-eminence, appeal is also made to the promise to Abraham in order to gain reassurance that behind Israel's existence and its tenure of the land of Canaan lay the divine purpose. The Abrahamic covenant is now referred to as made with all the three patriarchs[12] and is understood as exclusively concerned with the land of Canaan.[13] The land promised to Abraham has been promised to Israel as a whole, and the promise has found its fulfilment, both in the covenant at Horeb and in the conquest under Joshua.

Deuteronomy, then, fused together the promise of the land made to the early patriarchs and the tradition of the giving of the Law at Sinai. The relationship of the commandments to the land is regarded in Deuteronomy as twofold. On the one hand, the commandments are regulatory, that is, they are intended to provide guidance for the government of the land, for the conduct of the cultus, and for the arrangements demanded by the settlement.[14] On the other hand, the commandments are conditional; that is, only if they are observed can the land be received and possessed. According to Deuteronomy, under the terms of the covenant entered into at Sinai, Israel, if it disobeys the commandments, can be expelled from the

---

[12] G. von Rad, *The Problem of the Hexateuch*, p. 91, n. 30, points out that "the idea that Israel as a whole has a נַחֲלָה (an inheritance), is not found in pre-Deuteronomic writings, except in one single instance at Judges xx. 6. The notion that Israel is Yahweh's נַחֲלָה, however, was certainly current at an earlier date: cf. II Sam. xx: 9; xxi. 3." See also Clements, *Abraham and David*, pp. 64ff, and further F. Horst, "Zwei Begriffe für Eigentum," in *Verbannung und Heimkehr*, Tübingen, 1961, especially pp. 141ff. The notion of "inheritance" is important and inseparable from our theme. It has recently been examined by James D. Hester, *Paul's Concept of Inheritance*, Edinburgh, 1968.

[13] Deut. 4: 6, 14; 11: 31f; 12: 9ff; 17: 14; 18: 9; 9: 1; 21: 1; 26: 1. See G. von Rad, *The Problem of the Hexateuch*, p. 91.

[14] Deut. 4: 25f; 6: 18, 24; 16: 20. The strongest expression of this is in 29: 16–28. Compare Josh. 23: 16.

land: its occupancy of the land has a "legal" basis.[15] Yes: but Deuteronomy holds that by appeal to the promise to Abraham there can be reassurance for Israel. That promise was irrevocable: it could, therefore, become the ground for forgiveness even though the commandments had been broken. In this way, the promise to Abraham becomes a ground for ultimate hope. To put it perhaps too broadly or loosely, it is as if in Deuteronomy a covenant of "grace," that with Abraham, is a guarantee and safeguard against failure to observe the covenant of "the Law." To put it even more daringly, there is a "gospel" for Israel in the Abrahamic covenant.[16] Particularly revealing of this are the words of Moses to the people in Deut. 9: 24–29:

You have been rebellious against the Lord from the day that I knew you. "So I lay prostrate before the Lord for these forty days and forty nights, because the Lord had said he would destroy you. And I prayed to the Lord, 'O Lord God, destroy not thy people and thy heritage, whom thou hast redeemed through thy greatness, whom thou hast brought out of Egypt with a mighty hand. Remember thy servants, Abraham, Isaac, and Jacob; do not regard the stubbornness of this people, or their wickedness, or their sin, lest the land (*hâ-'âret̰*) from which thou didst bring us say, "Because the Lord was not able to bring them into the land (*hâ-'âret̰*) which he promised them, and because he hated them, he has brought them out to slay them in the wilderness." For they are thy people and thy heritage, whom thou didst bring out by thy great power and by thy outstretched arm.'"

When later we come to P, the priestly document, the strict historical origins and limits of the promise to Abraham become still further modified. The priestly document seeks to provide Israel with a renewed theological basis for its existence. Taking up J and E, P makes the divine promise to Abraham the bedrock on which all the subsequent history rests. P's understanding of that covenant is seen in Gen. 17: 1–14 [P]:

When Abram was ninety-nine years old the Lord appeared to Abram, and said to him, "I am God Almighty; walk before me, and be blameless. And I will make my covenant between me and you, and will multiply you exceedingly." Then Abram fell on his face; and God said to him, "Behold, my covenant is with you, and you shall be the father of a multitude of nations. No longer shall your name be Abram, but your name shall be Abraham; for I have made you the father of a multitude of nations. I will make you exceedingly fruitful; and I will make nations of you, and kings shall come forth from you. And I will establish my covenant between me and you and your descendants after you throughout their generations for an everlasting covenant, to be God to you and

---

[15] Clements, *Abraham and David*, p. 68.   [16] *Ibid.*, pp. 70ff.

to your descendants after you. And I will give to you, and to your descendants after you, the land (*'eretz*) of your sojournings, all the land (*'eretz*) of Canaan, for an everlasting possession; and I will be their God."

And God said to Abraham, "As for you, you shall keep my covenant, you and your descendants after you throughout their generations. This is my covenant, which you shall keep, between me and you and your descendants after you: Every male among you shall be circumcised. You shall be circumcised in the flesh of your foreskins, and it shall be a sign of the covenant between me and you. He that is eight days old among you shall be circumcised; every male throughout your generations, whether born in your house, or bought with your money from any foreigner who is not of your offspring, both he that is born in your house and he that is bought with your money, shall be circumcised. So shall my covenant be in your flesh an everlasting covenant. Any uncircumcised male who is not circumcised in the flesh of his foreskin shall be cut off from his people; he has broken my covenant."

Here Abraham is to be the father of a multitude of nations; Canaan is to be an everlasting possession; the god of the Abrahamic covenant (*El Shaddai* was probably his name historically) is to be the god of Abraham's descendants; and circumcision is to be a sign of God's people. The content of the covenant has thus been changed: its promissory character has been heightened; its inviolability affirmed—it is everlasting. P reveals what had already appeared in Deuteronomy—an appeal to the divine grace, the promise, as a bulwark against failure to observe the commandments of the Sinai covenant with which P, like Deuteronomy, had connected the Abrahamic covenant. The appeal to the Abrahamic covenant meant that Israel's election, and with it the possession of the land, could never, for P, become conditional on obedience to the Law; that election, resting upon the Abrahamic covenant, could not be annulled even by human disobedience. Israel, it follows, cannot be destroyed and the land *will* be hers.[17]

---

[17] G. von Rad, "The Form-critical Problem of the *Hexateuch*," in *The Problem of the Hexateuch*, p. 78. A section from P, Gen. 23, is particularly noteworthy. It describes very deliberate arrangements made by Abraham to secure burial for his wife, Sarah, in a cave, which he himself had securely purchased in the land. This purchase was before witnesses. Abraham not only refused to bury Sarah in a grave belonging to a native of the country in which at that time he was only a sojourner, but also in any grave given to him for the purpose. Similarly, P makes it quite clear that Abraham (Gen. 29: 9), Isaac and Rebecca, Leah (Gen. 49: 31), and Jacob (Gen. 50: 12f) were all buried in the land in the same cave, and so was it, it may be implied by P at Gen. 50: 24ff, in the case of Joseph. This concern with a grave in the land witnesses to the vitality of P's concern with the promise of the land to Abraham, as later to Jacob at Bethel in Gen. 35: 11f and again in Gen. 28: 3f.

But there is another emphasis on a promise which appears for the first time in P. According to this, Yahweh is to become the God of Israel and Israel his people as in Exod. 6: 66–67. Yahweh is to be actually present with his people in the tent of meeting, Exod. 29: 43–46;

So far we have presented the history of the reinterpretation of the promise to Abraham as it is traced by Clements. He ascribes to that promise a corrective, "evangelical" role in the Old Testament. Has Clements exaggerated its significance? We shall see that this is possible. But the importance of the promise cannot be ignored. Clements's concentration on this is parallel to that of von Rad, according to whom the whole of the Hexateuch in all its vast complexity was governed by the theme of the fulfilment of the promise to Abraham in the settlement in Canaan. "The chief purpose of this work," he wrote, "was to present in all its biblical and theological significance this one leading conception, in relation to which all the other conceptions of the Hexateuch assume an ancillary role."[18] Like Clements,[19] von Rad holds that it was the work of the

---

31: 12f. And at Sinai Yahweh became the God of his people, and his people knew him. See Exod. 6: 7; 16: 6f, 12; 29: 46. The promise made in P at Gen. 17 is fulfilled. Zimmerli, *Man and His Hope in the Old Testament*, trans., Naperville, Ill., n.d., German original, 1968, raises the question of how far this emphasis in P robs the hope for the land of its significance. "Before this mighty fulfilment of divine promise in which God in a visible order of worship becomes truly a God of his people, the lively expectation of the Yahwist tradition toward a possession of the land recedes noticeably into the background. Whether the priestly writer says anything further of the ownership of the land is a matter of dispute (p. 66)." Here Zimmerli's understanding of P is near to that of James Sanders, but he recognizes that the realized glorification of Yahweh among his people coexists with the promise of the land and that P still presents an open future.

[18] G. von Rad, *The Problem of the Hexateuch*, pp. 85ff, and also, especially in "The Theological Problem of the Old Testament Doctrine of Creation," pp. 132ff, where he discusses whether the doctrine of Yahweh as Creator is relevant to that of Redemption. He points out that: "The statement of Lev. 25: 23...is extremely ancient, and underlies the whole law of land tenure in the Old Testament. Nevertheless, it does not depend upon the doctrine of creation, but rests directly on belief in a historical act of grace on God's part. Nor does it lead on to a doctrine of creation, since so far as one can see it is quite unrelated to it (p. 132)." Later on in the history of Israel the doctrine of creation is incorporated into that of redemption (pp. 132ff). He refers to Ps. 136; 148; 33; Is. 40: 27ff; 42: 5; 43: 1; 44: 24; 44: 24–28; 51: 9f. etc. On p. 12 above we emphasized that the doctrine of the land is to be related to that of creation. According to G. von Rad, in the O.T. "the doctrine of creation was never able to attain to independent existence in its own right. Either it remained a cosmic foil against which soteriological pronouncements stood out more effectively, or it was wholly incorporated into the complex of soteriological thought (*The Problem of the Hexateuch*, p. 142)." On the other hand, James Barr, *Old and New in Interpretation*, London, 1966, p. 18, takes an opposite view. "Is there then any 'starting-point' for the understanding of the Old Testament? G. von Rad's reference to 'an historical act of grace' must not be unqualified. If we are to judge from Joshua 23, Yahweh proved or established his possession of the land through the conquest: this is grace for Israel, but not for its inhabitants. See also Josh 24: 8. In so far as the question is a real one at all, the only answer must be the creation story, because it is from here onwards that the story is cumulative." Compare also *Old and New*, pp. 74ff, where Barr rejects the views of von Rad and C. Westermann (*Der Schöpfungsbericht vom Anfang der Bibel*, Stuttgart, 1960, p. 6). It is difficult not to agree with Barr. Buber traces a cosmic dimension already in the Song of Deborah, Judg. 5; *The Prophetic Faith*, New York, 1949, pp. 8ff. On p. 10, Buber writes: "The going forth of the sun is not a mere poetic simile but a hint of the cosmic rule of God...God is the master of the world."

[19] Not all agree with R. E. Clements. For some Deuteronomy is wholly Mosaic and Northern in its outlook. Clements seems to offer the most convincing interpretation of the

Yahwist to fuse the whole complex of the patriarchal sagas together: for him the entry into Palestine under Joshua is the fulfilment of the promise. Later modifications of this basic pattern of J and E, in von Rad's view, were trivial.

Of all the promises made to the patriarchs it was that of the land that was most prominent and decisive. It is the linking together of the promise to the patriarchs *with* the fulfilment of it in the settlement that gives to the Hexateuch its distinctive theological character. For the Hexateuch the land is a promised land, and that inviolably. Whatever attitude one takes to the role ascribed to the promise by Clements, the significance of the promise as a fact in the Hexateuch, to which von Rad has so richly drawn our attention, is immeasurable: and that for a very simple reason. However much the Prophets and the Writings gained in significance, in later ages the Pentateuch remained the bedrock of revelation for Jews, so that the references to the promise of the land embedded in it must be accorded great weight in any assessment of Judaism.

2. The Land of Yahweh

We now turn to the second of the concepts that lend peculiarity to the understanding of the land in the Old Testament. G. von Rad lays great emphasis on Lev. 25: 23: "The land (*hâ-'âretz*) shall not be sold in perpetuity, for the land (*hâ-'âretz*) is mine; for you are strangers and sojourners with me."[20] This verse introduces a concept which von Rad refuses to connect with Canaanite ideas of the relationship between the

---

data over a wide range. Fascinating suggestions are made by J. A. Sanders, *Torah and Canon*, Philadelphia, 1972. He asks the simple question why it is the Pentateuch, not the Hexateuch which came to constitute the heart of Torah for Judaism. The "story," the memory of which alone kept "Israel" alive, in J and E (composed or collected between the 11th and 8th centuries B.C.) included the conquest of the land and stretched down further to include the monarchy of David. Sanders points out that the conquest of Canaan in the book of Joshua "culminated in the very place where Abraham first settled, at Shechem: the promise of the land, which was made to Abraham at Shechem was symbolically fulfilled at Shechem (from an unpublished paper, p. 24)." Would it not have been natural for Judaism to elevate the Hexateuch to a normative position? Apparently so. Yet it was Deuteronomy, a document from the 7th century that leaves Moses looking to the promised land but not entering into it (but on this see n. 16, p. 61), which formed the climax of the Torah of Judaism. Why? Sanders answers that the crisis of the sixth century B.C., in which the land, the city, and the Temple were lost and ceased to sustain "Israel", compelled the Deuteronomist, and later P (6th–5th centuries), to look back to the period before the conquest to the Mosaic age as that which supplied an authoritative norm, and to which both D and P ascribed the laws which were to give life. Sanders's case deserves serious examination. We simply ask whether he has not too rigidly separated "*torah*" as "law" from "*torah*" as "story," and that, although Judaism did elevate the Pentateuch, it did not isolate it. But such a question by no means adequately confronts his question. On the use of *torah* and *nomos* of the Pentateuch and other documents, see J. Bonsirven, *Le Judaïsme Palestinien*, Paris, 1934, vol. 1, pp. 248ff.
[20] *The Problem of the Hexateuch.*

Baalim and the land. In the rest of the Hexateuch the land is nowhere declared to have belonged to Yahweh, but rather to the nations whom Israel dispossessed. In the Hexateuch the land is referred to invariably as "the land of Canaan." Not until 1 Sam. 13: 19 does the phrase "the land of Israel" appear. Joshua 23 makes it clear that Yahweh himself only gained possession of the land through conquest.[21] The conquest gave him the land for the sake of Israel (23: 3), according to his promise (23: 5). But, despite her success in war which she owed to Yahweh (23: 9f: "for the Lord your God, he it is that fighteth for you, as he hath promised you"), Israel does not own the land. Disobedience to the commandments of Yahweh, through intermarriage with the inhabitants of the land, would inexorably incur the withdrawal of Yahweh's support and the loss of the land (23: 13f). Joshua 23: 15–16 deserves quotation.

But just as all the good things which the Lord your God promised concerning you have been fulfilled for you, so the Lord will bring upon you all the evil things, until he have destroyed you from off this good land (*hâ-'ᵃdâmâh ha-ṭṭôbâh*) which the Lord your God has given you, if you transgress the covenant of the Lord your God, which he commanded you, and go and serve other gods and bow down to them. Then the anger of the Lord will be kindled against you, and you shall perish quickly from off the good land (*hâ-'ᵃdâmâh ha-ṭṭôbâh*) which he has given to you.

There is evidence that Israel had a bad conscience about the act of expropriation, which we call the conquest or the settlement, and sought to justify its conduct. The following passages indicate this. In Josh. 24: 13 Israel is reminded that she had not developed the land herself:

I gave you a land (*'ereṣ*) on which you had not labored, and cities which you had not built, and you dwell therein; you eat the fruit of vineyards and olive-yards which you did not plant.

In Josh. 24: 8 the land is called unequivocally the land of the Amorites. Similarly in Judg. 11: 19ff the consciousness that Israel had dispossessed a people of its land is clear: it had avoided doing so in the case of the Moabites and the Edomites (Judg. 11: 17–18). According to 2 Sam. 7: 23

---

[21] Notice that in Exod. 23: 29–30 Yahweh is to drive out the Canaanites gradually lest the land should become desolate because of the lack of labourers to work on it. Contrast Wis. 12: 3–10, 19, where the Canaanites are driven out slowly. In the Mekilta, Pisḥa (Lauterbach, p. 157), Ch. 18, the Canaanites are said to have voluntarily evacuated the land before the Israelites. On the ambiguity of Israel's "conquest" and its effect on its thought and religion, see below, p. 50. On the Holy War, see F. M. Cross, *Biblical Motifs*, ed. A. Altmann, Cambridge, Mass., 1966, pp. 11ff. For a sociological approach to the "conquest," see G. Mendenhall, B.A., Vol. 25, 1962, pp. 66–87. See also p. 50 below for contrast referred to in Wis. 12: 3ff.

the conquest of Canaan was made possible only through "great and terrible things" wrought by God in driving out a nation and its gods. In Num. 33: 50ff the sole justification for the occupation is that Yahweh has seen fit to give Israel the land; the initial price of occupation is high in destruction (33: 52), and then the demands of safety take their human toll; 33: 55, in view of Israeli attitudes towards Arabs, has a strangely modern ring:

But if you do not drive out the inhabitants of the land ('*eretz*) from before you, then those of them whom you let remain shall be as pricks in your eyes and thorns in your sides, and they shall trouble you in the land ('*eretz*) where you dwell.

Compare with this Josh. 23: 13.

know assuredly that the Lord your God will not continue to drive out these nations before you; but they shall be a snare and a trap for you, a scourge on your sides, and thorns in your eyes, till you perish from off this good land ('*adâmâh ha-ttôbâh*) which the Lord your God has given you.

In Deut. 9: 4ff a reason for Yahweh's gift of the land is offered: it is "because of the wickedness of these nations that the Lord is driving them out before you": the conquest is, thereby, justified. The same justification appears in Deut. 18: 9–14: it is implicit in Deut. 29: 2ff. Can we also detect a need for justification in Ps. 44: 3? It is Yahweh, not the sword, who gave Israel the land: here it is as if the conquest were divorced from Israel's own volition:

We have heard with our ears,
O God,
our fathers have told us,
what deeds thou didst perform in
their days,
in the days of old:
thou with thy own hand didst drive
out the nations,
but them thou didst plant;
thou didst afflict the peoples,
but them thou didst set free;
for not by their own sword did they
win the land ('*eretz*),
nor did their own arm give them
victory;

> but thy right hand, and thy arm,
> and the light of thy countenance:
> for thou didst delight in them.

In Ps. 105: 44f the taking of another people's toil in the conquest is justified, without elaboration, in terms of observance of the law (is it implied here that only in the land can the law be observed?).

> And he gave them the lands (*'arẓôth*) of the
> nations;
> and they took possession of the
> fruit of the peoples' toil,
> to the end that they should keep his
> statutes,
> and observe his laws.
> Praise the Lord!

As late as 1 Macc. the "bad conscience" over or the need for a justification of the conquest remains: in 1 Macc. 15: 33 we read:

We have neither taken other men's land (*gên*), nor have we possession of that which appertaineth to others, but of the inheritance of our fathers...

But there coexists also, with the recognition in such passages that the land really belonged to the Canaanites, the very ancient notion—to which von Rad, as we saw, drew attention—that the land belongs to Yahweh and is his to dispose of, so that he can promise it to Abraham. This notion, that the land belongs to Yahweh himself, persisted throughout the Old Testament and beyond it. It emerges in several ways, which we now present, but with little attempt at an ascription of these various ways to different strata in the tradition or according to a chronological sequence. In time the notion with which we are concerned, although the intensity with which it found expression varied at different periods, as we shall see, entered into the very life of Israel and touched it at innumerable points, so that for our purposes it suffices merely to indicate its nature. The following are some of the ways in which it expressed itself.

First, in the conviction that the earth of Israel was not tribal property, but was given by Yahweh for cultivation by lot: the individual received his parcel of land by lot and so, too, did the tribe. The whole land was divided according to lot, as in Num. 26: 55:

But the land (*'ereẓ*) shall be divided by lot; according to the names of the tribes of their fathers they shall inherit.

27

It is difficult to trace the use of the lot. In Num. 27: 21 it was the Urim and Thummim that were the sacred lots. The priest cast forth these sacred lots from his ephod—a kind of sacred vestment with a pouch, perhaps—and they provided responses to questions seeking affirmative or negative answers. The judgment rendered by the lots was thought to be that of Yahweh himself.[22] Thus, when Yahweh commanded that the land be divided according to lot, it was he himself who decided upon its division. The choice was not that of the people of Israel. It is highly significant that in Ezek. 47, 48, even the sacred lots are ignored and the division of the land which surrounds the New Temple of the future age was to be at Yahweh's direct command, because the land was Yahweh's alone, and he alone could decide its allocation (47: 13f):

> Thus says the Lord God: "These are the boundaries by which you shall divide the land ('eret̩z) for inheritance among the twelve tribes of Israel. Joseph shall have two portions. And you shall divide it equally; I swore to give it to your fathers, and this land ('eret̩z) shall fall to you as your inheritance."

Secondly, the cultic statements about the harvest are to be understood in the light of Yahweh's ownership of the land. For example, this explains the demand for the offering of firstlings; of the first son in Exod. 22: 28; the tithe given to the Levites in Lev. 18: 24; the tithe of all the yield of the seed in Deut. 14: 22; and of all the produce in Deut. 26: 9–15. In the Hebraic mind the first of a particular series was the archetypal form, and as such represented the entire species. Thus the offering of the first fruits symbolized the offering of the entire crop or harvest. Since Yahweh was the owner of the land, the first-fruit offering was only a rendering to him of his proper portion. For as the land belonged to Yahweh so rightfully did all the produce. His ownership was symbolically acknowledged through the offering of first fruits. The same concept governed the custom of gleaning.[23]

Again, thirdly, Yahweh's possession of the land is acknowledged in the commandment that the land should keep a Sabbath to the Lord (Lev.

[22] On Urim and Thummim, see R. de Vaux, *Ancient Israel: Its Life and Institutions*, trans., New York, 1961, pp. 352f. Deut. 19: 14 reads: "Do not move your neighbour's boundary stone, Fixed by the men of former times in the patrimony which you shall occupy in the land the Lord your God gives you for your possession." The point is that the boundary stones had been set by the men of old at Yahweh's command and, thus, not even the Israelites, the elect of Yahweh, could alter the established pattern which he had imposed upon his land (see G. von Rad, *Studies in Deuteronomy*, trans., 1953, p. 59).

[23] See Buber, *Israel and Palestine*, pp. 3–6; J. Pedersen, *Israel: Its Life and Culture*, London, 1926, Vol. III–IV, p. 306. For criticisms of the work of Pedersen, see J. Barr, *The Semantics of Biblical Language*, Oxford, 1961.

25: 2, 4). Pedersen interpreted this commandment as an encouragement to the Israelites to show proper respect to the soil and to use it wisely to assure its continued productivity. Buber saw it as a validation of the covenant promise, a reiteration of the vow made by the Israelites to live faithfully under the statutes and laws of Yahweh.[24] But another explanation is possible. Lev. 25: 2 reads: "...the land (*há-'áretẓ*) shall keep a sabbath to the Lord." It is not the people who are commanded to allow the land to rest: rather the land itself, personified, seems to be addressed. The land, too, owes worship to Yahweh, to signify that special relationship which it enjoys with him. The land's rest recalls the seventh-day rest of the Lord himself after the creation, and came to symbolize Yahweh's creation and ownership of the land.[25]

And, fourthly, Yahweh's possession of the land was expressed in terms of "holiness," a conception which in its origin had little, if anything, to do with morality, but rather denoted a relationship of separation for or consecration to a god. Since the land was Yahweh's possession, it enjoyed a certain degree of closeness to him; for Yahweh dwelt in the midst of Israel. (Num. 35: 34 reads: "You shall not defile the land ('*eretẓ*) in which you live, in the midst of which I dwell; for I the Lord dwell in the midst of the people of Israel.") Because Yahweh was near to it, his own holiness radiated throughout its boundaries.[26] Note that the term "holy land," which suggests that the land itself was inherently "holy" seldom occurs in the Old Testament; that is, the holiness of the land is entirely derivative.[27]

---

[24] See Pedersen, *Israel*, Vol. I–II, p. 480; Buber, *Israel and Palestine*, pp. 4–6, 14ff.

[25] The injunction to keep the weekly Sabbath in Exod. 20: 8–10 is justified by reference to the Sabbath rest of Yahweh at creation. There is no reason not to transfer this justification to the Sabbath of the land (every seven years) and to the Jubilee year (every fifty years). Ancient oriental custom recognized the need to leave the land uncultivated to ensure its future fertility. In Israel this need was transferred to a theological plane: the Sabbath of the land signified the sole proprietorship of Yahweh. The basic principle is set forth in Lev. 25: 23. The idea that the Sabbath is designed to recall God's rest at creation emerges in Jos., *Antiquities*, 1: 33. "...and on the seventh [day] God rested and had respite from his labours, for which reason we also pass this day in repose from toil, and call it the Sabbath, a word which in the Hebrew language means 'rest' (Loeb, trans., p. 17)." See also Mekilta, Kaspa (Lauterbach, p. 177), Ch. 3.

[26] Pedersen, *Israel*, Vol. III–IV, pp. 264–295; Buber, *Israel and Palestine*, pp. 3–10. W. R. Smith, *Lectures on the Religion of the Semites*, New York, 1969, p. 140 ("while it is not easy to fix the exact idea of holiness in ancient Semitic religion, it is quite certain that it has nothing to do with morality and purity of life."); E. Durkheim, *The Elementary Forms of Religious Life*, New York, 1915, pp. 301–325.

[27] Ps. 78: 54 is instructive. The RSV renders: "And he brought them to *his* holy land, to the mountain which his right hand had won (our italic)." The land was holy because Yahweh had drawn near to it. The word אֶרֶץ (land) is missing. The M.T. reads: וַיְבִיאֵם אֶל־גְּבוּל. גְּבוּל But קָדְשׁוֹ הַר־זֶה קָנְתָה יְמִינוֹ (boundary) is used not only of a boundary, but of

29

Nevertheless, the potency of the concept of the holiness of the land, though only derived from its relationship to Yahweh, emerges particularly in those passages which so forcibly and vividly personify the land. Consider the following passages:

You shall therefore keep all my statutes and all my ordinances, and do them; that the land (*hâ-'âret̲z*) where I am bringing you to dwell may not vomit you out. And you shall not walk in the customs of the nation which I am casting out before you; for they did all these things, and therefore I abhorred them. But I have said to you, "You shall inherit their land (*'ad͏ᵉmâthâm*), and I will give it to you to possess, a land (*'eret̲z*) flowing with milk and honey." I am the Lord your God, who have separated you from the peoples. You shall therefore make a distinction between the clean beast and the unclean, and between the unclean bird and the clean; you shall not make yourselves abominable by beast or by bird or by anything with which the ground teems, which I have set apart for you to hold unclean. You shall be holy to me; for I the Lord am holy, and have separated you from the peoples, that you should be mine (Lev. 20: 22–26) (H: P).

In the above, the land is conceived of as itself ejecting Israelites when they are unfaithful to the commandments. One might conclude from this that it was the transgression of the specifically Israelite law, the Torah, that provoked the land and caused it to react violently. But Lev. 18: 24–30 reads as follows:

Do not defile yourselves by any of these things, for by all these the nations I am casting out before you defiled themselves; and the land (*hâ-'âret̲z*) became defiled, so that I punished its iniquity, and the land vomited out its inhabitants. But you shall keep my statutes and my ordinances and do none of these abominations, either the native or the stranger who sojourns among you (for all of these abominations the men of the land (*hâ-'aret̲z*) did, who were before you, so that the land (*hâ-'âret̲z*) became defiled); lest the land (*hâ-'âret̲z*) vomit you out,

a land within the boundary, and so becomes sometimes an equivalent for *'eret̲z*. See BDB, p. 148. There is no other instance of the term "holy land" in the Psalms. We find "holy ground" (MT אַדְמַת קֹדֶשׁ: LXX γῆ ἁγία) in Exod. 3: 5, but this is outside the land. Again it is the proximity of Yahweh alone that lends holiness to a place, or ground, or land. "Holy ground" appears in Zech. 2: 16: "And the Lord will inherit Judah as his portion in the holy land (RSV 2: 12, MT 2: 16)." There follow the words: "and will again choose Jerusalem." The Hebrew is:

וְנָחַל יהוה אֶת־יְהוּדָה חֶלְקוֹ עַל־אַדְמַת הַקֹּדֶשׁ וּבָחַר עוֹד בִּירוּשָׁלָ͏ִם

אֲדָמָה is here the equivalent of אֶרֶץ. The term "holy land" occurs in II Macc. 1: 7, and Wis. 12: 3 (thy holy land); 2 Bar. 63: 9–11; 84: 8 has "holy land"; Sib. Or. 111. 266–267 has "holy soil"; 4 Ezra 13: 48 reads "holy border," and "land of salvation." Ps. 106: 24 has "pleasant land"; Sib. Or. 111. 280 "fruitful land."

when you defile it, as it vomited out the nation that was before you. For whoever shall do any of these abominations, the persons that do them shall be cut off from my charge never to practice any of these abominable customs which were practices before you, and never to defile yourselves by them: I am the Lord your God (H: P).

In this passage the land had been defiled by its pre-Israelite inhabitants, who did not know the Torah, but had broken its demands. It was not the military prowess of the Israelites, nor even Yahweh's fighting for them, which had caused the expulsion of the inhabitants of the land. No! When it became defiled by the abominations of its inhabitants, the land itself thrust them out. It did this because of its holiness. The implication is that it is not even the presence of the Torah that lends it holiness. The land was already characterized by holiness before Israel brought the Torah: it was already holy in Canaanite days because Yahweh owned it and dwelt in the midst of it. This is the import of Num. 35: 34: "You shall not defile the land in which you live, in the midst of which I dwell, for I the Lord dwell in the midst of the people of Israel."

It was this very same relationship of the land to Yahweh that governed the relationship of the Law to the land, although the Law itself did not lend holiness to the land. If the Israelites were to live in Yahweh's land, in his very presence, they had to approximate to his holiness by following his Law: the verse "You shall be holy; for I the Lord your God am holy (Lev. 19: 1)" implies that Israel is to obey Yahweh's Law. And, in much of the Old Testament, obedience to the Law becomes the condition of occupying the land, as we have already seen. We shall return to this theme later. Suffice it here to refer to Is. 1: 19:

If you are willing and obedient, you shall eat the good of the land (*hâ-'âretẕ*);

And, again we read in Deut. 4: 40:

Therefore you shall keep his statutes and his commandments, which I command you this day, that it may go well with you, and that you may prolong your days in the land (*hâ-'ᵃdâmâh*) which the Lord your God gives you for ever.

Here it is important to recognize that Yahweh had imposed on the land— indeed upon nature—a sacred order or pattern or law, the violation of which produced a dissolution, a return to chaotic disorder and formlessness. This can best be illustrated from those laws which, when disobeyed, are specifically stated to pollute or defile the land of Israel. We note certain prohibitions:

31

(a) *Against harlotry*

Do not profane your daughter by making her a harlot, lest the land fall into harlotry and the land (*hâ-'áretz*) become full of wickedness (Lev. 19: 29) (H: P).

(b) *Against shedding blood*

And these things shall be for a statute and ordinance to you throughout your generations in all your dwellings. If any one kills a person, the murderer shall be put to death on the evidence of witnesses; but no person shall be put to death on the testimony of one witness. Moreover you shall accept no ransom for the life of a murderer, who is guilty of death; but he shall be put to death. And you shall accept no ransom for him who has fled to his city of refuge, that he may return to dwell in the land (*hâ-'áretz*) before the death of the high priest. You shall not thus pollute the land (*hâ-'áretz*) in which you live; for blood pollutes the land (*hâ-'áretz*), and no expiation can be made for the land (*hâ-'áretz*), for the blood that is shed in it, except by the blood of him who shed it. You shall not defile the land (*hâ-'áretz*) in which you live, in the midst of the people of Israel (Num. 35: 29–34).

And all the elders of that city nearest to the slain man shall wash their hands over the heifer whose neck was broken in the valley; and they shall testify, "Our hands did not shed this blood, neither did our eyes see it shed. Forgive, O Lord, thy people Israel, whom thou hast redeemed, and set not the guilt of innocent blood in the midst of thy people Israel; but let the guilt of blood be forgiven them. So you shall purge the guilt of innocent blood from your midst, when you do what is right in the sight of the Lord (Deut. 21: 6–9)."

> They poured out innocent blood, the blood of their sons and daughters,
> whom they sacrificed to the idols of Canaan; and the land (*hâ-'áretz*) was
>   polluted with blood.
> Thus they became unclean by their acts, and played the harlot in their doings
>   (Ps. 106: 38–39).

(c) *Against allowing a corpse to remain hanging on a tree*

And if a man has committed a crime punishable by death, and you hang him on a tree, his body shall not remain all night upon the tree, but you shall bury him the same day, for a hanged man is accursed by God; you shall not defile your land (*'ad^emáth^eka*) which the Lord your God gives you for an inheritance (Deut. 21: 22–23).

(d) *Against remarriage with a former divorced and remarried wife*

When a man takes a wife and marries her, if then she finds no favour in his eyes because he has found some indecency in her, and he writes her a bill of divorce and puts it in her hand and sends her out of his house, and she departs out of his house, and if she goes and becomes another man's wife, and the latter husband dislikes her and writes her a bill of divorce and puts it in her hand and sends her out of the house, of if the latter husband dies, who took her to be his wife, then her former husband, who sent her away, may not take her again to be his wife, after she has been defiled; for that is an abomination before the Lord, and you shall not bring guilt upon the land (*hā-'áreṯ*) which the Lord your God gives you for an inheritance (Deut. 24: 1–4, compare Jer. 3: 1).

To examine the background of these prohibitions in full is not possible here. Fundamental is what Pedersen[28] has emphasized as the concept of totality within the Israelite community. Everything within that community had its proper place: everything in the natural order was divided according to function or kind. For example, there could be no violation of species, no crossing of the boundaries set between differing groups. This explains the prohibitions expressed in Lev. 19: 19; 22: 5, 9, 10, 11. The first passage Lev. 19: 19 reads as follows:

You shall keep my statutes. You shall not let your cattle breed with a different kind; you shall not sow your field with two kinds of seed; nor shall there come upon you a garment of cloth made of two kinds of stuff (H).

[28] Pedersen, *Israel*, Vol. I–II, p. 485. Unfortunately the work of Morton Smith, *Palestinian Parties and Politics that Shaped the Old Testament*, New York, 1971, came too late for use. He dates H (Lev. 17–26), in 600–500 B.C. On p. 101 Smith seems to connect it with the period between 587 and 539: presumably this was when it was combined with strictly P materials. According to him, H carried to its "illogical conclusions" the position of what he calls the "Yahweh-alone party" that Israel was to be a holy people isolated by its peculiar purity. But, as Morton Smith recognizes, not all agree with this late dating of the Holiness Code. It is introduced by R. J. Faley, JBC, p. 78, as follows: "The earliest part of [Leviticus], this originally independent collection of laws, inspired much of the later Priestly teaching and legislation. It represents a compilation of the pre-exilic Jerusalem clergy. Collected and edited before 586, most of the laws proceed from an earlier period, with some added at a time of later editing during and after the Exile itself." N. H. Snaith favours a date for H between 600 and 570 B.C., between D and P, with "many traces of earlier material, and many traces of later (mostly P) material, *Peake*, p. 241." See further Smith, *Palestinian Parties*, pp. 140, 260, n. 70. Of extreme importance is Smith's treatment of Nehemiah, pp. 126–147. Understanding Nehemiah in the light of Greek "tyrants" of his period, and comparing his work with the codification of law going on in the contemporary Greece, he gives to him a special role in the history of Judaism. He writes: "[Nehemiah] seems to have won majority support for the program of the Yahweh-alone party. With this achievement the party position becomes that of the Judaeans generally; for the first time it becomes a territorial, if not a national, religion in fact, as well as in ideal...the separation from the neighbouring peoples was now a *fait accompli*...the position of the Yahweh-alone party may first be called 'Judaism'—that is, the religion of (most) Judaeans.... The national, political and territorial side of Judaism, by which it differed from the other hellenistic forms of oriental religions, was, as a practical matter, the work of Nehemiah. He secured to the religion that double character—local as well as universal—which made it endure, in fact, for five hundred years, and, in its terrible consequences, yet endures (pp. 144–146)." Smith is careful to note that the traditions and aspirations of the religion demanded a connection between Judaism and the worship of the restored Temple (p. 147), which made possible the development to which he refers. But contrast J. A. Sanders's understanding of the effect of the Exile with Smith's. They are antithetical. The Exile demotes the land in Sanders: through Nehemiah's work the territorial aspect of Judaism finds a surer hold in Smith.

There is a Yahweh-given order of the cosmos; a division is set between the sacred and the profane (Lev. 22: 5ff).

And it can safely be asserted that each of the prohibitions singled out above is directed against the violation of that order and the mixing of the sacred and profane which leads to the disintegration and profanation of the whole cosmos. Thus prostitution violated the concept of totality. The prostitute withdrew from the community as an integrated whole: she violated the sacred divisions set by Yahweh, by dissolving the boundaries between kinds.[29] Again, blood was especially holy to Semites: blood was life:[30] it was the possession of Yahweh as his portion of a sacrificial feast, and so was sacred. To shed blood was to handle what was sacred as if it were profane. So, too, because dead bodies were one of the major sources of uncleanness, to allow a corpse to lie in the land, and especially to hang it on a tree, was to subject the land, which in virtue of its relation to Yahweh was holy, to uncleanness.[31] From the corpse uncleanness spread like a contagion throughout the surrounding area: the totality of nature was thereby affected. And, finally, the prohibition against remarrying one's divorced wife who had remarried was governed by the recognition that such a woman was in a similar case to the prostitute: she had known two distinctive men. To return to her first husband was to mix diverse kinds and *ipso facto* to join together one who was clean (the first husband) with one who had, by her second marriage, become unclean. Again, such a violation of the natural order involved the whole cosmos, and is particularly manifested in the land itself.[32]

[29] Pedersen, *Israel*, Vol. I–II, p. 485.

[30] Lev. 17: 11ff; Pedersen, *Israel*, Vol. I–II, p. 172; Durkheim, *Elementary Forms*, p. 137.

[31] Deut. 21: 22–23. S. R. Driver's comment, *Deuteronomy*, ICC, Edinburgh, 1895, pp. 284f, is apt (note that the malefactor was hung not for the purpose of being executed, but after execution as an additional disgrace, compare Josh. 10: 26; 2 Sam. 4: 12): "probably the exposure of a malefactor's corpse by hanging was resorted to only in the case of heinous offences: it could be taken therefore as significant of the curse of God (Gen. 4: 11; Deut. 27: 24) resting specially upon the offender; and as murder, like other abominable crimes, was held to render the land in which it was perpetrated unclean (Num. 35: 33f; Lev. 18: 4f, 27f), so the unburied corpse, suspended aloft, with the crime as it were clinging to it, and God's curse resting visibly upon it, had a similar effect. Hence, as soon as the requisite publicity has been attained, the spectacle is to end: the corpse, at sunset, is to be taken down, and committed to the earth, as a token that justice has completed its work, and that the land has been cleansed from the defilement infecting it...."

[32] On the role of the land itself in casting out those that defile it, see Pedersen, *Israel*, Vol. I–II, pp. 454ff; Ellis, *The Yahwist*, p. 237. But Gen. 19: 28 does not illustrate this theme: "the smoke of the land" in the story of Sodom and Gomorrah. It is tempting to relate all the above to recent preoccupation, especially in the U.S.A., with problems of ecology. Primitive as much of the Old Testament ideas may appear, would not greater attention to them as they bear on the land have helped us earlier to acknowledge the ecological dangers that now threaten? It would appear that those who discuss ecology generally neglect these Old Testament concepts. See, for example, Lynn White, "The Historical Roots of our Ecologic Crisis,"

But it is merely for the sake of clarity that we have concentrated on the above four prohibitions. What is true of them holds true of every violation of Yahweh's commandments. Yahweh dwells in Israel. Through the contagion of his holiness the land becomes clean. Violation of Yahweh's Law is a profanation of the order which he has implanted in the cosmos. And when, through the violation of that Law, Israelites have profaned themselves, they can no longer remain in the holy-clean land; either the land itself ejects them, as in some passages, or the land suffers under the wrath which they have brought upon it, in which case, as Is. 24: 4–5 puts the matter:

The earth (hâ-'áretz) mourns and withers, the world languishes and withers; the heavens languish together with the earth (hâ-'áretz). The earth (hâ-'áretz) lies polluted under its inhabitants: for they have transgressed the laws, violated the statutes, broken the everlasting covenant.

In the above pages we have separated two peculiar emphases in the Old Testament understanding of the land. The first is an historical one, centred on the promise to Abraham and appearing chiefly in the narrative portions of the Hexateuch, in J and E. The second is a cultic one, concentrating on the conception of the land as Yahweh's own possession and appearing chiefly in the legislative portions of the Hexateuch, D and P. Although derived from different sources, these two emphases became merged in the cultic life of Israel and in its transmission of various traditional documents, so that, as the Old Testament now stands, they have to be carefully disentangled. The proper assessment of the role they played throughout the history of Israel is difficult of achievement. We shall postpone such an assessment and, at this juncture, simply refer to the treatment of the land in passages outside the Hexateuch.

Science, Vol. 155, March 1967, pp. 1203–1207; Philosophy of Religion and Theology: 1971, American Academy of Religion, 1971, pp. 3–13, 14–28. Contrast Barr, BJRL, vol. 55, 1972, pp. 9ff. But he too does not refer to our passages. For the emphasis on shedding blood in Hellenistic circles, see H. D. Betz, "Religio-Historical Understanding of Apocalypticism," Journal for Theology and the Church, Vol. 6, Apocalypticism, ed. R. W. Funk, pp. 143–150.

III. THE LAND IN THE PROPHETS: DOOM
AND RESTORATION

One thing seems clear: concern with the land and hope for the land emerges at many places in the Old Testament outside the Hexateuch. While the promise was regarded as fulfilled in the settlement, that settlement was not regarded as a complete fulfilment. Deuteronomy makes it clear that there is still a future to look forward to: the land has to achieve rest and peace.[1] This points to what von Rad calls one of the most interesting problems of Old Testament Theology. He expresses it thus: "Promises which have been fulfilled in history are not thereby exhausted of their content, but remain as promises on a different level, although they are to some extent metamorphosed in the process. The promise of the land was proclaimed ever anew, even after its fulfillment, as a future benefit of God's redemptive activity."[2] Promise and fulfillment inform much of the Old Testament, and the tradition, however changed, continued to contain the hope of life in the land.

Thus it is arguable that it was as inconceivable to the prophets as to the people as a whole that Israel should finally be deprived of her land. At this point, we encounter a notorious problem of proportion in the interpretation of the prophets. It has been easy and, indeed, almost customary, to assert that the impact of the prophetic sources is to suggest something as follows: the prophets insisted on Yahweh's freedom to choose and to reject Israel from the beginning, but they recognized that Israel as a whole had been unfaithful to her covenant with him, and maintained that Yahweh could exist without his people, that, indeed, it might become his will to destroy them. The prophets pronounced doom on people and land: it is this message of doom that rings like a knell most dominantly in their words. And the fact is pointed out that one, at least, of the greatest of the prophets seems to have been able to feel only a loose commitment to

---

[1] In one sense the very entry into the promised land was expected to be the achievement of rest (Deut. 12:9; 25:19), but the "rest" did not materialize. In Deut. 28:65ff the possible future "unease" of Israel is recognized with terrible clarity. Despite the centrality of the settlement in the land in Deuteronomy, it also looks forward to a future blessing—"rest." See G. von Rad's "A Rest for the People of God," *The Problem of the Hexateuch*, New York, 1966, pp. 94ff; for "rest" in later sources, see H. D. Betz, "The Logion of the Easy Yoke and of Rest", JBL, Vol. 86, 1967, pp. 10–24. See further, W. Zimmerli, *Man and His Hope in the Old Testament*, Naperville, Ill., 1968, pp. 74f. He refers to H. H. Schmid, "Das Verständnis der Geschichte im Deuteronomium," ZTK, Vol. 64, 1967, pp. 1–15.

[2] *The Problem of the Hexateuch*, pp. 92f.

the land, deep as was his love for it. The advice of Jeremiah to the exiles in Babylon deserves quotation.

These are the words of the letter which Jeremiah the prophet sent from Jerusalem to the elders of the exiles, and to the priests, the prophets, and all the people, whom Nebuchadnezzar had taken into exile from Jerusalem to Babylon. "Thus says the Lord of hosts, the God of Israel, to all the exiles whom I have sent into exile from Jerusalem to Babylon: Build houses and live in them; plant gardens and eat their produce. Take wives and have sons and daughters; take wives for your sons, and give your daughters in marriage, that they may bear sons and daughters; multiply there, and do not decrease. But seek the welfare of the city where I have sent you into exile, and pray to the Lord on its behalf, for in its welfare you will find your welfare. For thus says the Lord of hosts, the God of Israel: Do not let your prophets and your diviners who are among you deceive you, and do not listen to the dreams which they dream, for it is a lie which they are prophesying to you in my name: I did not send them, says the Lord (Jer. 29: 1, 4–9)."

A recent commentator on this passage writes:

. . . this letter reveals the most amazing combination of vision and commonsense. For the exiles, incited by their prophets, were refusing to settle down: their only thought was of speedy return to the homeland. Their hatred of Babylon led to riots which resulted in the summary "taking-off" of two of their most prominent and rabid prophets (22). Here Jeremiah lays a cool hand on hot heads lest by their rashness they should all perish in a pogrom in Babylon. All this is easily understood. Deuteronomy had made it impossible for a good Jew to live in an alien land. If Jerusalem be the only place where worship of Yahweh is possible, and if all life's activities such as building, planting, marrying and begetting children be associated with the religious cult, how could they escape a feeling of total frustration? For the cult was impossible in Babylon: only in Jerusalem could Yahweh be worshipped. Here Jeremiah writes to say that the world is God's world and God is not limited to Jerusalem and its Temple. Prayer is possible in Babylon (7) and the man who prayed for his enemies (18: 20) gives them the unique injunction to pray for Babylon. That was a "hard saying" for the Jews and it is without parallel in the O.T. God, too, has a plan and a purpose that embraces the Jews in Babylon and his plan is for good and not for evil. The vision may tarry—70 years it may tarry—but it will be fulfilled. And God can be found, or rather "lets himself be found," in Babylon: the "unclean land" becomes the sphere of revelation (12).[3]

In the popular mind the return from Babylon was an absolute necessity: for Jeremiah it was no urgent matter, although he was hopeful that some

[3] J. Paterson, *Peake*, p. 555.

day it would occur:[4] for the moment, to return to the land would be to follow false prophecy.

But not only in 29: 1, 4–9 does Jeremiah take a positive view of the exile. Jeremiah 29: 16–20 and 38: 2 make clear that those who were not deported, but remained in the land and in the city of Jerusalem, would know the sword and famine and pestilence. The words of Jer. 38: 2 are unequivocal: "Thus saith the Lord, He who stays in this city shall die by the sword, by famine, and by pestilence; but he who goes out to the Chaldeans shall live; he shall have his life as a prize of war, and live." Equally striking is the vision of the good and bad figs in Jer. 24: 1–30. The good figs are the exiles.

Thus says the Lord, the God of Israel: "Like these good figs, so I will regard as good the exiles from Judah, whom I have sent away from this place to the land of the Chaldeans (Jer. 24: 5)."

The evil figs are those who remain in the land.

But thus says the Lord: "Like the bad figs which are so bad they cannot be eaten, so will I treat Zedekiah the king of Judah, his princes, the remnant of Jerusalem who remain in this land ('*eretz*), and those who dwell in the land of Egypt. I will make them a horror to all the kingdoms of the earth, to be a reproach, a byword, a taunt, and a curse in all the places where I shall drive them. And I will send sword, famine, and pestilence upon them, until they shall be utterly destroyed from the land ('*adâmâh*) which I gave to them and their fathers (Jer. 24: 8–9)."

---

4 E. W. Heaton, *The Hebrew Kingdoms*, London, 1968, pp. 379f. He writes: "never was so far-reaching a religious revolution expounded in so short a document. Jeremiah knew from his own experience and now just takes it for granted that communion with God was independent of the religion of the Temple and, therefore, unaffected by the exiles' removal to a foreign land.... This insight represents not only a turning-point for the future development of Judaism, but the triumph of a faith grounded in history over the sanctuary-based religion of the ancient Near East." But Heaton recognized that Israel will not—in Jeremiah's mind— be finally separated from the land: see Jer. 32: 1–15; *The Hebrew Kingdoms*, pp. 383f, and below p. 43. On the distinction between the "historical" emphasis in the Old Testament and Judaism and other major religions where the re-enactment of myth in the cultus was central, see M. Eliade, *Cosmos and History*, New York, 1959, chapter 3, pp. 102ff. A. C. Charity, *Events and Their Afterlife: The Dialectics of Christian Typology in the Bible and Dante*, Cambridge, 1966, pp. 31ff, excellently shows how the belief in the promise is only possible because of Israel's experienced steadfastness of God in the past, hence the later Hebrew word for promise, see p. 167, n. 12, rests on the verb *bâtah*. Charity writes, "Faith in God's steadfastness finds in him the guarantee of the unity and continuity of history. It is thus too that Israel can make God's past action the bearer not only of present conditions...but also of promise for the future, of coming fulfilment....Yahweh's 'steadfastness'...makes prophecy possible." Note, however, Eliade's insistence, *Cosmos*, pp. 111–112, that, no less than non-Hebraic religions, Jewish Messianism also revolts against history but by abolishing it in "the end of the days."

For Jeremiah the exile is the fulfilment of the purpose of God: the exiles are blessed in their disaster.

The same theology re-emerges in Ezek. 17 in the parable of the eagle and the cedar.

Tell them that these are the words of the Lord God: A great eagle with broad wings and long pinions, in full plumage, richly patterned, came to Lebanon. He took the very top of a cedar-tree, he plucked its highest twig; he carried it off to a land of commerce, and planted it in a city of merchants. Then he took a native seed and put it in a nursery-ground; he set it like a willow, a shoot beside abundant water. It sprouted and became a vine, sprawling low along the ground and bending its trailing boughs towards him with its roots growing beneath him. So it became a vine, it branched out and put forth shoots.

Over against this picture is another: a picture of those in the land of Israel who forsake the covenant and perish. But the top of the tree transported in the first picture stands for those who are to go into exile. There, according to 17: 14, they are to be able to keep the covenant and, therefore, stand. As in Jeremiah, the exile proves a blessing.

But no other prophet provides such unequivocal testimony to the possibility of the good life apart from the land, and we may well ask whether the attitude of Jeremiah and Ezekiel indicated above was as unclouded as we have suggested. As the prophetic books now stand, alongside prophecies of doom against the land because of Israel's sin, there are promises of restoration. This is particularly conspicuous in Amos. After the most dire predictions of doom throughout the body of the oracles, at the very end in Amos 9: 14–15 we read:

"I will restore the fortunes of my people Israel, and they shall rebuild the ruined cities and inhabit them; they shall plant vineyards and drink their wine, and they shall make gardens and eat their fruit. I will plant them upon their land ('ad^emâthâm), and they shall never again be plucked up out of the land ('ad^e-mâthâm) which I have given them," says the Lord your God.

Compare also the incidence of prophecies of restoration in Hos. 1: 10; Is. 2: 1–5; 9: 1–9 (both possibly Isaianic); 9: 10–16; 24–27; 26: 15–20; 29: 16–21; 32: 15–20; Jer. 3: 18–19; 11: 4–5; Ezek. 4: 15. There can be little doubt that many such messages of restoration in the prophetic sources, as they now stand, are due to editorial processes operative after disaster had befallen. These were aimed at the domestication of the prophets so as to draw their sting. Like the generality in Israel, stung to the quick by prophetic denunciation and foreboding, pious scribes could not reconcile

THE GOSPEL AND THE LAND

themselves to the severity of the prophets. So they provided addenda to the prophets' oracles to soften their implacable stance against Israel. The prophets' messages of doom could not possibly have been their last word! They had to be muffled. The question, however, is whether *all* the prophecies of restoration to the land are to be so understood.⁵

There seems to be a paradoxical "nationalism," or rather attachment to Israel and her land, in the prophets, and, if we exclude Amos and Isaiah, they reveal a persistent yearning for the ingathering of the dispersed of Israel into one national entity in their own land. A quick glance at the major prophets is necessary.

⁵ The claim of S. Schechter that there was a bias against the acceptance of passages of restoration in modern critical scholarship is still worth pondering. If such a bias existed, it was not unrelated to what we wrote on pp. 3ff, above. It has now been eliminated, and the tendency toward the domestication of the "independent" prophets is noted by Heaton, *The Hebrew Kingdoms*, p. 241. He writes of "the tendency in popular tradition to approximate the independent prophets to the more familiar institutional prophets." His treatment of the prophets in recent scholarship is illuminating. While emphasizing the independence of the canonical prophets, Heaton also recognizes that they were not "isolated individuals detached from the mainstream of Israel's religious tradition...the content of their message proves beyond any doubt that they were heirs to and representatives of the continuing tradition of Mosaic Yahwism, as it found expression in the ministry of the priests at loyal sanctuaries and in the teaching given both in the schools of wisdom and in the domestic circle of the family..." But he adds: "There is equally no doubt, however, that their reinterpretation of Mosaic Yahwism was radical in the extreme—so radical, that the preservation of their preaching will never cease to be a source of wonder (pp. 243f)." Heaton refers to the "shocking" character of the independent prophets' words, which was matched by their shocking exploitation of all sorts of familiar forms in their style. He further refers to an "intellectual tradition" on which Amos and others drew. But he refuses to contemplate circles of disciples around the individual prophets. He thinks rather of the preservation of their written words. Heaton's presentation must now be compared with that of L. Finkelstein, *New Light from the Prophets*, London, 1969. Mr J. R. Lundbom drew my attention to Wellhausen's words, "Roses and lavender instead of blood and iron (*Die kleinen Propheten*, 1898, p. 96)," to describe the change which occurs at Amos 9: 8–15. Wellhausen set the pattern for the dating of the passages of hope. The "doxologies" in Amos 4: 13; 5: 8–9; 9: 5–6, and, more importantly, for our purposes, Hos. 11: 8–11; 14: 2–9 were considered late (see O. Eissfeldt, *The Old Testament: An Introduction*, trans., Oxford 1965, p. 387). Recent commentators, H. W. Wolff and Victor Maag, indicate the current trend toward treating such passages as authentic.

A cycle seems apparent in the prophets' thoughts on the land—an emphasis on its fertility as Yahweh's land (Amos 2: 10; Hos. 12: 9; Jer. 2: 7; 27: 5; Ezek. 36: 20); on the defilement of the land by Israel's sin (Hos. 10: 4; Is. 2: 7–8; 5: 8; Jer. 2: 7; 3: 2; 16: 18); on the anger of the Lord (Amos 1: 2; 4: 6; Micah 1: 3–5; Jer. 10: 10–13; Hos. 4: 3; Is. 7: 23–25; Ezek. 5: 16–17); on the barrenness and the loss of the land (Hos. 5: 7; Micah 2: 2–4; Is. 1: 7; Jer. 8: 16; Ezek. 7: 22); on the loss of the land as the ultimate punishment (Amos 6: 7; Hos. 9: 17; Is. 6: 11–12; Jer. 23: 12); on restoration after purification. This last takes two forms: (*a*) Yahweh protects the land when it is invaded and promises retribution to those who harm it, Amos 1: 13; Micah 5: 6; Is. 13: 5; 9: 14: in these passages the reference is *not* to the land of Israel. So, too, in Jer. 25: 38. See also Is. 10: 14; 14: 2, 18, 20, 25; 19: 17; 22: 18; 23: 13; 34: 7, 9; Jer. 12: 16–17; 25: 12–14. (*b*) Restoration to the land of Israel from exile: Amos 9: 13–15 (if permissible); Hos. 14: 7 (if permissible); Is. 16: 4; 26: 9–10, 15, 18; 30: 24; Jer. 32: 38–44; 29: 14; 30: 3ff. The pre-exilic prophets dwell heavily on famines, earthquakes: the exilic prophets, naturally, on exile and restoration. It is Jeremiah who most frequently speaks directly of the land.

40

At first sight there is nothing in Amos to suggest the recognition of a peculiar relationship between Israel and her land. But it is significant that Israel's punishment for her sins takes the two forms, among others, of a redistribution of the land and exile from it.

Therefore thus says the Lord: "Your wife shall be a harlot in the city, and your sons and your daughters shall fall by the sword, and your land (*'ad'māth'kā*) shall be parceled out by line; you yourself shall die in an unclean land (*'ªdāmāh*), and Israel shall surely go into exile away from its land (*'ad'māthô*) (7: 17: compare 5: 26)."

This verse, where the word "land" recurs three times, implies that the land is holy as divided by Yahweh, but it is to be rendered unclean through being profaned by a redistribution not according to his will. The horror of death in the land of Israel rendered unclean is set in parallelism with exile from the land itself. The verse, 7: 17, is instinct with the awareness of the significance of the land. There may be a glimmer of hope for people in the land expressed in 5: 14, but the closing words of Amos 9: 11–15 speaking of a coming salvation cannot certainly be derived from the prophet, so that any future restoration of the people and its land can only be very tenatively found, if at all, in Amos.[6]

It is otherwise when we turn to Hosea. The words of hope in Hos. 1: 10–11 can only very doubtfully be ascribed to the prophet, but those of 2: 14–23 may be taken as his:

Therefore, behold, I will allure her, and bring her into the wilderness, and speak tenderly to her. And there I will give her her vineyards, and make the Valley of Achor a door of hope. And there she shall answer as in the days of her youth, as at the time when she came out of the land (*'eretẓ*) of Egypt. And in that day, says the Lord, you will call me, "My husband," and no longer will you call me, "My Baal." For I will remove the names of the Baals from her mouth, and they shall be mentioned by name no more. And I will make for you a covenant on that day with the beasts of the field, the birds of the air, and the creeping things of the ground (*'ªdāmāh*); and I will abolish the bow, the sword, and war from the land (*'eretẓ*); and I will make you lie down in safety. And I will betroth you to me for ever; I will betroth you to me in righteousness and in

---

[6] Amos 3: 12 has been taken to mean that a remnant would be preserved, see A. Benson, CBQ, Vol. 19, 1957, pp. 199–212; J. P. Hyatt, *Peake*, p. 617, section 541 d., refers without documentation to an expectation of a remnant in Amos, presumably on the basis of the same text. But 3: 12 may equally be taken to indicate utter destruction, as by P. J. King, JBC. Equally ambiguous is Amos 5: 15, where it is not clear whether the prophet anticipates the doctrine of the remnant emphasized later by Isaiah (11: 11) and Micah (4: 7) or only recognizes that Israel is now only a remnant (cf. 4: 2, 5)—because of the calamities which she had already suffered (2 Kings 10: 32; Amos 4: 6–11)—for which there can be no great hope.

justice, in steadfast love, and in mercy. I will betroth you to me in faithfulness; and you shall know the Lord.

And in that day, says the Lord, I will answer the heavens and they shall answer the earth (*hâ-'áretẓ*); and the earth (*hâ-'áretẓ*) shall answer the grain, the wine, and the oil, and they shall answer Jezreel; and I will sow him for myself in the land (*bâ-'áretẓ*). And I will have pity on Not pitied, and I will say to Not my people, "You are my people" and he shall say, "Thou art my God (Hos. 2: 14–23)."

Here Yahweh is to entice his unfaithful Israel (2: 2–15) back to himself in the wilderness. But notice: it is *not* in the wilderness that Israel is to enjoy new fertility, but as she re-enters the promised land, through the Valley of Achor, where Achan sinned (Josh. 7: 24ff): this has now become a door of hope.[7] Unlike the Rechabites, whom we shall mention later, the prophet does not wish for a return to the desert: such a return as is envisaged in 2: 2–14 is merely a prelude to a new entry to the land. And that land is Yahweh's land; that the land of Canaan is the land of the Lord appears in 9: 3. The attitude toward the land in Hosea is a positive one: despite its apostacy Israel is to dwell in the land.[8]

The role of the land in Isaiah is less easy to assess. But one thing is clear: that the reward of sin is thought of in terms of the land indicates its significance (see 24). There is no doubt that the land is the land of Emmanuel (8: 8, cf. 14: 25). The seminal passage is 1: 5–9 (compare 5: 13, where exile is the punishment for sin and 7: 23–24; 9: 19), which reads:

Why will you still be smitten, that you continue to rebel? The whole head is sick, and the whole heart faint. From the sole of the foot even to the head, there is no soundness in it, but bruises and sores and bleeding wounds; they are not pressed out, or bound up, or softened with oil.

Your country (*'ar'tẓ'kem*) lies desolate, your cities are burned with fire; in your very presence aliens devour your land (*ªd'math'kem*); it is desolate, as overthrown by aliens. And the daughter of Zion is left like a booth in a vineyard, like a lodge in a cucumber field, like a besieged city.

[7] See P. R. Ackroyd, *Peake, ad rem.*

[8] Hosea 2: 7 does, however, imply that, in an earlier, more primitive and severe time, things were different and also better. But Hosea's hankering after this period, although reminiscent of the Rechabites and Elijah, indicates merely "a desire for change, because change is expected to bring relief." So W. R. Harper, *Hosea*, ICC, New York, 1915, p. 237. Dennis J. McCarthy, JBC, p. 257, goes deeper: he points out that, in 2: 8–9, 11–14, although Israel is to return to the desert, Hosea is really concerned, not with geography, but with Israel's need to re-establish contact with Yahweh: "The desert is not a place for permanent withdrawal, but an ideal place to seek God (compare 11: 2; J. Mackenzie, *The Way, I,* 1961, pp. 27–39). It is a necessary discipline, an opportunity to find Yahweh again; the final promise is a return to the fertile land." (It is doubtful whether Hos. 7: 14 supports the view that Hosea contemplates an Israel returned to its land. The NEB renders "my shadow," but notes that the probable reading is "its shadow.")

If the Lord of hosts had not left us a few survivors, we should have been like Sodom, and become like Gomorrah.

Three motifs emerge here: the destruction of the land, the isolation of Zion, that is, Jerusalem, and the recognition of the remnant. Because the two latter themes—Zion and the remnant—emerge elsewhere in Isaiah, and have received so much scholarly attention, they have had the effect of overshadowing the former in interpretations of the prophet.[9] But these two striking motifs should not be allowed to obliterate the hope for the land; for beyond the destruction of the land, Isaiah looks forward to a renewal of Zion[10] and the perpetuation of the remnant. True, unlike Hosea, he makes no reference to an exile and a return, but he does look forward to a new king and his kingdom.

Of the increase of his government and of peace there will be no end, upon the throne of David, and over his kingdom, to establish it, and to uphold it with justice and with righteousness from this time forth and for evermore. The zeal of the Lord of hosts will do this (Is. 9: 7).

Here the land is not explicitly mentioned, but the kingdom of the new David implies the restored land—restored in justice and righteousness, not in its old sinful form.

When we turn again to Jeremiah the evidence leads to the same attitude. Born in Anathoth, which is situated in the territory of Benjamin, it was perhaps natural that Jeremiah should have been concerned not merely with his own kingdom of Judah but also with the fate of the northern kingdom exiled in 722 B.C.,[11] because ethnologically Benjamin belonged to Israel.[12] At any rate his prophecies reveal an absorbing interest and a constant love for the Rachel tribes; it is his heart's desire that the northern Israel as well as Judah should ultimately return from exile.[13] Here we must emphasize his purchase of a portion of his family inheritance: this

[9] For the Remnant, see Herntrich, TWZNT, Vol. IV, pp. 200ff, and for a convenient summary of the doctrine, T. W. Manson, *The Teaching of Jesus*, 1945, p. 236. For a warning against overemphasis upon it, E. W. Heaton, JTS, N.S., Vol. III, pt. 1, pp. 27ff; Paul Minear, *Images of the Church in the New Testament*, Philadelphia, 1960, pp. 81, 273f.

[10] The striking passage in Is. 4: 2–6, standing in marked contrast to the surrounding contexts, is probably from a later hand than Isaiah's. But the notion of the fruitfulness of the land beyond catastrophe occurs in Is. 7: 15–16, 21–22; 37: 30–31 (the remnant). Is. 4: 2–6, however, shows that such a hope as it expresses is not considered by the redactor of Isaiah to be inconsistent with the thought of that prophet. See R. B. Y. Scott, IB, Vol. 5, p. 194. Compare Is. 16: 14; 26: 9–10, 15, 18; 30: 24; Micah 7: 11.

[11] S. A. Cook, *The "Truth" of the Bible*, Cambridge, 1938, p. 44.

[12] J. Skinner, *Prophecy and Religion*, Cambridge, 1922, p. 19.

[13] Jer. 3: 12f; 31: 4–15; 31: 9, 15–20. Skinner, *Prophecy and Religion*, p. 82, regards 3: 14–18, which also speaks of the restoration of Israel and Judah, as post-exilic.

is symbolic of his belief in the ultimate salvation of all his people and their establishment upon their own soil.[14]

Jeremiah said, "The word of the Lord came to me: Behold, Hanamel the son of Shallum your uncle will come to you and say, 'Buy my field which is at Anathoth, for the right of redemption by purchase is yours.' Then Hanamel my cousin came to me in the court of the guard in accordance with the word of the Lord, and said to me, 'Buy my field which is at Anathoth in the land of Benjamin, for the right of possession and redemption is yours; buy it for yourself.' Then I knew that this was the word of the Lord. And I bought the field at Anathoth from Hanamel my cousin, and weighed out the money to him, seventeen shekels of silver. I signed the deed, sealed it, got witnesses, and weighed the money on scales. Then I took the sealed deed of purchase, containing the terms and conditions, and the open copy; and I gave the deed of purchase to Baruch the son of Neriah son of Mahseiah, in the presence of Hanamel my cousin, in the presence of all the Jews who were sitting in the court of the guard. I charged Baruch in their presence, saying 'Thus says the Lord of hosts, the God of Israel: Take these deeds, both this sealed deed of purchase and this open deed, and put them in an earthenware vessel, that they may last for a long time. For thus says the Lord of hosts, the God of Israel: Houses and fields and vineyards shall again be bought in this land (*bā-'āreṭ ha-ẓẓôth*).' After I had given the deed of purchase to Baruch the son of Neriah, I prayed to the Lord, saying, 'Ah Lord God! It is thou who hast made the heavens and the earth by thy great power and by thy outstretched arm! Nothing is too hard for thee, who showest steadfast love to thousands, but dost requite the guilt of fathers to their children after them, O great and mighty God whose name is the Lord of hosts, great in counsel and mighty in deed; whose eyes are open to all the ways of men, rewarding every man according to his ways and according to the fruit of his doings; who hast shown signs and wonders in the land of Egypt, and to this day in Israel and among all mankind, and hast made thee a name, as at this day. Thou didst bring thy people Israel out of the land of Egypt with signs and wonders, with a strong hand and outstretched arm, and with great terror; and thou gavest them this land (*hā-'āreṭ ha-ẓẓôth*), which thou didst swear to their fathers to give them, a land flowing with milk and honey; and they entered and took possession of it. But they did not obey thy voice or walk in thy law; they did nothing of all thou didst command them to do. Therefore thou hast made all this evil come upon them. Behold, the siege mounds have come up to the city to take it, and because of sword and famine and pestilence the city is given into the hands of the Chaldeans who are fighting against it. What thou didst speak has come to pass, and behold, thou seest it. Yet thou, O Lord God, hast said to me, "Buy the field for money and get witnesses"—though the city is given into the hands of the Chaldeans (Jer. 32: 6–25).'"[15]

[14] See Skinner, *Prophecy and Religion*, p. 298.

[15] The passage is cited in full because in a very clear way it shows both how the land is understood against a doctrine of creation and redemption and also how it finds its quintessence in the city (see below, pp. 131ff).

If we accept Jer. 31: 2–6, 18–26, as authentic and accept the literal interpretation of them that Skinner[16] favours, they reveal the same longing.
This means that for Jeremiah the nation was still the sphere, if not the
unit, of religion. As Skinner put it: "the main point is that in some sense
a restoration of the Israelite nationality was the form in which Jeremiah
conceived the Kingdom of God."[17] In the very vision of the figs in
Jer. 24, it is essential to note that the "good figs," the exiles, will be
brought again to the land (Jer. 24: 6) (compare Jer. 12: 14b–15; 16: 15;
24: 6; 29: 14; 30: 3; 31: 9, 12, 14, 23–25, 33–34).

In Ezekiel we find the idea that Yahweh is a jealous god who can
brook no rivals.[18] He therefore inflicts punishment on Israel because of her
apostasy,[19] but the restoration of Israel is assured, because Yahweh's
name must be upheld among the nations; the failure of his people would
bring dishonour upon himself.[20] The ingathering of all scattered Israelites
in the land is a constant theme of Ezekiel; the reassembled nation will be
purified in heart and spirit; there will be one flock under Yahweh as the
shepherd.[21] Again to return to the eagle and the cedar, the end of the
parable reads as follows:

Thus says the Lord God: "I myself will take a sprig from the lofty top of the
cedar, and will set it out; I will break off from the topmost of its young twigs a
tender one, and I myself will plant it upon a high and lofty mountain; on the
mountain height of Israel will I plant it, that it may bring forth boughs and bear
fruit, and become a noble cedar; and under it will dwell all kinds of beasts; in the
shade of its branches birds of every sort will nest." (Ezek. 17: 22–23).

(Compare Ezek. 20: 42; 36: 9–12; 39: 26. The end of Ezek. 47: 15 –
48: 35 describes the redistribution of the land among the tribes of Israel.)

The same motif runs through Deutero-Isaiah. True Israel is to be a
missionary to the Gentiles, but its first task, before turning to them, is to
seek the return of the lost sheep of the house of Israel (Is. 49: 5f). There is
a core of particularism in the most universal of the prophets.[22]

[16] Skinner, *Prophecy and Religion*, pp. 300f.　　[17] *Ibid.*, p. 308.

[18] Ezek. 16: 38; 20: 9, 22; 36: 5f; 39: 25.　　[19] *Ibid.*, 5: 13.

[20] *Ibid.*, 39: 25f.

[21] *Ibid.*, 36: 16–38; 37: 24. See G. A. Cooke, *Ezekiel* (ICC), Edinburgh, 1936, p. 372. See
his index under "Restoration." Compare Micah 2: 12; 4: 6f; Zeph. 3: 19; Zech. 10: 8–10;
Neh. 1: 9.

[22] N. H. Snaith, "The Servant of the Lord in Deutero-Isaiah," *Festschrift for T. H.
Robinson, Studies in Old Testament Prophecy*, Edinburgh, 1950, pp. 187–200; P. A. H. de
Boer, *Second-Isaiah's Message* (Oudtestamentische Studien, Deel xl), Leiden, 1956; R.
Martin-Achard, *Israël et les nations: la perspective missionaire de l'Ancient Testament*, Paris,
1959, have all argued that Second Isaiah was a nationalist. For J. Lindblom, *Prophecy in
Ancient Israel*, Oxford, 1962, p. 428, Second Isaiah only became a universalist after 539 B.C.

That the futuristic aspect of the prophets' messages are not to be neglected is confirmed by recent studies. We see, first, those which point to the note of promise in the words of the prophets. This note is preserved even when the promise seems obliterated in the announcement of doom. Beyond the prophetic threat lies always the prophetic hope. The "Day" of Yahweh, which spelt judgment, would also witness the outpouring of his mercy. This hope comes to explicit expression in much-noticed concepts; that of the remnant in Isaiah,[23] that of the new covenant in Jeremiah,[24] and that of the spirit revivifying the dry bones in Ezekiel.[25] These concepts have so often been treated that we need merely pinpoint the pertinent. The remnant which is envisaged, not only by Isaiah but also by Amos, assures not only survival but continuity with the old community, and it exists not for its own sake, but for the sake of all of the community: within the perspective of Israel itself it is *always* a saving remnant.[26] Likewise, although the new covenant of Jeremiah suggests a radically new beginning, it is with Israel, albeit a changed people, that this new covenant is to be ratified; just as it is the people of Israel who is to be reconstituted when, in Ezekiel's vision, the spirit revivifies the dry bones.[27] It might be objected that neither the remnant nor the new covenant nor the spirit specifically referred to the land. But this might be questioned in Is. 7: 3, where clearly the remnant (*She'ar yâshûb*) is

The debate is reviewed by Harry M. Orlinsky. His conclusion is: "Israel will be 'a light of nations' in the sense that Israel will dazzle the nations with her god-given triumph and restoration: the whole world will behold this single beacon that is God's sole covenanted people. Israel will serve to the world at large as the example of God's loyalty and omnipotence." H. M. Orlinsky, "The So-Called Servant of the Lord and 'Suffering Servant' in Second Isaiah," *Studies on the Second Part of the Book of Isaiah*, pp. 3–128. See VT, Vol. 14, Leiden, 1967, p. 117. In the same studies, see also N. H. Snaith, "A Study of the Teaching of the Second Isaiah and its Consequences," pp. 137ff. But it is difficult to go the whole way with these scholars when we recall the cosmic setting of Isaiah's thought. The glory of God is to return for all men to see—nature itself is to be transformed and the nations are to be converted (Is. 45: 20–23; 51: 4–5; cf. 49: 6). On the other hand, the restoration of the land, a counterpart of the gift of the land, is clearly expected; Is. 44: 26; 49: 8, 19. See J. Muilenburg on Second-Isaiah, *ad rem*, IB, Vol. 5.

[23] Is. 10: 20ff; 11: 11 (*she'âr*); 37: 32 (*she'êrîth*). On the element of promise in the prophets, see J. A. Sanders, *Suffering as Divine Discipline in the Old Testament and Post-Biblical Judaism*, Rochester, 1955, in which he faces the relationship between calamity and the prophetic hope (see p. 64, n. 18, on Jeremiah): this is rich in materials and insight. Sanders establishes that for the prophets punishment is often discipline: from it shall come salvation (p. 62). This work should be read in connection with all the above discussion. See also J. Moltmann, *Theology of Hope*, trans., New York, 1967, pp. 124ff.

[24] Jer. 31: 31–34.   [25] Ezek. 37.

[26] Herntrich, TWZNT, Vol. IV, pp. 200ff. The remnant is related to the election of Israel by Yahweh and his judgment upon it, and is especially connected with Jerusalem; Herntrich, p. 210f, writes: "Das *leimma* ist nicht der Endzweck, sondern das Ziel ist Wiederannahme, Rettung von ganz Israel."

[27] See PRJ, pp. 82f.

involved in the very physical existence of the nation, and, in any case, in view of the passages we have cited in this connection, such a reference is not to be ruled out. Despite the difficulty of their precise delimitation, if we bear in mind the passages presenting promises of restoration in the prophets, together with references to the remnant, the new covenant, and the spirit, it is difficult not to recognize with Sifre[28] that the prophets first addressed hard words to Israel, but in the end spoke words of consolation, preceded by judgment though they were.

This is a convenient point to turn to the second emphasis in the understanding of the prophets which has been presented in a recent brief, but seminal, study by Finkelstein entitled: *New Light From the Prophets*, 1969. In Finkelstein's own words, it is this:

...all we have known about these supreme geniuses (i.e., the prophets as rhetoricians and poets who inaugurated by their moral teaching etc., a revolution in human thought) was peripheral to their fundamental task, that of teaching in their academies, raising disciples, and transforming them into teachers of other disciples. Behind the great addresses and poems preserved in the Scriptures, and differing from the generalised ethical appeals to the public, there was oral instruction, intended to create an unshakeable inner nucleus of devotion to truth, to learning, and human betterment, as complete as might realistically be attainable among men....The Prophets emerge as institution-builders, teachers, religious statesmen, authors of prayers on the one hand and learned tracts on the other. Beyond denouncing the evil in their time they were founders of a better society. The Messianic Age, which they predicted and for which they longed, was expected to burst upon the world after slow and prolonged preparations, through gradual but realistic emancipation of their followers from the enticements of the common corruption... in addition to their public labours, which were known to the whole community, the Prophets conducted academies for their immediate disciples, where teachings were not written but were studied by rote. The memorised texts entered the heritage of the Prophetic schools. Handed down from master to disciple for centuries, they were integrated ultimately into what became Pharisaic and Rabbinic works, and—perhaps thirteen centuries after their composition—were put into writing (pp. 2f).

Finkelstein's controversial work has not yet been assessed so that it cannot be used with confidence, so startling is it in its newness. But if he has successfully connected the prophets with the legal tradition that came

---

[28] Cited by Finkelstein, *New Light from the Prophets*, p. 14, without the exact reference. He translates: "And '*all*' the Prophets learned from him (Moses who first spoke harsh words to Israel but gave them his blessing before his death), at first addressing harsh words to Israel, but in the end turning about and speaking words of consolation." Finkelstein notes as examples: Hosea, Joel, Amos, Micah, Jeremiah.

after them, that is, with the development of the Rabbinic tradition (just as Alt, Buber, von Rad, Zimmerli, and others[29] have connected them with the Law in Israel before their day), then the concern of the prophets with and their anticipation of the future life of their people in the land becomes exceedingly probable however dark the doom they proclaimed. Under Finkelstein's hands the prophets become, to use Rudolf Otto's phrase, architects of the future, as well as heralds of destruction: they reveal the essential irrationality of the eschatological type, who can hold doom and future in living tension.[30]

Finally, before we leave the prophets, it must be borne in mind that, as still today, in the ancient Synagogue their words were read in their totality as they are presented in the scriptures. The distinctions that critical scholarship draws, and which we necessarily note in such a study as this, between the authentic words of a prophet and later, modificatory scribal additions to them, were not recognized. Prophecies of restoration would be given equal weight with those of doom, and, given the hope that springs eternal in the human breast, probably more weight. Our critical dissection does not, indeed, lead to murder of the text *for us*; on the contrary. But it does lead to the murder of it as it was understood in the ancient Synagogue if we imagine that that Synagogue was influenced by such dissection. The dissection that might compel us to de-emphasize the prophecies of restoration is irrelevant to the effective role played by the totality of the prophetic texts in moulding the thought of Judaism.

[29] See W. Zimmerli, *The Law and the Prophets, A Study of the Meaning of the Old Testament*, trans., Oxford, 1965.

[30] R. Otto, *The Kingdom of God and the Son of Man*, trans., London, 1938, pp. 59ff.

IV. THE LAND IN EXTRA-BIBLICAL SOURCES

1. THE APOCRYPHA AND PSEUDEPIGRAPHA

After the cessation of prophecy,[1] the hope for the land is taken over into later eschatological thinking in Israel. The problem of how far Apocalyptic is an outgrowth of prophecy or is a new emergence primarily instigated by the influence of Iranian and other factors on the life of Israel need not directly concern us. What does need recognition is that eschatological thinking was not alien to the main currents in Judaism. The antithesis drawn between Pharisaism as the heir of the Law and Apocalyptic as the heir of prophecy, so that, with the increasing significance of Pharisaism, Apocalyptic became correspondingly peripheral in Judaism, has had to be abandoned. This means that concepts that appear in the Apocalyptic sources need not be regarded as insignificant fringe elements in Judaism.[2] And we shall find that in these sources, the land is given, although less frequently, the kind of attention that is accorded to it in the Old Testament and in the Rabbinical sources.

The incidence of specific references to the land in the Apocrypha, the Pseudepigrapha, and the Qumran scrolls, especially in comparison with that in the Hexateuch, is meagre. But the awareness of the land—its holiness, its possible pollution by sin, and consequent need for purification—is unmistakably clear. The connection of Israel with the land is an assumption. The term "holy land" appears (Wis. Sol. 13: 3, 4, 7; 2 Baruch 65: 9, 10; 71: 1; Sib. Or. 3: 266f), and "goodly land" (Tobit 14: 4, 5; Jub. 13: 2, 6; 1 Enoch 89: 40), and "the land which is in thy

---

[1] The notion of the cessation of prophecy expressed in T. B. Yoma 21b; Num. Rabbah 15: 10 (see PRJ, p. 208) is connected by Rudolf Meyer especially with the needs of canonization. (See *Der Prophet aus Galiläa*, Darmstadt, 1970.) Contrast Jeremias and others. See also R. Meyer, TWZNT, Vol. VI, pp. 812–828, "There never was in Israel a prophetic age in the sense of a fixed historical period (p. 828)."

[2] See my "Apocalyptic and Pharisaism," first published in ET, Vol. LIX, 1948, now in *Christian Origins and Judaism*, Philadelphia, 1962, pp. 19–30. See also S. Sandmel, *The First Christian Century in Judaism and Christianity*, New York, 1969, pp. 63ff. D. Rössler, *Gesetz und Geschichte*, Neukirchener Verlag, 1960, holds that the Apocalyptic groups had a quite different conception of Torah from that of the Pharisees. This view is exaggerated; see B. Gerhardsson, *Memory and Manuscript*, Uppsala, 1961, p. 20, n. 1; H. D. Betz, *Apocalypticism, Journal for Theology and the Church*, Vol. 6, 1969, pp. 195ff. But see also K. Koch, *The Rediscovery of Apocalyptic, Studies in Biblical Theology*, Second Series 22, trans. 1970; he rejects the position indicated, pp. 54f. Contrast D. S. Russell, *The Method and Message of Jewish Apocalyptic*, Philadelphia, 1964, *ad rem*. On the history of the interpretation of Apocalyptic, see Johann Michael Schmidt, *Die Jüdische Apokalyptik*, Neukirchener Verlag, 1969. For D. Daube on Apocalyptic, see p. 354, n. 53.

sight the most precious of all lands" (Wis. Sol. 13: 3, 4, 7). In 1 Enoch 89: 40 the phrase "pleasant and glorious land" occurs, and in the Letter of Aristeas, line 107, the land is "extensive and beautiful."[3] The notion of the land of promise occurs in Jub. 12: 22; 13: 3; 22: 27; Sirach 46: 8; Ass. Mos. 1: 8f; 2: 1. The connection between Israel's conduct and the land is marked. In Jub. 6: 12–13 the failure to observe the demands of Yahweh is incompatible with occupation of the land: "The man who eats the blood of beasts or of cattle or of birds during all the days of the earth, he and his seed shall be rooted out of the land." Again, in Jub. 15: 28, the reward of those who observe circumcision is that "they will *not* be rooted out of the land." The cultic recital of Yahweh's acts in history was the vehicle for the transmission and perpetuation of the understanding of the relationship between people and land, as of other motifs. Even the rationalization of the conquest as a punishment for the sins of the pre-Israelite inhabitants reappears in the Wisdom of Solomon.[4] The insistence, however, on the mercifulness of Yahweh, even in the conquest, breaks through in the following:

For verily the old inhabitants of thy holy land,
Hating *them* because they practised detestable works of enchantments and
    unholy rites
(Merciless slaughters of children, And sacrificial banquets of men's flesh and
    of blood),
Confederates in an impious fellowship,
And murderers of their own helpless babes,
It was thy counsel to destroy by the hands of our fathers;
That the land which in thy sight is most precious of all *lands*
Might receive a worthy colony of God's servants.
(ἵνα ἀξίαν ἀποικίαν δέξηται θεοῦ παίδων ἡ παρὰ σοὶ πασῶν τιμιωτάτη γῆ)
Nevertheless even these thou didst spare as *being* men,
And thou sentest hornets as fore-runners of thy host,
To cause them to perish by little and little;
Not that thou wast unable to subdue the ungodly unde the hand of the right-
    eous in battle,
Or by terrible beasts or by one stern word to make away with them at once;
But judging them by little and little thou gavest them a place of repentance,
Not being ignorant that their nature by birth was evil, and their wickedness
    inborn,
And that their manner of thought would in no wise ever be changed,

   [3] See also 1 Enoch 27: 1 (Blessed land); holy mountain at the middle of the earth, that is, Jerusalem, 1 Enoch 26: 1; in 1 Enoch 90: 26 Gehenna is in the centre of the earth.
   [4] Wis. 2: 7; 1 Enoch 90: 20.

For they were a seed accursed from the beginning:
Neither was it through fear of any that thou didst leave them *then* unpunished
for their sins (12: 3–11).

The understanding of the land found in the Old Testament reappears in the Apocrypha and Pseudepigrapha, and our purpose here is to indicate how, for the most part, there is a continuity between these sources and the Old Testament in this area.[5]

The Apocrypha and Pseudepigrapha show that the idea grew in intensity that Yahweh must vindicate his choice of his people by restoring them to their land according to their tribes as a united people. Perhaps the most well-known expression of this idea is found in Psalms of Solomon (first century B.C.). Speaking of the Son of David, whom the Lord shall raise up, the author writes:

And he shall gather together a holy people, whom he shall lead in righteousness,
And he shall judge the tribes of the people that has been sanctified by the Lord
his God.
And he shall not suffer unrighteousness to lodge any more in their midst.
Nor shall there dwell with them any man that knoweth wickedness
For he shall know them, that they are all sons of their God.
And he shall divide them according to their tribes upon the land
And neither sojourner nor alien shall sojourn with them any more.

In 4 Ezra 13: 48 (first century A.D.) we read of the End that: "The survivors of thy people, even those found within thy holy border (shall be saved)." The same thought occurs in 2 Bar. 9: 2 (first century A.D.). In the last days, Yahweh will protect only the people who live in Israel: that land will be surrounded by his holy presence:

For at that time I will protect only those who are found in those self-same days
in this land.

In 71: 1 the author asserts that the land itself will act on behalf of Israel:

And the holy land shall have mercy on its own and it shall protect its inhabiters
at that time.

Only by such protection as God and the land itself provides can the name of Israel be remembered. As 2 Bar. 3: 4–5 expresses it:

What, therefore, will there be for these things (that is, at the End)? for if thou

---

[5] But it is to be fully recognized that the notion of the fulfilment of Old Testament prophecy plays little part in the Apocrypha and Pseudepigrapha, see J. L. Zinz, *The Use of the Old Testament in the Apocrypha*, Duke University, unpub., 1966.

destroyest thy city[6] and deliverest up thy land to those who hate us, how shall the name of Israel be remembered?

It agrees with the "active" role ascribed to the land itself in Baruch that in 4 Ezra the land becomes "holy" or sanctified in the last days because Yahweh draws especially near to it. The Israelites will escape from the dangers and terrors of the End through no merit of their own. Their only guarantee of salvation will lie in one fact: their actual dwelling in the land, which Yahweh will save for his own sake alone, as his own possession. 4 Ezra 9: 7–9 makes this clear:

And everyone shall survive from the perils aforesaid and shall see salvation in my land, and within my borders which I have sanctified for myself eternally.

Even in 1 Enoch (first century A.D.?), at 90: 20, cosmic and supraterrestrial as are its visions of the future, at the End it was in the pleasant land of Israel that the throne of Yahweh was finally to be erected.

2. THE QUMRAN WRITINGS

The high evaluation and significance of the land is also present in the documents from Qumran. In these the land is understood as Yahweh's own possession. In IQS 1: 5 we read that the members of the sect are:

to practice truth and righteousness and justice *in the land...(wᵉlaᶜᵃsôth 'ᵉmeth wẓᵉdâqâh wmishᵉppât bâ 'âretẓ).*

The council of the community is characterized as follows in IQS 8: 3:

In the Council of the Community (there shall be) twelve laymen and three priests who are perfect in all that is revealed of the whole Torah, through practicing truth and righteousness and justice and loving devotion and walking humbly each with his fellow *in order to maintain faithfulnsss in the land (lishᵉmôr 'ᵉmûnâh bâ 'âretẓ)* with a steadfast intent and with a broken Spirit (our italics).

Further in IQS 8: 4b–7 we read:

When these things come to pass in Israel, the Council of the Community will
    have been established in truth:
As an eternal planting, a holy house for Israel,
A most holy institution for Aaron,
Witnesses of truth concerning judgement,
And the chosen of grace to atone for the land (Brownlee "earth") (our italics)
(wbᵉhîrê râtẓôn lᵉkappêr bᵉ 'ad hâ-âretẓ).
And to render to the wicked their desert.

[6] Note here the collocation or even the equation of land and city (see below pp. 131ff). Jerusalem is the mother, 2 Bar. 3: 1.

The Council of the Community is to be "accepted to make atonement for the land (*wᵉhâyû lᵉrâtⱬôn lᵉkappêr bᵉʿad hâ-âretⱬ*) (IQS 8: 10)." The life of the community, in accordance with its own understanding of the Law, is designed to fulfil the function which the sacrificial system had in vain sought to accomplish, that is, the acceptance of the land by Yahweh. IQS 9: 3ff reads as follows:

> When these things come to pass in Israel according to all these regulations, for a foundation of a holy spirit, for eternal truth, *for a ransom for the guilt of transgression and sinful faithlessness, and for acceptance for the land*...(our italics) (*lᵉkappêr ʿal ʾashᵉmath peshaʿ wmaʿal ḥattʾâth wlᵉrâtⱬôn lâ ʾaretⱬ...*).

Part of the purpose of the community is to restore a land, made unclean, to acceptance. There is an "order" of the land which the Law recognizes and which is to be observed in human habitations (CDC ix: 6b). The tribal organization of the land is assumed (IQM 2): even in war the Jubilee of the land is to be honoured (IQM 2). The relationship between human conduct and the land, which we so often discovered in the Old Testament, is assumed throughout the Scrolls. Sin leads Yahweh to hide his face from the land (CDC 2: 9cf., 11) and causes the land to become desolate (CDC 4: 10). One significant mark of sin is the removal of the boundaries of the land, which, as we saw previously, were regarded as set by Yahweh himself (CDC 1: 16; 8: 1). But, however deep the consciousness of the corruption of the land through sin, it is of the very genius of the Qumran community that it recognizes that the condition of the land is not totally hopeless, because a "remnant," the sect itself, has been spared to atone for it. The awareness of the peculiarity of Israel, and its stance against other lands, is clear: Israel stands against the nations. At the End warriors from its tribes are to go out against the Gentile lands (IQM 2). The influence of Ezek. 40–48 is heavy in IQM. For the author (we need not here enter into the history of the development of the War Scroll into its present form), at the time of the return of the exiles from the desert of the peoples (Col. 1: 3, compare Ezek. 20: 35) the Sect, the true Israelites, would occupy the land, according to their tribes, and instigate an offensive war against those outside. This offensive war, with the land as its base, was to be a holy war much more intense and widespread than holy wars conceived in the Old Testament, which were defensive. What concerns us here is the centrality of the land of Israel in the thought of the author, who is in line with Is. 2: 1–5 and especially Ezek. 38 ff.[7]

---

[7] For details see the excellent edition by J. Van der Ploeg, *Le Rouleau de la Guerre, Traduit et Annoté Avec Une Introduction*, Leiden, 1959, and further below pp. 99ff. See also the

Our survey of the Apocrypha, Pseudepigrapha, and Qumran writings is over. Can our treatment—so brief is it—adequately cover these? At least it reflects the comparative infrequency of references to the land in these sources. This infrequency, however, must be qualified. After the Exile the sentiment concerning the land became concentrated in Jerusalem and the Temple, references to which in the sources used are very numerous. The absence of direct references to the land can, therefore, be misleading, because the land is implied in the city and the Temple, which became its quintessence. (See e.g., Tobit 13: 13, 17; and especially 14: 5, which looks forward to a future Temple to which the exiles will return as to a rebuilt house. At the same time, 14: 7 claims that all the children of Israel shall dwell forever in the land of Abraham in safety, and it shall be given over to them. See below pp. 131 ff.) Moreover, brief as it is, our treatment has brought into focus two factors. First, the difference in the approach to the land in the Apocrypha and Pseudepigrapha from that in the Qumran writings, which we shall enlarge upon and seek to explain below (see pp. 99 ff), and, secondly, the relationship between the events of history and the approach to the land. We saw in dealing with the Hexateuch how D and P reacted to the collapse of the state in the sixth century B.C. The same reaction is traceable *mutatis mutandis* in 2 Baruch and 4 Ezra where, after A.D. 70, there emerges an almost desperate concentration on the efficacy of life in the land. Indeed, these documents seem to go further than D and P. There are passages in the Old Testament where the land expels unworthy inhabitants: in 2 Baruch and 4 Ezra, as we saw, that land acts, not only negatively, but positively on behalf of "Israel." Such a note could only emerge out of desperation, which was probably more typical of apocalyptic circles than of the Rabbinic ones, to which we turn next.

3. THE RABBINIC SOURCES

In many apocalyptic and "sectarian" groups, then, the question of the land remained a living issue up to the first century. Such groups, as we saw above, have often been claimed to be outside the dominant or significant stream of Judaism, the Pharisaic, so that their concern with the land might be discounted by some as a mark of insignificant currents. But,

---

penetrating remarks of Friedrich Nötscher, *Zur Theologischen Terminologie der Qumran-Texte*, Bonn, 1956, pp. 192f. Of the Sect he writes that their most significant task was to atone for the land. They were the elect of the grace of God (IQp Hab. 5: 4; IQS 8: 6). Their judgment on the sons of darkness and the punishment of these was part of the process of cleansing the land. "Die Strafe für die Frevler würde dann als Voraussetzung zur Sühne für das land gehoren (p. 193)."

as we also saw above, such an approach to first-century Judaism is no longer possible. The customary picture of first-century Judaism before A.D. 70 as dominated by the Pharisees, who constituted the representatives of what was called normative Judaism, is not tenable: differences of emphasis there were between apocalyptists and Pharisees, but no cleavage. We shall find that on the question of the land the Pharisees largely shared the views of the groups referred to.[8]

In fact, Pharisaism so cherished the view that there was an unseverable connection between Israel and Yahweh and the land that this view has been referred to as a "dogma" of the Pharisees. The emphasis on this view has been connected with the destruction of the land by the Romans in the war from A.D. 66–70. Conditions in Palestine after A.D. 70 were economically difficult. As a result there developed an increasing tendency for Jews to emigrate from Palestine to neighbouring countries, especially to Syria. So serious did this become that it threatened to depopulate the land. The need to encourage Jews to remain in it was so urgent that the Pharisaic leaders after A.D. 70 adopted a policy of extolling the virtues of the land and encouraging settlement in it.[9] Conservative Sages, such as Rabbi Eliezer the Great or ben Hyrcanus (A.D. 80–120), in order to protect Palestinian agriculture wanted to subject Syrian agriculture to all the requirements of tithing and the sabbatical year so as to check the emigration of farmers to Syria. R. Gamaliel II (A.D. 80–120), while he opposed such extreme measures, also shared in this purpose. The following passage from Mishnah Hallah iv: 7–8 is instructive:

7. If Israelites leased a field from gentiles in Syria, R. Eliezer declares their produce liable to tithes and subject to the Seventh Year law; but Rabban Gamaliel declares it exempt. Rabban Gamaliel says: Two Dough-offerings [are given] in Syria. But R. Eliezer says: One Dough-offering. [Beforetime] they accepted the more lenient ruling of Rabban Gamaliel and the more lenient ruling of R. Eliezer, but afterward they followed the rulings of Rabban Gamaliel in both things.

8. Rabban Gamaliel says: Three regions are distinguished in what concerns Dough-offering. In the land of Israel as far a Chezib one Dough-offering [is given]: from Chezib to the River [Eastward; to the Euphrates] and to Amanah, [Northward, to the river Amanah (2 Kings 5: 12), which rises in the Antilebanon and flows through Damascus] two Dough-offerings....From the River and from Amanah, inwards, two Dough-offerings [are given]. . .

---

[8] For references, see PRJ, Chapter 1.

[9] For bibliographical details, see SSM, pp. 295ff. On the term "dogma" see below p. 390. Strictly speaking, there is no "dogma" of the land in Judaism. It is more accurate to speak of a doctrine. But the term dogma is often applied to this doctrine.

Legislation thus affected Syria. R. Akiba's rule, "the like of whatsoever is permitted to be done in the land of Israel may be done also in Syria," implies much discussion of this point. Akiba died in A.D. 132.

But it is not necessary to emphasize economic factors exclusively in this connection, important as they are. The roots of the emphasis on the land are deep in the Old Testament, as we have seen: it was the land of milk and honey (Exod. 3: 8 etc.), Israel's lasting resting place (Deut. 12: 9), and God's own land (Josh. 22: 19 etc.). After the horrors of the war with its subsequent dispersion, it was natural for Rabbis to idealize the old life in the land before the war—to engage in "myth," as we do today in idealizing the nineteenth century. The Tannaitic and other Rabbinic sources, building on the Scriptures, even if stimulated by economic and political realities, point to the significance of the land in the most unambiguous way. There is a kind of "umbilical cord" between Israel and the land. It is no accident that one-third of the Mishnah, the Pharisaic legal code, is connected with the land. Nine-tenths of the first order of the Mishnah, *Zeraim* (Seeds), of the fifth order, *Kodashim* (Hallowed Things), and of the sixth order, *Tohoroth* (Cleannesses), deal with laws concerning the land, and there is much of the same in the other parts of the Mishnah. This is no accident, because the connection between Israel and the land was not fortuitous, but part of the divine purpose or guidance, as was the Law itself. Consider the following passage, ascribed to a Rabbi flourishing between A.D. 140 and 165, from Lev. Rabbah 13: 2:

2. R. Simeon b. Yohai opened a discourse with: *He rose and measured the earth* (Hab. III, 6). The Holy One, blessed be He, considered[a] all generations and he found no generation fitted to receive the Torah other than the generation of the wilderness; the Holy One, blessed be He, considered all mountains and found no mountain on which the Torah should be given other than Sinai; the Holy One, blessed be He, considered all cities, and found no city wherein the Temple might be built, other than Jerusalem; the Holy One, blessed be He, considered all lands, and found no land suitable to be given to Israel, other than the Land of Israel. This is indicated by what is written: "*He rose and measured the earth*"— *And He released[b] nations (ib.).*

a. Lit. "measured," "assessed the comparative merits."
b. the verb *hittir* is understood here in its Rabbinic meaning, *viz.* "to permit," "to declare a thing permitted."[10]

The choice of Israel and the Temple and of the land was deliberate, the result of Yahweh's planning; R. Simeon b. Yohai's thought goes back to

[10] The Soncino translation with notes.

the beginning of things and finds Yahweh's purpose at work then. The connection between Yahweh, Israel, the land, Sinai, the Temple is primordial: it is grounded in a necessity of the divine purpose and is, therefore, inseverable. And it is no wonder that the Rabbis heaped upon the land terms of honour and endearment. For them the land of Israel is called simply *Hâ-âretz*, The land; all countries outside it are *ḥûtz hâ-âretz*, outside the land. In T. B. Berakoth 5a we read: "It has been taught: R. Simeon b. Yohai says: The Holy One, blessed be He, gave Israel three precious gifts, and all of them were given only through sufferings. These are: The Torah, the Land of Israel, and the World to Come..."[11]

We have seen that behind the glorification of the land stood passages in the Scriptures. But, in addition to this, two factors could not but unceasingly stamp the land upon the consciousness of Israel. The first is that the Law itself, by which Jews lived, was so tied to the land that it could not but recall the land. As we have already stated, one-third of the Mishnah deals with the land and all the agricultural laws in it, as those of Scripture itself do. Consider the following verses:

When you come into the land (*wkî-thâbôw 'el hâ-'âretz*) and plant all kinds of trees for food, then you shall count their fruit as forbidden; three years it shall be forbidden to you, it must not be eaten. And in the fourth year all their fruit shall be holy, an offering of praise to the Lord. But in the fifth year you may eat of their fruit, that they may yield more richly for you. I am the Lord your God (Lev. 19: 23) (H.).

Say to the people of Israel, *When you come into the land* (*hâ-'âretz*) which I give you and reap its harvest, you shall bring the sheaf of the first fruits of your harvest to the priest: (Lev. 23: 10) (H.).

And when you reap the harvest of your land (*'areʦʦekem*), you shall not reap your field to its very border, nor shall you gather the gleanings after your harvest; you shall leave them for the poor and for the stranger: I am the Lord your God (Lev. 23: 22) (H.).

Say to the people of Israel, *When you come into the land* (*hâ-'âretz*) *which I give you*, the land (*hâ-'âretz*) shall keep a sabbath to the Lord (Lev. 25: 2) (H.).

When you come into the land (*hâ-'âretz*) which the Lord your God gives you for an inheritance, and have taken possession of it, and live in it...* (Deut. 26: 1).

The words emphasized in each of the above verses make it clear that the

[11] See G. Cohen, *Zion in Jewish Literature*, ed. A. S. Halkin, New York, 1961, p. 41. Similarly Jerusalem is simply *ha'îr*, the city. For passages glorifying the land, see Halkin, *Zion in Jewish Literature*, pp. 18–37 and J. Gutmann, *'Eres Israel ba-Midrash u-ba-Talmud* in *Festschrift zum 75 jährigen Bestehen des Jüdisch-Theologischen Seminars Fränkelscher Stiftung* (2 vols. Breslau, 1929), Vol. 1 (Hebrew), pp. 9f. It is in the Mishnah that *hâ-âretz* first appears as the term to designate the country or land of Israel.

agricultural laws are to apply "in the land."[12] Further, only in Palestine could there be cities of refuge, which were so important in the civil law (Num. 35: 9f; Deut. 4: 41f; 19: 1f).[13] True there are laws not contingent upon the land; and the distinction between these and their opposite was clearly recognized. But the reward for the observance of the laws was "life in the land," as is implied in Mishnah Kiddushin 1: 9–10.

9. Any religious duty that does not depend on the Land (of Israel)[a] may be observed whether in the Land or outside of it; and any religious duty that depends on the Land[b] may be observed in the Land (alone); excepting the laws of *Orlah*-fruit[c] and of Diverse Kinds.[d] E. Eliezer says: Also the law of new produce.[e]

10. If a man performs but a single commandment it shall be well with him and he shall have length of days and shall inherit the Land; but if he neglects a single commandment it shall be ill with him and he shall not have length of days and shall not inherit the Land. He that has a knowledge of Scripture and Mishnah and right conduct will not soon fall into sin, for it is written, *And a threefold cord is not quickly broken.*[f] But he that has no knowledge of Scripture and Mishnah and right conduct has no part in the habitable world.

    a. Sabbath, circumcision, and all laws affecting personal conduct.
    b. Such as Heave-offering, Tithes, the Seventh Year law, Gleanings.
    c. App. I. 32 (Danby).
    d. See p. 28, n. 1 (Danby).
    e. Lev. 23. 14.
    f. Eccles. 4. 12.

The Law itself, therefore, to use current terminology, might be regarded as an effective symbol of the land: it served as a perpetual call to the land.

But, secondly, precisely because it was the land to which the Law most applied, the land gained in sanctity. Consider the following passage from Mishnah Kelim 1: 6–9:

6. There are ten degrees of holiness. The Land of Israel is holier than any other land. Wherein lies its holiness? In that from it they may bring the Omer,[a] the Firstfruits,[b] and the Two Loaves,[c] which they may not bring from any other land.

[12] It is puzzling, however, that in the Midrashim comparatively little emphasis is placed on the phrase: "When you come into the land." In Deut. Rabbah there is no comment on Deut. 26: 1. In Lev. Rabbah there is extensive comment on Lev. 19: 23, but little emphasis on the land as such, but rather on Torah: so, too, in the comments on Lev. 23: 10 attention centres, not on the land, but on the significance of the sheaf of the first fruits: the fulfilment of the commandment of the sheaf was the first demand in the land, hence its importance. The emphasis is diverted from the land to the commandment. No comment is offered on Lev. 23: 22 or 25: 2.

[13] For cities of refuge, see R. de Vaux, *Ancient Israel: Its Life and Institutions*, New York, 1961, trans., *ad rem.*

7. The walled cities[d] (of the Land of Israel) are still more holy, in that they must send forth the lepers from their midst; moreover they may carry around a corpse therein wheresoever they will, but once it is gone forth (from the city) they may not bring it back.

8. Within the wall (of Jerusalem) is still more holy, for there (only) they may eat the Lesser Holy Things[e] and the Second Tithe. The Temple Mount[f] is still more holy, for no man or woman that has a flux, no menstruant, and no woman after childbirth may enter therein. The Rampart[g] is still more holy, for no gentiles and none that have contracted uncleanness from a corpse may enter therein. The Court of the Women is still more holy, for none that had immersed himself the selfsame day (because of uncleanness) may enter therein, yet none would thereby become liable to a Sin-offering. The Court of the Israelites[h] is still more holy, for none whose atonement is yet incomplete may enter therein, and they would thereby become liable to a Sin-offering.[i] The Court of the Priests is still more holy, for Israelites may not enter therein save only when they must perform the laying on of the hands,[j] slaughtering, and waving.[k]

9. Between the Porch and the Altar is still more holy, for none that has a blemish or whose hair is unloosed may enter there. The Sanctuary is still more holy, for none may enter therein with hands and feet unwashed. The Holy of Holies is still more holy, for none may enter therein save only the High Priest on the Day of Atonement at the time of the (Temple)-service. R. Jose said: In five things is the space between the Porch and the Altar equal to the Sanctuary: for they may not enter there that have a blemish, or that have drunk wine, or that have hands and feet unwashed, and men must keep far from between the Porch and the Altar at the time of burning the incense.[l]

a. Lev. 23: 1of; App. I. 31 (Danby).
b. Deut. 26: 2ff.
c. Of Pentecost. Lev. 23: 17.
d. See. Arak. 9: 6.
e. See Zeb. 5: 6ff; 14: 8.
f. The whole square (see Danby, p. 589, n. 11) of the Temple Area.
g. Surrounding the rectangular group of inner courts, containing the Temple structure to the west and the Court of the Women to the east (see Midd. 2: 3).
h. Midd. 2: 5.
i. See Shebu. 2: 1.
j. Lev. 3: 2.
k. Lev. 7: 30.
l. See Tam. 6: 3 (end).

In each case—in the reference to the land, the walled cities of the land, the wall of Jerusalem, the Temple Mount, the Rampart, the Court of Women, The Court of the Israelites etc.—it is the connection with an enactment of the Law that determines the degree of its holiness. And, for our purposes especially, it is noteworthy that it is the applicability of the

Law to the land in 1:6 that assures its special holiness. The implication is that Jewish sanctity is only fully possible in the land: outside the land only strictly personal laws can be fulfilled, that is, the moral law, sexual law, Sabbath law, circumcision, dietary laws, etc. Of necessity, outside the land, the territorial laws have to be neglected. The exiled life is, therefore, an emaciated life, even though, through suffering, it atones.[14] A passage in T. B. Sotah 14a expresses this point of view in dealing with Moses' failure to enter the land.

R. Simlai (third century A.D.) expounded: Why did Moses our teacher yearn to enter the land of Israel? Did he want to eat of its fruits or satisfy himself from its bounty? But thus spake Moses, "Many precepts were commanded to Israel which can only be fulfilled in the land of Israel. I wish to enter the land so that they may all be fulfilled by me." The Holy One, blessed be He, said to him, "Is it only to receive the reward (for obeying the commandments) that thou seekest? I ascribe it to thee as if thou didst perform them"; as it is said, *Therefore will I divide him a portion with the great, and he shall divide the spoil with the strong; because he poured out his soul unto death, and was numbered with the transgressor; yet he bare the sins of many, and made intercession for the transgressors.*[a] "*Therefore will I divide him a portion with the great*"—it is possible (to think that his portion will be) with the (great of) later generations and not former generations; therefore there is a text to declare, "*And he shall divide with the strong,*" i.e., with Abraham, Isaac and Jacob who were strong in Torah and the commandments. "*Because he poured out his soul unto death*"—because he surrendered himself to die, as it is said, *And if not, blot me, I pray thee* etc.[b] "*And was numbered with the transgressors*"—because he was numbered with them who were condemned to die in the wilderness. "*Yet he bare the sins of many*"—because he secured atonement for the making of the Golden Calf. "*And made intercession for the transgressors*"—because he begged for mercy on behalf of the sinners in Israel that they should turn in penitence; and the word *pegi'ah* ("intercession") means nothing else than prayer, as it is said, *Therefore pray not thou for this people, neither lift up cry nor prayer for them, neither make intercession to Me.*[c]

a. Is. 53:12.
b. Ex. 32:32.
c. Jer. 7:16. (It is suggested that the application of these verses to Moses was a tacit parrying of the use made of that passage by Christian apologists. See Moore, *Judaism*, Vol. III, p. 166, n. 254.)

Moses, outside the land, is a suffering servant who atones.

[14] In T. B. Sanhedrin 37b, exile is said by Rabbi Johanan (probably A.D. 279–320) to atone for *all* sins. This is the measure of the suffering it involves: but views differed on this as the same passage shows. (That "exile" is often, if not almost always among nations, regarded as an emaciation is suggested by the Welsh word for emigration [*ymfudo*]—the emigrant or exile becomes a mute.)

In the light of the above, it is not surprising that both the gift of prophecy—the gift of the Holy Spirit, and the gift of resurrection of the dead—were by some connected with the land. A passage from Mekilta Pisḥa I reads:[15]

You could say: "I cite the case of those prophets with whom He did speak outside of the land of Palestine."[16] True, He did speak with them outside of the land, but He did so only because of the merit of the fathers.[a] For thus it is said: "A voice is heard in Ramah, lamentation and bitter weeping. Rachel weeping for her children, because they are not. Thus saith the Lord: Refrain thy voice from weeping and thine eyes from tears; for thy work shall be rewarded, saith the Lord, and they shall come back from the land of the enemy. And there is hope for thy future saith the Lord (Jer. 31: 15f)." Some say: Even though He did speak with them outside of the land, and because of the merit of the fathers, He did so only at a pure spot, near water, as it is said: "And I was by the stream Ulai (Dan. 8: 2)." Again it says: "As I was by the side of the great river, which is Tigris (Dan. 10: 4)"; "The word of the Lord came expressly unto Ezekiel the priest the son of Buzi, in the land of the Chaldeans by the river Chebar (Ezek. 1: 3)." Some say: He had already spoken with him in the land, and then He spoke with him outside of the land, for thus it is said: "The word of the Lord had come and came to Ezekiel." "Had come" indicates that He had spoken with him in the land; "and came"[b] indicates that He spoke with him outside of the land. R. Eleazar the son of Zadok [A.D. 90–130] says: Behold it says: "Arise go forth into the plain (Ezek. 3: 22)"; this declares that the plain was suitable for divine revelation. You can learn from the following that the Shekinah does not reveal itself outside of the land. It is said: "But Jonah rose up to flee unto Tarshish from the presence of the Lord (Jonah 1: 3)." Could he have thought of fleeing from the presence of God? Has it not been said: "Wither shall I go from Thy spirit? Or whither shall I flee from Thy presence? If I ascend up into heaven Thou art there; if I make my bed in the nether world, behold, Thou art there. If I take the wings of the morning, and dwell in the uttermost parts of the sea; even there would Thy hand lead me, etc.? (Ps. 139: 7ff). And it is also written: "The eyes of the Lord, that run to and fro through the whole earth (Zech. 4: 10)"; and it is also written: "The Eyes of the Lord are in every place, keeping watch upon the evil and the good (Prov. 15: 3)"; "Though they dig into the netherworld...though they climb up to heaven...though they hide themselves

[15] Lauterbach's translation, Vol. 1, pp. 5ff, with his notes. See further a forthcoming article where I write on this passage.

[16] That Moses died before entering the land could not but puzzle the Rabbis. If we follow Daube, the puzzle strongly invaded the text of the Old Testament itself. By showing the land to him, according to legal usage, Yahweh did, in fact, give Moses all the land in possession (Deut. 3: 27; 34: 1ff). The scene on Mt. Pisgah, on this view, is one way to come to terms with the death of Moses outside the land. Is the claim that his burial place was unknown another (Deut. 34: 6)? See D. Daube, *Studies in Biblical Law*, Cambridge, 1947, pp. 28ff.

in the top of Carmel...though they go into captivity, etc. (Amos 9: 2–4)";
"There is no darkness, nor shadow of death, where the workers of iniquity
may hide themselves (Job 34: 22)." But Jonah thought: I will go outside of the
land, where the Shekinah does not reveal itself. For since the Gentiles are more
inclined to repent, I might be causing Israel to be condemned.[c]

  a. The expression "merit of the fathers", *z*ᵉ*kûth 'abôth*, here is not to be taken
  literally, but rather in the sense of merit of parents or ancestors, for here it refers
  to the merit of Rachel who was regarded as the mother of all Israel (see Gen.
  Rab. 71. 3). The passage from Jeremiah cited here as proof was interpreted to
  mean that Rachel cried to God about her children who were exiled and God
  promised her that He would return them to their own land (see Pesikta Rabbati,
  Friedmann, 11b). It was because of Rachel, then, that God communicated with the
  prophets in the Babylonian Exile to tell them about the return, when and how it
  was to take place.
  b. The infinitive absolute הָיֹה in this passage is considered as having the force of
  a pluperfect [Ezek. 1: 3 reads: ...אֶל־יְחֶזְקֵאל הָיָה דְבַר־יהוה הָיֹה].
  c. By contrast with the Ninevites who would readily listen to the prophet and
  repent, Israel would stand condemned for not so readily listening to the prophets.

This passage reveals both the affirmation of Israel as the only land fit for
prophecy and the dwelling of the Shekinah, and efforts made to deal with
the difficulties such a position confronted: for example, the fact that
Yahweh had appeared outside the land.[17]

  Again, in the view of some Rabbis, the resurrection was to take place
first in the land, and the benefits of the land in death are many.[18]

Our teachers said two things in Helbo's name [A.D. 320–359]. Why did the
Patriarchs long for burial in Eretz Israel? Because the dead of Eretz Israel will be
the first to be resurrected in the days of the Messiah and to enjoy the years of the
Messiah. R. Ḥanina [A.D. 219–279] said: He who dies without the Land and is
buried there experiences a twofold death... (Jer. 20: 6). [I.e. as though the

[17] L. Finkelstein, *New Light From the Prophets*, London, 1969, pp. 26ff considers Sifre
Deut. 135 on Deut. 18: 15 to be of pre-exilic origin, because it interprets the term מִקִּרְבְּךָ
"from the midst of thee" to mean: "And not from outside the land of Israel." Finkelstein
concludes that the writer could not have known of Jeremiah's prophecies in Egypt (Jer.
43: 8ff), or those of Ezekiel, or the story of Jonah, or of Job 38, where God spoke outside the
land. In this view, the statement in Mekilta Pisḥa 1 (Lauterbach p. 4) is a quotation of that
preserved in Sifre. "The compilers of Mekilta," he writes, "made an effort to reconcile the
norm of Sifre with the historical fact that Ezekiel did prophesy in Babylonia and Jeremiah in
Egypt. The most natural suggestion was that once a person had become a Prophet in the
Holy Land, he could also prophesy elsewhere. However, the transmitters of the Mekilta,
feeling that this was a forced explanation which did not account for Prophets who had never
prophesied in the Holy Land and yet had prophesied outside it, suggested other explanations
to meet the difficulty (p. 27)."
[18] Gen. Rabbah 96: 5: on the resurrection, see G. F. Moore, *Judaism*, Vol. II, pp. 379f.
The Rabbis in the passages cited are later than the beginning of the third century. But they
only make explicit what was implicit much earlier.

burial counts as an additional death when it is without the land.] If so, said R. Simon [date unknown], the righteous who are buried without the land have lost thereby? [Surely not.] But what does God do? He makes cavities like channels for them in the earth [the channels are in the earth, and therefore like long caves stretching to Eretz Israel], and they roll along in them until they reach Eretz Israel, when the Holy One, blessed be He, will infuse into them a spirit of life and they will arise. How do we know this? Because it is written... (Ezek. 37: 12, 14). Resh Lakish [A.D. 279–320] said: There is a text explicitly teaching that when they reach Eretz Israel God will put a soul into them, for it says... (Is. 42: 5).

Rabbi and Rabbi Eliezer [A.D. 165–200] were once walking by the gates outside Tiberias, when they saw the coffin of a corpse which had been brought from without the Land to be buried in Eretz Israel. Said Rabbi to R. Eliezer: What has this man availed by coming to be buried in Eretz Israel when he expired without the Land? I apply to him the verse, *Ye made thy heritage an abomination*—during your lifetime—*And ye defiled My Land* (Jer. 11: 7)—in your deaths. Yet since he will be buried in Eretz Israel, God will forgive him, he replied, for it is written *And his land maketh atonement for His people* (Deut. 32: 43) (... ‏וְכִפֶּר אַדְמָתוֹ עַמּוֹ.‏).

Some urged that those who died outside the land would not rise: but even an alien (Canaanitish) slave girl who dwelt in the land might expect to share in the resurrection. A passage from T. B. Ketuboth 111a reads as follows:

R. Eleazar stated: The dead outside the Land[a] will not be resurrected; for it is said in Scripture, *And I will set glory*[b] *in the land of the living*,[c] [implying] the dead of the land in which I have my *desire*[d] will be resurrected, but the dead [of the land] in which I have no desire will not be resurrected. R. Abba b. Memel [A.D. 320–359] objected: *Thy dead shall live, my dead bodies shall arise*;[e] does not [the expression] "*Thy dead shall live*" refer to the dead of the Land of Israel, and "*My dead bodies shall arise*" to the dead outside the Land;[f] while the text,[g] *And I will glory*[h] *in the land of the living* was written of Nebuchadnezzar concerning whom the All-Merciful said, "I will bring against them a king who is as swift as a *stag?*"[i] The other replied: Master, I am making an exposition of another Scriptural text: *He that giveth breath unto the people upon it*,[j] *and spirit to them that walk therein.*[k] But it is not written, *My dead bodies shall arise?*[l] That was written in reference to miscarriages.[m] Now as to R. Abba b. Memel [A.D. 320–359], what [is the application] he makes of the text,[n] "*He that giveth breath unto the people upon it?*"—He requires it for [an exposition] like that of R. Abbahu [A.D. 320–359] who stated: Even a Canaanite bondwoman who [lives] in the Land of Israel is assured of a place in[o] the world to come, [for in the context] here it is written, *Unto the people*[p] *upon it*,[q] and elsewhere it is written,

Abide ye here with[r] the ass[s] [which may be rendered][t] "people that are like an ass."[u]

And Spirit to them that work therein[q] [teaches], said R. Jeremiah b. Abba [A.D. 320–359] in the name of R. Johanan [A.D. 279–320], that whoever walks four cubits in the Land of Israel is assured of a place[v] in the world to come. Now according to R. Eleazar,[w] would not the righteous outside the Land[x] be revived?[y] R. Elai replied: [They will be revived] by rolling [to the Land of Israel]. R. Abba Sala the Great demurred: Will not the rolling be painful to the righteous? Abaye [died A.D. 339] replied: Cavities will be made for them underground.

Thou shalt carry me out of Egypt and bury me in their burying-place.[z] Karna remarked: [There must be here] some inner meaning. Our father Jacob well knew that he was a righteous man in every way, and, since the dead outside the Land will also be resurrected, why did he trouble his sons?[aa] Because he might possibly be unworthy to [roll through] the cavities.[bb]

Similarly you read in Scripture, *And Joseph took an oath of the children of Israel,* [*saying...ye shall carry up my bones from hence*],[cc] and R. Hanina remarked: [There is here] an inner meaning. Joseph well knew himself to be a righteous man in every way, and, since the dead outside the Land[dd] will be revived, why did he trouble his brothers [with a journey of] four hundred parasangs? Because he might possibly be unworthy to [roll through] the cavities.[ee]

a. Of Israel.

b. צְבִי (= glory). Cf. *infra* notes d, i.

c. Ezek. 26: 20.

d. צביון containing the three letters of צבי (compare *supra* note b). God's care for Palestine is taken for granted. Cf. e.g., *A Land which the Lord thy God careth for; the eyes of the Lord thy God are always upon it* (Deut. 11: 12).

e. Is. 26: 19.

f. Of Israel.

g. Lit., "and what."

h. V. *supra* note b.

i. צְבִי also means "stag" (cf. *supra* note b).

j. The land of Israel.

k. Is. 42: 5.

l. Is. 26: 19.

m. Even they will be resurrected but only in the Land of Israel.

n. Lit., "that."

o. Lit., "daughter of."

p. עַם.

q. Is. 42: 5.

r. עַם.

s. Gen. 22: 5.

t. The consonants עם being the same (compare *supra* nn. p and r).

u. Sc. slaves who are considered the property of the master. As the "*people*" spoken of in Is. 42: 5 are assured of a place in the world to come, so are the "people" referred to in Gen. 22: 5. Moore describes this as "a specimen of exegetical whimsicality, rather than an eccentricity of opinion." (*Judaism*, Vol. II, p. 390.)

v. Lit., "sons of."

w. Who based his view on Ezek. 26: 20, *supra.*

x. Of Israel.

y. But this, surely, is most improbable.

z. Gen. 47: 30.

aa. To carry him to Canaan?

bb. *Var. lec.*, "because he did not accept the suffering of the pain of rolling through the cavities (Yalḳuṭ and עין יעקב)."

cc. Gen. 50: 25.

dd. Of Israel.

ee. See n. bb.

At the end of the second century Rabbi Meir, at his death, required that his remains should be cast into the sea off the Palestinian coast, lest he be buried in foreign soil. There is no space or necessity here to enlarge further. The desire to die in the land, to possess the soil, to make pilgrimages to it, all these manifestations of attachment to the land history attests.[19]

Throughout the centuries, beginning with the fall of Jerusalem in A.D. 70, the conscious cultivation of the memory of the land, concentrated in Jerusalem and the Temple, has continued in Judaism.[20] The

[19] See E. M. Meyers, BA, Vol. XXXIII, Feb. 1970, No. 1, pp. 1–29 on "Secondary Burials in Palestine." And now *Jewish Ossuaries: Reburial and Rebirth, Biblica et Orientalia*, Rome, Institute Press, 1971, especially pp. 72ff. It is replete with examples. The necropolis at Beth Shearim—presenting arcasolia, kokhim, and pits, all in simultaneous use—was a centre for the reburial of Jews from all over the Diaspora. The matter is dealt with interestingly and thoroughly by Meyers, BA, p. 26. He appeals not only to the necropolis at Beth Shearim, but to the ossuary inscriptions at Jerusalem. There can be no doubt that from the first century up to the fourth century A.D. many Jews arranged to be buried in Palestine. Burial in the land wrought atonement—Deut. 32: 43 being cited in support of this in the passage from Gen. Rabbah 96: 5 (Soncino translation p. 890), cited above. On pilgrimages, see S. Safrai, "Pilgrimage to Jerusalem at the End of the Second Temple Period" in *Studies in the Jewish Background of the New Testament*, Assen, 1969, pp. 12–21. For R. Meir [A.D. 140–165] and the land, see T. J. Kilaim 9: 6: the section is translated by Schwab as follows:

"R. Meir, sur point de mourir à Esyou (près d'Antioche), recommanda de dire aux habitants de la Palestine: 'Voice votre corde [Avec elle, au jour de la Resurrection, le cadavre serait tiré en Terre-Sainte. Aussi, les gens pieux avaient soin de faire munir leurs pieds d'une corde]; et malgré cela, il ajouta aussitôt après son décès, on mit sa bière au bord de la mer (afin de toucher ainsi à la Terre-Sainte), selon ces mots (Psaume 24: 2): Il l'a fondée sur les mers...'"

The whole section in T. J. Kilaim is extremely important for the land. Pilgrimage can be understood as a vicarious offering in substitution for life in the land.

[20] With such a cultivation are to be associated the following data which are noted by A. Heschel, *Israel: Echo of Eternity*, 1969, pp. 60ff, although they are not precisely dated by him.

1. The sages at Jamnia issued decrees that were designed to recall the city, for example, "Before time the *Lulab* was carried seven days in the Temple, but in the provinces one day

Rabbis at Jamnia, in demanding that the *Tefillah* or *Shemoneh Esreh* should be said three times a day, morning, afternoon, and evening only. After the Temple was destroyed Rabban Johanan b. Zakkai (first century A.D.) ordained that in the provinces it should be carried seven days in memory of the Temple; also (he ordained) that on the whole of the Day of Waving it should be forbidden to (eat new produce) (Mishnah Rosh Hashanah 4: 3)."

2. Similarly personal—not only national—mourning came to be associated with Jerusalem. "Like one whom his mother comforteth, so will I comfort you, and in Jerusalem shall ye be comforted (ADPD, p. 324)." These words are part of a prayer in which the heavenly "future" and earthly Jerusalem are strangely intermixed. Their date eludes me.

3. The extreme of joy is also connected with Jerusalem. At the conclusion of the Jewish wedding service a prayer is spoken for the city of Jerusalem:

> May she who was barren (Zion) be exceeding glad and exult, when her children are gathered within her in joy. Blessed art thou, O Lord, who makest Zion joyful through her children (ADPB, p. 299).

This is followed by the breaking of a glass by the bridegroom in remembrance of the destruction of Jerusalem. Among the prayers for the occasion (see Heschel, *Israel*, p. 62) is the following:

> May Zion rejoice
> as her children are restored to her in joy.
> Praised be Thou, O Lord,
> Who causes Zion to rejoice at her children's return...
> O Lord our God,
> May there soon be heard
> in the cities of Judah
> and in the streets of Jerusalem
> the voice of gladness...

(Heschel gives no date for this prayer.)

4. On ordinary, no less than extraordinary, days, Jerusalem is to be remembered. After meals, daily, the prayers include the following words:

> Have mercy, O Lord our God, upon Israel thy people, upon Jerusalem thy city, upon Zion the abiding place of thy glory, upon the Kingdom of the House of David thine anointed, and upon the great and holy house that was called by thy name... (ADPB, p. 281).

Attachment to the land of Israel, among certain circles at least, is claimed to have so dominated Jewish liturgical development that prayers for dew and for rain "accord with the seasons of the Holy Land rather than with the climates of the lands in which the worshippers recite the prayers." (See Heschel, *Israel*, pp. 64f: but the point is not clear from his reference.)

Of the desire of pious Jews to connect the birth of their children with the land and their own deaths with the same, so that they sought if possible to be buried in the land or to have a clod of heavy soil from the land thrown on their coffins, symbol of their return to Zion, or to receive water from the land as a gift—of all this there is a living tradition but it is difficult to document and date every detail: but the significance of Gen. 23, must not be overlooked (see above p. 22, n. 17). While the incidence of the motifs we have traced in this note has been widespread in Judaism, the extent to which they have been spiritualized, especially in certain quarters, is open to question.

Like many others, Heschel, in earlier works had emphasized that the Old Testament and Judaism are primarily concerned with time or events, and that space was secondary. In his work *Israel*, he does not depart from this position, but reconciles it with an emphasis on "space" also. Compare his *God in Search of Man: A Philosophy of Judaism*, Philadelphia, 1956, pp. 200ff with the later volume, *Israel*, where he recognizes the role of space and time. For example on pp. 28–30 of the latter work he writes, "Jerusalem is a place to which we all turn when we pray, of which we all think when we hope, to which our hearts go to weep. *On the eve of the Sabbath, at the decisive moment, about to enter holiness in time, in the midst of calling on the soul to welcome the Sabbath, we become engrossed in what is holy in space. What is*

(Mishnah Berakoth 4: 1ff), had in mind, among other things, the perpetual remembrance of Jerusalem and the land. The *Shemoneh Esreh* for the morning and afternoon service corresponded to the morning and afternoon daily whole-offerings in the Temple. There was no time fixed for the evening *Shemoneh Esreh*, but on Sabbaths and Festivals the *Shemoneh Esreh* was to be said four times (there being demanded an Additional *Tefillah* corresponding to the "Addition Offering" presented on those days in the ancient Temple). Three times daily, then, the Jew was required to pray; among other things, he was required to repeat the 14th Benediction (dated by Dugmore in 168–165 B.C.), the 16th (possibly pre-Maccabean), and the 18th (A.D. 40–70). These read as follows:

Benediction 14

רחם יי אלהינו	Be merciful, O Lord our God, in Thy
ברחמיך הרבים	great mercy, towards Israel Thy
על ישראל עמך	people, and towards Jerusalem Thy
ועל ירושלם	city, and towards Zion the abiding
עירך ועל ציון	place of Thy glory, and towards Thy
משכן כבודך	temple and Thy habitation, and to-
ועל היכלך ועל	wards the kingdom of the house of
מעונך ועל	David, Thy righteous anointed one.
מלכות בית	Blessed art Thou, O Lord God of
דויד משיח	David, the builder of Jerusalem.
צדקך ברוך	
אתה יי אלהי	
דויד בונה	
ירושלם:	

Benediction 16

רצה יי אלהינו	Accept [us], O Lord our God, and
ושכון בציון	dwell in Zion; and may Thy servants
ויעבדוך עבדיך	serve Thee in Jerusalem. Blessed art
בירושלם ברוך	Thou, O Lord, whom in reverent fear
אתה יי שאותך	we serve [*or*, worship].
ביראה נעבוד:	

holy in time, has left its imprint on the land, on Jerusalem," whose "excellence is in her being an event in the form of a city (our italics)." Or again Heschel writes: "Her stones became monuments, space became time (*Israel*, p. 32)." If what we have dealt with above be accepted, "space," as well as time, was always important in the Old Testament, and the caution voiced by J. Barr in his brilliant chapter on "The Concepts of History and Revelation" in *Old and New in Interpretation*, London, 1966, pp. 65ff is reinforced by this study also. The emphasis on Israel as a people of time goes back especially to Hegel. See also 'Abd Al-Tafahum, *Religion in the Middle East*, Cambridge, 1969, p. 369.

Benediction 18

שים שלומך   Bestow Thy peace upon Israel Thy
על ישראל   people and upon Thy city and upon
עמך ועל   Thine inheritance, and bless us, all of
עירך ועל   us together. Blessed art Thou, O
נחלתך   Lord, who makest peace.
וברכנו כולנו
כאחד ברוך
אתה יי עושה
השלום :

That there was a deliberate concern with Jerusalem appears from the text in Mishnah Berakoth 4: 1ff, where the rules concerning the *Shemoneh Esreh*, indicated above, are set forth, and where Mishnah Berakoth 4: 5 states that, according to R. Joshua (A.D. 80–120),

If [a man] was riding on an ass [when the time for the prayer is upon him] he should dismount [to say the Tefillah: Danby]. If he cannot dismount he should turn his face [toward Jerusalem]; and if he cannot turn his face, he should direct his heart toward the Holy of Holies.

The centrality of the land is clear. The same is also emphasized in the following passage from Num. Rabbah 23: 7 on Num. 34: 2. The phrase "Our Rabbis taught" suggests an early tradition:

WHEN YE COME INTO THE LAND OF CANAAN (34: 2). *Halachah:* Before they entered the Land, what blessing did they say after meals? Our Rabbis taught: Before they entered the Land of Israel they used to recite one blessing, viz. "Who feedeth all [ADPB, p. 280]." When they entered the Land of Israel they recited also the blessing, "For the land and for the food [ADPB, p. 281]." When the Land was destroyed they added the blessing, "Who rebuildest Jerusalem [ADPB, p. 282]." When the people slain at Bethar[a] were given burial the blessing, "Who art good and doest good [ADPB, p. 283]," was added, "Who are good" being said because the bodies did not decay, and "Who doest good" because they were given burial. Of all the blessings there is none more precious than the one "For the land and for the food." For our Rabbis have said that any one who does not mention in the Grace after Meals the blessing, "For the land and for the food," "a desirable land," the covenant of circumcision, the Torah and life [ADPB, p. 280], has not fulfilled his duty. The Holy One, blessed be He, said: "The Land of Israel is more precious to Me than everything. Why? Because I sought it out." In this strain it says, *In that day I lifted up My hand unto them, to bring them forth out of the land of Egypt into a land that I had sought out for them, flowing with milk and honey, which is the beauty of all lands*

(Ezek. 20: 6). And in the same strain it says, *And give thee a pleasant land, the goodliest heritage of the nations* (Jer. 3: 19). You find the same to have been the case when Joshua slaughtered the [Canaanite] kings. R. Jannai the priest says that there were sixty-two kings in the land. There were thirty-one at Jericho and thirty-one in the days of Sisera. When the latter went to fight against Israel they were also slain with him. Why did they go? Because they longed to drink of the water of the Land of Israel, and so they begged of Sisera, saying to him: "We beg of you, let us come with you to the war!" Every king who desired to go to war himself laid out money and hired mercenaries to assist him. These kings said to Sisera: "We do not ask anything of you. We will come with you for nothing, because we long to fill our stomachs with the water of that land." This may be inferred from the text which says, *The kings came, they fought, then fought the kings of Canaan, in Taanach on account of the waters of Megiddo; they took no gain of money* (Judg. 5: 19). This serves to inform you that no land was so precious as the Land of Israel. Said the Holy One, blessed be He, to Moses: "The Land, surely, is precious to Me"; as it says, *A land which the Lord thy God careth for...always* (Deut. 11: 12); and Israel are precious to Me; as it says, *Because the Lord loved you* (ib. 7: 8). "I shall," said the Holy One, blessed be He, "bring Israel, who are precious to Me, into the Land that is precious to Me"; as it says, WHEN YE COME INTO THE LAND OF CANAAN.

a. During the Bar Cochba revolt, 132–135 C.E.

The deliberate recalling of the Temple and, thereby of Jerusalem and the land, in the liturgy also appears from the following. Mishnah Rosh-ha-Shanah 4: 1–3

If a Festival-day of the New Year fell on a Sabbath they might blow the *shofar* in the Holy City but not in the provinces. After the Temple was destroyed Rabban Johanan b. Zakkai [first century] ordained that they might blow it wheresoever there was a court. R. Eliezer [first century: A.D. 80–120] said: Rabban Johanan b. Zakkai ordained it so only for Jabneh. They replied: It is all one whether it was Jabneh or any other place wherein was a court.

In this also Jerusalem surpassed Jabneh in that they could blow the *shofar* in any city that could see Jerusalem and that could hear [the *shofar* in Jerusalem] and that was near, and that was able to come; but at Jabneh they could blow it only in the court.

Beforetime the *Lulab* was carried seven days in the Temple, but in the provinces one day only. After the Temple was destroyed, Rabban Johanan b. Zakkai ordained that in the provinces it should be carried seven days in memory of the Temple (*ẓêker lammiqᵉddâsh*).

In other ways the same purpose was achieved, as recorded in the following passage from T. B. Baba Bathra 60b:

Our Rabbis taught: When the Temple was destroyed for the second time,[a] large numbers in Israel became ascetics, binding themselves neither to eat meat nor to drink wine. R. Joshua got into conversation with them and said to them: My sons, why do you not eat meat nor drink wine? They replied: Shall we eat flesh which used to be brought as an offering on the altar, now that this altar is in abeyance? Shall we drink wine which used to be poured as a libation on the altar, but now no longer? He said to them: If that is so, we should not eat bread either, because the meal offerings have ceased. They said: [That is so, and] we can manage with fruit. We should not eat fruit either, [he said,] because there is no longer an offering of firstfruits. Then we can manage with other fruits [they said]. But, [he said,] we should not drink water, because there is no longer any ceremony of the pouring of water.[b] To this they could find no answer, so he said to them: My sons, come and listen to me. Not to mourn at all is impossible, because the blow has fallen. To mourn overmuch is also impossible, because we do not impose on the community a hardship which the majority cannot endure, as it is written, *Ye are cursed with a curse,*[c] *yet ye rob me* [*of the tithe*], *even this whole nation.*[d] The Sages therefore have ordained thus. A man may stucco his house, but he should leave a little bare. (How much should this be? R. Joseph [A.D. 320–375] says, A cubit square; to which R. Hisda [A.D. 320–375] adds that it must be by the door.) A man can prepare a full-course banquet, but he should leave out an item or two. (What should this be? R. Papa [died A.D. 395] says: The hors d'œuvre of salted fish.) A woman can put on all her ornaments, but leave off one or two. (What should this be? Rab [circa A.D. 240] said: [Not to remove] the hair on the temple.)[e] For so it says, *If I forget thee, O Jerusalem, let my right hand forget, let my tongue cleave to the roof of my mouth if I remember thee not, if I prefer not Jerusalem above my chief joy.*[f] What is meant by "my chief joy?"[g]—R. Isaac [circa A.D. 320] said: This is symbolised by the burnt ashes[h] which we place on the head of a bridegroom. R. Papa asked Abaye [A.D. 375–427]: Where should they be placed? [He replied]: Just where the phylactery is worn, as it says, *To appoint unto them that mourn in Zion, to give them a garland* [*pe'er*] *for ashes* [*epher*].[i] Whoever mourns for Zion will be privileged to behold her joy, as it says, *Rejoice with Jerusalem etc.*[j] It has been taught: R. Ishmael ben Elisha (a pupil of R. Neḥoniah ben Haḳana; a Tanna) said: Since the day of the destruction of the Temple we should by rights bind ourselves not to eat meat nor drink wine, only we do not lay a hardship on the community unless the majority can endure it. And from the day that a Government has come into power which issues cruel decrees against us and forbids to us the observance of the Torah and the precepts[k] and does not allow us to enter into the "week of the son"[l] (according to another version, "the salvation of the son"),[m] we ought by rights to bind ourselves not to marry and beget children, and the seed of Abraham our father would come to an end of itself. However, let Israel go their way: it is better that they should err in ignorance than presumptuously.

a. In 70 C.E.

b. On the Feast of Tabernacles. See Mishnah Sukkah 4.

c. This is taken to mean: "You have laid on yourselves an adjuration (to bring the tithe)."

d. Malachi, 3: 9. It is assumed that the adjuration would not have been effective unless the *whole nation* had taken part in it; which is taken to show that we do not impose a hardship unless we are sure that the majority can stand it.

e. Which was usually removed as a mark of elegance.

f. Ps. 137: 5, 6.

g. Lit., "Head of my joy."

h. Lit., "ashes from the hearth."

i. Is. 61: 3. The word *pe'er* is supposed to refer to the phylacteries on the basis of the verse, *Bind thy headtire (pe'erka) upon thee* (Ezek. 24: 17).

j. Is. 66: 10.

k. The reference is to the persecution instituted by the Emperor Hadrian after the revolt of Bar Kochba, 135 C.E.

l. שבוע הבן. I.e., the rite of circumcision. [So Rashbam (died 1174) and Rashi (died 1105); Sanh. 32b. This term is said to have been adopted by the Jews as a disguise during the Hadrianic persecutions when the rite was prohibited in order to remove any suspicion that they were engaged in a religious observance. Others explain the term as denoting the seven days of festivities that followed the birth of a child. The expression "the week of the daughter," שבוע הבת also occurs in Nahmanides's *Torath Ha'adam*, 35b. This is to be taken as a proof against the usual identification of "the week of the son" with "the rite of circumcision."]

m. [ישוע הבן], "The redemption of the son (Rashi)"; or "The birth of a son (R. Tam)"; Tos. B.K. 80a, s.v. לבי.] (See further for bibliographical references the Soncino translation, p. 246.)

Again other elements in the Jewish liturgy came to be *zêker l<ĕ>ḥôr<e>bbân*, that is, in memory of the destruction. For three weeks of sorrow, ending on the ninth day of the month of Ab, which is given over entirely, for twenty-four hours, to fasting, Jews annually recall the destruction of their land. So much has that event become the quintessence of the suffering of Jewry that the 9th of Ab is recognized as a day on which disasters recurred again and again to the Jewish people. Connected with it, significantly, was the decree that the fathers should not enter the promised land. The passage in T. B. Ta'anith 29a, which states this, cannot easily be dated. But it is traced to an unknown Rabbi whose words are explained by R. Ḥama b. Ḥananiah (A.D. 279–320). The pertinent passage in Mishnah Ta'anith 4: 6–7 reads as follows:

...On the 9th of Ab it was decreed against our fathers that they should not enter into the land [of Israel],[a] and the Temple was destroyed the first and the second time,[b] and Beth-Tor[c] was captured and the City was ploughed up. When Ab comes in, gladness must be diminished.

In the week wherein falls the 9th of Ab it is forbidden to cut the hair or wash the clothes; but it is permitted on the Thursday because of the honour due to the Sabbath. On the eve of the 9th of Ab let none eat of two cooked dishes, let none eat flesh and let none drink wine. Rabban Simeon b. Galamiel says: A man need but make some difference.[d] R. Judah says: A man must turn up his couch.[e] But the Sages did not agree with him.

  a. Num. 14: 29ff.
  b. By Nebuchadnezzar and by Titus.
  c. Or Bethar; the present Bittir, south of Jerusalem, the scene of Bar Cocheba's final defeat in A.D. 135.
  d. E.g. eat somewhat less than is his custom.
  e. And sleep on the ground. A sign of mourning. Jer. 14: 2. Cf. Mishnah Moed Katan 3: 7.

As a matter of history only the fall of Betar (the Beth Tor of the text), the last stronghold of Bar Cocheba, captured by the Romans in A.D. 135, possibly occurred on the 9th of Ab. The first Temple was burnt on the 7th of Ab (2 Kings 25: 8–9) or on the 10th of that month (Jer. 52: 12): the second Temple fell on the 10th (see the dictionaries). The essential feature of the liturgy for the 9th of Ab (which is the only twenty-four-hour fast, apart from the Day of Atonement) was the reading of Lamentations and dirges. Later, on the fast of the 9th of Ab, an addition which concentrates on Jerusalem still further was made to the service. The prayer, as used today, begins with the words:

> O Lord God, comfort the mourners of Zion;
> Comfort those who grieve for Jerusalem.

It ends with:

> Praised are You, O Lord, who comforts Zion
> Praised are You, who rebuilds Jerusalem.

Unfortunately the date at which this addition was introduced eludes me: it is printed in its entirety in ADPB, pp. 121ff. But in the Jerusalem Talmud at Berakoth 8a, an addition to the Eighteen Benedictions is suggested for use, apparently in all services, not only in the afternoon where the additional prayer referred to above is customarily used. The passage in T. Jer. Berakoth 8a traces the prayer in its revised form to R. Ḥiyya of Sepphoris (third century or later): it was inserted into the Eighteen Benedictions—at the point which in the Palestinian Version is the Fourteenth Benediction. This Fourteenth Benediction is dated by Dugmore in 168–165 B.C. (*The Influence of the Synagogue on the Divine Office*, London, 1941, p. 121). But in T. Jer. Berakoth 8a we read, in Schwab's translation, the following:

R. Aḥa bar-Isaac, au nom de R. Iliya de Sephoris, dit:ᵃ Au jour d'Ab (anni-
versaire de la destruction des deux temples), il faut insérer (dans les dix-huit
bénédictions) des paroles relatives aux événements; voici ce que le particulier
doit dire: "Éternel notre Dieu, étends ta miséricorde infine et ta bienveillance,
qui ne se dément jamais, sur nous, sur ton peuple Israël, sur Jérusalem, ta ville,
sur Sion, résidence de ta gloire, sur cette ville en deuil, détruite, bouleversée,
désolée, livrée entre les mains des superbes, dévastée par les méchants, dont les
légions (legiones) se sont emparées, que les idolâtres ont profanée; tu l'avais
donnée à ton peuple Israël, comme un héritage pour la postérité de *Yeschouroun*;
elle a été détruite par le feu, et c'est par le feu que dans l'avenir tu la reconstruiras,
comme il est dit: Je serai pour elle, dit l'Éternel, *une muraille de feu tout autour, et
je résiderai dans son sein pour sa gloire* (Zacharie, II, 9)."

a. Ci-après, IX, 4.

See further I. Elbogen, *Der Jüdische Gottesdienst*, Frankfurt A.M., 1931,
pp. 53ff, 128f, 181; A. Büchler, JQR, Old Series, Vol. XX, pp. 799ff.

So far, in showing how the sentiment for the land remained powerfully
active in Judaism after A.D. 70, we have mostly adduced materials from
the Haggadah and the liturgy of Rabbinic Judaism. There was also a more
specifically halakic approach to the question of the land, some evidence
for which we used above on p. 55. The ramifications of this development
we are unfortunately not competent to trace. We can only refer to two
items. In the Jerusalem Talmud, in a tractate whose importance for our
theme we noted previously, in Kilayyim VII: 5, ed. Krotoshin (or Venice)
31a, line 32 (Venice, line 25), Orla 1: 2, ed. Krotoshin 61a, line 11 (Venice,
line 9), there is a law which is quoted as giving to Israel, under Jewish law,
a legal right to the land. The law states: אעפ"י שאין קרקע גזול יש ייאוש
לקרקע. This is translated by Lieberman as: "Though soil cannot be stolen,
a man can forfeit his right to this soil by giving up hope of ever regaining
it." The argument is that "Israel" "never for a moment gave up hope of
regaining the soil of Palestine. Never did they renounce their right to
Palestine and never have they ceased claiming it in their prayers and in
their teachings. It is on this foundation that [Jews] now claim that Eretz
Israel belongs to [them] (S. Lieberman, *Proceedings of the Rabbinical
Assembly of America*, Vol. 12, 1949)." Not unrelated to this law is that of
חֲזָקָה (prescription) in which the legal right of Israel to the land was sought.
(See *Baba Bathra* 28a, and notes in Soncino translation for חֲזָקָה.) But how
early such attempts were and how significant in the discussion of the
relationship between Israel and Eretz Israel in the period of our concern

we cannot determine. The history of the halakic understanding of that relationship lies beyond the scope of this study.[21]

Be that as it may, it is in the Haggadah and the liturgy that the full force of the sentiment for the land is to be felt. It cannot properly be seen except through Jewish eyes, nor felt except through Jewish words, such as those so powerfully uttered by Abraham Heschel in a book, *Israel: An Echo of Eternity*, New York, 1969, which is more a lyrical outburst than a critical study.

[21] The implication of the view that the true life was only fully possible in the land was that life outside the land was unclean. The Temple was in the land. True there was a cultic life in Yeb (Elephantine), Egypt, at the beginning of the sixth century B.C., and Onias built a Temple at Leontopolis (Jos. *Antiquities*, XIII. 3. 1, *Jewish Wars*, VII. 7. 3), which persisted till after 70 A.D. (*Jewish Wars*, VII. 10. 2), and Mishnah Menahoth 13: 10 at the least does not condemn it out of hand, even though one has to agree with Tcherikover, *Hellenistic Civilization and the Jews*, pp. 275–281, that Onias's temple was politically grounded. But at best these temples outside the land were dubious shadows of the Temple at Jerusalem. Where outside the land could authentic priests be found? Yet the uncleanness of the land of the peoples was not given legal expression till late. References to this uncleanness in Amos (!) 7: 17 and Josh. 22: 19 are not legal. L. Ginzberg traced the decree concerning the uncleanness of the land of the peoples and of glassware to Jose ben Joeser and Jose ben Johanan; their date is uncertain, but given by Ginzberg as early Maccabean. See T. B. Shabbath. 14b–15a. The text reads, "Jose ben Joeser of Zeredah and Jose ben Johanan of Jerusalem decreed [the capacity to receive] uncleanness upon the land of the peoples and on glassware."

According to Ginzberg, who follows others, this decree was aimed at stopping emigration by condemning those outside the land to perpetual impurity, and was imposed when, as a result of persecution under Antiochus Epiphanes, emigration from the land began (*On Jewish Law and Lore*, Philadelphia, 1955, p. 80). The decree on the uncleanness of glassware, which because it was imported caused loss to those producing earthen and metal ware in the land, was economically motivated: imported glassware declared ritually impure could not compete so effectively with the clean products of the land. The desire to curb foreign competition also influenced pronouncements on wheat, metal vessels, garlic, cattle (Ginzberg, pp. 79–86).

But Neusner appealing to the Jer. Talmud Shabb. 1: 4; Pesaḥim 1: 6; Ket. [sic] 8: 11 urges that there was no well-established tradition about who was responsible for the decree on the land of the peoples and glassware till the fourth century A.D. The text of Jer. Talmud Shabb. 1: 4 is not as clear to us as to Neusner, and in view of the decrees on the sale of large cattle in C.D.C. to which Ginzberg refers (p. 83), the other decrees are likely to be early also despite the confusion of the traditions. See J. Neusner, *The Rabbinic Traditions*, vol. 1, pp. 69ff).

Related to all this is the interpretation of M. Berakoth 5: 1: "Even if a king salutes a man [when he is saying the *Tefillah*] he may not return the greeting," and the saying in T. B. Baba Kamma 113a that the law of the land where a Jew lives is law. The former was referred only to a Jewish king in the land (T. B. Ber. 32b), the latter only to Babylonia and other lands of the Dispersion. In the land itself the Torah alone applied. According to Ginzberg (pp. 86ff), "gentile rulers who held sway over the Holy Land, whom the sages regarded as robbers and extortioners [were] without any rights whatsoever either in the land or over its inhabitants (p. 88)." This has a bearing on our discussion of Maccabees and "Zealots" and reinforces our view that they assumed the importance of the land. For Neusner's criticism of Ginzberg, *The Rabbinic Traditions*, vol. III, pp. 338–341.

V. CAUTIONARY CONSIDERATIONS

Our survey of the doctrine of the land in Israelite religion and in Judaism is over. It is now necessary to turn to what may easily be forgotten. Concentration on the land, such as we have exhibited in the above pages, *ipso facto* tends to a certain distortion, and needs to be corrected by the recognition of what, for convenience, we shall divide into three considerations, interrogatory, factual, and contextual.

1. INTERROGATORY

At this point it is necessary to deal with two questions concerning groups or currents which present complexities not easily resolved. First, is there not evidence that a nomadic ideal persisted in the Old Testament and in Judaism which regarded the wilderness (which played such a significant role in the life of the covenanters at Qumran and otherwise in Israel), rather than the land, as the proper sphere for the people of God? And, secondly, how far, in fact, did loyalty to the land, as such, play a part in the two great revolts against foreign occupation in post-exilic Jewish history—by the Maccabeans, and the "Zealots," with whom the covenanters of Qumran have sometimes been identified, against the Seleucids and the Romans respectively?

a. A NOMADIC IDEAL?

Let us first examine whether there is a persistent nomadic ideal in the Old Testament and Judaism.

Certain protests against, or modifications of, emphasis on the land, implicit and explicit, have to be recognized. The rightness of Israel's conquest of Canaan did not go unquestioned, as we have already seen. But, the cruelty of the conquest apart, the antipathy which is endemic and universal between those who follow the nomadic life and those who "indulge" in the sedentary, agricultural way is evident in the Old Testament. In Gen. 4: 1–17, Cain, the tiller of the soil, who first built a city, is at a disadvantage against Abel, the keeper of sheep: the offering of the firstlings of the flock is more acceptable than that of the fruit of the ground. It is the nomadic patriarchs who represent the classic simplicity of the ideal human life.[1]

[1] R. de Vaux, *Ancient Israel: Its Life and Institutions*, New York, 1961, pp. 3–15, notes the survival of relics of nomadism in the language of Israel (p. 13), and the reaction against the

And further, the role of the wilderness[2] in the history of Israel has to be carefully noted. There are verses where the wilderness period, as such, seems to be regarded as the decisive phase of that history (Hos. 9: 10; Ezek. 16: 5; Jer. 31: 2; and less clearly, Deut. 32: 10), that is, the period of its election. But usually the "wilderness" is bound up with the Exodus, the events at Sinai, and the wanderings, in an inextricable complex. In the wilderness Israel had experienced danger in obeying God's word and help in that danger (Exod. 13: 17 – 14: 31; 19: 4 etc., etc.): there, according to J and E, it had received the revelation of God's name (Exod. 3: 13 [E]; Exod. 3: 1 [E]; Exod. 33, 34 [J]), on the knowledge of which depended the possibility and validity of Israelite worship. There also the covenant had been established and the Law given, the foundations, along with the revelation of the Name, of Israelite religion and of Judaism. Through the covenant, with which the Law was inextricably bound, Israel became the people of Yahweh. As Deut. 27: 9f puts it:

Hear, O Israel, this day you have become the people of the Lord your God. You shall therefore obey the voice of the Lord your God keeping his commandments and his statutes, which I command you this day.

The desert is, therefore, the place of revelation and of the constitution of "Israel" as a people: there was she "elected (Exod. 4: 22f)."[3]

It is not surprising, therefore, that prophets looked back to the period in the wilderness for inspiration. Elijah, in order to renew his resolution, returned to the wilderness, to the mountain where Yahweh had spoken to Moses, outside the land (1 Kings 19: 4–8). The time in the wilderness is regarded with nostalgia. Redemption is to be preceded by a return to the wilderness where the old status of love and trust, broken by the "harlotry" of life in the land, will be restored. This is expressed in Hos. 2: 14–15 (MT 2: 16–17):

Therefore, behold, I will allure her, and bring her into the wilderness (*mid⁰bbâr*), and speak tenderly to her. And there I will give her her vineyards, and make the

---

sedentary civilization of Canaan with its risks of moral and religious perversion (p. 14), but recognizes that nomadism itself is not an Old Testament ideal: also Marvin Pope, IDB, *ad rem*. The idealization of the patriarchal life crops up in strange ways; see, for example, Ignaz Maybaum, *Creation and Guilt*, London, 1969, p. 12: the patriarchs "stand not in the beginning from which history starts, but in the midst of history: to the world of the fathers [patriarchs] the Christian doctrine of original sin is not applicable."

[2] On terms for "wilderness," "desert," etc., see U. W. Mauser, *Christ in the Wilderness*, London, 1963, pp. 18ff, חָרְבָּה, עֲרָבָה, שְׁמָמָה, מִדְבָּר. There are subtle distinctions in the connotation of these terms which we cannot pursue here. For example, מִדְבָּר refers strictly "to open pasture land as distinct from cultivatable land." So J. Gray, *The Legacy of Canaan*, p. 193.

[3] On the above, see Mauser, *Christ in the Wilderness*, pp. 15ff.

Valley of Achor a door of hope. And there she shall answer as in the days of her youth, as at the time when she came out of the land of Egypt.[4]

The return to the wilderness is a return to the grace of God. Such a return is not envisaged by Jeremiah, who also regards the time of the wilderness as one of mutual love between Israel and Yahweh. Jer. 2: 1f reads:

The word of the Lord came to me, saying, "Go and proclaim in the hearing of Jerusalem. Thus says the Lord, I remember the devotion of your youth, your love as a bride, how you followed me in the wilderness (*mid᷾bbâr*), in a land not sown. Israel was holy to the Lord, the first fruits of his harvest. All who ate of it became guilty; evil came upon them, says the Lord."

The time of the wilderness was one in which Israel had found grace (Jer. 31: 2, compare Exod. 33: 12f, 16f). There is also an appeal to that time as the norm against which to judge the corruption of the sedentary life, a corruption that was bound up with a cultus that had evolved in the land. Amos asks:

Did you bring me to sacrifices and offerings the forty years in the wilderness (*mid᷾bbâr*), O house of Israel (5: 25)?

And in the same way and for the same purpose—that of elevating moral over cultic demands—Jeremiah writes in 7: 21–23:

Thus says the Lord of hosts, the God of Israel: "Add your burnt offerings to your sacrifices, and eat the flesh. For in the day that I brought them out of the land of Egypt, I did not speak to your fathers or command them concerning burnt offerings and sacrifices. But this command I gave them, 'Obey my voice, and I will be your God, and you shall be my people; and walk in all the way that I command you, that it may be well with you.'"

---

[4] Compare de Vaux, *Ancient Israel*, p. 14. On Hosea H. M. Lutz, *Jahwe, Jerusalem und die Völker, zur Vorgeschichte von Sach. 12, 1–8 und 14, 1–5*, Neukirchener Verlag, 1968, pp. 190f, writes: "Der Vorgang der 'Umkehrung' von Heilstraditionen Israels in Gerichtsankündigen über Israel ist in der Prophetie nicht selten. An erster Stelle muss in diesem Zusammenhang Hosea gennant werden. Bei ihm findet sich mehrfach die der geläufigen Exodus—Überlieferung schärfstens entgegengesetzte Drohung, Israel müsse wieder 'zurück nach Ägypten' [Hos. 8: 13; 9: 3, 6; 11: 5 und deutlich vorausgesetzt 7: 16; 11: 11;...ferner ebenso Deut. 28: 68]. In gleichem Sinne ist die ähnliche Ankündigung zu verstehen, dass Israel wieder in die Wüste müsse [Hos. 2: 16] und wieder Zelten wohnen werde [Hos. 12: 10]. Eine ausdrückliche Umkehrung der Bundesschlussformel liegt vor, wenn Jahwe Israel 'Nicht-mein-Volk' nennt und sich selbst, unter Anspielung auf Ex. 3: 14, als der 'Nicht-ich-bin' vorstellt [Hos. 1: 9]. Schliesslich ist auch im angedrohten Entzug der Kulturlandgüter [Hos. 2: 10f] und in der verheissenen Unfruchtbarteit des Volkes [Hos. 9: 11, 14, 16] eine polemische Verkehrung der der Erzväterüberlieferung zugehörigen Landnahme—und Nachkommenschaftsverheissung [Gen. 12: 1–4a; 15: 18; Gen. 15: 5 vgl. Deut. 26: 1, 2, 3, 9, 11; 11: 14; 7: 13] zu sehen."

In Is. 63: 10–14 the time in the wilderness had been marked by the presence of the Spirit.

Then (Yahweh) remembered the days of old, of Moses his servant. Where is he who brought up out of the sea the shepherds of his flock? Where is he who put in the midst of them his holy Spirit, who caused his glorious arm to go at the right hand of Moses, who divided the waters before them to make for himself an everlasting name, who led them through the depths? Like a horse in the desert (*mid^ebbâr*), they did not stumble. Like cattle that go down into the valley, the Spirit of the Lord gave them rest. So thou didst lead thy people, to make for thyself a glorious name.

But more important still, the response to the challenge of Canaanite religion to Yahwehism in some circles took the form of a complete rejection of the settled agricultural life as the will of Yahweh for his people. This was the position of the Rechabites,[5] who appear as a vital group as late as the sixth century B.C. They would not grow cereals, cultivate the vine, or live in houses. True they did live in Judah, but the Hebrew text at Jer. 35: 7 makes it clear that they regarded themselves merely as sojourners who had no original rights in the land. That they lived in tents, not in houses, marks them as deliberately nomadic: the tent is the nomadic abode, a symbol of nomadic opposition to sedentary culture, which was deemed to be unmanly and degrading (compare the attitude revealed in the story of the blessing of Jacob and Esau, Gen. 27: 11: Esau is a hairy man and Jacob a smooth man). The Rechabites' total abstinence from wine was not a moral protest against drunken Canaanite orgies connected with fertility rites (although such a protest is not to be excluded) so much as an affirmation of the nomadic life in which wine was unknown: their protest was not in "the name of" the desert. There are counterparts to the Rechabites among the Nabataeans.[6]

The Rechabites had a long history before the days of Jeremiah (2 Kings 10: 15): their ultimate origin may, indeed, have been with the Kenites, who claimed kinship with Moses (1 Chron. 2: 55).[7] They continued their

5 G. W. Anderson, *Peake*, pp. 162ff (section 132a), notes four possible responses to the Canaanite challenge. (1) Rejection; (2) appropriation; (3) compromise; (4) syncretism. Rechabitism was the clearest example of (1): it was a religious *cul-de-sac*: it limited Yahweh's rule by excluding it from urban and agricultural life.

6 M. Pope, IDB, *ad rem*. Note the emphasis on *the tent* in the story of the murder of Sisera, a Canaanite king, in Judg. 4: 11–22 (see also *vv*. 18, 20, 21, 22). Even after the Rechabites did come to live in houses, they called them "tents."

7 R. de Vaux, *Ancient Israel*, p. 15, thinks that the Chronicler has "used the fiction of a genealogical link to connect two communities who lived more or less the same kind of life." He emphasizes that the Rechabites were not a *survival* of primitive nomads, but a reactionary *emergence* in the ninth century B.C. On this view the existence of the Rechabites does not point

semi-nomadic life long after Israel's settlement in the land (Judg. 1: 15; 1 Sam. 15: 6; 27: 10; 30: 29), mainly on the southern borders of Judah. By the time of Jeremiah, although admirably active, they had dwindled to a few: the prophet could invite them all to meet him in a chamber in the Temple (Jer. 35: 2). There is meagre evidence that they did survive the exile, but it is likely that they increasingly succumbed to the ways of the majority in Israel. There are no traces of them in the New Testament itself.[8]

It is not impossible, however, that the Rechabites stood in some connection with the Nazirites about whom we do read in the New Testament.[9] The origins and purposes of the Nazirites are obscure. Some ancient evidence suggests that they were charismatic figures enjoining ritual fitness to fight the holy wars of Yahweh: note Samson (Judg. 13–15), the tribe of Joseph (Gen. 49: 26; Deut. 33: 16), and even Samuel (1 Sam. 1: 11). But they have also been understood as representatives of the opposition to the Canaanization of the cult of Yahweh. The Nazirite avoidance of wine was possibly bound up with a suspicion of the land of the vine, the vine being the symbol of agricultural as over against nomadic life (Amos 2: 11–12; Num. 6). But the requirement of the presentation of a cereal offering in Num. 6: 17 on the completion of the Nazirites' time of separation should warn us against pressing this.[10]

---

to a long-standing, continuous "nomadic" movement from the earliest times in Israel. There does not seem to be in the Old Testament the kind of tenderness toward the earth which, among some primitive peoples, for example, makes ploughing its surface seem cruel. J. Frazer refers to some aboriginal inhabitants of central India who, upon rising in the morning, ask pardon of the earth before stepping on the ground: "O Goddess who is clothed (surrounded) by the sea, whose breasts are mountains and who is the wife of Vishnu, I bow down to thee. Please forgive the touch of my feet... (*The Worship of Nature*, New York, 1926, p. 377)." A prophet, Smohalla, among the American Indians, in Oregon and Washington, on being asked by whites to till the ground, replied (and his reply was dictated not only by his hatred of the whites): "You ask me to plow the ground! Shall I take a knife and tear my mother's bosom? Then when I die she will not take me to her bosom to rest (V. Lanternari, *The Religions of the Oppressed: A Study of Modern Messianic Cults*, New York, 1963, pp. 110–111)."

[8] See M. Pope, IDB. That the Rechabites survived the Exile may appear from: (1) Neh. 3: 14, but the reference implies that Malchijah, the son of Rechab, no longer dwelt in a tent. He was probably merely of Rechabite descent; (2) 1 Chron. 2: 55: in later Jewish tradition the Rechabites contracted priestly marriages; and (3) there is evidence for the existence of Rechabites in El Jubar in Arabia in the twelfth century A.D. But were these continuous with those in the Bible? See now Frank S. Frick, "The Rechabites Reconsidered," JBL, Vol. XC, Part III, Sept. 1971, pp. 279–287. He suggests that those Rechabite traits which are normally taken to point to a nomadic society in fact can also point to a guild of craftsmen, "probably in this case a guild of metal-workers involved in the making of chariots and other weaponry p. 285)," in which case the Rechabites afford no support for a nomadic ideal.

[9] Matt. 2: 23 (possibly); Acts 18: 18; 21: 23–24; 24: 5. In 1 Macc. 3: 49–51, the Nazirites could not observe the rites for ending their vows because the Temple was profaned.

[10] R. de Vaux, *Ancient Israel*, pp. 465–467 for further details. Only if the Nazirite vow was for life could it be taken as a rejection of the nomadic life as such. In Num. 6: 1–21 it is

In any case the significance of the Rechabites and Nazirites should not be overemphasized. They were few in number and at no time did they represent the mind of a majority or of a very considerable number in Israel.[11] Jeremiah's commendation of the Rechabites (35: 18–19) referred not to their way of life as such but to their fidelity to that to which they were committed: he cherished a like fidelity for Israelites generally to the commandments to which *they* were committed. And the attempt to claim on the basis of the material we have presented above, and of other factors which we cannot consider here, that Israel had a nomadic ideal of life must be rejected.

To begin with, the passage from Amos which has been taken to suggest this has been otherwise explained. Thus Amos 5: 25 does not necessarily mean that Amos questioned the Mosaic origin of the sacrificial system. The prophet was aware of material in the Book of the Covenant—which combines cultic and moral requirements. Compare Amos 2: 8 with Exod. 22: 25–47, and 4: 5 with Exod. 23: 18. What Amos asks, in intent, is: "Was it only sacrifices and offerings that you offered to me in the wilderness and not also moral obedience?" He expected a negative answer. Or again it is possible that he expected an affirmative answer. The fathers did offer sacrifices, but offered them in faith, in the context of keeping the rest of the covenantal demands. Or yet again, in the light of Stephen's use of this verse in Acts 7: 35–43 and the reference to foreign deities in Amos 5: 26, it is possible to interpret Amos 5: 25 as challenging the fidelity of the Israelites to Yahweh during the period of the wilderness. In this case the emphasis would be on the pronoun in the verse: "Did you bring *me* sacrifices...?" Whichever of these alternatives be taken, it is clear that Amos 5: 25 probably involves no idealization of the period in the wilderness.[12]

The last alternative mentioned for the interpretation of Amos 5: 25 affords a convenient point of transition to other passages which present

temporary, but in Amos 2: 11–12 the Nazirite seems to have a life-long standing—he is not one who has taken a vow for a time, but one possessed of a God-given charisma for life. Thus Samson has a life-long consecration (Judg. 13: 4–5, 7, 13–14). It should be noted that the earliest Nazirites did not abstain from wine.

[11] In Jer. 35: 1ff "the whole house of the Rechabites" could be accommodated in "the chamber of the sons of Hanan...." They cannot have been numerous.

[12] On Amos 5: 25; see H. H. Rowley, BJRL, Vol. 29, 1945–6, pp. 340ff. Rowley's view was that Amos intended to claim that Israel did not only bring flesh-sacrifices and meal-offerings to Yahweh in the wilderness, but also true worship. So R. J. Thompson, *Penitence and Sacrifice in Early Israel*, Leiden, 1963, pp. 165f; S. Amsler, *Osee, Joel, Amos, Abdias, Jonas*, Neuchâtel, 1965, p. 215. P. Hyatt, *Peake*, p. 622 thinks that Yahweh demanded the renunciation of sacrifice. Contrast P. J. King, JBC, p. 250.

the time of the wilderness and the wilderness itself in a cold light, without any idealization.

First, we find a clear-eyed recognition of the period of the wilderness as marked by rebellion. It was a time of "murmuring."[13] The long and dangerous journey through the wilderness had not been the free choice of Israel, but the outcome of a command by Yahweh (Exod. 3, 4): it had not been voluntary but obedient. In the course of it there were trials to Israel's faith—Pharaoh and his army (Exod. 14: 10f), lack of water (Exod. 15: 24; 17: 2), of bread (Exod. 16: 2f), the giants barring entrance to the land (Num. 14: 2f). These all led to disobedience to Moses, the leader, to Aaron, his mouthpiece, and to Yahweh himself (Exod. 15: 24; 16: 2; 17: 2; Num. 14: 2): Israel tired of the wilderness life (Num. 21: 5). The "murmuring" reached its culmination in the worship of the golden calf (Exod. 32), the significance of which is manifold. The bull or calf is a central image of Canaanite fertility worship: the seduction of the latter, so we are to understand, had already exerted itself in the time of the wilderness. By the worship of the golden calf Israel revealed her preference for the worship of many gods (Exod. 32: 4) and practically revoked her covenant with Yahweh. The election of Israel was all but annulled (Exod. 32: 10); it was preserved only by the renewal of the covenant in Exod. 34. The point is that the wilderness was as much a scene of sin as of election.[14]

Secondly, it agrees with this that in Deuteronomy the time of the wanderings is used parainetically. Deut 8: 2–5 reads:

And you shall remember all the way which the Lord your God has led you these forty years in the wilderness (*mid^ebbâr*), that he might humble you, testing you to know what was in your heart, whether you would keep his commandments, or not. And he humbled you and let you hunger and fed you with manna, which you did not know, nor did your fathers know; that he might make you know that man does not live by bread alone, but that man lives by everything that proceeds out of the mouth of the Lord. Your clothing did not wear out upon

[13] See G. W. Coats, *Rebellion in the Wilderness: The Murmuring Motif in the Wilderness, Traditions of the Old Testament*, Nashville, 1968. If Coats be followed, the development of the theme of murmuring in the wilderness is not concerned with "the wilderness" as such, but rather with the rivalry between Judah and the Northern kingdom; "the northern rights to election were forfeited when the fathers in the wilderness rebelled. And in the place of that election, a new election is now enjoyed in Jerusalem through the Davidic heir (p. 251)." The *Sitz im Leben* for the murmuring tradition on this view is the cult in Jerusalem. In Deuteronomy the polemic disappears: the northern kingdom had ceased. Yahweh gives his aid in spite of the rebellion of Israel, and Israel continues to rebel in spite of Yahweh's aid. Yahweh reveals his intention to reject his people completely, but, through Moses' intercession, they are spared.

[14] See Mauser, *Christ in the Wilderness*, pp. 15ff.

you, and your foot did not swell, these forty years. Know then in your heart that, as a man disciplines his son, the Lord your God disciplines you.

Here there is no idealization of the time of the wilderness. Rather it was then that Yahweh had tested, disciplined, and humbled Israel: then had he led her to the knowledge that she lived solely by his word and to the humility that springs from this. There is no glorification of the simple nomadic life nor of the wilderness in themselves. Rather a *time* is remembered which, as Deut. 8: 7ff makes clear, prepared Israel for life in the land.

The emphasis on the time of the wilderness as one of terrible punishments and discipline and warning appears in the Psalms. It has been pointed out that that time is seldom referred to—as might be expected in view of Yahweh's providential succour, guidance, and election in it— in Psalms of praise and thanksgiving. Where it is referred to, rebelliousness is to the fore. Psalms 78, 95, and 106 are particularly instructive. Psalm 78 warns against falling into the sins of the fathers exemplified in the wilderness (78: 40); for the author of Ps. 95 the generation in the wilderness is the supreme example of sinfulness:

Harden not your hearts, as at Meribah, as on the day at Massah in the wilderness (*mid°bbâr*), when your fathers tested me, and put me to the proof, though they had seen my work. For forty years I loathed that generation and said, "They are a people who err in heart, and they do not regard my ways." Therefore I swore in my anger that they should not enter my rest (Ps. 95: 8–11).

And, again, in Ps. 106: 24–27 the exile itself is probably seen in the light of the sins in the time of the wanderings.

Then they despised the pleasant land, having no faith in his promise. They murmured in their tents, and did not obey the voice of the Lord. Therefore he raised his hand and swore to them that he would make them fall in the wilderness (*mid°bbâr*), and would disperse their descendants among the nations, scattering them over the lands.

In verses 22–23 fault is found even with the "rash" Moses.

The connection between the period of the wilderness and the exile is made also by Ezekiel in 20: 23. The prophet goes so far as to claim that at that time, in order that Israel might know that he was the Lord, Yahweh had given her "statutes that were not good and ordinances by which they could not have life (20: 25)": he had deliberately defiled and horrified his people (20: 26).[15] But in Ezekiel there is also an echo of

[15] On this in later Judaism, see H. J. Schoeps, *Theologie und Geschichte des Judenchristentums*, 1949, pp. 147–187.

Deuteronomy's view of the time of the wilderness as a painful preparation for life in the land. For him, in the future, before the redemption of Israel, the wilderness is to be the place of judgment, as it had been in the past. Ezekiel 20: 33–38 reads:

As I live, says the Lord God, surely with a mighty hand and an outstretched arm, and with wrath poured out, I will be king over you. I will bring you out from the peoples and gather you out of the countries where you are scattered, with a mighty hand and an outstretched arm, and with wrath poured out; And I will bring you into the wilderness of the peoples (*mid'bbar há-'ámmîm*), and there I will enter into judgement with you face to face. As I entered into judgement with your fathers in the wilderness (*mid'bbâr*) of the land of Egypt, so I will enter into judgement with you, says the Lord God. I will make you pass under the rod, and I will let you go in by number. I will purge out the rebels from among you, and those who transgress against me; I will bring them out of the land where they sojourn, but they shall not enter the land of Israel. Then you will know that I am the Lord.

Thirdly, the note struck in the last quotation from Ezekiel is seminal. A period in the wilderness, both for the rebellious and the obedient in Israel, is to precede the final redemption (20: 40ff).

For on my holy mountain, the mountain height of Israel, says the Lord God, there are all the house of Israel, all of them, shall serve me in the land; there I will accept them, and there I will require your contributions and the choicest of your gifts, with all your sacred offerings. As a pleasing odor I will accept you, when I bring you out from the peoples, and gather you out of the countries where you have been scattered; and I will manifest my holiness among you in the sight of the nations. And you shall know that I am the Lord, when I bring you into the land of Israel, the country which I swore to give to your fathers. And there you shall remember your ways and all the doings with which you have polluted yourselves; and you shall loathe yourselves for all the evils that you have committed.

We have previously noted in Hosea the notion of a return to the wilderness as a condition of renewal before entry into the land. But there a return to the time when Israel enjoyed a filial status with Yahweh is signified: it provided a "door of hope." In Ezekiel, as we have seen, the wilderness is a place of judgment: the infidelity of the people in the period of the wanderings is reiterated unsparingly. But in Ezekiel, also, the return to the wilderness is a prelude to life in the land and is, in this sense, a sign of hope. The way to the land is through the wilderness. And this motif persisted.

In Deutero-Isaiah the return of the dispersed to the land is to be through a wilderness, the difficulties of which, have been smoothed (Is. 40: 3f; 35: 1f, 6ff; 41: 18f; 49: 9ff): a way will appear through the wilderness (40: 3; 43: 19; 49: 11). There is to be a new exodus, incomparably greater, even though the counterpart of the first. This notion is so familiar that it needs no elaborate documentation. It later emerges in 1 Enoch 28: 1; 29: 1; The Martyrdom of Isaiah 2: 8–12. That it was understood not merely oratorically or metaphorically is clear from three sources.[16]

First, the Dead Sea Scrolls. The community of the new covenant, which bequeathed the Scrolls to us, by the location of its headquarters at Qumran in the desert, a location dictated by the text of Is. 40: 3, by its organization—into tribes, thousands, hundreds, fifties, and tens, which parallel the subdivision of Israel under Moses—and by the regulation of its life in camps (compare 1QM 7: 3–7 with Num. 5: 1–4) shows its concern to "return" in repentance to the wilderness in preparation for the redemption that would lead it to the purified land.[17]

Secondly, in Josephus certain groups who *may* have had Messianic pretensions, since they promised to repeat the "signs" or miracles of the first exodus, went into the desert to prepare for a coming redemption. So, too, a prophet from Egypt, and Theudas, and a weaver, Jonathan—all had recourse to the desert to prepare for their assault on Jerusalem.[18] And, in the last desperate hours of the war against Rome, the Jews asked for permission to leave the Temple with their wives and children for the desert, probably because they expected the final deliverance to be inaugurated there.[19] It should not too easily be assumed that all the figures referred to in Josephus were Messianic claimants,[20] but in the light of the Dead Sea Scrolls it seems clear that a retreat to the desert could easily be understood in Messianic terms—as preparation for the Messianic age.

This is, thirdly, indicated in the New Testament itself by John the Baptist's preparatory ministry in the wilderness and explicitly in Matt. 24: 26:

[16] See SSM, p. 349, n. 2. P. Volz, *Die Eschatologie der jüdischen Gemeinde im neutestamentlichen Zeitalter*, Tübingen, 1934, pp. 370f.

[17] F. M. Cross, *The Ancient Library of Qumran*, New York, 1958, p. 78, n. 36a.

[18] Jos. *Antiquities*, XX. 5. 1.

[19] Jos. *Jewish Wars*, VI. 6. 3: "they asked permission to pass through his [Titus] line of circumvallation...undertaking to retire to the desert and to leave the city to him (Loeb trans. pp. 478f)."

[20] See further SSM, p. 118. The murmuring in the wilderness is important in Heb. 3, citing Ps. 95.

So, if they say to you, "Lo, he is in the wilderness," do not go out... (ἰδου ἐν τῇ ἐρήμῳ²¹ ἐστιν).

It is now necessary to recall our purpose in presenting all the above details: it was to point out how precarious, indeed untenable, is the view that the Old Testament sets up a nomadic ideal. The period of the wilderness is ambiguous: it could boast of the divine succour and guidance, of the revelation of the Name, of the election of the people, of the giving of the Law. Yes: but it was marked also by rebellion and judgment. At best it was only a transitional period: it was "on the way" to the land: its value was preparatory not final. And at this point a distinction must be made clear. We have spoken above of the *time* of the wilderness. What lent it significance was not the quality of the wilderness itself, but the events that happened in it; not the *space* of the wilderness but the *time* of the wilderness. We discovered no glorification of the wilderness as such. It is of the utmost importance that the New Covenanters at Qumran, like John the Baptist and the figures mentioned by Josephus, did not go into the wilderness because they valued it, as such, but because they were thereby fulfilling what had become a kind of eschatological dogma that a time in the wilderness would precede the End. Their "return" to the wilderness, was *not* governed by a rejection of "cultured" life in the land in favour of a more simple nomadic existence in the desert; not by a geographic preference for the wilderness over the land, but by an eschatological schema; not by considerations of space but of time; not by the cult of the primitive but by the observation of the times.²²

²¹ ἔρημος customarily translates מִדְבָּר in the LXX. See Hatch and Redpath.

²² J. W. Flight, JBL, Vol. 42, 1923, pp. 158–226 has set forth a nomadic ideal in the Old Testament: it includes opposition to city life, civilization and culture, cult and sacrifice, temple and idolatry. These oppositional factors *can* be found in the Old Testament. But it is difficult not to agree with Y. Kaufmann, *The Religion of Israel*, trans., Chicago, 1960, p. 339, n. 13. "There is no nomadic ideal in the Bible. Israel was never a genuine desert people; the desert was but an episode in its history. It originated in culture lands, and never aspired to nomadic life; at the Exodus it is promised 'a land flowing with milk and honey.' The Rechabites were a peculiar order; no prophet or any other biblical writer takes them as ideal types of the people as a whole. In all eschatological visions the land is central. The ultimate ideal is a people farming its land and enjoying its fruits in peace (Mic. 4: 4). Once upon a time, Israel was 'a fugitive Aramaean,' wandering in the culture lands without national territory; thanks to God they were delivered from that wretched status (Deut. 26: 25ff). The 'terrible desert' of the wandering was remembered, despite its hallowed religious associations, for the suffering and privation that were endured there. Hosea 2: 4ff warns of a return to the desert as part of Israel's punishment for idolatry. God will withhold the land's wealth, will put an end to Israel's festivals and Sabbaths, and take the people out again into the desert there to purge them. Israel will return and resettle the land." S. Talmon, in *Biblical Motifs: Origins and Transformations*, ed. A. Altmann, Cambridge, Mass., 1966, writes on "The 'Desert Motif' in the Bible and in Qumran Literature," pp. 31–63. Unfortunately this work came

This is still further to be emphasized when the understanding of the physical wilderness in the Old Testament is recognized. In the above, we repeat, we have spoken of the *time* of the wilderness, that is, we have interpreted "the wilderness" in the Old Testament historically not geographically. Even such a historical interpretation lends little support to the existence of a significant nomadic ideal. Much less does the geographic realism of the Old Testament allow for such. We can only touch upon certain aspects of this theme.

By "the wilderness" the Old Testament generally denotes unsown land: it stands over against the sown land, designated '*adâmâh*,[23] which was inhabited (Gen. 2: 5; 47: 23; 2 Sam. 9: 10). We have already indicated the pride with which the Israelite regarded the '*adâmâh* which had become his land ('*eretz*): it flowed with milk and honey, corn, young wine, and oils; it had pastures for cattle and, above all, enjoyed the gift of rain. There the blessing dwelt: hence the horror with which Cain contemplated Yahweh's punishment upon him: "Cain said to the Lord, 'My punishment is greater than I can bear. Behold, thou hast driven me this day away from the ground (*hâ-'adâmâh*) and from thy face I shall be hidden; and I shall be a fugitive and a wanderer on the earth (*bâ'âretz*), and whoever finds me will slay me' (Gen. 4: 13f)."

Outside the sown land the curse prevails. Pedersen,[24] who has most illumined it, expresses the matter, exaggeratedly it is true, as follows:

The opposite of the land of man is the *desert-land*. It is the *evil* place "where

---

to my notice after I had written the above. Talmon's excellent study confirms it. For him no return "to an original nomadic status was possible, because (*a*) there was never a time when Israel could be called a nomad society, and (*b*) even the Rechabites, like other desert types in the history of Israel, were outlaws, fugitives or at best virtuous primitives; they are not presented consistently in a positive light." Talmon examines the use of *mid^ebbâr* (desert, wilderness). He distinguishes, as we do above, between the desert and the time of the desert. Desert life was always but a preparation for the attainment of the ideal. P. Riemann, also, in a Harvard dissertation, unpublished, takes a cautious attitude to "the nomadic ideal."

Contrast with the emphasis in Talmon and Kaufmann that of V. Maag, *Malkût Yahweh, Congress Volume, Supplements to VT.*, Leiden, 1959, Vol. VII, pp. 129–153. Unlike other peoples, who left behind a nomadic life for a sedentary agricultural one, Israel continued to cherish the memory of the traditions of its nomadic past. As a result its original conception of its nomadic God as not bound to place, continued to influence Israel's thinking. The nomad God was a *Führer*, not a King, and this notion continued to colour Israel's understanding of its God. The religion of promise is the religion of the nomad God. But see W. Zimmerli's justifiable rebuttal of Maag, *Man and his Hope in the Old Testament*, p. 57.

[23] See above p. 15, n. 1.

[24] J. Pedersen, *Israel: Its Life and Culture*, London, 1926, Vol. I–II, pp. 455f. Mauser, *Christ in the Wilderness*, p. 36, n. 2, notes the weakness in the treatment given by Pedersen, who appeals only to the prophets and the hagiographa. "The theologically relevant themes of the wilderness as the place of the revelation of God's glory and help and the passages concerning the prophets' expectation of a new exodus through the desert are entirely disregarded by him."

there is no seed, nor figs, nor vines, nor pomegranates, neither is there any water to drink (Num. 20: 5)." In the desert the good plants do not grow; its soil is full of stones and salt, covered with nettles, with thorns and thistle (Is. 5: 6; 7: 24; Zeph. 2: 9).... For the Israelites the wilderness is the home of the curse. Wicked demons are at work here (Lev. 16: 10, 21f), but for human beings it is uninhabitable. Not only normal humans, but also the animals belonging to the world of man keep far from it. There is no thoroughfare, no wayfarers, only the bellowing of animals which live far from the dwellings of man—wild asses, jackals, ostriches, owls and ravens. The wilderness is the land of chaos, because the law of life does not operate there: we hear several times that the desert is *tōhū* or *tōhū wābhōhū*, the characteristic expression of chaos, the lawless, the empty...[25]

However, no geographic line clearly separates the desert-land from the land of man: the former can insidiously invade the latter and is always a threat to it:[26] how sin can reduce the land of man to desert-land we have previously touched upon.

It is not surprising that the wilderness acquired a symbolic significance. When God's judgment is exercised, the land of man, including his cities, is reduced to a desert. The term thus becomes a symbol for the effects of the divine wrath, the outward devastation that inexorably follows human sin. For her sin Hosea warns Israel:

lest I strip her naked and make her as in the day she was born, and make her like a wilderness (*mid'bbar*), and set her like a parched land ('*eretz tziyyâh*), and slay her with thirst (Hos. 2: 3: compare Hos. 2: 9–13).

Joel speaks of Yahweh's visitation at the day of judgment:

Fire devours before them, and behind them a flame burns. The land is like the garden of Eden before them, but after them a desolate wilderness (*mid'bbar sh'mâmâh*), and nothing escapes them (Joel 2: 3).

"Their land" writes Jeremiah,

has become a waste (*shammâh*) because of the sword of the Lord, and because of his fierce anger (Jer. 25: 38).

And the city is not different from the land:

Be warned, O Jerusalem, lest I be alienated from you; lest I make you a desolation and uninhabited land (פֶּן אַשִּׂימֵךְ שְׁמָמָה אֶרֶץ לוֹא נוֹשָׁבָה) (Jer. 6: 8).

The same thought appears in Jer. 7: 34:

[25] On all this, see Pedersen, *Israel*, Vol. I–II, pp. 453–470. Mauser gives the list of "animals" occupying the desert, *Christ in the Wilderness*, p. 37, n. 2.

[26] As will have been noticed from quotations used above, the distinction between אֶרֶץ as "land" or "country" and אֲדָמָה as "soil" or "land" is not always clear.

And I will make to cease from the cities of Judah and from the streets of Jerusalem the voice of mirth and the voice of gladness, the voice of the bridegroom and the voice of the bride; for the land shall become a waste (*hor^ebáh*).

But the symbolism of the wilderness has another inner dimension: it can refer—as later in Dante, Bunyan, T. S. Eliot and others—not only to visible, physical devastation but to the desolation and poverty of the soul of the nation and of the individual. That the spiritual poverty of the nation can appear as a wilderness is implied in Ezekiel's vision of the valley of dry bones, which, significantly, lies outside the land of Israel (37: 12). Desert imagery to symbolize moral and spiritual realities occurs in Is. 41: 17–20:

When the poor and needy seek water, and there is none, and their tongue is parched with thirst, I the Lord will answer them, I the God of Israel will not forsake them. I will open the rivers on the bare heights, and fountains in the midst of the valleys; I will make the wilderness (*mid^ebbár*) a pool of water, and the dry land springs of water. I will put in the wilderness (*mid^ebbár*) the cedar, the acacia, the myrtle, and the olive; I will set in the desert (*'^arábáh*) the cypress, the plane and the pine together; that men may see and know, may consider and understand together, that the hand of the Lord has done this, the Holy One of Israel has created it.

And as for the dryness of the personal life, this too came to be symbolized in terms of the desert. Isaiah 44: 1–5 is addressed to Israel as a whole, but embraces the individual Israelite:

But now hear, O Jacob, my servant Israel whom I have chosen! Thus says the Lord who made you, who formed you from the womb and will help you: Fear not, O Jacob my servant, Jeshurun whom I have chosen. For I will pour water on the thirsty land (*t_záme'*), and streams on the dry ground (*'abbáshâh*); I will pour my Spirit upon your descendants, and my blessing on your offspring. They shall spring up like grass amid waters, like willows by flowing streams. This one will say, "I am the Lord," another will call himself by the name of Jacob, and another will write on his hand, "The Lord's," and surname himself by the name of Israel.

And, finally, the wilderness acquires a mythological dimension of cosmic proportions. Since the wilderness was associated with demons—hairy satyrs, storm devils, howling dragons and monsters, the winged night monsters, and Azazel, their corporate representative—such a mythological development was natural. In some Psalms imagery derived from the story of the wanderings in the wilderness is combined with mythological concepts, such as "the cords of death," "torrents of perdition," "many waters," and thus given a mythological connotation (see Ps. 18: 4–5, 7–16). So, too, in Deutero-Isaiah notions of creation and redemption co-mingle with or are, perhaps, even informed by those derived from the time of the wilderness (Is. 50: 2, compare 34: 8–15; 51: 9f). In Deutero-Isaiah the expectation of a new creation and a new exodus intermingle. Most striking for our purposes is Ps. 68, where the wilderness is understood as one of the powers of chaos which is defeated by Yahweh in his intervention on behalf of his people, the wilderness being set in a cosmic framework.

O God, when thou didst go forth before thy people, when thou didst march through the wilderness (*y'shîmôn*), the earth quaked, the heavens poured down rain, at the presence of God; yon Sinai quaked at the presence of God, the God of Israel. Rain in abundance, O God, thou didst shed abroad; thou didst restore thy heritage as it languished; thy flock found a dwelling in it; in thy goodness, O God, thou didst provide for the needy (Ps. 68: 8–10).

This last passage is important in more ways than one. It presents the wilderness not only as one of the powers overcome, like chaos, in the presence of the Lord, but restored and renewed by that same presence; "the heavens poured down rain" in the wilderness. This should warn us against the overemphasis about which we hinted in Pedersen's treatment of the wilderness as under the curse. It is so: but in Ps. 68 at least that curse is regarded as lifted. And, at this point, we must recall yet again that, however much the wilderness geographically, symbolically, and mythologically is such as we have described above, it could be and also was the scene of the Divine Presence, of the revelation of the Name, of the Covenant and the giving of the Law. There can be little question that Pedersen's presentation of the evidence is too much governed by the Prophets and the Writings and too little informed by the positive aspects of Israel's wandering in the wilderness. He has, to some extent, allowed his concern with the geographic and mythological and symbolic aspects of the wilderness to overshadow the historical, and thereby deprived the wilderness of any possible positive aspects. To this it might be rejoined that he has rightly kept distinct the *time* of the wilderness and the wilderness itself as a *geographical* reality.[27]

[27] In assessing the significance of the wilderness it cannot be sufficiently re-emphasized that it was there that Israel received the Torah—outside the land. The location of the giving of the Torah much occupied the Rabbis. It denoted that the Torah was offered to all (Num. Rabbah 1: 7 on Num. 1: 2; Mekilta, Baḥodesh V [Lauterbach, p. 237]); it ensured that there would be no dissension among the tribes of Israel, since the Torah was not given in the territory of any one tribe (Mekilta, Baḥodesh V [Lauterbach, p. 236]), and that other nations

The outcome of our discussion is clear. There is no justification for positing a nomadic ideal in the Old Testament and Judaism. Efforts to do so on the grounds of an idealization of the desert cannot be substantiated. The other grounds for doing so do not carry conviction, for reasons which cannot be set forth here. Our rejection of a nomadic ideal can be carried over into Judaism. True, the wilderness reappears in the eschatology of Judaism, which is thought of, among other things, as a new exodus which would witness a new Moses and the return of the manna, etc. But in that eschatology also, the wilderness is not the goal but a stage on the way to the land, the glorification of which we have already illustrated from Rabbinic sources.

b. MACCABEES AND "ZEALOTS" AND THE LAND

We now turn to the second question raised above. How far, in fact, was it loyalty to the land as such that inspired the Maccabean and Zealot revolts?

First, we shall examine the Maccabean revolt. Most of the exiles in Babylon did not choose to return to the land when Cyrus (538 B.C.) made this possible:[28] clearly the land as such had little appeal for them (it was not the returned exiles whom Haggai and Zechariah called upon to rebuild the Temple, but native Israelites).[29] And it should be empha-

---

could not say "Because it was given in Israel's land, therefore we have not accepted it (Mekilta, *ibid.*)." For other explanations, see RA, pp. 166f. In this connection (see p. 148 below), also the Canaanite origin of the city of Jerusalem is to be noted. Despite its location near the centre of the Israelite tribes the city had until the time of David been alien, a foreign city held by Jebusites. As Judg. 19: 10 states: it was "a city of foreigners who do not belong to the people of Israel." Ezekiel could remind Jerusalem "Your origins and your birth are of the land of the Canaanites; your father was an Amorite, and your mother a Hittite (16: 3)." As Noth points out, Jerusalem, which later became the quintessence of the land, was not associated with the promise and the giving of the Torah. M. Noth, "Jerusalem und die israelitische Tradition," *Gesammelte Studien zum Alten Testament*, 1957, p. 174. The absence of a nomadic ideal in Israel makes it difficult to find a clue to her history in her geography as H. Trevor-Roper, for example, recently held, *Men and Events*, Harper, New York, 1957, pp. 1–5, where he writes: "The Old Testament so far as it is history, is the history of a great ideological struggle: a struggle between the invading gods of the desert and the native gods of the sown [land] (p. 3)". Doubtless Israel's history in an unusual degree was coloured by its critical geographic setting (Palestine was the junction of two cultures, that of settled agricultural Syria and that of nomadic Bedouin Arabia), but within that setting an infinite variety of non-geographic factors were at work. The Rechabites were oddities. Trevor-Roper's treatment of the Dispersion in the same volume, pp. 146–150, points to the intricacy of Jewish history and supplies a corrective to Ardrey's single overarching principle of the territorial imperative (see pp. 405ff), as it does, indeed, to his own simplistic treatment of Israel's history in his essay on the land.

[28] J. Bright, *A History of Israel*, Philadelphia, 1959, p. 344. He points out that Palestine was far away; the future in the land uncertain, and many Jews well established in Babylon. Compare Jos., *Antiquities*, XI. i. 3.

[29] P. R. Ackroyd, *Peake*, p. 644, on Haggai 1: 12–14. The claim of Ezra 1–6 that it was the returned exiles who rebuilt the temple is a reinterpretation of the message of Haggai.

sized that, after the return from the exile, Jews in Palestine itself were a "dispersion." During the period after Nehemiah (432 B.C.) and before Alexander's conquest in 332 B.C., the district of Judaea consisted simply of Jerusalem and a small area, about thirty-five miles long and twenty-five to thirty miles broad, surrounding it. Within this tiny area and outside it Jews came to be surrounded by Hellenistic influences.[30] The temptation to assimilate was real and ubiquitous. What was the attitude to the land in this period among Palestinian Jews thus exposed? Had it been of vital significance it is surprising that so little of direct appeal to the land was made in the Maccabean revolt, particularly since the land itself had become so reduced. In 1 Macc. 1: 7 we find the reasons why Mattathias, the father of Judas Maccabeus, initiated the revolt, and no mention is made of the land. Similarly when the same Mattathias, on his deathbed, spoke to his sons, he made no appeal to their loyalty to the land. When he did refer to Abraham, it was to recall, not the promise of the land given to that patriarch, but his faithfulness in temptation.[31] No pre-eminence was given to Abraham: he was listed along with many other notables who were loyal—with Joseph, Joshua, Caleb, and others. It was the commandments of the Law, not the occupation of the land, that concerned the dying Mattathias. It was so throughout his life. His rallying cry was simple: "Whosoever is zealous for the Law and maintaineth the covenant, let him come forth after me."[32] And it was in this spirit that the volunteers, "a company of Hasidim," who have been regarded as the fathers of the Pharisees, offered themselves.[33] The absence of an appeal to the land is striking because of the vividness of the awareness of the unity of the People of Israel in 1 Macc.[34] It agrees with this that when appeal is made to history it is not, as we have seen, to the promise to Abraham but to the Exodus, the event that gave birth to the people.[35] Later on, territorial considerations did enter into the Maccabean move-

[30] See Elias J. Bickerman, *From Ezra to the Last of the Maccabees*, New York, 1962; see also my essay on the Aboth in *Christian History and Interpretation: Studies Presented to John Knox*, eds. W. R. Farmer, C. F. D. Moule, R. R. Niebuhr, Cambridge, 1967, pp. 138ff, especially p. 138, n. 1, and my article "Paul and Judaism," in *The Bible in Modern Scholarship*, ed. J. Philip Hyatt, Nashville, 1965, pp. 178–183. And now the massive work of Martin Hengel, *Judentum und Hellenismus: Studien zu ihrer Begegnung unter besonderer Berücksichtigung Palästinas bis zur Mitte des 2. Jh. v. Chr.*, Tübingen, 1969. It is interesting to note that only at two minor points does Hengel turn his attention to the land, at pp. 33, 66. Important also is Morton Smith, *Palestinian Parties and Politics that shaped the Old Testament*, New York, 1971.

[31] 1 Macc. 2: 52.

[32] 1 Macc. 2: 27, 49–61.

[33] See G. F. Moore, *Judaism*, Vol. 1, *ad rem.*; 1 Macc. 1: 42.

[34] 1 Macc. 1: 64; 3: 2, 8, 14, 46; 4: 11, 30f; 5: 3, 45.

[35] 1 Macc. 4: 1–11.

ment, but these were motivated more by political ambition than religious concern with the Promise.

But the matter is even more puzzling. One item is frequently passed over in treatments of the Maccabean revolt. Tcherikover[36] urges that the Hasidim had been in rebellion before Mattathias slew a Hellenizing Jew, and that political and social factors and, indeed, international currents (a series of uprisings on the part of oriental countries against their western rulers) lay behind that event. For our purposes he points to one significant fact—the threat of the confiscation of Jewish lands under the Seleucids. According to 1 Macc. 3: 36, Antiochus Epiphanes ordered Lysias "to settle aliens in all their borders (that is, of Judaea) and to divide their land into allotments." According to 2 Macc. 11: 2, Lysias's aim was to make Jerusalem a place of Greek settlement, to levy taxes on the Temple, and to convert the High Priesthood into a post open to annual auction. In short, Jerusalem was to become a model Hellenistic city. The rural Jews, especially, would be sensitive to the threat to their land, and not only they but all Jews in Judaea. This makes it all the more difficult to understand the absence of an appeal to the land as such in our sources.[37]

We note, in the second place, that a similar phenomenon, absence of a direct appeal to the land, confronts us when we turn to the revolt against the Romans culminating in the fall of Jerusalem in A.D. 70. In his *Antiquities*, XVIII. 1–6, Josephus connects the emergence of those who were "zealous to draw them (the people of Judaea or the Jews) to revolt" with Judas, a Gaulonite, of a city whose name was Gamala, who had with him a Pharisee, Sadduc. Judas objected to the census imposed on Judaea by Cyrenius, the Roman senator, and Coponius, a man of the equestrian order, in A.D. 6–9, on the command of the Emperor. Their followers, to whom the name "Zealots" is generally given, are credited by Josephus with being the source of the misfortunes which fell upon the Jewish people and culminated in the destruction of the Temple. They acted, in the view of Josephus, "in pretence indeed for the public welfare, but in reality for the hopes of gain to themselves." Josephus regards them as a new emergence, a new "philosophy" which "we (the Jews)," writes Josephus, "were before unacquainted with." For him the "new philosophy" constitutes a madness, and throughout his presentation of the revolt its leaders are depicted as "lawless" men. The reasons for his depiction of them as

---

[36] *Hellenistic Civilization and the Jews*, trans., Philadelphia, 1959, pp. 204ff.

[37] Tcherikover, *Hellenistic Civilization*, p. 211. He seems to assume such an appeal, but supplies no evidence for it (p. 212).

newly emergent sons of darkness need not detain us.[38] Recent scholars[39] have discovered in them the conscious counterparts of the Maccabean rebels, with whom they shared a consuming zeal for the covenant and the Law, for which they were prepared to kill and die or commit suicide, an insistence on circumcision for those in "Israel," on the observance of the Sabbath, and on extreme loyalty to the Temple. A "theology" which regarded a possible return to the wilderness as a prelude to the End governed them, as it did the Maccabees, the memory of whose religious zeal and military exploits they consciously cherished.[40]

So much it is easy to document. But as in the case of the Maccabees so with the "Zealots"; there is a baffling lack of direct appeal to the promise of the land and to the land itself. A few passages appeal to the "laws of the country" or of "the land,"[41] but social, political and religious motives spurred the rebels not only the direct concern of the Sicarii with the land. Is this to be interpreted in both the revolts, against the Seleucids and the Romans, as an indication that the land as such was not a primary focus of concern?

To judge by the almost total silence of the sources, loyalty to the land as such, it has to be admitted, was not a factor in the two revolts. But in this context the argument from silence is particularly precarious. There are several considerations to suggest this.

During both the Maccabean and Roman revolts the people of Israel were dwelling in the land, so that preoccupation with any conquest or occupation of it was not their immediate concern. Rather it was the terms on which they were to live in the land. What were these terms to be? Two desiderata had to be met to satisfy those in Israel who were "zealous."

[38] On the term "Zealots," see below p. 336, n. 3. The lumping of all revolutionaries under that term is now untenable. There was probably no unified revolutionary movement from 6 A.D. on, but variously motivated persons and groups. Only the Sicarii explicitly connect their revolt with the land; see p. 95, n. 46. Social, economic, and political factors were at least as important as the religious. See D. Rhoads, "Some Jewish Revolutionaries in Palestine A.D. 6–73," unpublished dissertation, Duke University, 1973.

[39] Farmer, *Maccabees, Zealots and Josephus.*

[40] *Ibid.*

[41] It is not an accident that direct concern with the land appears after A.D. 70, see above p. 55. The parallel between the Maccabean and "Zealot" revolts cannot be pressed; the nationalists of the first century revolted when they were not provoked by the Romans as a matter of policy, although there was unavoidable religious provocation. The mere presence of the Romans in the land was sufficient to incite some to rebellion. See A. Fuks, "Aspects of the Jewish Revolt in A.D. 115–117," in *Journal of Roman Studies*, London, 1961, pp. 98ff. Compare M. Simon et André Benoit, *Le Judaïsme et le Christianisme Antique d'Antiochus Epiphane à Constantin*, Paris, 1968, pp. 215f. In *Jewish Wars*, VI. 5. 4, Josephus regards as the chief instigation to the revolt a prophecy that a Jew was to rule the world, in an ambiguous oracle, which Josephus himself interpreted of Vespasian.

First, it will be clear from what we have said before that Israel, as the covenant people, could only occupy the land securely if the commandments were observed. The occupation of the land presupposed loyalty to the Torah. Loyalty to the latter was a form of loyalty to the land. Torah and land are, even if not inextricable, closely related. The threat to the Torah was in a tangible, though indirect, sense a threat to the land. And in periods when Israel actually dwelt in the land, as in the Maccabean and Roman periods, the explicit concentration was naturally on the former.

Equally real was it, secondly, that the land was involved in any threat to the Temple. It cannot be sufficiently emphasized that life in the land, at least since the days of Josiah, was regarded as integrally related to the cultus at the Temple in Jerusalem. Changes in that cultus were particularly resented by the farmers in the rural areas, for whom the productivity of the soil was compromised by changes in the Temple worship. It is no accident that the leadership in the Maccabean revolt was from the rural priesthood: they recognized that on the observance of the Law, which included the observance of the Festivals and Temple ritual, depended the wellbeing of the land.[42] It follows that, in periods when Israel actually dwelt in the land, it was at the point of observance of the Torah and reverence for the Temple that the concern for the land came, albeit indirectly, to expression.

In this connection, it is pertinent to point out that in the Apocrypha and Pseudepigrapha the notion of the fulfilment of Scriptural prophecies and promises plays little part.[43] The reason is clear: in a real sense the promise of life in the land had been fulfilled in the return. There was, therefore, a shift of preoccupation from the land as such to those conditions on which it could be truly occupied—the observance of the Torah and reverence for the Temple—to the terms on which it could be enjoyed. This explains the centrality of Torah and Temple in the Maccabean and "Zealot" revolts: but that centrality throughout in the minds of the rebels assumes the essentiality of the land.

[42] The outbreak of the Maccabean Revolt, led by a priest, was in a small rural town, Modin. It should be recalled that the foundation stone of the Temple (resting on the original threshing floor) held the waters of chaos in check. The continued existence of the temple guaranteed the existence of the ordered and inhabited world. For example, see Pss. Sol. 29: 10; 46: 1ff; 93: 1ff. In Haggai 1: 9ff; 2: 14ff the rebuilding of the temple is conceived of as ensuring the end of drought and famine. Zech. 14: 17 notes that without worship in Jerusalem "no rain shall fall." Compare Joel 3: 18 which pictures the future when Jerusalem is holy and Judah full of water (Egypt a desert!). See Theophane Chary, *Les Prophètes et le culte à partir de l'exil*, Tournai, Belgium, 1955, p. 197.

[43] J. L. Zinz, *The Use of the Old Testament in the Apocrypha*, Duke University Dissertation, unpub. 1966.

But, apart from the weaknesses of the people of Israel themselves, what was it that most threatened the due loyalty to Torah and Temple through which the covenant people could enjoy life in the promised land? It was the threat of an "alien," occupying power to both Torah and Temple.[44] So long as the Seleucids or the Romans—or, indeed, any other powers— ruled the land, which belonged to Yahweh, so long would observance of the Torah and reverence for the Temple be precarious. It is in the light of this fact that the following description of "the fourth philosophy," by Josephus, should be read:

But of the fourth sect of Jewish philosophy, Judas the Galilean was the author. These men agree in all other things with the Pharisaic notions; but they have an inviolable attachment to liberty; and they say that God is to be their only Ruler and Lord. They also do not value dying any kinds of death, nor indeed do they heed the deaths of their relations and friends, nor can any such fear make them call any man Lord; and since this immovable resolution of theirs is well known to a great many, I shall speak no further about that matter; nor am I afraid that anything I have said of them should be disbelieved, but rather fear, that what I have said is beneath the resolution they shew when they undergo pain; and it was in Gessius Florus's time that the nation began to grow mad with this distemper, who was our procurator, and who occasioned the Jews to go wild with it by the abuse of his authority, and to make them revolt from the Romans; and these are the sects of Jewish philosophy.[45]

History had taught the Jews in the Maccabean period, as in the Roman, that a foreign ruler could disrupt the conditions under which alone the covenant people could live in the promised land. Even Josephus, despite his hatred of the Jewish nationalists, had to admit that they were very like the Pharisees. That is, although Josephus presented them in terms of "madness," they revered the Law and the Temple. The Sicarii's emphasis (which doubtless the Pharisees shared *in principle*, although *in practice* they urged patience and long-suffering) that God alone was to be their Ruler and Lord,[46] sprang from the bitter history of Israel and the clear-eyed recognition that they could only dwell securely in the promised land when it was not occupied territory.

The story of the conquest and occupation of the land was vivid in the Maccabean mind and in that of the nationalists of the first century. One feature, common to both, points to this; that is, the return to the wilder-

[44] Farmer, *Maccabees, Zealots, and Josephus.*

[45] Jos. *Antiquities*, XVIII. 1. 6. The prophecy referred to above has been interpreted of Dan. 7: 13f (Meyer, Michel) or Num. 24: 17f (Hengel). It is mentioned by Tacitus, *Hist.* 5: 13; Suetonius, *Vesp.* 4.

[46] Jos. *Ibid.*; *Jewish Wars*, II. 8. 1; VII. 10. 1; VII. 8. 6.

ness in both revolts. It is only touched upon briefly in 1 Macc. 2: 29–30: "Then many that sought after justice and judgement went down into the wilderness, to dwell there (εἰς τὴν ἔρημον, καθίσαι ἐκεῖ), they and their sons, and their wives and their cattle; because evils were multiplied upon them." The return is noted in far more striking circumstances in Josephus's account of the fall of the Temple: it is probably that of an eyewitness. After suicidal resistance, the rejection of Titus's plea for surrender before he set fire to the Temple, the actual burning of the sanctuary and its desecration by the setting up of the Emperor's standards, and finally, the rejection of Titus's offer to enter into negotiations, the rebels wanted only "permission to pass through his line of circumvallation with their wives and children, undertaking to return to the desert and to leave the city to him."[47] What is the explanation of this strange request? In all probability the rebels were governed by the eschatological belief that before the final redemption, even after the Temple itself had been forsaken by the Lord, the Lord himself would not forsake his people, but continue his presence with them in the wilderness to lead them again into the promised land. Like the Maccabees who withdrew to the wilderness, the "Zealots" also in their final request showed how the story of the conquest of the land informed their thinking and activity.

Moreover, in the Maccabean period, at two points in Daniel, the interest in the land may be claimed indirectly to break through. First, in Dan. 7: 25–26, as part of the description of the Fourth Beast, to be identified with Antiochus Epiphanes, we read:

> He shall speak words against the Most High,
> and shall wear out the saints
> of the Most High,
> and shall think to change the
> times and the law;
> and they shall be given into his
> hand
> for a time, two times, and half
> a time.
> But the court shall sit in judgment,
> and his dominion shall be taken
> away,
> to be consumed and destroyed
> to the end.

[47] Jos. *Jewish Wars*, VI. 6. 3. (ἔξοδον δ' ἠτοῦντο διὰ τοῦ περιτειχίσματος μετὰ γυναικῶν καὶ τέκνων· ἀπελεύσεσθαι γὰρ εἰς τὴν ἔρημον καὶ καταλείψειν αὐτῷ τὴν πόλιν . . .).

The saints of the Most High are to endure the domination of the Fourth Beast "for a time, two times, and half a time." These words have been understood as a vague indication of a brief time, and as a remarkable forecast, in fact, of either the period from the desecration of the Temple 15 Chislev 167 B.C., to 25 Chislev 164 B.C., the rededication of the Temple by Judas Maccabeus, or of the period from the visit of Apollonius to Jerusalem in the summer of 168 B.C. (1 Macc. 1: 54, 59) to 25 Chislev 164 B.C. It has been assumed that "a time, two times, and half a time" meant three-and-a-half years.

The process of thought by which this notion of three-and-a-half years or a very brief period arose has eluded commentators. But a suggestion by Bickerman[48] is convincing. In three-and-a-half years the Enemy of the saints of the Most High would be "consumed and destroyed to the end." On this Bickerman comments: "Three years and half is a half of the Sabbatical period. According to the Law the land of Israel had to have a solemn rest every seven years and lie fallow. In Leviticus (26: 34–43) the desolation of the land under foreign domination appears as reparation for the lack of the Sabbatic rest under national rule. The Jews will have to suffer a half of a Sabbatic septennium in payment for their disobedience of God's law." If this suggestion be followed, the awareness of the land, its reactions and demands, was living in the Maccabean period. The same is also implied in another passage in Dan. 11: 26–12: 4. When the coming Kingdom of God is described, after the destruction of the powers that have succeeded each other in history, it is in terms of the triumph of Michael. But Michael is the patron angel of Israel and its land, and that land is "the fairest of all lands (NEB)," (11: 16, compare 8: 9). There is no doubt that at the End the land remains central despite the cosmic horizons of Daniel. Antiochus Epiphanes is to meet his end, apparently, "between the sea and the holy hill," that is, between Jerusalem and the sea (11: 45), which Ezekiel (38: 14–16; 39: 2–4) had foretold as the scene

---

[48] 1 Macc. 1, 2. See especially, E. Bickerman, *Four Strange Books of the Bible*, New York, 1967, p. 101. Bickerman's treatment of the Maccabean revolt in *From Ezra* should be compared and contrasted with that of Tcherikover, *Hellenistic Civilization*. See the dissertation by David Rhoads, Duke University, 1973, on "Some Jewish Revolutionaries in Palestine, 6–73 A.D." for the later period. On the Sicarii he writes, "The significance of the land for the Sicarii is rooted in the popular reaction against the Roman census in A.D. 6," and points out, following Hengel, that there were ancient traditions opposing such censuses, based on the notion that assessment connotes ownership. As such, the census implied a slavery to Rome (Jos. *Jewish Wars*, VII. 8. 1; *Antiquities*, XVIII. 1. 1). See Hengel, *Die Zeloten*, p. 138; for other bibliography, see Rhoads. To the Sicarii the war against Rome was a "holy war." On this question, see also F. X. Malinowski, dissertation, Duke University, 1973, who shows how Josephus could not regard the war against Rome as "holy."

of the climax of all things. And it was in the land that the resurrection would take place (Dan. 12: 1–3).

How, then, shall we assess the role of loyalty to the land in the Maccabean and Zealot revolts? Despite the silence of the sources it cannot be doubted that that loyalty was a primary axiom for the rebels (our deepest axioms or assumptions are often most unexpressed). But it was unexpressed because in both revolts also it took a religious form, so that in the sources it is loyalty to the Torah and to the Temple that receive the accent. One thing, however, does emerge in both revolts. The essence of the Maccabean revolt is clear. It was not a popular revolt of the whole people, the majority of whom seemed to have been ready to assimilate: the land cannot have meant much to them. The revolt was the work of a small minority of enthusiasts for the Law and, implicitly, for the land, who were as incensed by the apostates among their own people as they were with Antiochus. It seems that the majority of the tiny Jewish political unit around the city of Jerusalem as well as the Jews in the rest of Palestine who were surrounded by a sea of Hellenistic influences cannot have been moved by loyalty to the land. And as for the Hasidim who joined the Maccabean revolt, it is a familiar, but for our purposes a highly significant, fact that as soon as the religious aims of the revolt had been achieved, that is freedom to observe the Law, they withdrew from further participation.[49] They had no territorial ambitions. So also, although Josephus for many reasons too much isolated the extremist leaders of the revolt against Rome from others, in their ideology and activity, it cannot be doubted that they constituted a minority, as did the Maccabean rebels.[50] First-century Judaism is the century of Hillel and Rabbi Johanan ben Zakkai, lovers of peace, no less than of the Zealots.[51]

But the situation in Israel between the exile and the first century was even more complicated than we have indicated. Let us return to the sectarians at Qumran who revealed a concentration on the land and the need for its purification. As we saw, the Maccabees and the Zealots hardly ever refer to the land directly, whereas the sectarians regarded it as part of their very purpose to "atone for the land." This difference probably has deep roots. Those who returned from Babylon, when Cyrus made this possible, were not a monolithic group.[52] For many among them the

<hr />

49 G. F. Moore, *Judaism*, Vol. 1, pp. 59f, 61f.

50 Although much points to a wider popular base to the revolt against Rome.

51 The infinite variety of first-century Judaism must be emphasized.

52 See O. Plöger, *Theokratie und Eschatologie*, Neukirchener Verlag, 1959, whom I follow here, and H. M. Lutz, *Yahwe, Jerusalem und die Völker*, Neukirchener Verlag, 1968, pp. 205–212.

return to the land and the rebuilding of the Temple signified Yahweh's favour. His judgments against Israel had now run their course. The restored community, devoted to the Law and the Temple, could count on his blessing. Life in the land was the seal of divine favour. To the early days of the return, if we follow Wanke,[53] belong those psalms which emphasize Jerusalem as the dwelling place of Yahweh, the centre of the theocracy of Israel.

To those who thought in this way belonged the core of the Maccabean and later first-century rebels. They do not refer to the land: they silently assume its importance and their right to it. They are not troubled by any sense that the people of Israel themselves had been responsible for defiling the land from within. The land needed no purification or atonement, only defence, when the Torah and its Temple were threatened from outside. Their devotion to the land, so deep that it needed no expression, was fanatic; it was not made coward by any bad conscience, that they themselves might have defiled it.[54]

But there were others in post-exilic Israel who differed. For these, although Israel had been given the opportunity to resettle in the land, the divine displeasure against Israel for its sins had not been exhausted. These still anticipated a dread future of further judgment upon Israel before the End should come. For the way in which vengeance against sinful Israelites is often associated with the concept of the land, see Jub. 15: 28; 20: 4; 21: 22; 36: 9; 50: 5; 2 Baruch 66: 2, 5. They did not consider Israel as a static theocracy that had achieved a desired status in the land, a land undefiled, but as a community still standing under the wrath of God. There thus coexisted, in post-exilic Israel, those for whom Israel was a theocracy, which had "arrived," and those for whom it was still under the shadow of eschatology.

It is in the light of this distinction that the difference between the Maccabean and later nationalist movements and the sectarians at Qumran is to be understood.[55] Let us recall the sectarians' understanding of them-

---

[53] G. Wanke, *Die Zionstheologie der Korachiten in ihrem traditionsgeschichtlichen Zusammenhang*, ZAW, Beih. 97, Berlin, 1966. See the critique of his late dating of this material by Lutz, *Jahwe, Jerusalem*, pp. 213ff. M. Noth, *The History of Israel*, trans., pp. 292, 296, perhaps, does not do justice to the significance of the exiles in Judaism.

[54] Signs of a bad conscience concerning "zeal" to root out the wicked from the land do emerge in the Pseudepigrapha. The "zeal" of Levi in executing vengeance on Shechem because of Dinah (Test. Levi 5: 3; 6: 3) is justified because it is commanded by an angel of God (5: 6). More clear is Test. Asher. 4: 2–5, which seeks to justify evil acts by zealous men. See also Pss. Sol. 4: 3.

[55] Plöger, *Theokratie*, finds in Daniel a representative product of those emphasizing eschatology and connects the attitude revealed in it with that of the Hasidim (1 Macc. 2: 31ff)

selves and of those around them. They were governed by their memory of the exile,[56] in which they found the model or parallel to their own experience.[57] In that first exile in a foreign land, Yahweh had spared a remnant which had confessed its faults and returned to the land under Ezra and Nehemiah.[58] But the community which had developed in the land since their day had not remained true to the demands of the covenant revealed by them: it had forsaken the revelation given to the remnant in and from Babylon. What followed? The land had become polluted or defiled. Loyal to the commandments of the covenant of the remnant from the Exile, the sectarians, who continued the remnant,[59] viewed the life of their countrymen, the sanctuary, and priesthood at Jerusalem, with horror. Separation from Judah and Jerusalem became imperative.[60] They must go into "exile."[61] Exile was preferable to life in the defiled land. Ephraim, in exile,[62] became a revered prototype. The sectarians chose to leave Judah to go to "the land of Damascus" into exile.

It is best to interpret "the land of Damascus" as referring to Qumran, not to Babylon.[63] But Qumran was not simply a geographic centre. In fulfilment of Zech. 11: 1 and Amos 7: 15 it was a symbol of the land of deportation, "the land of the North,"[64] the country of exile. There,

who withdrew their support from the Maccabees: he asks whether this attitude in turn is to be traced back to Isaiah himself and to Sech. 12–14 and Joel 3f.

[56] A. Jaubert, RB, Vol. 65, 1958, pp. 214–248 on "Le Pays de Damas."

[57] CDC 1: 3–9. Jaubert points to parallels for the schema: Sin, Exile, Return, indicated here, in Dan. 9; Bar. 1: 15–3: 8, and the Testament of the Twelve Patriarchs, but also in earlier documents Ezek. 6: 6–10; 36: 16–32; Lev. 26: 30–45; 2 Chron. 6: 36–39; Neh. 9: 30–37. She points especially to Jub. 1: 13–17. Whereas Jubilees speaks of "removing" or "transferring" "the plant of uprightness," that is, the true occupant, to Palestine, CDC speaks of the "germination" of it to inherit his land. Jaubert points to what is significant: "dans les deux cas la racine de plant *a germé en exil* (our italics, p. 218)." See further CDC 3: 10^b–4: 4 (note 4: 3 "who went out from the land of Judah"). Compare CDC 7: 14; 20: 22; 5: 16–6: 11, especially 6: 5. Notice the emphasis on the desolation of the land in CDC 3: 10a and 5: 20–21. In these texts there is a reference to the ruin of Jerusalem in 586 B.C. It is seen as a parallel to the experience of the Sect.

[58] Compare Ezek. 6: 8; Bar. 2: 30–32; Lev. 26: 39–45, A. Jaubert traces the calendar of the Qumran sect to the remnant returned from Babylon, *La date et la Cène. Calendrier biblique et liturgie Chrétienne*, Paris, 1957, pp. 31–41. W. F. Albright and C. S. Mann, RB, Vol. LXXVII, 1970, argue in favour of the Babylonian origin of the Essenes. So J. Murphy O'Connor, RB, Vol. LXXIX, 1972, p. 215, n. 45, who however rejects Albright's geographical understanding of "Damascus," in favour of a symbolical one.

[59] CDC 3: 18ff. for the remnant—the sure house in Israel: The false returnees have "removed the landmarks," CDC 8: 3.

[60] CDC 4: 3 and n. 5 above; 6: 18–19.

[61] CDC 7: 14 etc. Compare 4: 2–3; 6: 5.

[62] CDC 7: 12.

[63] See Jaubert, "Le Pays de Damas," pp. 25f. For the variety of views on the meaning. "Damascus," see a convenient note by J. H. Charlesworth, *John and Qumran*, ed. J. H. Charlesworth, London, 1972, p. 104, n. 125.

[64] Compare Zech. 6: 8; Jer. 31: 7; CDC 7: 14.

Yahweh now had his sanctuary, not at Judah or Jerusalem; there he now gave his revelation and, there, in the end of the days, a Star,[65] a leader, was to appear to lead the remnant back to a Jerusalem purified through punishment. Through "the diaspora," "the exile" of the sectarians, salvation would come for the land. The sect called itself "the exile"[66] and saw Judah and Jerusalem, the land, as profaned and in dire need of atonement. And this atonement was to come, not from Jerusalem, but from outside it.[67]

Two things follow from the above quick sketch of the self-understanding of the sectarians. We may ask two questions? First, was there a critical dialogue between the sectarians and those extreme nationalists in Israel who emphasized the evil of foreign occupation and underestimated the defilement of the land? We may assume an affirmative answer. But, secondly, and more important, what are we to make of the positive evaluation of "exile" among the sectarians? They apply the term "exile" to themselves: the true community of God was a diaspora through which alone the land was to achieve atonement.

Such an evaluation of exile had antecedents. As we saw, the sectarians could have appealed to Jeremiah and Ezekiel.[68] Moreover, it is not impossible that those Jews who were still geographically exiles, in the time of the sectarians, influenced them.[69] In the "War of the Sons of Light and the Sons of Darkness," there is a clear indication of the sectarians' very wide range of concern. We quote at length to make the point clear:

At the beginning of the undertaking of the sons of light, they shall start against the lot of the sons of darkness, the army of Belial, against the troop of Edom and Moab and the sons of Ammon, against the people of Philistia, and against the troops of the Kittim of Assyria, and with them as helpers the violaters of the covenant. The sons of Levi, the sons of Judah, and the sons of Benjamin, the exiles of the desert [גולת המדמר], shall fight against them and their forces with all their troops, when the exiles of the sons of light [גלות בני אור] return from the desert of the peoples [ממדבר העמים] to encamp in the desert of Jerusalem [במדבר ירושלים]. And after the battle they shall go up from there against the king of the Kittim in Egypt; and in his time he shall go forth with great wrath to fight against the kings of the north; and his wrath shall destroy and cut off

---

[65] CDC 7: 18f.

[66] Explicitly in M. 1: 1f "the Sons of Light who are now in exile."

[67] This could be held even though individual members of the Sect lived in Jerusalem; see S. E. Johnson, *The Scrolls in the New Testament*, ed. K. Stendahl, 1957, p. 142.

[68] Jer. 24: 1–13; 29: 16–20; 38: 2, 17; Ezek. 17.

[69] Jaubert, "Le Pays de Damas," p. 243; M. Smith, NTS, Vol. 7, 1961, pp. 347–360.

the horn of their strength. That will be a time of salvation for the people of God, and a period of dominion for all the men of his lot, but eternal destruction for all the lot of Belial. And there shall be a great tumult against the sons of Japheth; and Assyria shall fall with none to help him. And the dominion of the Kittim shall come to an end, so that wickedness shall be laid low without any remnant; and there shall be no survivor of the sons of darkness... (1: 1–7).

During the thirty-three years of war that are left the men of renown, those acclaimed in the assembly, and all the chiefs of the fathers of the congregation shall choose for themselves men of war for all the lands of the Gentiles from all the tribes of Israel; men of valour shall be equipped for them, to go out for warfare, according to the testimonies of war, year by year...

And as for the war of the divisions during the twenty-nine years that are left, in the first year they shall fight against Mesopotamia, and in the second against the sons of Lud; in the third they shall fight with the remnant of the sons of Syria, with Uz and Hul, Togar and Mashsha who are across the Euphrates; in the fourth and fifth they shall fight with the sons of Arpachshad; in the sixth and seventh they shall fight with all the sons of Assyria and Persia and the people of the east as far as the great desert; in the eighth year they shall fight against the sons of Elam; in the ninth they shall fight against the sons of Ishmael and Keturah; and in the ten years after these the war shall be distributed against all the sons of Ham (2: 1ff).

Unfortunately, in his otherwise excellent treatment of the theology of the War Scroll in his work *Le Rouleau de la Guerre*, Leiden, 1959, L. van der Ploeg O.P. does not deal with the word *galuth*, exile, nor the idea. But the exiles in Babylon are included in the final war. Not all had returned to the land from Babylon. Were those who remained there influenced by the words of Jeremiah and Ezekiel on the positive aspects of life in the Exile? Was it they who retained the traditions and thoughts of Baruch and Ezra? Some of them were of Davidic descent,[70] some were priests of ancient lineage.[71] They continued to infuse new blood into Palestinian Judaism right down to the first century[72] and much later. What was their

---

[70] Hillel—from Babylon—was a descendant of David. T. B. Pesaḥim 66a. See N. Glatzer, *Hillel the Elder: The Emergence of Classical Judaism*, New York, 1966, p. 24.

[71] Jos. *Antiquities*, XV. 2. 4; XV. 3. 1.

[72] There is evidence that the Jews in Babylon were the most significant in the first century. Jaubert refers to Jos. *Antiquities*, XI. 5. 2, where, speaking of the return of the exiles from Babylon he writes: "But the Israelite nation as a whole remained in the country. In this way has it come about that there are two tribes in Asia and Europe subject to Romans, while until now there have been ten tribes beyond the Euphrates—countless myriads whose number cannot be ascertained." (Loeb trans. pp. 377ff.) So too in *Antiquities* XV. 3. 1. In *Antiquities* XVIII. 9. 1, we read that the Jews in Babylon in the first centuries had treasure cities at Nearda and Nisibis, where they used to deposit "the two drachma—coins which it is the national custom for all to contribute to the cause of God, as well as any other dedicatory offerings." So much money would thus be deposited that "Many tens of thousands of Jews shared in the

attitude to the developments in Judah and Jerusalem after the Return? We know that they regarded the Second Temple as tainted,[73] and the question becomes inevitable whether there were continuing connections between the sectarians at Qumran, who regarded themselves as "exiles," and those others exiled in Babylon and elsewhere in the Diaspora. Was it to such connections that the sectarians owed the Iranian elements which their documents reveal?[74] And was it to Babylon that those regulations in CDC which seem to envisage a foreign country apply?[75] Were

convoy of these monies...." We can guess at the large numbers of Jews in Babylon from this. See further Acts 2: 9, and Jos., *Antiquities*, III. 15.3, which suggests the loyalty of Babylonian God-fearers to the Law: "...only recently certain persons from beyond the Euphrates, after a journey of four months, undertaken from veneration of our temple and involving great perils and expense, having offered sacrifices, could not partake of the victims, because Moses had forbidden this to any of those not governed by our laws nor affiliated through the customs of their fathers to ourselves...." Babylonian Jewry had its admirers.

Babylonian Jews continued to be of significance in later times. We note here only a few points. Babylonian Jews, like other Jews in every part of the world, contributed to the maintenance of the Patriarchate; Babylon gave a High Priest [Hanalil] to Herod; Judah the Prince, from fear of their predominance, withheld ordination from teachers who came from Babylon: Eliezer ben Pedat (A.D. 120–140) studied in Babylon; Abba (A.D. 165–200) was from Babylon; there were efforts in the late second century to establish a separate Sanhedrin for Babylon; the Patriarch Simeon ben Gamaliel had an assistant from Babylon in Rabbi Nathan (A.D. 140–165); Babylonian Jews had their own institutions and leaders—the chief of whom was the Exilarch (*Resh Galuto*); the Babylonian Jews regarding themselves as *bnê haggôlâh*, a community of exiles. Several exilarchs, although regarding Babylon as their home, desired to be buried in Palestine. In the early second century A.D., there was even a tendency to assign the Patriarchate to some kinsman of the Babylonian exilarchs. Rabbi Nathan aspired to the office. The relations of Babylonian Jews to the land can only be touched upon here: I hope to deal with this elsewhere. See Judah Goldin, in *The Jews*, 3rd ed., L. Finkelstein, New York, 1960, Vol. 1, pp. 169ff (The Period of the Talmud 135 B.C.E.–1035 C.E.), and S. Dubnov, *History of the Jews*, Vol. 2, rev. ed. by M. Spiegel, Brunswick, N.J., 1967, pp. 148ff; J. Neusner, *Development of a Legend*, Leiden, 1970, p. 292.

73 Malachi 1: 6–2: 9; 3: 3–4; 1 Enoch. 89: 73; Ass. Moses 4: 8; 2 Bar. 68: 7; 69: 1; Test. Levi 9, 10, 14, 16.

74 These Iranian elements are of three kinds: conceptual, lexicographical, textual. To document the discussion is impossible here. See, for example, A. Dupont-Sommer, *The Jewish Sect of Qumran and the Essenes*, trans., London, 1954, pp. 118ff; K. G. Kuhn, "Die Sektenschrift und die iranische Religion," in *Zeitschrift für Theologie und Kirche*, Vol. 49, 1952, pp. 296–316. See my essay in *The Scrolls and the New Testament*, ed. K. Stendahl, New York, 1957, pp. 164f. G. Widengren, " Quelques rapports entre Juifs et Iraniens à l'époque des Pathes," Volume du Congrès, Supplements to VT, Vol. IV, 1957, pp. 197–241. On lexicography, J. P. de Menasce, "Iranien Naxcir," in VT, Vol. VI, 1956, pp. 213–214. C. Rabin takes דֵּין to be a Persian loan word, *The Zadokite Documents*, 2nd ed., Oxford, 1958, p. 13, on 3: 18. For Iranian textual connections see W. F. Albright, "New Light on Early Recensions of the Hebrew Bible," BASOR, Vol. 140, 1955, p. 30; D. N. Freedman, BASOR, Vol. 145, 1957, pp. 31ff on "The Prayer of Nabonidus."

75 CDC 11: 2, 14; 12: 7. So, Jaubert, "Le Pays de Damas," p. 245. Rabin makes no comment on these verses to this effect. In CDC 13: 8 Rabin, *The Zadokite Documents*, p. 65, leaves the word בפרתיה untranslated: for him it is an "unintelligible, probably corrupt, word, forming part of a missing hemistich. It has been connected with פָּתַר, 'to solve' or פָּרַט 'to set out in detail.'" Dupont-Sommer renders it by "in the land of the Parthians" (*Evidences*,

there Essenes in Babylon also, and did they share in a theology which gave a positive evaluation to life outside the land as making possible the emergence of a remnant to atone for the land?

One thing may be regarded as certain. The uncritical and implicit devotion to the land which emerged in the Maccabean and "Zealot" mind was not unchallenged. True, for the sectarians also, life in a purified land and a purified city and Temple was the final goal, but they saw with clear eyes that in their present state land and city and Temple were defiled. And for them exile was the price of the atonement for the land. Exile, therefore, no less than land, has a role in the life of the people of the New Covenant. It is this that accounts for the marked difference between the treatment of the land by the Maccabees and the "Zealots" and by the sectarians.

2. FACTUAL

a. ABRAHAM OUTSIDE THE HEXATEUCH

Does the Old Testament support the ascription of a controlling significance to the promise to Abraham?

One serious difficulty is this: outside the Pentateuch the promise to Abraham as such is seldom referred to. Is it likely, therefore, to have played such a significant, reassuring part in the faith of Israel? Even in Deuteronomy, where Clements finds the fusion of the Abrahamic covenant with that established at Sinai, the land is said to be promised either, vaguely enough, to the fathers (1: 35; 7: 13; 10: 11; 26: 15; 31: 20) or to Isaac and Jacob as well as to Abraham (1: 8; 34: 4). In Deut. 29: 12 the covenant into which the children of Israel enter makes no mention of the land: the aim of the covenant is simply to establish a people unto the Lord. Again in Deut. 34: 1–12, despite its emphasis on the land sworn to the patriarchs (Deut. 34: 1–4), is it not significant that Moses, the servant of the Lord, whom the Lord knew face to face, like whom there had arisen no other prophet in Israel (34: 10ff), was not allowed to enter (34: 4), but died in Moab in a place unknown (34: 6)? No appeal to the promise for leniency is made even in the case of Moses.[76]

No. 60, p. 35, n. 66). Jaubert, "Le Pays de Damas," p. 245, n. 5, points out, also, how documents with Babylonian connections were preserved at Qumran. She notes fragments of Tobit (RB, Vol. LXIII, 1956, pp. 65–66), a fragment of the letter of Jeremiah (RB, *ibid.* p. 572). She takes 1 Baruch to be probably of Babylonian origin, and 2 Baruch, which emphasizes the Babylonian captivity, to have affinities with Qumran writings.

[76] That Moses died outside the promised land constituted a real problem for Israel. D. Daube, *Studies in Biblical Law*, Cambridge, 1947, pp. 28ff, interpreted the significance of the view of the land from Pisgah in terms of the prevailing legal customs: by viewing the land,

In the rest of the Old Testament there are few explicit references to the Abrahamic covenant. In Jer. 33: 24–26 the inviolability of the covenant with the patriarchs is affirmed and its reference to the land implied (33: 26): the passage reads:

The word of the Lord came to Jeremiah: "Have you not observed what these people are saying, 'The Lord has rejected the two families which he chose'? Thus they have despised my people so that they are no longer a nation in their sight. Thus says the Lord: If I have not established my covenant with day and night and the ordinances of heaven and earth, then I will reject the descendants of Jacob and David my servant and will not choose one of his descendants to rule over the seed of Abraham, Isaac, and Jacob. For I will restore their fortunes, and will have mercy upon them (Jer. 33: 23–26)."[77]

Ezekiel 33: 23ff contains a reference to the inheritance of the land by Abraham:

The word of the Lord came to me: Son of man, the inhabitants of these waste places (*heḥᵒrâbôth hâ-'êlleh*) in the land (*'adᵉmath*) of Israel keep saying, "Abraham was only one man, yet he got possession of the land (*hâ-'áretz*); but we are many; the land (*hâ-'áretz*) is surely given us to possess." Therefore say to them, Thus says the Lord God: You eat flesh with the blood, and lift up your eyes to your idols, and shed blood; shall you then possess the land (*hâ-'áretz*)? You resort to the sword, you commit abominations and each of you defiles his neighbour's wife; shall you then possess the land (*hâ-'áretz*)? Say this to them, Thus says the Lord God: As I live, surely those who are in the waste places (*bbeḥᵒrâbôth*) shall fall by the sword; and him that is in the open field I will give to the beasts to be devoured; and those who are in strongholds and in caves shall die by pestilence. And I will make the land (*hâ-'áretz*) a desolation (*shᵉmâmâh*) and a waste (*wmᵉshâmmâh*); and her proud might shall come to an end; and the mountains of Israel shall be so desolate (*wᵉshâmᵉmû*) that none will pass through.

Moses possessed the land even though he did not enter it. In Num. 20: 12 another explanation of Moses' failure to enter the land is offered: Moses and Aaron had failed to show forth God's sanctity (compare Deut. 32: 51). The context is not clear. Is it incomplete? Was it that Moses showed a certain lack of faith in striking the rock twice? R. E. Murphy, JBC, p. 93, *ad rem* suggests that Moses' anger (compare Ps. 106: 24–27) had changed a joyful manifestation of God's power to a scene of bitter denunciation. (He refers to E. Arden, "How Moses failed God," JBL, Vol. 76, 1957, pp. 50–52.) Deut. 1: 37 makes the divine wrath against the rebellious people, despite what Yahweh had done for them in Egypt and the wilderness, fall also on Moses and kept him outside the land. The claim that his burial-place was unknown (34: 4) may be a subtle way of avoiding a Moses cult outside the land. See further E. M. Meyers, *Jewish Ossuaries*, Rome, *Institute Press*, 1971, p. 15.

[77] In this passage the relationship between Yahweh and his people is as certain as that between him and the creation itself. In Jer. 11: 4–5 the Exodus motif is connected with the "oath which I have sworn to your fathers, to give them a land flowing with milk and honey." The references to the land given to the fathers in Jer. 16: 5; 30: 3 are too vague to be significant. With Jer. 33: 16–33, where the same kind of recital occurs, we have dealt above.

Then they will know that I am the Lord, when I have made the land (*hâ-'âreṯ*) a desolation (*sh^emâmâh*) and a waste (*m^eshammâh*) because of all their abominations which they have committed.

The section is interesting for two reasons: it implies that both Abraham's inheritance of the land, and, we may presume, though this is not explicitly stated, the promise of the land to Abraham were discussed widely by the exiles in Babylon as they contemplated their own relationship to the land. They argued—naïvely?—that, if one, Abraham, could be promised the land and be given it as an inheritance, *many* surely could expect the same. But in answer to this, Ezekiel makes explicit that the Israelites' abominations make their inheritance of the land impossible. The importance of this is clear: there is here no appeal from Israel's disobedience to the grace of the covenant. The covenant with Abraham provides no reassurance against failure to keep the commandments. Nor is there a reference to Abraham, but only to Jacob, in Ezek. 37: 25–27. In Ezek. 36: 16–38 the reference to "the land that I gave your fathers" is vague (in 36: 28), and its renewal is in terms of the new creation, not of the promise (36: 36).

In Deutero-Isaiah there are references to Abraham in 41: 8 and 51: 2–3. But in the former there is no more than a reference to Jacob (Israel) as the chosen, "the seed of Abraham, my friend," in a general way, and again in 51: 2–3 Abraham is the father of Israel, the rock whence she is hewn. Abraham has been called, has been blessed, and has been increased (51: 2), but there is no reference to the promise of the land to him, and in the following section 51: 9–16 the appeal is not to the activity of Yahweh in the promise of the land to Abraham, but in the creation and in the Exodus. The following two verses alone need quotation, from 51: 9–10:

> Awake, awake, put on strength, O arm of the Lord;
> awake, as in days of old, the generations of long ago.
> Wast it not thou that didst cut Rahab in pieces,
> that didst pierce the dragon?
> Was it not thou that didst dry up the sea,
> the waters of the great deep;
> that didst make the depths of the sea a way
> for the redeemed to pass over?

Three other references to the Abrahamic covenant appear at Ps. 105: 6 and 9, and 42. Their significance can only be seen in the totality of the Psalm. Here the promise to Abraham is really fused with the story of the Exodus. But it is so fused in the context of a survey of the "deeds" of Yahweh "among the people," his "wondrous works (Ps. 105: 2, 5)."

The promise has become an item—however significant—in a list of the
mighty works of God which culminate in the Exodus. On the other hand,
this Psalm does establish that the promise to Abraham is part of the
kerygmatic recitals of Israel.

And in Neh. 9: 5ff the recital of God's mighty works again includes
references to the promise of the land in the same manner, and gives
prominence to Abraham as such. With Jer. 33: 16–33, where the same
kind of recital occurs, we shall deal below. But it is to be noted that in
Chronicles neither at David's installation as King at Hebron (1 Chron. 11)
nor at the installation of Solomon by David (1 Chron. 28) is there a
reference to the Abrahamic covenant. At 1 Chron. 28: 8, especially, a
reference to Abraham might have been expected. In 2 Chron. 33: 8 the
Exodus and Abrahamic traditions are appealed to, but whereas explicit
reference is made to Moses, Abraham is not mentioned: the land has—
again vaguely—"been appointed for your fathers." If we are to judge by
the omission of the name of the patriarch and the inclusion of that of
Moses, here certainly the specifically Abrahamic emphasis has been subordinated. The paucity of explicit references to the promise in much of the
Old Testament appears to be striking and to cast doubt on Clements's
emphasis.

The same paucity marks the Apocrypha and Pseudepigrapha. We
previously noted that the sources dealing with the Maccabees seldom refer
to Abraham, and that not in connection with the Promise. The same is
true of the Apocrypha and Pseudepigrapha in general; these rarely
mention Abraham. In the Apocrypha, in Jubilees[78] alone—naturally in
view of its character as a kind of commentary on Genesis—is there any
lengthy treatment of the patriarch. Surprisingly the same must be asserted
even of the Rabbinic sources. In the Mishnah there are hardly twelve
references to Abraham, and among the early Midrashim, apart from
Genesis Rabbah, where discussion of Abraham is inevitable, the patriarch
is rarely discussed.[79] It agrees with this that the covenant itself—because
of the emphasis upon it in Christianity?[80]—was seldom directly treated

[78] It is significant that in *Abraham, Père des Croyants*, "*Cahiers Sioniens*," Editions du Cerf,
Paris, June, 1951, there is no separate section devoted to the Apocrypha and Pseudepigrapha.
[79] In the Mishnah there are only twelve references to the patriarch (Taan. 2: 4, 5; Ned.
3: 11; Kidd. 4: 14; B.K. 8: 6; B.M. 7: 1. All the other references are in Aboth at 3: 12;
5: 2, 3, 6, 19; 6: 10). Abraham came to his own in later mediaeval sources; see *Abraham, Père
des Croyants*. The treatment of Abraham in the Old Testament by R. Le Déaut, despite his
desire to emphasize it, supports ours. See *La Nuit Pascale*, Institut Biblique Pontifical, Rome,
1963, pp. 100–110, especially pp. 107f.
[80] Compare J. Bonsirven, *Le Judaïsme Palestinien*, Paris, 1934, Vol. 1, pp. 79f. His words
deserve quotation: "Cette idée de l'alliance domine toute la pensée juive: nous sommes

in early Rabbinic sources. We noted above passages in 1 Macc. where
Abraham is referred to, and it must not be inferred from the paucity of
references with which we are dealing that the significance of Abraham
and veneration for him were lost to those who wrote the Apocrypha and
Pseudepigrapha.[81] The covenant with Abraham was at the foundation—
assumed and unexpressed—of the people of Israel. Like the foundation of
a building it was often hidden from view and not actively discussed. But it
is erroneous[82] to claim that Abraham and the covenant were a preoccupation of Judaism: the sources do not support such a claim.[83]

b. ISRAEL: COVENANTED COMMUNITY

Our treatment of the relationship of the law to the land may have
created the impression that Israel in the Old Testament is to be under-

d'autant plus surpris de constater que la littérature rabbinique a relativement peu exploité
cette donnée biblique primordiale." J. Bonsirven asserts that there are very few places where
rabbis speculate on the covenantal idea: in the Midrashim comments on the Biblical texts
dealing with the Covenant are few. He also points out how sectarian movements remained far
truer to the Old Testament in this; for example, the Dead Sea Sect governed its life on the
covenantal principle. Thus not only Christian concentration on covenantal ideas, but other
sectarian tendencies also would tend to reinforce the surprising neglect of the explicit treatment of such texts in the Rabbinic sources. To judge from the extant works of Philo the same
neglect of the covenantal idea might be found in Hellenistic Judaism, but G. F. Moore
pointed out that Philo wrote two lost treatises on the Covenants (see R. Marcus—citing
G. F. Moore—*Law in the Apocrypha*, New York, 1927, p. 14 n). (The view expressed by
H. J. Schoeps in *Aus frühchristlicher Zeit*, Tübingen, 1950, p. 228, that Diaspora Judaism or
Septuagint-Judaism, as he describes it, had a false conception of the covenantal relation between
Yahweh and Israel, as did also Paul, to speak very mildly, is to be very seriously questioned.
Compare, for Paul, H. Conzelmann, "Current Problems in Pauline Research," in *New
Testament Studies*, ed. R. Batey, New York, 1970, p. 135.) In his *Theologie und Geschichte des
Judenchristentums*, p. 90, the same scholar offers parallels to the above-mentioned neglect of
the covenant concept in the rabbis, parallels which are illuminating. Schoeps is concerned to
show the way in which Judaism reacted to the Jewish-Christian emphasis on Christ as the New
Moses. He writes: "Welchen Rang und welche Verbreitung dieses Dogma, vielleicht auf
essäische Ursprünge zurückgehend, Christus Jesus-Novus Moses in der jüdischen Christen-
heit gehabt haben muss, lassen uns auch zwei weitere Umstände erkennen....Zum anderen
der auffällige Verzicht der Tannaiten und frühen Amoraer, Deut. xviii. 15 und 18 auszulegen
[see especially p. 90, n. 3, for evidence]. Es begegnet uns hier dieselbe Erscheinung wie bei
der Auslegungsgeschichte von Jes. liii; Ps. ii. 7; cx: 1; Jer. xxxi. 31f.; Hos. ii. 25 usw. *Die
jüdische Theologie der ersten Jahrhunderte n. Chr. fand diese Schriftsteller bereits durch die
christliche Auslegung präokkupiert und verzichtete daher auf ihre Verwendung innerhalb mes-
sianischer Diskussionen oder legte sie betont uneschatologisch aus* (our italics)." Compare also
G. Quell, TWZNT, II, *ad loc*. For the way in which Judaism closed its ranks against
Christianity, see S. W. Baron, *A Social and Religious History of the Jews*, Vol. II, Philadelphia,
1952, pp. 130ff, and the bibliographical details he supplies.

[81] See, for example, Pss. Sol. 11: 17; 18: 4.

[82] As does J. Jeremias, TWZNT, I, pp. 7–8; L. Cerfaux, *La Théologie de l'Église suivant
Saint Paul*, Paris, 1948, p. 21. See further C. K. Barrett, *From First Adam to Last*, New York,
1962, pp. 22–45.

[83] As we saw, Clements seeks to meet all the above by claiming that the Abrahamic
covenant was taken up into the Exodus tradition and, therefore, assumed. But we are not
wholly convinced. The silence is too significant to be thus explained away.

stood as a community bound to a land and governed by a law, much as a modern national state might be so tied and governed. But one thing has emerged clearly from studies on law in the Hebrew Scriptures. The laws were not related primarily to the political organization of a state, but rather to a community of men in which the common allegiance to Yahweh was the constitutive element. The context or setting in life in which Israel had received the Law was the covenant, a sacral act, and the communication of the Law was connected with the celebration of the covenant which bound Israel to its God. To maintain the validity of this covenant— of which the proclamation of the Law was an essential part—Israel celebrated or commemorated it in regular feasts. In this religious act lay the foundation of Israel. "The Israelite nation, then, had its true existence apart from and prior to the erection of their political, social and economic order in Canaan."[84] The community is to be understood as a corollary of the covenant.

It is this that explains why it is impossible to discover any Israelite idea of the State.[85] The Israelites did not imitate the Canaanite principalities whom they ousted. These principalities were made up of fortified cities surrounded by small territories: they were under a king, often of foreign birth, who led an army drawn from his own people and from mercenaries. But Gideon refused to be a King (Judg. 8: 22f) (the Kingdom of Abimelech, based on non-Israelite elements, was short lived; Judg. 8: 31; 9: 1f). In Canaan, Israel at first formed a federation of twelve tribes: these owed a common loyalty to Yahweh and shared a common law. But, in the light of the Book of Judges, they had no organized government. The judges themselves were charismatic figures called by Yahweh for specific missions: they were not rulers of all Israel. In time, the Israelite federation became a national monarchical state under Saul, a charismatic figure. But such a state was not unopposed. The attitude toward the monarchy was divided.[86] To some it was initiated by God: to others it was due to a reprehensible desire on Israel's part to be like other nations who supported their kings. But, nevertheless, under David and Solomon unity was achieved between Israel and Judah: the latter two areas were subsumed under one sovereign. But this state of affairs lasted only for two generations. On Solomon's death Israel and Judah separated, and two kingdoms emerged. Sometimes they were allies: some-

---

[84] R. B. Y. Scott, *The Relevance of the Prophets*, New York, 1968, p. 189.
[85] R. de Vaux, *Ancient Israel*, 1961, pp. 91ff.
[86] How opposition to the monarchy persisted is shown by Schoeps, *Aus frühchristlicher Zeit*, pp. 242ff.

times enemies. What is significant is that they acted independently, and that other nations treated them as two distinct powers. Political unity, a single statehood, eluded the people. But at the same time, throughout the separation of the monarchy, the religious idea of the unity of the people, of the federation of the Twelve Tribes,[87] remained. And the prophets, as we saw, looked forward to their reunion. "Israel" and the political organization or organizations of its people are to be distinguished.

After 587 B.C., when Jerusalem fell, the idea of a state declined. The Jews became again a purely religious community: in time priests came to rule them under God.[88] Israel is the people of Yahweh alone. In Ezra and Nehemiah the primary, if not the only, concern is that the people should obey the Law.[89] If we follow the traditional view of the origin of the Pharisees it was loyalty to the Law alone that governed them, and initially it was this that moved the Maccabees also. After the Exile, the Jews became a people of the Torah. How they concentrated on the Torah as such and not on the land in which they lived appears from the next section. But, before we turn to this, it must be emphasized again how much more the whole history of Pharisaism is necessarily concentrated on the Torah than on the political control of the land.[90]

C. POST-EXILIC WRITINGS

In many documents of the Old Testament, the precise dating of most of which is difficult, but all of which are post-exilic—Job, Proverbs, Ecclesiastes, Song of Songs, Esther, Jonah, and even parts of Daniel— the land of Israel as such hardly plays any part. This is noteworthy. The loss of control over the land, if as fact and idea the land played any significant role among Jews, especially since many of them lived in it, might have been expected to lead to a concern with, if not concentration

[87] R. de Vaux, *Ancient Israel*, p. 97; on the emphasis on the "one-ness" of "Israel," see PRJ, pp. 78ff. Note that the cultic status of Jerusalem could survive apart from adherence to the House of David. The prophets think of Yahweh, not David, as the founder of Jerusalem. See M. Noth, "Jerusalem und die israelitische Tradition," *Gesammelte Studien zum A.T.*, 1957, pp. 172–187, especially pp. 177–179.

[88] Such a statement needs qualification, see Bickerman, *From Ezra*, pp. 8ff. The priests were *under* Persia; Ezra 9: 9.

[89] In Cyrus's decree the Jews are to return "to build (Yahweh) a house in Jerusalem (Ezra 1: 2ff)." This decree was confirmed by Darius (Ezra 6: 1ff) and Artaxerxes (7: 1ff, 21): Ezra was concerned first and foremost with the Law, 7: 10ff, 25ff; 9: 10ff, although there is the clear recognition that only through obedience to the law can the land itself become clean, as in Neh. 1: 7ff. The centrality of the Law is clear in Neh. 8: 1ff. But the appeal to the promise to Abraham is also present in Neh. 9: 6–7, 35. See above, p. 107.

[90] Bickerman, *From Ezra*, pp. 174f; J. Neusner, *A Life of Rabbi Johannan ben Zakkai, 1–80 C.E.*, Leiden, 1962, p. 157, especially n. 2 for bibliographical details; *The Development of a Legend*, 1965, pp. 16, 99f. But see p. 128, n. 130.

upon it. Among many, however, to judge from the literature to which we have referred, this did not happen. Instead a concern with broad human, rather than specifically Israelitish, problems is more in evidence.

This is true of Job (600–450 B.C.?), whose main character, although from the land of Uz, was "blameless and upright (1: 1)," "the greatest man in all the East (1: 3, NEB)."[91] Uz was in Edom (Gen. 36: 28; Lam. 4: 21), south and east of Israel, although some have placed it in northeast Transjordan. Job suggests the nomadic patriarchs, not the settled Israelites, and the problem he deals with, after the manner of Egyptian and Babylonian models, is a universal one; that of the suffering of the righteous. One is tempted to suggest that the application of the adjective *tam*, "perfect," to a man living outside the land is not insignificant: "perfection" for the author of Job was not only possible in the land but outside it.[92] Similarly Ecclesiastes, probably written in the third century in Jerusalem, under the Ptolemies, does not concern itself with the land. Indeed to inherit the land or anything else is futile.

So I came to hate all my labour and toil here under the sun, since I should have to leave its fruits to my successor. What sort of man will he be who succeeds me, who inherits what others have acquired? Who knows whether he will be a worse man or a fool? Yet he will be master of all the fruits of my labour and skill here under the sun. This too is emptiness (2: 17–19, NEB).

Ecclesiastes reflects the economic, intellectual, and moral preoccupations (that is, questions of competitive business, Providence, Hedonism, Immortality) of the Greek enlightenment which had invaded the Jerusalem of its day. Its horizons are universal and timeless.[93] Equally so are those of the love-lyrics, comparable with those of Ancient Egypt perhaps, termed The Song of Songs. (So R. E. Murphy, JBC, p. 506.) And, in still another way, the outlook of the book of Jonah, usually dated in the fifth century B.C., is universal. It is customary to find in Jonah a protest against those in Israel (represented by Jonah) who would confine the mercies of God to the Chosen People. The refusal of Jonah to go to Nineveh at the command of the Lord, his dismay at the repentance of that city, and God's sparing of it bespeaks such a protest. The anger of Jonah at the perishing of the gourd is made the occasion of God's moving rebuke.

[91] H. H. Rowley, *Job*, 1971, *ad rem*, emphasizes that Job was a Gentile. The book invokes ancient *cosmic* mythology against Deut.

[92] All the commentators whom I have consulted do not connect *tam* with the observance of the Law and this should not be expected in dealing with a Gentile who was "perfect."

[93] See Bickerman, *Four Strange Books*.

"Are you so angry over the gourd?" "Yes," he answered, "mortally angry."
The Lord said, "...And should not I be sorry... (Jonah 4: 9–11)."

Most have interpreted the purpose of Jonah in the light of this passage
and have contrasted the wideness of God's mercy, with the grudging
narrowness of Jonah, Israel.[94] Even if it be admitted that the people of
Israel as such are not in the author's mind, because God, Jonah (the
prophet), and Nineveh alone are mentioned in the book, the central
emphasis remains on the divine mercy to all men.[95]

One small item in Jonah can lead us on to the next point. In 3: 6ff it is
noted that the edict for penance issues from the King of Nineveh who, at
the preaching of Jonah, had repented, "removed his robe and covered
himself with sackcloth, and sat in ashes." A pagan king appears in a good
light.

It is not always recognized that in Esther the attitude to a pagan ruler
is positive. The Persian ruler Ahasuerus did not hate "Jews" as a group:
he did not even know the name of the people whom Haman desired to
destroy: he did not ratify the decrees against them.[96] Not the ruler himself but an underling, Haman, caused ill to the Jews, and that out of
personal revenge, despite the warnings of his wife and advisers.[97] Nor
is there hatred of Gentiles in Esther. We may detect in that book a certain
pride in the attainment by Jews of high office in a pagan state. Both
Mordecai and Esther, whose names are not Jewish, achieved distinction
among Gentiles.[98] Mordecai became a Persian courtier, and Esther a
queen among a people whose queens were usually of royal blood or from
one of seven princely houses.[99] Although Esther did not observe the food
laws, and fitted, apparently without too much difficulty, into a heathen
harem, and although later Rabbis might well be embarrassed by Esther
and Mordecai, the author clearly holds them up for veneration.[100] Perhaps
this is what we might expect, because the excellence of the Greek in Esther
speaks much of its author's attitude to pagan culture in Jerusalem in the
second century B.C. The work records that the city of Susa, where Jews

[94] See JBC, ad rem; H. H. Rowley, Israel's Mission to the World, London, 1939, ad rem;
The Faith of Israel, London, 1956, p. 186.

[95] Bickerman, Four Strange Books, pp. 158ff.

[96] 8: 5; in 1: 1–9: Ahasuerus treats all alike (1: 5): no one was "compelled" but everyman
could do as he desired (1: 8). It was Haman who desired the destruction of the Jews (3: 6):
Ahasuerus did not know who these were (3: 8ff).

[97] 6: 12ff.

[98] Esther is called in Hebrew, Hadassah: the name "Mordecai" is Babylonian, after the
god Marduk.

[99] See Bickerman, Four Strange Books, pp. 171ff.

[100] Ibid.

were numerous and proud, grieved (3: 15) at the publication of Haman's edict and rejoiced at Mordecai's appointment (8: 15). Certainly there is here no racial anti-Semitism such as the twentieth century has known, even though Esther may be a political pamphlet designed to suggest to Gentile rulers that persecution and annihilation is not as profitable in the treatment of Jews—despite the counsel given by advisers such as Haman (and they pepper the pages of Jewish history)—as sensible taxation.[101]

The book of Esther evolved slowly: we need not trace its evolution. Its final form emerged in the second century B.C. and speaks to the Jews of the Diaspora. Esther is the only Biblical work that does not mention the land. To Diaspora Jews it brought the assurance that, not only within the land, as in the achievements of the Hasmoneans, but outside the land also, in such a city as Susa, God's intervention on behalf of his people— although God is never mentioned by name in Esther—was sure. "The promise given to the Chosen People in the Holy Land (Exod. 23: 27) was also fulfilled in the Diaspora: if you will obey God's commandments, God will lay the fear of you upon the nations."[102] In Esther the pagan ruler not only allows Jews to live according to their own laws, but also demands of his subjects that they defend the Jews in their affliction. "It would be difficult to push further the identification of a heathen ruler with the Jewish case."[103] Lysimachus is not without concern for Jerusalem, but it is a concern that allows him to look not with disfavour on life outside the land also.

The possibility of Jews coming to pleasant terms with kings outside the land is reflected also in Daniel, where, in the first chapters, Shadrach, Meshach, and Abednego are rulers in Persia, and Daniel a governor at the King's court (2: 48f): Daniel was made master of the magicians (4: 6). As in Esther, so in Daniel, a Gentile ruler, Darius, favours a Jew, Daniel: it is the King's "lords" who oppose him (6: 14ff). The evolution of the book of Daniel into its present form has been variously understood. But its division into two main parts, one containing stories about Daniel, a Jewish captive, and his three compatriots at the court of Nebuchadnezzar and his successors in the first six chapters, and the other, from chapters 7–12, containing a series of visions, is clear.[104] The land does break through in the second part, as we have indicated (see pp. 96f), but the stories in the first part originally may have had the Jews of the Diaspora in mind. They reflect the conflict which monotheistic Jews in positions of authority

---

[101] So Bickerman. [102] Bickerman, *Four Strange Books*, p. 205.
[103] *Ibid.* p. 230.
[104] See N. W. Porteous, *Daniel: Commentary*, Philadelphia, 1965, pp. 13ff.

were likely to experience in Gentile states and are admirably suited to encourage such in their loyalty. Daniel and his three compatriots served as examples for their people in their dispersion. In this light also, the efficacy ascribed to the diet which Daniel, Shadrach, Meshach, and Abednego subscribed to as Jews is to be understood: it was better than that of the Gentiles (1: 5–16). To observe the food laws was advantageous—a lesson frequently needed to help Jews in the Diaspora persevere in their observance. Moreover, amidst a sea of Gentiles, the power of whose rulers and, therefore, of whose gods, was all too evident, the assurance of the interventions of Yahweh on behalf of Daniel and his compatriots was highly necessary. Nor is concentration in the stories narrowly on the Jews in the Dispersion. There is a universal range to the stories in the first part (see 3: 31; 6: 26); and even in 7: 12, while the Greek empire is to be destroyed, the Oriental kingdoms are to be allowed to continue for a time. Bickerman writes: "This solicitude for the entire Levant is a testimony to Oriental solidarity in the face of the Greeks."[105] The last-named scholar finds the original intent of the stories in the first part of Daniel, then, which he claims emerged between 245 and 219 B.C., to be to address the Jews living among Gentiles. If Bickerman be followed there is, then, evidence for a Judaism adjusting to or coming to terms with life outside the land and with Hellenism. That the stories referred to came to be used later in the struggle against Antiochus Epiphanes in the mid-second century B.C. does not negate their earlier significance as evidence for currents in Judaism in which the land was not a preoccupation.

In the same context, the Book of Ruth is to be considered. Its date and purpose are disputed. As the emphasis on the Moabite origin of Ruth (1: 22; 2: 2, 6, 21; 3: 3, 5, 10) suggests, one possibility is that it was designed to counteract the policy of Ezra and Nehemiah, who sought to root out marriages with aliens. Ruth, in this view, is a polemic in post-exilic Israel against "exclusivism" or "isolationism" and it fits well into those other post-exilic documents with which we have dealt. But does the view indicated take into account the importance of the genealogy of David in 3: 18–22? Is it enough to claim in its favour that the introduction of Moabitic blood into the Royal Davidic line is designed to combat exclusivism? And does Ruth—described by Goethe as "the loveliest little epic and idyllic whole that tradition has given us"—suggest a political pamphlet? These and other questions cannot be pursued here:

---

[105] Bickerman, *Four Strange Books*, p. 105. For the date of the stories, Bickerman, pp. 61ff; H. H. Rowley, ZATW, Vol. 9, 1932, pp. 256–268.

but even bearing these questions in mind, at least the possibility that Ruth points to a universal dimension in post-exilic Judaism in which other lands than Judah are accorded great significance must be noted.

The broad human concerns to which we have referred in the post-exilic writings are not necessarily to be understood as precluding attachment to the land. The post-exilic period witnessed the work of the Priestly "School," which formulated P; this certainly concentrated on Temple and land, as had Ezekiel (although it is to be recognized that in Ezekiel and P there is also traceable a tendency to deny that the presence of Yahweh is to be associated with any single place). The Psalms witness to the love of the land and the author of 1 and 2 Chronicles enlarged the role of David (1 Chron. 17: 14; 28: 5; 29: 23). But the fact remains that in the literature of the post-exilic period there is an undeniable relocation of interest away from the land to the broadly human. And this relocation, surprising as it is at first, fits into another development, frequently noted, in the post-exilic period.

d. INDIVIDUALISM

In that period there emerged, not a new, but a deepened awareness of the dimensions of specifically personal religious experience: the spiritual pilgrimage of the individual as such, not only as a member of the group, gained in significance.[106] Jeremiah had prepared the way for this at the cost of the loneliness of his ministry: he seems to have felt at times that "the whole cause of Yahweh in the world hung on his individual life."[107] Ezekiel had come to recognize that, however much part of the group, each Israelite stood alone. And in Deutero-Isaiah an interesting phenomenon already begins to confront us. The vocabulary of entry into the land, that is, the vocabulary of national promise begins to be applied to the just man, the saint: consider Is. 57: 13b:

> But he who takes refuge in me
> Shall possess the land,
> And shall inherit my holy mountain.

And again Is. 65: 13–16:

> Therefore thus says the Lord God:
> "Behold, my servants shall eat,
> but you shall be hungry;

106 This is well brought out by Jacques Guillet, *Thèmes Bibliques*, Paris, 1951, pp. 192ff. "L'heritage attendu est parfois vraiment intérieur." He refers to Prov. 3: 35; Job 27: 13; compare 20: 29; 21: 2; Prov. 28: 10; 8: 20–21; Ps. 25: 13. Not the descendant of Abraham but "the man who fears the Lord" inherits "the land." Guillet's emphasis must be taken in conjunction with P below. Guillet is aware of the ambiguity of the texts, p. 193.

107 See J. Skinner, *Prophecy and Religion*, Cambridge, 1922, p. 223.

behold, my servants shall drink,
> but you shall be thirsty;

behold, my servants shall rejoice,
> but you shall be put to shame;

behold, my servants shall sing for
> gladness of heart,

but you shall cry out for pain of
> heart,

and shall wail for anguish of spirit.

You shall leave your name to my
> chosen for a curse,

> and the Lord God will slay you;

but his servants he will call by a
> different name.

So that he who blesses himself in
> the land

> shall bless himself by the God of
> truth,

and he who takes an oath in the land
> shall swear by the God of truth;

because the former troubles are
> forgotten

and are hid from my eyes.

The Wisdom literature, on the one hand, as we should now put it, has a curiously "international" flavour (and, indeed, draws upon Egyptian sources), while, on the other, it applies appeals and warnings uttered by the prophets of Israel to the individual Israelite. It is not only that the fate of the individual is bound up with that of his people, Israel, but that the experience of Israel, as a people, is reproduced on an appropriate scale in that of the individual Israelite. This appears in Prov. 1–9 which have been called "tissues de réminiscences deutéronomiques et prophétiques,"[108]

[108] André Robert, RB, Vol. XLIII, 1934, pp. 42–68, 172–204, 374–384; Vol. XLIV, 1935, pp. 344–365, 502–525, "Les attachés littéraires bibliques de Prov., I–IX," p. 152. On the international affinities of Proverbs, see R. B. Y. Scott, *The Way of Wisdom in the Old Testament*, New York, 1971, pp. 23–47. It is to be noted that centuries later, in reaction partly to the Crusades, the "crusade" for the land becomes a crusade for holiness within—withdrawal from the world. Still later in some Black spirituals—it is interesting to note—"the land," which Black Christians, like other Christians had often treated as a symbol of the transcendental, was rehistoricized. "The land" was made to refer to Africa, Canada, and states north of the Mason–Dixon line. Frederick Douglass wrote: "A keen observer might have detected in our repeated singing of

O Canaan, sweet Canaan,
I am bound for the land of Canaan,

something more than a hope of reaching heaven. We meant to reach the *North*, and the North was our Canaan." (*The Life and Times of Frederick Douglass*, New York, Collier

and "une perpétuelle transposition de leur doctrine, une application à la vie individuelle des appels adressés à la communauté d'Israël." Thus Prov. 1: 24–28 reads:

> Because I have called and you
>   refused to listen,
> have stretched out my hand and
>   no one has heeded,
> and you have ignored all my
>   counsel
> and would have none of my
>   reproof,
> I also will laugh at your calamity;
>   I will mock when panic strikes
>   you,
> when panic strikes you like a storm,
>   and your calamity comes like a
>   whirlwind,
> when distress and anguish come
>   upon you.
> Then they will call upon me, but I
>   will not answer;
>   they will seek me diligently but
>   will not find me.

Compare Is. 65: 2, 12; 66: 4 with Prov. 1: 24; Is. 66: 4 with Prov. 1: 26b; Is. 64: 13–14 with Prov. 1: 27c; Is. 65: 24 with Prov. 1: 28.

Later still, in the Maccabean period, the martyrs further imprinted the significance of the individual Israelite on Judaism. The martyrs in the Book of Daniel and elsewhere stand to the majority of their own people as the "apostates," in a relationship comparable to that in which Israel as a whole had often been thought to stand to the Gentile nations. The singularity of the people of Israel in the midst of the nations is now experienced by the martyr in the midst of Israel. The triumph of the individual martyr demanded the doctrine of the resurrection of the dead. True this doctrine never became primarily individualistic, but

---

Books, 1962, p. 159. Cited by James H. Cone, "Black Spirituals: A Theological Interpretation," *Theology Today*, No. 1, April 1972, p. 67.) In recent Black movements, land, either as a return to Africa or as a separate state in the United States, has continued to be a central concern. See, for example, *The Speeches of Malcolm X at Harvard*, ed. Archie Epps, New York, 1968, pp. 82ff, and especially *Message to the Grass Roots: Malcolm X Speaks*, Merritt Publishers and Betty Shabaz, 1965, cited in *Phase Blue: A Systems Approach to College English*, ed. J. B. Hogins, R. E. Yarber, Chicago, 1970, pp. 388ff. See a forthcoming saga *Roots* by Alex Haley.

neither was it purely communal.[109] In part at least, it was the concern to vindicate the individual martyrs that inspired the growth in the belief in the necessity of resurrection. Here, as in every sphere, Judaism preserved both a communal and an individual emphasis. Consider the following words from the Wisdom of Solomon 5: 1–2 which describe the triumph of the righteous in the resurrection and the discomfiture of the wicked:

> Then the righteous man (*ho dikaios*) will
> stand with great confidence
> in the presence of those who have
> afflicted him,
> and those who make light of his
> labors.
> When they see him, they will be
> shaken with dreadful fear,
> and they will be amazed at his
> unexpected salvation.

The concern with the fate of the individual as such, which we have indicated above, was not exclusive of concern with the land, because, as we have previously seen, the resurrection itself came to be tied to the land. But the individualization and internalization of religious concern could not but lead to a relocation of emphasis. And this was furthered by the major factor with which we next deal, the influence of the Dispersion.

e. THE DISPERSION

The condition and distribution of Jews in the post-exilic period deserves attention. We saw above that few of the exiles in Babylon chose to return to the land when Cyrus made this possible (538 B.C.). There continued in Babylon for a thousand years after Cyrus a well-organized Jewish community, which eventually gave the Babylonian Talmud to the world. The Jews had early spread to the West also. As is made clear in the Elephantine papyrii, there was a colony of Jewish soldiers in the city of Yeb (Elephantine) in Egypt at the beginning of the sixth century B.C. Alexander the Great stimulated the spread of Jews, and throughout the Greek and Roman periods various reasons contributed to further this.[110] Josephus quotes Strabo, the geographer (c. 41 B.C.–A.D. 24) "This people has already made its way into every city, and it is not that easy to

---

[109] PRJ, pp. 83f.
[110] See my article "The Jewish State in the Hellenistic World," *Peake*, pp. 686–692.

find any place in the habitable world which has not received this nation and in which it has not made its power felt (*Ant.* XIV. 7. 2)." The evidence confirms Strabo's view. The Dispersion was, and is, an impressive fact.

Few have written as perceptively on this Dispersion as Bickerman: he notes the continued attachment of Diaspora Jews to Jerusalem. He writes: "...the post-biblical period of Jewish history [that is, that following Nehemiah]...is marked by a unique and rewarding polarity: on the one hand, the Jerusalem center and, on the other, the plurality of centers in the Diaspora. The Dispersion saved Judaism from physical extirpation and spiritual inbreeding. Palestine united the dispersed members of the nation and gave them a sense of oneness. This counterpoise of historical forces is without analogy in antiquity.... The Jewish Dispersion continued to consider Jerusalem as the 'metropolis' (Philo), turned to the Holy Land for guidance, and in turn, determined the destinies of its inhabitants."[111]

But the experience of living outside the land over a length of time could not but tend to detach Jews from it. In this sphere, as in others, absence made the heart grow fonder, but the Babylonian exiles chose not to return to the land. Later, the Jews of the Dispersion on the whole refused to participate in the war against Rome in A.D. 66–70. They had their own life to live outside the land. And a form of religious association appropriate for such a life, the Synagogue, had already almost certainly emerged in the Babylonian exile and developed throughout the Dispersion to supply for Jews a rallying point other than the Temple, which was in the land.[112] In time, the Dispersion, which had been regarded as a punishment for sin, could be justified at least by two Rabbis. Rabbi Eleazar of Modiim (A.D. 120–140) said that "God scattered Israel among the nations for the sole end that proselytes should wax numerous among them." And although this was apparently a lonely voice, it is not without

---

[111] *From Ezra*, 1962, pp. 3f.

[112] The comparative significance of the Temple and the Synagogue in Jewish life in our period is hard to assess: certain it is that Judaism survived the destruction of the Temple. Could it have survived without the Synagogue? See S. Schechter, *Some aspects of Rabbinic Theology*, London, 1909, p. 208, n. 3; PRJ, pp. 258ff; F. C. N. Hicks, *The Fullness of Sacrifice*, London, 1930, p. 105; G. F. Moore, *Judaism*, Vol. II, pp. 11f; B. Gärtner, *The Temple and the Community in Qumran and the New Testament*, Cambridge, 1965, pp. 16, 99f. But see the caveat in Bonsirven, *Le Judaïsme Palestinien*, Vol. II, pp. 107ff. He refers to the Maccabaean zeal for the Temple, to the mourning after its fall in A.D. 70, to the *Letter of Aristeas*, 92–99. H. H. Rowley, *Worship in Ancient Israel*, Philadelphia, 1967, pp. 231–233 cites E. L. Sukenik, *Ancient Synagogues in Palestine and Greece*, 1934, p. 50, and F. Landsberger, HUCA, Vol. XXVIII, 1957, p. 183, to support the view that the Synagogues were built "towards" Jerusalem. Pilgrimages to Jerusalem continued.

significance: separation from the land could be regarded as a not un-mitigated evil.[113]

[113] T. B. Pes. 87b. Unfortunately, I have not been able to find an adequate treatment of the significance of the *galuth* in Judaism. On Jews in Damascus, see B. Z. Lurie, *Eretz Israel*, Vol. IV, pp. 111–118. J. F. Baer, *Galut*, Berlin, 1936, is unsatisfactory for our purposes. There are helpful references—dated from the second century to the modern period—scattered through H. J. Schoeps, *The Jewish-Christian Argument: A History of Theologies in Conflict*, trans., D. E. Green, New York, 1963. He notes the purpose of the *galuth* as punishment (but not rejection; Lev. 26: 44) (p. 31); as a part of the divine plan assuring the eternity of the nation (pp. 31ff); as due to sin and, therefore, justified (pp. 37, 160). The extremely long duration of the *galuth* after the fall of Jerusalem was explained as necessary to counteract not only the multiplicity of Israel's sins, but the neglect of the Sabbatical years (p. 74). The work of Franz Rosenzweig and Eugen Rosenstock-Huessey, indispensable as it is in this context, is too recent for our purposes. To the reference to Exod. Rabbah on p. 129, add T. B. Megillah 29a, where R. Simeon b. Yoḥai emphasizes the presence of the Shekinah with Israel in exile. For *galuth* in Mysticism, see Scholem, *The Messianic Idea in Judaism*, 1971, pp. 39–48, etc.

The full passage in T. B. Pes. 87b, cited above, makes the exile an act of Yahweh's compassion. R. Oshaia [mid-second century A.D.] said: "What is meant by the verse, *Even the righteous acts of His Ruler in Israel?* [Judg. 5: 11]. The Holy One, blessed be He, showed righteousness [mercy, צדקה] unto Israel by scattering them among the nations."

The full passage in T. B. Pes. 87b reads as follows:

R. Eleazer said: The Holy One, blessed be He, did not exile Israel among the nations save in order that proselytes might join them, for it is said: *And I will sow her unto Me in the land:*[a] surely a man sows a *seʾâh* in order to harvest many *kor*! While R. Johanan [died A.D. 279] deduced it from this: *And I will have compassion upon her that hath not obtained compassion.*[b]

a. Hos 2: 25.   b. *Ibid.* R. Johanan makes this refer to the Gentiles, who in God's compassion will be given the opportunity, through Israel's exile, of coming under the wings of the Shechinah. According to Rashi, R. Johanan deduces it from the concluding part of the verse, "And I will say to them that are not My people; you are My people."

This passage shows these two Rabbis in favour of proselytes: this enables them to regard exile, however undesirable, as having a purpose. This view found its exponent in the twentieth century in F. Rosenzweig, *The Star of Redemption*, trans., New York, 1971.

A passage in T. B. Sanhedrin 37b reads:

Rab Judah the son of R. Hiyya (A.D. 140–165) also said: Exile atones for the half of men's sins (גלות מכפרת עון מחצה:). Earlier [in the Cain narrative] it is written, *And I shall be a fugitive and a wanderer;*[a] but later, *And he dwelt in the land of Nod [wandering],*[b]

Rab Judah said (A.D. 165–200): Exile makes remission for three things (גלות מכפרת שלשה דברים...), for it is written, *Thus saith the Lord etc. He that abideth in this city shall die by the sword and by the famine and by the pestilence; but he that goeth out and falleth away to the Chaldeans who besiege you he shall live and his life shall be unto him for a prey.*[c] R. Johanan (A.D. 279–320) said: Exile atones for everything, for it is written (...גלות מכפרת על הכל). *Thus saith the Lord, write ye this man childless, a man that shall not prosper in his days, for no man of his seed shall prosper sitting upon the throne of David and ruling any more in Judah.*[d] Whereas after he [the king] was exiled, it is written, *And the sons of Jechoniah, – the same is Assir – Shealtiel his son etc.*[e]

a. נע ונד: Gen. 4: 14.   b. נוד· The other half of the curse, "to be a fugitive" was remitted because of his wandering, i.e., exile.   c. Jer. 21: 8–9. He that remained at home was subject to these three evils; but wandering and its consequent hardships outweighed them all.   d. Jer. 22: 30.   e. 1 Ch. 3: 17. Notwithstanding the curse that he should be childless and not prosper, after being exiled he was forgiven.

f. THE LAND AS SYMBOL OF THE TRANSCENDENTAL

The next to be noted is that, as indicated in both Hellenistic and Palestinian sources, Greek and Hebrew, in some quarters the land became a symbol for a transcendent order or for the age to come. The material can be divided into two kinds: first, that in which the land retains its geographic dimension and is yet used with a moral and a transcendental connotation; to this belong Philo's works and a section in the Mishnah: and, secondly, that in which the land is wholly transcendentalized, as in the Testament of Job.

First, then, Philo hoped for a restoration to the land in the Messianic Age, and yet the emphasis in his thought is *not* on the land. In the Messianic Age other nations will enjoy their own lands:[114] what Philo is concerned with is that they should recognize and accept the Law. It is in its possession of the latter that the peculiarity of the people of Israel lies, not in its connection with the land. The following passage from Moses 1: 278 makes this clear: the "wizard" or false prophet, whom King Balak (Num. 22–24) had asked to curse Israel, overcome by the divine inspiration ("for the craft of the sorcerer and the inspiration of the Holiest might not live together"), spoke as follows:

From Mesopotamia hath Balak called me, a far journey from the East, that he may avenge him on the Hebrews through my cursing. But I, how shall I curse them whom God hath not cursed? I shall behold them with my eyes from the highest mountains, and perceive them with my mind. But I shall not be able to harm the people, which shall dwell alone, not reckoned among other nations; and that, *not because their dwelling-place is set apart and their land severed from others, but because in virtue of the distinction of their peculiar customs they do not mix with others to depart from the ways of their fathers* (our italics; Loeb, trans., v. 4).[115]

Similarly Philo recognized that the root of anti-Judaism lay in the laws practised by his people. These were their glory but also their pain.[116]

[114] For Philo's understanding of the Messianic Age, see H. A. Wolfson, *Philo*, Vol. II, Cambridge, Mass., 1947, pp. 395ff. For Philo, as for Palestinian Rabbis, national and linguistic distinctions continue in the Messianic Age (p. 418): contrast Stoicism in which the disappearance of national differences is desired. For the conflict between "universalism" and "particularism," see Arnold Toynbee, *The Crucible of Christianity*, New York, 1969, pp. 37ff, especially p. 44. But see also N. Glatzer's response in *Hillel the Elder*, pp. 71ff.

[115] The Greek for the italicized section is: οὐ κατὰ τόπων ἀποκλήρωσιν καὶ χώρας ἀποτομήν, ἀλλὰ κατὰ τὴν τῶν ἐξαιρέτων ἐθῶν ἰδιότητα, μὴ συναναμιγνύμενος* ἄλλοις εἰς τῶν πατρίων ἐκδιαίτησιν. [*MSS συναναμιγνυμένων.] The term γῆ does not occur, but χώρα is well established as meaning "land": it frequently translates אֶרֶץ and מְדִינָה in the LXX (see Hatch and Redpath). For other usage, see Liddell and Scott and Jones, and Arndt and Gingrich.

[116] This is why, although they persist in the Messianic Age, the nations are all to abandon their "peculiar ways" and "ancestral customs" and accept the Torah: at this point there is

Moreover, although Philo retains the actuality of the Messianic hope for the land, he can also interpret the land symbolically.[117] In his *Questions on Genesis* he does not deal directly with Gen. 12: 1–3, but does offer comments on Gen. 15: 7, 8. In these the promised land is "fruitful wisdom."

What is the meaning of the words, "I am the Lord God[a] who led thee out of the land of the Chaldaeans[b] to give thee this land to inherit?" The literal meaning[c] is clear. That which must be rendered as the deeper meaning[d] is as follows. The "land of the Chaldaeans" is symbolically mathematical theory,[e] of which astronomy[f] is part. And in this (field) the Chaldaeans labour not unsuccessfully or slothfully. Thus He honours the wise man with two gifts. For one thing He takes him away[g] from Chaldaean doctrine,[h] which in addition to being difficult to seize and grasp, is the cause of great evils and impiety in attributing to that which is created with the powers of the Creator, and persuades men to honour and worship the works of the world instead of the Creator of the world.[i] And again, He grants him fruitful wisdom which He symbolically calls "land." And the Father shows that wisdom and virtue[j] are immutable and without change or turning, for it is not proper for God to reveal[k] that which is able to admit turning or change, because that which is revealed should be and remain unchangeable and constant. But that which is subject to change and is wont to be always fluid does not admit of true and proper[l] revelation.

a. LXX has merely "God," Heb. has merely "Lord (YHWH)." In the parallel passage, *Quis Rer. Div. Heres* 96, Philo follows the LXX in reading "God." Possibly the Arm. translator has here inserted "Lord" on the basis of Arm. O.T. which reads, "Lord God."
b. So LXX: Heb. has "Ur Kasdim (Ur of the Chaldaeans)."
c. *to rhēton.*

apparently an antinomy in Philo. See Wolfson, *Philo*, Vol. II, pp. 395ff. On the centrality of the Law in the life of Jews, compare Est. 3: 8. The Law, not their connection with or occupation of Palestine, is central.
[117] We have pointed to the less well-known passages in Philo. The most striking are the familiar ones in *The Migration of Abraham*. Commenting on Gen. 12: 1–3 Philo takes "thy land" to be a symbol of body, substance; "kindred" a symbol of sense-perception; "thy father's house" of speech (1: 1f). All these are to become strangers (11).
The work of S. Sandmel, *Philo's Place in Judaism: A Study of Conceptions of Abraham in Jewish Literature*, Cincinnati, O., 1956, is indispensable on Abraham. In the first part he traces the treatment of the patriarch in the Old Testament, the Apocrypha, and Pseudepigrapha, and other sources. His survey does not conflict with our treatment. He rightly emphasizes the apologetic motives at work. On the Alexandrian he writes: "It cannot be over-emphasized that Philo has little or no concern for Palestine, p. 117," and of the treatment of Abraham by Philo this statement is justified, as Sandmel convincingly shows. But the messianism of Philo is not to be neglected. Attention should also be drawn to the generalized, salutary treatment of the interpenetration of Hellenism and Judaism by S. Sandmel, *The First Christian Century in Judaism and Christianity*, New York, 1969, pp. 14–23. Important on Abraham also is G. Vermès, *Scripture and Tradition in Judaism*, *Studia Biblica*, Leiden, 1961, pp. 67–126.

d. Lit. "to the understanding of its nature"; Aucher more freely renders "ad sensus essentiam." In the *Quaestiones* the usual antithesis to *to rhêton* is *to pros dikaion*.

e. *sumbolikôs mathêmatikê theôria esti.*

f. *astronomia* in the sense of astrology.

g. Or "saves him."

h. Lit. "doctrine (or "school"—*dogmatos*) of opinions"; Aucher renders *ad hoc*, "de secta astrologorum videlicet de Chaldaeismi hallucinatione."

i. *ta tou Kosmou erga anti tou Kosmopoiou.*

j. *sophia kai aretê.*

k. Lit. "to show."

l. The Arm. translator seems to have taken *kurios* in the sense of "divine."

Philo's comment on Gen. 15: 19–21 reads as follows:

Who are "the Kenites and the Kenizzites and the Kadmonites and the Hittites and the Perizzites and the Rephaim and the Amorites and the Canaanites and the Girgashites and the Jebusites"?

These ten nations are reckoned (as) evils which he destroys[a] because of being neighbours,[b] since also a rejected and counterfeit denarius[c] (is a neighbour?) of acceptable ones.[d]

a. Or "which destroy," assuming that there was a neut. pl. subj. (*ethnê*) in the original; variant "which (he) likens."

b. The sentence is obscure and prob. corrupt; Aucher renders, "decem gentes numerantur malitiae quas destruit ob vicinitatem."

c. Arm. *dahekan* "denarius," "drachma," etc.

d. Lit. "of loved ones." The sentence is very puzzling; Aucher renders, "quoniam Denarius quoque falsus, et male signatus vicinus est bono ac amabili." The Arm. glossator explains, "The evil which is ten strives to be like the good, just as a rejected denarius, etc." (*Questions on Genesis*, ad rem.)

See also Philo on Gen. 15: 18. The point is that a meaning other than the territorial could be given to the land. And it does not come as a surprise, therefore, when we find that the land can be spiritualized in Pharisaism itself. In Mishnah Sanhedrin 10: 1 we read as follows:

All Israelites have a share in the world to come, for it is written, Thy people also shall be all righteous, they shall inherit the land for ever (*leʿôlâm yiyreshû ʾâretz*); the branch of my planting, the work of my hands that I may be glorified (Is. 60: 21).

Here "inheriting the land" is equated with having a share in "the world to come (*hâ-ʿôlâm ha-bbâʾ*)." The phrase "the world to come" is notoriously difficult to understand with any precision: sometimes it may be equated with the Messianic Age.[118] Here the context makes it clear that

118 See SSM, pp. 161f. The precise meaning of "The Age destined to Come" has to be largely determined by the context in each case. See P. Volz, *Die Eschatologie der jüdischen*

it refers to the final age beyond the resurrection of the dead.[119] The land is no longer territorial: it has become a symbol of the life of the Age to Come, what the Fourth Gospel refers to as "eternal life." This symbolism appears with a different connotation in the *gemara* on M. Sanhedrin 10: 3, where the land is interpreted, not as Palestine, but as "this world," and where the holy mount of Jerusalem is the equivalent of the future world, the Age to Come. The Soncino translation to T. B. Sanhedrin 110b reads as follows:

MISHNAH. THE TEN TRIBES WILL NOT RETURN [TO PALESTINE], FOR IT IS SAID, AND CAST THEM INTO ANOTHER LAND, AS IS THIS DAY:[a] JUST AS THE DAY GOES AND DOES NOT RETURN, SO THEY TOO WENT AND WILL NOT RETURN: THIS IS R. AKIBA'S VIEW. R. ELIEZER SAID: AS THIS DAY—JUST AS THE DAY DARKENS AND THEN BECOMES LIGHT AGAIN,[b] SO THE TEN TRIBES—EVEN AS IT WENT DARK FOR THEM, SO WILL IT BECOME LIGHT FOR THEM (Soncino trans., pp. 759f).

    a. Deut. 29: 28.
    b. Becoming dark in the evening and light in the morning.

GEMARA. Our Rabbis taught: The ten tribes have no portion in the world to come,[a] as it says, *And the Lord rooted them out of their land in anger, and in wrath, and in great indignation:*[b] *And the Lord rooted them out of their land,* refers to this world; *and cast them into another land*—to the world to come;[c] this is R. Akiba's view. R. Simeon b. Judah, of the Kefar of Acco,[d] said on R. Simeon's authority: If their deeds are as this day's,[e] they will not return; otherwise they shall. Rabbi said: They will enter the future world, as it is said, [*And it shall come to pass*] *in that day, that the great trumpet shall be blown,* [*and they shall come which were ready to perish in the land of Assyria, and the outcasts in the land of Egypt, and shall worship the Lord in the holy mount of Jerusalem*].[f]

    a. [I.e., not in the hereafter but in the Messianic days.]
    b. Deut. 29: 28.

Gemeinde, Tübingen, 1934, p. 71. It is interesting to note that *'eretz* could be used not only of the world to come, but of the nether world, Jonah 2: 7. See J. Gray, *The Legacy of Canaan*, p. 193. It bears this sense in Ugaritic texts.

[119] It is evidence such as we have cited above that makes it impossible to follow Messel's view that all Jewish eschatology was "this-worldly." But note that the transcendence to which we referred coexists with "this-worldly" expectations. Judaism is at home with such antinomies. See N. Messel, *Die Einheitlichkeit der jüdischen Eschatologie*, Giessen, 1915. The attitude of Josephus to the Messianic hope emerges in *Against Apion*, II. 1. 30; the *Jewish Wars*, II. 2. 11; II. 2. 14; III. 8. 5; *Antiquities*, XVIII. 1. 3. In him, according to A. Schlatter, *Die Theologie des Judentums nach dem Bericht des Josephus*, Beträge zur Förderung christliche Theologie, ed. by A. Schlatter and W. Lutgert, Series 2, Vol. 26, Gütersloh, C. Gertelsmann, 1932, p. 259. "Die Eschatologie wird zur Seelenlehre, und an die Stelle des Messianismus tritt die Unsterblichkeit." Revolutionaries were, to him, inspired not by the Messianic hope, but by that for immortality. Josephus avoided Messianism, and saw Providence at work in Roman rule. See especially *Jewish Wars*, VII. 8. 7; Schürer, *The Jewish People in the Time of Christ*, Division 1, Vol. 1, pp. 97f.

c. I.e., into a place other than the future world.

d. See p. 484, n. 7 of Soncino trans.

e. I.e., if they do not repent, "*this day*" referring to the time of their being exiled.

f. Is. 27: 13: "the holy mount of Jerusalem" is understood here to mean the future world.

We notice in this gemara both the concern with the reunification of all the tribes of Israel and the transcendental use of the land, and that, be it noted, by Akiba who certainly revered the geographic land.

This is the best place, secondly, to deal with a source in which the land seems to be wholly transcendentalized, the little noticed and examined *Testament of Job*.[120] Kohler[121] traced it to pre-Christian Essene circles and, oddly enough, found its eschatology and Messianic belief Jewish.[122] It is difficult to agree. The traditional eschatological terms—throne, kingdom, glory—do appear, but the substance of the future hope expressed in the *Testament of Job* suggests more the immortal world of souls than the resurrection of the dead. Job looks forward to an eternal order, beyond this present world, where he and his children will enter into glory. In one manuscript—probably the best—this eternal order is described as "the holy land," a term used in parallelism with "the imperishable world." The pertinent passage, in which Job replies to Elihu and others who had bemoaned the departure of his former glory in suffering, reads:

Be silent. Now shall I show you my throne and the glory and splendour which is among the saints. *My* throne is in the supernatural world, and its glory and splendour is at the right hand of the father. The whole cosmos will pass away and its glory *will be destroyed*, and all those who hold on to it will experience its catastrophe. My throne subsists in the holy land and its glory is in the world of the imperishable. The rivers will be dried up and the arrogance of their waves will descend to the depths of the abyss. But the rivers of my land, where is my throne, do not dry up, nor will they disappear, but they shall be for ever. These kings shall pass away and their officers [rulers] do pass away, and their glory and pride shall be as a mirror. But my kingdom is to the ages of ages, and its glory and splendour rests in the chariots of the father.[123]

The same anticipation of a life in a world to come emerges in Job's reaction to the request of his wife, Sitis, that the bones of his children be

---

[120] See the edition by S. P. Brock, *Testamentum Iobi*, Leiden, 1967, whose text I have followed here.

[121] K. Kohler, "The Testament of Job: An Essene Midrash on the Book of Job: re-edited and translated with Introductory and Exegetical Notes," *Semitic Studies in Memory of Rev. Dr. Alexander Kohut*, Berlin, 1897. This contains an introduction of great value. It was Professor David Flusser who showed me the relevance of *The Testament of Job* to my theme.

[122] *Ibid.*, p. 272.

[123] T. Job: 33; Brock, pp. 43f. There are many insignificant variants, but there is no fundamental difference in the ideology in the various texts. I give my own translations.

disinterred and rendered proper, decent burial. Job's words, when the kings gave order that this should be done, are:

Do not go into the trouble in vain, for you will not find my children, since they have been taken up into [the] heavens by their lord and king.[124]

On the protest of his friends that this was madness, Job further replied:

"Raise me that I may stand." And they raised me, lifting up my arms on both sides. Then standing I made confession to the Father: And after my prayer I said to them: "Look up with your eyes to the East and see my children crowned alongside the glory of the Heavenly one."[125]

And the reaction of Sitis was to fall on the ground and exclaim: "Now I have known that the memory of me remains with the Lord." That Sitis died without proper burial is of no consequence: she is remembered by God.[126] So, too, Job, who had set his hope, not on earthly things and an unstable earth, but on the living God,[127] was not concerned to hand on to his daughters earthly or worldly well-being and so gave them "three-stringed girdles" which transformed their existence from the earthly to the heavenly. And the worst fate that can befall Elihu, as all men, is that he should not be remembered by God or his holy ones or by the living. The reality of the supernal world is the ground of all hope and the reality of God's remembrance of us in that world.[128]

And this is set in a discussion between Job and his friends. They regard him as mad. Doubtless we hear the echo here of the way in which Sadducees and Samaritans and, perhaps, even Pharisees responded to those who were openly receptive to Hellenistic ideas, and prepared to mythologize "the land" or to turn it into a symbol of the transcendental. In fact, the *Testament of Job* recalls us in a startling way to the extent to which Judaism was being penetrated by Hellenism before the Christian era, and, was in some circles, gradually clothing traditional Jewish *realia* in a Hellenistic dress, so that the immortality of the disembodied soul could be substituted for the reunion of soul and body in the resurrection in the land. This process has been traced in the Book of Wisdom and in 4 Maccabees (see Wis. 3: 1–4; 4 Macc. 9: 21f).[129]

---

[124] T. Job: 39; Brock, p. 48.　　　　　　[125] T. Job: 40; Brock, p. 49.
[126] T. Job: *ibid*.　　　　　　　　　　　[127] T. Job: 40: lines 5–10; Brock, p. 50.
[128] T. Job: 36; Brock, p. 45.

[129] PRJ, pp. 302ff for evidence. Professor J. M. Robinson pointed out to me how in *The Paraphrase of Shem*, in the very last line, "the land" is used as a symbol of the blessed realm beyond. This indicates how tenacious and widespread was this usage. For *The Paraphrase*, see J. M. Robinson, NTS, Vol. XIV, 1968, pp. 378–380.

　　The *Testament of Abraham*, in which the patriarch is called φιλόξενος is too problematic in its

g. THE WITNESS OF HISTORY

This transcendentalizing of the land in Pharisaism leads naturally to a final and a major consideration. In previous pages, we have emphasized the strength of the sentiment (a term used here in its strict psychological connotation) for the land. But a striking fact confronts us. Judaism survived and came to terms with the loss of the land in A.D. 70, catastrophic as it was, with dignity and with comparative speed. It did so because Pharisaism, after A.D. 70, the dominant element in Judaism, was politically and otherwise prepared to adjust to the absence of the land, as to the loss of other symbols of its faith. This is not as surprising as at first encounter. The relations of the Pharisees to the Maccabees had foreshadowed their reaction to the fall of Jerusalem. Commenting on the estrangement of the Pharisees from the Maccabean dynasty, Bickerman writes:

to them [that is, the Pharisees] it must have appeared that a foreign domination respecting Jewish autonomy and recognizing the Torah as the binding law of Judaism would offer less hindrance to their work of education. Precisely because it was foreign, and hence concerned only for the prompt payment of tribute and for civil order, they assumed that the internal life of the people would remain outside the range of its interest.

. . . The Pharisees might justly expect foreign rulers scrupulously to follow the opinions of the scholars in all such [legal] matters whereas a Jewish King, as was the case with the Maccabees, would desire to shape even the internal and religious life of the people according to his own notions and not always according to the recommendations of the teachers of the law. In point of fact, it was the Roman rule which made possible and facilitated the development of Pharisaic Judaism to a high degree, until the great conflict between the two unequal powers set in. In this conflict the Jewish people lost its land, in order to win a historic

---

authorship and origin for use here. The subject is not the land, but the world beyond death, ἡ ἄνω βασιλεία (ch. 7: line 22, p. 84, in *Texts and Studies: Contributions to Biblical and Patristic Studies*, ed. J. Armitage Robinson, Cambridge, 1893, Recension A). There is a reference to God as ὁ εἰσαγαγών σε ἐν τῇ γῇ τῆς εὐαγγελίας (ch. 8, line 11, p. 85), but there seems to be an emphasis (ch. 9, p. 86) on the mortality even of Abraham to whom the promise had been given. He, too, is not ἀθάνατος but θνητός: death is the end of all. Even the land of promise is subsumed under mortality. This οἰκουμένη has witnessed good and bad (ch. 10, pp. 87ff). God's purpose is fulfilled in heaven, and Abraham is taken there ὅπως θεάσηται ἐκεῖ τὰς κρίσεις καὶ ἀνταποδόσεις . . . (ch. 10, p. 88). This document needs thorough examination. The text we followed is that of M. R. James in the volume cited, *The Testament of Abraham: The Greek text now first edited with an introduction and notes*, pp. 1–130, with Appendix by W. E. Barnes on the Arabic version of it. According to a report of Francis Schmidt on *Le Testament d'Abraham*, Dissertation, Strasbourg, 1971, by J. Smit Sibinga, at Los Angeles, 1972, the earliest recension (B) of the work was translated from an original Hebrew document in the first half of the first century A.D. "Its background is a popular Essenism, such as Dupont-Sommer postulates for the book of Tobith." (Private report Sept. 1972, p. 4.) The recension A, Schmidt dates in Alexandria before 115 A.D. The text and translation of Michael E. Stone, *The Testament of Abraham*, Society of Biblical Literature, 1972, came too late for use.

continuity such as was vouchsafed to no other people of antiquity, not even to their conquerors, the Romans.[130]

It was the Pharisaic understanding of Judaism that made this continuity possible—an understanding that placed Torah above political power and control of the land. This brings us to the achievement of the Rabbis at Jamnia. The question is: was it their aim and achievement so to reinterpret Judaism that it could persist without the land, Jerusalem, and the Temple? Nineteenth-century scholars gave to this question an affirmative answer. But the issue is not to be settled so simply. Rather, the ambiguity of the Rabbinic position has to be recognized. The Rabbis at Jamnia did deliberately seek to establish a sentiment for Torah (and *ipso facto* for the Synagogue) which would *comfort* Israel for its loss of the land, the city, and the temple. But this sentiment for Torah was not to be a final substitute for the latter triad. The Pharisees after A.D. 70, no less than in the Maccabean period were realists. In the latter period the Pharisees recognized that the Maccabees would not act as they desired, in accordance with the law, and, therefore, became estranged. In the Roman period they recognized political realities and after A.D. 70, while by no means abandoning ultimate hope for the land, the city, and the temple, sought comfort in devotion to the Torah with all that this implied for their personal and communal life. The fact that Rabbi Johanan b. Zakkai claimed for Jamnia the prerogatives of the Temple at Jerusalem (Mishnah Rosh Hashanah 4: 1; T. B. Rosh Hashanah 29b), and followed the policy of excluding former Temple officials from authority, did mean that "place" could be transcended. Some have argued that Johanan was trying to free Judaism from connection with Jerusalem and the Temple. But this is untenable. Johanan did not reject the Temple: he merely sought to provide an "interim" form for the religious life. (In Jewish history that interim has been variously understood—as preceding a return to the land or the End of all things.)

The following two groups of passages point out the ambiguity to which we referred.

---

[130] Bickerman, *From Ezra*, pp. 174f. All discussions of the Pharisees must now take account of the pioneering work of Jacob Neusner, *The Rabbinic Traditions About the Pharisees Before 70*, 3 vols., Leiden, 1971; this has been popularized in *From Politics to Piety: The Emergence of Pharisaic Judaism*, Englewood Cliffs, New Jersey, 1973. Neusner compels great caution in any description of the Pharisees before 70 A.D., and especially of their "peaceful," "non-political" character before the time of Hillel. But that it was the Pharisees who enabled Judaism to survive the loss of the land emerges even more strongly from Neusner's work. Bickerman's position must be balanced by that expressed on p. 74, n. 21, last paragraph.

CAUTIONARY CONSIDERATIONS

Group I

1. Passages showing that the loss of the Temple and city was keenly felt:
M. Taanith 4: 6.
Pesikta de Rab Kahanah 16: 128a.

2. Passages witnessing a continued interest among the Rabbis in the temple and its services, and a desire to preserve the tradition of worship against the time of the restoration of the Temple. Mishnah Aboth 1: 2; 6: 10 (the Temple has a status and sanctity of its own, apart from any future hope). M. Berakoth 9: 5; 4: 4. (See G. F. Moore, *Judaism*, Vol. 1, p. 96n.)

3. Passages pointing to the hope for a rebuilt Temple and a restored Jerusalem.
M. Pesahim 10: 6.
T. B. Megillah 17b–18a.

Pesikta Rabbati 162a–b; see W. G. Braude, Pesikta Rabbati, 52: 8, pp. 884, 554, 404. The rabbis cited in 52: 8 are from the fourth century.
Aboth de R. Nathan l. 35.
Num. Rabbah 1: 3.

4. Passages attesting that the divine presence through the Shekinah was still present at its site although the Temple itself was in ruins. Tanḥuma, Terumah 8; Num. Rabbah 12: 4. (See Moore, *Judaism*, Vol. 1, p. 369.)

But over against such passages are the following from:

Group II

1. Passages denying that the Shekinah had rested on the Second Temple at all. Pesikta Rabbati 160a. W. G. Braude, Pesikta Rabbati 35: 1, p. 670. The passages are undateable: the Rabbi cited is of the third to the fourth century.

2. Those stating that the Shekinah is everywhere, and, therefore, could not be confined to the Temple but might be in the humblest synagogue. Exod. Rabbah 2: 5; Deut. Rabbah 7: 2; T. B. Berakoth 10a; Lev. Rabbah 4: 8.

3. Passages pointing to the spiritualization of worship and sacrifice which enabled Pharisaism to overcome the loss of the city and the Temple.
Aboth de Rabbi Nathan l. 6: mercy not sacrifice is important;
Mishnah Aboth 3: 2, study of the Torah ensures the presence of the Shekinah;
Pesikta de Rab Kahana 60b, "if you study the laws about sacrifice that is to me as if you had offered them." See W. G. Braude, Pesikta Rabbati, 16: 7, p. 354 (fourth century, in the name of Rabbi Ḥanina bar Papa).
Megillah 16b "Greater is study of Torah than the rebuilding of the Temple";
T. B. Shab. 119b;
Deut. Rabbah 5: 3 ("The righteousness and justice you perform are dearer to me than the Temple"); Lev. Rabbah 7: 2, "Whence is it derived that if one repents, it is imputed to him as if he had gone up to Jerusalem, built the Temple, erected an altar and offered upon it all the sacrifices enumerated in the Torah?

From the text: 'the sacrifices of God are a broken spirit (Ps. 51: 17).'" (See further G. F. Moore, *Judaism*, Vol. II, p. 218.)

This second group of passages reveals that the Temple and the city, and, we may presume, the land, could be spiritualized even while the hope for their restoration was retained. It was its ability to detach its loyalty from "place," even while retaining "place" in its memory, that enabled Pharisaism to transcend the loss of its land. Nor was it unique in this. The same spiritualization of the realia of their faith emerges among the sectarians at Qumran. They interpreted the community itself as the Temple: the presence of God had moved for them from a physical building to the "spiritual" domain of the community itself. The spiritualization went further. As in Pharisaism, obedience to the Torah became the true sacrifice of the new Temple (1QS 3: 11–12; 4: 21; 5: 5ff; 8: 4–11; 9: 3–6; 4QFlor. 1: 6f). At the same time, as among the Pharisees so among the sectarians, the hope for a new and restored Temple and cult at Jerusalem, in the land, remained strong.[131] Religion, like philosophy, has its antinomies and paradoxes.[132]

3. CONTEXTUAL

In Philo and the Rabbis, then, and among others, the land was sometimes "spiritualized" or given a transcendent connotation. This fact provides a convenient point of transition to the third type of consideration with which we must deal, namely, that which concerns the total setting against which the significance of the land is to be assessed. This consideration is concentrated in three themes, that of Jerusalem, and of the Temple, as more than geographic entities, and that of the new creation. These themes raise acutely the question of how far in the course of time the expectations engendered by the promise to Abraham were so trans-

---

[131] See Gärtner, *The Temple and the Community*, p. 14. The role of the sacrificial system for the sectarians has been variously assessed. Probably they did not reject it in principle, but objected to its misuse: it was commanded in the Torah and, therefore, to be revered. It was the profanation of it that the sectarians objected to, not its observance. Compare J. van der Ploeg, *Le Rouleau de la Guerre*, pp. 28f. It was this profanation that spurred the Sect at Qumran to take over for itself, as a community, the functions and meanings previously attached to Jerusalem and the Temple. Thus the prophecy of Isaiah about the new Jerusalem was applied to the Qumran community in sections of the Isaiah commentary. The life of the community wrought the atonement hitherto associated with the Temple system through its expression of obedience. 1QS 9: 4–6.

[132] The de-absolutizing of the cult, as it has been called, achieved at Jamnia was not new in kind but only in degree. See, for example, The Prayer of Azariah, *vs.* 16 (first century B.C.); Ecclesiasticus 7: 8–9; 34: 18–19, 25–26; 35: 1–3 (second century B.C.). These documents were Palestinian. But we find the same "spiritualizing" of worship in The Letter of Aristeas 170, 234 (first century B.C., Alexandria) and Philo, *Quod omnis probus liber sit*, 75.

muted that the hope for the occupation of the land in history became a hope for an order beyond history. How far did the land become a symbol for a transcendent order, the promise of territory being absorbed, and thereby annulled, in the yearning for the future "Age to Come"?

a. JERUSALEM

We must first consider the understanding of Jerusalem in the Old Testament and in Judaism, because the hopes for the land became more and more concentrated in those cherished for that city, which seems to have become the quintessence of the land. As we saw, in the post-exilic period the life of Jewry was mainly centred in Jerusalem and in the area surrounding it, so that it was probably inevitable that the city should gather to itself the hopes of Israel. Geographic actualities demanded this. But it was not only, and not chiefly, the physical nodality of Jerusalem that accounted for its increasingly representative character. This was rooted in the history and religion of Israel more than in the facts of geography.[133]

Pre-Israelite Jerusalem need not concern us, and a detailed account of the development of the mystique of Jerusalem in the Old Testament would take us too far afield. Suffice that the city became the political and religious centre of Israel in the reign of David, who introduced the Ark, the symbol of Yahweh's presence, into it.[134] A covenant—the covenant at Sinai, adapted to changing circumstances—was formed between Yahweh and David, so that, through the latter, Jerusalem became the political centre of the people of God. And through the Ark, on the other hand, the

[133] See especially Tcherikover, *Hellenistic Civilization*, pp. 12ff. The emergence of the city of Jerusalem as the centre of Israel in this period is not an isolated phenomenon. A. T. Olmstead, wrote in *History of Assyria*, London, 1923, pp. 525ff, on "The Imperial Free City," "Urban economics were as highly developed in Babylonia or in Phoenicia as they were in the earlier Greece (p. 528)." On the significant cities in the Persian period, see A. T. Olmstead, *The History of the Persian Empire*, Chicago, 1948, pp. 162ff. Alexander the Great's work led to increased urbanization. See M. Rostovtzeff, *The Social and Economic History of the Hellenistic World*, Oxford, 1941, Vol. I, pp. 130ff. The Jewish concentration on the city of Jerusalem, therefore, fits into a common Near Eastern pattern in the post-exilic period. It should be recognized, however, that it took the Temple at Jerusalem three centuries to thrust all other temples out of its way. See T. C. Vriezen, *The Religion of Ancient Israel*, Philadelphia, 1967, p. 183.

[134] 2 Sam. 7. See R. de Vaux, "Jerusalem and the Prophets," in *Interpreting the Prophetic Tradition*, ed. H. M. Orlinsky, Cincinnati, 1969, pp. 278ff. "In receiving the ark Jerusalem had become the heir of all this past, and she must preserve it intact. The building of a temple in the manner of a royal sanctuary of the Canaanites could appear as a rupture of tradition which would put this heritage in danger. The sanctuary of the ark must remain what it had been for the Federation of the Tribes—the spiritual centre of 'all Israel.' Paradoxically, the refusal of the temple signified, and meant to preserve, the religious importance of Jerusalem (p. 281)."

religious and historical traditions of that people were preserved and grafted on to Jerusalem, as their repository, so that the city became the religious centre of Israel. That the traditions referred to were focussed in the Ark in part explains why Nathan, the prophet, opposed the building of a temple.[135] But, although the spiritual centrality of Jerusalem for Israel was thus originally conditioned by the presence of the Ark within its walls, in Solomon's reign a temple *was* built. This was acceptable to Yahweh, the God of Sinai, as a fit abode for his glory, and served, therefore, to increase still further the religious significance of the city within which it was built.

This significance survived events which might be expected to have diminished it. It survived the division of the Kingdom (Jer. 41: 5), it survived the decline of the dynasty of David, it even survived the loss of the Temple and of the Ark in 587 B.C. Why? Although the pre-Exilic prophets had linked Jerusalem to the dynasty of David, they had preferred to think of the city, as did the Psalmists, not as the city of David, but as that of Yahweh: they referred to it as Zion,[136] the archaic name of

[135] 1 Kings 5: 17f; 8: 10–11; 9: 1ff. On the other hand the Ark has been regarded as a miniature temple, see H. G. May, "The Ark—A Miniature Temple," *American Journal of Semitic Languages and Literature*, Vol. 52, 1936, pp. 222ff. G. von Rad characterized the concepts centring in the Ark as a "theology of presence," so that the transfer of the Presence to the Temple of Solomon was natural. See *Old Testament Theology*, Vol. 1, New York, 1962, pp. 234–238: for a different approach to the Ark, see de Vaux, *Interpreting the Prophetic Tradition*, p. 302. Nathan's attitude may be the perpetuation of the tradition of the "tent of meeting," which represented a "manifestation theology."

[136] On all this, see de Vaux, *Interpreting the Prophetic Tradition*, pp. 285ff. For the use of the name Zion for Jerusalem, see Amos 1: 12; Is. 8: 18. But it must be emphasized that the understanding of Jerusalem is related to that of the land of Canaan through the king. As Lord of the land Yahweh dwelt in it, but he had chosen David to be king over it and thereby sealed it and its central city as the inheritance of his people (Ps. 132: 11–14: compare 2 Sam. 7: 12–16). See R. E. Clements, *God and Temple*, Oxford, 1965, pp. 50f. Again in Is. 7, 8 and Exod. 15: 1–18 (The Song of Miriam) Yahweh's choice of Mt. Zion implies that the whole land of Canaan belonged to him: the conquest of that land finds its proper goal in the building of a temple. See Rost, *Das kleine Credo und andere Studien zum Alten Testament*, Heidelberg, 1965, pp. 76–101. M. Simon, "La Prophétie de Nathan et le Temple," *Revue d'Histoire et de Philosophie Religieuses*, Vol. 32, 1952, pp. 41–58, and M. Simon, "Saint Stephen and the Jerusalem Temple," *Journal of Ecclesiastical History*, Vol. 2, 1951, pp. 127–142, sees in Nathan the first expression of a trend opposed to the temple. With this are to be connected the Nazirites and, more, the Rechabites. The latter lived in tents, as we saw above, and did not want their God to dwell in a house. Did Jeremiah have to persuade them to accompany him to the Temple (Jer. 35: 2)? The opposition became explicit in Is. 8: 1. See de Vaux, *Interpreting the Prophetic Tradition*. Nor must the Samaritan opposition be overlooked. G. A. Barrois, IDB, Vol. IV, p. 959, relates the term צִיּוֹן to צִיָּה dryness, desert, steppe, parched land: so BDB Samuel Krauss, PEQ, Jan.–April, 1945 (no vol. number given), pp. 16–21, derives it from צְבִי, splendour, because of the prophetic and poetic allusions in the Old Testament to that characteristic of Jerusalem. For other derivations, presented without decision, L. Koehler and W. Baumgartner, *Lexicon in Veteris Testamenti Libros*, 1958, p. 802. They note צָוָה to erect, constitute, and צה יון, bleak hill.

the Jebusite acropolis that had *become* the city of David (2 Sam. 5: 7). It is, therefore, not altogether surprising that the fall of the Davidic dynasty did not loosen the religious hold of the city. And, although no pre-exilic prophet states that Yahweh had chosen Jerusalem, Is. 14: 32 does assert that he had founded it (and so was its creator); and there, in the Temple, Yahweh dwelt (Amos 1: 2; Is. 2: 2; 8: 18; 31: 9), seated on his throne, the Ark (Is. 6: 1 cf. 1 Sam. 4: 4; 2 Sam. 6: 2). The destruction of the Temple and the disappearance of the Ark could not but, therefore, have been traumatic experiences for the people of God. And yet Jerusalem remained its religious centre. How could this be?

It could be only because, as Jeremiah and Ezekiel make clear, apart from the Ark and the Temple, Jerusalem itself was believed to be peculiarly related to Yahweh.[137] In the future Jeremiah envisages the whole of Jerusalem as the throne of Yahweh; he mentions no temple. In Jer. 3: 16–17, Yahweh's presence, it is implied, has become independent of the Temple, as of the Ark.[138] This divorce of Yahweh from "holy space," centred in the Temple, is evident also when we compare Is. 2: 2 with Is. 27: 13 and 66: 20. The "mountain of the Lord's house" of the first passage has become in both the latter simply "the holy mountain of Yahweh." True Ezekiel[139] and Zechariah[140] do see a temple in the future, restored Jerusalem. But for Ezekiel, at least, the heart of that city is the presence of Yahweh himself. Its name will be: "Yahweh is there (Ezek. 48: 38)." Ark and Temple might pass away, but the presence of Yahweh in the city is still assured.

But for Israel, the year 587 B.C. was traumatic in another way. Jerusalem itself was then reduced to ruins. This event was traumatic because of the belief that the city, as the city of Yahweh, was inviolable. The origins of this belief need not detain us. Isaiah[141] and the Psalms[142]

[137] It should not be overlooked that David himself has sealed the religious character of the city also by offering sacrifice on the threshing floor of Araunah, thus selecting the site for the future Temple (2 Sam. 24).

[138] Note that in Jer. 3: 18ff the thought of the return to the land by both the house of Israel and of Judah is envisaged. There is no incongruity between the "spirituality" of a worship without Ark and Temple and this recognition of the importance of the land for Israel. The disloyalty of Israel to Yahweh has been doubly grievous because of the gift of the land; Jer. 3: 19f are especially poignant. On the possibility that Jer. 3: 14–18 are not from Jeremiah, see John Paterson, "Jeremiah" in *Peake*, p. 543.

[139] Ezek. 43: 1–5.

[140] Zech. 2: 14ff; 8: 3. In this connection it is important to remember that Jerusalem had not become Yahweh's dwelling place because the temple was there. Rather the temple had been built in Jerusalem because Yahweh had chosen it as his abode. Clements, *God and Temple*, p. 55. The temple was patterned after a residence—but one for Yahweh (2 Kings 19: 14; cf. Ps. 27: 4; 42: 4; 84; 122: 1–4).

[141] Is. 17: 12–14; 29: 1–8. [142] Ps. 46, 48, 76.

point to it. Isaiah did not wholly endorse it,[143] and Micah[144] and Jeremiah[145] rejected it. Its reality for the majority of Israel cannot be doubted.
Lamentations make this clear:

The kings of the earth did not believe, or any of the inhabitants of the world,
that foe or enemy could enter the gates of Jerusalem (4: 12).

And yet as Jerusalem survived the loss of the Ark and the Temple, so it
survived its own ruin to rise like a Phoenix in the hopes of Israel.

Lamentations itself expresses the hope for the restoration of the city.

For the Lord will not cast off for ever, but, though he cause grief, he will have
compassion according to the abundance of his steadfast love; for he does not
willingly afflict or grieve the sons of men (3: 31–33).

This hope emerges with power in the prophets of the Exile, in Ezek.
43: 1–5; Deut.-Is. 40: 1–2; 52: 1; 52: 8. Yahweh cannot forget Jerusalem.
"Behold, I have graven you on the palms of my hands, your walls are
continually before me (Is. 49: 16)." Deutero-Isaiah pictures the dispersed
Jews from many lands returning to the city (40: 11; 41: 17ff; 43: 5f).
Jerusalem will be greatly enlarged and exceedingly beautiful (49: 19ff;
54: 1–3, 11–12; 60: 13–18). Haggai asserts that: "The latter splendour
of this house (the rebuilt Temple) shall be greater than the former, says
the Lord of hosts (Hab. 2: 9)." Zechariah is assured that Yahweh "will
again choose Jerusalem (2: 12) (see also 1: 14b, 17; 3: 2)," and he describes
the future glories of that city (8: 3–8). The nations will flow to a city
rebuilt and elevated miraculously above the earth (14: 10ff). And in Is.
60–62 the hope for such a city in the future reaches full tide: this section
we shall discuss later.

So far, although they indicate miraculous elements in its constitution,
the passages to which we have referred envisage a renewal of the historical
or empirical Jerusalem. The future would see a new Jerusalem which would
essentially be a glorified version of the old Jerusalem. And it cannot be
sufficiently emphasized that in many sources the significance of such an

[143] See de Vaux, *Interpreting the Prophetic Tradition*, p. 289; J. Bright, *A History of Israel*,
Philadelphia, 1959, pp. 282–287; contrast Is. 14: 24–27; 17: 12–14; 29: 5–8; 31: 4–9 with
28: 14–22; 30: 1–7, 8–17; 31: 1–3.

[144] Micah 3: 9–12.

[145] Jer. 7: 9–10; 26: 5–6; compare 7: 12–14. Bright, *A History of Israel*, p. 283, seems to
find the origin of the dogma of the inviolability of Zion in the collapse of Sennacherib's army
in 701. Contrast J. H. Hayes, "The tradition of Zion's inviolability," JBL, Vol. 82, 1963,
pp. 419–426, who thinks the belief pre-Israelite: it was connected with the temple of El-Elyon,
who was worshipped in Canaanite Jerusalem. Compare von Rad, *Old Testament Theology*, Vol.
II, p. 157.

earthly Jerusalem, new as it might be, persists. It remains the place of salvation; it is built for eternity; it will be purified as at the beginning; it will be renewed in glory and become the mid-point of the earth, so enlarged that it can accommodate the multitudes that will in the end come to it. The religious centrality of Jerusalem in the future is indicated most significantly in that the nations that will converge upon it are not first converted in their own lands before proceeding to Jerusalem.[146] No! Their conversion takes place at Jerusalem. But the new Jerusalem, nevertheless, is not materially or substantially different from the old. We cannot pursue the evidence for this in detail; suffice to refer to *Tobit* (*c.* 200 B.C.), where in 1: 4 we read that Jerusalem is:

Chosen from among all the tribes of Israel, Where all the tribes should sacrifice and where the temple of the dwelling of the Most High was consecrated and established for all generations for ever.

Compare Ecclesiasticus, 36: 11–14; 51: 12 (*c.* 180 B.C.): Pss. Sol. 17: 22f (*c.* 70–40 B.C.): The Sibylline Oracles (*c.* 140 B.C.–A.D. 70) *passim*: Test. Lev. 10: 5. In 3 Macc. 2: 9–10 (first century B.C.) Jerusalem is elect from creation; in 4 Ezra (first century A.D.) it is connected with the election of the people of Israel itself (4 Ezra 5: 24ff); compare Num. 3: 2.

In Pharisaic sources the hope for the restoration and the glorification of Jerusalem is vivid. Written well before A.D. 70, the 14th Benediction in the Shemoneh Esreh, which we cited above, makes this clear. See further T. B. Megillah 17b–18a, and especially Aboth de Rabbi Nathan, 35, which, in Goldin's translation, pp. 143ff (with his notes added in part), reads thus:

TEN[a] *miracles were wrought for our ancestors in Jerusalem:*
No woman ever miscarried because of the smell of the sacred flesh;[b]
No man was attacked (by demons) in Jerusalem;
No man ever met with an accident in Jerusalem;
No fire ever broke out in Jerusalem;
No structures ever collapsed[c] in Jerusalem;
No man ever said to his fellow: "I haven't found an oven in Jerusalem to roast the paschal sacrifices";
No Man ever said to his fellow: "I haven't found a bed to sleep in in Jerusalem";
No Man ever said to his fellow: "Too strait is the place for me,[d] *that I should lodge in Jerusalem."*[e]

[146] Is. 2: 1ff. The date of this section is in dispute: see J. Bright, *Peake*, p. 491, who regards a post-exilic date as questionable.

Ten things were said of Jerusalem:[f]

Jerusalem's houses do not become unclean through leprosy;[g]

It is not to be declared a condemned city;[h]

Neither beams nor balconies nor sockets may project there over the public thoroughfare lest, by overshadowing,[i] they give passage to corpse uncleanness;

The dead may not be lodged there overnight;[j]

The bones of a dead man may not be carried through it;[k]

No place is made available there for a resident alien;[l]

No graves may be kept up there excepting the graves of the house of David, and of Huldah the prophetess, which were there since the days of the early prophets.[m] And when (all other) graves were cleared away, why were these not cleared away? They say: There was a tunnel here which gave passage to the uncleanness into the brook of Kidron;[n]

No plants may be planted there; neither gardens nor orchards may be cultivated there,[o] excepting rose gardens, which were there since the days of the early prophets;

Neither geese nor chickens may be raised there nor, needless to say, pigs;[p]

No dunghills may be kept there because of uncleanness;

No trial of a stubborn and rebellious son[q] may be held there—such is the view of Rabbi Nathan—for it is said, *Then shall his father and his mother lay hold on him and bring him out unto the gate of his place* (Deut. 21: 19), and this (Jerusalem) is not *his*[r] *city*, this is not *his place*;

No houses may be sold there save[s] from the ground up;[t]

The sale of houses is not valid there for longer than twelve months;[u]

No payment for a bed[v] is accepted there—Rabbi Judah says: Not even payment for beds (and)[w] coverings;[x]

The hides of the sacrificial beasts are not for sale there. What was done with them? Rabban Simeon ben Gamaliel says: They were given to the innkeepers. The guests would stay indoors and the innkeepers out of doors. The guest resorted to an evasion[y] by buying painted[z] sheep whose hides were worth four to five sela, and these were left as compensation for the men of Jerusalem.[aa]

a. Compare PA 5: 5; ARNB, pp. 103ff; see p. 145 in Goldin.

b. The lesser sacrifices could be eaten anywhere in Jerusalem.

c. In consequence of an earthquake.

d. Compare Is. 49: 20.

e. Compare PA 5: 5. Note that only eight miracles are listed in the ARNA version of these miracles; cf. the list of ARNB. See also MABO, pp. 89ff.

f. On the following passage cf. ARNB, pp. 107f; B. Baba Kamma, 82b. See Finkelstein in AMJV (Heb. section), pp. 351ff; see further Goldin.

g. See Lev. 14: 34f. Verse 34 reads, "When ye come into the land...which I give to you for a possession." To none of the tribes, however, was Jerusalem given as a possession.

h. See Deut. 21: 1ff. Verse 1 reads, "If one be found slain in the land which the Lord...giveth thee to possess it." Compare preceding note.

i. Compare Num. 19: 14; see Goldin.

j. See Goldin, p. 36. According to Baba Kamma, 82b, there is no reason for this; it was merely a tradition. See, Goldin.

k. See Goldin.

l. I.e. one who renounces idolatry in order to acquire limited citizenship in Palestine (see Moore, *Judaism*, Vol. I, 339ff). Cf. PTP, pp. 134ff; see Goldin.

m. Compare 2 Kings 22: 14ff. On Huldah, see *Legends* [L. Ginzberg], 6, 69, 249f. See Goldin.

n. Southeast of the city. In other words the uncleanness was given passage into the outskirts of Jerusalem. We must assume that the cubic space of the tunnel was at least one handbreadth; otherwise, according to rabbinic law, the uncleanness would penetrate perpendicularly upward and render those who passed over the grave unclean (for they would then be regarded as "overshadowing"; cf. preceding note).

If, on the other hand, there is a cubic space of a handbreadth, we do not say that the uncleanness penetrates upward; it can then pass through the tunnel, out to the river Kidron.

o. According to B. Baba Kamma, 82b, because of the foul air that would spread after the use of fertilizer and because of weed. See also Jos., *Against Apion*, I. 22; see Goldin.

p. They might defile hallowed things with the food they gather from refuse. On pigs, B. Baba Kamma, 82b, tells a story very much like that told by Jos., *Antiquities*, XIV. 2. 1.

q. See Deut. 21: 18ff.

r. Jerusalem was national territory; cf. above, note g. See Goldin.

s. See Goldin.

t. Only the structure on the ground, not the ground itself, could belong to an individual; compare preceding note.

u. See Goldin.

v. From the pilgrims who come for the festivals. See Goldin.

w. Compare Finkelstein in AMJV, pp. 355, 360.

x. Compare reference in note v above.

y. See below, note aa.

z. So *editio princeps*, and cf. HJP, p. 145, n. h; note aa below. ARNS reads *mtzrm* ("Egyptian"?).

aa. "Jerusalem's residents extended to the pilgrims every hospitality for which the guests did not pay. In order to show their gratitude, however, the guests resorted to an interesting evasion (*ha'ărâmâh*): often they had at their disposal large sums of second-tithe money, use of which was limited to the purchase of food, and then only in Jerusalem. If with such money an animal is bought, only the flesh is subject to second-tithe sanctity, not the hide (M. Ma'ăsér Sheni 1: 3). Taking advantage of this law the pilgrims would deliberately buy animals whose hides were worth more than their flesh. This, which is obviously an 'evasion' of the intent of the second-tithe law, the Mishnah finally legalized, for it states (*ibid.*) that second-tithe sanctity applies to the flesh only, even if the animal's hide is more valuable than its flesh. The guests left such hides as gifts for their hosts, and the latter could then trade with the hides profitably everywhere. To make the hides so valuable, the animals were no doubt painted in some way (on adorning of animals cf. HJP, pp. 145f) and the painted hides brought higher prices than ordinary hides. (I am indebted to Professor Saul Lieberman for the interpretation and understanding of this passage.) Note that more than ten things are said of Jerusalem (So Goldin)."

While the earthly Jerusalem stood, and after it had again fallen in A.D. 70, the hope for a New Jerusalem, then, persisted.[147]

But at this point we must note another evolution in the understanding of and hope for Jerusalem, which breaks the bounds of the earthly, historical Jerusalem, at least in part.

We begin with an aspect of the Old Testament presentation of Jerusalem hitherto unnoticed. The city had been connected with Mt. Sinai in Is. 2: 1-5:

> The word which Isaiah the son of
> Amoz saw concerning Judah and Jerusalem.
> It shall come to pass in the latter days
> that the mountain of the house of
>   the Lord
> shall be established as the highest of
>   the mountains,
>   and shall be raised above the hills;
> and all the nations shall flow to it,
>   and many peoples shall come,
> and say:
> "Come, let us go up to the mountain
>   of the Lord,
> to the house of the God of Jacob;
> that he may teach us his ways
>   and that we may walk in his
>   paths."
> For out of Zion shall go forth the law,
>   and the word of the Lord from
>   Jerusalem.
> He shall judge between the nations,
>   and shall decide for many
>   peoples;
> and they shall beat their swords into
>   plowshares,
>   and their spears into pruning
>   hooks;

---

[147] The precise interpretation of the passage from ARN is in dispute. A. Guttmann, HUCA, Vol. XL–XLI, 1969–1970, pp. 251–275 on "Jerusalem in Tannaitic Law," has argued that some of the details referred to are applicable only to the ideal Jerusalem of the future. In any case, they witness to an extraordinary idealization of a city. The passages giving the laws concerning Jerusalem are in ARN 1. 35 (p. 104); 11. 39 (p. 107), Tos. Negaim 6: 2 (Zuckermandel, p. 625); T. B. Baba Qamma 82b. For details on Jerusalem in the first century, see J. Jeremias, *Jerusalem in the Time of Jesus*, trans., Philadelphia, 1969.

nation shall not lift up sword against
    nation.
neither shall they learn war any more.
O house of Jacob,
    come, let us walk
in the light of the Lord.

The same connection occurs in Ps. 68: 15–17:

O mighty mountain, mountain of
    Bashan;
Why look you with envy,
O many-peaked mountain,
at the mount which God desired
    for his abode,
yea, where the Lord will dwell
    for ever?
With mighty chariotry, twice ten
    thousand,
thousands upon thousands,
the Lord came from Sinai into the
    holy place.

But these two passages also connect Jerusalem with a conception found in Canaanite mythology—that of the mountains of the gods, of which Bashan and Zaphon and the North (Is. 14: 12–13) are examples. There is a reference to Bashan as envious of Mt. Zion in Ps. 68: 15–17, but in Ps. 48: 1–3 Zion is identified with Mt. Zaphon. The RSV renders this passage as follows:

Great is the Lord and greatly
to be praised
in the city of our God!
His holy mountain, beautiful in
    elevation,
is the joy of all the earth,
Mount Zion, in the far north,
the city of the great King.
Within her citadels God
    has shown himself a sure defense (Ps. 48: 1–3).

But a more literal rendering of verse 3 would be:

Mount Zion, the remotest part of Zaphon,
the city of the great King.

Jerusalem has become the place of the highest mountain. The view re-emerges in Ezek. 20: 40; 40: 2. In the latter passage the prophet sees the future Jerusalem opposite "a very high mountain" in the land of Israel.[148]

The theme of the mountain to which we have referred re-emerges in a group of Psalms (belonging to the "Psalms of Korah," 42–49; 84–85; 86–88), which are preoccupied with Zion. According to the authors of these, Yahweh dwelt exclusively in Zion. There was the house and dwelling place of God (42: 4); from "the holy hill" came forth the light and truth of God (43: 3). The mountain of God is mentioned in 48: 2; 87: 1. With this mythological motif are combined that of paradise (46: 4) and of the conflict with chaos (46: 2ff). The city is endowed with the riches of mythology to give it a cosmic significance. No wonder that those born in her are especially blessed:

> And of Zion it shall be said,
> "This one and that one were born in her";
> for the Most High himself will establish her.
> The Lord records as he registers the peoples,
> "This one was born there (Ps. 87: 5)."

A day in the courts of her temples is better than a thousand elsewhere (Ps. 84: 10).[149]

One of the most direct testimonies to the continuing vitality of the veneration of Jerusalem has appeared in a document discovered at Qumran, at column XXII in IIQPsa.[150] The literary affinities between this column, generally referred to as "Apostrophe to Zion," and Is. 54: 60–62; 66, and other Old Testament passages have been pointed out. It has also been suggested that we have here a distinct stage in the theology of

---

[148] See de Vaux, *Interpreting the Prophetic Tradition*, p. 297; on the Temple as the summit of the earth in terms of a cosmology ultimately derived from Babylonia, see Eric Burrows, *The Labyrinth*, London, 1935, pp. 54f. On Tzaphon or Saphon, see Gray, *The Legacy of Canaan*, p. 209.

[149] On all this, see Günther Wanke, *Die Zionstheologie der Korachiten*, ZAW Beihefte, 1966.

[150] The text is printed conveniently in CBQ, Vol. XXIX; 1 January 1967, p. 60. See Conrad E. L'Heureux, "The Biblical Sources of the Apostrophe to Zion," pp. 60–74; James A. Sanders, *The Psalm Scroll of Qumran Cave II (IIQPsa)*, Vol. IV: Discoveries in the Judaean Desert of Jordan, Oxford, 1965. See further for the concern with Jerusalem, M. Baillet, "Fragments Araméens de Qumran 2: Description de la Jérusalem nouvelle," RB, Vol. 62, 1955, pp. 222–245. These fragments probably date from between the end of the first century B.C. and A.D. 70. The text is also found in M. Baillet, J. T. Milik, R. de Vaux, eds., *Les "petites Grottes" de Qumran*, Discoveries in the Judaean Desert, 2 vols., Oxford, 1962, pp. 84ff; 184ff. See also Yigael Yadin, "The Temple Scroll." in *New Directions in Biblical Archaeology*, eds. D. N. Freedman and J. C. Greenfield, New York, 1969, pp. 139–148.

Zion—the application to that city of terms usually applied to God
Himself: the glorification of Zion could hardly go further! The following
are the grounds for such a view.

The first verse of the Apostrophe reads:

a. I mention you (*w'azâkírkâh*) in blessing, O Zion;
b. I love you with all my strength.
c. Your remembrance is blessed for ever.

With line b compare Deut. 6: 5: "and you shall love the Lord your
God with all your heart, and with all your soul, and with all your might."
All this verse would be evoked by line b above. Significant also is the first
verb in line a: "I mention you (from *zâkar*, the Hiphil form)." The matter
is expressed by L'Heureux as follows: "The Hiphil of *zâkar* is a technical
cultic expression meaning to 'name the name.' That is, it is the deno-
minative of the noun *zkr*. Brevard Childs describes the use of the verb
in this way:

Especially in the later Hebrew the verb undergoes a decided broadening.
Is. 12: 4 still used the hiphil in conjunction with the name, but now with the
meaning of 'praise' or 'confess' and parallel to 'give thanks (*hôdhāh*).' The
object of the verb, used in this broader sense of 'praise,' now includes the
deeds of Yahweh (Ps. 77: 12), his righteousness (Ps. 71: 16), his steadfast love
(Is. 63: 7), etc. (Brevard Childs, *Memory and Tradition in Israel*, Naperville,
Ill., 1962, pp. 11–12 and 14).

What we have in the Apostrophe is a further development where the term
is applied, not to God, but to Zion. With this opening verb are to be
connected verse 15:

> Time and again I mention you in blessing;
> I bless you with all my heart

And again with this, verse 14:

> Sweet to the smell is the praise of you, O Zion,
> Above all the earth's expanse."[151]

Here, according to L'Heureux, the act of praising Zion is compared to
incense which covers the whole world. L'Heureux also finds the application to Zion of words usually used in respect to God in verse 18a.

> Be high (*rûmi*) and wide, O Zion.

The term *rûmi*, an imperative, is addressed to the Almighty in the Psalms.

[151] L'Heureux, "The Biblical Sources," CBQ, pp. 61f.

L'Heureux concludes that the Apostrophe marks a stage in the idealization of Zion. At first, Zion was praised because of the Lord who dwelt there. But Zion herself becomes more and more an object of praise until concepts previously applied to the Lord are applied to the city itself. L'Heureux admits, however, that the Lordship of Yahweh is never forgotten: the redemption of Zion, it is assumed, in the Apostrophe rests in his hands. But even if L'Heureux's exegesis may not convince entirely because in each verse to which he appeals he tends to overtranslate, while in one verse his translation is open to discussion,[152] there can be no question of the interest of the "Apostrophe to Zion" for our purposes. The earthly Jerusalem here again evokes the profounder response. The sentiment for the land is not mentioned. It is concentrated in Jerusalem, and in verse 13 a term elsewhere used in connection with the land is applied to Zion. Compare verse 13 (our italics):

> Your enemies have been *cut off* (*nkrthw*) about you, O Zion

with Prov. 2: 21–22.

> For the upright will inhabit the land,
> and men of integrity will remain in it;
> but the wicked will be *cut off* (*yikkârêthŵ*) from
> the land.

In the passages hitherto appealed to it would seem that Jerusalem is still *in* the land, but is so transformed and idealized that the question must be asked whether it is still *of* the land. This question is especially posed by the section in Is. 60–62 in which we claimed above that the hope for Jerusalem had reached full tide. Does it warrant the view that, already in the Old Testament, the city has become a transcendental entity, "mystic, wonderful," so that the earthly Jerusalem is taken up into a heavenly? R. de Vaux[153] does not hesitate to claim that in Is. 60–62 the dazzling description of the city "has no longer any connection with earthly realities: Jerusalem transcends history; in her is summed up the whole history of salvation." It is difficult not to agree with this verdict, because, although in most of Is. 60–62 the earthly city is surely envisaged, in one section at least we are pointed beyond the bourne of time and space: it reads, in Is. 60: 19–20:

---

[152] It should be noted that the interpretation of the "righteous" as "sacrifices" possibly suggests that the author(s) of the Apostrophe does not contemplate a re-institution of the sacrificial system: but this cannot be pressed.

[153] *Interpreting the Prophetic Tradition*, p. 296.

> The sun shall be no more
> your light by day,
> nor for brightness shall the moon
> give light to you by night;
> but the Lord will be your everlasting
> light,
> and your God will be your glory.
> Your sun shall no more go down,
> nor your moon withdraw itself;
> for the Lord will be your
> everlasting light,
> and your days of mourning shall
> be ended.

But not all have found a transcendent reference here.[154] The above passage may be taken as only metaphorical, and there are certainly in Is. 60 mundane verses in which Jerusalem is envisaged as a very earthly city to which the wealth of the nations is brought (Is. 60: 3, 5ff, 10, 13).

However, whether Jerusalem had already in the Old Testament gained a super-historical connotation or not, in later sources the duality of the city, if we may so put it, its earthly and "heavenly" affinities, are evident although highly complex.

The belief in a heavenly Jerusalem emerges clearly. If we reject the view that this idea is already present in Is. 60: 19–20, it probably first occurs in 1 Enoch 90: 28–38, where although the express phrase "heavenly Jerusalem" does not occur, its existence is presupposed. The passage follows a description of the judgment of the fallen angels, the unworthy shepherds and the apostates. It reads:

And I stood up to see till they folded up that old house; and carried off all the pillars, and all the beams and ornaments of the house were at the same time folded up with it, and they carried it off and laid it in a place in the south of the land. And I saw till the Lord of the sheep brought a new house greater and loftier than that first, and set it up in the place of the first which had been folded up: all its pillars were new, and its ornaments were new and larger than those of the first, the old one which He had taken away, and all the sheep were within it.

And I saw all the sheep which had been left, and all the beasts on the earth, and all the birds of the heaven, falling down and doing homage to those sheep

[154] S. Safrai, for example, "The Heavenly Jerusalem," in *Ariel: A Review of the Arts and Sciences in Israel*, No. 23, 1969, pp. 11–16, thinks that nowhere in the Old Testament is Jerusalem a supraterrestrial entity. N. W. Porteous, in *Verbannung und Heimkehr*, p. 249, finds a transcendent note especially in Is. 65: 17ff, but shows how the author even here falls back on the description of an earthly paradise for his purpose.

and making petition to and obeying them in every thing. And thereafter those three who were clothed in white and had seized me by my hand [who had taken me up before], and the hand of that ram also seizing hold of me, they took me up and set me down in the midst of those sheep†before the judgement took place†. And those sheep were all white, and their wool was abundant and clean. And all that had been destroyed and dispersed, and all the beasts of the field, and all the birds of the heaven, assembled in that house, and the Lord of the sheep rejoiced with great joy because they were all good and had returned to His house. And I saw till they laid down that sword, which had been given to the sheep, and they brought it back into the house, but it held them not. And the eyes of them all were opened, and they saw the good, and there was not one among them that did not see. And I saw that that house was large and broad and very full.

Here the new house is implied to have existed already before it is set up in what 1 Enoch 90: 20 calls "the pleasant land." It is conceived in very enlarged proportions to contain those beasts and birds—the dispersed and apostates[155]—who desire to enter it. But the meaning of the "new house" is ambiguous. Usually it has been taken, without discussion, to refer to the new Jerusalem; but it might be interpreted as the new Temple. This ambiguity of interpretation suggests what is frequently found in the sources, and is illustrated in quotations which follow, that is, the interpenetration or the identification of the City and the Temple and the indiscriminate transition from the one to the other. However, the magnitude of the "new house" contemplated suggests that the whole City, not merely the Temple, is in view, so that we may, though not with complete certainty, find here an implicit reference to a heavenly Jerusalem. But notice: this heavenly Jerusalem is to come down to the land. It does not remain "in heaven": however "heavenly," it is to become earthly.[156]

A more unambiguous reference to a pre-existent city appears in the

155 See R. H. Charles, *Apocrypha and Pseudepigrapha of the Old Testament*, Oxford, 1913, p. 259; R. J. McKelvey, *The New Temple: The Church in the New Testament*, Oxford, 1969, *ad rem.*

156 Perhaps this should be expressed more cautiously, although 1 Enoch 90: 29 speaks of the Lord bringing and setting up the new house, presumably on earth. McKelvey, who takes the house to refer to the Temple, not to Jerusalem, suggests that insofar as the heavenly Temple *is* the new Temple described in supraterrestrial terms, it follows that one day it must descend to earth, McKelvey, *The New Temple*, 1969, p. 40. 1 Enoch 90: 26 referring to "the right of that house" suggests Jerusalem (the south of the city). T. Levi 10: 5 which refers to this passage seems to understand "the house" to be Jerusalem. Probably the "tower" in 1 Enoch 89: 50 refers to the Temple. See also 89: 66; 89: 73: this favours taking "the house" to refer to Jerusalem. The fact is that as in 93; 91: 12–17 Temple and city cannot be separated. See D. Hill, *The New Temple in the Messianic Age*, unpublished STM Thesis, Union Theological Seminary, New York, n.d., pp. 32f. 1 Enoch 83–90 (The Dream Visions) are dated by Charles, *Apocrypha and Pseudepigrapha*, Vol. II, pp. 163f, in 164–163 B.C.; by Eissfeldt in 176–134 B.C.

Syriac Baruch at 4: 1–7. Probably written within forty years after the destruction of the second Temple in A.D. 70, and purporting to deal with visions of destruction of the First Temple and the City in the time of Jeremiah, the work makes a clear distinction between the earthly temple and another. The author depicts the coming destruction of the Temple and of Jerusalem and then in 4: 1–7 adds:

1 And the Lord said unto me:
   "This city shall be delivered up for a time,
   And the people shall be chastened during a time,
   And the world will not be given over to oblivion.
2 [Dost thou think that this is that city of which I said: "On the palms of My hands have I graven
3 thee?' This building now built in your midst is not that which is revealed with Me, that which was prepared beforehand here from the time when I took counsel to make Paradise, and showed to Adam before he sinned, but when he transgressed the commandment it was removed from him, as
4 also Paradise. And after these things I showed it to My servant Abraham by night among the
5 portions of the victims. And again also I showed it to Moses on Mount Sinai when I showed to him
6 the likeness of the tabernacle and all its vessels. And now, behold, it is preserved with Me, as also
7 Paradise. Go, therefore, and do as I command thee."][157]

We note here again the passage, without warning, from the City to the Temple. The City no less than the Temple existed before creation: the vision of it was granted to Adam, but withdrawn after the Fall, only to be renewed to Abraham, the father of the eschatological faith of Israel, and later to Moses. The vision of the City is granted to Abraham "by night among the portions of the victims." The reference is to Gen. 15: 9–21. The vision of the city—not present in that text—is mentioned, rather than the promise of the land: has it taken the place of the latter in the author's mind?

The same belief in a "heavenly Jerusalem" emerges in 4 Ezra written also after A.D. 70. Consider the following passages:

For behold the days come, and it shall be when
the signs which I have foretold

---

[157] On this see Charles, *Apocrypha and Pseudepigrapha, ad rem.* Verse 2, which derides the actual Jerusalem, may be an interpolation. Torrey dates 2 (Syriac) Baruch in A.D. 70. Rothstein, in E. Kautzsch, *Die Apokryphen und Pseudepigrapha,* in A.D. 70–96; Pierre Bogaert, *Apocalypse de Baruch* (2 vols.), Vol. 1, p. 293, in A.D. 95, and O. Eissfeldt, *The Old Testament, An Introduction,* trans., 1965, in A.D. 100–130.

unto thee shall come to pass,
[Then shall the city that now is invisible
appear, and the land which is now concealed
be seen;]... (4 Ezra 7: 26).

Most interesting here is that the city and the land are placed in parallelism and, thereby, perhaps equated. This explains, perhaps, why in 3: 13, 14 the promise of the land to Abraham is not mentioned, but is subsumed under his vision of "the end of the times":

...Thou didst choose thee one from among them
whose name was Abraham: him thou didst
love, and unto him only didst thou reveal
the end of the times secretly by night.

Here the last words unmistakably refer to Gen. 15: 9ff. Among the future glories of the redeemed there is no mention of the land, but there is of the City. 4 Ezra 8: 52–53 asserts of the seer, who is among the saved:

For you
is opened Paradise,
planted the Tree of life;
the future Age prepared,
plenteousness made ready;
a City builded,
a Rest appointed;
Good works established,
Wisdom preconstituted;
The (evil) root is sealed up from you,
infirmity from your path extinguished;
And Death is hidden,
Hades fled away;
Corruption forgotten,
sorrows passed away;
and in the end the treasures of immortality
are made manifest...

This passage is significant. Here unmistakably "the city builded" is classified with a future order which wholly transcends the historical order.[158]

But no passage makes the existence of a heavenly Jerusalem—the city

---

[158] There is less ambiguity about the descent of the heavenly city in 4 Ezra and 2 Bar. than in 1 Enoch. Compare McKelvey, *The New Temple*, pp. 32–34. But even in 4 Ezra the express language of a descent is not found.

of 4 Ezra 8: 52–53—more clear than the tantalizing section dealing with "The Vision of the Disconsolate Woman" in 4 Ezra 9: 38–10: 57.[159] We quote 10: 40–55.

The matter, therefore, is as follows. The woman who appeared to thee a little while ago, whom thou sawest mourning and begannest to comfort: whereas now thou seest no likeness of a woman any more, but a builded City hath appeared unto thee: and whereas she told thee of the misfortune of her son—this is the interpretation: This woman, whom thou sawest, is Sion, whom thou now beholdest as a builded City; And whereas she said unto thee that she was barren thirty years: the reason is that there were three thousand years in the world before any offering was offered in (it) (i.e. in the world). And it came to pass after three thousand years that (David) built the City, and offered offerings: then it was that the barren bare a son. And whereas she told thee that she reared him with travail: that was the (divine) dwelling in Jerusalem. And whereas she said unto thee: "My son entering into his marriage-chamber died," and that misfortune befell her—this was the fall of Jerusalem that has come to pass. And lo! thou hast seen the (heavenly) pattern of her, how she mourned her son, and thou didst begin to comfort her for what had befallen.

> Now, the Most High seeing
> that thou art grieved deeply
> and art distressed whole-heartedly on account
> of her;
> hath showed thee the brilliance of her glory,
> and her majestic beauty.

Therefore I bade thee remain in the field where no house has been builded; for I knew that the Most High was about to reveal all these things unto thee. (Therefore I bade thee come into the field where no foundation of any building is, for in the place where the City of the Most High was about to be revealed no building-work of man could endure.)

Therefore be not thou afraid, and let not thy heart be terrified; but go in and see the brightness and vastness of the building, as far as it is possible for thee with the sight of thine eyes to see!

Here, despite the complexities of the text, the distinction between the earthly Jerusalem (the Son) and "the (heavenly) pattern of her" (the woman) is unmistakable. The "wholly other" character of the heavenly pattern is emphasized, especially in the section which explains why the vision had only been granted in a field: it had to be placed in a fresh

---

[159] On 4 Ezra 9: 38–10: 57, see Hill, *The New Temple*. Compare 2 Enoch 55: 1a, 2 (first century A.D.). Between his first and second trips to heaven, Enoch is made to say: "My children, behold the day of my term and the time have approached...For tomorrow I shall go up to heaven, to the uppermost Jerusalem, to my eternal home."

setting. How important the vision of the heavenly city was for the author of 4 Ezra appears from the frequency with which he refers to it (see 7: 26; 13: 35f).

In the Rabbinic sources, discussion of the heavenly Jerusalem centres on two themes: first, its exact location in the heavens—for example, was it in the third heaven or the fourth? Apart from the materials to which we have referred, the New Testament also, for example, at Rev. 21: 2, 10, makes it clear that such speculation prevailed in the first century, although most of the Rabbinic material dealing with it is too late for our purposes.[160] One text, Gen. Rabbah 69: 7, places the heavenly Jerusalem eighteen miles above the earthly (so Simeon ben Yohai, A.D. 140–165). The same Rabbi in Gen. Rabbah 55: 7, on Gen. 22: 2, finds that, on earth, Moriah corresponds to the Heavenly Temple. In T. B. Ḥagigah 12b, Resh Lakish (Rabbi Simeon b. Lakish, A.D. 279–320) thinks that the Heavenly Temple is situated in the heaven $z^e b\hat{u}l$ (the fourth of the seven heavens). ($z^e b\hat{u}l$ is that in which "[the heavenly] Jerusalem and the Temple and the altar are built, and Michael, the great Prince, stands and offers up thereon an offering...." Reference is made to 1 Kings 8: 13 and Is. 43: 15 where $z^e b\hat{u}l$ is referred to as the habitation of God.) Secondly, how was this heavenly city to be made manifest? There is a sharp division between the earlier Rabbinic sources and the later at this point. That there was a correspondence between the structure of the heavenly Jerusalem and the earthly was generally recognized. But none of the earlier texts suggests that the heavenly Jerusalem will descend to earth to replace the earthly: the heavenly city remains transcendent.[161] The descent of the city envisaged in the Pseudepigrapha, to which we referred above, seems to be rejected: the Jerusalem on earth will be rebuilt with human hands: the heavenly Jerusalem remains above. But the two cities are connected.[162] In T. B. Ta'anith 5a we read as follows:

R. Naham [A.D. 279–320] further asked R. Isaac, how do you explain the verse

[160] On this, see Safrai, "The Heavenly Jerusalem," *Ariel*, 1969.

[161] Later Rabbinic texts do take up the theme of the descent of the heavenly city to earth. See Beth ha-Midrash 1: 23:

Let Jerusalem come down from heaven and never destroy it. Gather there the dispersed of Israel that they may live there in safety.

Cited by McKelvey, *The New Temple*, p. 35.

[162] At this point, Safrai introduces the influence of the interaction between Judaism and Christianity. Because of Christian emphasis on the descent of the heavenly Jerusalem to earth (Rev. 21: 1–4), Judaism increasingly insisted that the heavenly Jerusalem was not to descend. Rather, by human effort, under the Divine Blessing, the earthly Jerusalem was to be so elevated that it would eventually reach heaven, and become conjoined to the Jerusalem

(Hos. 11: 9): "*The Holy One in the midst of thee, and I will not come into the city?*" [Surely it cannot mean] because the Holy One is in the midst of thee, I shall not come into the city?! "Thus said R. Johanan, The Holy One, blessed be He, meant to say: I will not enter into the heavenly Jerusalem until I can enter into the earthly Jerusalem." Is there then a heavenly Jerusalem?—Yes, for it is written (Ps. 122: 3): "*Jerusalem, thou art builded as a city that is compact together.*"

אמר רבי יוחנן אמר הקדוש ברוך הוא לא אבוא בירושלם של מעלה עד
שאבוא לירושלם של מטה ומי איכא ירושלם למעלה אין דכתיב ירושלם הבנויה
כעיר שחברה לה יחדו:

As the editor of the Soncino translation shows, the argument is that the words *sheḥûbᵉrah* (joined, compacted), implies that Jerusalem has a *ḥᵉbûrâh* "companion," in heaven; both earthly city and heavenly proto-type are located opposite each other. And again in Mekilta, Beshallaḥ' the assumption seems to be that "Jerusalem" existed at the time of the Exodus. Since the Jerusalem on earth did not then exist, the reference must be to the heavenly Jerusalem. The pertinent comment on Exod. 14: 15 (see Lauterbach's edition, p. 216) reads as follows:

And the Lord Said unto Moses: "Wherefore Criest Thou unto Me? Speak unto the Children of Israel that They Go Forward."... R. Ishmael [A.D. 120–140]

above. That such a reaction may have arisen in Judaism is likely, although there is no direct or explicit evidence for it.

One question we have not asked is *why* Jerusalem, despite the vicissitudes of its history, became the symbol of Israel's transcendental hopes. Several answers may be given. The Second Temple had never been quite as glorious in Israel's mind as had the first, and certainly nothing like the new temple envisaged by Ezekiel and others. It had been defiled by Antiochus IV and the suspicion continued that, despite the purification of it by Judas Maccabeus, it had not been fully restored to holiness (1 Enoch. 89: 73). In fact, the second Temple was not complete: it lacked the Ark (according to 2 Macc. 2: 1ff, Jeremiah had hidden the tabernacle, the ark, and the altar of incense before the destruction). Some claimed that the Divine Presence had never dwelt in the second Temple (see Targum on Haggai 1: 8). But these, mainly negative, factors in themselves would not have created a hope for a new temple and a new Jerusalem. Let us recall deeper factors. We noted above the peculiar relationship that even the prophets recognized to exist between Jerusalem and Yahweh. It was a relationship which by its very nature seemed to demand or imply permanence. But N. W. Porteous has helped us to see even further. In his essay "Jerusalem-Zion: The Growth of a Symbol" in *Verbannung und Heimkehr*, Tübingen, 1961, pp. 235–252, he pointed out the association between the very name Jerusalem and "*peace*," "*righteousness*." This association made it natural for the city to become the focus of the eschatological hope of Israel and the symbol for the universal Kingdom of God. Some have held that there was a deity, *Tzedek* (righteousness), connected with Jerusalem; others that in pre-Israelite times its tutelary deity was *Salem* (peace). In any case, Jerusalem did evoke thoughts of peace and righteousness (Is. 1: 21, 26; Ps. 72; Is. 28: 16ff; Ps. 85; 122; Ezek. 13: 8–16 etc., etc.), and was, therefore, a fit and natural symbol for the eschatological hope. The impact of events in 587 B.C. and A.D. 70 cannot be exaggerated. Many Jews may have come to feel that an earthly city so often disrupted and profaned could not be the scene of the perfect worship. This feeling was combined with a profound sense of sin and an enlarged understanding of God. See Charles, *Apocrypha and Pseudepigrapha*, Vol. II, p. 482; A. Causse, "De la Jérusalem terrestre à la Jerusalem céleste," *Revue d'Histoire et de Philosophie Religieuses*, Vol. XXVII, 1947, pp. 13–14.

"For the sake of Jerusalem, I will divide the sea for them." For it is said: "Awake, awake, put on thy strength, O Zion; put on thy beautiful garments, O Jerusalem, the holy city; for henceforth there shall no more come into thee the uncircumcised and the unclean (Is. 52: 1)."

A pre-existent, heavenly Jerusalem, seems also to be implied elsewhere in the same passage (see Lauterbach, p. 222): "Israel" and "Jerusalem" seem to be regarded as having been designated to be before God "from the time of the six days of creation." According to R. Eliezar Jacob, a contemporary of the destruction of A.D. 70, "Jerusalem is destined to keep rising aloft until it reaches the throne of glory (Pesikta de Rab Kahana, end of section 20. Mandelbaum ed. p. 315. German trans. A. Wünsche, *Pesikta des Rab Kahana*, Leipzig, 1885, p. 203)." Does this mean that Jerusalem on earth is ultimately to be united with the heavenly, that is, to become wholly transcendent or simply that there is no fundamental difference between the earthly and the heavenly Jerusalem? This question must remain unanswered. Was Philo of Alexandria's understanding of the tabernacle built by Moses that it only *resembled* its heavenly prototype? In Moses 11: 74ff; in 11: 59 we read: ἡ μὲν οὖν σκηνή, καθάπερ νεὼς ἅγιος, τὸν εἰρημένον τρόπον κατασκευάσθη . . . This is translated in the Loeb series by F. H. Colson thus: "The tabernacle, then, was constructed to resemble a sacred temple in the way described." But perhaps such a translation does not do justice to the phrase τὸ εἰρημένον τρόπον "in the way described," because 11: 74 makes it clear that the tabernacle is not simply to resemble a sacred temple, but was to be according to divine pronouncements given to Moses, according to a heavenly model (11: 76) ("So the shape of the model was stamped upon the mind of the prophet, a secretly painted or moulded prototype, produced by immaterial and invisible forms; and then the resulting work was built in accordance with that shape by the artist impressing the stampings upon the material substances required in each case [Loeb, p. 487])." How much beyond Philo the Rabbis would go in connecting the earthly and the heavenly city remains problematic. The reference to the tabernacle naturally leads to our next subsection.

b. THE TEMPLE

Before our examination of the understanding of Jerusalem is closed, it is necessary to revert to the point adverted to earlier only in passing, namely, that the pertinent texts move without warning from the Temple to Jerusalem and *vice versa*, so that these two entities, in their earthly and heavenly forms, are in constant association.[163] So it is that a survey of the development of the understanding of the Temple would rest almost entirely on the same texts as those with which we have dealt in our

[163] According to L. R. Fisher, *The Journal of Semitic Studies*, Vol. 8, Jan.–Dec. 1963, pp. 34ff, in an article on "The Temple Quarter," the Hebrew word עִיר itself is "a flexible term meaning not only village, city, or state, but...also...temple quarter or even the inner room of the temple. This in turn can be equated with the mountain of God (p. 34)." He examines the term as used in connection with Jerusalem and finds the meaning "city," "temple quarter," "hill of God/altar" used of Jerusalem as a city. In Ezek. 40: 2–5 city stands for temple area; in 45: 6 the word city means city as distinguished from the holy district with the temple. In Is. 50: 7, 13, 14 God's temple is equated with "the city of the Lord." Compare Ps. 101: 8. In Zech. 8: 3 the city is "the Mountain of Jahweh of hosts." "It seems that, ideally, Yahweh does not have a temple quarter within a city, but the city is his temple quarter, temple and even the Hill of God (Fisher, p. 40)." That the double meaning of "temple quarter" and "city" for עִיר was alive in the first century is clear from Jos., *Antiquities*, XII, 11. 145–146.

This interchangeability of the city and the temple has an important bearing on a recent paper by E. Urbach in Hebrew: *Yerushalaim l\u02bedorotheiah*, 1968, pp. 156ff (English summary p. 64). Urbach by drawing a sharp distinction between the Heavenly Temple and the Heavenly City is able to argue that the concept of the Heavenly Jerusalem specifically appears only once in Talmudic literature, in the Babylonian Talmud (T. B. Ta\u02beanith 5a). He contrasts its use in Apocalyptic literature. The latter dwells on the Heavenly Jerusalem and on its descent to earth. Urbach writes: "The reasons for Heavenly Jerusalem having been passed over by the Tannaim and the Amoraim are explained as a reaction to the adoption of this motif by Christianity. This is to be rejected, for it does not explain the difference in attitude towards the Heavenly Temple and has no basis in the sources." Urbach fails to take into account that interchangeability of Temple and City to which we pointed. In addition, it is difficult not to agree with Werblowsky in the same volume, that Paul himself provides evidence that the notion was Pharisaic, as was the notion that Jerusalem was *metropolis*.

But is Urbach right when he refuses to find in the hesitancy of the Tannaim and the Amoraim in speaking of the descent of the Heavenly Jerusalem to the earth a reaction to Christian emphases? These emphases are familiar. Certain Christians held the view that the Heavenly Jerusalem would descend to the earth. Indeed, the New Jerusalem was already present in the Christian community on earth (Rev. 21). According to Paul, the Heavenly Jerusalem already finds an extension of herself on earth through her children, that is, Christians, whose mother she is (Gal. 4: 26). Safrai suggested that Palestinian Rabbis who were in contact with Christianity hesitated to speak of the descent of the Heavenly Jerusalem because of the Christian ideas we have indicated, whereas Babylonian teachers, who had no such contact, whose views emerge in later sources, show no such hesitancy. In the light of this it is tempting to urge that the notion of the Heavenly Jerusalem went through the following stages:

1. The beginnings of the transcendentalizing of the city in the immediate post-exilic period.

2. The insistence that the Heavenly Jerusalem would soon descend in certain circles.

3. A reaction against Christian claims among the Tannaim and Amoraim, who urged that the Heavenly Jerusalem was not to descend from above but that the earthly Jerusalem was to be built upwards to reach it in heaven.

But Urbach's point that there is no specific evidence for this reaction is reinforced by other considerations. 4 Ezra, which was not altogether removed from Palestinian Pharisaic circles, retains the notion of the descending Jerusalem after A.D. 70. But even more important, the debate as to whether the Heavenly Jerusalem was to descend or to be prepared for through the upbuilding of the earthly city has roots as far back as the exile. The evidence for this is clearly traced by R. Hamerton-Kelly in VT, Vol. XX, No. 1, 1970, pp. 1–15 in "The Temple and the Origins of Jewish Apocalyptic." He connects the notion of the descending Jerusalem with Ezekiel, and the opposite emphasis with P, and argues that Apocalyptic is rooted, among other currents, in a tradition stemming from Ezekiel, who himself draws on an ancient priestly

discussion of Jerusalem and would demand a repetitiveness in our treatment which we have chosen to avoid, without, we think, any undue loss. And, since the texts dealing with the Temple always implicitly, and usually explicitly, implicate the city, just as Jerusalem became the quintessence of the land, so also the Temple became the quintessence of Jerusalem.[164]

This identification of the Temple with the city stems from several causes. The return from the exile was both a return to the city and to rebuild the Temple; the Temple became the centre of both the religious and political life of the post-exilic community; the communal institutions, the Sanhedrin and the Synagogue, were established there. Even more important, in time the city came to be regarded as a veritable extension of the Temple. In the period of the first Temple and in the early days of the second Temple, edible portions of the sacrificial victims were permitted to be consumed only within the Temple area: this applied to peace offerings and the paschal lamb. But in Mishnah Zebahim 5: 8 they were permitted throughout the entire city.

The Firstling,[a] the Tithe (of Cattle),[b] and the Passover-offering are of the Lesser Holy Things; they were slaughtered anywhere in the Temple Court and their blood required to be sprinkled with but one act of sprinkling, provided that it was sprinkled against the (Altar-) base. There is a difference in their manner of eating: the Firstling was eaten only by the priests,[c] and the Tithe (of Cattle) by any man; they could be eaten anywhere in the City, and cooked for food after any fashion, during two days and a night; but the Passover-offering could be eaten only during that night[d] and only until midnight, and it could be eaten only by the number that were assigned to it,[e] and it could only be eaten roast.[f]

a. Num. 18: 17.
b. Lev. 27: 32.
c. Num. 18: 18.
d. Exod. 12: 8.

tradition of a heavenly sanctuary. If Hamerton-Kelly be right, and he has much of O. Plöger, *Theokratie und Eschatologie*, Neukirchen Verlag, 1959, on his side, the attitude of the Tannaim and Amoraim need not have been inspired by Christian emphasis: they were rooted in a long tradition that antedated Christianity.

164 In the text I have made no attempt to connect this theme—the "identity" of the Temple and the City—with the Ancient Near Eastern ideas referred to by Burrows, *The Labyrinth*, pp. 45ff. According to him: "One might almost formulate a law that in the ancient East contemporary cosmological doctrine is registered in the structure and theory of the temples (p. 45)." The natural centre of the naïve cosmologist is the temple which is the centre of his locality. His universe is "hierocentric." The temple, among other things, is "the bond of the land (p. 47)." The naïve temple-centred realism of Babylon was known in Israel: see the story of the Tower of Babel. And this was carried over to Jerusalem (pp. 53f).

e. Compare Pes. 5: 3.
f. Exod. 12: 9.

This means that the sanctity of the Temple was now extended to the whole city which became "holy" and the Temple was "holy." Laws were enacted which recognized this holiness. The dead were not to be buried within its walls: its streets were to be swept daily. The half-shekel tax, levied on every adult male Jew in Palestine and in the Dispersion, was used not only to cover the expense of maintaining the Temple—for example, to pay judges and proofreaders of the Torah-scrolls—but also to maintain "the city wall and the towers thereof and all the city's needs." So too in Mishnah Shekalim 4: 2 we read:

The (Red) Heifer[a] and the scapegoat[b] and the crimson thread[c] were bought with the *Terumah* from the Shekel-chamber. The causeway for the (Red) Heifer[d] and the causeway for the scapegoat[e] and the thread between its horns,[f] the (upkeep of the) water-channel,[g] the city wall and the towers thereof and all the city's needs were provided from the residue[h] of the Shekel-chamber. Abba Saul says: The causeway for the (Red) Heifer was built by the High Priests at their own charges.

a. Num. 19: 1ff. See tractate Parah.
b. Lev. 16: 10, 21ff.
c. To distinguish between the two goats; Lev. 16: 5ff. See Yom. 6: 4.
d. Par. 3: 6.
e. Yom. 6: 4.
f. Yom. 6: 6.
g. That flowed through the Temple Court. Yom. 5: 6; Zeb. 8: 7ff; Tem. 7: 6; Tam. 5: 5; Midd. 3: 2.
h. What was left after the *Terumah* had been taken.

Jerusalem and the Temple, then, became almost inseparable realities. For our purposes, it is essential to recognize that they became the point of concentration, or the depositories for the hope of the land, with which we have been concerned. That hope continued to find strong expression, as we have seen, and that in an explicit manner. But even where it was not explicit it was always implied in the texts, which expressed the hope for Jerusalem and the Temple in their terrestrial and supra-terrestrial forms. To recognize this will be important when we turn to the New Testament, where the land itself is comparatively seldom mentioned, but Jerusalem and the Temple frequently. But to the extent that the hope for the land did often become absorbed in that for the city and the Temple, it could, in certain contexts, easily, if wrongly, be overlooked and deprived of that intensity which we discovered in the Old Testament. Above all, the terrestrial hope for the land could not but be modified or muted with the growth of those supra-terrestrial hopes for Jerusalem and the Temple to which we have referred. This cannot be pressed, because the Heavenly Jerusalem and the Heavenly Temple, until we come to the early Tannaitic sources, as we indicated, were expected to descend to the land. But at least we can say that in some circles the hope for the land had been taken up along with Jerusalem and the Temple, into a more than ordinarily terrestrial context.[165]

C. THE NEW CREATION

This enlargement of the context of the hope for the land, even though concentrated in the hope for Jerusalem and the Temple, was further enhanced by the other element in its eschatological setting to which we referred above, that is, the expectation of a new creation at the end of the days.

We urged previously that at no point should the doctrine of the promise of the land be separated from that of Yahweh as creator of the universe. And in the eschatology of Israel that promise must more and more be understood in a larger context, against the eschatological doctrine

---

[165] The recognition of the close relationship between Jerusalem, the city, and the land—not to speak of their apparent identification in some quarters—adds weight to the cautionary considerations, with which we are concerned, for a simple reason. Nothing is clearer that, however much revered Jerusalem and the Temple, the latter especially was the object of criticism and even rejection by many throughout the centuries. Those currents which were critical of the Temple were likely also to have been disinclined toward any doctrine or tendency which would over-emphasize the significance of the land. The literature on the criticism of the Temple is vast. See R. Dowda, unpublished thesis on "The Temple in the Synoptic Gospels," Duke University, 1972, for bibliography.

From another angle also, the understanding of the Temple is important for our thesis. The way in which Yahweh's relationship to the Temple was interpreted went through several stages. First, Jerusalem and the Temple are conceived as the actual habitation of God (1 Kings 8: 13; the Temple is called a house(בַּיִת) or palace(הֵיכָל);Jer. 7:1;Ps. 43: 3; Ezra 7: 27 etc.); secondly, they become the place where God's name dwells (Deut, 16: 6; 12: 5 etc.; 1 Kings 8: 27, 29; see von Rad, *Studies in Deuteronomy*, pp. 38–39, *Theology*, Vol. II, p. 346); his transcendence being thereby preserved. Thirdly, they are the abode of God's glory (כָּבוֹד) (Ezek. 11: 3; 43: 4, 7). In P the place of God on earth is his מִשְׁכָּן where the glory tabernacles. By using the category of a glory tabernacling P suggests that the presence of God is not permanent. He can depart from Jerusalem. (See R. de Vaux, *Israel*, p. 295; G. von Rad, *Studies in Deuteronomy*, pp. 39–43.) Finally, this understanding of a tabernacling glory prepared the way for the later Rabbinic doctrine of the Shekinah which preserved the transcendence of God over against any exclusive limitation of his presence to Jerusalem and the Temple. See Klaus Baltzer, "The Meaning of the Temple in the Lukan Writings," HTR, Vol. LVIII, 1965. The Rabbis recognized the presence of God everywhere through his Shekinah so that they could survive the fall of Jerusalem and the Temple, even while they still recognized that they had consituted the special place of his abode and would be so again. What was true of God's relationship to the City and the Temple was true of his relationship to the land of which they were the quintessence.

of a new creation. No detailed account of this doctrine need be given here, /
but only its bare structure.

Is. 11: 6 reads as follows:

> The wolf shall dwell with the lamb,
>   and the leopard shall lie down
>   with the kid,
>   and the calf and the lion and the
>   fatling together,
>   and a little child shall lead them.

Already in this passage, usually referred to as Messianic, the End is |
conceived as the restoration of the beginning: the Messianic Age in cosmic
terms over against the fall of Adam: a return to the paradisal conditions
existing before that event. By the time of Trito-Isaiah the belief that
cosmic changes would mark the end becomes explicit:

For, behold, I create new heavens and a new earth (Is. 65: 17).

But there is a parallel thought, not only in Is. 66: 22, but in Deutero-
Isaiah at 51: 6. The latter passage contrasts this passing material world
with God's salvation, which is to be for ever:

> Lift up your eyes to the heavens,
>   and look at the earth beneath;
> for the heavens will vanish like
>   smoke,
> the earth will wear out like a
>   garment,
> and they who dwell in it will die
>   like gnats;
> but my salvation will be for ever,
>   and my deliverance will never be
>   ended.

Later sources reveal a bewildering variety of views on the End: it would
be by fire, the final destruction by fire corresponding to the initial
destruction by the flood: it would occur sometime after the Messianic
Age or before the final judgment of God. If there was to be a "place" for
salvation, where was that to be, in heaven or on earth after that earth had
been scorched? Or again what was meant by the "new heaven"? Was the
old earth to be undone and then remade out of a new substance? Or was
the earth in its present material form to undergo a transformation? Or was

the earth, without undergoing dissolution, to be purified? Or was "the new" to be wholly unrelated to the old? Such questions are reflected in the Apocrypha and Pseudepigrapha, the Qumran writings, and in the Rabbinic sources. And speculation about the end also occurs in another frame of reference, in Hellenistic sources which also reveal that the future might lead to a fiery end of all things.[166]

What is pertinent in all this for our purpose is that the promise of the land, living as we have seen it to be, must be considered over against the kind of speculation to which we have referred. This speculation could not but have depressed the doctrine of the land to a less central position than it would otherwise have occupied. In certain circles the flames of the End, feeding on a cosmos afire, would probably have diminished interest in the land as such. And, even in circles not fervently preoccupied with the cosmic End, the land would have been viewed in a new perspective which, to the extent that it was cosmic, tended to minimize the hope for it as such.

[166] See especially Volz, *Die Eschatologie, ad rem* for the references to the sources in full. A passage in Test. Dan. 5: 12–13 shows especially how intimately the New Jerusalem is related to the creation in Gen. 1, 2 (compare also Is. 65: 17ff):

> And the saints shall rest in Eden, and in the New Jerusalem will the righteous rejoice. And it shall be the glory of the Lord for ever, and no longer shall Jerusalem endure desolation, Nor Israel be led captive For the Lord shall be in the midst of it (living amongst men).

"This is the earliest occurrence of the expression New Jerusalem in Jewish literature (Charles, *Apocrypha and Pseudepigrapha*, p. 334)." The reference is to the renewed earthly Jerusalem. The thought is governed by the maxim that the last things are to be as the first. The last sentence of the paragraph raises the question how far Apocalyptic is to be related to Hellenism. H. D. Betz in a stimulating article "On the Problem of the Religio-Historical Understanding of Apocalypticism" in *Journal for Theology and the Church*, 1969, ed. R. W. Funk, Vol. 6, *Apocalypticism*, pp. 134ff, dismissing H. H. Rowley's concentration on its Old Testament roots (*The Relevance of Apocalyptic*, 3rd ed., New York, 1963; compare D. S. Russell, *The Method and Message of Jewish Apocalyptic*, Philadelphia, 1964) and pointing out how formal has been the recognition of Iranian influences on Apocalyptic, urges that Apocalyptic is the Jewish form of answers to questions which plagued the entire period of Hellenism (p. 138). Jewish apocalyptic is an example of Hellenistic syncretism. Betz illustrates his case from Rev. 16. Points of interest to our thesis in Hellenistic sources mentioned, with a wealth of detail, by Betz, are the following: 1. "The elements of the world," which can be used at creation beneficially, can be transformed by God for the purpose of punishing the godless: see Wis. 12ff, especially 15: 15ff; 19: 18ff; Philo, *Moses* 96–146. 2. Sin (here the sin of giants, but man also is guilty) pollutes the elements, *Corpus Hermeticum* XIII, 53ff, where redemption means "purification" of the elements. Compare Ethiopic Enoch 7: 4–6, where we read that in response to sin ἡ γῆ 'ενέτυχεν κατὰ τῶν ἀνόμων (The earth laid accusation against the lawless ones). 3. In the *Corpus Hermeticum, ibid.* God's saving act results in the "purification" of the earth, the restitution of righteousness and true worship and the announcement of an era of paradise. 4. Bloodshed especially pollutes the earth (Betz, "On the Problem," pp. 147f). See also *Pseudo-Clementine Homilies*, viii–ix. How far such phenomena indicate an interaction between Judaism and Hellenism, as Betz urges, and how far merely parallelism we cannot discuss here. F. M. Cross, "New Directions in the Study of Apocalyptic," in *Journal for Theology and the Church*, Vol. 6, *Apocalypticism*, pp. 157–165, finds the main impulse to Apocalyptic in the Old Testament understanding of the history of salvation, p. 158, and questions Betz's emphasis (p. 161, n. 8). See further W. L. Knox, *St. Paul and the Church of the Gentiles*, Cambridge, 1939, chapter I.

Our survey of elements which must condition the understanding of our theme in a cautionary direction is over. Taken in conjunction with our earlier discussion it indicates the complexity which envelopes the question of the land, and the vicissitudes of its history. Previously we noted the significance for it of the collapse of the state in the sixth century B.C. and the first century A.D. It is now further to be suggested that a consideration of the dates of the various passages cited, especially the Rabbinic ones, and the general impact left by the perusal of the sources indicate that there was after A.D. 70, as before, a duality in the understanding of the land. After that date there was, at first, both a reassertion, especially in the more Apocalyptic circles, of the importance of the land, and also a strong concern to assert the viability of Judaism apart from the land. But as time passed, already in the second century, the sentiment for the land seems to have increased in vigour. A passage in Sifre 11. 80 (ed. Finkelstein, p. 116) is instructive. It lists the names of scholars who left Palestine for the Diaspora to establish academies. When they approached the border of Palestine they turned back in the direction of their land and wept. They tore their garments and returned to Palestine. They finally, however, left for the Diaspora, but not before showing how hard it was to do so. All this needs no comment to illumine the duality about which we write. It leads on naturally to the general conclusion to the first part of our study.

There was no one doctrine of the land, clearly defined and normative, but, as is usual in Judaism, a multiplicity of ideas and expectations variously and unsystematically entertained. It should be clearly recognized that there were currents which would temper any concentration on the land, but belief in the promise of the land to Israel by Yahweh, to whom it belonged, also persisted. Among many Jews the certainty of the ultimately indissoluble connection between Israel and the land was living and widespread in the world within which Christianity emerged. And, while the view that all Jewish eschatology was this-worldly cannot be accepted, because so many sources anticipate a transcendent order or supernatural changes "in the end of the days," this connection is not always to be "spiritualized," but accorded its full terrestrial or physical and historical actuality. The belief in the "umbilical" nature of the relationship of Israel to the land contributed to the tensions that prevailed in the early decades in first-century Palestine: it helped to kindle the fire of the war against Rome. The mystique of the land inevitably confronted early Christianity. That that same mystique remains in our own day and can be illuminated by our Jewish contemporaries appears from words penned in New York City, *centrum mundi*. Finkelstein describes his understanding of his own work as follows:

We at the Seminary regard ourselves and American Jewry neither as one of the foci of a great ellipse nor the center of a circle with only mystic connections with a similar circle surrounding Jerusalem. We recognize that we stand on the periphery of Jewish inspiration; and if we are content with our position, it is only because we believe that the service we can render God, Torah, and mankind from this stance is one to which we have been called and which we cannot neglect. Yet always we turn to Zion not only in prayer but also in the hope of instruction. We gladly assume the role of amanuensis to our brethren who have been given the superior privilege of serving God and studying Torah in the land in which both were uniquely revealed. If the experiences we have garnered in our efforts to weave the tapestry we have mentioned may prove of use, they are at the disposal of our masters and teachers in Israel and Zion.[167]

Not all Jews have shared the veneration thus movingly indicated, but many have done so and still do. Under often harsh realities and vicissitudes, far-flung exile and the blandishments of assimilation, in many a Babylon, the sentiment for the land of Israel has often been tempered, suppressed, and even ignored and rejected by many Jews. Yet, rooted in the Scriptures, and, therefore constantly meditated upon, nourished by the liturgy of the Synagogue and the home, stimulating and in turn being stimulated by pilgrimages and funerary customs, that sentiment has remained tenaciously present in the depth of the consciousness of many Jews across the centuries. And, because it could draw inspiration from the potent blend of religion and peoplehood—not to speak of nationalism—which is a mark of Judaism, it has in times of necessity been easily awakened to influence powerfully the course of history.

In the following pages we shall examine the Pauline Epistles, the Synoptic Gospels, Acts, and the Fourth Gospel for traces of the way in which the early Christian movement came to terms with the mystique expressed in the above quotation in the twentieth century, as it might well have been in the first. And, finally, we shall ask in what relationship Jesus himself stood to this mystique.

[167] L. Finkelstein, *Israel: Its Role in Civilization*, ed. Moshe Davis, New York, 1956, p. 16, on "Israel as a Spiritual Force." In the same volume, R. T. Handy points to the significance of the motif of "Zion" in American history. See also his article "Studies in the Inter-relationships between America and the Holy Land," *Journal of Church and State*, Vol. 13, No. 2, Spring, 1971, pp. 284–301. The quotation from Finkelstein I owe to a former student at Fordham University, Father Huckle.

PART II

THE LAND IN THE
NEW TESTAMENT

"...those holy fields
Over whose acres walk'd those blessed feet
Which fourteen hundred years ago were nail'd
For our advantage on the bitter cross."
                    Shakespeare, *Henry the Fourth, Part I.*

"Counsel the brethren to be absent from the body to go to our Lord
rather than to be absent from Cappadocia to go to Palestine."
                    Gregory of Nyssa (A.D. 335–394).

VI. INTRODUCTORY

How did early Christians come to terms with the convictions and expectations about the land of Israel which we have sought to assess in the preceding pages? Christianity arose in that land at a time when, in varying degrees of emotional intensity and geographic distribution, these were the constant concern, if not preoccupation, of many Jews, inside the land especially, and also outside it. The tensions of the decades before the fall of Jerusalem in A.D. 70 made this inevitable. The earliest Christians, Jews convinced that the "end of the ages" had come upon them and that the promises of God were being fulfilled, could not have escaped the convictions and expectations to which we refer. They met them, not only in highly charged actions and words of their fellow Jews, but also in their own breasts and minds, because these convictions and expectations were rooted in and evoked by the agelong yearnings of the Jewish people. Did early Christians simply ignore or suppress or reject these? Did they confront them deliberately, to sublimate or transcend them? Or did they at times succumb to them? Such questions can only be answered by looking afresh at the documents of the New Testament from an unusual point of view.

Here it is imperative to recall what we wrote in the introductory pages of this volume. Christians have usually understood Judaism in too theological and, therefore, too intellectual terms. And they have also usually looked at their own foundation document, the New Testament, in the same way. In their proper concern to unravel theological developments and subtleties in primitive Christianity, they have neglected to search for evidences of an encounter between it and the *realia* of Judaism and for any possible resolutions of such an encounter.[1] In particular, they have failed to inquire after the place of the land in the thought and lives of early Christians. Marshall McLuhan has stated recently that: "Thingness is a scandal to conceptualists."[2] For many Jews part of the "thingness" of

---

[1] This is why it is that only recently has the full significance of the festivals of Judaism for the understanding of some of the New Testament documents been recognized, for example, in the Fourth Gospel. Concentration on doctrine has often been accompanied by a neglect not only of the festivals, but of the pilgrimages, the liturgy, as well as the land, that is, of *realia* in Judaism.

[2] Cited by J. S. Whale, *Christian Reunion: Historic Divisions Reconsidered*, Grand Rapids, Mich., 1971, p. 59. Whale's comment on that of McLuhan's is: "It illustrates his antithesis of 'percept' and 'concept': religion dies when the former is made to yield to the latter; that is, when theology takes over from revelation. Here McLuhan is in line with Kierkegaard and Luther."

Judaism was and is the land. It is not surprising, however, that Christian scholars and theologians, who are perhaps by nature and certainly by tradition conceptualists, have not so much failed to do justice to this "thingness" as ignored it. In the following chapters we shall concentrate on one aspect of this "thingness" of Judaism, the land, as it emerges in the major documents of the New Testament—beginning with the Pauline Epistles, as the earliest, and working through to the Fourth Gospel, and then attempting to relate our findings, however tentatively, to Jesus of Nazareth himself.

Unfortunately, not only because of limitations of space, but also because it has been more frequently dealt with so that the literature upon it is vast—a significant fact because it offers an escape from "thingness"—there is one extremely important aspect of our theme which, in this volume, we must pass by in order to concentrate on less scrutinized aspects. We refer to the transference of Christian hope from the earthly Jerusalem, the quintessence of the land in Judaism, to the heavenly.[3] This transference we can only refer to programmatically here, in the hope that we may deal with it elsewhere. With this limitation of our task we turn to the Epistles of Paul.

[3] The question has been dealt with exhaustively elsewhere and we are, therefore, the less uneasy about postponing any discussion of it here, and the more justified in merely pointing out—programmatically—the areas that would demand investigation. There are passages in the New Testament where "Jerusalem" signifies not an earthly city but a heavenly, and becomes a symbol of the final or ultimate community where God dwells with his own. Only the briefest notice of these passages is possible here.

The symbolism appears in Hebrews at 12: 18–24. Here the earthly Mt. Zion—traditionally the hill of Moriah where Abraham sacrificed Isaac, where David was victorious over the Jebusites, where Solomon's temple, the second Temple, and Herod's temple were sited—becomes a symbol of the society of the New Covenant, the sphere of the spiritual fulfilment of the eschatological hope, the city of the living God, whence he exercises his rule. It is because God has his seat there that Zion is the city with foundations. But God's habitat is not on earth: he is in heaven, and Zion, therefore, must be a heavenly reality. It is not so clearly implied as in Galatians that the Church is part of the heavenly Zion. Rather Christians "stand before" or have drawn near to the heavenly city. Compare chapters 3–4 where the rest of God, not achieved for Jews through the conquest of the land by Joshua, still remains a possibility for Christians. In fact, for the author of Hebrews it was to this heavenly city that even the heroes of faith in the Old Testament had looked (11: 13–16). Christians similarly have no permanent home on earth but are seekers for a city to come (13–14), a city that cannot be touched, eternal in the heavens.

And there remains further the last book of the New Testament, where the new Jerusalem plays a climactic role. We cannot here assess the extent to which Revelation, like Paul, thinks of Christians as already participating in the heavenly Jerusalem or to what degree that heavenly city is constituted by the Church. It is, however, difficult not to ascribe to it a transcendental dimension. It comes down. Yes. But it is *from heaven* that it comes and that to a *new* earth. Surely the earthly Jerusalem has here lent its name to a spiritual, transcendental reality.

I have found the following works most pertinent:

The commentaries by R. H. Charles (ICC, 1920), E. Lohmeyer (Tübingen, 1926),

W. Bousset (Göttingen, 1906), E. Lohse (NTD, 1960), Th. Zahn (Leipzig, 1926), A. Farrer (Oxford, 1964), E. F. Scott (London, 1939), G. B. Caird (London, 1966), SB, *ad locum*; C. Brütsch (*La clarté de l'Apocalypse*, 5th ed., Genève, 1966), and on Galatians by Schlier. Also J. Comblin, "La Liturgie de la Nouvelle Jérusalem," ETL, 1953, Vol. 29, pp. 15–40. *Le Christ dans l'Apocalypse*, Paris, 1965. A. Causse, "Le mythe de la nouvelle Jérusalem, du Deutéro-Esaie a la IIIe Sibylle," RHPR, 1938, Vol. 18, pp. 377–414. K. L. Schmidt, "Jerusalem als Urbild und Abbild," *Eranos-Jahrbuch*, 1950, Vol. 18, pp. 207–248. R. Poelman, "Jérusalem d'en haut," *Vie Spirituelle*, 1963, Vol. 108, pp. 637–659. R. Halver, *Der Mythos im letzten Buch der Bibel*, Hamburg, 1964. M. Rissi, *Time and History: A study on the Revelation*, Richmond, 1966. H. Bietenhard, *Die himmlische Welt im Urchristentum und Spätjudentum*, Tübingen, 1951. R. Poelman's work is popular; A. Causse has a lengthy presentation of Jerusalem's place in the history of the Ancient Near East, of its importance as a centre of pilgrimage, and of the hope in the Exile of a renewed (earthly) Jerusalem. K. L. Schmidt's work is more important: he emphasizes that the theme of a future city is more frequent in the New Testament than is usually assumed. See Phil. 1: 27 (*politeuesthe*); Eph. 2: 12 (*politeia*); and Eph. 2: 19 (*sympolitai*) ("Jerusalem," p. 211), in addition to the first and clearest passage in Gal. 4: 26 (p. 212). Schmidt discusses whether the heavenly city is to be understood against an apocalyptic or Platonic background and favours the former, because the Platonic idea is connected with the image of the Greek city not with the name Jerusalem, which is important in its Greek form in Philo and Origen, but not in the NT (pp. 213ff). What is important in Galatians is not the name, but the contrast between an earthly and heavenly expression of the city (p. 217). In Christ the Kingdom of the upper, future Jerusalem has already come into the present lower world (p. 220). Jewish texts frequently refer to the Heavenly Jerusalem but they all derive, according to Schmidt, from Is. 54: 10–13; 60–62 (in Is. 60: 1 Jerusalem is expressly mentioned in the LXX); Ezek. 40ff, Zech. 1; 2: 1; 8: 3; 9–14 (p. 222f).

J. Comblin's essay in ETL is very valuable for the distinction to be made between the heavenly Jerusalem in Christianity and Judaism, and should be read in connection with pp. 148 above. Extremely valuable is H. Bietenhard, *Die himmlische Welt*, pp. 192–204 both for its treatment of Judaism and of Gal. 4: 26 and Rev. 21. For him, what we find in Gal. 4: 26 is the conviction that the heavenly Jerusalem is not a transcendent reality but a future one which already exists (pp. 198–201). Invaluable is his discussion of the idea of the new Jerusalem in Revelation. The idea of a new Jerusalem without a Temple is impossible in Judaism. The New Testament separates itself from the earthly Jerusalem. Contrast Comblin and Bietenhard. M. Rissi, *Time and History*, builds on the ideas already noted. Very rich is G. B. Caird's commentary. "The whole point of the descent of [the city] is that now God's dwelling is with men... (p. 263)." The heavenly Jerusalem is, therefore, a present reality, of pastoral relevance to the needs of the seven churches. In the phrase "I am making all things new" he finds "the process of recreation by which the old is transformed into the new p. 265)." This approach agrees with Caird's general understanding of eschatology, see pp. 206 below.

See, for further bibliographical details, a forthcoming volume by R. Hamerton-Kelly on *The Idea of Preexistence...* on Gal. 4: 26. He favours an apocalyptic background: only in Jewish apocalyptic, he asserts, is the heavenly city called "our mother": 1 Bar. 3: 1ff; 4 Ezra 10: 6. Valuable also is the more conservative work of J. C. De Young, *Jerusalem in the New Testament: The Significance of the City in the History of Redemption and in Eschatology*, J. H. Kok, N. V. Kampen, 1960.

VII. THE LAND IN THE PAULINE EPISTLES

The earliest extant documents produced by primitive Christianity are the work of Paul. Opinions differ as to which of those usually designated as his epistles are to be attributed to the Apostle himself. Galatians, 1 and 2 Corinthians, Philippians, Philemon, 1 Thessalonians, and Romans are almost universally taken to be genuinely Pauline. But strong doubt has been expressed, especially, about Ephesians and about Colossians and 2 Thessalonians. Hebrews, 1 and 2 Timothy, and Titus—apart from minor fragments of these last three—are widely and rightly regarded as non-Pauline. In addition, the value of Acts as a guide to Paul's life and thought has been radically challenged. In this chapter we need not examine the problems raised by the question of the authenticity of the various epistles, but wherever necessary we shall indicate our judgment upon them. Suffice that we accept those epistles as authentic which are generally so regarded, and still consider the authorship of 2 Thessalonians, Colossians and, to a lesser degree, Ephesians an open question. Colossians and Ephesians, even if non-Pauline, are within the ambience of Paulinism. Acts we shall use with a respectful reserve.

What makes the works of Paul so important for our purpose is not only that they are early, but that their author, before he joined the Christian community, was a Jew. True, he was born in Tarsus, the Hellenistic capital of the province of Cilicia, a busy commercial and cultural centre. True, his writings reveal Hellenistic influences in their terminology, form, and content and a mastery of Greek which makes them literary classics.[1] But, whether he had spent a long or a short time in Tarsus or had been taken very early as a child to Jerusalem,[2] he had joined the Pharisees. He recalls to his Galatian converts his pre-Christian zeal for Judaism: "how in the practice of our national religion I was outstripping many of my Jewish contemporaries in my boundless devotion to the traditions of my ancestors (Gal. 1: 14, NEB)." Long after his conversion his pride in his own people lurks ever ready to spring forth, as in Phil. 3: 4–5: "If any other man thinks he has reason for confidence in the flesh, I have more:

[1] See the quotation from Wilamowitz-Moellendorf in G. Bornkamm, *Paul*, trans., New York, 1971, p. 9.

[2] See W. C. van Unnik, *Tarsus or Jerusalem*, trans., London, 1952; G. Ogg, *Scottish Journal of Theology*, Vol. 8, 1955, pp. 94ff. Gal. 1: 21 may be taken to be against van Unnik's view that although born in Tarsus, Paul was not perhaps brought up there, but may have left Tarsus at a very early date and spent his youth entirely in Jerusalem. On this view it is hardly credible that he could be unknown by sight to the churches of Judaea.

circumcised on the eighth day, of the people of Israel, of the tribe of Benjamin, a Hebrew born of Hebrews; as to the law a Pharisee. ..." In self-defence against opponents who boasted of their Jewish privileges he wrote: "Are they Hebrews? So am I. Are they Israelites? So am I. Are they descendants of Abraham? So am I (2 Cor. 11: 22)."[3] The same pride breaks forth in Rom. 11: 1–2. "I ask, then, has God rejected his people? By no means! I myself am an Israelite, a descendant of Abraham, a member of the tribe of Benjamin. God has not rejected his people whom he foreknew." Paul belongs to the Jewish people; in Rom. 9: 4 he speaks of them as his flesh: he and they are one body. The use of the names "Hebrew," "Israelite," and "Abraham" in Rom. 11: 1f and Phil. 3: 5 points not only to his ethnic but to his religious pride in his Jewishness. Despite the widespread anti-Judaism that existed, the terms "Hebrew" and "Israelite" were honoured in Paul's day. They had not then acquired those undertones of hostility and contempt with which, alas, history has often invested them. The far-flung success of the Jewish mission in the Dispersion is evidence enough of the respect which Jews could evoke in the first century.[4] Paul, who was educated in Jerusalem, probably at the feet of Gamaliel,[5] at every point strikes us as the kind of Jew who, rejecting the lax conformity of so many in the Dispersion and the lofty coldness of the established traditional priesthood, shared in the dedicated enthusiasm of the Pharisees. And this enthusiasm, which after A.D. 70 became more reserved in its attitude towards Messianic speculation and eschatological dreams, before that date certainly shared in and cherished the apocalyptic hopes of the Jewish people.[6]

[3] On these titles, see D. Georgi, *Die Gegner des Paulus im 2 Korintherbrief*, Neukirchener Verlag, 1964, pp. 51–60. "*Hebraios*" (Hebrew), he thinks, emphasizes the authority and distinctiveness and superiority of the Jewish tradition, not necessarily Palestinian origin. "Hebrew" refers to the outward distinctiveness of the Jew; but "Israelite" to the content of the Jews' faith. The point for us is that both terms emphasize "Jewishness" with pride in some form or another.

[4] Compare Bornkamm, *Paul*, p. 4; see my work "The Jewish State in the Hellenistic World," *Peake*, pp. 686ff.

[5] Much scepticism has been applied to Paul's education under Gamaliel. See, for example, John Knox, *Chapters in a Life of Paul*, Nashville, 1950, pp. 34f; Bornkamm, *Paul*, p. 11. But T. R. Glover, *Paul of Tarsus*, New York, 1925, p. 57, may well have long ago been right that Paul was hardly likely to have remained on good terms with such a "judicious" person as Gamaliel I, hence his silence about him. But is it credible that many of the Christians for whom Luke was writing would have heard of Gamaliel? What reason could there be for introducing him? See D. Daube, "Dissent in Bible and Talmud," in *California Law Review*, Vol. 59, No. 3, May 1971, pp. 784–794, who shows how Gamaliel's attitude is understandable at the advent of a Messianic movement, and natural within the Jewish expectation. The Sabbatian movement confirms Daube's point that Jews would expect not to be sure when a genuine Messiah had appeared and would caution against a too hasty confirmation or rejection of a Messiah. [6] See above, pp. 49ff.

All this is repeated here to make it clear that such a Jew as Paul, we can be sure, would have *felt* the full force of the doctrine of the land, Jerusalem, and the Temple which we have traced above. His epistles might be expected to reveal how he came to terms with it. The measure of the seriousness with which he regarded the doctrine may well be safely taken as a fair indication of the reaction of Christians to it, because few would be likely to deal with it more empathatically, even passionately, than he. Paul was nothing if not passionate.

1. THE ABSENCE OF EXPRESS REFERENCES TO THE LAND

At first, one might conclude that Paul was not concerned with the land at all. In his presentation of the content of his message, which he shared with other Christians, in 1 Cor. 15: 3–8, we read:

For I delivered to you as of first importance what I also received, that Christ died for our sins in accordance with the scriptures, that he was buried, that he was raised on the third day in accordance with the scriptures, and that he appeared to Cephas, then to the twelve. Then he appeared to more than five hundred brethren at one time, most of whom are still alive, though some have fallen asleep. Then he appeared to James, then to all the apostles. Last of all, as to one untimely born, he appeared also to me.

In this central recital there is no interest at all in geography. Paul is unconcerned with the location of the various appearances of the Risen Lord.[7] They were a series of occurrences, unique in character, unrepeatable, and confined to a limited period, but not geographically located. No mention is made of Galilee, Jerusalem or, in the case of Paul himself, of Damascus.

The omission of the latter location might be taken to be especially significant. The prominence ascribed in Acts to the so-called "conversion" of Paul on the road to Damascus may have given to that event a disproportionate prominence in interpretations of Pauline theology.[8] But of its significance there can be no question. Even though Paul himself does not explicitly locate his conversion, it is clear from Gal. 1: 17 that that location was clearly fixed in his memory. But he does not find it necessary to pin it down geographically. It might be argued that, since in Judaism the activity of the Holy Spirit was often deemed to be confined to the land,[9] it was of theological significance to Luke that Paul should have seen

---

[7] This means that the earliest evidence reveals no influence of locality on the presentation of the resurrection.

[8] Bornkamm, *Paul*, pp. 13–25, especially pp. 24f.

[9] See H. Parzen, JQR, Old Series, Vol. xx, pp. 51ff on "The Ruaḥ Haḳodesh in Rabbinical Literature"; L. Finkelstein, *New Light from the Prophets*, London, 1969, pp. 26ff.

the Risen Lord outside the land in Damascus, a "haven of heretics," and there received the Spirit (Acts 9: 17). If so, Paul himself did not think in the same way. The question whether the Lord had appeared to him within or outside the land did not, apparently, occur to him, or was brushed aside as insignificant. The resurrection had nothing to do with locality as such. Paul either knew nothing of or else ignored any distinction between a Galilean and Jerusalemite emphasis in accounts of the Resurrection.

Similarly, in his list of the advantages enjoyed by the people of Israel in Rom. 9: 4, the Apostle does not mention the land as one of these. The verse reads: "They are Israelites: they were made God's sons; theirs is the splendour of the divine presence, theirs the covenants, the law, the temple worship, and the promises (NEB)." True, Paul refers here to the promises (*epangeliai*) but he does not define them. The noun "promise" and its cognate verb do occur in the Septuagint, but not in the technical sense of the great promises made by God to Israel.[10] A passage from the Pss. Sol. 12: 8, is illuminating:

And the sinners shall perish together from before the face of the Lord: and the saints of the Lord shall inherit the promises of the Lord.

These words express the wistful expectation of Jews in the first century B.C. The term "promises" in Rom. 9: 4 is best understood as summarizing messianic predictions of various kinds. T. W. Manson[11] comments on the term as follows: "The 'promises' express God's good purposes for Israel. They spring from great men; and from them is sprung one who is greater than all men, God's Anointed." These promises included the items mentioned in Rom. 9: 4 and would doubtless refer also to the land. It may also be, as has been suggested, that the reference to "Christ after the flesh" implies a side glance at the land, as implied in the Davidic Messiahship. But this is very tenuous. It is surely noteworthy that the land itself is not singled out for special mention. Some scribes may have felt this gap when they changed the plural to the singular "promise":[12] certainly the singular "promise" would make the

[10] A glance at Hatch and Redpath, *A Concordance to the Septuagint*, reveals how very infrequently ἐπαγγελία (promise) and its verbal form occur: ἐπαγγελία occurs six times in the Old Testament and Apocrypha and ἐπαγγέλλειν eleven times. Even in these few instances there are ambiguities as to the meaning, see SB, Vol. III, pp. 206–208.

[11] T. W. Manson, *Peake*, p. 947. So C. K. Barrett, *A Commentary on the Epistle to the Romans*, New York, 1957, p. 178.

[12] The singular is read in P46 D E F Boh. (Compare the change of διαθήκη in P46 B D F G.) The change to the singular is more likely than the reverse. The Rabbinic equivalent of ἐπαγγελία is הַבְטָחָה which suggests that it is the certainty and reliability of the promise that is its foremost characteristic. SB, Vol. III, pp. 206–208. See above p. 38, n. 4.

reference to the land more clear. As the text originally stood, however, it contained no explicit reference to the promise to Abraham as such. That no side glance to the land is present is made certain from other passages.

2. ABRAHAM AND THE PROMISE

Elsewhere Paul deals explicitly with the promise to Abraham. But how? The Apostle certainly shared in the deep veneration of the Jewish people for Abraham (Gal. 3; 4: 2; 2 Cor. 9: 22; Rom. 4; 9: 7; 11: 28). However, apart from 2 Cor. 9: 22, which largely corresponds in sentiment with Rom. 9: 1, it is only in Romans and Galatians that the Patriarch appears. At first sight, this is surprising. But apart from Romans, which in this regard is betwixt and between, and Ephesians, which many have regarded as non-Pauline partly for the very reason that it is addressed to everybody in general and to nobody in particular, the Pauline epistles are directed to concrete situations and are strictly occasional. It is, therefore, understandable that only in the two epistles where he confronts the question of the terms of salvation or of inclusion in the people of God truly descended from Abraham, a question raised by his Jewish and Jewish-Christian opponents especially, but also by Gentile Christians, does the foundation figure of Judaism directly engage Paul.

In Galatians and Romans the Apostle faces those Christians who claimed that physical descent from Abraham, or physical incorporation into the children of Abraham through circumcision (even though for Judaism such incorporation still preserved the distinction between those born Jews and those converted to become Jews),[13] and the observance of

---

[13] See SB, Vol. I, p. 119. Participation in the merit of Abraham was conditioned by birth: even proselytes were wanting at this point. M. Bikkurim 1: 4, 5:

These [the Men of Mount Zeboim] may bring the First-fruits but they may not make the Avowal [Deut. 26: 5ff]: the proselyte may bring them but he may not make the Avowal since he cannot say, *Which the Lord sware unto our Fathers for to give us.*[a] But if his mother was an Israelite he may bring them and make the Avowal. And when he prays in private he should say, "O God of the fathers of Israel"; and when he is in the synagogue he should say, "O God of your fathers." But if his mother was an Israelite he may say, "O God of our fathers."

R. Eliezer b. Jacob [A.D. 80–120 or A.D. 140–165?] says: A woman that is the offspring of proselytes may not marry into the priestly stock unless her mother was an Israelite; it is all one whether [she is the offspring of] proselytes or freed slaves, even to the tenth generation: [her like may not marry into the priestly stock] unless their mother was an Israelite.[b]

a. Deut. 26: 3.   b. Compare Kidd. 4: 7. According to Num. R. viii (which is difficult to date) (Soncino trans. p. 232), the proselyte must achieve his own merit. The proselyte "should not say, 'Woe is me, for I have no distinguished ancestry to rely on [for a share in the World to Come]! All the good deeds that I shall store up will only yield me reward in this world.' Scripture announces to the proselyte that by virtue of his own merit he will enjoy the fruit of his actions both in this world and in the next. . . .." Not all shared this

the commandments of the Law were necessary for justification before God and, therefore, to salvation. The intensity of their claim can be gauged in the light of such a passage as Pss. Sol. 9: 17.

For thou hast chosen the seed of Abraham rather than all the Gentiles.

With this may be compared 18: 4.

Thy judgements are upon all the earth in mercy: and thy love is upon the seed of Israel, the son of Abraham. (Thy chastisement is) upon us as upon an only first-born son: to turn away the soul...which is not instructed...(May God purify) Israel for the day in blessing for His mercy....

In such passages national and religious fervour blend. Rabbinic sayings pointing to Abrahamic descent as a condition of salvation are numerous. Abraham was pre-eminently the "father" of Jews.[14] That fatherhood, in the minds of many, in itself conferred salvation. The saying in Mishnah Sanhedrin 11: 1, although not universally received, probably expressed the view of the majority of religious Jews:

All Israelites have a share in the world to come, for it is written, "*Thy people also shall be all righteous, they shall inherit the land for ever; the branch of my planting, the work of my hands, that I may be glorified.*"[15]

The New Testament itself bears witness to this belief and to its vitality in the first century. Consider the following passages from Matt. 3: 7–10 (with its parallel in Luke 3: 7–9) and compare John 8: 1–40. Matt. 3: 7–10 reads:

But when he saw many of the Pharisees and Sadducees coming for baptism, he said to them, "You brood of vipers! Who warned you to flee from the wrath to come? Bear fruit that befits repentance, and do not presume to say to yourselves, 'We have Abraham as our father'; for I tell you, God is able from these stones to raise up children to Abraham. Even now the axe is laid to the root of the trees; every tree therefore that does not bear good fruit is cut down and thrown into the fire."

These verses are from Q: the thought in them had, almost certainly, engaged the Baptist and Jesus. They both asked the question, which

---

attitude, see SB, Vol. I, p. 119. There was also the recognition of the reliance on the Merit of the Fathers, see PRJ, pp. 268ff. The Adiabenes, a royal family converted, are called by a higher name than proselytes, that is, by *homophuloi* (Jos. *Jewish Wars*, 11. 16. 4).

14 SB, Vol. I, p. 116.

15 This is 10: 1 in the Jerusalem Talmud. My insistence there that the words are not a "dogmatic" statement is confirmed by I. Epstein in the Soncino translation p. 601, n. 2. The text reads:

כָּל־יִשְׂרָאֵל יֵשׁ לָהֶם חֵלֶק לְעוֹלָם הַבָּא...

The term "all Israel" includes even those condemned to death by the *bêth din*.

occupied the early Church from the first: "Who are the true sons of Abraham?" And as Gentiles were increasingly admitted into the Church it became acute. It was this question, among others, that came to a head in the epistles to the Galatians and the Romans. For the sake of clarity, we summarize the ramifications of the question in terms of two groups.

First, there were those Gentile Christians who could not claim physical descent from Abraham, because they had neither been circumcised nor observed the Law. How could they claim Abraham as their father, that is, belong to the people of God? How could such as they possibly partake in the heritage promised to Abraham? At this point, apart from the endemic pride of such men as Paul in their Jewish "national" descent, it is essential to recognize one thing, that is, the envy which the ancient lineage of Israel could inspire among Gentiles. In the rootless, Hellenistic world of the first century pride in pedigree was cherished: the desire to share in the Jewish genealogical tree understandable.[16] Moreover, the prominence of the people of Israel in the Septuagint and the recognition of their significance by Christian leaders, as those who had cradled the Gospel, would further inspire Gentile Christians with eagerness to ensure their incorporation into the people of Abraham.[17] This eagerness Paul could well understand.

And, secondly, there were those Jews, physically descended from Abraham, who had accepted Christ as the ground of their salvation. Were they still to be considered the children of Abraham? Had they, thereby, that is, by their acceptance of Christ, forfeited their claim to be such? Was to be "in Christ" to give up being "in Israel"? What, in short, was the decisive criterion for membership in the chosen people? This question drove Paul to the heart of the relationship between the Gospel and Judaism. If such membership was now rooted in the response to the Gospel or incorporation "in Christ," what was the relationship of the community formed through such a response to the Israel that claimed physical descent from Abraham?

It was with these questions, then—raised by Gentile and Jewish Christians—that Paul wrestled in Galatians and Romans. They explain the desperate seriousness and tortured passion with which he discussed

[16] See my "Reflexions on Tradition: The Aboth Revisited," in the *Festschrift for John Knox*, Cambridge, 1967, pp. 140ff for bibliography and evidence.

[17] See J. Munck, *Paulus und die Heilsgeschichte*, Aarhus, 1954, trans., 1959. H. J. Cadbury, "Overconversion in Paul's Churches," in *The Joy of Study*, ed. S. E. Johnson, London, 1965, pp. 43ff; my review of Munck, in *Christian Origins and Judaism*, Philadelphia, 1962, pp. 179ff.

matters which can superficially be regarded as trifling. To the unsympathetic mind, the observance of the Law, centring in the minutiae of dietary laws and table-fellowship, could not but appear, at worst, antiquated superstition and, at best, annoying, and antisocial priggishness: circumcision to such a mind could only suggest a barbaric survival. But often in history, as, for example, in the Puritan controversy over vestments, great issues have been fought in terms of trivia. So in the early Church, battles for principles often centred around apparent peccadilloes. Throughout his treatment of circumcision and the Law, remote and pettifogging as they may seem, Paul was concerned with a central question: the nature or constitution of the people of God—its continuity and discontinuity with the Jewish people of history. And so he had to come to terms with the father of that people. He had to do so in the last resort simply because he himself was a "Hebrew of the Hebrews" whose whole nature and training compelled him to take seriously the Scriptures and the people of the Scriptures, for whom the conduct of the Patriarch was of fundamental significance. This is another way of saying that the questions raised by Jewish and Gentile Christians were those that Paul himself faced as a Jew: they were not intellectual conundrums posed to him by others but—to use current language—existential questions for the Apostle himself, whose solution for him, as for his opponents, had to lie in the Old Testament: he confronted those opponents not only in the churches but in his own breast.

Like Marcion later, who claimed to understand Paul only to misunderstand him, the Apostle might have answered the questions with clean simplicity. He could have cut the Gordian knot by declaring that a New Israel had emerged to replace the Old. But he resisted this solution, if it ever presented itself to him, which is unlikely. Paul abjured the phrase "The Old Israel" to describe the Jewish people.[18] Instead he took seriously his own principle or assumption of the givenness of the authority of the Scriptures as the revealed will of God, and sought by an examination of them, employing Rabbinical and other methods, to do justice

---

[18] See Peter Richardson, *Israel in the Apostolic Church*, Cambridge, 1969, who emphasizes that for religious and sociological reasons, the name "Israel" is not applied to the Church before Justin Martyr's *Dialogue with Trypho*, about A.D. 160. Justin Martyr's *Dialogue*, 140: 1; 142: 3, implies a much closer relationship between Jews and Christians right up to the middle of the second century A.D. than has been commonly accepted (Richardson, *Israel*, p. 12). It may be objected that the fact, if not the name, of the New Israel is present in the New Testament, where the ecclesia is the $q^e hal\ Yahweh$ in a new phase of its existence: and that Gal. 6: 16 includes Christians is hard to refute. But Richardson has effectively pointed to the ambiguity of the evidence.

both to the new emergence, the Church, and to its matrix, the Jewish people. He could do no other without betraying his roots. And so he came to terms with Abraham. He did so with penetration, even though, as we shall see, without falling into an insidious simplicity, as did Marcion, nor allowing the clarity of his logic unfettered sway.

How does Paul deal with Abraham? He concentrates with directness on one thing, that is, on the Patriarch's role in history as the one who had received the divine promise, had responded to it by faith, and had thereby been justified and become the father of many nations. The justification of Abraham was the result of God's grace and free election and, of the believing appropriation of this grace by faith and obedience. But what exactly was this faith of Abraham's? Various answers were given to this question in the early Church. The author of the Epistle to the Hebrews turned to Gen. 12 (Abraham's "obedience" to his call) and Gen. 22 (the offering of Isaac) for the understanding of it as the virtue of utter (blind) faithfulness, even to the point of the sacrifice of an only son (Heb. 11: 8, 17). The author of the Epistle of James—possibly, in reaction against Paul—resting on Gen. 15: 6 (emphasizing faith) and Gen. 22 (the offering of Isaac) respectively, combined faith with works in his under-standing of the Patriarch and concluded that "man is justified by works and not by faith alone (Jas. 2: 24)." Paul goes on his own more radical way. Unlike Hebrews and James, he makes no appeal to Gen. 12 and 22, but concentrates on one text only, Gen. 15: 6 ("And he believed the Lord; and he reckoned it to him as righteousness"). This verse could be and was interpreted, as we have seen, in terms of "faithfulness." But by employing a rabbinical, technical, exegetical device called the ge$z$erah shawa, which connects passages employing the same terms for the purposes of inter-pretation, Paul has recourse to Ps. 32: 1f to illumine Gen. 15: 6, because the term "reckon" occurs in both. Since in Ps. 32: 1f, that is, 31: 1, 2, in the Septuagint, which Paul follows, the verb "to reckon" connotes that God refrains from attributing a man's sin against him, Paul employs it to justify finding the same meaning for it in Gen. 15: 6. The two passages read in the Septuagint:

And he (Abraham) believed in the Lord; and he [God] *reckoned* it to him as righteousness (καὶ ἐπίστευσεν Ἀβραμ τῷ θεῷ, καὶ ἐλογίσθη αὐτῷ εἰς δικαιοσύνην) [Note the use of the passive verb for the activity of God.] (Gen. 15: 6).

Blessed are those whose transgressions are forgiven, and whose sins are covered. Blessed is the man to whom the Lord will not *reckon* sin and in whose mouth there is not guile (Μακάριοι ὧν ἀφέθησαν αἱ ἀνομίαι, καί, ὧν ἐπεκαλύφθησαν αἱ ἁμαρτίαι. Μακάριος ἀνὴρ ᾧ οὐ μὴ λογίσηται Κύριος ἁμαρτίαν, οὐδέ ἐστιν ἐν τῷ στόματι αὐτοῦ δόλος) (Ps. 32: 1, 2) $\overline{(LXX\ 31: 1, 2)}$ (our italics and translation).

The justification of Abraham is apart from any achieved righteousness and denotes his free acceptance by God on the basis of his faith. This faith is expounded by Paul particularly in Rom. 3: 21–4: 25,[19] where it is set over against works, and illustrated from Abraham's relations with his wife Sarah. The God in whom Abraham believed "gives life from the dead and calls into existence the things that do not exist (4: 17)," and so he

[19] The passage is dealt with by E. Käsemann, *Perspectives on Paul*, trans., London, 1971, pp. 79–101. (He rightly dismisses G. Klein, "Römer 4 und die Idee der Heilsgeschichte," *Rekonstruktion und Interpretation*, 1969, pp. 145–179, who regards the history of Israel as "radically profaned and paganized [p. 148]," in an essay on "The Faith of Abraham in Romans 4.") He identifies the faith of Abraham in the promise with the faith of Christians in the Resurrection, because both imply creation out of nothing. This, in turn, makes it possible to identify both faiths with belief in the justification of sinners, that is, those who are and have nothing. Paul deliberately by-passes Moses to go back to Abraham, the prototype, not of Christ, but of Christian faith, and finds the continuity between the Gospel and Judaism, at least primarily, not in a historical sequence of a salvation-history but in the promise (not the Law). The promise does not find its fulfilment in Christ (the notion of "promise and fulfilment" was born of the idea of development and must here be abandoned). Rather, to quote Käsemann's own words, "the promise, according to Gal. 3: 8 for example, is to be understood as the anticipation or complement of the gospel, is substantially identical with it, and is termed only another aspect of the revelation in the Word. It is the gospel pre-given in salvation-history, its historical concealment, whereas the gospel itself is the promise eschatologically revealed and open to the day. The gospel replaces the law but not the promise; indeed it has itself the character of promise...expectation of final redemption. The co-ordination of promise and gospel brings out the fact that eschatological happening breaks into real history thus designating the latter as the sphere in which the divine creativity and providence have always ruled.... The promise entered history by concealing itself in the Scriptures. The gospel, with its universal proclamation and revelation of the depths of history, liberated the promise from its concealment (p. 90)." Continuity in history, salvation-history, and ecclesiology are secondary for Paul to the call of the Word, the confrontation with the Lord who justifies the ungodly (pp. 93, 101).

If we have understood Käsemann aright, we are puzzled at certain points. 1. Can we identify belief in a promise for what has not happened (Abraham) with one in an "event" which has at least incipiently happened, the Resurrection, (Paul)? 2. How can we reconcile the sharp distinction between promise and Law in the light of Rom. 3: 21 without careful definition of Law: the promise is part of the Law for Paul? 3. Can the radical dismissal of "fulfilment" be accepted if Rom. 9–11 be taken seriously? Käsemann himself, in dealing with the catchword "heir of all things" recognizes that, by the nations referred to in Gen. 17: 5, Paul understands the Gentiles who have become Christians. He writes that "the promise to Israel, which is valid and has been fulfilled through the Jewish Christians is not abrogated," and goes on to emphasize that "the stress lies unmistakeably on the point that the promise bursts apart this circle of receivers (p. 89)." But, we ask, is not this in itself a fulfilment? Has Käsemann, in his concentration on Rom. 4, which is concerned with the condition on which Jews and Gentiles are to be redeemed, that is, with justification by faith, neglected too much Rom. 9–11 which is more directly concerned with the problem of continuity? For our purpose we emphasize that whether Paul thinks in terms of promise and fulfilment or, as Käsemann urges, in terms of the explication of the meaning of the promise or of its "liberation from its concealment (p. 90)," the content of the promise is for him deterritorialized and acquires "universal dimensions (p. 89)."

trusted in God's promise that he should be "the father of many nations" when this seemed—because of his and Sarah's age—impossible.[20] As Paul expresses it:

In hope he believed against hope, that he should become the father of many nations; as he had been told, "So shall your descendants be." He did not weaken in faith when he considered his own body, which was as good as dead because he was about a hundred years old, or when he considered the barrenness of Sarah's womb. No distrust made him waver concerning the promise of God, but he grew strong in his faith as he gave glory to God, fully convinced that God was able to do what he had promised. That is why his faith was "reckoned to him as righteousness."

Perhaps we may express Paul's thought as follows. Man may approach life and its many demands in the belief that he himself in his own strength can meet these demands and fulfill them: he can, in short, work out his own salvation: he can stand four-square to all the winds that blow, and by his own achievement prevail. To live in this belief is to court self-righteousness, pride, and, at the last, despair. This is true of all men; it is true particularly of the religious man who counts on his own obedience to the Law. On the other hand, man may recognize his own insufficiency to meet the demands of life and particularly the demands set before him in the Law and yet, in the light of the mercy revealed in Jesus Christ, trust life to work in and through him to his good. Faith is trust in life as coming from God, the All-Sufficient, who is also the All-Merciful revealed in Jesus. Faith is self-knowledge and self-abandonment. It is that attitude in which, "acknowledging our complete insufficiency for any of the high ends of life, we rely utterly on the sufficiency of God. It is to cease from all assertion of the self, even by way of effort after righteousness, and to make room for the divine initiative."[21] Paul recognizes in

---

[20] The reference to the ages of Abraham and Sarah as beyond that of normal procreation must not be superstitiously interpreted, as if God "miraculously" caused certain physical changes in Sarah to make possible the birth of Isaac, although such changes are doubtless implied. This would reduce "faith" to credulity. What Paul has in mind is *creatio ex nihilo*—exemplified in the birth of Isaac, as at the Resurrection (see Rom. 4: 24–25). So T. W. Manson, *Peake*, p. 944; Käsemann, *Perspectives on Paul*, p. 92. So, too, Bornkamm, *Paul*, p. 144, insists that Abraham was not "blind to realities and [did not take] refuge in illusions." Sanday and Headlam, ICC, *Romans*, SB, Vol. III, New York, 1911, p. 115, seem to follow the view taken in Num. Rabbah 11: 2 (Soncino trans. pp. 415ff) that the nature of Abraham was renewed by his faith so that he became a new creature. The passage in Num. Rabbah connects the seven benedictions conferred upon Abraham with the seven verses connected with the work of creation. Sanday and Headlam take 'ενεδυναμώθη τῇ πίστει to mean "empowered by faith," that is, recreated by faith not "in respect to faith," and seem to think of a miraculous empowering of Abraham sexually (pp. 112f).

[21] C. H. Dodd, *Romans*, New York, 1932, p. 41.

Abraham's trust in the promise the same quality of faith that he knew for himself. The centre of Abraham's faith was his trust that God "gives life from the dead and calls into existence the things that do not exist (Rom. 4: 17)," and this is also the faith of those who trust in Christ, because they have believed that God raised him from the dead—that is, gave life from the dead and called into existence things that did not exist. In this way Abraham's faith is linked with the faith of Christians in the Resurrection. It was as a man of such a faith that Paul interpreted Abraham, in whose trust in God's promise Paul recognized a faith comparable to his own. But if such a man was the father of the people of God, then certain circumstances followed.

1. *Salvation is apart from circumcision and the Law.* According to the Scriptures, Abraham had been justified, as a matter of history, apart from circumcision and the Law. Both of these were, therefore, unnecessary to justification and salvation. In Rom. 4: 10–12, Paul insists that Abraham received the promise *before* he had been circumcised (Gen. 15: 6), because circumcision was first commanded and practised after the promise had been given (Gen. 17: 9–14; 23–27). In fact, circumcision came to symbolize a status which Abraham had already acquired or been granted through faith. Similarly Abraham had been justified long before the Law had even been given (Gal. 3: 10–24; Rom. 4: 13–15).

2. *Salvation is grounded in the promise and in faith.* Since the fatherhood of Abraham rests on the promise and on faith, these are also the grounds of sonship to Abraham. It is those who share in the Patriarch's faith who inherit the promise and the divine blessing (Gal. 3: 9, 14, 18, 22; Rom. 4: 11–13, 16): Abraham is the father of all—whether circumcised or un-circumcised—who believe in the promise (Rom. 4: 10–12). Conversely, even among the circumcised, that is, Jews, only those who share in Abraham's faith are truly descended from him (Gal. 3: 8, 14). In Gal. 4: 21–31 Paul uses an allegory—that of the two women, Hagar and Sarah, and their offspring—to bring his meaning home. Abraham had two sons; one born after the flesh (that is, by the ordinary processes of nature) to Hagar, his slave; the other born after the promise (that is, by the divine intent and contrary to the natural processes) to Sarah, his wife, who like Abraham himself had become aged. But natural generation signifies not: what matters is that one should be a child of the promise by faith. Such are those who are "in Christ" and they, therefore, are the true inheritors of the promise, the true children of Abraham. Through faith in Christ they share in the faith of the Patriarch himself and thus become

his sons (Gal. 3: 29; 4: 31; compare 4: 7). For Jews and Gentiles, there-fore, faith is the condition of sonship. To Gentile-Christians anxious to acquire status and to be sure that they were engrafted on the family-tree of the ancient people of God, and, therefore, too easily open to the suggestion that circumcision and observance of the Law were desirable as passports to Abrahamic privileges, Paul declares these passports un-necessary: the one, but indispensable, passport is faith. To Jewish-Christians, suffering from pride of pedigree, anxious not to lose their birthright status as sons of Abraham, he gives the assurance that faith in Christ, not physical birth, is the condition of any status that matters. Since the promise finds fulfilment through faith not birth, their faith in Christ assures their sonship.

3. *Salvation is pan-ethnic*. But, thirdly, what is the content of the promise thus fulfilled? Paul understands the promise under a particular aspect. He uncovers his understanding of the content of the promise by appeal to two Old Testament passages, Gen. 12: 3 and 18: 8. The pertinent texts are the following:

Thus Abraham "believed God and it was reckoned to him as righteousness." So you see that it is men of faith who are the sons of Abraham. And the scripture, foreseeing that God would justify the Gentiles by faith, preached the gospel beforehand to Abraham, saying, "In you shall *all the nations* be blessed." So then, those who are men of faith are blessed with Abraham who had faith (Gal. 3: 6–9) (our italics).

That is why it depends on faith, in order that the promise may rest on grace and be guaranteed to all his descendants—not only to the adherents of the law but also to those who share the faith of Abraham, for he is the father of us all, as it is written, "I have made you the father of *many nations*"—in the presence of the God in whom he believed, who gives life to the dead and calls into existence the things that do not exist. In hope he believed against hope, that he should become the father of *many nations*; as he had been told, "So shall your descen-dants be (Rom. 4: 16–18) (our italics)."

Paul discovers in the promise to Abraham a supra-national hope for salvation apart from circumcision and the Law: the promise is pan-ethnic not pan-halakic. It had been initially fulfilled in the miraculous birth of Isaac to Sarah in her old age (Rom. 4: 19ff), and now "in the fullness of time" had brought forth "a seed," Christ, through incorporation in whom, a society, the true people of God, in which there was neither Jew nor Greek, slave nor free, male nor female, had emerged: its members, without distinction, were the heirs of the promise and, like Christ himself and in unity with him, constituted the "seed" of Abraham (Gal. 3: 27–29; Rom. 4: 13–16). There seems no doubt that in Rom. 4: 13–16 Paul takes "the seed" or "offspring" to refer both to Christ himself and then to the Church, including both Jewish and Gentile Christians: it has no territorial boundaries.

We have above cursorily treated Paul's appeal to Abraham—an appeal for him neither mythological nor theological but historical. To grasp its full impact it would be necessary to set it over against the interpretation of Abraham in Judaism.[22] Since this would prolong our discussion inordinately, however, only the special aspect of it that concerns us can be treated.

We saw in the previous chapter that the promise to Abraham in the Old Testament had an unmistakable territorial reference which was variously interpreted at different periods; usually the territorial dimension of the promise was retained even though it was often "eschatologized" or "spiritualized." To this inviolate promise and to this "national," territorial reference within it many Jews came to appeal, especially in times of crisis, as a ground of security. The universal dimension of the promise was often neglected or transformed. Abraham had forsaken the idolatry and astrology of Ur and had, in fact, called himself a proselyte; he was, therefore, preeminently the father of Gentiles.[23] But in Judaism he was regarded as the father of Jews. Even proselytes were not allowed to call Abraham "our father," and in the liturgy of the Synagogue substituted "your father" for "our father" in referring to the Patriarch. Nor could proselytes, as could all Israel, share in his merits. Sometimes the Abrahamic blessing upon all nations was generalized to refer simply to monotheism or providence, sometimes weakened so that Abraham would serve simply as the standard of blessing or, again, sometimes confined only to proselytes.[24] The exigencies of Jewish history—not surprisingly—had pressed upon the Abrahamic promise a "national," territorial stamp which often tended to obliterate its universal range.[25]

[22] See *Abraham: Père des Croyants. Cahiers Sioniens*, Paris, 1951. SB, Vol. I, pp. 117–121; C. K. Barrett, *From First Adam to Last*, New York, 1962, pp. 30ff.

[23] See references in n. 22. The fact that Abraham was a Gentile when he received the promise must never be overlooked in the interpretation of Paul. See Rom. 4: 11. Compare Bornkamm, *Paul*, p. 143.

[24] See Barrett, *From Adam to Christ*, pp. 31f. See n. 12 above.

[25] Barrett, *From Adam to Christ*, p. 34 quotes J. Bonsirven, *Le Judaïsme Palestinien*, Paris, 1934, Vol. I, p. 76. "It seems that the universalist promise, 'In thee shall all the families of the earth be blessed' was scarcely ever taken up [in Jewish circles]. The commentaries do not develop it, or else it undergoes this significant transformation—all the blessings that God bestows upon the earth, the rain and even creation itself, were given for Abraham's sake."

Paul's treatment of Abraham, as we have seen, runs against the grain of all this. It has been claimed that he anticipated modern criticism by discovering a stratum of the Pentateuch in which grace was emphasized, a stratum "which took form under the influence of the earlier prophets before the intense legal development of the period of the Exile and after."[26] Certainly he rejected the development, traced in the first chapter above, which appealed to the promise in order to establish the inviolable status of the people of Israel. For Paul the promise did not so much confirm status as require faith, a faith that provided not security in privileges of birth but trust in what seemed to offer no security. But it is not this aspect of the Pauline revolution that concerns us directly, although it is implied or is a corollary to that which does. It is this. Paul ignores completely the territorial aspect of the promise. The land is not within his purview. Why?

In writing to the Roman Church it might have been politically wise for the Apostle to avoid discussion of the question of the land.[27] There is a probability that he was anxious not to cause any misunderstanding that might disturb Rome. Thus he used the phrase "The Kingdom of God" very sparingly for this reason. Political considerations did enter into Jewish-Christian relations in the first century. Paul counselled respect for the powers that be (Rom. 13: 1f).[28] But political considerations would probably not be as directly relevant when he was writing to the Galatians, and in the epistle to them we might expect him to be uninhibited. The suggestion seems to have been made that the Judaizers who harassed Paul in the Galatian churches were Zealots, in which case the question of the land would certainly have occupied him.[29] But even if the Judaizers were not Zealots it is likely that they were "territorially" conscious. The view that the Judaizers were Gentiles and, therefore, unlikely to be concerned with the land, we have elsewhere rejected.[30] In Galatians we can be fairly

[26] Dodd, *Romans*, p. 65.

[27] PRJ, pp. 36f.

[28] See *Peake*, pp. 880. For a sober assessment, D. R. Griffiths, *The New Testament and the Roman State*, Swansea, 1970, pp. 87ff.

[29] D. Georgi, *Die Geschichte der Kollekte des Paulus für Jerusalem*, Hamburg–Bergstedt, 1965, p. 15, speaks of "judaistische Eiferer." But see Robert Jewett, "Agitators and the Galatian Congregation," NTS, Vol. 17, No. 2, Jan. 1971, pp. 198–212. His thesis is that "Jewish Christians in Judaea were stimulated by Zealotic pressures into a nomistic campaign among their fellow Christians in the late forties and early fifties... p. 205." This is a rich treatment making use of the historical setting effectively and drawing on the work of Hengel and Bo Reicke. But see p. 93, n. 38, for caution in the use of "Zealots."

[30] See n. 17. That a "political" Messianism was present and even widespread among some Jewish-Christians is likely. See J. Daniélou, *Theologie du Judéo-Christianisme*, Vol. 1, p. 58. M. Borg has very forcefully urged that Paul has in mind to counteract such Messianism

certain that Paul did not merely ignore the territorial aspect of the promise for political reasons: his silence points not merely to the absence of a conscious concern with it, but to his deliberate rejection of it. His interpretation of the promise is a-territorial.

And the Apostle's silence on the land is in keeping with the role he ascribes in Galatians and Romans to the Law. The Law—the guide for life and especially, as we saw in Part I, the condition for peaceful life in the land—Paul interprets as having been an intervention between the promise to Abraham and its fulfilment in Christ. Its role had been a particularized one, that is, directed only to Israel, which had thus been set apart from other peoples, but only in order to bring Israel to Christ, and that for the sake of all peoples. But even the particular role of the Law had been purely provisional (Gal. 3: 19ff). Now, in the coming of Christ, the promise had been fulfilled and the Law was no more necessary (Gal. 3: 10–14, 23–26). The children of the promise had achieved maturity and entered into their inheritance (Gal. 4: 17). The preparatory, particularized time of the Law had now given place to the universalism of grace manifested in the fulfilment of the promise to Abraham "in Christ" (Gal. 3: 15–18; Rom. 4: 16). With the coming of Christ the wall of separation between Israel and the Gentiles was removed. This wall, usually interpreted of "the Law," or of "the veil in the Temple," in the passage in Ephes. 2: 11–22, which here, whether written by him or by a member of his school or not, brings Paul's thought to its full expression, we may also interpret implicitly to include the geographic separation between those in the land and those outside the land. Because the logic of Paul's understanding of Abraham and his personalization of the fulfilment of the promise "in Christ" demanded the deterritorializing of the promise. Salvation was not now bound to the Jewish people centred in the land and living according to the Law: it was "located" not in a place, but in persons in whom grace and faith had their writ. By personalizing the promise "in Christ" Paul universalized it. For Paul, Christ had gathered up the promise into the singularity of his own person. In this way, "the territory" promised was transformed into and fulfilled by the life "in Christ." All this is not made explicit, because Paul did not directly apply himself to the question of the land, but it is implied. In the Christological logic of Paul, the land, like the Law, particular and provisional, had become irrelevant.

in Rom. 13. See "A New Context for Romans xiii," NTS, Vol. 19, No. 2, Jan. 1973, pp. 205–218. He convincingly notes the principles, but not the sentiments, which governed the Apostle. See p. 220.

3. The Pauline Mission

No less than his Christology, Paul's life points to the same conclusion. Converted outside the land near Damascus, Paul possibly worked as a missionary in Arabia, in Damascus itself, and certainly in Syria and Cilicia before he was called to Antioch by Barnabas.[31] His missionary journeys took him to Asia Minor and Greece; he set his heart on going to Rome and Spain. The main bases for his operations were Antioch and Ephesus: the world was his parish: his gospel spread, we read in Rom. 15: 19, "from Jerusalem and as far round as Illyricum," that is, through the whole Eastern Empire right to its western edge in Illyricum.[32]

At what point Paul consciously set before himself a world-wide goal is disputed. In the references to his conversion, in Gal. 1: 15–16, Acts 9: 15, 22: 15 (see also 22: 21), 26: 17f, the awareness of the necessity to preach to the Gentiles is presented as immediate. But to judge from reliable materials from the diary presumably preserved in the "We" sections of Acts, Paul's first missionary journey was very tentative. On the second journey this tentativeness gives way to deliberate descent, under the guidance of the Spirit active outside the land, upon Europe; but it is by the third journey that all tentativeness is gone. That Paul's world consciousness impinged immediately on his conversion may be doubted.[33]

The progress of the missionary work of Paul, who, perhaps significantly, seems always to have preferred to use his Roman name rather than the Jewish, Saul, has suggested that he came to think of it in terms coloured by the Roman Empire. His missionary strategy was to concen-

---

[31] Gal. 1: 15–16, 21; Acts 11: 22–26. On the basis of Gal. 5: 11 it may be argued that Paul, as a Pharisee, before his conversion had been a missionary for Judaism to the Gentiles. Compare Bornkamm, *Paul*, p. 12; *Peake*, p. 874 for the details of Paul's life.

[32] Note that Jerusalem, not Antioch, from which Paul first started with Barnabas on his "official" missionary work, is put as the Eastern term of his work. This is important for our later treatment. The Gospel for Paul begins from Jerusalem (compare Luke 24: 27). The reading at Rom. 15: 19 varies considerably. The generally followed text is B: ὥστε με ἀπὸ Ἰερουσαλὴμ καὶ κύκλῳ μέχρι τοῦ Ἰλλυρικοῦ πεπληρωκέναι τὸ εὐαγγέλιον τοῦ Χριτσοῦ, that is, "so that from Jerusalem and round about as far as Illyricum I have completed the Gospel of Christ." But D G it read: ὥστε πεπληρῶσθαι ἀπὸ Ἰερουσαλὴμ μέχρι τοῦ Ἰλλυρικοῦ καὶ κύκλῳ, that is, "so that the Gospel of Christ is completed from Jerusalem as far as Illyricum and round about." The former reading provides strong evidence for Paul's work among the Jews in Judaea before he worked among the Gentiles (compare Acts 26: 20). According to J. Munck, *Paul and the Salvation of Mankind*, trans., Richmond, 1959, p. 52, n. 1, the patristic expositors took the verse to mean that Paul preached "all over the many countries lying between Jerusalem and Illyricum, not simply along the shortest route." Munck supplies the evidence. The claim in Rom. 15: 19 seems to be exaggerated unless it be recognized that Paul thinks that each of the churches he founded stands for a whole district. See Bornkamm, *Paul*, pp. 53.

[33] See my article "The Apostolic Age and the Life of Paul," *Peake*, pp. 875ff. Compare Bornkamm, *Paul*, p. 49.

trate on centres of imperial significance: Roman imperial policy, Sir W. M. Ramsay urged, found its counterpart in Pauline missionary policy.[34] Paul set the kingdom of God over against the Empire of Rome; Christ against the Emperor; the Christ Myth against the Emperor Myth. Paul, on this view, may have laid the foundations of the Constantinian settlement. The Empire had ousted the Chosen Land.

But this is to misunderstand Paul. Certain facts are inescapable. Paul never refers to an Emperor by name; never mentions the Roman senate, the provinces of the Empire, and their officers. Romans 13 suggests a distance from the political realm, although this is not to be confused either with Stoic superiority nor the abhorrence and disgust of the cultured Greek for the uncultured, and for the lust for power of the Romans, nor with the world-denial of the Apocalyptists of Judaism. Nothing human was alien to Paul. But his purpose was not to be confused with any imperial-political aims however much baptized into Christ.[35] This appears from his actual missionary practice, glossed over as it can so easily be with the geographical structure of the Empire. Clearly Paul did centre his work in certain cities—Tarsus, Damascus, Antioch, Corinth, Ephesus, Rome, not to speak of Jerusalem. But, on the other hand, we saw, first, that he also visited, apparently for personal reasons in the case of Cyprus, less significant places. It is not clear that Antioch in Pisidia, Lystra, Iconium, Derbe were "significant" centres of Roman penetration: authorities differ on this and these cities were regarded by some as out of the way. And, secondly, that Paul should have gone to the chief cities was natural, if not inevitable, but this must not be taken to mean that he was necessarily thinking of a "divine commonwealth" set over against or parallel to the Roman. The only thing certain is that Paul first approached the Jews: he therefore sought out synagogues. After his experience on the first journey, the tentativeness of which we noted, he became more deliberate and geographically conscious. Thus the second journey up to Troas was largely a prelude to the descent upon Europe. As his deliberateness grew, his work followed more and more the pattern laid down by the imperial government, but not because he had become the Christian counterpart of an imperial strategist. This was due merely to the fact that his work could thus be most efficiently executed. Thus Spain, not Rome, was his goal in the West. Paul was thinking not of capturing

---

[34] *St. Paul the Traveller and Roman Citizen*, London, 1898.

[35] Compare Bornkamm, *Paul*, p. 55: "with Paul there is no question of a political, imperial understanding of the inhabited world such as the late Greeks conceived ideally and the Romans translated into the realm of politics."

the Empire but the whole known world. Acts has perhaps made him more "Roman" than he was. To think of him as a calculating strategist either bent on Jerusalem or Rome is erroneous. Rather he was bent, whenever and wherever he could, on building the body of Christ. Sometimes this demanded speedy passage from city to city; sometimes, as at Corinth and Ephesus, a prolonged stay in one place; sometimes retracing his steps. But shortened as he thought the time to be before the End, Paul's speed was unhurried, dictated by no eschatological dogma or imperial policy. To build the body of Christ in places mean and not mean, among Jews first and, when they rejected his message, among the Greeks—this was his aim, to create a body wherein was neither Jew nor Greek, bond nor free, male nor female "in Christ." What is noteworthy is that that body knew no geographic limitation or even concentration: Pauline ecclesiology is a-territorial.

The logic of Paul's Christology and missionary practice, then, seems to demand that the people of Israel living in the land had been replaced as the people of God by a universal community which had no special territorial attachment. But as we have seen, Paul never refers to the Church as the New Israel or to the Jewish people as the Old Israel. In addition, he never without qualification calls Gentile Christians "the children of Abraham." The italicized words in the following quotation from Gal. 3: 27–29 are not an unimportant addendum or designed to downgrade the Jews. They are a qualification of weight to emphasize that Gentile Christians are of the seed of Abraham only in virtue of the promise.

For as many of you as were baptized into Christ have put on Christ. There is neither Jew nor Greek, there is neither slave nor free, there is neither male nor female; for you are all one in Christ Jesus. And if you are Christ's, then you are Abraham's offspring, *heirs according to promise*.[36]

All this might be taken merely to be a logical inconsistency in the declared universalism of Paul's faith. But Paul did not think so. It is an inconsistency only if we concentrate on Paul's Christology to the neglect of his Theology. To take the latter seriously is to recognize that Paul's refusal to sacrifice the existence of his own people to Christological consistency is

[36] It is easily possible to ignore the point made in the text. It is not even noted by P. Richardson, *Israel in the Apostolic Church*, London, 1969, in his important treatment of "Old and New in Galatians in Relation to Israel," pp. 97ff, although he notes that for Paul: "The complete fulfilment of the original promise is possible now through its universal application; Gentiles are included as sons of Abraham as God intended (3: 7). This can now be effected by being 'of Christ (3: 29).' But Abraham had two sons, two kinds of children (4: 22), and these two characterize two ways of life... (p. 100)."

not illogical. This is made clear in Rom. 9–11. Whether this section be regarded as a sermon on the Jewish question previously fashioned and used by Paul as occasion demanded,[37] or a commentary applying the message of justification by faith alone, set forth in Rom. 1–8, to the Jewish people,[38] or as the intended climax of the epistle, we need not decide.[39] What is clear is that, while Paul never tries to justify the ways of God with men (Rom. 9: 19ff), his Theology does enable him to deal with the destiny of his own people in a way which his Christology alone does not.

After stating in Rom. 9: 1–3 his intense concern for Jews and recognizing their many and great advantages, Paul urges that they have a continued place in the purpose of God. It is incredible that God's declared purpose for them should become a dead letter (Rom. 9: 6). Is the Jewish people replaced as the people of God? In answering this question Paul has recourse to two concepts: that of the remnant, and that of God's sovereignty, which he assumes and refuses to impugn (Rom. 9: 14–29). Throughout history a principle of selection has been at work which has issued in an ever-emerging remnant: God has "chosen" some, such as Isaac (Rom. 9: 7) and Jacob (9: 13), and "hated" or rejected others, such as Esau (9: 13). See also Rom. 11: 1ff: in the time of Elijah 7000 did not bow the knee to Baal. So too in the time of fulfilment there are those among the Jews who hear and accept the Gospel and those who do not (Rom. 9: 24; 11: 17, 25). True, in Rom. 10, Paul recognizes that it is the Gentiles who are now ready to accept the Gospel and are being incorporated into "Israel," while the Jewish people itself is being disobedient. He implies that the mission to the Jews is over: they have "heard" the Gospel, that is, it has been preached to them but they have rejected it (Rom. 10: 18ff). But it cannot be said that the Jewish people as a totality has been disobedient and has, therefore, been replaced as the people of God by a Gentile community, the Church. No! A remnant has believed and it remains true that the nucleus of the people of God, the Church, is still Jewish—as Jewish as Paul himself! God has not rejected his people (Rom. 11: 1).

Moreover, the Jews who have refused the Gospel may change. Paul thought that his own Gentile mission, not by frontal assault, but in-

[37] Dodd, *Romans*, pp. 148ff—on grounds of content and style.
[38] Bornkamm, *Paul*, p. 149.
[39] This view goes back to F. C. Baur. For the recent discussion, see Käsemann, *Perspectives on Paul*, pp. 60ff, for whom the doctrine of justification by faith "dominates Rom. 9–11 no less than the rest of the epistle (p. 75)." On Rom. 11: 15, see PRJ, p. 298 n. 1.

directly, would be the means of bringing about that change: its results among the Gentiles would show his fellow countrymen what they were missing by rejecting the Gospel, and spur them to envy (Rom. 11: 13f). So Paul looked forward to a time when they would all be saved (Rom. 11: 25–32). The Jews' rejection of the Gospel for Paul, then, was a Phyrhic rejection: through their very rejection of it, they would ultimately be reconciled to it and thereby reconcile the world. That event—the reconciliation of the Jews to "Israel," the Church, and *ipso facto* of the world to God—would be "the resurrection of the dead." This enigmatic phrase must not be diluted to mean merely the greatest moral and spiritual blessings in a general way: it denotes rather the inauguration of the End (Rom. 11: 15).

All this Paul can believe because for him the whole process of history, past, present, and future, is under the mysterious and sovereign control of God: this does not imply that the Apostle is committed to determinism, because the challenge of God's word is always near (Rom. 10: 8) and can win response—a free response. But God's "gifts and call are irrevocable (Rom. 11: 29)." God has consigned all men (including the Jews) to disobedience, that he may have mercy on all (including the Jews) (Rom. 11: 32). Thus Paul holds that within God's purpose the Jewish people remain the Chosen People: their rejection of the Gospel has affected only part of Israel and is temporary. The Apostle seems to leave their reconciliation to the infinite wisdom of God and no longer regards it as a direct charge or task laid upon him. But that reconciliation is finally assured, and will prove to be the prelude to the End, when God's supreme mercy will be shown to all. In the meantime, it is implied, the continued existence of the Jewish people as an ethnic or "national" entity is affirmed.[40]

Paul's tortuous discussion thus leads to a paradox: in Christ there is neither Jew nor Greek and yet a continued place for the Jewish people as such. This paradox is not to be weakened. It cannot be explained away as arising merely from Paul's constant shuffling from an ethnic to a spiritual level in his understanding of the people of God and *vice versa*. It has rather a basis in the stubbornness of history itself. As a matter of simple fact, a remnant of the Jewish people was in the Church supplying a solid continuity between those "in Christ" and the Jewish past, rooting the Gospel in Judaism despite its transcendence of the ethnic limitations of the latter, and thus preserving it from the perils attendant upon its too rapid expansion into the Graeco-Roman world. Paul's insistence on the continued

---

[40] The comment by T. W. Manson, *Peake*, p. 949 is excellent.

significance of the Jewish people was historically grounded and historic-ally necessary: his instinct was right when he refused to follow the clarity of his Christological logic and was—in true Rabbinic fashion, we may note—content to rest in a paradox. But he himself was aware, as we are, of the tensions and ambiguities of this paradox; the unravelling of Rom. 9–11 testifies to this, and in the end he grounds the paradox, not only in history, but in the mystery of the divine grace, whose wisdom is past finding out, but which forbids God to cast off his ancient people or to revoke his covenant with them. Hence the conclusion of Rom. 11 in a grand doxology, which recalls Deutero-Isaiah and Job and the Psalms, is inevitable, and it is not an accident that this doxology is not Christo-logical but strictly Theological (Rom. 11: 33–36).[41]

But the question that now confronts us is this: does the paradox to which we have referred extend to the land? In affirming that God had not revoked his covenant with the Jewish people, does Paul also assume that he had not revoked the territorial aspect of the promise to them? One thing is clear: he avoids any direct discussion of this question: he speaks no unambiguous word about the land. Explicitly he does not include the Jewish land in the paradox. Does he do so implicitly?

4. THE TEMPLE

We saw in Part I that the thought of the land in Judaism is inextric-ably bound up with that of the Temple and Jerusalem. Do Paul's references to these throw any light on our question? At first sight, the a-territoriality of the Apostle's treatment of the Jewish people seems to reemerge in his interpretation of the Church as the temple of God: holy space seems to have been "transubstantiated" into a community of persons, the Body of Christ. Since this theme has been frequently treated the briefest statement will suffice here.

The concept comes to clearest expression in 2 Cor. 6: 14–7: 1 which, if it is a part of the letter mentioned in 1 Cor. 5: 9ff, may also be the earliest statement of it. The passage reads:

Do not be mismated with unbelievers. For what partnership have righteousness and iniquity? Or what fellowship has light with darkness? What accord has Christ with Belial? Or what has a believer in common with an unbeliever?

---

[41] J. Munck, *Christ and Israel: An Interpretation of Romans 9–11*, Philadelphia, 1967, pp. 141f, sets the doxology in Rom. 11: 33–36 over against the description of God's love in Christ at the end of Rom. 8. He is right in finding the clue to the doxology in the struggle of the Apostle "to trace God's working in the world," neither to late Jewish (Sanday and Headlam, ICC, *Romans*, SB, Vol. III, pp. 294f) nor to Hellenistic parallels (Kühl and Lietzmann). For further details, see Munck.

What agreement has the temple of God (*naô theou*) with idols? *For we are the temple of the living God (êmeis gar naos theou esmen ẑôntos)*; as God said,

> "I will live in them and move
>   among them,
> and I will be their God,
> and they shall be my people,
> Therefore come out from them
> and be separate from them, says
>   the Lord,
> and touch nothing unclean;
> then I will welcome you,
> and I will be a father to you,
> and you shall be my sons and
>   daughters,
> says the Lord Almighty."

Since we have these promises (epangelias), beloved, let us cleanse ourselves from every defilement of body and spirit, and make holiness perfect in the fear of God.

The first sentence in italics is the key one: it begins with an emphatic "we": the whole community constitutes the shrine or temple (*naos*) of God. Like the *naos* (the shrine and temple) in Jerusalem, this new *naos* is to be set apart from idolatry and pagan defilement. Paul applies to the new community passages from the Old Testament applied to the tabernacle and to the future temple in the land: first, Lev. 26: 12 and then Ezek. 37: 27; then, Is. 52: 11, which has reference to priests "who bear the vessels of the Lord," the whole community being a priesthood; then, 2 Sam. 7: 14 from the chapter promising that God would make a house for David. The reference to Lev. 26: 12 is particularly telling in 2 Cor. 6: 16b. Lev. 26: 11, 12 in the MT reads:

> And I will make my abode among you
> and my soul shall not abhor you.
> And I will walk among you, and will be your God, and
> you shall be my people.

The text in the LXX at Lev. 26: 11–12 may be translated as follows:

> And I will set my tabernacle (*tên skênên*)
> among you (*en humin*), and my soul shall not abhor you,
> and *I will walk (emperipatêsô)*

186

among you (en humin), and be your god, and ye shall be
my people.[42]

For the italicized English words in these verses Paul has substituted:

"I will live *in them (en autois)*" and "*move among them*...."

He has departed from the LXX, which he normally follows, and fallen
back on the Hebrew text.[43] In doing so he uses a verb (*enoikeô: I will live
in them*) which is never found in the LXX. He seems anxious to emphasize
that God no longer dwells *with* his people in a tent or temple, but actually
dwells *in* them.

The next passage to notice is 1 Cor. 3: 16–17.

Do you not know that you are God's temple (*naos*) [God's temple not a temple
of God] and that God's Spirit dwells in you (*en humin oikei*)? If any one destroys
God's temple (*naon*), God will destroy him. For God's temple (*naos*) is holy,
and that temple are ye.

The concept is here introduced as if already known to the Corinthian
Christians, probably through Paul's previous preaching. That the new
temple is a corporate entity appears from the plural pronouns and verbs
and from the images of the building and of the field, 1 Cor. 3: 9ff. The new
temple is constituted by the indwelling of the Spirit. In the context, the
implication is that schism destroys a unity which has its source in the
Spirit.[44] The application of the adjective "holy" to the new temple has
been taken to imply that Paul here has an almost "spatial" view of the
Church as a holy preserve into which evil cannot enter.[45] This view is not
impossible; but it is important not to press it. It is not the totality of the
new temple that the Spirit indwells directly so much as every individual
in the totality (compare 2 Cor. 1: 22); the "holiness" to which Christians
have been called evokes not spatial but moral undertones (1 Thess. 4: 17).

---

[42] The reading τὴν σκηνήν is that of F: H. B. Swete *The Old Testament in Greek*, Vol. 1,
Cambridge, 1925, p. 245, prefers to accept τὴν διαθήκην (I will set my covenant). Rahlfs does not
even note the reading τὴν σκηνήν. Is there a misprint in Swete at 26: 11? Should the text read
ἐμπεριπατήσω as in Rahlfs? Swete has ἐνπεριπατήσω.

[43] The Hebrew in Lev. 26: 11–12 is translated as follows in the RSV:

11 And I will make my abode among you

וְנָתַתִּי מִשְׁכָּנִי בְּתוֹכְכֶם

and my soul shall not abhor you.

12 And I will walk among you

וְהִתְהַלַּכְתִּי בְּתוֹכְכֶם

and will be your God, and you shall
be my people.

[44] A. Plummer, ICC, 1 Cor., p. 66.

[45] Compare R. J. McKelvey, *The New Temple*, Oxford, 1969, pp. 93ff.

The individual dimensions of the new temple come to the fore especially in 1 Cor. 6: 12–19. Here, although the precisely plural or corporate reference is retained, the body of each Christian is a shrine (*naos*) of the Holy Spirit which must not be corrupted by immorality. How "the body" became related to the Temple need not detain us here. At this point we need only notice that in Ephesians, which if not Pauline is deutero-Pauline, the concept of the Church as a temple comes to full flower (Eph. 2: 21). Jew and Gentile, on the basis of the redemptive blood of Christ, have become united in one body in the Church. They now both have access to the Father, through the spirit. The temple, which in 2 Cor. 6: 14ff had appeared exclusive, now is emphasized as inclusive.

On the basis of the above texts, it is legitimate to ask whether Paul was the earliest Christian to develop the view that the Jerusalem Temple had now been replaced as the dwelling place of God by the Christian community. As a Christian did he, like the Stephen of Acts, radically reject the Holy Sanctuary at Jerusalem? This question has been answered in the affirmative. The Church is for Paul the fulfilment of the hopes of Judaism for the Temple: the presence of the Lord has moved from the Temple to the Church, which now bears the dangerous holiness once associated with the former, and the life of the Church replaces the temple cult through its own spiritual sacrifices (Rom: 12: 1ff) and the foundation stone (*eben shetiyyâh*) of the old temple is replaced by Christ, the foundation of the new temple (Eph. 2: 20). It is easy to conclude that there was a deliberate rejection by Paul of the Holy Space in favour of the Holy People—the Church.

Before such a position is accepted, however, it should be reiterated that, both in Qumran and in Pharisaic circles, it proved possible to combine attachment to the Temple in Jerusalem with a spiritualized understanding of the Divine Presence in communal and personalized terms respectively. In the sectarian documents the community is regarded as the temple of the Lord, although it is clear that, once suitably cleansed, the existing Temple at Jerusalem would be the dwelling place of the Lord. The following passages reveal the role of the community itself as the Temple: 1QS 5: 5ff; 8: 4–11; 9: 3ff; 4Q Flor. 1: 1–13; 4Qp Isa, fr. 1; 1QHab. 12: 1ff. The second of these passages reads:

When these are in Israel, the Council of the Community shall be established in Truth. It shall be an Everlasting Plantation, a House of Holiness for Israel, an Assembly of Supreme Holiness for Aaron. They shall be witnesses to the Truth at the Judgement, and shall be the elect of Goodwill who shall atone for the

Land and pay to the wicked their reward. It shall be that tried wall, that *precious cornerstone*, whose foundations shall neither rock nor sway in their place (Isa. 28: 16). It shall be a Most Holy Dwelling for Aaron, with everlasting knowledge of the Covenant of justice, and shall offer up sweet fragrance. It shall be a house of Perfection and Truth in Israel that they may establish a Covenant according to the everlasting precepts. And they shall be an agreeable offering, atoning for the Land and determining the judgement of wickedness, and there shall be no more iniquity.[46]

That on the probable interpretation of 1QSa,[47] the Sect expected that the High Priest would be the head of the congregation, reveals how far from Qumran Paul was removed, but it also warns against the automatic assumption that Paul rejected the Jerusalem Temple because he conceived the Christian community in terms of it.

Similarly, Pharisaic Judaism was able to survive the fall of Jerusalem and the Temple because it could conceive of the Divine Presence apart from holy space. The Shekinah had been especially associated with the Temple, but R. Eleazer b. Azariah (A.D. 120–140) urged that: "The Holy Spirit should reside in that man who cleaves to the Shekinah,"—the latter is associated with men not with a place.[48] The Divine Presence is not confined to the Temple but found in every place which God chooses for the remembrance of his name: that is, it is ubiquitous, unconfined by space.

[46] See B. Gärtner, *The Temple and the Community in Qumran and the New Testament*, Cambridge, 1965, pp. 16–46: the community as Temple is over against that of Jerusalem. For criticism of McKelvey, see V. Nikiprowetzky, *Revue des Études Juives*, Vol. cxxx, 1970, pp. 5–30.

[47] *Qumran Cave I*, Discoveries in the Judaean Desert, I, eds. D. Barthélemy O.P., and J. T. Milik, Oxford, 1955, p. 117 (1QSa 2: 11–22). J. Muilenburg translated this as follows:

> This is the sitting of the distinguished men invited to the communal council. When God begets [sic!] the Messiah with them the priest will come as head over all the congregation of Israel and all the fathers of the sons of Aaron, the priests who are invited to the feast..., and they shall take their place, each according to his rank. And afterward shall enter the Messiah of Israel.... When they solemnly unite at the communion table or to drink wine, and the communion table is arranged and the wine (mixed) for drinking, no one shall stretch out his hand on the first portion of the bread or of the wine before the (Messiah) priest, for he shall bless the first portion of the bread and wine, and (stretch out) his hand on the bread first of all. Afterwards the Messiah of Israel shall stretch forth his hands on the bread; and (having given a blessing) all the congregation of the community (shall partake) each (according) to his rank. And they shall follow this prescription whenever the meal is arranged, when as many as ten eat together (USQR, Vol. xi, No. 3, 1956, p. 10).

[48] Eleazer b. Azariah [A.D. 120–140] in other places emphasized that God wants the heart. See RA, pp. 492ff. The success with which Pharisaism survived the fall of the Temple and of Jerusalem in A.D. 70 is already noted, see p. 127 above. For the substitutions which it came to find for Jerusalem and the worship at the Temple, see, for the Torah as centre, *Tanḥuma*, ed. S. Buber, Ahare Mob 35a; Pesikta de R. Kahana 60b (R. Huna, a second generation Babylonian Amora); T. B. Makkoth 10a; T. B. Berakoth 8a; M. Aboth 3: 2; T. B. Megillah 16b; for righteousness, Deut. R. 5: 3; T. B. Berakoth 55a; Lev. R. 7: 2. See further G. F. Moore, *Judaism*, Vol. i, p. 218.

The personal provenance of the Holy Spirit appears in the well-known saying of Rabbi Phinehas b. Jair (A.D. 165–200):[49]

The Torah leads to watchfulness, watchfulness to strictness, strictness to sin-lessness...sinfearing to holiness, holiness to the Holy Spirit and this last to the resurrection of the dead.

Every sin puts the Shekinah to flight. The communal aspect of the ex-perience of the Holy Spirit in Judaism we have emphasized elsewhere.[50] The loss of the Temple was not an insuperable difficulty for the Pharisees. But at the same time, there is no indication that they desired its super-session: the "spiritual" and "the spatial" Presence could coexist in the mind of the Pharisees: they lived without the Temple and at the same time prayed for its rebuilding. The Essenes, then, thought of their community as the Temple because, in their day, the Temple at Jerusalem was corrupt: the Rabbis at Jamnia personalized and spiritualized cultic forms because, in their day, the Temple had fallen.[51]

What of Paul? Nothing can be gained from his vocabulary. When he writes of the Church as the temple of God, he uses the term *naos*, best rendered, perhaps, as shrine. Only in 1 Cor. 9: 13 does he use the term *hieron* (temple) at all, and there it can mean simply the area around the altar of burnt offering, just outside the Temple building itself. This suggests that he is not thinking of the Christian community over against the temple as a totality, but (waiving for the moment whether the term *naos* in Paul always evokes the *naos* of the Jerusalem temple, its shrine) is concerned with replacing the very heart of the Temple with a new shrine—a living community in Christ. There is no interest in cleansing the Temple as in the ministry of Jesus: it is not with the reform of the Temple (*to hieron*) that Paul is concerned, but with the substitution of a new shrine (*naos*) for the old.

Not only is there no parallel in Paul to the cleansing of the Temple by Jesus, but (although in Rom. 9: 4f he does not mention it as one of the privileges of Israel) he was not wholly negative toward the Temple and its

---

[49] Mishnah Sotah 9: 15; T. B. Abodah Zarah 20b. W. Bacher thought that this saying was of Essene provenance, but A. Büchler disagreed. See W. Bacher, *Die Agada der Tannaiten*, Strassburg, 1902, Vol. 11, p. 497; A. Büchler, *Types of Jewish-Palestinian Piety*, New York, 1968, pp. 42f, according to whom (p. 62), "the originality of R. Phinehas lay in the systematic gradation of the various moral qualities to lead up the pious, by a natural progress in self-education, to the highest perfection, the possession of the Holy Spirit." See also JE, Vol. V, p. 225.

[50] PRJ, pp. 201ff.

[51] On all this, see McKelvey, *The New Temple*, and literature there cited, and Gärtner, *The Temple and the Community*.

services. This may be deduced from 1 Cor. 9: 13ff. In discussing the right of those who proclaim the Gospel to live by it, Paul cites the example of the priests in the Temple.

Do you not know that those who are employed in the temple service get their food from the temple, and those who serve at the altar share in the sacrificial offerings? In the same way, the Lord commanded that those who proclaim the gospel should get their living by the gospel (1 Cor. 9: 13–14).

Actual Temple practice is not frowned upon, but supplies a model for Christian forms. There is no hint of criticism of the priesthood or the Temple system.

It is precarious to use Acts for the understanding of Paul, but at this point the Epistles are not contradicted. In Acts 22: 17ff, in a speech before the Roman tribune and the crowd, Paul is made to declare that after his conversion he had returned to Jerusalem, and that, as he was praying and in a trance in the Temple, he had had a vision. Acts assumes that, like other early Christians, the early Paul at least found no difficulty in frequenting the Temple for prayer. Such speeches as those in Acts 22: 17ff, however, have been increasingly rejected as clues to the historical Paul, and Luke's tendency to present a figure friendly to Judaism is possibly to be detected here.[52] But what of the preceding verses in 21: 17ff where there is an even more surprising presentation?

There Paul's activity in Jerusalem, on what was to prove his last visit, is described. After reporting the history of his mission among Gentiles, he agreed, on the request of James and the elders, who were anxious to avoid trouble, to a noteworthy act. There were four Christians in the city under a temporary Nazirite vow. Such a vow could be discharged at the appropriate time, that is, at the end of the period for which it was taken, by the shaving of the head and the offering of prescribed sacrifices. To assist in the payment of the expense of such sacrifices was an act of merit. This Paul agreed to do. Not only so. He was also requested to "purify" himself along with the Nazirites. Probably the Jerusalem leaders felt that Paul had contracted uncleanness during his time among the Gentiles: such uncleanness demanded a cleansing on the seventh day (compare Num. 19: 12). This also Paul consented to do, thereby acknowledging the impurity of the Gentile world: he submitted to the ritual practices of Jewish piety in order to avoid offending Jewish Christians and, possibly, Jews (when trouble did break out, as recorded in Acts 21: 27, it was Diaspora Jews, not Jewish Christians, who caused it).

[52] See most recently Bornkamm, *Paul*, pp. xviif, following Dibelius.

This chapter of Acts belongs, perhaps, to the "We" sections, being possibly derived from the diary of an eye-witness:[53] to some this would lend it a certain historical reliability. Paul recognized the Temple and its observances in the land, and honoured the sensitivities of Jewish-Christians, more conservative than he, about the "pollution" of life among Gentiles outside the land (and even in the land). How is his conduct to be understood? It is possible to dismiss it as expediency. It was necessary to placate Jewish Christians and Jews and to disabuse them of their false understanding of Paul as a notorious antinomian; to convince them that he was capable of reverence for traditional forms; to disarm their suspicions about receiving a collection from a lawless Paul. Again, it may be urged that here Paul was acting in his private capacity and for the sake of private persons—four impoverished Nazarenes, and that, therefore, there was no ecclesiastical significance to his acts.[54] That the Apostle no longer recognized the authority of the Jewish Law did not signify that every legal observance was closed to him when he was among Jews: his very freedom from the Law enabled him to submit to it when he so desired. His was an "unprincipled" morality that enabled him to trim his sails to the wind. He was merely practising in Acts 21: 17ff his policy, or rather strategy, as revealed in 1 Cor. 9: 19ff.

To the Jews I became as a Jew, in order to win Jews; to those under the law I became as one under the law—though not being myself under the law—that I might win those under the law. To those outside the law I became as one outside the law—not being without law toward God but under the law of Christ—that I might win those outside the law. To the weak I became weak, that I might win the weak. I have become all things to all men, that I might by all means save some. I do it all for the sake of the gospel, that I may share in its blessings.

In the light of Galatians especially, however, it is difficult to think of Paul as a "trimmer."[55] The recognition of the Temple and the laws of purity in the Gentile world remain puzzling. But the point is that Acts does not contradict the Epistles on Paul's attitude to the Temple. The assessment of the texts with which we have already dealt, 2 Cor. 6: 14–18 and 1 Cor. 3: 16–17, is difficult in this connection. How are we to understand

[53] 21: 17–18 are certainly "We" passages, but it should be noted that after verse 18 there is no first person plural in 21. For the caution necessary in using the "We" materials as sources, see Bornkamm, *Paul*, p. xx.

[54] See the various commentaries.

[55] See H. Chadwick, NTS, Vol. 1, 1954–1955, pp. 261ff on "All things to all men." It should be recognized that Paul's letters point to ambiguities—was Titus circumcised? (Gal. 2: 3). Timothy, according to Luke, was (Acts 16: 3).

them? Do they imply a deliberate antithesis to the Temple at Jerusalem? Such an antithesis, it is true, seems implicit in the light of the quotations from the Old Testament in 2 Cor. 6: 14–18, but the express antithesis made is between the Church (The Temple of God) and idols, that is, temples with idols. Christians do constitute the eschatological temple: the *"we"* of 2 Cor. 6: 16 is emphatic. But this eschatological temple is not expressly opposed to the Jerusalem Temple of which it is the "fulfil-ment." To detect a rejection of the Jerusalem Temple here would be to go beyond the evidence. Like the Sectarians at Qumran and the Pharisees themselves, Paul might well have been able to recognize the Temple in Jerusalem even while he had substituted for it the new shrine of the Church.

Similarly the context in 1 Cor. 3: 16–17 offers no explicit rejection of the Temple at Jerusalem, although the abode of the Spirit, it is implied, is no longer there but in the Church. Is it likely that Paul in writing to Corinthian Christians would expect them to read into his words there a rejection of the Temple at Jerusalem? Two possibilities are open: (1) that Paul is employing language familiar in the Hellenistic world to assert that God dwells in the human heart, not in stone temples; or (2) that he is thinking of the Christian community as the eschatological temple of Jewish hope—a temple regarded as new or as a renewal of the old in various Jewish sources.[56] Even if we accept the second alternative—as better fitted for the communal emphasis in 1 Cor. 3: 16f—it does not necessarily follow that Paul intends to dismiss the Jerusalem Temple out-right here. At least he has left that dismissal unexpressed: Paul never speaks of a new temple, although his understanding of the Church logically seemed to demand such terminology.

In accordance with all this ambiguity there is one passage where the Temple in Jerusalem does seem to remain for Paul a centre of eschatological significance. It is 2 Thess. 2: 3–4.

Let no one deceive you in any way; for that day will not come, unless the rebellion comes first, and the man of lawlessness is revealed, the son of perdition,

[56] See McKelvey, *The New Temple, a* rem. We have elsewhere dealt at length with Rom. 3: 25, where Christ is set forth as *hilastêrion*. It is tempting to see here Christ as the replacement of the *Kappôreth* of the Temple, but the difficulty of interpreting *hilastêrion* is very great. Does Paul here regard Christ as the place of atonement and the victim (the refer-ence to his blood suggests this) at one and the same time? Dodd still thinks this unlikely (USQR, in a review of my *Invitation to the New Testament*): Christ cannot be the place of expiation and the means of expiation. But it is not impossible that it is this paradox that Paul had in mind. In this case, Rom. 3: 25 would lend support to the view that Paul has directly dismissed the Temple as a centre of reconciliation (see PRJ, pp. 237ff). But the absence of the article before *hilastêrion* suggests that Paul is not thinking of an antithesis to *the Kappôreth* of the Temple.

who opposes and exalts himself against every so-called god or object of worship, so that he takes his seat in the temple of God, proclaiming himself to be God.

Here Paul anticipates two preludes to the Parousia which have not yet eventuated: (1) the rebellion, that is, the apostasy which in Jewish eschatology was anticipated before the End; and (2) the man of lawlessness or the man of sin, the son of perdition. The exact connotation of the phrase, "the man of lawlessness," is a matter of dispute. What concerns us is that the final expression of this figure's opposition to God is that he takes his seat in the temple (*naos*) of God, and proclaims himself to be God. But to what does the temple of God here refer? The interpretations proposed are numerous and sometimes fantastic.[57] The reasons in favour of understanding by it the Temple at Jerusalem are convincing. The verb "to sit" points to a specific location; the natural meaning of the phrase "the temple of God" for Paul, when the Jerusalem Temple was still standing, is clear; the imagery of the whole passage rests on Daniel, where the time of rebellion has reference to the Holy City; the parallels in Matthew and Mark point to the Jerusalem Temple. What is significant is that for the Apostle the desecration of that Temple is the penultimate act of impiety leading on to the claim to replace God himself, the ultimate impiety. The passage speaks eloquently of Paul's sentiments about the Temple.[58]

However, since doubts have been cast about the authenticity of 2 Thessalonians, the passage to which we have appealed will not carry conviction to many. Moreover, even if Pauline, 2 Thessalonians must be regarded as a very early epistle, the thought of which, his other epistles attest, he outgrew. Our examination of Paul's attitude to the Jerusalem temple concludes, therefore, with ambiguities and possibilities only. If the evidence of Acts (we have preferred to confine our treatment to the epistles) and 2 Thess. 2: 3–4 be admitted, he retained for the Temple the reverence he had had as a Jew, albeit a reverence that came to be overshadowed by his overwhelming conviction that the Church was the temple of the Living God.

But the validity of such a view cannot be assessed without consideration of the place of Jerusalem in the Apostle's thought, because the Temple and the City are inextricable in Judaism, as we saw, and serve as the quintessence of the land.

[57] For these see B. Rigaux, *Les Épitres aux Thessaloniciens*, Paris, 1956, *ad rem.*
[58] Rigaux, *Les Épitres*, p. 337.

5. JERUSALEM

In a previous reference to words in Rom. 15: 9 in which Paul claimed to have fully preached the gospel of Christ "from Jerusalem and as far round as the Illyricum," we noted the implication of the centrality of Jerusalem for the Apostle as the point of departure for his work. Although by his arrangement of his material the author of Acts has created the impression that Paul undertook three distinct missionary journeys which had their base at Antioch, he too presents a Paul eager to be in touch with Jerusalem as his ultimate geographic base (Acts 19: 21; 20: 22; 21: 11ff), so that again Acts confirms the Epistles. Paul's visits to Jerusalem, however those mentioned in Acts are to be reconciled with those noted in the Epistles, were significant. Both Rom. 15: 19 and Acts justify us in pursuing the question of what role Paul ascribed to Jerusalem.

Let us begin with a text where the term "Zion" is explicit, Rom. 11: 26. After referring to the "mystery" that, after the fullness of the Gentiles had accepted the Gospel, Israel also would finally be saved, Paul quotes words from Is. 59: 20–21; 27: 9; and Jer. 31: 33f. In Rom. 11: 26f we read:

> ...and so all Israel will be saved; as it is written,
> "The Deliverer will come from Zion,
> and he will banish ungodliness from Jacob";
> "and this will be my covenant with them.
> when I take away their sins."

The above is the rendering of the RSV. The reference seems to be to Jerusalem, and, in the light of 2 Thess. 2: 3–4, to the Temple in Zion, where in a more ruthless vein, Paul seems to think that the Lord Jesus will destroy the lawless one in the Temple, which he has desecrated. The appearance of Jesus coincides with that destruction and then, presumably, he will come from Zion as the Deliverer. But whether it be legitimate thus to create a logical sequence from such disparate sources, including an Old Testament quotation, or not, Paul seems to regard Zion, that is, Jerusalem as the source of the eschatological Deliverer. In view of the role of Jerusalem in the world of Paul such an interpretation is most likely. For the Apostle the geographic centre of the world, Jerusalem, would be the centre of salvation.

This interpretation may be supported by a significant change in the Old Testament text cited by Paul in Rom. 9: 25–26, where the Apostle refers to the calling of the Gentiles. The text in Romans reads:

> As indeed he says in Hosea,
> "Those who were not my people

> I will call 'my people,'
> and her who was not beloved
> I will call 'my beloved.'"
> "And in the very place where it was
> said to them, 'You are not my
> people,'
> they will be called 'sons of the living
> God.'"

The RSV and the NEB ignore the *ekei* (there) in the Greek text, which literally reads: "*there* they will be called sons of the living God." The underlined *there* is missing in our Septuagint text at Hos. 2: 1 (MT 1: 10); did Paul's Septuagint text have *ekei* in it? Or did Paul himself insert it? In any case, it is very emphatic in the text as Paul understood it: it is unlikely that Paul is merely quoting loosely. But what does *ekei* (there) refer to? Either to the land or to Jerusalem, a distinction which, as we have seen, by the first century, is a distinction without a difference in Judaism. What is illegitimate is to ignore the plain geographic emphasis of the text at Rom. 9: 25–26 in favour of a generalized reference to the call of the Gentiles or of lapsed Jews.[59] The full weight of the doctrines which we dealt with in Part I are in favour of giving to Zion a geographic connotation. Zion or Jerusalem was for the Jew, Paul, the centre of the world, the symbol of the land itself and the focal point for the Messianic Age. The likelihood is that, at first at least, it occupied the same place in his life as a Christian. 2 Thess. 2, and possibly Rom. 11: 26, and, probably Rom. 9: 26 confirm this.

And yet the matter is not so simple. Some have "spiritualized" the term "Zion" in Rom. 11: 26 so as to make it refer to the Heavenly Jerusalem and, derivatively, to the Church. In Rom. 9–11 Paul is not thinking at all of the earthly city as the scene of the End. The precise nature of the connotation of terms in apocalyptic passages is always difficult to assess. The term "Zion" can be notoriously ambiguous, and especially so in Rom. 11: 26, which is partly a quotation from Is. 59: 20. True in the MT at Is. 59: 20 the redeemer is to come "*to* Zion," לְצִיּוֹן and the reference is unmistakably to Jerusalem. But Paul does not follow or is not directly dependent on the MT here. Nor is he on the LXX, which reads at Is. 59: 20: καὶ ἥξει ἕνεκεν Σιὼν ὁ ῥυόμενος, that is, "and the Redeemer will come for the sake of Zion." Is Paul's divergence from both the MT and the LXX deliberate and significant?

---

[59] Barrett, *Romans*, does not deal with the geographic reference in Rom. 9: 25–26 or 11: 26.

Does he refuse to contemplate a Messiah coming to Zion, or for her sake or on her account? Since the Apostle usually follows the LXX, must we not assume that he does not give to Jerusalem the significance that that translation ascribes to that city? And does he, also, want to remove the Redeemer from such a connection with the earthly Jerusalem as is made in the MT?

Gal. 4: 26, which contrasts the earthly with the heavenly Jerusalem, suggests, at first sight at least, that these questions should be answered in the affirmative, and that in Rom. 11: 26 Paul is thinking of the heavenly Jerusalem from which the Redeemer will come. Here he has cast off the Messianic significance of the earthly Jerusalem, with which we dealt above, in favour of the heavenly, as in Gal. 4: 26. In this Galatian passage Paul writes to enlighten Gentile Christians who want to adhere to the Torah, that is, to become Jews in becoming Christians. He uses an allegory to bring his point home. He thinks of those who adhere to the Law, represented by Hagar, as the children of servitude, and of those who are in Christ as the children of Sarah. In the course of his allegory Paul contrasts the *homes* to which these two belong. His argument may be tabulated as follows:

Hagar	*Sarah*
the Covenant of Law.	the Covenant of Promise.
She corresponds to the	She corresponds to the
present Jerusalem	Jerusalem on high

The children of Hagar have their home in the earthly city where God dwells in the Temple made with hands. But the children of Sarah, Christians, who acknowledge a risen and exalted Lord, know that their home is not on earth, but in heaven. Their mother is the Jerusalem on high. Paul shares in the apocalyptic view that the heavenly Jerusalem already exists in heaven. But those who live by faith in Christ *already* live the life of the new Jerusalem; they are already citizens of heaven, Gal. 2: 19–21; Phil. 3: 20ff. In this view, the Church belongs to an already existing heavenly city. Notice that Paul does not say that this heavenly city will be established as a visible city on earth. But Christians on earth already do share in its glories: it belongs to that realm "which eye hath not seen nor ear heard," that is, it is transcendental.

The view that the Church here and now is part of the heavenly Jerusalem does not conflict with Rom. 11: 26: in fact it fits in well with Rom. 11: 25–26. In Rom. 11: 25, Paul asserts that when the fullness of the Gentiles has "come in," then, in this way (καὶ οὕτως) Israel also will "come in," because, presumably from out of the fullness of the Gentiles, constituting the heavenly Jerusalem, Zion, in accordance with the Scriptures, the Redeemer will come (ὅτι πώρωσις ἀπὸ μέρους τῷ Ἰσραὴλ γέγονεν ἄχρι οὗ τὸ πλήρωμα τῶν ἐθνῶν εἰσέλθῃ, καὶ οὕτως πᾶς Ἰσραὴλ σωθήσεται...).

It is understandable, therefore, that commentators who deal with the "geographic" dimensions of Rom. 11: 26 at all, and they are few, refer "Zion" to the heavenly Jerusalem. This interpretation becomes even more persuasive if there were among Paul's opponents in Galatia, Corinth, and Rome those who emphasized the role of Jerusalem in the present and future: there is some evidence that there were such. And the outcome of our discussion of Rom. 11: 26 is at best that Paul may have given a special place to Jerusalem in that text, but that this is by no means certain. Is there other evidence that he did so?

Any detailed treatment must begin with Galatians. In Gal. 1: 16f Paul emphasizes his independence of the apostles in Jerusalem. After his conversion he did not confer with flesh and blood, nor did he go up to Jerusalem to those who were apostles before him. He went away instead to Arabia and again returned to Damascus. The first visit to the city recorded in Gal. 1: 18, three years later, was to visit Cephas, when Paul remained for fifteen days. The Greek word translated "to visit" in the RSV is *historêsai*, from which our term "history" derives. Its precise meaning has evaded us. Did it mean simply "to visit" or "to get information from" or "to inquire of"? The RSV translates "to visit Cephas"; the NEB is stronger and renders "to get to know Cephas." But perhaps even this is not strong enough. The use of such an unusual verb as *historêsai* prompts us to seek an Aramaic word behind it. It may translate an Aramaic term denoting "to seek after a tradition" or "to inquire after a tradition" or "to visit an authoritative teacher."[60] The most that can certainly be claimed is that the verb *historêsai may* have implied that Paul visited Peter as a depository of the tradition of Jerusalem. The Jerusalem Church at large did not directly concern him and, apart from Peter, he only saw James, the Lord's brother, not even the other apostles. Paul seems anxious to emphasize his independence of the Jerusalem leaders.

But that this view is not to be pressed appears from the second visit

[60] For the evidence, see SSM, Appendix IX, pp. 453ff. Bornkamm, *Paul*, p. 28, allows for a certain "discussion of the understanding of the Gospel on which the Jerusalem church based its life and which Paul was preaching in his own way."

recorded in Gal. 2: 1ff. The view has been held that it implies a juridical relationship between Paul and Jerusalem. The visit of Paul, Barnabas, and Titus was designed to give an account of their work before the central authorities at Jerusalem, as "inferiors" before "superiors," submitting their Gospel to examination and expecting an authoritative ruling as to its validity: the visit was Paul's Canossa![61] True the right hand of fellowship was given to Barnabas and Paul, and their sphere of labour among Gentiles recognized, as was that of James, Cephas, and John among the Jews. But the juridical relationship found expression in the imposition of a tax in its own interest by the Jerusalem Church on the Gentile Churches, after the manner of the Temple tax levied by Judaism on all Jews.

Such an approach to Gal. 2 is untenable.[62] If it be assumed that all references to a collection in the Pauline epistles point to that instituted, by implication, at Gal. 2: 10,[63] then it is clear that a voluntary gift from the Gentile Churches to the Church in Jerusalem is meant, not a tax. The terms used for the collection (*logeia*, 1 Cor. 16: 1f; *eulogia*, 2 Cor. 9: 5) are the following: contribution (*koinonia*, 2 Cor. 8: 4; Rom. 15: 26); material blessings (*sarkika*, Rom. 15: 27); fruit (*karpon*, Rom. 15: 28); service (*diakonia*, Rom. 15: 25; 15: 31; 2 Cor. 9: 1; 9: 12); grace (*charin*, 2 Cor. 8: 6); "a remembrance of the poor" (μόνον τῶν πτωχῶν ἵνα μνημονεύωμεν, Gal. 2: 10). None of these terms or phrases are juridical. Indeed, it is not to be ruled out that the term "the poor (*ptôchoi*)," in Gal. 2: 10, may not refer to the Church as a whole, but to those who were in actual poverty.[64]

But even apart from these considerations, Paul went up to Jerusalem, not at the command of any central "authorities," but "by revelation." He confesses his own concern to make sure that this work had the approval (not the authorization) of the Jerusalem "pillars." When he first refers to

[61] Karl Holl, "Der Kirchenbegriff des Paulus in seinem Verhältnis zu dem der Urgemeinde," *Sitzungsberichte der Preussischen Akademie der Wissenschaften*, Vol. 53, 1921. For the reference to Canossa, see E. Stauffer, "Petrus und Jakobus in Jerusalem," *Begegnung der Christen: Festschrift für O. Karrer*, 1960, pp. 361ff: see p. 369.

[62] Bornkamm, *Paul*, p. 28, calls it fantastic. See for a full critique, R. N. Flew, *Jesus and His Church*, London, 1938, pp. 185ff. For a criticism of Stauffer's position, Georgi, *Die Geschichte der Kollekte*, p. 17, n. 28.

[63] See below pp. 214ff.

[64] The difficulty in dealing with "the poor" (πτωχοί) is that the corresponding term in Hebrew אֶבְיוֹנִים can refer both to the economically poor and to "the spiritually poor." See Georgi, *Die Geschichte der Kollekte*, pp. 22ff who takes "the poor" to be a title for the Christians of Jerusalem in Gal. 2, but in Rom. 15 understands it to refer to the economically poor, Paul being no longer interested in Jerusalem Christians as such (pp. 81ff).

"the pillars" in Gal. 2: 2, it seems implied that he had "a deep instinctive respect" for them; but that this did not compromise his freedom in any way is clear in Gal. 2: 6—where he refers more coldly "to those who were reputed to be something." The tone of the whole of Gal. 2: 1ff is ambiguous. It suggests both respect for and independence from the Jerusalem Church on the part of Paul. The Apostle is almost truculent in demanding equal status for Jewish and Gentile Christians. And yet, independent as he presumed his work to be, he was glad to have the right hand of fellowship extended by the pillars of the Jerusalem Church, and fervently agreed to arrange a collection on behalf of the "poor" in Jerusalem.

Can we understand why? The reason he gives is that he fears that by neglecting the link with the Jerusalem Church he might have run "in vain" (Gal. 2: 2). Does this mean that he was eager that his churches should be united with the Jerusalem Church? If we consider references to a collection in other Pauline epistles and interpret these, with most scholars, in terms of the collection inaugurated, by implication, in Gal. 2: 10, the answer is clearly in the affirmative. In commenting on 1 Cor. 16: 1–4, Barrett[65] finds the reasons why Paul undertook the collection to be quite simple. "He made the collection because he had been asked to do so, because, no doubt, he felt a genuine compassion for the needy, and probably because he hoped that it would cement together the two divisions of the church, which already were showing signs of at least uneasy partnership." Certainly 2 Cor. 9 at least makes the third reason suggested by Barrett clear (it does much more as we shall see below). The pertinent verses (2 Cor. 9: 1, 6, 10–15) read:

1 About the provision of aid for God's people, it is superfluous for me to write to you.

6 Remember: sparse sowing, sparse reaping; sow bountifully, and you will reap bountifully.

10–15 Now he who provides seed for sowing and bread for food will provide the seed for you to sow; he will multiply it and swell the harvest of your benevolence, and you will always be rich enough to be generous. Through our action such generosity will issue in thanksgiving to God, for as a piece of willing service this is not only a contribution towards the needs of God's people; more than that, it overflows in a flood of thanksgiving to God. For through the proof

---

[65] *The First Epistle to the Corinthians*, pp. 385ff. K. F. Nickle, *The Collection: A Study in Paul's Strategy*, London, 1966, is invaluable for details and for the theological interpretation of its theme, especially pp. 100–143. He is near to Munck's position and not sufficiently aware of the paradox to which we refer in our treatment.

which this affords, many will give honour to God when they see how humbly you obey him and how faithfully you confess the gospel of Christ; and will thank him for your liberal contribution to their need and to the general good. And as they join in prayer on your behalf, their hearts will go out to you because of the richness of the grace which God has imparted to you. Thanks be to God for his gift beyond words! (NEB.)

In the light of this passage the purpose of the collection is at least to recognize equality between Gentile and Jerusalem Christians, the establishment of a true ecumenicity.

But the full scope of the intent of the collection goes much further than has been suggested above. Apart from compassion and ecumenicity, Paul was governed by other factors. In Rom. 15: 25–27 Paul refers to a debt that the Gentile Christians, who were contributing the collection, owed to the Christians in Jerusalem; from the latter the former had received spiritual blessings for which their material gifts were the payment of a debt. The collection was to be a recognition of the historical place of the Church in Jerusalem in the history of salvation: that Church was the beginning from whence the blessings of the Gospel had come. In part, therefore, the collection (we must not overlook the danger attending its presentation of which Paul was fully aware; Rom. 15: 31 makes it clear that both Jews and Jewish-Christians might be antagonistic) was for Paul a symbol of his very deliberate recognition of the continuity of Gentile Christianity with Jewish-Christianity and through it, located in Jerusalem, with Judaism as its matrix. In short, it served as an important indication of a theological truth.

But can we go further in ascribing significance to Jerusalem? In a well-known work, this has been urged by Johannes Munck.[66] We have elsewhere examined his thesis. Here it will suffice to state his understanding of the collection. For him, it is to be interpreted in the light of Rom. 9–11, where Paul is concerned with that historical continuity to which we have referred and with the Gentile mission. In that section it is asserted that the life of Gentile believers is to spur the envy of Jewry, and thus lead to their acceptance of the Gospel. And Munck has insisted that the collection can only be fully understood in the light of Paul's eschatology as set forth in Rom. 9–11. He removes the collection from any merely moral and ecumenical dimensions, and beyond the historical level suggested by Rom. 15: 25–27, to the eschatological. The large representation from the Gentile Church (covering major areas of the Pauline mission

[66] *Paul and the Salvation of Mankind*, trans., Richmond, 1959.

field, travelling at considerable, and, surely unreasonable, cost if their purpose was merely the relief of the poor), and the readiness of the Apostle to devote immense energy and time and even to risk death at Jerusalem (Rom. 15: 31) in taking the collection there are only comprehensible if the collection be connected with Rom. 9–11.[67] Paul was governed by an eschatological schema. By the presentation of the collection, he aimed at evoking the jealousy of the Jews and thus their acceptance of the Gospel which would inaugurate "life from the dead (Rom. 11: 15)." Thus would the prophetic expectations for the incursion of the Gentiles expressed in Is. 2: 2ff; Mic. 4: 1ff; and Is. 60: 5ff be fulfilled.

In Munck's judgment, then, Jerusalem as the centre of the world, on this evidence, governs Paul's mind: that city is to be for him the scene of the End. Even when he wrote Romans, according to Munck, despite his references to a projected visit to Spain, on which, in passing, he would visit Rome, Jerusalem was the focus of Paul's concern. True, at Jerusalem things did not follow according to Paul's hope. The Jews set in motion legal machinery against him. He appeared before the Sanhedrin, before Felix in Caesarea, then before Festus and King Agrippa, and, on appeal to Caesar, was finally taken to Rome as a prisoner. The Apostle of Liberty became a captive eagle. And like Milton, whose blindness taught him that "they also serve, who only stand and wait," so Paul through his imprisonment learnt a new patience. He recognized that he was being allowed providentially to witness before the Emperor and thus continue his ministry to the Gentiles. But the hope of the End at Jerusalem, when all Israel would be saved, did not forsake him. The geographic centre of Jewish eschatology remained significant for him: he never severed his tie with the land.

If we concentrate with Munck, on the apocalyptic geography of Paul, the picture of the Apostle that emerges is not unlike that of Jesus given by Schweitzer. Paul was governed by an eschatological dogma with a geographic structure, and dominated, like Jesus, by what turned out to be an illusion. But such a picture, convincing as it may seem when looked at in isolation, appears as a distortion when placed against the totality of Paulinism. Even at a superficial glance it occasions question. For example, if Paul were governed by the eschatological significance of Jerusalem and thought of the collection in the eschatological terms suggested by Munck, his appeal to Caesar becomes difficult to explain. This is especially so if he

[67] *Ibid.*, pp. 282ff.

saw in the necessity to go to Jerusalem a parallel to that Divine necessity which had led Jesus there.[68]

But more important still, Munck does not recognize an obvious difficulty in his approach. One striking fact encounters us in Paul's treatment of the collection in Rom. 15: 22–29. Paul is preparing to go to Jerusalem with the collection. On Munck's view, he then expected the Jewish people, spurred to jealousy by the fruit of the Gospel among the Gentiles, to accept that Gospel and to experience along with the Gentile believers what he vaguely refers to as "life from the dead (Rom. 11: 15)."[69] But what does the text of Romans attest? Paul, even as he prepares for Jerusalem, fixes his gaze beyond it on far away Spain, on the way to which, he will stay at Rome (Rom. 15: 24). This implies that "The End," which Paul anticipated, would not see the cessation of the present order and the establishment of a new order with the land of Israel and Jerusalem at its centre. No! He would still find it necessary to go to Rome. Munck has sought to minimize the attention paid to Rome in Rom. 15. Paul had to go to Rome to preach, but so had he to other cities also: he was under obligation to preach to Gentiles everywhere, not only in Rome. In any case, he is thinking of Rome, not as the centre of the Empire, but as a stage in his journey to Spain. He would break his journey at Rome for a short time in order to strengthen the Church there, but his goal lay beyond in the West, in Spain, for which Rome would serve as a temporary base. Not Rome, insists Munck, but ultimately Jerusalem was Paul's goal. With Munck's refusal to overemphasize the significance of the Apostle's visit to Rome we can agree. But he has not seen the force of the paradox created for his view by the references to Spain and Rome in Rom. 15 to which we have alluded. For the sake of clarity we repeat the two things which constitute that paradox. First, Paul, filled with eschatological expectations, actually travels to Jerusalem as the centre of the world. Secondly, *at the same time* his eyes are fixed, beyond Jerusalem, on Spain and Rome. How are these two things to be accounted for? Several ways of doing so are open for examination.

First, it is possible to take the futuristic statements of Paul as so confused or unsystematized, and so difficult to define with any precision, that the paradox to which we have referred can easily be ignored or treated as an unimportant, apocalyptic remnant which does not demand serious attention. This is virtually how Bultmann and, more recently, Bornkamm deal with the problem.

[68] See my review of Munck NTS, reprinted in *Christian Origins and Judaism*, pp. 179ff.
[69] The exact connotation of this phrase has been doubted; see PRJ, p. 298, n. 1.

Bultmann does not, in fact, deem it necessary even to discuss such a paradox as we have noted. For him, Paul was not interested in the history of the nation of Israel or of the world, but only in "the historicity of man, the true historical life of the human being, the history which everyone experiences for himself and by which he gains his real essence. The history of the human person comes into being in the encounters which man experiences, whether with other people or with events, and in the decisions he takes in them."[70] In the light of this it is not surprising that at no point in his *Theology of the New Testament* does Bultmann take seriously Rom. 9–11.[71] The futuristic elements in Paul's eschatology are only a symbolic mode of expressing man's self-realization, when the grace of Christ has freed him from himself and when he continually asserts himself as a free individual in decisions for God. In such acts he stands before the tribunal of Christ. The schemes of the future revealed in Rom. 9–11, and elsewhere in the epistles, are vestiges—flotsam and jetsam—of an apocalyptic view which no longer really governed the Apostle's mind. All this means that Paul reinterpreted eschatology in terms of anthropology. The Pauline view of history is the expression of his view of man. Romans 9–11 can, therefore, be ignored and the paradox to which we referred is unworthy of consideration: such inconsistencies are of no significance at all because they are accidental and incidental in Paul's thought.

Such a view does full justice to the crisis in the life of the individual constituted by a confrontation with Christ. But it abstracts Paul from that Jewish milieu within which he had emerged and largely operated. That milieu was one in which the Jewish people, as the people of God, was of central theological significance, and its salvation, as well as that of the cosmos, a matter of supreme concern. To a Jew such as Paul, his own people, its history and destiny, were of crucial importance both in this world and in the age to come, when the resurrection itself was to be a resurrection of the community, not merely of individuals. Concern with the future of Israel was not vestigial, but endemic and essential if not primary. Paul could wish himself accursed and cut off from Christ "for the sake of my brethren, my kinsmen by race (Rom. 9: 3)." For such a Jew, Jerusalem and the land were not naturally and easily dispensable. Bultmann's approach involves the kind of Christological and personalized concentration that neglects the wider theological dimensions of

---

[70] R. Bultmann, *The Presence of Eternity: History and Eschatology*, New York, 1957, p. 43.

[71] The only references to verses in Rom. 9–11 are on pp. 70, 81, 125, 229, 263, 267, 280, 312, 317 of Vol. 1, and they are all insignificant.

Paul's mind, a concentration which we saw that Paul himself avoided so as to be able to deal with "the Jewish question." For example, Bultmann interprets the phrase in Rom. 10: 4 that "Christ is the end of the law" to mean that history "has reached its end." In such an interpretation, Christology has been allowed to run rampant. Rom. 10: 4 means not that history has reached its end, but that salvation-history has entered upon a new phase, "the ends of the ages have met (1 Cor. 10: 11)."[72]

Bornkamm[73] is aware of the extreme individualism of Bultmann's interpretation of Paul. He deals more seriously with Rom. 9–11 and gives the Apostle's corporate or "national" sensitivity more weight. But he also insists on two things. First,[74] that Paul stood in opposition to the apocalyptic mentality which thought in terms of world-schemes and aeons and dealt with the rise and fall of nations and peoples. The Apostle, rather, concentrates on the individual as a responsible creature addressed by God, not as an insignificant cog in the chain of fate, be it either for damnation or salvation, as in Apocalyptic. Precisely the evaluation of the individual as free to choose or reject the challenge of God is what differentiates Paul from the Apocalyptists. Faith never has anything to do with collectivities. And, equally, precisely this individualism—which implies no limitation of Paul's horizons to subjectivism and existentialism in the modern sense—is the ground of a truly universal salvation, freed from any ethnic reference. And, secondly, Bornkamm emphasizes that Paul's apocalyptic statements are sporadic. They are evoked by specific questions posed by his churches and, therefore, admit of no systematization. To trace development in his anticipations of the future is extremely precarious.[75] Bornkamm is plainly embarrassed by the apocalyptic or futuristic elements in Paul except insofar as they preserve the convictions that salvation rests in the hands of God, whose is the ultimate victory, that it includes Israel and the cosmos, and that it is rooted in what has happened "in Christ." For us the point is that for Bornkamm, as for Bultmann, the paradox created by Rom. 15, with which we have been concerned above, need not be taken seriously: it arises simply from the

---

[72] Compare J. A. Fitzmyer, *Pauline Theology: A Brief Sketch*, Englewood Cliffs, N.J., 1967, p. 30. On Rom. 10: 4, see Ulrich Luz, *Das Geschichtsverständnis des Paulus*, München, 1968, pp. 139–158.

[73] *Paul*, pp. 196–200, 219ff; for his awareness of the cosmic in Paul's eschatology, p. 224.

[74] *Ibid.*, pp. 198, 200f.

[75] *Ibid.*, pp. 220, 222, 224. Bornkamm has to acknowledge that Paul definitely expected the conversion of Gentiles and the consequent return of the whole people of Israel to belief before the end (p. 221), but does not touch on the place of Jerusalem in this. On his interpretation of Pauline eschatology he cannot but regard it as remarkable that in Paul's last great letter, Romans, eschatological motifs become so prominent (p. 225).

vestiges of a discarded Apocalyptic: even to pose it as we have done is to give to Paul's futuristic statements a cohesion they do not justify.

But one thing must be made clear here. Even though in the light of the corporate and land-oriented tradition, which we have traced in Part I as the milieu within which Paul emerged as a Christian, we cannot readily accept the demotion of the "eschatological" data in the Pauline Epistles, nor the extreme, almost exclusive, concentration on the individual in Bultmann and Bornkamm, we shall, nevertheless, seek to do due justice to the emphasis on the individual as it relates to our theme at a later stage and hope to indicate its deep significance.

A second way to explain the paradox with which we deal is suggested by the provocative work of G. B. Caird on the nature of apocalyptic language.[76] Although he distinguishes between the usage of Jesus and that of the New Testament epistles, it is worth while asking how the application of his understanding of Apocalyptic bears upon the paradox which concerns us. According to him, individual eschatology must be sharply distinguished from national eschatology. The former deals with "the last" things of an individual's life: the latter with critical events in the people's life which are not necessarily the last events at all, but rather those which bring the forces at work in a given period of a nation's history to their inexorable, moral conclusion: thus the Day of the Son of Man has reference in the Gospels not to the ultimate, last judgment, but to the judgment on the nation of Israel in the war of A.D. 70. If such be the inner meaning of apocalyptic language, that is, if it designates the culmination of the process of the divine will in this world, how shall we understand Rom. 9–11? Caird himself does not deal with this question, but the logic of his position which we venture to pursue here would seem to demand some such interpretation of it as the following.

Paul looks at the actual situation of his people. The Gentiles are accepting the Gospel: the Jews are in part rejecting it. But he looks forward to a day when the Jewish people will recognize the spiritual blessings granted to the Gentiles and thus be led to join the Church. He is not thinking of this event as something at the end of all history, but as a process at work in his own day and as the prelude to a new stage in history. Romans 9–11 obviously deals with national eschatology. Yes! But these chapters, it is implied in Caird's view, do not, as Munck thinks,

---

[76] *Jesus and the Jewish Nation*, Ethel M. Wood Lecture, Athlone Press, London, 1965. For Caird eschatological language is never employed independently of its concrete, historical embodiment and realization. See ET, Vol. LXXIV, 1962–63, p. 84, "On Deciphering the Book of Revelation—III. The First and the Last."

look forward to the End but only to the full expression, in history, of the forces that Paul saw at work in the Church and among his own people.

To what does this lead us? The paradox to which we referred is only a paradox if we follow Munck in treating Rom. 9–11 as if they dealt with the end of all history and in connecting the collection with this end. But there is no reason—if we avoid the intolerable literalism of the conventional interpretation of Apocalyptic—to pin the hope for the entry of the Jews into the Church to the last stage of history and to connect the collection specifically with this. Paul did take up the collection to Jerusalem: he did regard that city as the geographic centre of the world and the scene where the drama of his nation was to be played out. But important as he thought the collection to be, when he wrote Romans he did not expect that the end of all things would coincide with the delivery of that collection. Hence the paradox is no real paradox at all. Paul could go up to Jerusalem with the collection, but, since he was not looking forward to the end of all history at that time, he could also look forward to a visit to Spain. The paradox disappears in the light of a reinterpretation of national eschatology.

Caird demands a drastic change in our understanding of Apocalyptic. Do the epistles warrant this? It should be noticed that his view helps to a solution of Rom. 11: 26. In the view we have expounded in the light of Caird's work, Zion, from which the Redeemer is to come, will be the Christian community coming into being in Paul's day in Zion as elsewhere. But the same view does not adequately explain the topographical reference in Rom. 9: 26, nor the reference to the resurrection of the dead, which is best taken to refer to the final resurrection, although Caird would "spiritualize" this event.

Even if we are not entirely convinced that Apocalyptic is an interpretation of the present national condition rather than a "fictionalized" premonition of the ultimate end of the nation and of the world, such an approach as is implied in Caird's interpretation of Apocalyptic applied to Rom. 9–11 should warn us against one thing: the too sure connection between the collection and the end of all history. In fact, popular as is this connection in recent scholarship, it is drawn by scholars, not necessitated by the text itself: it is merely based on an assumed probability. Nor should it be overlooked that if, as some have thought, Rom. 9–11 existed as an independent "sermon" on the Jewish question before Romans was composed, it is even more precarious to connect the collection with Paul's thoughts therein. And it is possible to understand the collection without recourse to Rom. 9–11, that is, to separate it from anticipations of the immediately expected End entirely. It is clear that when Paul took the collection to Jerusalem he was thinking of a time beyond the collection when he would be free to pursue his course. If, on the basis of 1 and 2 Thess. and 1 Cor., we ascribe to him an expectation of an imminent End of all things—an End, the events of which were to be centred in Jerusalem—by the time we come to Romans, although that city remains the city of the End, Paul is no longer governed by concern with it as the ultimate centre of his activity. Rather, Jerusalem has become for him the place where the unity of the "Israel of God," not the end of history, is to be revealed. How this is so we shall enlarge upon when we turn to Georgi's work below. The important point to make here is that despite Paul's concentration on the collection for the "poor" in Jerusalem, by the time he came to write Romans, his tie with the land does not appear to have been as compulsive as Munck's "apocalyptic" rigidity in the treatment of the Apostle demands.

6. DEVELOPMENT IN PAUL

Had that tie ever been compulsive? In much recent scholarship it has been emphasized that there was a change in Paul's eschatological concentration. The changes in the Apostle's eschatology as a Christian were traced by R. H. Charles,[77] but it was C. H. Dodd,[78] in a famous essay, who documented that these changes were a development from the apocalyptic concentration in 1 and 2 Thessalonians to a more restrained treatment of the End in 1 Corinthians and later epistles. The same emphasis on development re-emerged in Cerfaux's work. The briefest statement of it will suffice here.

Apart from his very early ones, Paul's epistles are less concerned with apocalyptic imagery as with such concepts as "in Christ," "dying and

---

[77] *A Critical History of the Doctrine of a Future Life in Israel, in Judaism and in Christianity*, London, 1899.

[78] "The Mind of Paul, Change and Development," BJRL, Vol. XVIII, Manchester, 1934. For a lucid and helpful survey of this question, see William Baird, NTS, Vol. 17, April 1971, pp. 314–327, "Pauline Eschatology in Hermeneutical Perspective." He recognizes change in Paul's eschatology but no gradual development from Jewish to Hellenistic forms. There is a reduction in Apocalyptic in Paul, as Dodd indicates. "Because apocalyptic language is used primarily to describe the indescribable future, the reduction of apocalyptic involves an increasing concern for the past and the present—a concern apparent even in Galatians (v. 1–12; vi. 7–10) and II Cor. x–xiii (cf. x. 3–4; xi. 12–33). At the same time, Paul's eschatological thought has become increasingly personal (p. 327)." On the relation between Paul and Apocalyptic, see my article "Paul and Jewish Christianity according to Cardinal Daniélou: A suggestion," *Recherches de Sciences Religieuse*, Janviers-Mars, Tome 60, 1972, pp. 69–80: Paul was a "reductionist" in Apocalyptic: his attitude to the land illustrates this.

rising with Christ," "in the Spirit." Despite its early traditional apocalyptic framework (with its geographic structure concentrated in the
Temple in Jerusalem) the centre of gravity of Paul's thinking shifted
away from such traditional, geographic eschatology. The real centre of
his interest moved to certain realities encountered "in Christ." Munck's
geographic emphasis, therefore, set over against the totality of the Pauline
corpus, even if Colossians and Ephesians be omitted from such a corpus,
seems exaggerated. It presents a distorted picture which should at least be
counterbalanced by other emphases in Paul to which we have referred.

And assuming that there was an increasing diminution or de-empha-
sizing of the apocalyptic, and, if we recognize Rom. 9: 26 and 11: 26 to
be isolated phenomena, of the apocalyptic-geographic element in Paul,
scholars have sought to explain an apparently growing lack of interest in
the *realia* of Judaism in the Apostle. There are three ways in which the
change has been dealt with—the personal, the intellectual, and the
ecclesiological.

1. The personal approach is associated especially with C. H. Dodd,[79]
whose position is so familiar that it need only be touched upon. According to this, two factors in particular impinged upon Paul's thought of
the End—his experience of the delay of the Parousia, and of spiritual
humiliation and reconciliation. At the beginning of his ministry, Paul
expected that the End was to come almost immediately. His preaching at
Thessalonica had created such a vivid or urgent expectation of the
imminent Parousia that many Christians had given up their work: they
seem to have fallen into a frenzy of anticipation which Paul had to correct.
But the Parousia was delayed. Some Christians at Thessalonica died.
What was to be their lot? Paul had now to reinterpret the End so that he
could come to terms with the fact that some Christians had already died.

The Apostle inevitably encountered the same problem at Corinth.
Again, he was instigated to deal with the resurrection of Christians who
had died or would die before the Parousia. The geographic schema of
Apocalyptic had to be modified in more complicated terms in 1 Cor. 15.
And death crept closer still. By the time 2 Corinthians came to be written,
the possibility of his own demise faced Paul. And at the same time he had
passed through a crisis of the spirit. An attempt at re-establishing his
authority at Corinth had failed, and Paul found himself incapable of
effective speech and action. He was humiliated: 2 Cor. 9: 1; 11: 7; 12: 21.
But in the depths of his humiliation he had gained firm ground. He came

[79] *Ibid.*

to accept his limitations; and 2 Cor. 1–9 reveals a chastened Paul. He apologizes for his previous letter, pleads for affection, and reveals an acceptance of life, a reconciliation to experience. God's grace has become sufficient for him.

From this probably, according to Dodd, was born the changed temper of all his later epistles. The impatience of the Apocalyptist, calculating the time and planning and, indeed, trying to manipulate the future, has left him. The future hope is retained, but there is increasingly a greater recognition that the substance of hope is a present possession: the imminence of the End is less emphasized. The later epistles reveal a gradual diminution of apocalyptic dualism, a growing appreciation of this world and, we may add, an unconcern with geographic apocalyptic. The Lord is now to appear, not in Jerusalem, but "from heaven." "From heaven we expect our deliverer to come. . . ." and "the commonwealth of Christians" is already "in heaven (Phil. 3: 20–21)." To be "in Christ" in the present and to be with Christ in the world to come has replaced any hope that Paul may ever have cherished of dwelling in the land.[80]

Not all have been convinced by this approach. Any reconstruction of Paul's experience, since based upon sporadic epistles, must be conjectural, and it is doubtful whether the reality of his personally profound spiritual experience alone would have sufficed to work such a deep change. But it is difficult not to agree with Dodd that, for whatever reason, there is a change in the epistles. In 1 and 2 Thess., 1 Cor., 2 Cor. 6: 14–7: 1, and 2 Cor. 10: 1 – 13: 10 there is a dwelling upon apocalyptic elements and an apocalyptic "mood" which are absent from Romans, 2 Cor. 1–9, and the Captivity Epistles. This change was naturally accompanied by the abandonment of geographic eschatology.

2. Secondly, Paul's deliverance from traditional Jewish apocalyptic forms of thought has been connected especially with the theological challenge which faced him when he came to present the Palestinian Gospel couched in geographic-apocalyptic terms to the Hellenistic world. This "deliverance" arose not so much out of a crisis of the spirit or of moral experience, as out of a crisis of thought. This view has recently been forcefully presented by Lucien Cerfaux.[81] He urges that the Pauline epistles reveal a development from an eschatology expressed in terms of

---

[80] The distinction on being "in Christ" in this world and "with Christ" in the world to come, which was emphasized by E. Lohmeyer "*Sun Christō*" in *Festgabe für Deissmann*, Tübingen, 1927, pp. 218–257, has not carried conviction. It is followed by A. Wikenhauser, *Pauline Mysticism: Christ in the Mystical Teaching of St. Paul*, trans., New York, 1960, pp. 206f.

[81] *Le Chrétien Dans La Théologie Paulinienne*, Paris, 1962, pp. 266ff.

Jewish apocalyptic to a more refined Hellenistic eschatology. Such a transition was not as violent as is often imagined. The expectations of Judaism existed within the more general anticipations of the Graeco-Roman world. Influences from ancient Babylonian and Persian religions and from the contemporary mysteries and religions, Judaism among them, had led to a faith in world renewal. Virgil's Fourth Eclogue bears witness to this. Early Greek philosophy had long since mused upon the unification of the world. The monotheism of Xenophanes (who had claimed that: "There is one God, sovereign over gods and men; he is not like mortals in bodily ideas, nor in thoughts") had persisted. The multiplicity of secondary gods was reabsorbed fairly easily into a principal divinity, sometimes Zeus or Serapis or Isis. And along with this monotheism had grown a belief in immortality and in future rewards and punishments.

The view of Cerfaux, and he has eminent predecessors, in particular W. L. Knox,[82] is that Paul gradually adapted his Gospel to this Hellenistic hope. The process of adaptation has begun even in 1 Thess. In 1 Thess. 1: 1–10, Paul gives a digest of the results of the preaching of the Gospel among the Thessalonians: he writes how "(they) turned to God from idols, to serve the living and true God, and to wait for his Son from heaven, whom he raised from the dead, Jesus who delivers us from the wrath to come." Here monotheism, future judgment, and the resurrection emerge as the central motifs of Paul's message, and these were motifs familiar to Gentiles.[83] In 1 Thess. 4: 13ff and 2 Thess. 2: 3–12 the commonplaces of apocalyptic literature appear in the listing of the premonitory signs of Christ's coming—the great apostasy and the revelation of the man of lawlessness ("The son of perdition, who opposes and exalts himself against every so-called god or object of worship, so that he takes his seat in the Temple of God proclaiming himself to be God"). But, note, it has been possible for modern scholars to detect even in the pictures of the Lord's return in 1 and 2 Thess. influences from the joyous entries of Hellenistic sovereigns, kings and emperors, into the cities of their possession; and they appeal to St. John Chrysostom for support. By the time we come to 1 Cor. 15: 24–26, Paul no longer describes the eschatological war in the panoply of Apocalytic, although traces of this remain. It is now in the realm of spiritual powers. At the last, Christ overcomes his enemies, including the last enemy, Death, the symbol of man's revolt against God. In 1 Cor. 15: 26–28, the End is described with classical simplicity.

[82] *St. Paul and the Church of the Gentiles*, Cambridge, 1939; *Some Hellenistic Elements in Primitive Christianity* (Schweich Lectures, 1942), London, 1944.
[83] Compare R. Bultmann, *Theology*, New York, 1951, Vol. I, Chapter 3, on this preaching.

The last enemy to be destroyed is death. "For God has put all things in subjection under his feet." But when it says, "All things are put in subjection under him," it is plain that he is excepted who put all things under him. When all things are subjected to him, then the Son himself will also be subjected to him who put all things under him, that God may be everything to everyone (ἵνα ᾖ ὁ Θεὸς πάντα ἐν πᾶσιν) (RSV).

At two places, then, Cerfaux discovers a profound Hellenization of Paul's thought: here, in the concept of eternal life (for so Cerfaux[84] understands the concept that "God is all in all," NEB), unrelated to any geographic dimension, as the end of the Christian life emerges, and at 1 Cor. 13: 12–13, which defines the vision of God as knowledge. ("For now we see in a mirror dimly, but then face to face. Now I know in part; then I shall understand fully, even as I have been fully understood. So faith, hope, love abide, these three; but the greatest of these is love.") From this point forward that Hellenization proceeds apace in Paul's development of the notion of a spiritual resurrection in 1 Cor. 15: 42–44, 53; Phil. 3: 21, and in that of an inner and outward man in 2 Cor. 4: 7–5: 10, and of course, in the notion of a dwelling not made with hands eternal in the heavens in 2 Cor. 5: 2ff.[85]

We need go no further. Paul, in this view abandoned Jewish eschatology, with its geographic structure, and embraced the perspectives of Hellenistic dualism. It follows inexorably that the *realia* of Judaism, and, especially for our purpose, the Temple, Jerusalem, and the land could no longer have the significance for the older Paul that they had for the younger.

The issue raised by Knox and Cerfaux over the Hellenization of Paul's understanding of the Gospel cannot be discussed here. I have urged elsewhere that the alleged Hellenization can be questioned at any rate in degree, and that the familiar dichotomy between the Semitic and the Hellenistic needs extremely sensitive assessment. The increasing recognition of the interpenetration of Judaism and Hellenism in the first century makes any dogmatism highly precarious.[86] In view of recent work on the opponents of Paul in Corinth and of Paul's almost conservative appeal to the eschatological realities in his attempt to combat them, it seems clear

---

[84] Cerfaux, *Le Chrétien*, pp. 212f. Contrast A. Schweitzer, *The Mysticism of St. Paul The Apostle*, trans., New York, 1968, p. 12. The translation of 1 Cor. 15: 28 is that of the RSV; that of the NEB is more exact: "and thus God will be all in all."

[85] *Le Chrétien*, pp. 495ff.

[86] For references see p. 91, n. 30 above.

that Cerfaux is guilty of two things:[87] (1) an overemphasis on the purely "intellectual" confrontation of Paul with Hellenism: Paul himself, indeed, seems to have abjured such a confrontation at least at Corinth (1 Cor. 2: 1ff); and (2) an underestimate of the pervasiveness of Apocalyptic in primitive Christianity and the tenacity of its hold upon Paul. Two reactions are provoked by Cerfaux's treatment. The first is in the form of a question. Granted that the *realia* of Jewish apocalyptic do recede in Paul's later epistles, was this because he moved more and more in the Gentile world, and was compelled to envisage the future in a cosmic, rather than a Palestinian setting, and to bring into prominence those aspects of Jewish eschatology which were most amenable to presentation and reinterpretation to the Hellenistic mind, without necessarily jettisoning other aspects of a more tangible, geographic kind? And the second is this. There is no doubt that, as he saw the Gentile Church grow, the centrality of Christ as Living Lord became more and more normative for the Apostle. It is no accident that, in 2 Cor. 5, and elsewhere, he does not speak of being gathered to his fathers, although he recognized Abraham and Isaac and Jacob as the fathers of Christians. No! He speaks of being "in Christ" and being "with Christ," and that in the company of those who with him had responded to the Gospel. Deissmann was not wholly wrong when he understood the phrase "in Christ" in a kind of locative sense. Christ has become for Paul the "locus" of redemption here and in the world to come. "The land" has been for him "Christified." It is not the land promised much as he had loved it that became his "inheritance," but the Living Lord, in whom was a new creation.

In the last few words I have noted that Paul thought of being "in Christ" and "with Christ" not as a solitary state of individual possession. It was no flight of the "alone to the Alone." It was rather a life shared with those who, with him, had responded to Christ. Without underestimating its intensely personal or individual dimension, to which we shall return,

---

[87] See the illuminating remarks by E. Käsemann, "Primitive Christian Apocalyptic," in *New Testament Questions Today*, trans., Philadelphia, 1969, p. 132. "If we try to see things through the eyes of his adversaries, we shall have to describe Pauline theology as a retarding, more a reactionary stage of development." D. Georgi, *Die Gegner des Paulus in 2. Korintherbrief: Studien zur religiösen Propaganda in der Spätantike. Wissenschaftliche Monographien zum Alten und Neuen Testament*, XI, Neukirchener Verlag, 1964, finds a strong Jewish element in the opposition that Paul faced, that is, the preaching of Jewish-Christian wandering preachers coming out of Hellenistic Jewish apologetic circles. Paul probably did not confront Hellenism head on, as Cerfaux assumes. See C. K. Barrett, NTS, Vol. 17, No. 3, April 1971, on "Paul's Opponents in II Corinthians." "The chief actors who appeared on the Corinthian stage, under the eye of a Corinthian audience, were Jews (p. 253)."

"in Christ" was for him a communal conception. In one passage Paul seems even to equate Christ with the *ecclesia* (1 Cor. 12: 12). And this brings us to the next factor which has to be reckoned with in understanding that diminution of the significance of the *realia* of Judaism which occupies us: the ecclesiological.

3. The ecclesiological approach can best be brought out by a return to the collection with which we dealt earlier and to Georgi's treatment of it.[88] Georgi claims that Paul undertook two distinct collections.[89] The first was in response to the request of "the pillars" of the Church as reported in Gal. 2: 10. There was a special theological reason for Paul's acceptance of that task. He feared that his churches might cease to be united with the Jerusalem Church. But why was such unity essential? Could not Paul allow his churches to develop in independence? If the Jerusalem Church perished meanwhile, would that make any fundamental difference? The answer to these questions turns on eschatological geography, on the centrality of the city of Jerusalem in the mind of Paul, as of other Christians. There—in the city of David—was the eschatological hope to be realized. The earliest disciples had returned from Galilee to Jerusalem for this reason.[90] They considered themselves not as a remnant, a concept which can be greatly exaggerated in the interpretation of the New Testament,[91] but as the people of God awaiting the End in the city of the End. Paul desired his churches to belong to that same people of God. The church of Jerusalem had an eschatological significance, and deserved to be remembered for this reason. Georgi even suggests that the verb *mnêmoneuô* in Gal. 2: 10 has the significance of "recognition." That is, "the poor," interpreted as the totality of the Church in Jerusalem, deserved the recognition of their eschatological significance in the eschatological city. The collection was a sign of this recognition.[92]

But despite the extended right hand of fellowship, Peter and Paul came into open collision in Antioch. Paul became estranged from the Antiochian Church and inaugurated his own mission. The aorists in Gal. 2: 10 (*espoudasa poiêsai*) signify that the zeal for the collection, requested by "the pillars," was a thing of the past, and there is no sign that Paul even organized this collection among the Galatians.[93] He had become disenchanted, both with those who had joined him in the agreement, and

---

[88] Georgi, *Die Geschichte der Kollekte.*   [89] *Ibid.*, pp. 39ff.

[90] *Ibid.*, pp. 25ff.   [91] See above p. 43, n. 9.

[92] *Die Geschichte der Kollekte*, p. 27. According to Georgi μνημονεύω has the meaning not, as has generally been held, of "remembering in order to help," but of "remembering in recognition." The Christians in Jerusalem wanted to be recognized as the holy remnant.

[93] *Ibid.*, pp. 31ff.

with the Jerusalem "pillars" with whom he had made it. He became increasingly critical of Judaism (1 Thess. 2: 14–16). In Gal. 4: 22ff he combats an over-evaluation of Jerusalem. He even equates that city with Hagar and calls it a place of servitude against which he opposes a Jerusalem above. The geographic Jerusalem and her Church have no longer a special place in his thought: his first theological, eschatological understanding of the Jerusalem "poor," that is, the Church there, is discarded.[94]

But what of the numerous references to a collection in other epistles? According to Georgi, these do not refer to that inaugurated by "the pillars," but to a wholly new collection which Paul himself started. This new collection had a different ground. The collection asked for by "the pillars" was designed to promote and even to create unity, which had been destroyed by the false understanding of the Gospel urged by Paul's opponents. The collection which Paul himself inaugurated was to be an expression of an already existing God-given unity, arising out of the grasp of the Gospel by the Gentile Churches or rather by God's grasp of the Churches in the Gospel.

The first reference to this strictly Pauline collection occurs in 1 Cor. 16: 1–4. In the *kerygma* outlined in 1 Cor. 15: 3ff, there is no explicit geographic concern. But immediately after the close of 1 Cor. 15, the chapter on the Resurrection, Paul turns to a collection again. Why? Because the witnesses to the Resurrection still lived in Jerusalem: it was to their witness that Christians everywhere owed their being. The collection asked for in 1 Cor. 16: 1–4 is in recognition of this fact. It is not in recognition of a community located in the eschatological city, but in recognition of the unity of all Christians with the original witnesses. This new collection is a token of gratitude for the *kerygma*, the foundation of the Church. But it is now a grace (*charis*), an expression of a will to unity and a living connection with Jerusalem Christians. Paul no longer sees the collection as his work, but as that of God in the communities. In 2 Cor. 8, he never mentions those who are to receive the collection in Jerusalem: he is interested not in them as such particularly, but more in the communities that organized the collection. In 2 Cor. 8: 1, the collection is a grace of God for the Macedonians; their sacrifice is not for the Jerusalem Church but for God and Paul (2 Cor. 8: 5). Their gift is abundant fruit of God's grace (2 Cor. 9: 10).

[94] *Ibid.*, pp. 33ff. Georgi finds in the Galatian communities an over-evaluation of law and history and of the earthly Jerusalem. This Paul had to oppose by pointing, among other things, to the Heavenly Jerusalem. Birger A. Pearson, HTR, vol. 64, 1971, pp. 79–94, "1 Thessalonians 2: 13–16: A Deutero-Pauline Interpolation," argues impressively that the passage concerned, to which Georgi appeals, is not Pauline.

That Jerusalem and the Jerusalem Christians are no longer the centre of Paul's interest, which has shifted to the Gentile Churches which have so wondrously come into being and borne fruit, appears in Rom. 15. As we have already indicated, for Georgi, the term "poor" here no longer signifies the whole Church of Jerusalem, as it had in Galatians, but the poverty-striken in its ranks.[95] Its eschatological reference is muted. Voluntarily the Churches of Macedonia and Achaia, in return for spiritual blessings which they had received through the Jerusalem Church, had been moved to contribute.[96]

But the eschatological dimension of the collection is not forsaken. Already in 2 Cor. 9: 9 the citation of Isaiah connects the collection with the theme of the eschatological procession of Jews and Gentiles to Jerusalem. And, like Munck, Georgi also understands the collection in the light of Rom. 9–11, where the salvation of the Gentiles is, if not the condition of, the prelude to the salvation of the Jews. The eschatological procession leading to that salvation begins with the collection, which will testify to the presence of God's eschatological salvation. But, note, delivery of the collection by a delegation of uncircumcised Gentiles is a complete reversal of Jewish expectation. The Gentiles now take precedence over the Jews. The centre of interest is no longer the Church of Jerusalem, but the eschatological significance of the emergence of the Gentile Churches, the character of which is revealed by the collection— a sure sign that God's grace is in *their* midst.[97]

Georgi's work does not always carry conviction. His case for a rigid separation of the collection asked for by "the pillars" in Gal. 2: 10 and a distinct, personal collection inaugurated by Paul himself rests on dubious grammatical grounds[98] and is a *tour de force*. Sometimes, as in his interpretation of *ex isotêtos* in 2 Cor., and his contrast of "the poor" with the Temple in the treatment of the delivery of the collection, his exegesis is forced. In much, also, he differs little from Munck. Both scholars retain a geographical-eschatological framework for Paul's activity. Both find the centre of the land and the world, Jerusalem, highly significant for Paul. But Georgi has brought into prominence a crucial, and extremely

---

95 *Ibid.*, pp. 81f.

96 *Ibid.*, pp. 39–85 for all the above.

97 *Ibid.*, pp. 40, 85ff.

98 Does the aorist in Gal. 2: 10 (ἐσπούδασα) necessarily imply that Paul is no longer interested in the collection? The translation offered for Gal. 2: 6 is not wholly convincing. Gal. 2: 6 has to be taken with Gal. 2: 9. Nor is the translation proposed for δεξιὰς ἔδωκαν ἐμοὶ καὶ βαρναβᾷ κοινωνίας without difficulty. For the treatment of ἐξ ἰσότητος, see Georgi, *Die Geschichte der Kollekte*, pp. 62ff, 97ff.

important, dimension in Paul's connection with the collection which neither Munck nor Dodd nor Cerfaux have emphasized, but which, as we suggested above, *might* be deduced from Caird's work. In his concentration on geographic eschatology, Munck fitted Paul into an apocalyptic mould. Georgi's treatment, in principle, frees Paul from this mould. His recognition of Paul's growing awareness of the grace of God at work in the quality of the response of the Gentile Christians to the Gospel makes clear that, despite its apocalyptic framework (that is, the geographic, eschatological structure centring in Jerusalem), the centre of gravity of Paul's ministry has shifted away from geographic eschatology. The real centre of his interest has moved from "the land," concentrated in Jerusalem, to the communities "in Christ." This is what the Pauline epistles as a whole attest. Passages that deal directly with eschatology in its apocalyptic form are few. Paul's epistles are mostly peppered, not with apocalyptic imagery, but with terms such as "in Christ," "dying and rising with Christ," "in the Spirit." The life "in Christ" is the life of the eschatological Israel, an Israel, which, through Christ, transcends the connection with the land and with the Law attached to that land.

Or, again, Christians constitute the Body of Christ, a phrase which emerges, in an ecclesiological sense, in the later epistles of Paul and finds its fullest expression in Ephesians, an epistle which according to many is not by Paul, and indicates, in its concentration on and interpretation of the Church, a non-Pauline development. Into the relationship between these two ways of thinking about the Christian community, that is, as the eschatological Israel and as the Body of Christ, their mutuality or incompatibility, we need not enter here.[99] The point is that they both emphasize the significance which Paul gave to the believers and point to his communal or societary understanding of those who are "in Christ." To be "in Christ"—interpreted in terms of the eschatological "people of God" and salvation-history or more "locatively" in terms of the Body of Christ—has replaced being "in the land" as the ideal life.

At this point we must, however, recall that there are those—perhaps the majority—who have concentrated on the individualism of Paul's understanding of the life "in Christ." Particularly the doctrine of justification by faith has been interpreted as concerned with the pangs of conscience and their alleviation.[100] The societary, not to speak of the

---

[99] The problem is discussed with penetration by Käsemann, *Perspectives on Paul*, pp. 102ff.

[100] See K. Stendahl, "The Apostle Paul and the Introspective Conscience of the West," HTR, Vol. LVI, 1963, pp. 199–215, reprinted in S. H. Miller and G. Ernest Wright, eds.,

ecclesiological, dimension of Paul's understanding of the Christian life has been questioned, or at best, set over against the individualistic. But it is not necessary to separate what in Paul is inseparable. Romans 7, the classic Pauline treatment of the individual, occurs in the same Epistle as his classic treatment of the fate of Israel, in Rom. 9–11. To set the reconciliation of the individual and the amelioration of his pangs of conscience rigidly over against the reconciliation of Israel and the nations is to fail to deal with Paul in the actuality and totality of his experience: it is to fall victim to an especially excessive theological conceptualization of Paul, as of other persons and phenomena in the New Testament. Because, in fact, it is precisely in the context of his confrontation with the fate of Israel and the nations that Paul's sense of his individual failures comes to expression. True, in Rom. 7[101] he seems specifically to refer to sexual failure, but this should not mislead us into thinking that his moral sense would not have been quickened and sensitized as he wrestled with the fate of Israel and the nations. Recent events, particularly in the U.S.A., have revealed how wrestling with social problems of a vast scope, in the Civil Rights Movement and otherwise, has a strange and sometimes devastating way of revealing personal moral failures in which "Liberals" and "Conservatives" share and by which they are equally humbled. Social involvement often leads to a personal or individual conviction of sin and a quickening of the pangs of conscience. What personal agony lies behind Rom. 9: 1–6? Did the inclusion of the Gentiles in "Israel" and the "failure" of Israel so shake the very "foundations" of Paul that his moral awareness was spurred into a new sensitivity, just as the current struggle for civil rights in this country has "awakened" many who previously "slept"? Whether this question be answered affirmatively or not, the intense personal dimension of the life "in Christ" has a real bearing on Paul's relationship to the land. The deeply personal nature of that life would, in itself, be not uncongenial to detachment from the land. Aldous Huxley in an essay entitled "Words and Behaviour," wrote as follows: "But *the moment we start resolutely thinking about our world in terms of individual persons we find ourselves at the same time thinking in terms of universality.* 'The great national religions', writes Professor Whitehead, 'are the outcome of the emergence of a religious consciousness that is universal, as

---

Ecumenical Dialogue at Harvard, Cambridge, 1964, pp. 236–256 and Käsemann's response, *Perspectives on Paul*, pp. 6off. See PRJ, p. xiii, and D. O. Via, *Sciences Religieuses: Studies in Religion*, Vol. 13, Canada, 1971, pp. 204–212 on "Justification and Deliverance: Existential Dialectic" for a critique and assessment of Stendahl. Via's article is especially important.

[101] Romans 7: 7 points to sex, but the total context in Rom. 7 points also the fall of Adam. See PRJ, p. 32.

distinguished from tribal and even social. Because it is universal, it introduces the note of solitariness.' (And he might have added that, because it is solitary, it introduces the note of universality.) *The reason of this connection between universality and solitude is that universality is a disconnection from immediate surroundings.* And conversely the disconnection from immediate surroundings, particularly such social surroundings as the tribe or nation, the insistence on the person as the fundamental reality leads to the conception of an all embracing unity (our italics)."[102] Notice particularly the words in italics. The moment the personal relationship with Christ became primary for Paul the process of his "disenlandisement," if we may use such a term, had begun. "Individualism" no less than "ecclesiology" would lead him to disconnect himself ultimately from the land.[103]

In the above pages we have sought to bring together the personal, theological, and ecclesiological factors that impinged upon Paul and led him not so much to look away from the land of his fathers as to discover his inheritance "in Christ"—the land of Christians, the new creation, if we may so express the matter. In conclusion, let us point out that apart from any such pressures as we have indicated, the Gospel, as Paul understood it, in itself implied such a development. Let us recall again that, although many Jews have regarded the Torah as itself a "portable land," and have deliberately chosen and justified living outside the land of Israel while remaining "observant," that is, obedient to the demands of the Torah, nevertheless, on its own terms, in principle and in its entirety, the Torah is inseparable from that land. The Gospel substituted for the Torah, Jesus, the Christ, who was, indeed born and bred in the land, but

---

[102] From Aldous Huxley's essay on "Words and Behaviour" in *Collected Essays*, by Aldous Huxley, New York, 1959. The quotation from Whitehead is not documented by Huxley.

[103] We have taken seriously and affirmatively the main thrust of Georgi's treatment. But the following comment by G. Stemberger needs to be taken into account also. "There certainly is a shift in emphasis from the position of the poor of Jerusalem to the place the Christian communities have in the collection. But does this include a new theological interpretation and understanding of the Jewish-Christian community at Jerusalem? The eschatological task of the Jerusalem community (to represent the whole Church at the site of the expected eschatological events) is not incompatible with the interpretation of the delivery of the collection as the eschatological procession to Jerusalem, even when the first point loses some of its importance. And the geographical Jerusalem has the same importance in the first and in the second stage of this development: it is always there where the signs of the end are to take place (in a private communication)." We go further in asserting that, in principle, more than Stemberger allows, Paul has broken away from his prior attitude to Jerusalem, although emotionally he failed to do so: it is not so much the role of the Jewish-Christian community at Jerusalem that now draws Paul's concern as the reality of the grace of God in the *Gentile* churches.

who became the Living Lord, the Spirit. "The wind blows where it wills, and you hear the sound of it, but you do not know whence it comes or whither it goes; so is it with every one who is born of the Spirit." So wrote the author of the Fourth Gospel (3: 8). Paul and John were here at one. For Paul, the Lord and the Spirit were almost exchangeable. And once Paul had made the Living Lord rather than the Torah the centre in life and in death, once he had seen in Jesus his Torah, he had in principle broken with the land. "In Christ" Paul was free from the Law and, therefore, from the land. It is arguable that he never completely and consciously and emotionally abandoned the geography of eschatology: it may have continued alongside his new awareness of the "ecclesiological" eschatology inaugurated by Christ. For a long time Paul apparently felt no incongruity between retaining his apocalyptic geography, centred in Jerusalem, even though, since he was "in Christ," it had become otiose. Theologically he had no longer any need of it: his geographical identity was subordinated to that of being "in Christ," in whom was neither Jew nor Greek.

VIII. THE LAND IN MARK AND MATTHEW

E. Lohmeyer and R. H. Lightfoot discovered in the Synoptics a connection between locality and doctrine, an emphasis (in Mark and Matthew) on Galilee as the sphere of revelation and redemption, and in both Gospels (though perhaps to a lesser degree in Matthew) an emphasis on Jerusalem as the place of rejection. With variations, their work has been continued by Marxsen. Here we assume Stemberger's survey of the debate on this matter in Appendix B, p. 409,[1] and in these pages we concentrate on one aspect of it, the contribution of Naphtali Wieder.

The explanation which Lohmeyer, Lightfoot, and Marxsen gave for the emphases referred to was that there were two centres of primitive Christianity, one in Galilee (Lohmeyer thinks of a Galilean Christianity existing from the very beginning, following immediately on the resurrection; Marxsen finds it emerging later, and regards it as especially contemporary with Mark), and the other in Jerusalem. These two centres imposed their respective interests on the tradition. The geographic patterns discovered by the three scholars mentioned are necessarily tentative, and are by no means clean cut. For example, as we shall indicate later, Lightfoot himself recognized that the pre-eminence of Galilee is not consistently kept in view by Matthew: the lament over Jerusalem in Matthew is an expression of love as well as of condemnation, and even in Mark there is a note of hostility toward Jesus in Galilee.[2] The question will insinuate itself whether the geographical references in the tradition, which, by much subtle exegesis, are made to yield the doctrinal interpretations proposed are not simply reminiscences or floating data, inaccurate or imprecise,

[1] In addition to the studies indicated by Stemberger, see E. Schweizer on "Eschatology in Mark's Gospel" in *Neotestamentica et Semitica: Studies in Honour of Matthew Black*, eds. E. E. Ellis and M. Wilcox, Edinburgh, 1969, pp. 114–118, where he subjects the view of Marxsen to convincing criticism. He follows H. Conzelmann, "Geschichte und Eschaton nach Mk 13," ZNW, 50 (1959), pp. 210–221, in insisting that Mark 13 did not expect the Parousia in the near future (see 13: 7f; 13: 3–8, 10, 14–23, 24). In addition, he notes (1) that eschatological or even apocalyptic passages are scarce in Mark; (2) that in view of the many references to the resurrection of Jesus, in 8: 31; 9: 9, 31; 10: 34, it is natural to expect not the Parousia at the end of the Gospel after 16: 8, but the resurrection appearance; (3) that "to see" can refer to the resurrection as much as to the Parousia (see below p. 230); (4) that Christians reading Mark 16: 1–8 would naturally think of the resurrection; in 13: 14 Christians are urged to flee not to Galilee, but to Judaean mountains; (5) that if Mark anticipated a very imminent Parousia he would not have bothered with problems such as marriage and divorce (as in 10: 1–12); (6) that for Mark the original expectation of a very near Parousia has vanished: the centre of his gospel is the *suffering* of the Son of Man which enables his disciples to follow him.

[2] R. H. Lightfoot, *Locality and Doctrine in the Gospels*, New York, date of preface, 1937, p. 130.

preserved in the tradition, which do not necessarily demand those interpretations. Apart from the precariousness of the highly original exegesis
in Lohmeyer, Lightfoot, and Marxsen, the difficulty in accepting their
theories of locality and doctrine has been twofold.

First, there has been no convincing evidence for the existence of a
distinct Galilean Christianity[3] such as could have imposed itself on the
tradition. It is particularly significant that attempts to prove that a
Galilean dynasty developed in the family of Jesus in early Christianity
have failed. And, secondly, according to Strack-Billerbeck[4] (and Lightfoot concedes this point),[5] in the ancient Jewish sources there is no
connection made between the Messiah and Galilee, so that any marked
eschatological or theological significance ascribed to Galilee by a primitive
Christian community would be extremely difficult to understand. True,
there are passages where Galilee may be referred to in Messianic contexts. These are Song of Songs Rabbah 4: 16, with parallels in Lev.
Rabbah 9: 6 and Num. Rabbah 13: 2. In these passages, if the term
"North" be taken to refer to Galilee, then the Messiah may be connected
with that area.

It is with this second difficulty in the theories of locality and doctrine
that we are concerned here, because it touches closely on our theme "the
Gospel and the Land." Recently Naphtali Wieder[6] has challenged the
view of Strack-Billerbeck that there was no connection made in ancient
sources between the Messiah and Galilee. He has sought to prove that
Galilee was well established in Jewish expectation as the place destined
for the Messianic redemption: he thereby supplies support, in his judgment, to Lohmeyer and Lightfoot. It will be recalled that, despite his
recognition of Strack-Billerbeck's view, the latter also urges that the
coming of the Messiah in Galilee for Mark rested on a divine choice of
that area as the sphere of revelation and for Matthew on a "dark promise"
that this would be so.[7] We shall, therefore, concentrate in this section on
Wieder's thesis and seek to show that it cannot confirm the position of

---

[3] See Stemberger below: L. Goppelt, *Jesus, Paul and Judaism*, trans., New York, 1964,
p. 100, is content merely to state without evidence that shortly after the crucifixion "in
Jerusalem and probably also in Galilee a *fellowship of these disciples of Jesus arose....*"

[4] SB, Vol. I, p. 160. "Der Messias wird in der älteren Literatur ausdrücklich nirgends mit
Galiläa in Verbindung gebracht...."

[5] *Locality and Doctrine*, p. 115.

[6] *The Judaean Scrolls and Karaism*, London, 1962.

[7] Lightfoot, *Locality and Doctrine*, p. 115. "Owing to our familiarity with the gospel
story," writes Lightfoot, "we are apt to forget how remarkable not to say impossible it is
likely to have seemed to Jewish thought that this should take place in Galilee." He refers to
John 7: 41–52 in support of this. For the dark promise, see p. 127.

Lohmeyer, Lightfoot, and Marxsen. That thesis is built on a series of tortuous steps.

1. Wieder begins by claiming that the Damascus, to which the Qumran Sect migrated,[8] is to be understood geographically.[9] Further, on the basis of IQS 8: 12–15 and 9: 19–20, and especially the War Scroll, IQM 1: 3, he equates Damascus with "the wilderness of the peoples." The passages read as follows:

IQS 8: 12–15

And when these things come to pass for the community in Israel (13) at these appointed times, they shall be separated from the midst of the habitation of perverse men to go into the desert to prepare the way of "Him"; (14) as it is written:

In the wilderness prepare the way of....Make straight in the desert a highway for our God.

[8] *The Judaean Scrolls*, pp. 1ff. See note 87. CDC 8: 6. "The well is the Law, and they who digged it are the penitents of Israel who went forth out of the land of Judah and sojourned in the land of Damascus... (Charles translation)."

[9] *Ibid.*, p. 3. The geographic connotation of Damascus in CDC 8: 6 has not been universally accepted. I. Rabinowitz, JBL, Vol. LXXIII, Pt. 1, March, 1954, pp. 11–35, denies that there was a post-Exilic withdrawal from Judaea to Damascus by the sectarians. He examines the references to "Damascus" and concludes that they refer to the migration of "the righteous, spared Remnants into Babylonian captivity; and 'Damascus' is merely the biblical tag (taken from Amos 5: 27 and quoted at CDC 7: 15 and all six other passages) [6: 5; 6: 19; 7: 19; 8: 21; 19: 34; 20: 12] used by the writer(s) to allude to the locale of the Assyro-Babylonian Captivity (p. 34)." (Rabinowitz uses the text of S. Schechter, *Fragments of a Zadokite Work*, Cambridge, 1910: his references are to it.) Why did the writer choose the term Damascus rather than Babylon? Rabinowitz answers: "because the former is not merely a geographical expression but a summary representation of his theological theories about the Exile [into Babylon] and the prophetic 'new Covenant.'" (*Ibid.*, n. 128.) J. M. Allegro, *The Dead Sea Scrolls*, Harmondsworth, 1956, p. 101, is not clear: "Damascus" is used "figuratively" of the place of exile of the Sect. T. H. Gaster, *The Dead Sea Scriptures*, New York, 1956, p. 4, takes the sojourn in the forbidding wilderness of Judaea to be described as exile "in the wilderness of Damascus" in fulfilment of Amos 5: 27. He notes that: "To emphasize the basic idea [that it was repeating in a later age the experience of their remote forefathers in the days of Moses] and to bring out more clearly its sense of continuity with previous 'remnants,' the community made a point of applying to itself a series of titles, styles and epithets charged with significant historical associations (p. 4)." This is the view of F. M. Cross, *The Ancient Library of Qumran and Modern Biblical Studies*, New York, 1958, pp. 59f, n. 46: "the land of Damascus," he writes, "is the prophetic name applied to the desert of Qumran." Like Wieder, he finds "the land of Damascus" parallel to "the desert of the peoples (Ezek. 20: 35)." (IQM 1. 2–3.) The most convincing treatment of the meaning of Damascus is the brilliant one by A. Jaubert in RB, Vol. 65, 1958, pp. 214–248, on "Le Pays de Damas": she shows how "the land of Damascus" is the place of the new alliance, Qumran; "Damascus" could come to bear this significance not because of the geographic Damascus (despite the Jewish influences there, Jos. *Jewish Wars*, II. 20. 2), but because of its use in prophecy in Amos 5: 27. Jaubert rightly emphasizes the Exile more than the Exodus (as does Gaster) in the typology of the Sect. A. Dupont-Sommer, *The Essene Writings from Qumran*, Oxford, 1961, p. 92, n. 2, takes the retreat into the desert in its literal sense in IQS 8: 12–15 (and presumably elsewhere), that is, it was to Qumran. See also above, p. 100, n. 63.

(15) This (way) is the study of the Law which He has promulgated by the hand of Moses...

IQS 9: 19–20

This is the time to *prepare the way* (20) to go into the desert...

IQM 1: 3

fo[r war] (shall be declared) on all their lands when the Deportation [Exile] of the Sons of light returns from the desert of the peoples to camp in the desert of Jerusalem (Translations of A. Dupont-Sommer in *The Essene Writings from Qumran*, 1962, Meridian Book: trans. by G. Vermès, pp. 92, 96, 169).

2. "The wilderness of the peoples" according to Ezek. 20: 35–37, was to be the scene of the eschatological covenant ("And I will bring you into the wilderness of the peoples...and I will cause you to pass under the rod, and I will bring you into the bond of the covenant"). The Sect migrated to Damascus "*in order to anticipate there the appearance of the Messiah or, in general, the inauguration of the Messianic drama* (Wieder's italics)." Wieder claims evidence in Rabbinic materials to support his claim that Damascus is to be the scene of Messianic events, that is, from Sifre Deut. ed. M. Friedmann, 65a; Song of Songs Rabbah 7: 5.[10] From Sifre Deut. ed. M. Friedmann, 79b, and Num. Rabbah 14: 4[11] he finds Tannaitic materials connecting Elijah, whose Messianic relationships are well known,[12] with Damascus. In other passages, Song of Songs Rabbah 4: 8 and Gen. Rabbah 78: 12 (a passage from a fourth-century Rabbi), the exiles are to be brought to the Messiah in Damascus in fulfilment of Is. 66: 20: ("And they shall bring all your brethren from all the nations as an offering to the Lord, upon horses, and in chariots, and in litters, and upon mules, and upon swift beasts"). This reference of the Messiah to Damascus is all the more striking here since in the Masoretic Text the nations are to be brought "to my holy mountain Jerusalem...," a portion of the verse which is omitted in the Midrash at Song of Songs 4: 8. In far later Karaite sources the same equation of Damascus with the scene of Messianic events occurs, supported by the very same text, Amos 5: 27, that is used in CDC 7: 14. But with this and much other later material

---

[10] In the light of the previous note, one of the weaknesses of Wieder's treatment is that he ignores other motifs than the Damascus one in the Scrolls. See the review by E. Wiesenberg, JSS, Vol. 11, 1965–66, pp. 264–268; he ignores the Exodus motif in CDC, 20: 13–15; C. Rabin, *The Zadokite Documents*, pp. 38f.

[11] This reads: "*Thy nose is like the tower of Lebanon, which looketh toward Damascus.*" This signifies: If you have fulfilled the Torah [And so elevated it like a tower], you may expect [As is implied by the words "*looketh toward*"] Elijah, to whom I said: *Go, return on thy way to the wilderness of Damascus* (1 Kings 19: 15)... (Soncino trans. p. 583).

[12] See SSM, pp. 158ff; R. B. Y. Scott, *The Canadian Journal of Religious Thought*, 1962, pp. 490–502; L. Ginzberg, *Eine unbekannte jüdische Sekte*, New York, 1922, pp. 303ff.

which Wieder adduces (from mediaeval Jewish Apocalypses, Qallir's religious poetry, and Islam) we need not stay. They are too late to be pertinent.[13]

3. The next step in Wieder's argument is that the land of Damascus included Lebanon and Anti-Lebanon (hence the designation of the community at Qumran as "Lebanon"; the Sect waited for the Messiah in Damascus-Lebanon).[14] But within Lebanon and Anti-Lebanon was Upper Galilee. The equation follows naturally, for Wieder, that Damascus can be identified with Galilee and that the Messianic expectations centred in the former pertained also to the latter. Upper Galilee, the land of Damascus, is the place for the ingathering of the exiles and the appearance of the Messiah. Wieder admits that only by tracing an eleventh-century source back to R. Levi, an Amora of the third century, can even such a late date be explicitly established for this belief. But even if geographically, perhaps, there is no impossible difficulty in equating Galilee with Damascus, because the former had a very widespread significance and stretched both to the Lebanon and the Anti-Lebanon,[15] it should be noticed that Josephus presents a very well-defined Galilee, which does not partake of the vagueness ascribed to the boundaries of the area in much recent writing.[16]

Wieder then brings all this material to bear on the Gospels. It is in the light of this connection between Galilee and the End that he understands the emphasis on the beginning of the ministry of Jesus in Galilee. One is reminded of Schweitzer's picture of a Jesus governed by an eschatological dogma. Jesus deliberately began his ministry in the region where some circles expected the Messianic Age to dawn. The time is fulfilled and the kingdom has drawn near *in Galilee*—as it was foretold. In addition to thus explaining the confession at Caesarea Philippi[17] (that place, "being situated on the slopes of Mt. Hermon, belonged to the territory where the prologue of the messianic drama was to be enacted," was the natural scene

[13] In fact the pertinent texts to which Wieder appeals are noted by SB, Vol. 1, pp. 160f. Out of the masses of Rabbinic sources, it must be emphasized, they are very few in number.
[14] *The Judaean Scrolls*, p. 20. He refers to IQHab on 2: 17: "The violence of Lebanon shall overwhelm thee... 'Lebanon' stands for the Communal Council... (T. H. Gaster's translation p. 255)." In fact, Lebanon does not stand for the whole community in the commentary on this passage. But Wieder refers to passages where the "council of the community" is equated with the community as a whole. He refers to IQS 3: 2; 5: 7; 6: 3, 10, 16; 7: 2, 22, 24; 8: 22. Only in one of these passages does it seem quite clear that this equation is justified, that is, in IQS 6: 14–16.
[15] G. A. Smith, *The Historical Geography of the Holy Land*, 25th ed., London, 1931, p. 417.
[16] See an unpublished dissertation by F. X. Malinowski, Duke University Library: "Galilee in Josephus."
[17] Mark 8: 27ff and parallel, Wieder, *The Judaean Scrolls*, pp. 14ff.

for the confessions of Jesus as Messiah), and the Transfiguration[18] (this is set on a High Mountain which Wieder equates with Mt. Hermon, which was closely identified with Galilee), Wieder particularly points to two aspects of the Galilean emphasis in Mark and Matthew. They are connected with the beginning and end of the Gospel of Mark. In Chapter 1, Mark set the initial programmatic appearance of Jesus in Galilee. Many scholars now claim that he intended to close his gospel at 16: 8 and anticipated a Parousia immediately in Galilee. And, even if we prefer to think of a lost ending for his Gospel, dealing with the resurrection, it is clear that Mark anticipated appearances of the Risen Lord in that region (14: 28).

First, let us look at Wieder's treatment of Galilee as the beginning of the Gospel.[19] The connection between Galilee and the beginning of the Gospel is attested not only in Mark, but seems integral to the Kerygma from the first. This emerges from Acts 10: 38 as well as from Matthew, and even from the Fourth Gospel, which places the beginning of the manifestation of the glory of the Lord in Galilee.[20] Wieder concentrates on the interpretation of the beginning of the Gospel in Galilee given by Matt. 4: 12–16, which draws upon Is. 8: 23–9: 2.

Now when he heard that John had been arrested, he withdrew into Galilee; and leaving Nazareth he went and dwelt in Capernaum by the sea, in the territory of Zebulun and Naphtali, that what was spoken by the prophet Isaiah might be fulfilled:

"The land of Zebulun and the land of Naphtali, toward the sea, across the Jordan, Galilee of the Gentiles—the people who sat in darkness have seen a great light, and for those who sat in the region and shadow of death light has dawned."

Wieder thinks that here Matthew reflects and uses an old tradition born naturally out of the ancient Isaianic text. Because Galilee had first suffered national disaster, in deportation and exile, it would be the first to be visited by the Messiah. Particularly striking evidence for this interpretation of the Matthaean citation is found in Jerome, who draws upon Jewish-Christians for it, in his commentary on Isaiah.

The Hebrews who believe in Christ interpret these passages as follows: "Of old these two tribes of Zebulun and Naphtali were taken captive by Assyrians and were led away into a strange country, and Galilee was deserted; but as the prophet said, they should be relieved by him [Christ], who should bear the sins

---

[18] Mark 9: 1ff; Wieder, *The Judaean Scrolls*, pp. 15ff, 23.
[19] Wieder, *The Judaean Scrolls*, pp. 23ff.
[20] John 2: 11.

of the people." Afterwards not only the two tribes, but the remnant who dwelt beyond Jordan and in Samaria, were likewise led away into captivity. And this they [the Judeo-Christians] affirm the Scripture to say: "In the selfsame region whose population had been led captive and had started to serve the Babylonians, and which was first tormented by the darkness of error, that same land should be the first to see the light of the preaching of Christ."[21]

Other Karaite and Zoharitic sources to which Wieder appeals, however interesting, are too late to be relevant.

But apart from the lateness of the sources to which Wieder appeals, difficulties remain. The precise words in the Hebrew text of Is. 9: 1 which refer to the *peripateia* of Zebulon and Naphtali are:

But there will be no gloom for her that is in anguish. In the former time he brought into contempt the land of Zebulun and the land of Naphtali, but in the latter time he will make glorious the way of the sea, the land beyond Jordan, Galilee of the nations...

These words constitute the ground for the view that Galilee was to be the first to be Messianically blessed, because it had been first brought into contempt. But note: Matthew omits these pertinent words. It may be argued that he is assuming the total context of the quotation which he gives, but it is a fair assumption that he cannot have wished to emphasize a point the words specifically referring to which he has omitted (although such an omission would not be unknown in Rabbinic quotations).

Another datum confirms this view. In the Masoretic Text at Is. 9: 1 we read:

> The people who walk in darkness
> MT   *hắ'ắm ha hôl'kîm baḥôshek*
> LXX *ho laos ho poreuomenos en skotei*

The LXX presents a confused translation from which the idea that, because Zebulun and Naphtali had first suffered, they were the first to be Messianically visited can hardly be extracted. But what is most note-worthy is that Matthew has changed the *ho poreuomenos* (he who walks) of the LXX to *ho kathêmenos* (he who sits). He has either followed the A text of the LXX at this point or given his own translation of the Masoretic Text.[22] And *ho kathêmenos* (he who sits) suggests that Matthew is thinking not of a people who have undergone exile, but of a static

---

[21] Wieder, *The Judaean Scrolls*, p. 28. The passage is from Migne, P.L. 24, 127: the translation that of H. J. Schonfield in *Secrets of the Dead Sea Scrolls*, London, 1956, p. 52. It is well, however, to remind ourselves of the date of St. Jerome: he lived between A.D. 348 and 420. The jump from this to the first century is considerable.

[22] See A. Rahlfs, *Septuagint*, Vol. II, *ad rem*.

people. The notion of a *peripateia* in terms of exile and Messianic compensation for this does not apply to them. Matthew here is not slavishly following any tradition, such as Wieder suggests, which led him to connect Jesus, the Messiah, with Galilee. His method of citation is not *pesher*.[23] The sacred text does not determine his understanding of the ministry of Jesus. Rather the geographic location of that ministry has led him to use a particular testimonium. He is governed by history not by an exegetical tradition. And, in view of the fact that both the LXX and the Targumim know nothing of the tradition to which Wieder refers, it may be doubted whether it existed in a well-defined pre-Christian form and was not, rather, a product of Christian reflection on Matthew as much as on the Masoretic Text.

Secondly, the same reserve is evoked by Wieder's treatment of Mark 14: 28. The passage in Mark 14: 27–28 reads:

And Jesus said to them, "You will all fall away: for it is written, 'I will strike the shepherd, and the sheep will be scattered.' But after I am raised up, *I will go before you to Galilee (alla meta to egerthênai me proaxô humas eis tên Galilaian).*"

Wieder connects the italicized sentence with traditions about the Messiah and about the Divine Presence. For him the crucial verb *proaxô* (I will go before) is *mutatis mutandis* simply the Greek term for *hâlak liph°nê* ("to go before"), in Exod. 13: 21:

And the Lord went before him by day (*hôlêk liph°nêhem yômâm*) in a pillar of cloud to lead them along the way...;

And, again, in Is. 52: 12:

> For you shall not go out in haste,
> and you shall not go in flight
> for the Lord will go before you (*kî-hôlêk liph°nêkem*),
> and the God of Israel will be your rear guard.

Further, *proagô* is the equivalent of "to go up before" or to "pass on before" and "to be at the head of" in Micah 2: 12f:

12 I will surely gather all of you, O Jacob
 I will gather the remnant of Israel:
 I will set them together, like sheep in a fold,
 like a flock in its pasture, a noisy multitude of men.
13 The breaker will go up before them (*'âlah ha-ppôrêṯ liph°nêhem*);

---

[23] The exact meaning of the term, *pesher*, is hard to define: we use it here to designate at least the use of Scripture which allows the text to dictate the presentation of an event.

They will break through and pass the gate,
going out of it.
Their King will pass on before them,
The Lord at their head.

The term "the breaker" in 2: 13, that is, *ha-ppôrêtz*, is interpreted of the Messiah in Gen. Rabbah 48: 10 and in Gen. Rabbah 85: 14 (which is undatable) and Lev. Rabbah 32 (the end). Thus in the latter passage, which again is undatable, the bowl (*gûllâh*), mentioned in Zech. 4: 2, in the description of the golden candlestick, is understood by one of the Amoraim as "the breaker,"[24] the Messiah, who here belongs to the "world to come." Other passages to which Wieder refers are too late to be pertinent.

But, further, Wieder connects Mark 14: 28 even more directly with Exod. 13: 21, which deals with the pillar of cloud, and Is. 52: 12, "The Lord will go before you . . .," which we have cited before. Both these verses had been Messianically interpreted in terms of the pillar of cloud as part of the complex which interpreted the Messianic Age as a New Exodus comparable to the first. Reference has already been made to Gen. Rabbah 48: 10. The Shekinah, in a cloud, together with "the breaker" will lead the dispersed nation back to its homeland. It is impossible to follow the intricacies of Wieder's statement here. He discovers on the basis of the key expression "go before" a whole tradition according to which the pillar of cloud was "to go before" the redeemed people accompanying the Messiah. And in the use of the phrase "I will go before you, *proaxô humas*," in Mark 14: 28 this whole tradition, he claims, is evoked.

But, apart from the lateness of the sources to which Wieder appeals, two obvious difficulties immediately stand out.

First, the term *proagô* (I go before) is not used in the LXX to translate *halak liph^ene*, either at Exod. 13: 21 or Is. 52: 12. The pertinent texts are as follows:

Exod. 13: 21:
MT   And the Lord went before them (*hôlêk liph^enêhem*) by day in a pillar of cloud to lead them (*lan^ehôthâm*) along the way. . . (RSV).
LXX   *Ho de Theos egeito (led) autôn hêmeras men en stulô nephelês, deixai autois tên hodon.* (Notice the use of *agô (egeito)* not *proagô*.)

---

[24] The passage reads: "Two amoraim differ on the meaning of '*gulah*' [Zech. 4: 2]. One reads *golah* and the other reads *go'alah*. He who reads '*golah*' explains it to mean that they had been exiled (*gulah*) to Babylon and the Shechinah had accompanied them into exile; as it says, *For your sake I have been sent to Babylon* (Isa. xliii, 14). He who reads *go'alah* renders '*redeemer*'; as it says, *Our redeemer* (go'alenu) *the Lord of hosts is His name.* (ib. xlvii, 14), and it is written, *The breaker is gone up before them* . . ." (Micah ii, 13).

Is. 52: 12:

MT *kî hôlêk liphᵉnêkem yehwâh*
for the Lord will go before you (RSV).

LXX *proporeusetai gar proteros humôn kurios*

Here we have *proporeuomai* not *proagô*. According to the Hexapla the other versions offer no variants. This is all the more striking because the simple *agô* (I lead) used in Exod. 13: 21 would, if Wieder be correct, suit Mark's purposes better than *proagô* which emphasizes prevenience rather than actual leadership. Similarly the *'âlâh* and *yya'ᵃbor liphᵉnêhem* of Micah 2: 13 is not rendered by *proagô* in the LXX. The texts are as follows:

MT:

עָלָה הַפֹּרֵץ לִפְנֵיהֶם פָּרְצוּ וַיַּעֲבֹרוּ שַׁעַר וַיֵּצְאוּ בוֹ וַיַּעֲבֹר מַלְכָּם לִפְנֵיהֶם
וַיהוָה בְּרֹאשָׁם:

LXX:

Ισραηλ, ἐπὶ τὸ αὐτὸ θήσομαι τὴν ἀποστροφὴν αὐτων· ὡς πρόβατα ἐν θλίψει, ὡς ποίμνιον ἐν μέσῳ κοίτης αὐτῶν ἐξαλοῦνται ἐξ ἀνθρώπων. ¹³διὰ τῆς διακοπῆς πρὸ προσώπου αὐτῶν διέκοψαν καὶ διῆλθον πύλην καὶ ἐξῆλθον δι' αὐτῆς, καὶ 'εξῆλθεν ὁ βασιλεὺς αὐτῶν πρὸ προσώπου αὐτῶν, ὁ δὲ κύριος ἡγήσεται αὐτῶν.

Secondly, the difficulty posed by the future *opsesthe* (you shall see) in Mark 16: 7 ("But go, tell his disciples and Peter that he is going before you to Galilee; there you will see him [*ekei auton opsesthe*] as he told you") is not dealt with by Wieder. If, as he holds, the term *proagô* evokes "the cloud" leading the way, then the leader would be visible during the whole of the journey to Galilee, and the phrase "there you shall see him" becomes inappropriate. This holds whether we follow Lightfoot's interpretation of *opsesthe* (you shall see) as referring to the Parousia, or not.[25] The text of Mark 16: 7 demands a "now" and a "then," or a "here" and a "there," for which Wieder's understanding of *proagô* does not allow.[26]

[25] In fact, although the verb ὁράω ("I see") can refer to the experience of the Parousia (Mark 13: 26; 14: 62; 1 John 3: 2; Rev. 1: 7; 22: 4), it can also refer to the encounter with the Risen One (1 Cor. 9: 1; John 20: 18). For Lightfoot's view of the use of the verb "to see" here, see *Locality and Doctrine*, pp. 61ff, 73–77.

[26] Lightfoot speaks of Jesus' "prevention" of his disciples to Galilee in Mark 14: 28 and 16: 7, *Locality and Doctrine*, p. 55. Eduard Schweizer recognizes that the phrase "before you" or "ahead of you" can be interpreted spatially, as by Lightfoot and Wieder, in the sense of going at the head of a procession like a leader, but rightly points out that it can also be interpreted temporally, with the meaning "to go first, with others following later" as in Mark 6: 45. The future tense of 14: 28 is changed in 16: 7 to the present tense: Jesus is already on his way to Galilee—before the disciples have begun to go there. There is no suggestion of a procession to Galilee and there is none elsewhere in Mark. See *The Good News According to Mark*, trans., Richmond, 1970, pp. 307, 365ff.

All in all, then, Wieder's thesis, which, as we saw, would be contrary to that held by Billerbeck, that Galilee was especially connected with the Messiah as the scene of the Messianic Age, must be treated with great reserve. It was not because they were guided by a long traditional belief, based on Scripture, that Galilee should be the first area illumined by the "light of the Messianic Kingdom,"[27] that Mark and Matthew ascribe a Galilean character to the ministry and anticipate a future beyond the cross in Galilee.

Further, consideration of the Rabbinic passages to which Wieder appeals to support the claim that Galilee and Damascus should be equated reveals the intent of these passages to be very different from what he finds. They indicate a strong awareness of the difference between North and South in the land of Israel, and a marked desire to connect the Messiah and the return of the exiles in the Messianic Age always with the South and especially with Jerusalem. We may suggest a reason for these emphases. Let us consider the passages used by Wieder, already mostly isolated by Billerbeck.

First, there is Song of Songs Rabbah 7: 3, which reads:

[THY FOREHEAD IS] LIKE THE TOWER OF LEBANON: as it says, That goodly hill-country and Lebanon (Deut. 3: 25)...WHICH LOOKETH TOWARD DAMASCUS. R. Johanan [A.D. 279–320] said: Jerusalem will in the time to come extend as far as the gates of Damascus, as it says, *The burden of the word of the Lord. In the land of Hadrach [and in Damascus shall be His resting place]* (Zech. 9: 1). What is *"Hadrach"*? R. Judah [A.D. 130–160] and R. Nehemiah [A.D. 130–160] gave different answers. R. Judah said: It is a place called Hadrach. Said R. Jose b. Durmaskis [A.D. 120–140][28] to him: By the [Temple] service! I am from Damascus, and there is a place there which is called Hadrach. R. Nehemiah said: It is the Messiah who is both sharp and soft (*had we-rach*)—sharp to the other nations and soft to Israel. Another explanation of Hadrach: this is the Messiah who will guide (*hadrich*) all humanity in the way of repentance before the Holy One, blessed be He. "*And in Damascus shall be His resting-place.*" Is Damascus His resting-place? Is His resting-place any other than the Temple, as it says, *This is My resting-place for ever* (Ps. 132: 14)? He replied: Jerusalem will one day expand on all sides until it reaches the gates of Damascus, and the exiles will come and rest under it, to fulfil what is written, "*And Damascus shall be His resting-place*"; as if to say, *As far as* Damascus is His resting-place. What does R. Johanan make of the verse, *And the city shall be builded upon her own mound* (Jer. 30: 18)? [He replies]: It will be like a fig-tree which is narrow below and

---

[27] On this phrase, see the references given by Wieder, *The Judaean Scrolls*, p. 29. SB, Vol. I, p. 161. The passages cited by Billerbeck are later than the third and fourth centuries.
[28] See W. Bacher, *Die Agada der Tannaiten*, Strassburg, 1902, Vol. I, pp. 425–432.

broad above (i.e. Jerusalem while expanding on all sides will still be based on the same site). So Jerusalem will expand on all sides and the exiles will come and rest beneath it, to fulfil what is said, *For thou shall spread abroad on the right hand and on the left* (Is. 54: 3). This proves expansion in length. What is the proof of breadth? Because it says, *From the tower of Hananel unto the King's winepresses* (Zech. 14: 10). R. Zakkai Rabbah [no date] said: Up to the pits of Ripa [another reading is Jaffa]; up to the winepresses which the supreme King of Kings, the Holy One, blessed be He, pressed [i.e., the Ocean]. So much for the length and breadth of it. What about the height? Because it says, *And the side-chambers were broader as they wound about higher and higher* (Ezek. 41: 7) (this refers to the Temple and is probably understood to indicate that Jerusalem, too, would rise higher and higher). It was taught: Jerusalem, is destined to expand and ascend until it reaches the Throne of Glory, until it will say, *The place is too strait for me;* [give place to me that I may dwell] (Is. 49: 20). R. Jose b. R. Jeremiah [A.D. 375–427] said: We have still not learnt the whole glory of Jerusalem. Whence do you learn its full glory? From [what is said of] its walls, as it says. *For I, saith the Lord, will be unto her a wall of fire round about her* (Zech. 11: 9).

This passage is exceedingly difficult to expound.[29] Certainly, as Wieder notes, Damascus is connected with the Messiah and the Messianic Age. But equally certain, Damascus is subordinated to Jerusalem. The midrashic claim is made that Jerusalem was destined in the Messianic Age to spread so as to encompass Damascus, which, on Wieder's terms, would include Galilee. The centrality of Jerusalem is thus preserved. This view is asserted by R. Johanan, a third-century Amora, but it is traceable to a Tanna, Rabbi Nehemiah, in the early or mid-second century. The view had to meet the opposition of Rabbi Judah (A.D. 130–160). But his interpretation of Zech. 9: 1 is easily countered by that of Rabbi Jose b. Durmaskis.

A consideration of the date of the view of Damascus and Jerusalem expressed in the passage must make us suspicious of applying it to the time of Jesus. We may venture to suggest how it arose. In the age of the Rabbis concerned, Jerusalem was out of bounds to Jews, who were scattered from that city as far away as Damascus. Such Jews lacked the comfort of living in the land, as its boundaries were understood in the first century, and lacked the consolation of living with easy access to

---

[29] In an oral discussion of this passage, Professor L. H. Silbermann suggested that another factor may have evoked the desire to link Galilee with Jerusalem, North with South. At a later date than the second century, in the time of Rabbi Judah and others, Galilee became the centre of Jewish learning in the second century and the third when schools were developed at Usha, Sepphoris, and Tiberias. The desire to lend the sanctity of the Holy City to the place where sacred learning was pursued would tend to reinforce and create attempts to connect Galilee with Jerusalem.

Jerusalem, the centre of their world. But, it was natural that they should want to claim that they, although scattered to Damascus, were still to be considered as belonging to the land where the Messiah was to appear. At the same time, they had no desire to question the age-long centrality of Jerusalem. Aware of this twofold aspect of the yearnings of Jews, did the Rabbis in their Messianic hopes, for their comfort, expand Jerusalem to include Damascus? These passages which Wieder takes to express ancient Messianic hopes going back to pre-Christian times are, in fact, we suggest, a witness to the hopes of uprooted Jews in the second century and later.

The same conditions produced the other passage in Song of Songs Rabbah 4: 16 referred to by Wieder. It reads:

What does R. Eleazar make of this verse, AWAKE, O NORTH WIND, AND COME, THOU SOUTH? He explains: When the exiles who are living in the north shall bestir themselves and come and encamp in the south, as it says, *Behold, I will bring them from the north country, and gather them from the uttermost parts of the earth* (Jer. 31: 8). When Gog and Magog who live in the north shall come and fall upon the south, as it says, *And I will turn thee about and lead thee on, and will cause thee to come up* (Ezek. 39: 2). When the Messiah who is in the north shall awake and come and build the Temple which is in the south, as it says, *I have roused up one from the north, and he is come* (Is. 41: 25).

It is interesting to note that in Gen. Rabbah 22: 5, which contains material parallel to Song of Songs Rabbah 4: 16, the above words by R. Eleazar are missing. In Gen. Rabbah 22: 5, as in Song of Songs Rabbah 4: 16, the words: "Awake, O North Wind, and Come, Thou South" are appealed to in a discussion between R. Eleazar (A.D. 279–320) and R. Jose b. R. Hanina (an older pupil of R. Johanan) concerning peace offerings and burnt offerings by the sons of Noah. But the verse is not applied to the exiles or to the Messianic Age. The discussion of these items appears in this context only in Song of Songs Rabbah. In the latter, the exiles from the North (shall we think here of Damascus and Galilee?) together with the Messiah himself are made to move from the North to the South. Again, we are probably to find the impact of those factors which we mentioned above in connection with Song of Songs Rabbah 7: 3—the desire among exiled Jews to assert both that they are within the ambience of the future Messianic activity and that the centre of their life is still Jerusalem.

There are further interesting passages. The following is again from Song of Songs Rabbah 4: 16, from a third-century Rabbi:

BLOW UPON MY GARDEN, THAT THE SPICES THEREOF MAY FLOW OUT. R. Huna said in the name of R. Joshua b. R. Benjamin b. Levi: In this world when the south wind blows the north wind does not blow, and when the north wind blows the south wind does not blow. But in the time to come God will bring a strong clearing wind on the world and drive on the two winds together so that both will be in action, as it is written, *I will say to the north: Give up, and to the south: Keep not back* (Is. 43: 6).

Again, in Song of Songs Rabbah 4: 14 the exiles from the North, together with the Messiah himself, are made to move from the North to the South, and it is clear that the rivalry between North and South is in view. Here we encounter the hope that North and South will be reconciled in the Messianic Age or in the Age to Come. The R. Joshua in the passage, if to be identified with R. Joshua b. Levi, lived at Lydda in the third century and R. Huna, who died in A.D. 297, was the principal of the Rabbinic School at Sura. They would both know of that twofold yearning about which we wrote above, although they do not make it explicit here. It is made explicit in the following passage from Num. Rabbah 13: 2, by R. Hunia (A.D. 375–427) in the name of R. Benjamin b. Levi (A.D. 320–359).

The expression, "*Awake, O north wind*" teaches that the winds will, in the Messianic era, enter into a spirit of rivalry with one another. The south wind will say: "I shall bring back the captivity of Teman and that of the Hagrites and the entire south," while the north wind will say: "I will bring back the northern captivity." And the Omnipresent will make peace between them, and both will enter by one door, in order to fulfil the words of the text, *I will say to the north: Give up, and to the south: Keep not back, bring My sons from far*, etc. (Is. 43: 6).

These texts may merely pinpoint what is known from other sources; that, however much significance was possibly ascribed to Galilee as the scene of a Messianic Age, much more was it the case with Jerusalem, which could brook no rival at that time. While this may merely reflect the age-long animosity which we know to have existed between the North and the South in the land of Israel, it is more probable that those forces which we previously referred to among exiled Jews were again at work here.

In view of the above discussion, the absorbing centrality of Jerusalem as the scene of revelation and redemption in eschatological speculation need not be doubted. At the end of the days it was Jerusalem that was to be the scene of the eschatological drama when Gentiles would come to Mount Zion to worship at God's Holy Mountain. Any area that might be desirous of inclusion in that drama (and after the Fall of Jerusalem and the scattering of Jewry there were many such), was simply taken over geographically into the orbit of the city. Any rivalry that might have arisen between such areas and Jerusalem was thereby cut at the root.

Finally, what does Galilean Judaism itself reveal about the relationship between Galilee and Jerusalem? There is no complete study of it available.[30] But to judge from Josephus, the history of Messianic or apocalyptic movements in Galilee confirms the view that it was Jerusalem, not Galilee, that was regarded as destined to be the scene of the Messianic revolution. Certain facts are difficult to understand if Galilee had been regarded as the Messianic centre even in a few circles. 1. The constant movement of Galileans on pilgrimages to Jerusalem (Jos., *Antiquities*, XX. 6. 1; XVIII. 10. 2) at the time of the festivals, when political-messianic hopes were alive and could easily be aroused. 2. The concentration of Galilean revolutionary leaders on Jerusalem; for example, Judas the Galilean, John of Gischala and Menahem, son of Judas the Galilean, who took their final stand in Jerusalem. 3. The prominence of Galileans among the most audacious Zealots in Jerusalem (Jos., *Jewish Wars*, IV. 9. 10). 4. The readiness of Galileans to accept the leadership of a priest (Jos., *Life*, 1: 43–47) and to support the priesthood in Jerusalem with tithes during even the exigencies of war (Jos., *Life*, 1: 12; 1: 15–16; 1: 42–43; 1: 45; 1: 49; 1: 51). 5. The conviction of the Galileans, rebels, expressed by John of Gischala that they "could never fear capitivity since the city was God's (*Jewish Wars*, VI. 2. 1)." There were differences between Southerners and Northerners, Judahites and Galileans, into which we cannot enter here, but these data suggest that in their recognition of the Messianic centrality of Jerusalem they were at one. Unlike the Samaritans, the Galileans did not set up any rival site to Jerusalem, the centre of their land.

It is, therefore, clear that the ministry of Jesus in Galilee ran counter to the dominant popular and learned expectation of Judaism that Jerusalem would be the centre for the advent of the age of the Messiah. Did Mark and Matthew, as Wieder implies, choose Galilee as the sphere of his work in order deliberately to reject that dominant expectation of his people for a

---

[30] There is no satisfactory treatment of the relations between Galilee and Judaea in the first century. The following books are helpful: S. W. Baron, *A Social and Religious History of the Jews*, Philadelphia, 1952, 1–11, pp. 278f; L. Elliott-Binns, *Galilean Christianity*, 1956, pp. 17–22; R. Otto, *The Kingdom of God and the Son of Man*, trans., London, 1938, pp. 13ff; W. Bauer, *Jesus der Galiläer*, in *Festgabe für A. Jülicher*, Tübingen, 1927; for the difference between Galilee and Judaea in language, M. Black, *An Aramaic Approach to the Gospels and Acts*, Oxford, 1946; W. R. Farmer, *Maccabees, Zealots, and Josephus*, New York, 1956, is invaluable in connection with the text above. See F. X. Malinowski, unpublished thesis, Duke University.

Messianic advent in the Holy City and in order to signify the fulfilment of a less marked, but no less real, expectation that that advent should be in Galilee? It is unlikely. For them, as for the Nazarene himself, human need in Galilee and elsewhere and his response to the divine will as he understood it, that is, as limitless love, not any arcane eschatological geography, motivated Jesus.

Lightfoot himself[31] is compelled to admit that his thesis of a connection between locality and doctrine is not without its difficulties. He notes[32] that already in Mark 2: 1–3: 6 dealing with the conflict between Jesus and the Jewish leaders in Galilee "the shadow of the final passion is already present (2: 19, 20; 3: 6)."[33] Indications of Jesus' popularity with the people are not confined by Mark to Galilee, but indicated in Judaea, among those from Jerusalem, and from Idumaea, and from beyond Jordan, and those who live in Tyre and Sidon (Mark 3: 7ff). This offsets Lightfoot's point that the hostility toward Jesus recorded in Galilee in Mark 3: 22 and 7: 1 was due to influences proceeding from Jerusalem.[34]

Moreover, there is an apparent inconsistency in Lightfoot's treatment of the scene in Mark 6: 1–5, and its parallels, describing the rejection of Jesus in Nazareth. In his work entitled *History and Interpretation*, Lightfoot recognized the importance of "The Rejection in the Patris," and devoted a full chapter to it.[35] Mark 6: 1ff reports the last appearance of Jesus in the synagogue in that Gospel. Lightfoot rightly contrasts it with the first such appearance recorded in 1: 21–27. In the latter, witness is at once given to the supernatural character of Jesus by a man possessed of an unclean spirit. In the former, Mark 6: 1ff, the wisdom of the teaching and the mighty works of Jesus are recognized, but they only call forth astonishment and resentment. The significance of Jesus as the "Son of Mary" is belittled.[36] This occurs in his *patris*, in Galilee. Lightfoot[37] carefully notes that, just as in the Fourth Gospel the last and greatest sign of Jesus, the raising of Lazarus from the dead, is followed by the direct

[31] *Locality and Doctrine*, p. 130.
[32] *Ibid.*, p. 118.
[33] *History and Interpretation, The Bampton Lectures for 1934*, London, 1935, p. 110.
[34] *Locality and Doctrine*, p. 130, n. 4.
[35] Pp. 182–205. For a full discussion of Mark 6: 1–6a, see E. Grässer, NTS, Vol. 16, October, 1969, pp. 1–23. He notes how, apart from the work of Lightfoot, Robinson, and Burkill, the pericope has been strangely neglected. Grässer, like Lightfoot and Austin Farrer, finds the shadow of the cross already in Mark 6: 1–6 (p. 3). Compare A. Farrer, *A Study in St. Mark*, London, 1951, p. 147.
[36] In a Semitic milieu the failure to note the father of Jesus is striking, "most unnatural... presumably meant to be derogatory, in the highest possible degree." Lightfoot, *Locality and Doctrine*, p. 187.
[37] *History and Interpretation*, p. 190.

threat of death (John 11: 45ff, especially 11: 53), because Jesus is seen to be life itself, the rejection of Jesus recorded in Mark 6: 1ff occurs immediately after three acts of power: the casting out of demons in the land of the Gerasenes (5: 1–20); the healing of the woman with the issue of blood (5: 25ff); the raising of the daughter of Jairus (5: 21–24, 35–43). In the last act—his greatest—Jesus is the giver of life. Lightfoot notes that in the story of the rejection at Nazareth "the evangelist sees the symbol and explanation of his lack of success also in the larger world of Galilee, and perhaps even of Israel itself."[38] The culmination of the Galilean ministry, then, ends with a dramatic presentation of the rejection of Jesus.[39]

Mark, however, in Lightfoot's view,[40] was not sufficiently master of the sayings and incidents at his disposal to attempt any fully systematic treatment of them, so that, by implication, we should not place too much emphasis on his location of the story of the rejection. But Matthew— much more a master of his materials—has also chosen as the climax of the Galilean ministry itself the rejection of Jesus in his native place (13: 53–58).[41]

Lightfoot's analysis in the first of his volumes, *History and Interpretation*, is convincing, but he is unaware what this does to his view of Galilee as the sphere of salvation[42] as expressed in his later work *Locality and Doctrine in the Gospel*, 1937 (preface). True his main emphasis is that, for Mark, Galilee is the sphere of revelation and Jerusalem that of judgment, but he also thinks of Galilee as the land where the revelation began to be accepted, as the seat of the gospel of fulfilment (for example, note Lightfoot's contrast of the acceptance of Jesus by Galileans in 11: 9 and his rejection by the people of Jerusalem).[43] He fails to deal with the significance of the rejection of Jesus in his native place in Mark 6: 1ff as he himself had previously urged in his understanding of its location at

---

[38] *Ibid.*, p. 191.

[39] It is not altogether clear what precisely Lightfoot regards as the climax of the Galilean ministry. He propounds the view indicated in the text, but elsewhere suggests that "the picture of the great multitude of Israel assembled on the shore of the Sea of Galilee to greet the Lord of Israel... (*Locality and Doctrine*, pp. 119f)" from Mark 3: 7–19 and Matt. 15: 29–31 is that climax—"the close of the ministry in Galilee proper." The fact that so often, as our treatment above and below makes clear, Lightfoot has to modify his main emphasis by various concessions and implied inconsistencies itself makes it suspect.

[40] *History and Interpretation*, pp. 189ff. Jeremias is very emphatic on this. He urges that Mark is a composition of independent complexes of tradition so that "the search for a systematic structure of the Gospel is a lost labour of love, *New Testament Theology*, New York, 1971, p. 38." The discussion of Mark 6: 1–6, in these pages, from Jeremias's point of view is misplaced.

[41] *History and Interpretation*, p. 195.

[42] *Locality and Doctrine*, p. 111.

[43] *Locality and Doctrine*, p. 124.

the culmination of the Galilean ministry. In *Locality and Doctrine* he only deals with Mark 6: 1ff in two places. On page 130, he finds it to be merely an indication of disaffection and hostility in the Galilean section of Mark, and in pages 145ff deals with it, exceedingly briefly, only in connection with John 1: 1–18; 4: 43. The fact is that Lightfoot's treatment of Mark 6: 1ff and Matt. 13: 53ff in *History and Interpretation* is inimical to his thesis in his *Locality and Doctrine*, which could hardly be maintained if the Galilean ministry is seen to culminate in the rejection in Nazareth.

The significance of Mark 6: 1–6 is, in fact, inimical to any elevation of Galilee to "holy land" in Mark, as in Matthew. Despite its apparent simplicity, Mark 6: 1–6, on examination, turns out to be a highly developed unit of tradition with a telling meaning. We need not consider that an originally successful visit of Jesus to Nazareth has been changed into an unsuccessful one. Rather Mark has taken a tradition of Jesus' rejection by his fellow citizens or countrymen in Nazareth and used it for his purpose. As it stands Mark 6: 1–6 presents a series of difficulties.

1. Was there a minority and majority group in the synagogue—(6: 2: "and the many hearing...")?
2. In 6: 2 "the many" are *amazed*: in 6: 3 they are *scandalized*. Is there a distinction to be drawn here: did something cause the amazement to turn into offence?
3. In 6: 2 Jesus is a teacher of wisdom and a worker of wonderful works (*dunameis*), but in 6: 4 a prophet.
4. In 6: 5 it is emphasized that he is simply a carpenter; contrast 6: 2 and 6: 4.
5. What are we to make of the collocation of *patris* ("country") *sungeneis* (kin) *oikia* (house) in 6: 4?

There are clearly here wheels within wheels. Mark has used a story to bring out the outcome of the encounter between the carpenter Jesus, who was also the Jesus powerful in word and deed in Mark 5, with his own people. Assuming the content of his preaching, in 1: 14f; 2: 16; 4, Mark shows how increasingly his own had rejected Jesus—his family in 3: 21, 31ff (recalled by *sungeneis* and *oikia* in 6: 4) and now his countrymen in his *patris*. The references to the *sungeneis* and *oikia* do not serve to demote in any degree the rejection in the *patris*, but only to reinforce it as further examples of Jesus' rejection by his own.

The appearance of Jesus in Nazareth did compel questions: whence is he (*pothen toutô tauta*); what wisdom has been given him; what his powers (6: 2)? But his own were "*scandalized*" (*eskandalizonto*: 6: 4) in him and showed "*unbelief*" (*apistia*: 6: 6). These two terms must be given their full force. "To be scandalized" did not simply signify "offence," but, as elsewhere in the Gospels, a denial of faith which has eschatological importance. There is here a heightening of the responsibility of the people in the synagogue at Nazareth; it is not merely that they have despised a prophet, but have been scandalized by the eschatological figure who has appeared among them. In 6: 5 Jesus is a human being, but he is the one who in 5: 33ff had raised the dead. Their "unbelief" is a form of blasphemy: they have passed eschatological judgment upon themselves.

The significance of this unbelief in Nazareth is emphasized by Mark by the place which he gives to this pericope in his gospel. The pericope 6: 1–6 has been taken by some to end the first part of the Gospel, 1: 1–5: 43, and to begin the second 6: 1–9: 50: others have found a parallel between the structure of 1: 14–3: 6 and 3: 7–6: 60, revealing the increasing rejection of Jesus. The rejection at Nazareth culminates the rejection of Jesus by his very own and points forward to his rejection by "Israel." Whatever view be taken of the place of 6: 1–6 in the total structure of Mark, its importance for Mark is unmistakable. And it makes it impossible to think that Galilee for him was holy land.

We are now free to look afresh at the place of Galilee in Mark and Matthew as objectively as possible, that is, without any conscious attempt to ascribe a theological dimension to it. In his comment on Mark 1: 9–11, Eduard Schweizer makes an astute assessment: "The characteristics which distinguish Jesus from the masses are not biographical data—his family, his particular training, his early abilities and successes. A "Life of Jesus" similar to the biography of some great personality is not found here. All we are told is his name. The reference to his home town serves the same function as our family names, and Nazareth is so insignificant that it is not mentioned in any other source...."[44] People born in small countries will understand at once the force of Schweizer's point. In Wales, for example, locality is mentioned along with personal and other names for identification, not to indicate significance. Had Mark's aim been to emphasize Galilee, he would not merely have used it to qualify Nazareth. The first occurrence of Galilee in Mark, therefore, cannot be taken to be theologically significant.[45] Elsewhere the geographical data provided by Mark concerning Galilee are extremely scanty. There is a broad geographic division in Mark between Galilee (1: 13–10: 52) and Jerusalem (11–16), but it is by no means absolute. In Mark 6: 1–9: 50, Jesus is at times outside Galilee in Tyre (7: 24), Tyre and Sidon (7: 31), Bethsaida

[44] *The Good News According to Mark*, trans., Richmond, 1970, p. 37.
[45] Nazareth itself was so geographically insignificant that it had to be identified simply by the addition "of Galilee." See the commentaries.

(8: 22), Caesarea Philippi (8: 27), the country of the Gerasenes (5: 1). Other topographical details are most vague. We read of "a mountain," or "the mountain (3: 13; 6: 46; 9: 2, 9)"; "the sea of Galilee," "the water's edge (1: 16; 2: 13; 3: 7; 4: 1)"; "the other side (4: 35; 5: 21)"; "a boat," "the boat (4: 1, 36, 37; 5: 2, 18, 21; 6: 32–54; 8: 10)"; "at home," "the house (2: 1; 3: 20; 7: 17, 24; 9: 28)"; "a desert place (1: 35, 45; 6: 31, 32)"; "the synagogue (1: 21–39; 3: 1; 6: 2)". When we turn to actual placenames in Mark, Capernaum is mentioned three times only, at 1: 21; 2: 1; 9: 33. In the latter the reference to Capernaum is casually introduced as part of a journey in Galilee (9: 30ff). As we saw, Nazareth is referred to once only at 1: 9, and is not mentioned, although it is implied, in 6: 1–6. Bethsaida is mentioned twice at 6: 45; 8: 22. When we note that Matthew and Luke connect many miracles with Bethsaida and Chorazin (Matt. 11: 20–24; Luke 10: 12–15), it is significant that Bethsaida (6: 45; 8: 22) gets such slight notice in Mark, and that Chorazin is ignored completely. It seems that, although the necessity that Jesus should go to Jerusalem is strongly implied in Mark, Galilee, as such, can hardly have interested him significantly (Mark 10: 32f.).

What of Galilee in Matthew? The Q passage already cited in Matt. 11: 20–24 pronounces doom on the cities of Galilee:

Then he began to upbraid the cities where most of his mighty works had been done, because they did not repent. "Woe to you, Chorazin! woe to you, Bethsaida! for if the mighty works done in you had been done in Tyre and Sidon, they would have repented long ago in sackcloth and ashes. But I tell you, it shall be more tolerable on the day of judgment for Tyre and Sidon than for you. And you, Capernaum, will you be exalted to heaven? You shall be brought down to Hades. For if the mighty works done in you had been done in Sodom, it would have remained until this day. But I tell you that it shall be more tolerable on the day of judgment for the land of Sodom than for you."

For Matthew it is clear that the mission of Jesus in Galilee produced only a few true disciples. Many in Galilee were interested in and attracted by Jesus: the crowds always and everywhere followed him. Yes! But they remained unmoved by his proclamation and largely uncommitted. Despite his recognition of the eschatological significance conferred upon Galilee in the coming of Jesus, a significance which in 4: 12ff he rested on the Old Testament, Matthew assesses it—"demotes" would be too strong a word perhaps—realistically. True, he retains Galilee for the final scene of his gospel, and that scene, in 28: 16–20, is a proleptic parousia. But he modifies any possible emphasis on Galilee as a whole, that this might be taken to imply, by concentrating on a mountain—a single spot in Galilee ordained by Jesus. It is clear that to Matthew this mountain was not on any map. And he goes still further. In the very last scene in Matthew all geographic bounds become insignificant: the gospel is for all nations. The Risen Lord transcends Galilee and Jerusalem: his audience is universal.[46] I have elsewhere noted that Matthew wrote at a time when there was an increasing emphasis among the Sages at Jamnia on the land and on the necessity whenever possible to remain in it.[47] This makes it all the more striking that Matthew, who was much exercised over confrontation of the Gospel with Jamnia and Judaism, issues this challenge of his last verses. Not for him nor for Mark was Galilee *terra Christiana*; it was no Messianic holy land in either Gospel. Failure as well as success marked the Galilean ministry from the start. That failure knew no geographic boundaries. There is no Galilean idyll for Jesus in Mark or Matthew. For them both, Galilee found much to object to in Jesus, as he found much to condemn in it. Lohmeyer and Lightfoot too easily overlooked the fact that even when the Galileans "understood" Jesus they misunderstood him: for this reason, at the very height of his popularity there, Jesus found that he had to escape from Galilee.[48]

What of Jerusalem? We find in Mark and Matthew the unexpressed assumption, which governs Judaism, that Jerusalem was the "inevitable" Messianic centre. We have already noted the necessity which Mark seems to imply (10: 31f) that Jesus should go to die in Jerusalem. This necessity emerges explicitly in Matthew. Mark and Luke make no such explicit reference to the city. (Contrast Matt. 16: 21 with Mark 8: 31; Luke 9: 22.) As Jesus entered the city for his passion, Matthew is careful

[46] See especially G. Bornkamm, "Der Auferstandene und der Irdische, Mt 28: 16–20," *Zeit und Geschichte, Dankesgabe an Rudolf Bultmann*, hrsg., von Erich Dinkler, Tübingen, 1964, pp. 171–191.

[47] See SSM, p. 295; B. Z. Bokser, *Pharisaic Judaism in Transition*, New York, 1935, pp. 98ff.

[48] See below, p. 342. G. Strecker, *Der Weg der Gerechtigkeit*, FRLANT, Göttingen, 1962 takes an opposite view to that of Lightfoot. In accordance with his interpretation of the Gospel of Matthew as concerned to emphasize the "pastness" of Jesus in history and to pin down his historicity by geographic precision, Strecker finds the references to Galilee in Matthew to be strictly geographical, without trace of symbolism of any kind. The location of Jesus's house in Capernaum (4: 13; 9: 1) is governed by a strictly geographical and histori- cizing aim, over against Mark's use of "house" in a typological way as the place of revelation. The fact that Matthew used mountain in a special way (5: 1; 15: 29; 28: 16), not of a geo- graphical place, but as a means of presenting events and teaching in an eschatological light, implies, so Strecker curiously holds, that "Galilee" itself was intended to have a geographical rather than a symbolical meaning. In his insistence on the simply geographic connotation of Galilee in Matthew, Strecker is to be followed, even though one may dissent from his reasons for holding this. See G. Strecker, *op. cit.*, pp. 93ff. See also G. Strecker, AARJ, Vol. xxxv, 3, 1967, p. 225 on "The Concept of History in Matthew."

to note that the whole city was disturbed at his advent, while neither Mark nor Luke are concerned to refer to the reaction of the city as such. (Matt. 21: 10 has no parallel in Mark and Luke.) In the account of the Resurrection the custodians at the tomb "went into the city to report what had happened (Matt. 28: 11)"; the dead raised at the time of the crucifixion "went into the holy city (Matt. 27: 53) and appeared to many." There is no doubt that Jerusalem is for Matthew the city of the great king, the setting of the eschatological drama.

But there is no uncritical elevation of it. The sin of the city is particularly real to the Evangelist. Throughout his passion narrative even its crowds appear hostile, in marked contrast to those of Luke, who tend, at least on occasion, to sympathize with Christ in his hour of death. The Passion evokes "emotion" in Luke as it does not in Mark and Matthew; for example, at Luke 22: 43; 23: 27. For Matthew, the Holy City has become the guilty city.[49] This emerges clearly in his references to the fall of Jerusalem which particularly occupied the Evangelist. In two passages, he introduces what can hardly be other than direct references to this event. In the parable of the wedding feast, in 22: 1ff, the anger of the King with the recalcitrant elect, that is, the Jews, is expressed in what is almost certainly a reference to the siege and fall of the city. "The King was angry, and he sent his troops and destroyed those murderers and burned their city (22: 7)." This means that Matthew discusses the rejection of Israel particularly in the light of the fall of Jerusalem. Equally significant and consonant with this is it that Matthew places the poignant cry of Jesus over Jerusalem at the very close of his anti-Pharisaic discourse. The culmination of that indictment and its vindication he states in 23: 37f: "O Jerusalem, Jerusalem....Behold, your house (temple) is forsaken and desolate (RSV)." This is followed immediately in chapter 24 by the discussion of the Parousia:[50] the fall of the city is an eschatological event. The Parousia in Matthew has been interpreted by Feuillet as the divine judgment on Judaism in the fall of Jerusalem: in any case, it includes that event (24: 1–3).[51] There is in Matthew the awareness that the geographic dimensions of Jewish expectation, both Galilean and Judaean, have been shattered. We have already referred to Matt. 28: 16–20, where the Risen

---

[49] It should, however, be noted that the crowds in Jerusalem as over against the priests and elders were not always unfavourable to Jesus: not the city but its leaders were against him (see Mark 14: 2; Matt. 26: 5; Luke 20: 19; 22: 2; and Matt. 21: 45).

[50] See SSM, pp. 298ff.

[51] A. Feuillet in *The Background of the N.T. and its Eschatology*, eds. W. D. Davies and D. Daube, Cambridge, 1956, pp. 261; RB, Paris, 1949, no. 1, p. 85, no. 2, p. 85.

Lord breaks all such dimensions in the command to a universal mission to all peoples.

But one thing might be regarded as possible. Christians of Galilean origin, like Northerners in every country one has known, would be unlikely to be loosely attached to their native heath and would, perhaps, tend to magnify and emphasize their own Galilee, as over against Judaea, as the sphere where historically the Messiah had appeared. Such an emphasis could have drawn upon an ancient tradition of tension between Israel and Judah, North and South, which persisted in Judaism, as is attested by the passages cited above. But evidence for such a tension between Christians of a Judaean and Galilean origin is hard to come by. If such a tension did exist, it need not be connected with any developed Galilean Christianity as such. Local loyalties might naturally have entered the Christian movement, but that local geographic loyalties came to control, in any appreciable degree, the presentation of the ministry of Jesus in Mark and Matthew (on the grounds of Jewish expectations and historical probability) is unlikely. Certainly the two gospels lend little, if any, support to the view that preoccupation with Galilee had led to its elevation to *terra Christiana*.[52]

---

[52] See Stemberger's excellent appendix for a positive evaluation of Galilee in Mark. E. Trocmé, *Jesus as Seen by His Contemporaries*, trans., Philadelphia, 1973, pp. 16f, recognizes the historical actuality of Jesus's ministry in Galilee, although he speaks of the use of Galilee as "normally symbolic," as is that of Jerusalem, the "Sea" of Tiberias, the desert, and desert places.

IX. THE LAND IN LUKE-ACTS

There has recently been much emphasis on geographical factors in Luke-Acts, as on those in Mark and Matthew. The best starting point is the influential[1] work of H. Conzelmann, who devotes the first part of *The Theology of St. Luke*, translation 1960, pp. 18–94, to "Geographical Elements in the Composition of Luke's Gospel." This work is important for our purpose because, after dealing with Luke 17: 11 ("In the course of his journey to Jerusalem [Jesus] was travelling through the boundaries of Samaria and Galilee [NEB]"), Conzelmann touches on our theme by claiming that: "To this picture of the scene of Jesus' life must be added the 'typical' localities, mountain, lake, plain, desert, the Jordan, each especially employed in a way peculiar to Luke. *In a word the process by which the scene became stylized into the 'holy Land' has begun.*"[2] The term "holy Land" is here left undefined. Presumably we are to understand, *mutatis mutandis*, that the land of Israel achieved incipiently in Luke a significance comparable to that which it held in Judaism: it began to acquire peculiarity as a geographic area having theological significance. Can this be substantiated?

1. A HOLY LAND IN LUKE?

Let us first set forth Conzelmann's position. He readily recognizes that Luke's knowledge of the land of Israel was vague,[3] but insists that that Evangelist introduced into this geographical unity (Galilee and Judaea are for him one entity[4]), theological considerations similar to those with which we dealt in the works of Lohmeyer, Lightfoot, and Marxsen. According to Conzelmann,[5] Luke was the first to bring to expression the distinction between "then" and "now" in the Christian dispensation, the first to look back to the ministry of Jesus as constituting a timeless "salvation," which was to be distinguished from the present. He recognized the uniqueness of the time when Jesus was active, a uniqueness

---

[1] In particular, E. Haenchen in his commentary on Acts endorses Conzelmann's position and builds upon it.

[2] *The Theology of St. Luke*, London, 1960, p. 70. On the symbolic connotation of the lake as the place of manifestations see p. 42 on Luke 5: 1; on the mountain, as the place of revelation pp. 44ff on 6: 12.

[3] *Ibid.*, pp. 20, 39 (Luke gives the impression that Capernaum is in the middle of the land), p. 41, n. 1; on p. 45 we read: "the country seems to be seen from the perspective of one living abroad."

[4] *Ibid.*, pp. 40ff; 43, n. 3; pp. 60, 69, 86 n.

[5] *Ibid.*, pp. 13ff.

which meant that that time was neither normative for his own day nor merely a reflection of his own day. In this way, Luke fits the figure of Jesus—now a historical phenomenon—into a larger framework as follows:

1. The period of the gathering of "witnesses" in Galilee, opening with the proclamation of Jesus as the Son of God (4: 14–9: 50).
2. The journey of the Galileans to the Temple, opening with the narrative passage containing the disclosure that Jesus must suffer, and the Transfiguration (9: 51–19: 28).
3. The period of the teaching in the Temple and of the Passion in Jerusalem, opening with the revelation of his royalty at the Entry. This period closes with the dawn of the new epoch of salvation with the Resurrection and Ascension (19: 29–23: 49; 23: 50–24: 53).

It is over against this schematization that Conzelmann's geographical emphasis operates. To begin with, to establish the above threefold sequence, he separates John the Baptist clearly from Jesus, and uses geography to this end. He points out that the Baptist worked at the Jordan and is not associated either with Galilee or Judaea, the areas of Jesus' ministry. The region of the Jordan was the region of the old era; people from Judaea did not come to be baptized by John, and after his baptism Jesus had no more contact with the Baptist. The latter was *historically* in the old dispensation, before the Rule of God drew near in Jesus, and, correspondingly, he was *geographically* merely on the borders of Galilee and Judaea, never inside them. Luke uses geography to set forth his non-eschatological or merely preparatory view of the Baptist, as over against that of Mark.[6] This is further seen in the role ascribed to the desert, where John dwelt and Jesus was tempted, between the Jordan and Galilee. That desert, so located, symbolizes the separation of the Baptist from Jesus, the Galilean.[7]

The Baptist, then, geographically and theologically, belonged to the old era. Galilee is the region of the new era inaugurated by Jesus. It is the scene of his ministry, which Luke looks back to as an ideal phenomenon in the past, and, we may add, in a distant land. As Jesus worked in Galilee, there were around him those who witnessed his work and who were later to accompany him to Jerusalem. They recognized the salvation

---

[6] *Ibid.*, pp. 18ff.

[7] *Ibid.*, p. 20, n. 3. There is still a larger framework—three epochs: the period of Israel (The Law and the Prophets reaching up to and including John the Baptist [16: 16], and the early history of Jesus); the central period free from Satan, ending with the Last Supper; the third period of the Church, beginning at Pentecost (Acts 2: 1ff; Luke 24: 49). See Conzelmann.

of the Lord because the time of Jesus in Galilee, including that of his journeys there on the way to Jerusalem (9: 51ff), had a salvific quality, which lent it uniqueness.[8]

To emphasize this fact Conzelmann fixes on the statement in Luke 4: 13, that after Jesus' temptation in the desert the devil departed from him *achri kairou*—which used to be rendered "for a season." The RSV translates the verse as follows: "And when the devil had ended every temptation, he departed from him until an opportune time": the NEB reads: "Lo, having come to the end of all his temptations, the devil departed, biding his time." Throughout the Galilean ministry Jesus was not open to the attacks of Satan, who only returned to the field of battle in Luke 22: 3, when the Passover was approaching. "Then Satan entered into Judas Iscariot...." The "opportune time" anticipated in Luke 4: 13 had now arrived, and the disciples became subject to "temptations" which had not troubled them during the Galilean idyll.[9]

But Conzelmann attaches much significance to something that happens on the way to Jerusalem—on the journey from Galilee. There is a "tour" of Galilee from 6: 1 onwards: Jesus "travels" there before beginning the "journey" to Jerusalem, which occupies 9: 51–19: 27.[10] The scene of the journey also is Galilee: locations outside that area, mentioned by Mark in the appropriate places, Luke omits.[11] It is emphasized that the journey is not inherent in the material Luke employs, but is imposed upon it by him. The journey itself, in Galilee, is a ministry: it is not a simple passage. Here is no rapid ascent to Jerusalem, but a slow progress in ministry toward it.[12]

When we turn to Jerusalem, the end of the journey, we are on less ambiguous ground as we seek to understand Conzelmann, because, in his expressed view, Luke ascribes to Judaea and especially to Jerusalem, as the place of the Temple, a significance of its own.[13] Conzelmann's presentation is complicated. He sharply separates the "Entry" of Jesus from the city itself, and again separates the Temple from the city, and rightly emphasizes that Luke presents a protracted ministry of Jesus in the Temple.[14] Above all, like others before him, he urges that Luke differs from Mark and Matthew in his understanding of the significance of the

[8] *Ibid.*, p. 14.

[9] *Ibid.*, p. 27ff. "'Galilee' has beyond its geographical meaning, a symbolical meaning which brings out its true significance as expounded by Lohmeyer... (p. 30)." Conzelmann's emphasis on Luke 22: 3 would be more convincing had Luke more emphasized the time indicated by the use of such a term as καὶ τότε or ἐν ἐκείνῃ τῇ ὥρᾳ. The notion that Satan impelled Judas is not peculiar to Luke, see John 13: 2.   [10] *Ibid.*, p. 47.

[11] *Ibid.*, p. 55.   [12] *Ibid.*, pp. 62, 67f.   [13] *Ibid.*, p. 41.   [14] *Ibid.*, pp. 75ff.

events that transpire at Jerusalem. For Mark and Matthew the cleansing of the Temple and the occurrences at the Holy City are of eschatological import: Jerusalem for them is the city of the End. For Mark and Matthew especially, the close of the ministry of Jesus in Jerusalem is associated with the End of all things. But for Luke, although it is at the City that the Risen Lord appears, it is above all the place where the Jewish leaders rejected Jesus, the scene of his Passion, and it is, therefore, understood not so much in an eschatological light as in that of the Cross. For Luke, Jerusalem was not the city of the Parousia but of the Passion. It was there, and by its hand, that Jesus *had* to die (13: 33, 34); to this extent Luke implies the mystique to which we referred above. But emphatically Conzelmann declares: "Jerusalem has nothing to do with the Parousia, though it has with the Resurrection."[15] The geographical and religious centre of Judaism, where again as Luke 22: 3 indicates, Satan became active, is separated from the End.

Inadequate as it is, the above summary[16] may enable us to assess Conzelmann's claim that in Luke we find the inauguration, embryonically, of the concept of the Holy Land in Christendom. Certain considerations, sometimes recognized by Conzelmann himself, are pertinent.

First, the murkiness in Luke's geography, as Conzelmann understands it, stands in sharp contradiction to the clarity of his geographical-theology. Conzelmann's work suggests that for Luke the land of Israel as a geographic area, that is, as *Eretz Israel*, had little if any intrinsic significance. Luke did not know the land at first hand; he wrote as an outsider who did not even know that Galilee was separated from Judaea by Samaria, but believed that all three regions were adjacent.[17] Where indications of an accurate topographical knowledge do emerge, as in the story of the Risen Lord at Emmaus, they are accounted for by Luke's use of local sources, not by his own awareness.[18]

Particularly difficult, since Conzelmann's thesis demands a distinction between Galilee and Judaea, is his insistence, frequently expressed, that Luke, while he did distinguish these two regions, nevertheless regarded them geographically, nationally, and religiously as a unit.[19] Thus, as in the Fourth Gospel, passage from Galilee to Judaea or the reverse can be

[15] *Ibid.*, p. 74. For a criticism of Conzelmann, see Robert Dowda, unpublished dissertation, Duke University, 1972.
[16] Only a detailed reading of Conzelmann's work can do justice to it: we have here merely reminded the reader of its main lines as they concern us.
[17] *The Theology of St. Luke*, p. 69.
[18] *Ibid.*, p. 94.
[19] See n. 4 above.

indicated without the recognition of any transition from one well-defined locality to another.[20] Such cloudiness militates against any ascription to Luke of a well-defined geographical interest: does it not obviate any serious geographical "symbolism" he may have wished to entertain?

Let us take one example. Conzelmann makes quite clear that, for Luke, the Galilean ministry is significant because of what happened during it, not because of its location. He contrasts the understanding of Galilee expressed in Matt. 4: 14ff, where that region as such seems to have significance, with what we find in Luke. He writes: "'Galilee' has no fundamental significance for Luke as a region (cf. by contrast Matt. iv, 14ff), but only on account of the Galileans."[21] And it is not their geographical origins that lends the Galileans their significance, but their character as "witnesses."[22] In fact, they are not mentioned as being present in Galilee and are known as Galileans even in Jerusalem. It was the *time* of Galilee, we might infer, not the *region* that was significant. But, as we already noted, it is otherwise with Judaea and Jerusalem. "Judaea has a significance of its own as a locality, especially Jerusalem, as the place of the Temple."[23] All this means that while Galilee shares in no "holiness"— to use the term loosely for the moment—Judaea, and Jerusalem especially do. But this is hardly possible if, for Luke, there is no real distinction between Galilee and Judaea.

Secondly, a similar contradiction is involved if Luke, as Conzelmann holds, is capable of moulding his sources at will in the interests of his own itinerary, and yet retains certain episodes in the tradition, almost unaltered in their geographical setting, which contradict those interests. Conzelmann recognizes that

the insertion of material into a plan of a journey for which it was not originally intended creates a certain lack of harmony. In only one passage is the journey context inherent in the material, in ix, 51–6, where the arrival in a Samaritan village is an essential part of the story. Only two other reports contain a place-name as part of the original material xviii, 35–43 and xix, 1–10. Finally, there is one further passage xiii, 31–3 which requires a local setting, that of Galilee. By its very nature it could be used to provide the motivation for the start of a journey, but in its present position it comes in the middle.[24]

We note that after the departure in 9: 51ff, Jesus is still in Galilee, and he is no nearer Jerusalem in 17: 11 than in 9: 51: this is a strange "journey."[25]

[20] *The Theology of St. Luke*, p. 69.   [21] *Ibid.*, p. 41.
[22] *Ibid.*, p. 38.   [23] *Ibid.*, p. 41.   [24] *Ibid.*, p. 61.
[25] Conzelmann himself recognizes that many scholars—Wellhausen, Schmidt, Bultmann— have been unable to recognize a "journey" in 9: 51–19: 27; others have failed to agree on the beginning and the end of the journey. See *The Theology of St. Luke*, pp. 61ff for details.

Similarly, the scene of the rejection of Jesus by the Samaritan villagers in 9: 51–6 becomes an embarrassment for Conzelmann. He wants to locate the journey in Galilee, and yet Luke presents him with a Samaritan scene, so that he has to insist that: "This locating of the Journey in Samaria, which is almost universally accepted (with significant exceptions), is based not on the text but on the map. Passages such as xvii, 2 ['In the course of his journey to Jerusalem he was travelling through the borderlands of Samaria and Galilee. NEB.'], however, make us wonder whether Luke might not have had an inaccurate picture of the country."[26] But it is precisely this kind of geographical inconsistency that makes any precise geographical-theological interest so questionable.

And the text of Luke is awkward in other ways. The rigid separation insisted upon by Conzelmann between John the Baptist and Jesus, which is necessary for his schematization, and which he roots in geographical data, is only possible by the rigid exclusion of chapters 1–3 from the body of the Gospel. Such a distinct separation cannot be maintained. The infancy narratives are an essential part of the Gospel and there are back-references to them in 3: 1–20; 7: 18–35; 16: 16, while the motif of prophecy in Luke 1–2 finds a sequel in the last division of the Gospel in 9: 45–24: 53, where there is a return of Jesus to the Temple, where Luke began his story, and the recognition of the fulfilment of prophecy (23: 26–24: 53) which was emphasized in the infancy narratives (1: 5–2: 40; compare Acts 2: 17f. Luke emphasizes the coming of the Messiah as calling forth a fresh outpouring of prophecy.) True, the importance of the contrast between John and Jesus for Luke is clear in Luke 1–2, and also their relationship. It is with Jesus that the Rule of God comes for Luke, not with John, who is merely a preparer and not a precursor of Jesus, but this distinction, which Conzelmann rightly makes, should not be made absolute.[27] This again calls into question the discovery of that marked geographical symbolism which he insists upon in dealing with the scene of the Baptist's labours.

And, thirdly, the schematization suggested by Conzelmann seems at times, despite the wealth of detail and brilliance with which it is supported, to do violence to certain texts. The interpretation of 4: 13 which gives to *achri kairou*, "until the opportune time," such weight, must be regarded as

[26] *The Theology of St. Luke*, p. 66.

[27] The criticism of Conzelmann's treatment of the Baptist by P. Minear in *Studies in Luke–Acts*, eds. L. E. Keck and J. L. Martyn, Nashville, 1966, pp. 111ff is convincing; see also E. E. Ellis, *The Gospel of Luke*, London, 1966; and W. Wink, *John the Baptist in the Gospel Tradition*, Cambridge, 1968, pp. 46ff.

uncertain because, though Satan was especially active during the Passion, he was also active, as we saw, in the Galilean period. What are we to make of passages such as 10: 18; 11: 14–28; 13: 10–17, where Satan, though otherwise named, is presumed to be active? The Galilean period was not free of the demonic nor does Luke seem to emphasize that Satan was at work in the period of the Church, after the Resurrection. (Satan appears in Acts only twice as a tempter at 5: 3; 13: 10.) The words in Luke 22: 28, "You are the men who have stood firmly by me in my times of trial (NEB)"; "You are those who have continued with me in my trials (RSV)," are not without difficulty. Conzelmann, in accordance with his interpretation of 22: 3, finds the perfect, "who have continued," to refer to the trials endured by the disciples since they had arrived in Jerusalem. This is not unlikely if the proposed interpretation of 22: 3 be accepted with its full implications, but, if the activity of Satan in the Galilean period be not excluded, the perfect tense can equally well be taken to refer to the whole period of the ministry. The perfect is best taken to refer to "the successful endurance of a long test."[28] Similarly, although Conzelmann's case for emphasizing the period of the Passion as that when the trials by Satan would be active (that period, we repeat, was certainly such; see in addition to 22: 3; 23: 28, 31, 53, and, especially, 23: 35, which might be taken to refer to an ideal period before the resumption of Satan's attacks, and 23: 36 which warns of this) is strongly supported, the interpretation of 23: 38 which he proposes in its light must be regarded as forced: the context, Conzelmann thinks, "suggests a symbolical interpretation of the sword, in connection with the Christian's daily battle against temptation, particularly in times of persecution. . . . What the disciples have to face is not battle and victory, but temptation."[29] But such symbolism is unlikely: are the purse, bag, sandals symbolical? If not, why should the sword be? Luke has here to deal with the tradition that at the time of the arrest at least one sword was used by the Lord's disciples (Mark 14: 47; Matt. 26: 51; Luke 22: 49–51; John 18: 10). This caused him embarrassment, since he was eager to attest the political harmlessness of Christians; but if the Messiah's followers looked and acted like lawless men, their conduct could be explained in terms of the fulfilment of prophecy.[30]

In the light of the above, the claim that Luke tends to that process

[28] B. S. Easton, *The Gospel According to St. Luke*, New York, 1926, p. 325. The Greek of Luke 22: 28 is: ὑμεῖς δὲ ἐστε οἱ διαμεμενηκότες μετ' ἐμοῦ ἐν τοῖς πειρασμοῖς μου. . . .

[29] *The Theology of St. Luke*, pp. 81–83.

[30] A. R. C. Leaney, *A Commentary on the Gospel According to St. Luke*, New York, 1958, p. 271.

which led to the concept of the "Holy Land" in Christendom must be suspect. But Conzelmann's treatment has pointed again to two long-recognized aspects of Luke which are very important for our purposes.

2. THE WAY

First, he has redirected attention to the itinerary interest in Luke. While Mark supplied Luke with the reason for the journey (Mark 9: 30; 10: 1, 17, 32, 46; 11: 1, 11) it is Luke himself who provided the notices of movement and destination (Luke 9: 57; 10: 1, 17, 38; 11: 1; 13: 10; 14: 1, 25; 9: 51; 13: 22, 33; 17: 11; 18: 35; 19: 1, 11), and he did so in material from all the sources that he used—Mark, Q, and special material. This presentation of Jesus' activity in terms of a journey, fits into the overall understanding of the Christian dispensation which Luke offers in the whole of Luke-Acts, where it emerges as a way. In Acts 9: 2; 19: 9, 23; 22: 4; 24: 14, 22 the Christian movement is called "The Way," and this interpretation of it is implied in Acts 13: 16ff; 20: 18ff. The ministry of Jesus himself is a way, Luke 13: 33; 22: 22; 9: 31.

And Luke's story is a pilgrim story, beginning at Nazareth (4: 16), proceeding to Capernaum (4: 31), and further to Judaea (4: 44). He avoids the disjointed presentation of Mark and leads on to Jerusalem, and then *from* Jerusalem (Luke 24: 47; Acts 1: 8); and the Way is under God's purpose and his Holy Spirit.[31]

But Luke has to present evidence for or to substantiate "this Way." In Luke 1: 4 he asserts that he has "decided to write a connected narrative..., so as to give you authentic knowledge about the matters of which you [Theophilus] have been informed (NEB)." To do this he has to provide witnesses. Conzelmann himself recognized that the function of the Galileans who accompanied Jesus was to be witnesses of his activity,[32] and this necessity for witnesses is traceable throughout Luke-Acts. It is this necessity, not geographical-theology, that accounts for the pro-traction of the journey in Luke 9: 51–19: 27. That journey is briefly described in Mark, but much expanded in Luke. Why? Why did not Luke make the journey short? The answer is: because during that journey, as in the rest of Jesus' activity, there should be witnesses who could testify to the nature of his Way, who could be taught by him. The section 9: 51–19: 27 is extraordinarily rich in materials that are appropriate for preparing the disciple-witnesses to be apostles.[33] This preparation of the apostles

---

[31] See especially W. C. Robinson Jr., JBL, Vol. LXXIX, 1960, Pt I, pp. 20ff, on "The Theological Context for Interpreting Luke's Travel Narrative."

[32] *The Theology of St. Luke*, p. 38.

[33] See references to literature in Robinson Jr., "The Theological Context," JBL.

was all the more imperative in Luke's mind, because his perspective was that the Parousia was not imminent, and that the apostles faced the long task of bringing salvation to the Gentiles. From this point of view, Luke's strange indifference to geographical realities or activities, as Conzelmann understands the matter, need occasion no surprise. His threefold pattern for Luke-Acts is not the only possible division for it: some have found a simpler twofold division—a life of Christ and a history of the beginnings of the Christian mission to Jerusalem and from Jerusalem.[34] But within the broad outline of his schema—whichever be followed—which centred geographically in Jerusalem, what concerned Luke was that there should be present during the activity of Jesus "authentic witnesses," who had the knowledge and the preparation for leading the Church from Jerusalem, even though, at the same time, the geographical localities which Luke specifically mentions in this section, for example Samaria, should be taken with the utmost seriousness. Although the term "witness" and its cognates seldom occur in Luke, and not at all in 9: 51–19: 27, and seldom in Acts, except for the noun *martus* which occurs thirteen times, in view of the prominent role that the idea of witness plays in Luke-Acts, we cannot doubt that "both the form and content of the travel narrative are part of Luke's presentation of the certainty of the authentication and preparation of the apostolic witness on which the Church was built."[35] The Way of Jesus was one that was attested. Here we emphasize, however, that that Way was a living one. Whatever places Jesus passed through, when he mentions them at all, are significant, or derive their interest for Luke, from his ministry.

3. JERUSALEM: HONOURABLY DEMOTED?

But secondly, Conzelmann has reminded us, there was one place that Luke did recognize as central. As we saw, Conzelmann set Judaea, and especially Jerusalem, in a category apart from Galilee. However, although he seems to presuppose it in 13: 33f, he does not explicitly refer to the mystique of that city, as we traced it in the Old Testament and in Judaism. This is part of the price Conzelmann pays for not taking seriously the first three chapters of the Gospel in particular, because they do introduce us to that mystique.

These chapters constitute the beginning of Luke's work and point to the importance of Jerusalem in his mind. They locate the very beginning

---

[34] See, for example, G. W. H. Lampe, "Luke," *Peake*, p. 820.
[35] Robinson Jr., "The Theological Context," JBL, p. 31.

of the life of Jesus, not only in Nazareth and Galilee, but in the Holy City. In Luke 1: 5ff we are in the centre of the life and land of the people of Israel, in the Temple itself, and in 1: 39ff in the hill country of Judaea (1: 65), and in 2: 22ff, 36ff, we are again referred to Jerusalem and the Temple. There the time of the fulfilment of prophecy is announced, and there too the shadow of the Cross already falls (2: 33ff). For Luke the beginnings of the life of Jesus are intertwined inextricably with the age-long centre of Jewish hope. The city of Jerusalem haunts his Gospel; the beginnings of Jesus, like the beginnings of the Church (Acts 1, 2), were there, informed by the piety of the Old Covenant, within the context of the revival of prophetic inspiration. The first two chapters come to a climax in the story of Jesus at the age of twelve in the Temple: this is his proper sphere, "surrounded by the teachers, listening to them and putting questions." He was "bound to be in my Father's house [NEB: so RSV.] (Luke 2: 41ff)."

Outside the two opening chapters, Jerusalem continues to occur throughout Luke. The statistical record is interesting. While the word "Jerusalem" occurs six times in Luke 1–2, it occurs also twenty-four times in the rest of Luke (three times in its Greek and twenty-one times in its Hebrew form), and sixty-four times in Acts. In the Gospel of Luke there are twice as many occurrences as there are in each of the other Gospels. It is not simply that Luke, a Gentile-Christian, has an emotional satisfaction in using the term "Jerusalem," such as a Roman Catholic outside Italy might have in using "Rome." There is more than this to Luke's usage, as appears from certain central places where he introduces Jerusalem.

In his account of the "temptations" of Jesus, Luke changes the order, or offers a different order from that found in Matthew. In Matt. 4: 8f the final temptation is that on "the high mountain"; the temptation on the Temple in Jerusalem being placed second. But Luke 4: 9 has as his last temptation that: "The devil took [Jesus] to Jerusalem and set him on the parapet of the Temple." Why has Luke preferred to place the temptation at Jerusalem as the climax of the temptations?[36] It is not adequate simply to claim that Luke has preferred a geographical arrangement, "the only change of locality, from the desert to Jerusalem, occurring last," which, incidentally, would also provide a culminating contrast to the desert scene of the first temptation. Almost certainly, Luke did see the concentration of Satan's onslaught on Jesus taking place in the city of Jerusalem,

---

[36] A. H. McNeile, *The Gospel According to St. Matthew*, 1915, p. 37; Matthew has a psychological climax, Luke a geographical one.

which he explicitly names. (Matthew simply has "Holy City.") There by destiny, and historically, Jesus was to be tried and was to suffer. It is no accident that Luke does not locate any temptation at Caesarea Philippi (contrast Mark 8: 27–30 and Matt. 16: 13–20 with Luke 9: 18–21): for him temptation is concentrated especially in Jerusalem.

Similarly at another critical moment, the Transfiguration, in Luke 9: 28ff, the name Jerusalem emerges. Moses and Elijah are reported in Mark and Matthew to be conversing with Jesus, but Luke alone supplies their words: "Suddenly there were two men talking with him; these were Moses and Elijah, who appeared in glory and spoke of his departure, the destiny he was to fulfil in Jerusalem (9: 31 NEB)." The RSV renders the pertinent words of the verse thus: ". . . spoke of his departure, which he was to accomplish at Jerusalem." The "departure (tên exodon autou)" has been taken to refer, improbably, to the Resurrection of Jesus. But this is not to be separated thus distinctly from the Passion: in Luke 24: 46 Passion and Resurrection are inextricable. Luke regards the Passion and the Resurrection as the "Exodus" of Jesus. Whereas Matthew and Mark find parallels to the Exodus in the beginnings of the life of Jesus, Luke does so in its close.[37]

After the Transfiguration, Luke presents the journey of Jesus to Jerusalem. A series of redactional notices make Luke's view of Jerusalem as the city of destiny clear (9: 51, 53; 13: 22; 17: 11; 19: 11). Especially significant are 13: 33 ("However, I must be on my way today and tomorrow and the next day, because it is unthinkable for a prophet to meet his death anywhere but in Jerusalem") and 18: 31 ("He took the Twelve aside and said, 'We are now going up to Jerusalem; and all that was written by the prophets will come true for the Son of Man . . .'"—a verse much fuller than the corresponding one in Mark 10: 33). The city of Jerusalem was to see him rejected who had been destined so to be (Luke 2: 34f).

And, finally, that city was also to be the scene of the Risen Lord's appearances. Luke can hardly have been ignorant of the Galilean appearances.[38] He chose to ignore them, and concentrate on those in Jerusalem.[39] Those women who had companied with Jesus in Galilee had

[37] See J. Dupont, Die Versuchung Jesu in der Wüste, Stuttgart, 1969, pp. 75ff: he cites the pertinent literature.

[38] Ellis, The Gospel of Luke, p. 272, writes: "Luke's selection of episodes arises not from ignorance of or antagonism toward Galilean traditions but rather from his theme. In the Gospel the scene moves from Jerusalem to Galilee to Jerusalem. . . ."

[39] See on this P. Schubert, "The Structure and Significance of Luke 24," Neutestamentliche Studien für Rudolf Bultmann, Bh. ZNW, Vol. XXL, Berlin, 1957, pp. 165–186.

witnessed his death also ("they watched it all": 23: 49 NEB). They are reminded by the two men at the tomb of what Jesus had told them. "Remember what he told you while he was still in Galilee, about the Son of Man; how he must be given into the power of sinful men and be crucified, and must rise again the third day (Luke 24: 6)." There is no reference here to the words in Mark 14: 28 (contrast Luke 24: 6 with Mark 16: 7). Not Galilee but Jerusalem concerns Luke: *there* is the Resurrection. Luke has deliberately modified Mark, and emphasized that all the prophecies of the Scriptures (Luke 24: 25–27, 32–35, 44–49) were fulfilled in Jerusalem, and that the centre of the new movement was to begin there (Luke 24: 47). The closing words of Luke's Gospel are the following:

And he said to them, "This is what I meant by saying, while I was still with you, that everything written about me in the Law of Moses and in the prophets and psalms was bound to be fulfilled." Then he opened their minds to understand the scriptures. "This," he said, "is what is written: that the Messiah is to suffer death and to rise from the dead on the third day, and that in his name repentance bringing the forgiveness of sins is to be proclaimed to all nations. Begin from Jerusalem; it is you who are the witnesses to it all. And mark this: I am sending upon you my Father's promised gift; so stay here in this city until you are armed with the power from above."

Then he led them out as far as Bethany, and blessed them with uplifted hands; and in the act of blessing he parted from them. And they returned to Jerusalem with great joy, and spent all their time in the temple praising God (Luke 24: 44–53 NEB).

They are taken up, with variation, in Acts 1: 1–13, and the motif of prophecy becomes clear again in Acts 1: 15ff; 2: 1ff.[40]

Luke, then, was fully aware of Jerusalem as the centre of Jewish eschatological hope. The beginnings of Luke and Acts reveal how, more perhaps than any other writer in the New Testament, Luke, a Gentile concerned above all with the Gentile mission, was aware that Christianity arose out of the boiling cauldron of eschatological anticipations of first-century Judaism,[41] and emphasized the significance for its beginning of the city around which those hopes had clustered.

But there is another dimension to Luke's awareness: his recognition of what we might call a demotion of Jerusalem as a necessity for the Church of his day. In Jewish expectation Jerusalem was the city of the End: an eschatological mystique surrounded it. Early Christians could easily succumb to this mystique, and some, as we shall see in Acts, were tempted

---

[40] *The Theology of St. Luke*, pp. 75ff. In Luke 24 the name Jerusalem occurs five times. And equally frequently in Acts 1.

[41] See below, pp. 261ff.

to do so. Luke was aware of that mystique and of its accompanying seduction. He saw that it was necessary, quite deliberately, to transcend it. To do this, while, as we have recognized, he gives to that city its due importance as the city of the beginning, as the scene of the Passion and of the Resurrection, he separates it from the End. It is not to be linked to the Parousia.

Conzelmann rightly emphasizes that Luke develops his eschatology in relation to Jerusalem.[42] Early in the Gospel, Luke refers to the disciples' misunderstanding of the relation of Jesus to that city. They had failed to grasp that Jesus was not going there to establish his Kingdom, but to suffer: for them the eschatology of Judaism, in which Jerusalem was to be the scene of the Parousia, was still normative. According to Luke, it was not so with Jesus (9: 45; 18: 34).

The clue to Luke's mind emerges in 19: 11, where we read that "because [Jesus] was near to Jerusalem and because they supposed that the Kingdom of God [centred in Jerusalem] was to appear immediately," Jesus told the parable of the pounds or talents. This parable in a different form is found in Matt. 25: 14ff. Whether Luke depended on Matthew, or on another independent source, we need not decide. Either he has modified Q directly or used a source in which the parable of the talents seems to have been combined with another concerning the acquiring of a Kingdom. The outcome of Luke's use of the material is clear. By removing the parable of the talents from its marked eschatological setting in Matthew,[43] and by introducing or using modifications to it, he has removed the impression left by Matthew that the Kingdom was to appear immediately.[44] Christ must first leave his own land (19: 12) in order to receive it. This departure involves his rejection by his own people, Israel, and on his return (19: 27) the destruction of those who have rejected him. His Kingdom will be administered by his disciples: it will not be narrowly confined and self-complacent but will continually expand. His disciples are to promote the world-wide mission entrusted to them (19: 23). To cling to privileges and possessions will be to lose them and bring judgment upon Judaism (19: 27).[45]

---

[42] *The Theology of St. Luke*, pp. 73ff.

[43] It is preceded by the Parables of the Good Servant and the Wicked Servant (Matt. 24: 45–51), and of the Ten Virgins (25: 1–13), and followed by The Parable of the Last Judgment (25: 31–46).

[44] In Luke 19: 11 the implication is that the occasion for the parable is twofold: (1) they are nearing Jerusalem; (2) the disciples are under the [false] impression that the Kingdom of God is about to appear (ὅτι παραχρῆμα μέλλει ἡ βασιλεία τοῦ θεοῦ ἀναφαίνεσθαι).

[45] That the defaulters are to be punished in the presence of the returned Master does not necessarily mean that they are to experience this soon.

This parable—which Luke so clearly applies to his own day—is placed immediately before the Entry into the city: it indicates in advance that that event was not to be understood eschatologically or politically. Jesus did not go to Jerusalem to set up his Kingdom. The purpose of the Entry is to introduce not the End, but the Passion. It is not to the city, as such, that Jesus goes but to the Temple (19: 45). Conzelmann is possibly too subtle in insisting that the Entry is not connected with the city at all, but it is significant that it was to the religious centre of the nation's life that Jesus went; it was not with the eschatological destiny of Jerusalem that Jesus was concerned, but with the possession of the centre of Israel's worship: Luke was concerned to indicate, not that the End was at hand for the city, but that Jesus was seeking to found the true Israel. To reduce the political aspect further, Luke makes, not the people, but the disciples rejoice in his entry (19: 37), and in 19: 38 omits the words in Mark 11: 10: "Blessed is the Kingdom of our father David that is coming." Similarly, later, Luke makes it clear that while he admits the Davidic descent of Jesus, he is not, for him, merely the Son of David (20: 41–44). There is no anointing at Bethany, and the extreme political position over taxes to Caesar is rejected (20: 19–26).

As for the cleansing of the Temple, it is to be understood in the light of Luke's presentation of an implied protracted period of teaching in the Temple, with, presumably, nightly visits to the Mount of Olives (19: 47; 21: 37).[46] The cleansing is reported in two brief verses (Luke 19: 45, 46):

> Then he went into the temple and began driving out the traders, with these words: "Scripture says, 'My house shall be a house of prayer'; but you have made it a robbers' cave."

The Markan criticism of the cult and ascription of eschatological significance to the cleansing is modified radically. To this end apparently, Luke even omits the reference to "the house of prayer for all nations": he suppresses reference to acts of violence as much as possible. For Luke the cleansing is not eschatological, but designed simply to purify the Temple for Jesus' presence and teaching. Is Luke here already suggesting that the Temple is to be identified with Jesus himself? Is he "gradually developing the theological notion that the physical city and the material temple are no longer sacred places of God's presence?" Has Jesus "taken over the prerogative and honour in himself"?[47]

[46] See B. Gerhardsson, *Memory and Manuscript*, Uppsala, 1961, and the critique in SSM. Appendix, pp. 464ff.

[47] See Carroll Stuhlmueller, C.P., JBC, p. 153b, *ad rem.*

This reference to the city takes us back more directly to the theme that occupies us. What of Jerusalem itself and the End? This is part of the theme of Luke's discourse in the Temple in chapter 21: 5–36. The sources of that chapter have much occupied scholars: is Luke here dependent on a text different from Mark 13 in our present text? Had he before him a Proto-Lukan document? Or again did he merely change Mark in his own interests? The latter seems most probable. And one of those interests was to make clear that the fall of Jerusalem is to be separated from the Parousia: that Jerusalem is not the city of the End. This interest Luke has already exemplified in 17: 20–37, where the fall of Jerusalem and the Parousia, which are combined in Matthew 24 and Mark 13, are kept distinct, the Parousia being there described without reference to Jerusalem.[48] So, too, in Luke 21, teaching is given publicly in the Temple, whereas in Mark 13: 3ff it is given privately to the disciples on the Mount of Olives, as if it concerned them particularly and was not for all men.

The question concerning the overthrow of the Temple in Mark 13: 1ff leads on to the eschatological concern in 13: 4: "Tell us, when will this be, and what will be the sign *when these things are all to be accomplished?*" Luke expresses the question in less eschatological terms: "Teacher, when will this be, and what will be the sign *when this is about to take place?*" There is a subtle change in the Lukan version of the words in italics: the fall of the Temple in the latter is not the End. Similarly, to Mark's catalogue of those who raise false eschatological hopes, Luke adds those who claim that "the time is at hand (21: 8 NEB: 'The Day is upon us')." Such a declaration is false: the Parousia is not at hand. For Mark's words "the end is not yet (13: 7)," Luke substitutes a stronger expression, "but the end does not follow immediately (Luke 21: 9 NEB)," and in Luke 21: 24, the statement of Mark 13: 20, "And if the Lord had not shortened the days...but for the sake of the elect, whom he chose, he shortened the days"; is changed. Luke introduces the thought of the Gentile destruction and domination of Jerusalem (compare Zech. 12: 2–3).[49] In 21: 2ff Luke had already emphasized what was to happen before the End, giving seven verses to this theme over against Mark's four. Luke 21: 20ff also interprets Mark's reference to "the desolating sacrilege (Mark 13: 14)" of the destruction of Jerusalem by enemy forces and spells out the evacuation of the city implied in Mark 13: 15ff. The reference in Mark 13: 14 to "the

[48] True there is a reference in 17: 25 to the suffering. This would be in Jerusalem, but Luke does not mention the city, and the term "first" suggests that that suffering precedes and is separated from the End.

[49] See below, pp. 259 ff.

desolating sacrilege" of Daniel 9: 27; 11: 31; 12: 11 is phrased in Luke 21: 20 in these words: "But when you see Jerusalem surrounded by armies, then know that its desolation has come near." Luke thereby makes it clear that the desolation of Jerusalem is not to be confused with the End, but regarded as an expression of Divine retribution. The same is the thrust of Luke 21: 23–24: "For there will be great distress in the land [that is, the land of Israel] [RSV wrongly 'earth'] and a terrible judgement upon this people [that is, the people of Israel]. They will fall at the sword's point; they will be carried captive into all countries; and Jerusalem will be trampled down by foreigners *until their day has run its course* (NEB)." Much is to happen between the fall of Jerusalem and the End.

Consonant with this is the change Luke gives to the position of the reference to Dan. 7: 13–14 which Mark placed in the trial scene (Mark 14: 62). Luke introduces it to the discourse at Luke 21: 27. Unlike Mark he understands that passage to refer to the distant, future Parousia, and finds it appropriate in a context dealing with that Parousia. He changes the "you will see" of Mark 14: 62 to "they will see." The fig tree to which Luke draws attention in 21: 29, in a parable, there being no curse, is conjoined with other trees to show, perhaps, that the words of Jesus apply not only to Judaism, but have a wider eschatological reference. In the same context Luke softens Mark's words "you know that he is near, at the very gates (13: 29)" to "you may be sure that the kingdom of God is near (21: 31)." And in the final section, Luke 21: 34–36, the Evangelist makes it clear that he is not merely thinking of a localized End, centred in Jerusalem, but of "a day that will come on all men wherever they are, the whole world over (NEB)." That day is not at hand: first many things have to come to pass (Luke 21: 9): the term "first" is emphatic and is absent in Mark 13: 7. Before that day comes there will be need for enduring perseverance in prayer (Luke 21: 34–36), prayer before, and in, imminent troubles, and in the more distant time when Christians are to stand in the presence of the Son of Man (see the distinction in Luke 21: 36). There are things that belong to the final end (21: 25–28) and others to the immediate future (21: 20–24): they are not to be confused.

These details are presented to establish that Luke refuses to confuse the End with the fate of Jerusalem.[50] It is to be recognized that Luke, perhaps,

[50] In addition to Conzelmann, so H. J. Cadbury, *The Making of Luke-Acts*, New York, 1927, p. 292; J. M. Creed, *The Gospel According to St. Luke*, London, 1930, p. 292; E. Grässer, *Das Problem der Parusieverzögerung . . .*, Berlin, 1957, pp. 178f for the delay of the Parousia. The understanding of the cleansing of the Temple in Luke as compared with that found in Mark and Matthew, who differ in this matter more than Conzelmann seems to allow, is

does not carry through his separation of these with rigid consistency. In 21: 31–32 it would be natural to link the fall of Jerusalem with the redemption of the elect and the coming of the Kingdom.[51] But the full impact of the details presented above must not be ignored: probably it is familiarity with the Markan text that makes it difficult for us to see how marked is the separation of Jerusalem from the Parousia in Luke. And the full significance of this separation must be grasped: it is this—Luke fully recognizes Jerusalem as the geographic centre of Christian beginnings; he also knows its mystique. But he deliberately and clinically transcends this spatial dimension. Christianity is a Way which began at Jerusalem, but passes through it. True, Luke retains the cry of Jesus over Jerusalem in 19: 41–44. But, despite the weeping, it is clear-eyed and unsentimental: Luke recognized that Jerusalem had chosen the way of political nationalism which led to war with Rome. In the coming of Jesus, God had decisively visited Jerusalem, but it was in judgment. Despite his awareness of the mystique of Jerusalem, Luke was not as susceptible to it as was Paul. A Gentile, even a Gentile Christian, Luke could be clinical about Jerusalem in a way that Paul never achieved.

4. The Land and Rome

But, it will be urged, even though we recognize the full force of that tradition in Judaism which had come to see in Jerusalem the quintessence of the land, can we move from Luke's treatment of Jerusalem to the land of Israel?

That the old hope for a restored Israel on the land of Israel survived till his day Luke clearly reveals in 24: 18–21. Even the Lukan Paul shares this hope, as the remarkable words in Acts 26: 6f reveal: "And it is for a hope kindled by God's promise to our forefathers that I stand in the dock today. Our twelve tribes hope to see the fulfilment of that promise, worshipping with intense devotion day and night; and for this very hope I am impeached...." The reference to the twelve tribes, in these words of Paul before Agrippa, indicates the national concentration of the

---

instructive and confirms our treatment of Jerusalem. See Dowda, unpublished dissertation, Duke University, 1972.

[51] A. L. Moore, *The Parousia in the New Testament*, Leiden, 1966, pp. 162f, draws attention to two passages in Luke which suggest an imminent Parousia. First, 13: 6–9: "It is not yet too late to repent; but the time is limited." But the reference here seems to be strictly to Israel, that is, it contemplates the national disaster imminent not the End. There is direct reference to the men of Jerusalem immediately before in 13: 4 and to Jerusalem in 13: 33, 34–35. A. R. C. Leaney, whom Moore refers to in support of his view, specifically refers the parable to the inhabitants of Jerusalem, *A Commentary on the Gospel According to St. Luke*, p. 207. Secondly, and more difficult not to recognize, is 18: 1–8.

hope.[52] And in Acts 1:6 the disciples themselves reveal their perplexity, if not their minds. "So when they were all together, they asked him, 'Lord, is this the time when you are to establish once again the sovereignty of Israel?'" Hopes of the control of the land by Israel are here unmistakable. These Luke had to combat.

At this point a glance at the Birth Narratives is instructive. We shall assume that Luke 1 and 2 are an integral part of Luke-Acts. There Luke draws on previously existing sources, but the material he uses has been made his own, so that the same hand is traceable in the Birth Narratives as in the rest of Luke-Acts. The date of the materials upon which Luke draws in Luke 1–2 is early: it has been traced by some even to the time of the ministries of Jesus and the Baptist, by others to the very early days of the Church in Jerusalem.[53] Certainly the hopes they express would be familiar to Luke.

Can we precisely describe those hopes? In their present form the Birth Narratives in Luke 1 and 2, as indicated, reflect Luke's mind. But the peculiarly Christian or Lukan emphases in them are, in fact, few. Thus there is only one reference to the salvation of the Gentiles, in 2:29–32, where Simeon proclaims, on receiving the child Jesus:

This day, Master, thou givest thy servant his discharge
    in peace; Now thy promise is fulfilled.
For I have seen with my own eyes
the deliverance which thou hast made ready in full view of all the nations:
A light that will be a revelation to the heathen,
    and glory to thy people Israel (NEB).

And even here, as the last verse indicates, strictly speaking it is the salvation of Israel before the nations that we find. The background for 2:29–32 is Gen. 15:15; the promise to Abraham is in Luke's mind. The well-known words in Luke 2:14, through the mistranslation of the King James Version, have been given a universal ring which the Greek does not warrant.[54] They speak not of "peace among men" but of "peace for men on whom his favour rests." True in 1:58 Zechariah predicts that John the Baptist would "...lead his [God's] people to salvation through knowledge of him, by the forgiveness of their sins..." and that a salvation conceived in such terms is more than political. Yet, the dimensions

---

[52] It is not sufficient to find in the reference to the twelve tribes merely a rhetorical touch.

[53] Ellis, *The Gospel of Luke*, p. 65; Minear, *Studies in Luke-Acts*, p. 126.

[54] See J. A. Fitzmyer, *Essays on the Semitic Background of the New Testament*, London, 1971, pp. 101–104, on "Peace On Earth Among Men of His Good Will" (Lk 2:14).

of the salvation even here are national. Similarly in the passage where Luke makes clear that the shadow of the Cross is over the birth of Jesus in 2: 35, the horizons are still national. "This child," said Simeon to Mary, "is destined to be *a sign which men reject*;[55] and you too shall be pierced to the heart. Many in Israel will stand or fall because of him, and thus the secret thoughts of many will be laid bare." This translation in the NEB suggests by the words in italics a universal rejection, but the Greek has no such suggestion: its ambience is Israel. All this means that in the Birth Narratives we encounter little that is specifically Christian in "tone" but rather a glimpse into the cauldron of excited eschatological hopes fulfilled, but still concentrated on Israel.[56] It is no accident that English Bishops often referred, in the thirties, to the Magnificat as being "more revolutionary than the Red Flag," and, we may add, less universalistic. The atmosphere of piety pervading Luke 1–2 can easily hide the nationalistic intensity. E. E. Ellis, writing of the last half of the Magnificat, writes: "...[it] describes God's victory in terms of national deliverance from human oppressors. This is a recurrent note in pre-Christian messianism. The New Testament writers do not deny it, but they redefine it and transfer it to Messiah's *parousia*."[57] Can it be said that that note is redefined in Luke 1–2? Hardly.

Consider the following emphases in them. First, the prediction that Jesus would occupy the throne of David. Gabriel says to Mary:

...the Lord will give to him the throne of his father David and he will reign over the house of Jacob forever, and of his kingdom there will be no end (Luke 1: 31–33).

Zechariah the father of John the Baptist cries:

> Praise to the God of Israel!
> For he has turned to his people, saved them and set them free,
> and has raised up a deliverer of victorious power
> from the house of his servant David.
> (Luke 1: 68 NEB; compare 1: 27; 2: 5; 2: 11).

---

[55] The Greek in Luke 2: 35 simply has: εἰς σημεῖον ἀντιλεγόμενον: the order of the Greek text is changed in the NEB.

[56] It is pertinent to note the many parallels that have been drawn between the ideology of the Birth Narratives and the Qumran documents. The "nationalism" of both is not dissimilar.

[57] *The Gospel of Luke*, p. 72. Compare with our position, 'Abd Al-Tafahum, "Doctrine" in *Religion in the Middle East*, ed. A. J. Arberry, Vol. 2, Cambridge, 1969, p. 383: "Mary's own *Magnificat*, sweet hymn as it is of the reversal of values, could be taken or mistaken, in the usual sense of the great hope: 'He hath scattered the proud...He hath put down the mighty....'"

Simeon is described as one who had waited for the "consolation of Israel" (2: 25 RSV, which the NEB renders "the restoration of Israel") (compare Acts 1: 6).[58]

Secondly, Luke 1 and 2 frequently express the fulfilment of God's word in the coming of Christ. Behind 1: 37, 38, lies the promise of God to Abraham in Gen. 18: 14 (although the word "promise" is not used), as Gen. 17: 7; 18: 18; 22: 17 lie behind 1: 58f. The NEB introduces the word "promise(s)" at 1: 37 and 1: 55: this is not justified by a literal translation, but it does do justice to the intent of the texts concerned. So, too, in Luke 1: 70–75 the idea of promise, introduced again in the NEB, lies behind the text. In 1: 73 Abraham is named as in 1: 55.

And, thirdly, as we have previously noted and need not here document, the notion of the fulfilment of the prophecies is ubiquitous in Luke 1 and 2.

Our purpose in thus pointing to certain repeated elements in the Birth Narratives is to suggest that we catch a glimpse in them of an aspect of primitive Christian anticipation which, in the tendency to recognize the extent to which the Gospel transformed Jewish eschatology by spiritualizing it, we easily overlook. For example, Easton spoke of the anti-Zealotic character of Luke 1, 2; but it is difficult to agree.[59] Certainly in the Magnificat at 1: 51, as Easton himself recognizes: "In the context the verbs must refer to the conception of the Messiah. God's Anointed is in the world, even though not yet born, and the destruction of the powers of evil is so certain that it may be regarded as already accomplished. The 'proud' are the enemies of Israel, primarily the Romans and (perhaps) the Sadducees...."[60] Here we are probably in touch with an early (and not defunct) Palestinian mentality in the Church which, while not Zealot, was concerned with the national hope based on the promise to Abraham. There were Christians whom Luke knew, who did think, we cannot but assume, of the land, concentrated for them in Jerusalem. For them the work of the Messiah was inseparable from God's help to his servant Israel (1: 54). Easton significantly comments on Luke 2: 33: "Luke doubtless felt that this explicit prediction of the Messiah's illumination of the Gentiles was a new feature in the prophecies of the Nativity."[61] It can rightly be implied that Luke stood against much popular Palestinian piety which could easily have been exploited by Zealots.[62] How he countered

---

[58] The Greek has παράκλησιν τοῦ Ἰσραήλ. The term παράκλησις in the LXX renders: תַּחֲנוּן, נֹחַם, נַחוּמִים, תַּנְחוּמִים which do not suggest such a strong term as "restoration."

[59] The exact page reference eludes us here.

[60] *The Gospel According to St. Luke*, p. 15.   [61] *Ibid.*, p. 28.

[62] Compare our treatment of Paul, "Paul and Jewish Christianity in the light of Cardinal Daniélou..." in *Recherches de Science Religieuse*, Tome 60, 1972, pp. 69–80.

"the atmospheric pressures" of the popular Christian eschatology we encounter in Luke 1 and 2, we can see in Acts 1.

The opening verses of Acts put these anticipations in proper perspective at the very outset. Acts 1: 3–11 reads as follows:

> He showed himself to these men after his death, and gave ample proof that he was alive: over a period of forty days he appeared to them and taught them about the kingdom of God. While he was in their company he told them not to leave Jerusalem (*mê chôrizesthai*). "You must wait," he said, "for the promise made by my Father, about which you have heard me speak: John, as you know, baptized with water, but you will be baptized with the Holy Spirit, and within the next few days."
>
> So, when they were all together, they asked him, "Lord, is this the time when you are to establish once again the sovereignty of Israel?" He answered, "It is not for you to know about dates or times, which the Father has set within his own control. But you will receive power when the Holy Spirit comes upon you; and you will bear witness for me in Jerusalem, and all over Judaea and Samaria, and away to the ends of the earth."
>
> When he had said this, as they watched, he was lifted up, and a cloud removed him from their sight. As he was going, and as they were gazing intently into the sky, all at once there stood beside them two men in white who said, "Men of Galilee, why stand there looking up into the sky? This Jesus, who has been taken away from you up to heaven, will come in the same way as you have seen him go (NEB)."

First, Acts 1: 4 at least implies that there had been a desire on the part of the disciples, the Galileans of Acts 1: 11, to return to Galilee. Had some of them actually gone back? According to some, if the present tense of the verb "to leave (*chôrizesthai*)" be pressed, this is implied. In classical Greek *mê chôrizesthai* denotes "to stop moving away" over against *mê chôristhênai*, which means "not to begin to move away."[63] In Mark and Matthew and John 21 the disciples had gone back to Galilee. If so, we can only assume that their anticipation of the End in Jerusalem, in accordance with Jewish expectations, had caused them to return thither. Luke knew of the tradition that Jesus had instructed the disciples to go to Galilee (Mark 14: 28; 16: 7), but had corrected it already in Luke 24: 6. Luke 24: 50–53 is, however, also corrected in Acts. That passage had left the impression that Jesus had finally parted from his disciples on Easter night. Acts in 1: 3 speaks of appearances for forty days and describes what the Risen Lord spoke. It is best not to press the distinction between *chôrizesthai* and

---

[63] See E. Haenchen, *Die Apostelgeschichte*, Göttingen, 1957, p. 112. He rejects the possibility referred to in the text.

chôristhênai, and to assume that Luke did not understand some of the disciples to have already returned to Galilee. The disciples are advised to remain in Jerusalem. The reason given for this advice is that they are to wait there for the fulfilment of the promise of the Spirit (Acts 1: 5; compare Luke 24: 49; Acts 2: 33). Any attachment to Galilee is discouraged: nostalgia for "the good old days" there, at least on Conzelmann's view, is ruled out. It is in Jerusalem that the destiny of the disciples lies to begin with. But only to begin with![64]

Because, secondly, Luke in these opening verses faces at once the expectations cherished by the earliest members. In Acts 1: 6 the words *hoi men oun* (so when they...) signify that Luke no longer contemplates only the Apostles, but a more indefinite group. He refers to a generalized anticipation among the earliest Christians for the imminent restoration of Israel's national independence, when they would have positions of authority (compare Mark 10: 35ff; Luke 1, 2, 22: 24ff). Such a restoration, they expected, would accompany the gift of the Spirit, and would ensure their centrality. Luke insists that whatever purposes of his own God might have for such a national restoration, that is, for Israel after the flesh, the messengers of Christ were not to be concerned with these things. The disciples' expectation of an *imminent* Kingdom is rejected, although the expectation of the Kingdom of God as such is not annulled. They are enjoined to eschew concentration on an imminent end of the world. Luke makes use of words in Mark 13: 32 and Matt. 24: 36, which he had not used in his Gospel, for this purpose: not for them the calculation of the times. Their task is defined for them. They are to be witnesses, and the scope of their witness is not to be confined to the land of Israel. The geographic span of that witness is to include "Jerusalem, all Judaea, Samaria and then the end of the earth (1: 8)." Many have seen in this sequence the plan which Luke followed in the presentation of his materials, thus: Acts 1–7: Jerusalem; 8, 9: Judaea and Samaria; 10–28: mission to the end of the earth. There is no mention of Galilee, and, if even Luke possibly included Galilee in Judaea, he pays no attention to any Christianity of any special significance in Galilee.

In the opening verses of Acts, then, two questions are squarely faced,

---

[64] Given the mystique of Jerusalem to which we have so constantly referred it was natural for the disciples to stay in Jerusalem when their initial dismay was overcome. And it is possible to overemphasize that dismay, particularly in Luke, which, in chapter 24, suggests, on their part, more a wistful disappointment or even expectation than deep dismay. John Knox, *Chapters in a Life of Paul*, Nashville, 1950, pp. 25f, does not do justice to the role of Jerusalem in Jewish expectation: this rather than a *Tendenz* in Luke-Acts accounts for the concentration upon it.

the imminence of the Parousia and "nationalistic" concentration. They are both challenged. The Church is to venture forth into the large world confined neither to Galilee nor Jerusalem, but facing the end of the earth. Jerusalem and the land are important as the scene of the beginning and they continue important to preserve the historical roots of the Gospel and its continuity with the ministry of Jesus. But the Gospel is not to be tied to them. In the choice of a successor to Judas (Acts 1: 15–26), the qualifications for apostleship are defined in terms of a relationship to the historical Jesus and of witness to the Resurrection. But the location of the life of Jesus in Galilee, although assumed (Acts 1: 21ff) is not mentioned: as such it is unimportant. The reception of the Spirit is the centre of gravity, rather than the hope for the Parousia, and becomes also the mark of the witness.

For our purposes two questions arise. First, could not what we find in Luke-Acts, as far as the geographic spread of Christianity is concerned, be due to the purely historical sequence of events as Luke understood them? Apart from the desire to check Messianic fervour for the restoration of Israel which we have already noticed among the earliest Christians, is it necessary to find in Luke-Acts an additional unmistakable theological concern to emancipate the Gospel from attachment to the land, be it Galilee or Jerusalem or the totality of the land? Did the question of the land, as part of the promises of God in the Old Testament, occupy Luke? And the second question is this: did Luke, as many hold, find in Rome "the climax of the Gospel"? Did he, while detaching the Gospel from one land and city prepare the way, either deliberately or unconsciously, for its attachment to the Eternal City?

To begin with the first question. Is there evidence that Luke was concerned with the question of the land? One fact might lead us to expect an affirmative answer. We already noted that in the Birth Narratives Abraham and the promise to him figure. These narratives, however, are pre-Lukan and primitive and we suggested that there was much nationalistic sentiment in them which Luke opposed. But the importance of Abraham and the promise is marked also in Luke-Acts generally. The name Abraham occurs only once in Mark, seven and eleven times in Matthew and John respectively, but fifteen times in Luke, and seven times in Acts. Noteworthy for our direct purpose are Acts 3: 12–26 and 13: 16–41. In the former we have Peter's speech: "You are the sons of the prophets," he tells the Jews, "and of the covenant which God gave to your fathers, saying to Abraham, 'And in your posterity shall all the families of the earth (*hai patriai tês gês*) be blessed . . . (3: 25).'" Haenchen takes the term "families" here to refer to all the tribes of the country, that is, of Israel. Be that as it may, 3: 26 gives a universal scope to the promise. The change of "the nations (*ethnê*)" of the LXX of Gen. 18: 18; 22: 18, and the "tribes (*phulai*)" of Gen. 12: 3 to "the families (*patriai*)" of Acts 3: 25 may be due to Luke's desire not to anticipate the story of Cornelius in Acts 10, but it may also simply be that the text Luke used translated the Hebrew *mish*ᵉ*pp*ᵉ*hôth* more accurately than did the LXX. The point is that the Jews are included in the posterity of Abraham to be blessed. But their blessedness is not defined in terms of the possession of the land, but of turning from wickedness (3: 26).

Similarly in Acts 13: 16–41, Paul's speech at Pisidian Antioch, the background to the Apostle's thought is the election of Abraham (13: 17) and God's promise to him (13: 26, 32–33). The promise to Abraham reiterated variously to the fathers, made operative through David, has been fulfilled in Jesus (13: 23, 26ff), and the resurrection (13: 32ff). But here again the result of the fulfilment has nothing to do with the occupation or possession of the land, but all to do with the forgiveness of sins (13: 38), even though Paul is addressing "the family of Abraham and god-fearers (13: 26)." The passages from the speeches by Peter and Paul attest that Luke-Acts do find in the life, death, and resurrection of Jesus the fulfilment of the promise and of prophecy, but they also ignore what was as a constitutive element of the promise, that is, the land.

Does Luke-Acts at any point confront the question of the land, and not simply ignore it? This brings us to one of the most difficult problems in Acts, the interpretation of Stephen's speech in Acts 7. Two approaches are possible. The first, the most recent, is to recognize that, unlike many of Paul's speeches in Acts, that of Stephen is not essentially related to its context, that its main section at least is irrelevant to this. Paul's speeches, on the contrary, reveal a sensitivy to the audiences to which they are addressed. In this view, Luke has borrowed a homily from the Synagogue and inserted it at a point in the history which he deemed suitable, in order to expound his own attitude to or estimate of Judaism. It follows that it is fruitless to try to relate any of the details of the speech to the situation confronting Stephen, because they are not directly addressed to it. Dibelius and Haenchen have followed this approach. It is not surprising that Haenchen finds no theology of the land in the speech. In favour of this approach is the fact that the direct charges of the false witnesses in Acts 6: 13 that Stephen spoke against "this holy place and the law" can hardly be claimed to be refuted by the speech, which is largely a survey of the history of Israel and only touches briefly on the Temple in 7: 44–50, and on the Law, only incidentally almost, in 7: 35ff.

The second approach refuses to regard the speech of Stephen as irrelevant to its context. An example of such an approach is provided by N. A. Dahl's essay "The Story of Abraham in Luke-Acts."[65] He takes seriously the context, that is, the situation of Stephen, and seeks to find lines of contact between it and the details of the speech. He begins by emphasizing the first section of the speech 7: 1–8, and particularly Acts 7: 7, where there is a quotation from Gen. 15: 13–14, the text of which in the MT reads:

> Then the Lord said to Abram, "Know of a surety that your descendants will be sojourners in a land that is not theirs, and will be slaves there, and they will be oppressed for four hundred years; but I will bring judgment on the nation which they serve, and afterward they shall come out with great possessions."

The text in Acts 7: 7 substitutes for the last words, "they shall come out with great possessions," the words "And after that they shall come out and worship me in this place." These latter words are a part of Exod. 3: 12: "He [God] said [to Moses], But I shall be with you; and this shall be the sign for you, that I have sent you: when you have brought forth the people out of Egypt, you shall serve God on this mountain." According to Dahl, Stephen's speech is a commentary on this prophecy and its fulfilment. For Stephen, the goal of the Exodus is not the worship of God at Sinai, nor the possession of the land of Canaan, nor the erection of the Temple by Solomon. It was, however, now achieved in the worship of the disciples, here represented by Stephen, gathered in the Name of Jesus in the Temple in Jerusalem and in their homes. The promise is fulfilled. But in the very moment when the prophecy comes to pass, its fulfilment, as always in the history of Israel, is violently rejected. The account of Stephen's martyrdom and speech constitutes the end of the initial movement centred in Jerusalem: his speech is the last preaching of the apostles and evangelists in that city. Henceforth in Acts the preaching takes place elsewhere, in Samaria and beyond. The concentration on Jerusalem has been broken.

In this way Dahl connects Stephen's speech with its context. But Dahl is surely right to emphasize the opening section of the speech and to point to an aspect of it which Dibelius and Haenchen too easily neglected, its

[65] In *Studies in Luke-Acts*, eds. L. E. Keck and J. L. Martyn, pp. 139ff.

concentration on the land. Dahl[66] notes, almost in passing, the theological significance of the insistence in Acts 7: 2–5 that when God promised the land to Abraham he had no land of his own. The verses read: "The God of glory appeared to Abraham our ancestor while he was in Mesopotamia, before he had settled in Haran, and said: 'Leave your country and your kinsfolk and come away to a land that I will show you.' Thereupon he left the land of the Chaldaeans and settled in Haran. From there, after his father's death, God led him to migrate to this land where you now live. He gave him nothing in it to call his own, not one yard; but promised to give it in possession to him and his descendants after him though he was then childless." Unfortunately, Dahl tantalizingly does not explain this theological significance.

We now ask whether discussion of the land such as implied in Acts 7: 2–7 is not unrelated to the preceding section in Acts 6: 1–15. In Acts 6: 1–6 we encounter "Hellenists." It is unlikely that these were Greeks: they were Jews who probably spoke Greek and had interest in the Greek world in some way.[67] They reveal a growing variety in the Church, a crisis which led to the choice of seven leaders with Greek names, among whom was Stephen. Acts 6: 7, a summary statement, looks backwards and forwards; it reads: "The word of God now spread more and more widely; the number of disciples in Jerusalem went on increasing rapidly... (NEB)." Some in the "diaspora" synagogues in Jerusalem (Acts 7: 9) became alarmed at Stephen and instituted proceedings against him. Stephen's speech is in defence against these: a Hellenist speaks to the Diaspora Jews in Jerusalem. Their charges, as we saw, centred in the Temple, the Law, and the words of Jesus. Perhaps in the total complex, Acts 6: 1–15, we can see a crisis in the Church, spilling over to the Diaspora Jews, foreshadowing the emancipation of the Christian movement from "Palestinian" domination. Was that movement as Hellenists entered it, beginning to kick against its geographic limitations and to strain at the leash of the Temple, symbol of Judaism? This may be so, but it has to be admitted that it is conjectural, if probable.

But even if we cannot with confidence connect the discussion in Acts 7: 2–7 with a problem that had explicitly emerged concerning the land in Acts 6: 1–15, because there is there no reference to the land, that Luke in Acts 7: 2–7 was so concerned can hardly be doubted, and that he had

---

[66] *Ibid.*, p. 143.

[67] J. A. Fitzmyer, *Studies in Luke-Acts*, pp. 237f: he follows C. F. D. Moule's view that the Hellenists were "Jews who spoke only Greek": see "Once More, Who Were the Hellenists?", ET, LXX, 1958–59, pp. 100–102.

reason to be so concerned he has made clear in Acts 1: 1ff. The evidence is as follows.

The term "land" occurs five times in Acts 7: 2–7. In Acts 7: 2 it is emphasized that the revelation of God came to Abraham in Mesopotamia outside the land, before he had settled down at the first stop even (that is, when he was travelling), at Haran. The addition of "before he had settled in Haran" (which is in modern Turkey) adds force to the extra-territorial nature of the revelation. And the command of God to Abraham was: "Leave your country and your kinsfolk and come away to that land that I will show you (Acts 7: 3)." True, Abraham is not asked to be without a land. In fact, he is promised the land. But Luke next emphasizes that God "gave him nothing in it to call his own, not one yard (Acts 7: 5 NEB)." Further, by God's will Abraham's descendants were to live as aliens in a foreign land (Acts 7: 6). God's people have encountered him in and been led by him to a foreign land.

That the presence of God can be known "outside the land" is further made clear in 7: 9ff. Joseph was sold into slavery in Egypt, but "God was with him and rescued him from all his troubles" and gave him "presence and powers of mind." Egypt befriended Joseph, and Jacob, who ended his days there, was buried, of all places in Shechem, honoured by the Samaritans. There is a confusion here regarding Jacob's burial place. According to Josh. 24: 32, Joseph was buried in Shechem in the tomb which Jacob bought of the sons of Hamor (Gen. 33: 19), whereas Jacob was buried at Hebron in the field Abraham had bought for a burying place (Gen. 50: 13; 23: 19). But the point is all the more clearly made that Jacob, Israel's eponymous ancestor, like Joseph, was a stranger in a Gentile country and that he and other patriarchs died having no inheritance in the promised land, except for a tomb bought from heathen Canaanites in an area where they were later buried, which was near Mt. Gerizim, the antithesis of Jerusalem (7: 15).

Similarly God intervened through Moses in Egypt (7: 17ff). But who was this Moses? He was not brought up in the "holy land," but by a foreigner (Pharaoh's daughter herself) in a foreign court, and "was trained in all the wisdom of the Egyptians, a powerful speaker and a man of action (7: 21f)." This is not the only "foreign" aspect in Moses's life: he spent forty years, as an exile, in the alien land of Midian (7: 29), and it was outside the land in Mt. Sinai that the supreme call came to him. There was "holy ground" outside the "holy land (7: 33)." "It was Moses who led them out working miracles and signs in Egypt, at the Red Sea, and for forty years in the desert.... It was he again who when [the Israelites] were assembled here in the desert, conversed with the angel who spoke to him on Mount Sinai, and with our forefathers... (7: 36ff NEB)." The desert outside the land saw the redeeming activity of God: and later, for their sins, it was God's purpose to send Israel into Babylon; the Exile was according to his will (7: 43).

And, finally, what are we to make of Acts 7: 44–50? There is an abrupt transition at 7: 44 to a discussion of the Tent of Testimony in the desert, which is contrasted with the "dwelling-place," the house eventually built for God by Solomon, that is, the Temple. While the Tent is noted as having been built after the pattern commanded by God (7: 44), and its movements to the time of David are traced without adverse comments (7: 45ff), the Temple built by Solomon is, by implication, condemned, as man-made, and unworthy to "contain" the Lord. The implication seems to be that the Lord does not have "a resting place" like the Temple. The passage 7: 49–50 reads:

Heaven is my throne and earth my footstool. What kind of house will you build for me, says the Lord; where is my resting-place? Are not all these things of my own making?

While the direct connection between 7: 44–50 and 7: 1–44 is not obvious, its thrust is clear. There is a glance toward the Temple at Jerusalem. The foundation of that static edifice was, it is implied, misguided. Such a structure is not after the divine pattern, but the movable tent, transitory and impermanent, is.

Enough has been written to indicate that the land was much in Luke's mind as he wrote Acts 7, and while the speech does not directly answer the charges made against Stephen, it does fit into the general situation described in 6: 1ff which implies that already the question of the relationship of the Gospel to non-Palestinian Jews, if not to Gentiles, was being raised in the conflict between the Hebrews and the Hellenists. William Manson, to whom we are indebted in the above, finds the concentration in Acts 7 on the extra-territorial dimension of God's activity a direct challenge to the Jewish community and to the early Christian community, "huddled" around the Temple in Jerusalem and in the land, to move forward, to cease to cling to the securities of the institutions of the past— the Temple, the Law. The purpose of God has always called upon his people to "go forth." William Manson asks:

whereas the original Apostles and witnesses thought that Jesus would come back to *them*—"Lord, is it at this time that you restore the Kingdom to Israel?"

—did Stephen say that they must go out and, so to speak, anticipate the Son of Man's coming by proclaiming Him to every nation and people of that larger world *which was now included in His* dominion?*. . . Israel has been tempted to identify its salvation with historical and earthly securities and fixtures, and Stephen cannot but see the same danger in the attitude of the "Hebrew" brethren in the Church.* His words are, indeed, to the Jews, but his animadversions on Moses and the Law, and on the Holy Place and Tradition, could not but have oblique reference to the conservatism of a section of the Christian community (italics Manson).[68]

If we substitute Luke for Stephen in the above quotation, we may agree. There is little doubt that what we have in Acts 7 is Luke's important statement—a lengthy one—of his attitude to a Christianity too narrowly and rigidly bound to Judaism, the Temple, and Jerusalem and the land. There are many motifs he desires to emphasize—the parallels between the history of the leaders of Israel in the past (Moses, Joseph etc.) with Jesus; the parallel between the rejection of Jesus and other frequent rejections of God's emissaries in Jewish history. We have concentrated on one theme—the extra-territorial dimension of God's challenge and presence in the history of Israel.

One difficulty in thinking that it is Stephen's mind, not Luke's, that we encounter in Acts 7 on this theme is that, as Luke presents the matter, it requires an exceedingly early emergence of the question of the land in Jerusalem itself. In a charged Messianic atmosphere such as that of the early Christian movement, ideas, like events, are likely to have moved very rapidly, as we shall point out below (and there were Diaspora Jews in the Church perhaps from the beginning). But even so is it likely that it was in Jerusalem itself that the question of the land first emerged? It is probably best to look elsewhere for the historical origin of the express concentration on the question of the land.

It is significant that as Acts relates the story of Stephen it presents grave difficulties. The account of disputes in Acts 6: 1ff runs counter to the picture elsewhere drawn by Luke of the earliest church at peace. Presumably Acts 6: 1ff, therefore, is based on a tradition that Luke had received. From whom? Wendt[69] and Jeremias[70] argued for a source derived from the archives of the Church at Antioch! Trocmé[71] for a travel diary;

[68] *The Epistle to the Hebrews*, London, 1951, pp. 32, 35.
[69] H. H. Wendt, "Die Hauptquelle der Apostelgeschichte," ZNW, Vol. 24, 1925, pp. 293–305.
[70] J. Jeremias, "Untersuchungen zum Quellenproblem der Apostelgeschichte," ZNW, Vol. 36, 1937, pp. 213–220.
[71] E. Trocmé, Le "Livre des Actes" et l'histoire, Paris, 1957, pp. 134–140.

Haenchen suggests other ways in which Luke might have gained knowledge of the Hebrews and the Hellenists and their conflict in Acts 6: 1ff.

"How," asks Haenchen, "did [Luke] come to learn of the background to the Stephen episode, and the subsequent persecution, as it is sketched in 6: 1ff? From Jerusalem or from Hellenists driven out (say) to Antioch? The unexpected light thrown on the state of the Jerusalem Church by the mention of the two groups, betrays an intimate knowledge of the situation such as one expects only from participants. On the other hand, the conflict of 6: 1ff has been minimized. Is Luke simply transmitting, without important alterations, the view of things bequeathed to him by former members of the Jerusalem Church? Has he himself rubbed down the most jagged points of a 'Hellenistic' recollection? Or had the original tradition mellowed, even in Gentile circles, into a harmonious overall picture?"[72]

We need not settle this question. We suggest that the concern with the land was brought to focus on the expulsion of the Hellenists from Jerusalem, and that the discussion of it in Acts 7 reflects considerable speculation about it in a centre such as Antioch. Luke has used traditions about such speculation at the crucial point when the Gospel, presented at Jerusalem by Stephen, was found to be incompatible with Judaism and that religion was brought to a point of decisive challenge. The precise challenge, as Luke presents it, centred on the Law and the Temple, but as the Hellenists went outside the land it became also concerned with the land. In this account of the Jerusalem Church, and in his explanatory speech, Luke combines these foci of interest and, indeed, by beginning his speech with the question of the land gives to this a certain priority—the priority which it had for him as he was tracing the Way out of its chrysalis in Judaism to the larger Gentile world.

The emphasis on the question of the land, in Luke, is to be held in close contact with those Jewish expectations to which we referred in Part I on pp. 61ff. The Spirit was to be experienced in the land. It is from this point of view that we should regard the references to Christians in Samaria in Acts 8. As a result of Philip's preaching here and his miracles "in many cases of possession the unclean spirits came out with a great outcry; and many paralysed and crippled folk were cured; and there was great joy in that city." But despite their baptism, converts in Samaria who had accepted the word of God (8: 12, 13) had not received the Spirit (8: 15, 16). This came with the prayers of Peter and John (8: 17). Outside the land—if Samaria be considered as non-Jewish territory—the Spirit

[72] Haenchen, *Die Apostelgeschichte*, Introduction, Section 6.

now descended. There was a new territorial phase in the mission, a Samaritan Pentecost; Samaritans are joined to the People of God, and that by emissaries from hated Jerusalem. Geographic limits to "the Spirit" are transcended. This is part of the significance of the conversion of the Ethiopian eunuch (Ethiopian means not Abyssinian, but belonging to Merre, the modern Sudan): the emphasis is not on his being a eunuch, but on his being an Ethiopian. The reception of the Spirit is explicitly mentioned only in the Western Text, but it is implied in Acts 8: 36–39. The Ethiopian had *not* received the Spirit at Jerusalem (8: 28). Similarly Paul himself was given the Spirit, not in the land, but in Damascus, a famous "haven for heretics (Acts 9)." The emphasis in Acts 10, describing the amazement that filled those who accompanied Peter, men of Jewish birth (10: 45), at the coming of the Spirit in Joppa is on the reception of the Spirit by Gentiles; Joppa was in Judaea. But the territorial implications are not to be overlooked. Caesarea, the home of Cornelius, was in Samaria, and Luke seems anxious to make clear that the Gospel has here entered non-Jewish lands. This is the force of his reference in 10: 37, 39: what had previously been confined "to the land of the Jews" is no longer so confined. And, finally, the presence of the Spirit at Antioch reached the ears of the Church in Jerusalem. The disciples there are fully conscious that they belong geographically to another world from that of their fellow Christians in Judaea (Acts 11: 39). But they share in the gift of the Spirit: the approval of the work there is prompted by the Holy Spirit in Barnabas (11: 24). From this point forward the geographical question need not concern us: the territorial limits of Jewish expectation have been transcended.

We have concentrated in the above on one motif which is more often implied than made explicit by Luke, who couches the progress of the Way in terms of the Gentiles, not of geography. To isolate the question of the land, as we have done, is to magnify it. But Luke's presentation, we emphasize, must constantly be placed against the background of those eschatological expectations about the land which we saw informed first-century Judaism and, as Luke himself makes clear, earliest Christianity also. We assume that, in the crisis which the Gospel precipitated, the place of the land was seriously discussed. To this we shall return later.

At this point, we turn to the second question that we posed. What is the significance of Rome for Luke? According to some, although Jerusalem remains for Luke the primordial centre of the Faith, its goal for him is Rome. Rome had been chosen as the city where the Church would recover its true role in the world after having been rejected in Jerusalem. Acts begins there: it ends in Rome.[73] Others have pointed out how the last eight chapters of Acts leads on to the triumphal note of Acts 28: 14: "And so we came to Rome." Luke in short may, it is implied, have taken part in the inauguration of the Christian mystique of Rome, which played such a fateful part in later history.[74]

1. To begin with let us note a fact which our emphasis on the freeing of the Gospel from its geographic origin, Jerusalem, caused us to mute. It is notorious that Paul in Galatians, while he showed due respect to "the pillars" at Jerusalem, insisted also on his independence from them. But even Paul, as we saw before, never emotionally at least, overcame the mystique of that city, nourished as it was by past experience and the future hopes of his people.[75] It is now essential to recognize that, throughout Acts, Luke emphasizes the connection between The Way and Jerusalem. The shadow of Jerusalem persists after Acts 7. It has been held that, after Stephen, Jerusalem ceased to be the *centrum mundi* for Luke and became merely the *point de départ*, preserving indeed the continuity of the Gospel with its historical origins, but above all becoming the springboard to Rome: O'Neill has gone so far as to claim that after the martyrdom of Stephen, although it continues, the mission of the Jerusalem Church does not concern Acts.[76]

But such a view does not do justice to a continuous emphasis in Luke. Acts opens in Jerusalem. As we saw, no appearances of the Risen Lord in Galilee are recorded: it was in Jerusalem that the new movement began and, at first, settled. The Temple was apparently central to it (Acts 3: 1; 5: 12). The Church was extremely successful in Jerusalem in its missionary work: 2: 9; 2: 41, 47; 4: 4; 5: 14; 6: 7; 21: 20. Luke is careful to note at each decisive step in the history of The Way that the approval of the Jerusalem community was sought. Acts 8: 14–15, 25, make it clear that for Luke the Jerusalem Church is the controlling headquarters of the Church's mission. It sets the seal of approval on Philip's extension of the mission to Samaria. After his call, Paul remained in Damascus until he went up to Jerusalem (9: 20f; contrast Gal. 1: 17). Luke insists on the

73 See especially J. C. O'Neill. *The Theology of Acts in its Historical Setting*, London, 1961.
74 H. Chadwick, *The Circle and the Ellipse*, Oxford, 1959.
75 See above p. 220.
76 *The Theology of Acts in its Historical Setting*; see the convincing criticism by H. Conzelmann, *Studies in Luke-Acts*, eds. Keck and Martyn, p. 309. See also H. Flender, *St. Luke Theologian of Redemptive History*, Philadelphia; M. D. Goulder, *Type and History in Acts*, London, 1964.

close association of Paul with the Jerusalem apostles and their authoriza-
tion of his ministry (Acts 9: 26–30; contrast Gal. 1–2). He thinks of the
Twelve (the apostles here seem to be identified with these) as the governing
body of the Church, in residence at Jerusalem (9: 27). (In Acts 22: 17–21
Paul leaves the city on the Gentile mission under divine commission: not
Christian, but Jewish opposition caused him to do so.) Peter's activity at
Joppa and Caesarea is recognized by the Jerusalem Church (11: 1–18), as
had been that of Philip in Samaria (8: 14). Peter reported to that Church.
Later at 11: 22 the Jerusalem Church recognized the creation of a mixed
Jewish-Christian Church at Antioch. The Gentile mission in Luke's eyes
was authorized officially by Jerusalem: the Judaizers who dog Paul are not
representatives of the Church in Jerusalem. The Christian prophets at
Antioch, on the other hand, seem to be associates of the Jerusalem apostles
(11: 27); one of them inspired a contribution for the relief of fellow
Christians in Judaea (11: 30). There is solidarity between the Church at
Antioch and at Jerusalem. (The reading in Acts 12: 25 is difficult.)[77] In
Acts 14: 26 Luke seems anxious to explain why Paul and Barnabas, after
their first missionary journey, did not report to Jerusalem: it was because
they heard it was the Church at Antioch that had commissioned their
work! Into the historical problems presented by Acts 15, describing the
Apostolic Council, we need not enter here. The significant point is that in
a bitter crisis over the admission of Gentiles into the Church the leaders
of the Jerusalem Church, with James as their spokesman, recognized that
it was God's purpose to include Gentiles in the People of God, provided
only that they observed four precepts which were required of all men. Luke
seems to be governed throughout by the desire to affirm that the Gentile
mission (11: 18), and the admission of Gentiles without circumcision into
the Church (provided they observed certain Noachian Laws) were under
the blessing of the Jerusalem leaders. Paul was no rebel from Jerusalem.
The authority of the Jerusalem Church emerges also in the decision of the
whole assembly to send envoys back to Antioch along with Paul and
Barnabas (15: 22); the unity is reaffirmed implicitly by the return of Judas
and Silas to Jerusalem (15: 33). In Acts 16: 4, on the visit to Derbe and
Lystra, Paul seems to act as a representative of the Jerusalem Church in
delivering the council's decisions. Later in Acts 18, after the second
missionary journey, Luke again makes Paul first visit Jerusalem to pay
his respects before going down to Antioch (18: 22), 18: 21 having already

[77] In Acts 11: 1 the verb "heard" implies official congnizance. See Lampe, "Luke,"
Peake, p. 900b. The Western Text at 11: 22 has a considerable introduction to this narrative
which makes Peter's subordination to the Jerusalem Church less clear.

foreshadowed more fateful visits to the Holy City. (The historical improbability of a visit by Paul to Jerusalem such as is implied in 18: 22 only makes Luke's anxiety to connect the second missionary journey with Jerusalem more marked.) So during the third missionary journey Paul's mind is occupied with Jerusalem (as with Rome) (Acts 19: 21): he will go there to report. From this point on there was a divine necessity that he should go on his "passion" to Jerusalem, under the constraint of the Spirit (Acts 20: 22–24; 21: 4 does not contradict this; compare 20: 36–7; 21: 11ff).[78] The welcome of the Jerusalem Church, despite opponents of Paul, is real (21: 18ff). Paul's fate in Jerusalem does not concern us here. How far he was prepared to recognize the guidance of the Jerusalem Church, in Luke's mind, appears from 21: 23ff where he undertook to discharge the dues of four Christians who were under temporary Nazirite vows: he notes in his defence before the Jerusalem mob that he had received a vision in the Temple; his commission originated in the centre of Judaism, the Temple itself: he was no apostate (Acts 22: 17). His speech before the Sanhedrin affirmed his attachment to Judaism (23: 1–10); he was, he declares before Felix in Caesarea, on a pilgrimage in Jerusalem; he worshipped "the God of our fathers (24: 10ff)." Again, at Caesarea before Festus, he maintained his innocence of any offence against the Law or the Temple (25: 6–12), and before Agrippa insisted on his loyalty to the promise of the God of Israel (26: 6). He was not hostile to the religion centred in Jerusalem.

Such a quick survey calls into question any lack of interest on the part of Luke in the city of David after Acts 7. But the nature of this interest has to be defined. It was not geographical or strictly historical. Two important reasons made it necessary for Luke to emphasize the continuity of Christianity with Judaism. First, the Gentile mission which concerned Luke involved or demanded the abandonment of the Jewish Law and, thereby, endangered the continuity of Christians with Judaism by separating them from their root. And, secondly, in addition to this theological reason, there was a political reason, that is, the desire to secure for the young Christian movement, through its associations with Judaism, the legal recognition of the Roman government. One way of meeting both these considerations was to emphasize the continuities of Christianity with Jerusalem: this emphasis we have traced above. Luke was anxious to maintain a continuity between the witness to and understanding

---

[78] On the similarity between Paul and Jesus, compare Acts 21: 11ff; 28: 17. There is a close parallel between Paul's journey to Jerusalem and that of Jesus. See especially J. Munck, *Paul and the Salvation of Mankind*, trans., Richmond, Va., 1959, pp. 319ff.

of the Gospel on the part of Paul and the first "witnesses" in Jerusalem. The continued assertions of the authentication of the Pauline mission by those in Jerusalem, where Acts opens, and of Paul's anxiety to retain the good will of the Jerusalem Church show that the centrality that that city has for Luke in Acts is not so much geographical and historical as theological. Jerusalem was important as the seat of the primary witnesses to the salvation wrought by Christ. To the extent that the concern with it in Acts is not strictly geographical, it should not be allowed to detract from any centrality of a geographical kind that Luke may have ascribed to Rome.

2. Other factors in Acts should warn against a too hasty acceptance of a Lukan concentration on Rome.

First, Luke in Acts has a quick sensitivity to geography, a fondness for noting small ports of call on Paul's voyages, but above all for lingering with cities that stir his (and our) imagination. Jerusalem, Damascus, Corinth, Athens, Ephesus, Antioch—all these and others he deals with. He had an acute awareness of the point at which the Gospel passed over to Europe from Asia (Acts 16: 6–10). As in the story of Cornelius, where the turning to the Gentiles is traced to a divine purpose, not to any merely human plan, so here the entry upon a new area of the Christian mission is due to a vision. This does not preclude psychological and other considerations which may have helped to lead to such an entry, but Luke is not concerned with these.[79]

That Luke should, therefore, be interested in the city of Rome was inevitable. But certain considerations are to be recognized. In view of his interest in other cities, that in Rome should not be automatically emphasized. Luke could clearly give to cities other than Rome a highly symbolic significance. This is particularly true of Athens, which, in Acts 17: 16–21, stands for the Greek philosophical world. At that time, it was politically and economically insignificant. But it is at Athens that Luke makes Paul, for the first and only time, seriously address a Gentile audience directly (apart from a minor episode at Lystra [14: 8–18]), and introduces Epicurean and Stoic philosophers (17: 17). Because of the speech on the Areopagus, Athens acquires a symbolic importance for Luke as the scene of the confrontation between the Gospel and Hellenism, Christ and Culture. Was it in some such symbolic sense—not at all emphatic or peculiar—that Luke thought of Rome also as the symbol of the Gentile world? If so, it should be given no undue significance in

[79] Haenchen, *Die Apostelgeschichte*, pp. 223ff.

Luke's purpose. In fact, while in a general sense, Acts does set forth the progress of Christianity to Rome, such a march does not illumine or absorb all the contents of Acts. There is much, for example the story of Ananias and Sapphira and the many speeches of Paul before he finally arrives at Rome, which cannot profitably be connected with such a march. Acts is not simply a straightforward history of the way Christianity reached Rome.[80]

Secondly, the interest of Acts in Rome seems to be confined to the last chapters. It never shows how the Gospel reached Rome. But it does assume that the Church had been established there before Paul's arrival. This makes that arrival, if the purpose of Acts was to trace how the Gospel came to Rome, anti-climactic. In fact, at no point does Acts explicitly state that it was designed to trace the advance of Christianity to Rome. The verse most often quoted as supporting Luke's concern, if not preoccupation, with that city is not without difficulty. Acts 1: 8 reads as follows:

But you shall receive power when the Holy Spirit has come upon you; and you shall be my witnesses in Jerusalem and in all Judaea and Samaria and to the end of the earth.

The phrase *eôs eschatou tês gês*, "to the end of the earth," has usually been taken to refer to Rome and the whole verse to indicate the geographic plan to be followed by Luke in Acts. Trocmé[81] understood the phrase to look to the complete evangelization of the land of Israel. But this is unlikely, because the phrase recurs in 13: 47 as part of a quotation from Is. 49: 6, where it refers certainly to extra-Israelite lands. In 13: 47, at Antioch of Pisidia, Paul uses that passage to justify the turning to the Gentiles. (One scholar—whose view is mentioned as a curiosity—was constrained to the forced idea that because *eschatou* was masculine, it referred to the last man to be evangelized!)[82]

The passage cited in favour of understanding "to the end of the earth"

---

[80] To judge from E. Haenchen's survey of interpretations of Acts in his commentary, the concentration on the arrival at Rome as central for the understanding of Luke's purpose did not emerge in the earliest modern commentators. By today it has become almost a "dogma." The most notable critic of this is W. C. van Unnik in two excellent articles to which I am much indebted: "'The Book of Acts' the confirmation of the Gospel," *Novum Testamentum*, Vol. iv, 1960, pp. 26–59; "Der Ausdruck '*eôs eschatou tês gês*' (Apostelgeschichte 1: 18) und sein alttestamentlicher Hintergrund," in *Studia Biblica et Semitica*, Wageningen, 1966, pp. 335–349.

[81] On this view *tês gês* is *hâ-'âretz*—the stock term for the land of Israel. See Trocmé, *Le Livre des Actes*.

[82] For bibliographical references see van Unnik, *Studia Biblica et Semitica*.

as Rome occurs in the Pss. Sol. 8: 16. But van Unnik convincingly points out that the reference there is more plausibly to Spain.[83] Luke was a man of culture: Rome might be for him the centre of the world, but hardly its end. It is far better to interpret "to the end of the earth" in a general sense of the salvation of the whole world. Luke probably took the expression from Old Testament passages such as Is. 52: 10; 48: 20; 49: 6; 62: 11. In Acts 1: 8, the Risen Lord sends his apostles out to be witnesses to all the world, not specifically to Rome. Because Luke ended Acts with a scene in Rome it is a ready temptation to read Rome back into the first chapter; but this temptation must be resisted. It is implied at Acts 27: 24 that Luke was aware that Paul did appear before the Emperor. It is odd, if the confrontation of the Gospel with Rome, symbolic of the Gentile world, was the centre of his interest, that Luke did not, if he knew of it, describe this appearance and provide an appropriate speech for the occasion. Instead, he presents a summary of a speech not before Roman authorities, but before Jewish leaders (28: 23ff). As we shall indicate later, the significance of Rome does not seem to occupy him so much as the rejection of the Gospel by Jews and its reception by Gentiles.

3. To what extent can it be claimed that Luke, centring on bringing the Gospel to its climax at Rome, aimed at conciliating Roman authorities by showing that the spread of the Gospel had not been hindered by Roman officials, but rather furthered and protected? The extreme claim that Acts was prepared as a source of information for the defence of Paul before the imperial tribunal in Rome[84] need not detain us, because so much in Acts would be irrelevant to such a purpose, for example the story of Pentecost, to note only one item. But that Luke does reiterate the comparatively favourable treatment accorded to Christians by Romans as opposed to Jews is undeniable. In Acts 3: 2, it was a Jew who delivered up Jesus to the Romans; 13: 4–12 presents Sergius Paulus, the first Roman Governor outside Judaea to be mentioned, as favourable. A Jew, a false prophet, has tried to hinder a friendly Gentile, representative of the Roman government, who was anxious to hear the Gospel, and who was, in the end, converted; Acts 16: 19–25 carefully explains that the hostile action of the Roman authorities at Philippi was based on a misunderstanding of the situation; a pagan gaoler was converted (16: 25–34). The magistrates apologized for their conduct (16: 35–40); in Acts 17 Roman authorities

---

[83] *Ibid.*, pp. 346ff.

[84] See F. F. Bruce, *The Acts of the Apostles*, London, 1951, p. 30, for bibliographical details. On the attitude to the Roman state in Acts, see D. R. Griffiths, *The New Testament and the Roman State*, Swansea, 1970, pp. 72ff.

recognize that the charge of sedition brought by Jews against Christians was false; in the appearance before Gallio at Corinth in 8: 12–17 Paul is vindicated; 19: 23–41 emphasizes the good relations between Paul and the civil authorities; a Roman tribune saves Paul from torture (22: 22–29), and Romans rescue Paul in 23: 10; and hold Paul in high favour and keep him only in open arrest (23: 16); from the Roman point of view Paul is innocent (23: 25). Felix was not inclined to treat Paul as a criminal and allowed him a large measure of freedom and visiting privileges (24: 22); Festus and Agrippa and Bernice (25: 6–27) were convinced of Paul's innocence, and, finally, at Rome itself after 28: 9ff the centurion is no longer mentioned. Paul's captivity being thus played down. So too the military escort is not mentioned at Acts 28: 15, nor the Roman authorities at 28: 16. At 28: 18 the Romans desire to set Paul free but he had to appeal to Caesar because of the Jews. Paul preached unhindered (Acts 28: 31).

But here again it is easy to exaggerate. The Roman authorities made some mistakes for which they had to apologize. They did not always intervene to protect Christians (17: 13 at Beroea); Gallio is hardly sympathetic or protective, he is aloof and unconcerned (18: 12ff); at Acts 22: 22–29 only the fact that Paul was a Roman citizen, not that he was a Christian, hindered a tribune, frightened by the mob (22: 23), from torturing him; Felix was not above a bribe (Acts 24: 26), and Festus thought Paul "mad (26: 24–29)."

Roman officials are pictured, it might be urged, as more neutral than favourable to the Faith, and sometimes in a dubious light. There are passages, moreover, which would strike disturbingly on Romans' ears. "We must obey God rather than men (Acts 5: 30)," although uttered to a Jewish Council and the High Priest, who under the guidance of Gamaliel came to terms with the sentiment, would not ingratiate Christianity with Rome. The desire to present a favourable picture of the new Faith to Rome is a very subordinate motif in Acts.[85]

4. Do the last chapters in Acts support a very marked concentration on getting to Rome? The shipwreck at Malta was followed by a three months' stay on that island (Acts 28: 11). This three months' delay on the way to Rome may have been unavoidable because of the season, sailing being perhaps impossible. But there is no expression of impatience at that delay. Rather Acts 28: 7ff gives a strange impression of a leisurely stay:

[85] Bruce, *The Acts of the Apostles*, p. 30. Lampe, "Luke," *Peake*, p. 884a, finds the motif secondary but important. R. J. Dillon and J. A. Fitzmyer, JBC, pp. 165ff, do not deal with the matter.

Paul and his companions were entertained. Three days were spent at Syracuse, a day at Rhegium, and a week at Puteoli. There is in 28: 1ff little if any suggestion of a majestic speed, a deliberate urgency in getting to Rome. On the contrary, there is almost a "tourist" air about the voyage.

Throughout Acts, then, considerations that have usually been brought forward to indicate how significant Rome was for Luke cannot certainly be ascribed the importance that is usually accorded to them. But we have yet to consider the weight which should be given to the incidence of the term "Rome" in the last eight chapters of Acts. There are five references to the city in these chapters, as in the whole of Acts: at 18: 2, which for our purposes is unimportant, and at 19: 21; 23: 11; 28: 14, 16. Let us look at these closely.

In Acts 19: 21, the reference to Rome comes after those to Macedonia, Achaia, and Jerusalem. The words follow: "After I have been there [Jerusalem], I must also see Rome (*dei me kai Hrômen idein*)." Here it is difficult not to recognize that Paul is not going so much to Jerusalem as to Rome, which would hereafter be his centre of operations, as first Antioch and then other cities had been (Acts 19: 21 is Paul's first recorded mention of Rome in Acts). Ramsay saw in this verse the clear conception of a far-reaching plan to proceed via the Imperial City "to evangelize the chief seat of Roman civilization in the West [Spain]."[86] The verse does mark a crisis in Paul's career. He is turned now irrevocably to Rome. Though *idein* (to see) is not a strong verb, full weight must be given to the verb *dei* (it is necessary). Luke regards it as the divine purpose that Paul should take the Gospel to Rome.

The reference to Rome in 23: 11 is equally impressive. After a furious attack on Paul by the Jews of Jerusalem following his defence before them, which led to a great clamour, when the Roman tribune became afraid that Paul would be torn in pieces, the Apostle is consoled by a vision of the Lord. "The following night the Lord stood by him and said 'Take courage, for as you have testified about me at Jerusalem, so you must bear witness also at Rome.'" Jerusalem has finally rejected the Gospel. Paul is to look forward to bearing witness—more promisingly?—at Rome. The reaction against his speech among the Jews in 22: 22 is expressed as follows. "Up to this word they listened to him; then they lifted up their voices and said: *aire apo tês gês ton toiouton ou gar kathêken auton zên.*" This is usually rendered: "Away with such a fellow from the

---

[86] *St. Paul the Traveller and Roman Citizen*, London, 1898, pp. 254f, 274.

earth." But a better translation probably would be: "Away with such a fellow from the land." Paul defiled "the land," that is, the land of Israel; as unclean, he is treated with contempt—"they threw dust into the air." In 21: 36 the mob who attacked Paul merely shouted "Away with him *(aire auton)*": this might suggest that the *apo tês gês* of 22: 22 is emphatic, though I do not press this. Is Luke suggesting that, in fact, what the Jews desire—the separation of Paul from the land—was, under divine providence, to take place, and that the consolatory vision, in which Paul is pointed forward to Rome by the Lord himself, looks back to this, that is, to 22: 22. Again the end of his journey in Rome is foreshadowed, and again the *dei* of divine necessity is used: Paul must now move on to Rome.

Finally, we come to the references to Rome in the very last chapter, in 28: 14: *kai houtôs eis tên Hrômen êlthamen*. Attempts have been made to play down the force of this. The NEB rendering, consciously or unconsciously, has this effect. It gives simply: "And so to Rome"—as it were without ceremony. Again the *houtôs* may be taken to refer to the course of the journey to Rome and might have the force of: "and in this leisurely way we came to Rome." Ramsay regarded *tên Hrômen* in 28: 14, because of the article, as referring to the district of Rome, not to the city itself. But 28: 15 rules this out. And there can be little question that the phrase *êlthon eis apantêsin hêmin* has a dramatic character, as Harnack long ago noted. The description of the brethren coming to meet Paul "as far as the forum of Appius and the Three Taverns" adds force to this view. The scene has been called a triumphal entry.[87] Certainly Luke plays upon Paul's arrival. The phrase *êlthon eis apantêsin hêmin* is significant. "*Apantêsis*" has been regarded as a technical term for the official welcome of a newly arrived dignitary by a deputation which went out from the city to greet him and to escort him there; there is thus deep significance in the use of this word to describe the welcome received by Paul from the Roman Church. Bruce[88] refers to Matt. 25: 6; 1 Thess. 4: 17, and the synonymous *hupantêsis* in Matt. 8: 34; 25: 1; 12: 13, and other extra-Biblical sources. The meeting is a solemn introduction of the Apostle to his city of destiny. We may also, I think, argue that the reply of the Jews to Paul in 28: 21f serves to emphasize the significance of Paul's arrival at Rome. "They said to him, 'We have received no letters from Judaea about you, and none of the brethren coming here has reported or spoken any evil about you. But we desire to hear from you what your views are;

---

[87] Lampe, "Luke," *Peake*, p. 925b, on Acts 28: 15.
[88] *The Acts of the Apostles*, p. 475.

for with regard to this sect we know that every where it is spoken against.'" Lampe[89] notes that it is strange that the Jews in Rome are so ignorant of the Christian movement; there was a church in Rome containing many Jewish members, as the Epistle to the Romans makes clear, and there had been disturbances in Rome caused by Christian missionaries which had led to the expulsion of Jews from the city (Acts 18: 2). In any case it is clear that Luke presents the Jews in Rome as *noncommittal*; they had not really been presented with the challenge of the Gospel. This may be Luke's way of enhancing the role of Paul as *the* witness to Rome. Before he came, Rome had not faced the full challenge of Christianity. In any case Luke could not be unaware of what he had written in 18: 2.

Before we attempt to draw any conclusions it should be recognized again that Acts is inseparable from Luke's Gospel, and the part of Rome in Acts can only be fully grasped in the light of the Gospel. And Luke 2: 1ff, in presenting the birth of Jesus, had linked it with the enrolment of the whole world by Caesar Augustus. The significance of this has been expressed by Lampe as follows: "although Luke does not anticipate post-Constantinian writers in connecting the empire of Christ with the *pax Romana*, he is clearly anxious that the reader should be reminded of the relevance of the birth of Christ to the whole of Caesar's world, since he is to be 'a light for revelation to the Gentiles,' as well as 'for glory to Israel.' Luke's eyes are already looking ahead from the Jerusalem of the beginning of his Gospel to the Rome of the last chapter of Acts."[90] Those passages which place Rome in a favourable light in Acts are given an added significance when the conduct of Pilate at the trial in the Gospel of Luke is recalled, Luke 23: 4; 23: 13-25 (nor is the toning down of Mark's account of Barabbas in Luke 23: 19 irrelevant). The Gospel adds force to the contention that Acts leads to Rome and finds in that city "the climax of the Gospel."

But the nature of that climax has to be carefully assessed. Was Luke concerned with Rome as the geographical centre of the Roman Empire? True Paul had appealed to Caesar, and Luke implies, as we saw in 27: 24, that he did appear before the Roman court, and that there was a divine necessity that this should be so. Are we to conclude because of this that Rome as such was of crucial or climactic significance in Luke's mind? The difficulty in precisely defining the place of Rome in Luke-Acts is that the course of the Word of God, of salvation, has been set down by

[89] "Luke," *Peake.*   [90] *Ibid.,* p. 825.

Luke as a history. His history was, however, not like a modern scientific history, fully integrated, but rather impressionistic. There is no continuous march of Christianity from Jerusalem to Rome in Acts, but a number of episodes revealing how, and with what results, the Gospel was preached and received or rejected in various places, in Jerusalem, Samaria, Gentile cities and, finally, the greatest Gentile city, Rome itself. These various episodes are often connected by generalizing summaries or set in an itinerary framework. The "history" is a "loose" history. Not the precise presentation of historical and psychological and other factors normally presented in a history in terms of cause and effect, and not the geographic locations where the Gospel was preached, in themselves, are important for Luke, so much as the witness borne to the Faith in them: it is the vicissitudes of the Word of God that concern Luke, not primarily their geographic incidence.

So is it when Paul reached Rome. Not the city itself, great as that was and great as was Luke's sense of an "occasion," not the fate of Paul himself even—much as he seems to have regarded Paul as a *theios anêr*—is important for Luke, so much as the witness borne to the Word of God in Rome and the direction of that witness facing the larger Gentile world. For example, there is no reference to the actual appearance of Paul before the Emperor, although Acts 27: 24, as we stated before, implies that he did so appear under divine necessity. There is no speech by Paul before the Emperor or before Roman authorities: Luke may have felt that such a speech could only have been a virtual repetition of what Paul had already uttered before Festus, Felix, and Agrippa. The death of the Apostle is not recorded and his tomb—if such existed—is left unnoticed. These were not Luke's concern: he had no desire to make Rome a place of pilgrimage to the tomb of the Apostle. No! what Luke describes in Rome, in Acts 28, is parallel to what he had previously presented in the Gospel and in Acts—the proclamation of the Gospel to Jews, their rejection of it, and its offer to the Gentiles. Rome witnesses no special turn in Luke's story, even if he ends it there. It was Paul's witness in Rome, as elsewhere that concerned Luke, a witness made "quite openly and without hindrance."

And does he, in fact, *end* a story in Rome? Even if we reject the view that Luke intended a third volume after Acts, there is a sense—a crucial sense—in which Luke thought that his story of the progress of the Word of God had no end. He closes Acts as follows: "He [Paul] stayed there two full years at his own expense, with a welcome for all who came to him, preaching the kingdom of God and teaching the facts about the Lord Jesus Christ (*kerussôn tên basileian tou theou kai didaskôn ta peri tou kuriou Iêsou Christou*) quite openly and without hindrance (*meta pasês parrêsias akôlutôs*) (NEB)." To make Luke, who had seen and grasped the significance of the movement of the Word of God from Jerusalem and from the land to the Gentile world, leading outward and onward to the "end of the earth," tie it to another city or ascribe to that city anything more than a significance as a crucial geographical centre for witnessing to the Gospel and to say that he provided the ground for the later mystique of Rome in Christendom, would be to make him inconsistent with himself. There is no doubt that Rome, especially, had a strange, a natural, fascination for Luke: but, while it informs, it does not dominate his presentation in Luke-Acts. No! Once the Gospel had been preached there, for Luke doubtless all roads led not *to* Rome but *from* Rome, because that Gospel was that of the kingdom of God, which was always dynamic: it called Christians not to settle down, even in Rome, but to continue on their pilgrim way. The Living Word which Paul preached at Rome, was not bound: Acts is open-ended: it subordinates all geography, even Rome, to theology.

We may now sum up. There is no justification for thinking that Luke initiated that process which led to the concept of the "Holy Land" by any idealization of Galilee or otherwise. His real concentration on Jerusalem can be understood in terms of theological and political concerns. He deliberately opposed hopes for the restoration of Israel; the land was not to bind the Gospel. Neither was the city of Rome to do so, although he finds in that city the symbol of the Gentile world, and deliberately ends his work, though not his theme, on Paul's arrival there. The question of the land as such, which surfaced, we suggested, when the Hellenists left Jerusalem, probably at Antioch, finds only cursory recognition at Acts 7, where it is submerged by other concerns. Why? By the time Luke came to write, Gentiles, who would have little interest in the land, had far outnumbered Jews in the Church. The importance of this basic fact cannot be overemphasized. But, in addition, may there not have been another factor at work? For Luke to have discussed the separation of the Gospel from the land directly would have undermined two of the purposes which he dearly cherished, and which led him to concentrate so much on Jerusalem—first, the recognition of the theological continuity between Gentile Christianity and Judaism, and, secondly, the political necessity to emphasize this. The same factors which led him to give Jerusalem a full measure of attention would have led him to minimize that given directly to the land. As a Gentile he probably did not share the common Jewish awareness, which we recognized in Part I above, that Jerusalem was the quintessence of the land, and so he could separate his treatment of that city from that of the land.[91]

[91] At this point a suggestion made to me, orally, by Professor J. A. Sanders is noteworthy, namely, that one reason why Paul was effective among Gentiles was that he did not deal directly with the problem of the land: the same might have been true of Luke. It should be noted that the mystique of Rome, whenever and however it arose, did not long remain un-challenged within Christendom. The Eastern Empire rejected it as a Christian capital because of its pagan origins and associations. Constantinople was a new Rome free from a pagan past. But to pursue this theme is beyond our competence and purpose. See, for example, Sozomen, *Eccl. Hist.* 2: 3; Augustine, *The City of God*, 5: 25. Constantine's emphasis on Jerusalem as the centre of the Christian Mystery is also pertinent here. For all this, see J. Vogt, on 'Con-stantinople,' *Reallexikon für Antike und Christentum*, Stuttgart, 1955, Lieferung 17–24, pp. 348–353: Constantinople was a second Rome, but Christian; and G. Downey, *The New Catholic Encyclopedia*, London, 1967, Vol. IV, pp. 231–236.

X. THE LAND IN THE FOURTH GOSPEL

As we turn to the Fourth Gospel, certain preliminary remarks are in order.

First, ever since Clement of Alexandria used the phrase, the Fourth Gospel has often been understood as "the spiritual Gospel," over against the "carnal" Synoptic Gospels. This has usually been taken to imply that, whereas the Synoptics were primarily concerned with the recording of data about the Lord's life, death, and resurrection, the Fourth Gospel was designed to set forth the spiritual dimensions of those data: it is no chronicle but a theological interpretation. Were John thus peculiarly "spiritual" in its intent, two contradictory conclusions might be drawn in connection with our attempt to trace the part played by the land of Israel in the New Testament. It might be urged that such a Gospel would hardly be concerned with any geographical motifs, so that any interest in the land would be unlikely to appear in it. On the other hand, it might be expected that precisely in such a spiritual Gospel would a theological significance be given to geographical realities. As it turns out, the choice between these two contradictory conclusions has become unreal, because the understanding of John as a "theological" Gospel to be sharply distinguished from the Synoptics has now been abandoned. The Synoptics are now recognized to be no less governed by "theological" concerns than John, so that if geographical-theological concerns may have governed the former they may equally well have governed the latter.

Secondly, the Fourth Gospel has often been understood as an essentially Hellenistic document, to be connected particularly with Ephesus in Asia Minor. The question is inevitable whether such a comparatively late document, emanating from such a quarter, is likely to have preserved a concern with Palestinian geographical considerations of any other than the strictest historical or traditional kind. Would not the remove in time and space indicated by the Fourth Gospel have blurred any Palestinian geographical-theological considerations—if ever such existed—and rendered them irrelevant?

The answer to such a question is not difficult. The approach to the Fourth Gospel which emphasized its Hellenistic affinities almost exclusively has been largely abandoned. Few would not now concede that the Fourth Gospel is rooted both in Judaism and in Hellenism, and that to deny it an interest in the land of Israel on the ground of the Hellenistic mould of its thought would be unjustifiable. Recent study has revealed that however Hellenistic its spread, the Fourth Gospel has drawn upon sources of a Palestinian origin, which might be expected to preserve "primitive" tendencies, traces of which at least it would be reasonable to expect in the Gospel in its present form. Indeed, it is now clear that the Fourth Gospel was in living dialogue with Judaism,[1] and possibly, if not probably, Palestinian or Syrian Judaism; and that, we must insist, at a time when the relationship of Judaism to the land was of particular concern to its leaders, so that echoes of that concern might perhaps be overheard in the Gospel.[2]

A third, even more positive preliminary note is necessary. The Fourth Gospel reveals a well-marked practice of ascribing two meanings or even more to certain phenomena. Sometimes an event is treated on two levels: it may refer to an incident in the life of Jesus himself or in that of the believer. At other times, a temporal notation is clearly designed to suggest a "spiritual" dimension: the "night" when Judas departed from the Last Supper was a spiritual "night" for mankind and the cosmos, or, as St. Augustine thought, stood for Judas himself as "night." Again, by a play on the word "lifted up" (elevated), the crucifixion signifies both humiliation and glorification. The point is, that in a Gospel where such double meanings occur it is not unnatural to ask whether spatial or geographical terms, like others, might have a double significance.[3]

This leads to the fourth preliminary consideration. There is evidence that the Fourth Gospel was concerned with the question of "holy space," or, at least, with a tradition that was so concerned and did impose a double-connotation on certain spatial realities. The following data are pertinent.

1. THE TEMPLE

Let us begin with the "holy space" *par excellence*, the Temple in Jerusalem. John places the Cleansing of the Temple very early in his Gospel, in 2: 13–22, to signify that a New Order had arrived. The "Holy Place" is to be displaced by a new reality, a rebuilt "temple (*naos*)," which John refers to as "the temple of his body (*tou naou tou sōmatos*

---

[1] This is brought out most forcefully recently in J. Louis Martyn, *History and Theology in the Fourth Gospel*, New York, 1968.

[2] See SSM, pp. 295f. The Gospel has been connected with Syria.

[3] O. Cullmann, "Der johanneische Gebrauch doppeldeutiger Ausdrücke als Schlüssel zum Verständnis des vierten Evangeliums," *Theologische Zeitschrift*, Vol. 4, Basel, 1948, pp. 360–372.

autou (2: 21))." This phrase refers either to the Resurrection, that is, to the Living Reality of Christ in the midst or to the Church, which, elsewhere in the New Testament, is called "the body of Christ." The phrase "the temple of his body" designates either a person or a community or both that is to replace the "holy space" of the physical temple. The Gospel is destined to personalize or Christify that space, or, rather, holiness is no longer to be attached to space at all.[4]

This attitude to the Temple may be carried further in another passage. Chapters 7 and 8 describe the manifestation of the Messianic presence at the Temple in Jerusalem during the Feast of Tabernacles. At the end of the eighth chapter the claims of Jesus to be the Messiah, the Light of the World, are carried to the utmost. He designates himself as "I am (8: 58)."[5] And, immediately following this, in escaping from the Jews, he departs from the Temple (*kai exêlthen ek tou hierou*) (8: 59).

Most commentators either ignore or pay scant attention to the reference to this departure from the Temple: it merely signifies, it is implied, that the activity of Jesus at the Feast of Tabernacles is over. Jesus had gone up to the Temple in 7: 14, and now in 8: 59, naturally, he leaves it. No profound intent should be read into the references to the departure. This is consonant with the view that the sequence of time and space in Chapters 7 and 8 (as elsewhere in John) are insignificant.[6] But it is possible to give to the narrative setting of these two chapters a special significance. It reveals the characteristic irony of the Fourth Gospel. Outwardly, in these chapters, a rustic prophet makes his appeal to the centre of the nation,

---

[4] So R. E. Brown, *The Gospel According to John*, New York, 1966, pp. 115ff. He rightly does not follow O. Cullmann, *Early Christian Worship*, trans., London, 1953, p. 74, and A. M. Dubarle in finding a eucharistic, sacramental symbolism here ("wine" in John 2: 1ff [The Wedding at Cana] and "Body" in 2: 12ff). But A. M. Dubarle's "Le Signe du Temple," in RB, Vol. 48, 1939, pp. 21–44, is right in connecting John 2: 12 with John 1: 51. Compare C. K. Barrett, *The Gospel According to St. John*, London, 1955, "the human body of Jesus was the place where a unique manifestation of God took place and consequently became the only true Temple, the only centre of the true worship; cf. 4: 20–24. It is possible that John's thought goes further and that he includes in his conception of the body of Christ the thought of the Church, as in the Pauline metaphor (Rom. 12: 5; Col. 1: 18 *et al.*)." Barrett rightly connects 2: 12ff with 4. For fuller discussion, see below.

[5] See E. Schweizer, *Egô eimi...*, Göttingen, 1939, 2nd ed., 1965; C. H. Dodd, *The Interpretation of the Fourth Gospel*, Cambridge, 1953, pp. 93ff; Philip Harner, *The "I Am" of the Fourth Gospel*, Philadelphia, 1971.

[6] R. E. Brown, although fully aware of the connection between the cleansing of the Temple and the break with Judaism, and finding subtly but probably rightly even in 2: 17 a reference to the death of Jesus, *The Gospel*, p. 24, ignores the sentence, except to say that 8: 59 is merely an inclusion designed to hold together 7 and 8, looking back to 7: 10, p. 360. Barrett, *The Gospel*, speaks of the suggestion of a supernatural disappearance, but otherwise does not enlarge. R. Bultmann, *Johannesevangelium*, Göttingen, 1950, p. 249, n. 5, refers to the same motif of disappearance or removal in Philostratus, *Vit. Apollonios*, 8. 5. He rightly rejects the nationalistic interpretations of the verse, but fails to recognize its symbolism.

Jerusalem. But on a deeper level, the incarnate Logos manifests himself to the world. C. H. Dodd has expressed the matter as follows:

The narrative setting of the series of dialogues is itself a *sēmeion* in the sense which that word bears in the Fourth Gospel. It might have been given as a simple narrative of an occurrence during the ministry of Jesus. After a period of retirement in Galilee, He went up to Jerusalem for the Feast of the Tabernacles, and there made a public appeal in the temple. The result was that the crowd threatened to stone Him, and the authorities ordered His arrest. He therefore left the temple, and went into retirement again. But every stage of this narrative has symbolic meaning. The Logos was in the world unknown. He came to His own place (Jerusalem is the *patris* of Jesus in the Fourth Gospel, iv. 44), and those who were His own received Him not. As a result, the manifestation of the Word is withdrawn from Israel: *ekrubē kai exēlthen ek tou hierou*. The whole episode, from this point of view, might be taken as a large-scale illustration of the way in which this evangelist understands the primitive Christian doctrine of the blinding or *pōrōsis* of Israel, to which he has given a prominent position in the epilogue to the Book of Signs, xii. 37–41.[7]

The point which particularly concerns us is the departure from the Temple at 8: 59, which Dodd does not emphasize. Is any symbolic significance to be attached to this explicit reference to a departure from the Temple as such? Can we claim that this departure particularly connotes the turning away of Jesus from Judaism, and that the departure from the Temple—"the holy space"—has become the symbol of that rejection? There are obvious objections to such a view. The verse in 8: 59 may be taken, as by Dodd,[8] for example, as a closure for the whole section beginning at 7: 1, the words "not publicly but in private" of 7: 10 being recalled by the words "but Jesus hid himself" in 8: 59; the departure from the Temple may be taken simply as a natural geographical detail (as we have previously noted, he went up to the temple in 7: 14 and he left it in 8: 59). Again, if the departure from the Temple in 8: 59 were symbolic of the definitive rejection of Judaism and its "holy place," is it likely that Jesus would have gone back again into the Temple, as is stated in 10: 22ff? This would seem to rule out, at first sight, any final significance for 8: 59 in the relationship between Jesus and the Temple.

But the matter is not so simple. The visit of Jesus to the Temple is described in 7: 14 as follows:

---

[7] *The Interpretation*, pp. 351–352.

[8] *Ibid.*, p. 348. Note that E. Schweizer thinks that Mark 13: 1 "As Jesus was leaving the Temple...(καὶ ἐξελθων ὁ Ἰησοῦς ἀπο τοῦ ἱεροῦ)" "may represent for Mark the definitive schism." *The Good News According to Mark*, trans., D. H. Madvig, Richmond, Va., 1970, p. 267. Compare John 8: 59.

About the middle of the feast (of Tabernacles) Jesus went up into the temple and taught...

Here Jesus takes the initiative: he taught. Similarly in 7: 37 we read:

On the last day of the Feast, the great day, Jesus stood up and proclaimed, "If any one thirst... (the words translated 'proclaimed' are strong: the Greek is: *heistêkei ô Iêsous kai ekraxen legôn*...)."[9]

In both passages Jesus deliberately issues a challenge to the Jews: he invites a confrontation.

Contrast with these passages the description of Jesus in 10: 22f, which reads:

It was the feast of the Dedication at Jerusalem; it was winter, and Jesus was walking in the temple in the portico of Solomon. So the Jews gathered round him and said to him, "How long will you keep us in suspense? If you are the Christ, tell us plainly." Jesus answered them, "I told you, and you do not believe..."

Here Jesus issues no challenge; he provokes no confrontation. Rather the Jews confront him: he refers to a challenge that he has already issued (*eipon humin*) ("I told you"), and which has been rejected. Moreover, whereas in 7: 14ff and 7: 37ff Jesus seems engaged in or involved with the Feast of Tabernacles, having gone up to it with great deliberateness at its middle, in 10: 22f it is merely stated that he was walking about (*periepatei*) in the Temple: he seems disengaged; he is at best a kind of onlooker. The reference to the portico of Solomon is significant here. As is made clear in the Western variant at Acts 3: 11 ("As Peter and John came out (of the Temple)... the people stood astonished in the portico which is known as Solomon's"), this portico was outside the Temple proper, constituting the boundary of the latter. Jesus cannot, therefore, be said to be "in the temple" in 10: 22, as he *was* in 7: 14 and 7: 37. And it agrees with this that, at the conclusion of the section 10: 22–39, there is no reference to a departure from the Temple, but only to Jesus' escape from the hands of the hostile Jews. Contrast the explicit reference to such a departure at 8: 59. Throughout 10: 22–39, the movement is on the fringe of the Temple.

Can we find a reason why Jesus should be found thus "walking in the portico of Solomon," if already in 8: 59 John had suggested a final

---

[9] Is the use of ειστηκει here significant? In the Mekilta Beshallah on Exod. 14: 3 (Lauterbach, p. 210), it is stated that wherever the verb "he stood" occurs, the presence of the Holy Spirit is indicated.

rejection of "the holy place" and the departure of the "*I am* (*egô eimi*)" from it? Perhaps the answer lies in the nature of the Feast of Dedication, That feast, called Hannukkah in Hebrew, of the month of Chislev (December) (2 Macc. 1: 9), celebrated the Maccabean victories. From 167–164 B.C. the Syrians had profaned the Temple: they had erected the idol of Baal Shamem (the oriental version of the Olympian Zeus) on the altar of holocausts (1 Macc. 1: 54; 2 Macc. 6: 1–7). The "holy place" was cleansed of this pollution when Judas Maccabeus drove out the Syrians, built a new altar, and rededicated the Temple on the 25th of the month of Chislev (1 Macc. 4: 41–61). It was this event, the reconsecration of the altar and Temple, that the Feast of Dedication annually commemorated. The Feast, as we saw in John 10: 22 was designated by the Greek term *Enkainia*, literally "Renewal." The Greek term, in its substantive and verbal forms, was used in the Septuagint to describe the dedication of the altar in the original tabernacle (Num. 7: 10, 11), of the Temple of Solomon (1 Kings 8: 63; 2 Chron. 7: 5), and of the new Temple which was built after the return from the Babylonian captivity (Ezra 6: 16). The Festival called *Enkainia*, then, evoked the history of the reconsecration and renewal of the "holy place" in Jewish history. But Jesus walking on the fringes of the Temple during this feast of reconsecration knows that the hour of true renewal has passed; the *egô eimi* ("I am he") has departed from the Temple and the real dedication is the dedication of himself by God to fulfil the role of the Temple, that is, to mediate the presence of God to men. This is made explicit in 10: 37, which speaks of the sanctification of Christ. Jesus counters the Jews' claim that he is blaspheming when he claims that: "I and the Father are one," by referring to the Scriptures. The passage reads:

33 The Jews answered him, "We stone you for no good work but for blasphemy; because you, being a man, make yourself God."
34 Jesus answered them, "Is it not written in your law, 'I said, you are gods'?
35 If he called them gods to whom the word of God came (and scripture cannot be broken),
36 do you say of him whom the Father consecrated and sent into the world, 'You are blaspheming,' because I said, 'I am the Son of God'?
37 If I am not doing the works of my Father, then do not believe me."

The Father has consecrated Christ (*hon ho patêr hêgiasen kai apesteilen eis ton kosmon humeis legete hoti blasphêmeis, hoti eipon huios [tou] Theou eimi*). The Greek term translated "consecrated (*hêgiasen*)" is not that used of the Festival itself (*enkainia*), but it *is* used of Moses' consecration of the Tabernacle in the LXX of Num. 7: 1, *enkainizein* being used in Num. 7: 10–11 of the dedication of the altar. Both terms *hagiazein* and *enkainizein*, therefore, occurred in a passage read at the Feast of Dedication in the Synagogue, and in a sense which appears to be synonymous. The implication is that for John, Christ has taken the place previously occupied by the Tabernacle and the altar and the Temple. He has become "the place" for the Divine Presence and reconciliation: the separation from the old "holy space" symbolized by the departure from the Temple in 8: 59 has been "consummated": may we say that, for John, Christ has replaced the Holy of Holies by himself? After the walking in the portico of Solomon there is no further reference to Jesus in the Temple. At Passover in 11: 56 the Pharisees were in the Temple wondering whether Jesus would come to the Feast. He did come to the city; but by that time his attitude to the Temple in John had been determined and made clear. Any cleansing of the Temple in John's Passion narrative for this reason would be otiose or anachronistic.[10]

The purpose of this long excursion on 10: 22ff has been to show that the visit to the portico of Solomon in 10: 22 does not of itself deny finality to the departure recorded in 8: 59: here also John has been concerned to utilize a geographical or spatial note—"departure from the Temple"—to signify a spiritual dimension.

But is there any intrinsic reason why 8: 59 should be given such finality as we have suggested for it? Does John intend to indicate that Jesus there deliberately and finally broke with "Holy Space"? One factor might suggest this. The discussion between Jesus and the Jews ends with the following words in 8: 56–59:

56 Your father Abraham rejoiced that he was to see my day; he saw it and was glad.
57 The Jews then said to him, "You are not yet fifty years old, and have you seen Abraham?"
58 Jesus said to them, "Truly, truly, I say to you, before Abraham was, I am."
59 So they took up stones to throw at him; but Jesus hid himself, and went out of the temple.

Jesus makes here the affirmation that as "I am" he was before Abraham.

---

[10] John's attitude to the Temple is like that implied concerning Israel in the cursing of the Fig Tree in Matthew and Mark—the judgment upon it is passed. The *egô eimi* has departed. Contrast the patience we noted in Luke 13: 6ff. R. E. Brown rightly recognizes a heightening of hostility toward the Temple in John as compared with all the Synoptics, *The Gospel*, p. 122, and connects John with the Hellenists, Hebrews, and Acts 7: 47–48, and even the Samaritans (John 8: 48). See also O. Cullmann, "L'opposition contre le Temple de Jerusalem," NTS, Vol. 5, 1958–59, pp. 157–173.

Into the history of the phrase "I am" we cannot enter here: suffice that "I am" here probably, as in many other places, signifies the Divine Presence. The recognition of himself as "I am" by Jesus is the clearest implication in the New Testament of the Divinity of Christ.[11] The Jews recognize this: they proceed to stone Jesus because in the light of Lev. 24: 16 he is guilty of blasphemy (He who blasphemes the name of the Lord shall be put to death; all the congregation shall stone him; the sojourner as well as the native, when he blasphemes the Name, shall be put to death).

For our purposes, the point to be emphasized in this context is that the Divine Name "I am" probably occupied a prominent role in the liturgy of the Feast of Tabernacles. The pertinent section of it is described as follows in the Mishnah, Sukkah 4: 5:

How was the rite of the Willow-branch fulfilled? There was a place below Jerusalem called Motza. Thither they went and cut themselves young willow branches. They came and set these up at the sides of the Altar so that their tops were bent over the Altar. They then blew (on the shofar) a sustained, a quavering and another sustained blast. Each day they went in procession a single time around the Altar, saying, "Save now, we beseech thee, O Lord! We beseech thee, O Lord, send now prosperity." R. Judah says: '*Ani waho!* Save us we pray! '*Ani waho!* save us we pray! But on that day they went in procession seven times around the Altar. When they departed what did they say? "Homage to thee, O Altar! Homage to thee, O Altar!" R. Eliezer says: "To the Lord and to thee, O Altar! To the Lord and to thee, O Altar!"[12]

The use of the phrase or formula "I am ('*Ani hu*; '*Ani wahu* or *waho*)" by Jesus, therefore, in 8: 58 is eminently fitting: the Feast of Tabernacles itself evoked it. And, if what we have written above be anywhere near the intent of the Evangelist, in 8: 59 we find the implication that, for John, "I am" has departed from the Temple, that "holy space" is no longer the abode of the Divine Presence. The Shekinah is no longer *there*, but is now found wherever Christ is, because later (10: 36 makes this probable, if not unmistakably clear) Christ himself is the Sanctified One, the altar and Temple, the locus of the Shekinah. The consecration of Jesus referred to in 10: 36 is to be associated with the theme of the new Tabernacle

<hr/>

[11] So Brown, *The Gospel*, p. 367; "Does the New Testament call Jesus God?" TS, Vol. 26, 1965, pp. 545–573.

[12] Unfortunately there is no clear certainty about the Hebrew אני והו in this passage, but it is usually taken as referring to God on the grounds that its numerical value is equal to that of אנא (the tetragrammaton corresponding to the abbreviation 'ה being given its full form for the purpose). So P. Blackman, *Mishnayoth*, 2nd ed., Vol. II, p. 337, n.

(1 : 14) and the new Temple (2 : 21). In this view, 10 : 37 is the culmination of a series of replacements associated with the feasts of Judaism in John. In chapter 5 the Sabbath feast is subordinated to the activity of Jesus in doing the work of life and judgment entrusted to him by the Father. In chapter 6 the manna of the Passover story is replaced by the multiplying of bread as a sign that Jesus was the bread come down from heaven. At Tabernacles, in Chapters 7–8, the water and light ceremonies are replaced by Jesus, the true source of living waters and the light of the world. And, finally, at the Feast of Dedication the old tabernacle and Temple are replaced by the consecrated Christ. And we have suggested that within this sequence belongs another step, indicated in the geographical reference to the departure of Jesus from the Temple, which symbolizes the departure of the Divine Presence from the old "Holy Space."

2. Other Holy Places

a. bethel

Not only is the central place for Jewish worship to be replaced "in Christ," but John shows an interest in other "holy places" which are also replaced, or rather transcended. Two passages reveal this, one in 1 : 51 and the other in 4.

In the very first chapter of the Gospel the question of "holy places" is at least one motif among others that emerge. We are concerned with the dealings of Jesus with Nathanael. The latter was sceptical of the Messiahship of Jesus on geographical grounds. "Can anything good come out of Nazareth?" he asked (1 : 46). Nevertheless, he is called "Israelite indeed in whom is no guile." This should not be watered down simply to mean that "he was 'a Jew' without guile." The last verse in Chapter 1, verse 51, implies clearly that John is thinking of Nathanael in terms of Jacob (Israel) and his vision at Bethel. "And (Jesus) said to him, (Nathanael) 'Truly, truly, I say to you, you will see heaven opened, and the angels of God ascending and descending upon the Son of Man.'" These words are recognized generally to refer to Gen. 28 : 10–17, the story of Jacob at Bethel. But beyond this general agreement there is a wide diversity of interpretations.

It would be arbitrary to fix on any single interpretation of 1 : 51 as the right one: the verse is kaleidoscopic. But at least among its many possible connotations we may legitimately find a contrast drawn between the holy *place* of Jacob's vision which was for him "the house of God and the gate of heaven" and, therefore, in Jewish tradition associated with the Temple and the *eben shetiyyâh*, and the *person* of Nathanael's vision, the Son of Man. The passage in Gen. 28: 10–17 reads as follows:

10 Jacob left Beersheba, and went toward Haran,

11 And he came to a certain place, and stayed there that night, because the sun had set. Taking one of the stones of the place, he put it under his head and lay down in that place to sleep.

12 And he dreamed that there was a ladder set up on the earth, and the top of it reached to heaven; and behold, the angels of God were ascending and descending on it;

13 And behold, the Lord stood above it and said, "I am the Lord, the God of Abraham your father and the God of Isaac; the land on which you lie I will give to you and your descendants;

14 and your descendants shall be like the dust of the earth, and you shall spread abroad to the west and to the east and to the north and to the south; and by you and your descendants shall all the families of the earth bless themselves.

15 Behold, I am with you and will keep you wherever you go, and will bring you back to this land; for I will not leave you until I have done that of which I have spoken to you."

16 Then Jacob awoke from his sleep and said, "Surely the Lord is in this place; and I did not know it."

17 And he was afraid, and said, "How awesome is this place! This is none other than the house of God, and this is the gate of heaven."[13]

[13] John makes the angels ascend and descend upon the Son of Man. In Gen. 28: 12 they do so on the ladder. The Hebrew term for ladder, used in the MT, is סֻלָּם, which is masculine. It follows that in Gen. 28: 12 the Hebrew masculine pronoun is used בֹּו (above it, masc.). But in the LXX the female pronoun is used here at Gen. 28: 12 because ladder (κλῖμαξ) in Greek is feminine. John has substituted "the Son of Man" for "the ladder"—a masculine for a feminine—side-stepping the LXX. Strictly this is no violation of the Hebrew. The pronoun in Gen. 28: 12 in the Hebrew text could refer to Jacob: "the angels went up and down upon him." Later Rabbis did take Gen. 28: 12 (בֹּו) to refer to Jacob in this way (H. Odeberg, *The Fourth Gospel Interpreted in its Relation to Contemporaneous Religious Currents in Palestine and the Hellenistic–Oriental World*, Uppsala, 1929, pp. 33–42). But the sense of Gen. 28: 12 is surely against this. R. E. Brown, in an excellent treatment, rightly resists efforts to disassociate the interpretation of John 1: 51 from Gen. 28 (W. Michaelis, "John 1: 51, Gen. 28: 12 und das Menschensohn-Problem," TL, Vol. 85, 1954, 210–211; C. K. Barrett, *The Gospel*, p. 156 is cautious: he enumerates the various interpretations proposed). We follow I. Fritsch, ". . .videbitis. . .angelos Dei ascendentes et descendentes super Filium hominis, Io. 1, 51," *Verbum Domini*, Vol. 37, 1959, pp. 3–11. J. Jeremias's view that the reference is to the *rock* at Bethel on which Jacob slept (Gen. 28: 18), which became a ceremonial pillar, and which Jesus has now replaced, might appear to be over-subtle, but see an illuminating article by A. Jaubert, "Le Symbolique Des Douze," *Hommages à André Dupont-Sommer*, Paris, 1971, pp. 453ff, who points out how in Jewish tradition the stone at Bethel represented the unity of all the twelve tribes of Israel. (Is there an emphasis on *one* stone in Gen. 28: 11?) Since the place where Jacob had slept was the house of God, it was possible to connect the stone at Bethel with the Temple, and with the *eben shetiyyah*. The transition from John 1: 51 to the cleansing of the Temple in 2: 12ff is not so abrupt as at first it appears. Jaubert gives the pertinent texts. On the difficulty of interpreting 1: 51, see

The point of John 1: 51, in part at least, is that it is no longer the place, Bethel, that is important, but the Person of the Son of Man. It is in his Person that "the house of God and the gate of heaven" are now found. Where the Son of Man is the "heaven will be opened" and the angels will ascend and descend to connect that heaven with earth, that is, in 1: 51 Jesus is not to be set over against Jacob or the ladder of his dream, but over against the sanctuary at Bethel itself, which had been a link between heaven and earth and the place of God's habitation on earth. This interpretation has the advantage over many others proposed of relying simply on the Biblical text at Gen. 28. Furthermore, it comports well with the idea of the humanity of Christ as the dwelling place of God with men and as the new temple with which we have already dealt, and especially with the concept of the Logos becoming flesh in 1: 14.

b. SAMARITAN HOLY PLACES

Chapter 4, where the encounter between Jesus and the woman of Samaria is described, a chapter with which we deal further below, presents us with two holy places in Samaria as well as Jerusalem itself.

The first holy place occurs in 4: 1–15 which concentrates on the water drawn by the woman from the well of Jacob near Sychar, a city of Samaria. Almost all the manuscripts read Sychar in 4: 5, but there are no traces of the name Sychar in Samaria. One Syriac text (Syˢ) reads Shechem, however, and, since Shechem, near which Jacob's well stands, at a distance of only 250 feet, fits the requirements of the scene, it is best to accept the Syriac text. Although the well of Jacob is not mentioned in the Old Testament and does not appear outside the New Testament in Christian sources before the fourth century, there is no reason to doubt the existence of such a well.

But is it justifiable to regard it as "holy space"? There is no reference to this well in the Old Testament. But in the Palestinian Targum on Gen. 28: 10 we read: "Five signs were performed for *our father Jacob* at the time he went forth from Beersheba to go unto Haran...the fifth sign: after *our father Jacob* had lifted the stone from the mouth of the well, the well rose to its surface and overflowed and was overflowing twenty years: all the days that our father dwelt in Haran."[14] We have already

---

W. A. Meeks, JBL, Vol. 91, No. 1, March 1972, "The Man from Heaven in Johannine Sectarianism," pp. 50f. He finds most important "the *pattern* of ascending and descending." He does not deal with our question.

[14] See D. José Ramon Díaz, "Palestinian Targum and New Testament," *Novum Testamentum*, Vol. VI, 1963, pp. 75–80. I follow his translation on pp. 76f.

seen that John is occupied with Gen. 28, and, although we are dealing with a town in Samaria, whereas Haran was outside the land, it may be that we have an echo of this tradition in John 4. Certainly the association of Jacob with the well would automatically lend it a certain sanctity. The connection of patriarchs with wells is well established.[15] Moreover, the general site with which we are concerned is also associated by John with another patriarch, Joseph. Is Jacob's well regarded as being actually situated in the field given by Jacob to his son Joseph (4: 5)? It is at least near to it. And the connection of Joseph with Shechem is clear from the Old Testament. According to Josh. 24: 32 "The bones of Joseph which the people of Israel brought up from Egypt were buried at Shechem [see Exod. 13: 19] in the portion of ground which Jacob bought from the Sons of Hamor the father of Shechem for a hundred pieces of silver; it became an inheritance of the descendants of Joseph." More important, according to Gen. 33: 18–20, in the same portion of ground Jacob had built an altar at Shechem and, according to Gen. 48: 22, he had given a certain mountain slope—the same portion of ground, on the slopes of Mt. Gerizim?—to Joseph. That the awareness of the association of Shechem with Joseph was a living one appears from Jub. 46: 5–6 and Heb. 11: 22. There is, therefore, considerable justification for regarding the well of Jacob as a "sacred place."[16]

The evangelist's interest in the story of Jacob in chapter 1 of the Gospel has already been noted. Especially in 1: 51 the focus is on the replacement of the "holy place" Bethel by the Son of Man. Here in chapter 4, again, it is not so much Jesus over against Jacob as the water provided by Jacob's well and that provided by Jesus that constitute the real centre of interest. This appears not only from the broad sense of the passage as from the subtle variation in the vocabulary. In 4: 6 the well of Jacob is designated by *pêgê tou Iakôb*. Normally in the LXX *pêgê* translates the Hebrew word *'ain*, which denotes a fountain. At 4: 6 the well of Jacob, then, by the very term used to particularize it, is thought of as a fountain of fresh living or flowing water—as we have seen it was in some Jewish circles. Later on, at 4: 11 the woman of Samaria refers to the well of Jacob, no longer as a

---

[15] For details see F. M. Braun, *Jean Le Théologien: Les Grandes Traditions d'Israël: L'Accord des Ecritures l'après Le Quatrième Évangile*, Paris, 1964, pp. 181ff. He refers to Gen. 21: 30; 26: 15, 18–31, 25, 32; Jub. 16: 11, 15, 20; 18: 17; 21: 1; 29: 17–19; 36: 12; 44: 1, 8; 24: 1; CDC 3: 16; 6: 3; 19: 34; and Targum Yerushalmi (Codex Neofiti 1) on Num. 26: 18–19. Braun also connects Wisdom with John 4, p. 183.

[16] See Braun, *Jean Le Théologien*, pp. 184ff. Barrett, *The Gospel*, p. 196, notes that the fact that Jacob himself drank of the well "lends it distinction—even he needed no better water; that his cattle did so indicates the copiousness of the supply."

pêgê, but as a *phrear* which translates the Hebrew *beʾêr*, something like a cistern. On the contrary, in 4: 15 it is the water that Jesus gives that is living and fresh and constitutes a *pêgê*.

Rather, the water that I shall give him, will become within him a fountain of water leaping into eternal life (R. E. Brown's translation).

In short, Jesus is the source of a fountain over against the old cistern of Jacob.[17]

It is customary to find in this antithesis, very naturally in the light of the way in which "wells" and "water" were both used as symbols of the Torah, a contrast intended by John between the Torah of Judaism and Christ. The verses 4: 1–15 simply carry forward a symbolism already used in the story of the wedding at Cana with its reference to six water-pots, and in chapter 3 the story of Nicodemus.[18] The contrast indicated is clear. But it need not exhaust the significance of 4: 1–15. Whether based upon some historical reminiscence of Jesus' activity in Samaria[19] or merely an artificial construction to provide a suitable framework for the Johannine discourse, the setting at Jacob's well, in the field where Joseph's bones were reputed to be buried, is unlikely to have been wholly irrelevant to the evangelist's purpose. Was he not here, as elsewhere, concerned to demote a geographic focus of piety in Samaria in favour of the centrality of the Person of Jesus?

That this question should be answered in the affirmative is suggested by the "geographic" interest which emerges in the verses that follow 4: 1–15, in 4: 16–25. They read:

16 He told her, "Go, call your husband and come back here."

17 "I have no husband," the woman replied. Jesus exclaimed, "Right you are in claiming to have no husband.

18 In fact, you have had five husbands, and the man you have now is not your husband. There you've told the truth!"

19 "Lord," the woman answered, "I can see that you are a prophet.

20 Our ancestors worshipped on this mountain, but you people claim that the place where men ought to worship God is in Jerusalem."

21 Jesus told her:

"Believe me, woman,

---

[17] So Brown, *The Gospel*, p. 170. The NEB does not bring out the above nuances. Barrett, *The Gospels*, p. 193, notes that the absence of the article in πηγὴ τοῦ 'Ιακώβ is Semitic, but also not un-Greek. He does not pursue the distinction between πηγή and φρέαρ, though he mentions it on p. 196, only to state that "the use of synonyms is characteristic of [John's] style."

[18] So Dodd, *The Interpretation*, pp. 311f.

[19] Dodd, *Historical Tradition in the Fourth Gospel*, Cambridge, 1963, p. 237.

an hour is coming
when you will worship the Father
neither on this mountain
nor in Jerusalem.

22 You people worship what you do not understand,
while we understand what we worship;
after all, salvation is from the Jews.

23 Yet an hour is coming and is now here
when the real worshippers
will worship the Father in Spirit and truth.
And indeed, it is just such worshippers
that the Father seeks.

24 God is Spirit,
and those who worship Him
must worship in Spirit and truth."

25 The woman said to him, "I know there is a Messiah coming. Whenever he comes, he will announce all things to us." (This term "Messiah" means "Anointed.")

26 Jesus declared to her, "I who speak to you—I am he."

Here, without entering into a detailed examination of the whole section, we note a reference to the sacred mountains of the Samaritans and of the Jews, Gerizim and Jerusalem. According to the Samaritan Pentateuch, Joshua instructed that a shrine be set up on Gerizim, the sacred mountain of the Samaritans. See Deut. 27: 4, where the MT reads "Ebal," which almost certainly is a correction of Gerizim in order to oppose the Samaritans. (The same polemic against Samaritan worship appears in 2 Chron. 6: 6.)[20] The Samaritans had inserted into the Decalogue itself the obligation to worship on Mount Gerizim. Again it is customary, and rightly so, to find in 4: 19ff the dismissal of the temples[21] situated on the mountains concerned. This is, however, not to be made exclusive: the mountains themselves are to be included in the dismissal. In fact, although the reference to worship in 4: 21 implies the temples on Gerizim and Jerusalem, it is only in 4: 20 that there is explicit reference to temples, that is, in the word "place." But is the text certain in 4: 20? Most manuscripts, it is true, read "place (topos)" in that verse, but it is omitted in the Codex Sinaiticus and in 348. The inclusion of topos is understandable, since, as we have seen, the replacement of the Temple is a familiar theme in John, and it may have led to the insertion of topos: its omission is much more

[20] See Brown, The Gospel, pp. 171f.
[21] Dodd, The Interpretation, p. 314. (The reference to the five husbands in 4: 16–19 does not concern us here.) The NEB renders τόπον unequivocally as "temple" in 4: 19.

difficult to understand.[22] It is legitimate to see the replacement of the two mountains as well as the two temples in 4: 19ff. That replacement is the consequence of the presence of that Person who is the source of a Spirit in whom alone worship in "spirit and in truth" is possible. As R. E. Brown so well expresses it, in recognizing the present and future of the eschatological tension in the Fourth Gospel (contrast 4: 21 and 23), "The idea seems to be that the one is present who, at the hour of glorification, will render possible adoration in Spirit by the gift of the Spirit." The Divine Presence is to be experienced in Jesus, who is "I am he (*egô eimi*, 4: 26)," and his spirit is not geographically conditioned (John 3: 8).[23]

c. BETHZATHA

The next pericope to be referred to is John 5: 1–9 which reads as follows:

After this there was a feast of the Jews, and Jesus went up to Jerusalem.

2 Now there is in Jerusalem by the Sheep Gate a pool, in Hebrew called Bethza'tha, which has five porticoes.

3 In these lay a multitude of invalids, blind, lame, paralyzed.... [See *v.* 4 below.]

5 One man was there, who had been ill for thirty-eight years.

6 When Jesus saw him and knew that he had been lying there a long time, he said to him, "Do you want to be healed?"

---

[22] Barrett, *The Gospel*, p. 197, like R. E. Brown, simply takes "the place" as the temple, referring to John 11: 48. In 11: 48 the reference is so clear that the RSV can render τόπος by "holy place" but although the NEB renders τόπος, in both 11: 48 and 4: 19, by temple, the direct reference to the temple in 4: 19 should not be pressed, and τόπος, as we saw, may not have been in the original text.

[23] *The Gospel*, p. 172. The point of John 3: 8 is that "the Spirit, like the wind, is entirely beyond both the control and the comprehension of man. It breathes into this world from another (Barrett, *The Gospel*, p. 176)." This implies that it cannot be geographically anticipated. I have elsewhere sought to examine how far Judaism connected the land, which found its concentrated centre in Jerusalem and the Temple, with "the Spirit." C. K. Barrett's comments on 4: 23ff are excellent, *The Gospel*, pp. 198ff. But that the worship "in the spirit and in truth" is set over against that centred in Jerusalem and Gerizim is hardly merely incidental, as he notes on p. 200, because the contrast is given such prominence. On 4: 23 Barrett (p. 199) writes: "The 'true' worshippers are those who do in truth worship God, whose worship realizes all that was foreshadowed but not fulfilled in the worship of the Jesus at Jerusalem and of the Samaritans at Mount Gerizim, not because a higher level of worship has been reached in the course of man's religious development, in which the material aids of holy places can be dispensed with, but because Jesus is himself the 'truth,' the faithful fulfilment of God's purposes and thus the anticipation of the future vision of God." But is not the thrust of the passage 4: 19–24, given the geographic *realia* of first-century Judaism and Samaritanism, that "in Christ" geographic dimensions have been transcended and that "holy places," as such, can be dispensed with in the "holy Person." This does not mean that worship can be without material aids, but that these are all subordinated to the Person in a radical way.

7 The sick man answered him, "Sir, I have no man to put me into the pool when the water is troubled, and while I am going another steps down before me."

8 Jesus said to him, "Rise, take up your pallet, and walk."

9 And at once the man was healed, and he took up his pallet and walked. Now that day was the sabbath.

...waiting for the moving of the water;

4 For an angel of the Lord went down at certain seasons into the pool, and troubled the water: whoever stepped in first after the troubling of the water was healed of whatever disease he had. (RSV.)

This incident has sometimes been treated symbolically. The aim of the story has been claimed to be that the Torah, represented by the waters as well as by the five pillars of the pool, which denote the Pentateuch, had failed to provide the healing, which comes through the word of Jesus. The sick man represents Israel under the Law: his sickness lasted thirty-eight years to correspond to the period during which Israel wandered in the wilderness.[24] A variation upon this view is the fantastic one that the five pillars indicate the five-ineffective?-groups in Judaism, namely, the Pharisees, the Sadducees, the Disciples of John the Baptist, the Essenes and the Samaritans.[25] Scholars who have rejected the extremes of symbolical interpretation have nevertheless found in the pericope either a criticism of a powerless Judaism[26] over against a life-giving Gospel or a criticism of all religion and a mirror of what happens when the Revelation in Christ confronts the world.[27] On the other hand, there are those who have found in the pericope a sacramental significance. The sheep-pool stands for the sheep whom Jesus gathers and the pool for baptism.[28] So influential have been the symbolical and sacramental approaches to the pericope that it is difficult to look at it with fresh eyes.

But let us now attempt to do this. In form the story is similar to that of many stories of healing in the Synoptic Gospels. The introduction of the patient, the indication of the duration of his illness, the colloquy between him and Jesus culminating in a commandment leading to actions that establish the cure—all these elements are common in the Synoptic healing stories: some have argued for John's direct dependence on Mark

[24] For bibliographical details see Bultmann, *Johannesevangelium*, pp. 177ff.

[25] *Ibid.*

[26] Dodd, *The Interpretation*, p. 319.

[27] Bultmann, *Johannesevangelium*, pp. 177–179.

[28] See especially O. Cullmann, "Sabbat und Sontag nach dem Johannesevangelium, Joh. 5: 17," *In Memoriam Ernst Lohmeyer*, Stuttgart, 1951.

2: 1–12. So, too, although it does not lead to a simple pronouncement, as do so many of the Synoptic stories, John 5: 1–9 is followed by a discourse which can be regarded as a protracted pronouncement. As for the style of the pericope it reveals a "primitive" character in its so-called "Semitisms," which is also reminiscent of the Synoptic stories. More questionably, the absence of any developed psychological interest in 5: 1–9 has also been found to be characteristic of Synoptic healing stories. The point is that a story whose form is so similar to that of the Synoptic healing stories is unlikely to present any elaborate symbolism and sacramentalism. And as to the essential content of John 5: 1–9 there can be little question: it sets forth the efficacy of the word of Jesus in restoring health to a cripple. Jesus, the Word, speaks, and by his word, which calls for the obedience of the patient, works healing. Again, as far as its content goes, John 5: 1–9 remains within the ambience of the Synoptic stories.[29]

By itself, then, thus baldly analysed, John 5: 1–9 reveals nothing peculiarly Johannine, and a recent commentator has found it difficult to ascribe any purpose to the pericope taken in isolation. He urges that it is only as it leads on to the discourse in 5: 10ff that the story gains significance.[30]

Two possibilities are open to us, that is, to emphasize the connection between 5: 1–9 either with what follows it or with what precedes it. Fortunately the case for each of these alternatives has been set forth severally by two of the greatest interpreters of the Fourth Gospel. First, Bultmann[31] held that 5: 1–9 came from a special source, a collection of "signs": the story in the Gospel is a "sign" of the judgment upon "Religion"—and indeed the world—constituted by the coming of the Word. The present order of the text of the Gospel is a disarrangement. Originally chapter 5 followed chapter 6. The whole of 5: 1–47 is part of a subdivision of the Gospel, as originally arranged (4: 43–45, 46–54; 6: 1–59; 5: 1–47; 7: 15–24; 8: 13–20) which Bultmann entitles "The Revelation as Crisis." This means that he connects both the healing of the nobleman's son at Cana, in 4: 43ff, and of the sick man at the pool of Bethesda, in 5: 1–9, not with chapters 1–4, but with material that follows. This procedure has considerable impact on his understanding of 5: 1–9. He subordinates the story to the materials in 5: 9b; 4: 43ff; 6: 1–59, above: his treatment of 5: 1–9 reveals not only a lack of sympathy with any possible symbolical and sacramental motifs, but also an absence of any

---

[29] See Dodd, *Historical Tradition*, pp. 174–180. Compare Barrett, *The Gospel*, p. 208.
[30] Brown, *The Gospel*, p. 210.
[31] Bultmann, *Johannesevangelium, ad rem.*

attempt to utilize the specific geographical data of the pericope in the interpretation of it.

Now although it is not called such by John, there can be no question that 5: 1–9 is regarded by him as a "sign." But a sign of what? Whether it belonged to a book of "signs" or not, before it was taken over by the Evangelist, it is pertinent to ask whether the original intent of 5: 1–9 as a "sign" can be recovered by greater attention to its geographical actualities on their own terms, and whether this original intent was still operative, even though, in Bultmann's view, the "sign" had been further interpreted by John in terms of the discourse in 5: 9ff. In short, we must ask whether the very geographical setting of 5: 1–9 may have had originally, and still retains in the Fourth Gospel in its present canonical form or as rearranged by Bultmann, a peculiar significance? It is this question that is blurred in Bultmann's subordination of the pericope to the discourse.

Oddly enough, the same question as to the point of reference of John 5: 1–9, as a sign, that is, the question whether the geographical setting as such is significant, remains blurred in the other approach to the text to which we referred. This is represented by Dodd[32] who accepts the order of the text of the Gospel as it stands and connects 5: 1–9 closely both with 4: 43ff, the story of the healing of the nobleman's son, and with materials in chapters 2, 3, 4. True he regards the discourse which follows 5: 1–9 as growing naturally out of the story in that section, but it is in terms of what goes before, in 4: 43ff, that he understands the pericope 5: 1–9 itself.

According to Dodd, two motifs converge in this pericope. First, there is that of the life-giving word which governs both 4: 46ff, the healing of the nobleman's son, and 5: 1–9, the healing of the patient at the pool of Bethesda. Both healings witness to or are signs of the life-giving power of Jesus' words. Secondly, there is the motif of the replacing of water—symbolizing the ineffective ordinances of religion on the level of mere flesh, as opposed to religion in spirit and in truth—as a means of healing by the word: in the wedding at Cana (2: 1–12), the waters of purification of Judaism are replaced by the wine of the Gospel (2: 6ff); in the story of the woman at the well in Samaria the water provided by Jacob's well is contrasted with the water given by the Messiah: Jesus said to her, "Every one who drinks of this water will thirst again, but whoever drinks of the water that I shall give him will never thirst; the water that I shall give

---

[32] Dodd, *The Interpretation*, pp. 318ff.

him will become in him a spring of water welling up to eternal life (4: 13–14)"; and then in 5: 1–9 the "curative" water at the pool of Bethesda is replaced by the life-giving Word. Dodd understands the water in the narrative in 5: 1–9 as representing "the law given through Moses (or any religious system on that level)." He presses the symbolism as follows:

There lies the healing water, but the cripple remains unhealed: so the Torah promised life to men, but the Gospel tradition knew of "publicans and sinners" for whom it did nothing: the sick who needed a physician (Mark ii. 16–17). Of them the cripple of Bethesda may serve as representative. But how, it may be said, could the Torah, beneficent as it was, benefit those who refused to make use of its means of grace? The man might have been healed long ago, perhaps, if he had stepped down into the pool. Precisely; and that is why the first word of Jesus is, "*Have you the will* to become a healthy man?*" The reply is a feeble excuse. The man has not the will. The law might show the way of life; it was powerless to create the will to live. The will to live, together with the power to live, is given in the word of Christ. We have one more exemplification of the maxim, *ho nomos dia Môuseôs hê charis kai hê alêtheia dia Iêsou Christou.*

It is clear that in his earlier work, *The Interpretation of the Fourth Gospel* (1953), Dodd, like Bultmann, attaches little if any significance to the space, as such, where the healing took place in 5: 1ff; he concentrates on the water.[33] But in his later work, *Historical Tradition in the Fourth Gospel* (1963), he pays more attention to the topography of 5: 1ff. He notes there that the scene in which the healing is set is described fully. Even if 5: 3c–4 be regarded as a later insertion and omitted from the text (as by the RSV), the description of the pool of Bethesda is unusually long and elaborate. Such fullness of scenic detail is not altogether absent from the Synoptics (see Mark 2: 1–2; Luke 17: 11–12), but in 5: 1–9 the scenery is much more emphasized. Here "what is unlike the forms of traditional narrative known to us from the Synoptics is the communication of detailed topographical information in a style which is almost that of a guide book: 'There is in Jerusalem, near the Sheep-gate, a pool called in Hebrew Bethesda which has five colonnades.'"[34]

In this later treatment, Dodd does not go beyond pointing out how emphatic is the topography in 5: 1ff. Can we go further? We now point out what seems the clear implication of all this, namely, that the tradition

---

[33] Compare Barrett, *The Gospel*, p. 208: "The indications both of time and space are extremely vague; evidently John was not interested in them." Contrast R. E. Brown, *The Gospel*, p. 209: "The factual details found in the introduction...are very accurate. They betray a knowledge of Jerusalem that militates against a late or non-Palestinian origin of the story."

[34] Dodd, *Historical Tradition*, pp. 179ff.

used by John in 5: 1ff was directed, in part at least, specifically to the question of "holy space": it was designed to indicate that the efficacy of the holy place, Bethzatha, is transcended by the coming of Christ. The "holy space" is fully described. True, in the use made of the story by John the motif of the breaking of the Sabbath is introduced, but this is a secondary development and serves as a transition to the discourse in 5: 19ff, and can be ascribed to the evangelist. And even if in its present total setting in the Gospel, the "water" is given at least as much prominence as the "space," neither the motif of the breaking of the Sabbath nor of the replacement of the water by the life-giving Word should be allowed to obliterate the motif of the criticism of "holy space." This was original to the pericope and remains in force in its present wider context, even though it is necessarily less emphasized, and is, indeed, absent from the discourse.

But is there any evidence that the pool at Bethzatha was ascribed special significance in the first century before and during the time when John wrote? And an even more negative question may be asked. Is there not much in the text of John 5: 1–9 to suggest that we do not there encounter geographical and historical fact, but merely an imaginative geographical construction?

First, there is dispute over the precise translation of 5: 2. Is the reference to a Sheep-pool or a Sheep-gate? The NEB for example, renders 5: 2 as follows:

Now at the Sheep-Pool in Jerusalem there is a place with 5 colonnades. Its name in the language of the Jews is Bethesda. (In agreement is R. E. Brown, *The Gospel*, p. 206.)

The RSV on the other hand translates:

Now there is in Jerusalem by the Sheep Gate a pool, in Hebrew called Bethza'tha, which has five porticoes.

According to the former translation Bethesda is a place, that is, a building with five colonnades; according to the latter it is a pool called Bethzatha.

Secondly,[35] there is difficulty over the precise preposition to be read in 5: 2. Should we accept *epi* or *en* and translate accordingly either *at* or *in*

---

[35] The text at 5: 2 is attested as follows:
   ἐπι P⁶⁶, BCKpm (followed by Nestle)
   ἐν D G L θ a r.
On purely textual grounds ἐπί is the preferred reading. See on the text Barrett, *The Gospel*, p. 210, although he does not deal with ἐν and ἐπί.

(*at*)? It will be recognized that a building *in* a pool, which one text at least might demand, would not be easy to conceive.

Thirdly, even the name Bethesda is in question. The texts present as many as five possibilities for it—Bethesda, Bethscuda, Bethzatha, Belzetha, Bethezda. Can such a confused textual tradition about the very name of the phenomenon referred to in 5: 2 engender anything other than a profound suspicion of its geographical validity and significance? Moreover, that the nature of the healing water—an intermittent stream— invites comparison with the pool of Siloam, the only spring in Jerusalem and that an intermittent one, so that some have been led to identify the scene in 5: 2 with the pool of Siloam, only serves further to erode confidence both in John's geographical knowledge and in the significance he ascribes to geography. And, finally, though less forcedly, the varieties of traditions as to the exact location of the scene described in 5: 1ff in the history of the Church still further add to the suspicion referred to: the local tradition at Jerusalem is witnessed to by Eusebius in his *Onomasticon* written before A.D. 324, by the Pilgrim of Bordeaux writing in A.D. 333, and Cyril, Bishop of Jerusalem (A.D. 348–386). The factors indicated would seem to militate against pinning 5: 1ff to any certain geographical scenery and, therefore, against ascribing to "space" any significant role in its interpretation.

But at this juncture archaeology has come in to readjust the negative balance of the textual tradition, and, as we shall see, of the historical confusion as to the location of the site. The question as to the nature and location of the scene in 5: 1ff was recently thought to have been solved by archaeological discoveries near the Temple.[36] These were summarized and evaluated by Jeremias in an essay first published in German in 1949. Later in 1966 the same essay in an enlarged form was translated into English. It takes into account archaeological research of prime importance done since 1949, and literary evidence from the Qumran Copper Scroll. On archaeological ground, Jeremias takes Bethesda to be a building, of that name, situated partly *in* the Sheep Pool discovered near the Temple. The initial discovery of the pool was made at the restoration of St. Anne's Church in Jerusalem in 1856, and since 1888 it came to be recognized increasingly as the pool mentioned in John 5: 2. Subsequent excavation revealed that the pool was dual and trapezoidal in shape. The two parts of the pool were separated by a wall running west to east. The discovery of this band of rock was important. While no single complete column was

---

[36] See Barrett, *The Gospel, ibid.*; J. Jeremias, *Die Wiederentdeckung von Bethesda*, Göttingen, 1949, enlarged 1966, pp. 5–8.

found, there were many fragments of columns unearthed. The conclusion drawn by Jeremias was that there "were five magnificent galleries four of which surrounded the twin pool while the fifth cut across the pools": and it was in this middle portico that the lame man had lain and was healed. "Bethesda"—the building with five porticos—was "in the pool" in this sense. How is Jeremias so certain that Bethesda was the name of the building? This is on the evidence supplied by the Copper Scroll where the name Bethesda in a dual form, has appeared.[37] And, finally, a graffito —discovered by Jeremias himself—in Hebrew characters, inscribed on the wall on the southern side of the southern pool, is in a script which, in the judgment of F. M. Cross, belongs to the first century A.D. and is late Herodian.[38] For Jeremias there is no question that the scene described in John 5: 1ff can be precisely located, in porticos built by Herod the Great in connection with the enlargement of the Temple begun in 20–19 B.C. Fine specimens of Herodian buildings, these porticoes were designed not for practicality but for show: they constituted a landmark in Jerusalem. It seems impossible to establish how early the place came to be associated with healing. Its name suggests a more humble origin than the porticoes themselves would indicate. But, since its early history was associated with the Temple, this in itself would tend to lend to its waters healing power. Jeremias suggests that at some point sacrificial animals were herded near the area: hence its name. But the two pools themselves, he thinks, were designed to provide opportunities for visitors to the Temple to take the prescribed ritual baths, one being necessary to serve the needs of men and the other those of women.

If Jeremias—and most seem to accept this interpretation[39]—be correct, it is highly probable, surely, that, in its original intent in the tradition, there is here a replacement of a Jewish holy space, with its holy water, by the living Word. The episode belongs, since the holy place is so near to the Temple, to the Johannine theme of the replacement of the Temple, which we have already touched upon, by the Word. Other sacramental and symbolical connotations came to be read into it possibly by the Evangelist,[40] but part of its original concern was to indicate how the

---

[37] See J. T. Milik, *Discoveries in the Judaean Desert*, Vol. III, 1962, p. 271. According to Milik, in the area of the Temple, on the eastern hill of Jerusalem, treasure was buried (according to the tradition) "*en Bet 'Esdatayin*, in the pool at the entrance to its smaller basin." The area or pool was, therefore, called Bethesda: this was the singular form of the dual form found, because there were two basins, in the text. (*Beth Esda* means "the house of the flowing".)

[38] Jeremias, *Die Wiederentdeckung*, p. 31.   [39] So, C. K. Barrett, R. E. Brown.

[40] See the cautious remarks of R. E. Brown, *The Gospel*, p. 211. He is suspicious of symbolic and baptismal interpretations. But, if what we have suggested above be correct,

Living Word transcends "holy space." This fits in with the healing of the nobleman's son in 4: 43ff, where also the Word transcends distance, and healing is effected from afar.

The position taken by Jeremias, that is, the identification of the two basins near St. Anne's with the Sheep's Pool of John 5: 1ff has, however, been challenged recently by Antoine Duprez, who has engaged in archaeological research near the area of the two basins. He wrote a thesis at the Biblical Institute in Rome on the theme: "La guérison du paralytique en Jean 5: 1 et s., et les dieux guérrisseurs du Proche-Orient d'après les textes et l'archéologie." The thesis is now published in full; but it appeared also in a summary popular article in *Bible et Terre Sainte*, No. 86, January, 1966, pp. 5–15.[41]

Let us begin by noting difficulties in Jeremias's position, in part suggested by Duprez himself. First, there is little indication in Jeremias's description of the two basins, which were very deep, that there were adequate stairways to facilitate descent into them. But if there were no stairways how could the sick reach the waters? There may be an indication in 5: 7, if *balê* be given its full weight, that in fact the sick were thrown into the water (R. E. Brown translates: "I haven't anybody to plunge me into the pool") so that steps were not necessary, or at least not used. If such were the case drowning must have been a real possibility for the sick. But this difficulty cannot be pressed because at one point Jeremias does mention steps,[42] if vaguely, and commentators usually claim that *balê* should not here be given its full classical strength but rather be taken as meaning "put" rather than "plunge" or "throw." The NEB, like the RSV, renders it by "put."

Secondly, a more serious difficulty for Jeremias is the exceeding unlikelihood that water used for ritual baths by those frequenting the Temple was also used for healing the sick. This would have been tantamount to using contaminated, unclean water for ritual purposes.

Then, thirdly, the inevitable question is what purpose, apart from satisfying the building propensities of Herod, such an elaborate structure as Jeremias envisages could have served? The reconstruction conjectured by him in his diagram suggests about 125 pillars: Duprez estimates 136

---

his comment that "the theme of water is incidental to the story: it has nothing to do with the healing..." is to be challenged. Part of the very significance of the story is that water at a holy place does not and cannot have efficacy; to this Brown's comment unconsciously witnesses.

[41] See A. Duprez, *Jésus et les Dieux Guérisseurs à propos de Jean V*, Cahiers de la Revue Biblique, Vol. 12, Paris, 1970.

[42] *Op. cit. Die Wiederentdeckung.*

as necessary for his porticoes. Nor must it be forgotten that the basins were trapezoidal in form so that the erection of such a symmetrical structure as Jeremias envisages would have been exceedingly difficult.

But, apart from these possible difficulties in Jeremias's position, what of the positive case presented by Duprez? He points out that the two basins were discovered in the area north of the temple called Bezetha, which he takes to be the correct reading at 5: 2. The two basins, in which certain steps (*marches*) are clearly visible but no stairway (*escalier*), were used to supply the Temple, which needed a great deal of water. The basins are pre-Herodian: Duprez thinks that they are probably referred to in Ecclesiasticus 50: 3, so that they existed before the days of Simon, the High Priest, the Son of Onias (220–195 B.C.).[43] Were these basins the Sheep-pool of 5: 2 as Jeremias holds? We have already briefly indicated the reasons why Duprez rejects this view.

He asks the question why other neighbouring locations in Bezetha have not been explored; and instead of staying with the basins, Duprez turns to their surroundings. To the east of the two basins, in Bezetha, there is an area of great intricacy pierced by several natural grottos, pools, stairways, rooms, baths. Duprez has shared in the excavation of this area and as a result propounds the view that in it there was a cult of healing. The rooms and baths go back to a period before Aelia Capitolina (A.D. 135). Tubs and pools were discovered which may have served for libations and ritual baths respectively and there are suggestions of arrangements for sacrificial animals. In Bezetha, there seem to have been a series of baths around a central grotto. These cannot have been private baths because they present mosaics and frescoes unsuitable for such. The frequency of the baths is reminiscent of those at Qumran, except that the latter were used, apparently, solely for purificatory purposes while those at Bezetha were for the healing of the sick.

And now we come to the strikingly fresh suggestion of Duprez. He connects the healing cult with those associated with the healing gods in the ancient Orient and Greece. Often the centres of such cults were veritable "hospitals." It is to such a centre that Jesus comes in John 5: 1ff: the third verse refers to "a multitude of invalids, blind, lame paralyzed." And note, above all, that the centre is probably in the name of Serapis.

[43] In the book mentioned in note 41, Duprez suggests that they were constructed by Simon, the Son of Onias (220–195 B.C.). There are three stages in Duprez's argument which can only be mentioned here: first, the archaeological, in which the existence of a sacred place of healing is established before and after A.D. 70; second, the historical, in which the ubiquity of cults of healing, especially under Serapis in the pre-Christian and post-Christian period in the Near East is indicated; third, the exegetical.

Consider the audacity of Jesus. He came to a pagan cultic centre at Bezetha. This act is of a piece with his eating with sinners, talking with a Samaritan woman, calling a publican. He appears in John 5: 1 over against a pagan healing god. He is the sole healer: he gives life. Notice that this connects better with the discourse in John 5: 19ff than the polemic concerning the Sabbath in 5: 10ff, which John has introduced as a kind of transition.

One aspect of Duprez's approach is attractive. If the archaeological evidence and the interpretation of it which he offers be accepted, we might detect a progression in the kinds of "holy places" that are replaced in the Fourth Gospel by The Word. In chapter 2 the Jewish Temple at Jerusalem, in chapter 4 Jacob's well at Samaria, and in chapter 5 a pagan cultic healing centre at Bezetha. It is true that in the discourse in 5: 10ff it is pre-supposed that the man healed is a Jew and that it is Jews who are addressed in 5: 19ff. But there is nothing in 5: 1-9 itself to suggest that the healed man was a Jew. In the story as it came to the Evangelist in the tradition, he may well have been a Gentile. But this is a matter of indifference because in the centre at Bezetha, as Duprez envisages it, there would be Jews—'*âm hâ-âretz*—and Gentiles who were being healed.

This brings us to the difficulties in Duprez's case which he himself recognizes and seeks to answer. They are two.

First, Duprez offers no explanation of the five porticoes (*pente stoas*), which are so neatly explained by Jeremias.[44] But he points out that Eusebius[45] refers to their rapid destruction. They were, therefore, probably not as impressive as Jeremias envisaged them to be, but of modest dimensions to comport with customary structures around Jewish baths: they are not likely to have left any traces.

Secondly, is it likely that Jews would have tolerated a pagan sanctuary so near to the Temple? To meet this question, Duprez points out that the healing centre was outside the city and near the Roman barrack at Antonia. Roman soldiers had always venerated healing gods. Moreover, while official Judaism distrusted pagan cults, because they spread pagan customs and beliefs, it recognized that they could not easily be eradicated. Cults of healing were too deep rooted and widespread and popular to be radically rejected. So Jewish authorities tolerated many ill-defined

[44] Duprez points out that there is no archaeological evidence for their existence, *Jésus et les Dieux Guérisseurs*, p. 38.
[45] Eusebius of Caesarea (*c.* A.D. 330), *Onomasticon*, 240. So too St. Jerome in his translation at 5: on this text all other witnesses to the five porticoes depended. But no one had seen them. For further details, Jeremias, *Die Wiederentdeckung, ad rem.*

customs, giving them a pale cast of orthodoxy. John 5: 1ff supplies an excellent example of this. The act of healing in the pools was ascribed to an "Angel of the Lord." Duprez, against most scholars, argues that 5: 4 was in the original text and was later omitted by scribes who were uneasy about its "orthodoxy." Moreover it cannot be sufficiently emphasized that in the first century Jerusalem was a very mixed city. Jewish leaders were themselves divided: only after A.D. 70 did Pharisaism become dominant. And the leaders of Judaism were themselves more permeated by Greek culture than is usually recognized. And, again, the majority of the inhabitants of Jerusalem were like the crowd mentioned in John 7: 49 "who did not know the Law," the niceties of which they could not understand and the commandments of which they found heavy to be borne. Nor should the foreign soldiers and other Gentiles in the city be forgotten. At festival times, especially, the city was likely to be filled with "all sorts and conditions of men." In the light of all these factors a pagan healing site in Jerusalem is not inconceivable.[46]

It is impossible to examine further the evidence presented by Jeremias and Duprez. For our purposes the main point is this: the healing at Bethesda by Christ implies a critique of a "holy space," be it pagan or Jewish; and although the Evangelist has subordinated this motif it still shines through his text. God's creative activity in Christ is not tied to "place" or "time" (the precise feast is not important in 5: 1—the feast referred to there is unnamed and bears no article). In 2: 13ff and 4: 19ff, and perhaps in 8: 59, is made explicit what is also, at least, implicit in 5.

d. THE POOL OF SILOAM

At this point it is appropriate to turn to the healing of the blind man in 9: 1ff, a section reminiscent of 5: 1ff in many ways, but where, at first sight, Jesus recognizes a "holy place"—the pool of Siloam—favourably and even uses it in healing. The blind man, after treatment by Jesus, is sent to the pool of Siloam to wash himself and is thereby cured. The term used in John 9: 7 for the pool is "Siloam." The term is repeated in 9: 11 and is interpreted (the name means "sent" NEB) (9: 7). The form *Siloam*, as such, does not occur in the Hebrew text of the Old Testament, but it is the form used in the LXX to translate *Shiloah* in Is. 8: 6. The interpretation of Siloam given by the Evangelist in 9: 7 clearly indicates that he

---

[46] Duprez, *Jésus et les Dieux Guérisseurs*, pp. 57–127, gives a rich and convincing statement of the extent to which Hellenistic religious practices like this had invaded Judaism in our area. He adds one more nail in the coffin of Montefiore's theory of the rigid separation of Hellenistic and Palestinian Judaism.

understands the Pool of Siloam as the Pool of Siloah. In Is. 8: 6 the waters of Siloah refer to waters whose flow can be watched, that is, they refer either to waters conveyed in a conduit or to waters running naturally. In any case, they were waters flowing from the one spring to be found in the neighbourhood of Jerusalem, the Gihon spring, which rises in a cave on the eastern declivity of the eastern hill of Jerusalem, that is, the ancient Mount Zion.[47] Moriarty[48] thinks that these waters of Siloah led to the lower pool within the city. Later Hezekiah built a tunnel, over 1700 feet long, to bring water from Gihon to his newly built reservoir, known as "the Pool of Shiloah (Siloam)."

Such detailed distinctions as to the precise location of the pool of Siloam do not concern John. But the significance of its waters—whatever its exact location—in the Old Testament and in Jewish tradition may have been significant for him. Certain factors may be noted. First, in Is. 8: 6 the prophet contrasts "the gently flowing waters of Siloah with the mighty torrent of Assyria. The former symbolized divine aid, the latter the naked power of Assyrian arms."[49] The waters of Siloah were insignificant in outward appearance, as is the power of Yahweh. And they were rejected by Israel. Secondly, their source, in the spring of Gihon, meant that these waters were associated with Zion, the site of Yahweh's temple and the royal palace; they were the "living" waters of Jerusalem as contrasted with waters stored in cisterns. And thirdly, it must be emphasized that the waters of Gihon, from which the waters of Siloah came, had played a part in the coronation of Kings. David caused Solomon to be anointed King of Gihon (1 Kings 1: 33f). The waters of Siloah "may, therefore, have been associated with the theology of the Davidic dynasty." The Targum on 1 Kings 1: 33, 38, 45, identifies Siloah with Gihon. Fourthly, in the *Lives of the Prophets*, a collection of extra-Biblical Jewish traditions concerning the history and activities of these famous men, which is dated by C. C. Torrey[50] before A.D. 80, there is a play on the word Siloam strongly reminiscent of that in John 9: 7, so that the Evangelist *may* here be drawing upon an established interpretative convention.[51] And, fifthly, the waters of Siloah are used in the rites of the Feast of Tabernacles and are, therefore, highly pertinent to the setting of

[47] G. B. Gray, *Isaiah I–XXXIX*, ICC, pp. 144ff.
[48] JCB, p. 271.
[49] Gray, *Isaiah I–XXXIX*, p. 273, and, for what follows this note, pp. 146, 713.
[50] C. C. Torrey, *The Lives of the Prophets*, JBL Monograph Series, Vol. 1, Philadelphia, 1946.
[51] F. W. Young, "A Study of the Relation of Isaiah to the Fourth Gospel," ZNW, Vol. 46, 1955, pp. 215–233.

9: 1ff, if that setting is still the same as that of chapters 7 and 8, that is, the Feast of Tabernacles. But the waters of Siloah have cultic significance outside the Feast of Tabernacles also in the ritual of the Red Heifer. (See Mishnah Sukkah, 4: 9, 10; M. Parah 3: 2.)

Clearly the waters of Siloah were famous and significant as being associated with divine, messianic, and cultic power. If the *Lives of the Prophets* belongs to the period indicated above, those waters were associated especially in the Old Testament and popular Judaism with the prophet Isaiah who had prayed that he be given them as he was dying. "For the prophet's sake," we read in the *Lives of the Prophets*, "God wrought the sign (miracle) of Siloah; for before his death, in fainting conditions he prayed for water, and it was sent to him from this source. Hence it was called Siloah, which means 'sent.'" John was certainly aware of the ascription of such healing powers to the waters of Siloah, whether he knew of the specific tradition concerning Isaiah and the waters of Siloah or not. There are indications that the Evangelist has the Prophet Isaiah in mind in 9: 39. But whether any such reference to the prophet Isaiah be implicitly present in 9: 1f or not, the main point of the story is that the waters of Siloah are only truly enlightening if they can be equated with "the One sent." We encounter here again, admittedly less clearly, the notion that the place of healing water—associated with the Temple and its ritual—has been replaced by Christ himself. That Jesus was sent of God is a common theme in John (3: 17, 34; 5: 36, 38). The notion of his replacement of the waters of Siloah by himself is reinforced, if, as is possible, the context of 9: 1ff is the Feast of Tabernacles, because in 7: 37–38 it has already been made clear that Jesus is now the source of life-giving water, the unexpected fulfilment of the prayers uttered in the Feast of Tabernacles for rain. R. E. Brown puts the matter as follows: "we may well suspect that the Evangelist is playing on the idea that the man was born in sin (9: 2, 34)—sin that can be removed only by washing in the waters of the spring or pool that flows from Jesus himself."[52]

The replacement to which we have referred here must be carefully delimited. In chapter 5 we saw that the healing of the paralytic at the pool of Bethesda was by the word of Jesus: in chapter 9, although Siloam is equated with Jesus, nevertheless the cure is still by water. There is an efficacy retained for water, but for the water not of Siloah as such, but of Jesus. And many have understood this to mean that the reference is to baptism. The waters of Siloah are replaced by the waters of the One sent.

[52] Brown, *The Gospel*, p. 381.

The reasons for finding a baptismal motif in 9: 1ff are impressive. Chapter 9 appears seven times in early catacomb art, most frequently as an illustration of Christian Baptism; it served as reading material in the preparation of catechumens for baptism. But, as we have seen, it is not only the use of John 9: 1ff in this way in the later Church that suggests its baptismal symbolism but the details of the narrative itself: it is the "pool" of the One who has been sent which gives sight.[53]

The preceding pages make it possible to claim that in the Fourth Gospel the Person of Jesus Christ replaces "holy places." This motif of replacement, however, to a degree which our treatment may seriously ignore, has been taken up by the Evangelist and placed in larger contexts which hide its significance. Does this mean that, although aware of its presence in the materials which he used, the Evangelist himself was not particularly concerned with the motif referred to? Fortunately we are now in a position to examine, very briefly here, precisely this question: that is, to what extent the motif was present to John himself. This is so because we can look at the way in which he used his sources.

It has long been held that John drew upon what has been called a Signs Source, and recently an important work has been devoted to this. Fortna has urged that this source was a complete Gospel (SG), which he has been able to reconstruct. He has further suggested that John "while radically reinterpreting (SG)—out of all recognition, perhaps, in the eyes of its author—nowhere contradicts it."[54] He further suggests that the signs become in John "expressions of the incarnation." Assuming the results of Fortna's work, we now suggest that John has so used SG as to express his understanding of holy spaces. We can do this only summarily.[55]

To begin with, the verse 1: 51 had long been noted as an addendum to the preceding section dealing with Nathanael. The change from the singular pronoun and verb (*opsê*), (*autô*), to the plural pronoun (*humin*) and verb *opsesthe* between 1: 50 and 1: 51 indicated that 1: 51 was once a detached saying.[56] There are other reasons for coming to this conclusion.[57] 1: 51 was added by John to define his understanding of the words

[53] See Brown, *The Gospel*, ibid., for details.

[54] R. T. Fortna, *The Gospel of Signs*, Cambridge, 1970.

[55] See the salutary work of D. M. Smith, *The Composition and Order of the Fourth Gospel*, Yale University Press, 1965, and his review of Fortna, JBL, Vol. 89, Pt. iv, Dec. 1970, pp. 498–501; also that of C. K. Barrett, JTS, Vol. XXII, NS, Oct. 1971, pp. 571–574. More positively, J. M. Robinson, *American Academy of Religion Journal*, Review of D. M. Smith, Sept. 1971, pp. 339–348.

[56] In these passages SG refers to the "document" as presented by Fortna, *The Gospel of Signs*, pp. 235–295.   [57] For details see Brown, *The Gospel*, pp. 88–89.

"greater than these you [sing.] shall see" addressed by Jesus to Nathanael in 1: 50 in SG. 1: 51 was not in SG, according to Fortna. So the faith of Nathanael in the display of the supernatural knowledge of Jesus is not corrected by the addition of 1: 51. Instead, it becomes the occasion for John to point out through 1: 51 the significance of Jesus as the one who, through his signs and works, becomes "Bethel" for men.

As for the cleansing of the Temple, in SG[58] this (along with the death plot of 11: 47–53) stood immediately before the anointing at Bethany, that is, close to the Passion, as it does in the Synoptics. Its present radically changed position in chapter 2 is due to John. Originally the saying in 2: 19 in SG, that is, "Destroy this temple (*lusate tou naon touton*)," carried no explicit reference to the Temple at Jerusalem; it was left enigmatic. But John, although he retains *naos* and does not use *hieron* makes this reference clear by adding verses 20–22. These words placed on the lips of "the Jews" make explicit the contrast which may have been implied in SG. In this light the spatial dimension of John's thinking on the cleansing of the Temple becomes still clearer. If we follow Fortna, 2: 13, which makes explicit reference to Jerusalem, is also the editorial work of John. John again here makes unmistakably clear what is present, but not emphasized in SG, the spatial realities with which he was concerned. It is specifically the Jerusalem Temple which is to give way to another "Temple."

Next, in SG[59] the story of Jesus and the Samaritan woman, sandwiched, in Fortna's reconstruction, into the sign of the raising of Lazarus, in a position comparatively much later than it finds in the canonical Gospel, contained no dialogue concerning Gerizim and Jerusalem. The whole of 4: 10–16, 20–24 is added by John to SG. Thereby he uses SG to set forth his understanding of the replacement of holy space: the spirit is what matters, not the place, and that spirit, John has already explained in 3: 8, "blows where it wills."

The use of SG is equally clear in 9: 1ff.[60] In SG there is a simple, straightforward story of a man blind from birth being healed, through Jesus' act and advice. The purpose of the story is uncomplicated: it is to bear witness to the Messianic status of Jesus, who, by his power alone, works miracles. John follows SG, but in addition to dealing with the works of God in 9: 4–5 (not found in SG), explains the meaning of the word Siloam to indicate that it is not the physical waters of the pool of

---

[58] Fortna, *The Gospel of Signs*, p. 241.
[59] *Ibid.*, p. 239.   [60] *Ibid.*, p. 240.

Siloam that really heal, but those of him sent. The displacement of a holy space is here again suggested.

Of the sections where we found the motif of displacement above, only in the healing of the man ill for thirty-eight years at the pool of Bethzatha in 5: 2ff[61] is there no change made by John in SG. But here there was no need to introduce any change in order to indicate that Christ, rather than a holy place, is the mediator of divine healing. The story itself makes this clear. A man thirty years ill at a holy place, suddenly (*eutheôs*) became healthy (5: 9). Note the frequency with which the reference to health and healing occurs, in 5: 9, 10, 11, 13, 14, 15.

Where necessary and appropriate, therefore, into the signs of SG, John, among other things, introduces material to indicate that it is Jesus, not any holy space, that now mediates the Divine. His interest in making this clear is one concern that governed his use of SG. This motif was not absent in SG, as in 5: 2ff, but it was not emphasized. It merely emerged as SG presented his christological signs, which had as their simple aim that of bearing witness to Jesus as Messiah. John used these signs for more varied purposes, of which one direct use was that which we have indicated.

In this way, a consideration of John's use of SG confirms our previous treatment. In the Fourth Gospel the person of Jesus becomes "the place" which replaces all holy places. In the light of this, it is, therefore, not a gospel likely to ascribe theological significance to geographic entities. To do so it would seem, would be to contradict much of its concern. Yet the Fourth Gospel has appeared to many to do just this, that is, to use space in the interests of Theology. This in two ways, one minor and the other major, both of which we shall now examine.

3. THE GEOGRAPHY OF JOHN THE BAPTIST

First, does the area where John the Baptist practised his ministry have a theological significance for the Fourth Gospel? In 1: 28, although this could easily be deduced from the context, it is specifically, if redundantly, noted that the Baptist's ministry "took place in Bethany beyond the Jordan, where John was baptizing." Again in 3: 22ff the place of the Baptist's activity is carefully defined: "John also was baptizing at Aenon near Salim, because there was much water there, and people came and were baptized." The various spheres of the Baptist's ministry are noteworthy. The reason is clear. Although the Baptist was destined to decrease and Jesus to increase (3: 30), yet he is designated as "a lamp, burning

[61] Fortna, *Ibid.*, p. 240.

brightly (5: 35)," as a witness to Christ (1: 6f, 26; 5: 33). That the sphere, "Bethany beyond Jordan," where John had first baptized, was carefully noted appears from 10: 40ff, where we read: "He went away again across the Jordan to the place where John at first baptized, and there he remained. And many came to him; and they said, 'John did no sign, but everything that John said about this man was true.' And many believed in him there."

How is this reference to the place where John first witnessed to Christ to be understood? The context might suggest the following. As we have seen, in 10: 22–39 there is a kind of climax: Jesus has claimed to be the Son of God, just as in a section which 10: 22–39 strongly recalls, that is, 7–8, he had designated himself "I am." The enmity of the Jews had become intense (8: 59; 10: 39). The break with Judaism was clear. But was there any continuity to which Jesus could appeal? There was—in the ministry of John the Baptist. And at this point of great disjuncture between Jesus and Judaism, John turns to the Baptist and the place where his witness had been given. In the passage cited from 10: 40–42, it is implied that Jesus exercised a ministry in this region, but no description of it is given. The interest in the pericope does not lie in what Jesus did, but in the place where he did it—which was the place where witness to him had been given as the Lamb of God. In this view, 10: 40–42 looks back to 1: 28. The ministry of Jesus is attached geographically in this way to that of the Baptist, not solely because historically such may have been the case (a sojourn of Jesus in Perea before the Passion is recorded in the Synoptics, Mark 10: 1; Matt. 19: 1; Luke 15: 15), but because there is an anxiety to preserve the relationship between the Baptist and Jesus theologically. Topography subserves Theology.

Such an approach as we have indicated is largely followed by Hoskyns and Davey,[62] and R. E. Brown[63] in his recent commentary urges a somewhat similar position. The latter takes 10: 40–42 to be a closure for the whole public ministry of Jesus; and this geographic closure subserves two theological interests. First, because chapters 11 and 12 present indications that they are editorial additions, Brown suggests that in the original outline of the Gospel, *which John had prepared*, 10: 42 was followed by 13: 1. The pericope 10: 40–42 looks back to 1: 11 (He came to his own and his own received him not) which Brown interprets as referring to "the heritage of Israel, the Promised Land and Jerusalem." At 10: 40–42 the ministry of Jesus among his own, that is, in his own land, came to an

[62] *The Fourth Gospel*, Vol. 2, London, 1940, p. 458.
[63] Brown, *The Gospel*, pp. 414f.

end.[64] When, in 13: 1, Jesus is in Jerusalem, he has crossed the Jordan a second time and is going to his "own land" in another sense, that is, to be "with the Father." The departure from Judaea in 10: 40–42, in this view, signifies the fulfilment of 1: 11; it is a judgment on "his own land" which has rejected Christ. Geography subserves Theology. This is not essentially modified when John later inserts chapters 11 and 12 between 10: 42 and 13: 1 in order to provide a more dramatic conclusion to the public ministry in the raising of Lazarus.

But this last suggestion made by Brown betrays the uncertainty of what we have so far written about 10: 40–42. Westcott[65] long ago urged that 1: 28, and *ipso facto* 1: 11, were too remote from 10: 40–42 to be referred to by the latter, and Brown[66] himself implies that, as a closure to the public ministry, 10: 40–42 was, for John himself, too nondescript: it had to be reinforced by the raising of Lazarus. True, there are details in 10: 40–42 which evoke a symbolic intent. The use of *menô*, an ambiguous word which *may* suggest "spiritual abiding," is one such. And again Jesus had come to "his own land," but had to escape from it. But on the other side of Jordan, he found a faith which his own land had denied him: the repeated and, therefore, emphatic *ekei* (there) in 10: 40 and 10: 42 may be indicative of this. Moreover, a symbolic interpretation of John 10: 40–42 goes back at least to Cyril of Alexandria.[67] But Brown's uneasiness with 10: 40–42 is a clear warning against reading too much into these verses. Bultmann takes 10: 40–42 to be not a closure, as does Brown, but an introduction to a new section, 10: 40–12: 33 (along with the misplaced 8: 30–40; 6: 60–71). With 11: 54, they constitute a framework for the story of the raising of Lazarus, which Bultmann understands as a theophany.[68] In this view no geographical-theological significance is to be given to 10: 40–42. Similarly C. H. Dodd,[69] who recognizes the historical meaning of 10: 40, does not find any specifically geographic symbolism in 10: 40–42; for him the passage is a simple back reference to

[64] *Ibid.*, p. 10. Here Brown understands 1: 11 of "the heritage of Israel, the Promised Land, Jerusalem." On p. 414 he simply refers to "his land" as the equivalent of "his own."
[65] *The Gospel According to St. John*, London, 1908, p. 167.
[66] *The Gospel*, pp. 414, 427.
[67] For details, see Brown, *ibid.*
[68] Bultmann, *Johannesevangelium*, pp. 299f.
[69] *Historical Tradition*, pp. 277ff, 241ff. Dodd finds no "geographic-theology" here. John is writing on "information received (p. 244)." R. H. Lightfoot, *St. John's Gospel*, 1956, pp. 217ff, takes 10: 40–42 to introduce 10: 40–11: 53, dealing with "The Lord as the Resurrection and the Life." The mission of Jesus to the leaders of his nation is now over. The point of 10: 40–42 is to underscore, despite the rejection of Jesus by Judaism, the truth of John's words of witness. Here, however, Lightfoot makes no use of the "geographical-theological motif"; although 10: 40–42 recalls 1: 28, it more recalls 1: 31.

1: 28 to be accepted at face value. It is, in his judgment, derived from a source of information about John the Baptist, traceable in 1: 28; 3: 23, and here in 10: 40–42, which refers to activity by Jesus in Transjordan in a district where the Baptist had been active and his testimony to Jesus effective as a preparation for the Gospel, leading men to believe in Christ. The section is a suitable transition between 10: 22–39 and the story of Lazarus. Writing of 10: 40–42 and other topographical data, Dodd[70] claims that they "are such as cannot reasonably be accounted for except as fragments of historical information which the evangelist has incorporated. The attempt to treat them as symbolical cryptograms breaks down, and there is no ground for supposing that they subserved any special interest either of the evangelist or of his readers."

If we correctly assess the data provided by 10: 40–42, the function of which as a closure for the central ministry of Jesus or as an introduction or transition to the story of Lazarus in chapter 11 must remain open, the most that can be claimed with certainty is that the place where John the Baptist preached is not in itself given any profound symbolical meaning, and its significance is wholly derivative. At the most, it merely serves the concern to connect Jesus with the witness of the Baptist: 10: 40–42 is not essentially concerned with any geographical symbolism, but with historical continuity, and even this concern is not made explicit but has to be deduced. Here Barrett is probably more to be followed than Hoskyns. The latter places the emphasis on the topography of 10: 40–42: the former merely states that here John "means in effect that Jesus fulfilled the Old Testament in the person and predictions of its last and greatest representative (*The Gospel*, p. 321)." This forceful statement, ignoring topography, probably brings us to the heart of the matter in 10: 40–42.

4. GALILEE AND JUDAEA

We now turn to the second major way in which geography has been given a theological significance in John. We may begin with R. H. Lightfoot's treatment of locality and doctrine in the Fourth Gospel. The *patris*, that is, either the native country or the native town, of Jesus is not in Galilee or Nazareth, but in Judaea and Jerusalem, and there Jesus is not received (4: 43; 5: 43); Judaea is chiefly the seat of discipleship and of opposition to Jesus (7: 3; 1: 43; 4: 1; 18: 15); there is a consistent belittling of the Galilean and Nazarene origin of Jesus. "It is only an imperfect or superficial or hostile understanding which traces his origin to

[70] *Historical Tradition*, p. 249; Barrett, *The Gospel*, p. 321 .

Nazareth and Galilee and believes itself to know his parentage, cf. 7: 27f; 1: 46; 7: 41, 52; such an understanding fails and must fail to perceive his true origin 8: 14, 19; 9: 29; which is not from Galilee or Nazareth (p. 148)."[71] But only in Galilee is Jesus received, 4: 45; to be of Galilee seems almost identical with being an adherent of Jesus (7: 52); the signs in Judaea are not fruitful, as are those in Galilee (2: 14–22; 5: 2–47); only in Chapter 6 do we read of opposition to Jesus in Galilee, and even here the opponents of Jesus, in Lightfoot's view, turn out to be southerners; in Judaea there were frequent attempts to do away with Jesus (7: 1, 19f, 25; 8: 37, 40, 59; 10: 31; 11: 53). On these grounds, roughly enumerated here, Lightfoot finds Judaea to be the centre of John's concern. He, finally, notes that, as Galilee had been of little interest in John's presentation of the ministry of Jesus, it was also of no importance in his thought of the future. Jerusalem, especially, had been the scene of God's "mightiest working," of mankind's "supreme deliverance," but also of conflict and rejection. "Accordingly in St. John's gospel there falls on Jerusalem, as on the cross itself, not only light, but shadow; and Jerusalem holds the chief place in John's gospel because the cross stood there."

Certain modifications of this understanding of the role of Judaea must be noted. Lightfoot himself admits that the notion of Judaea as the *patris* of Jesus is not emphasized. But it must also be recognized that it is not altogether clear that John intends it to be taken as the *patris*. The notorious difficulty of interpreting 4: 44 cannot be easily resolved. In 4: 1–4 we read:

Now when the Lord knew that the Pharisees had heard that Jesus was making and baptizing more disciples than John (although Jesus himself did not baptize, but only his disciples), he left Judaea and departed again to Galilee. He had to pass through Samaria.

There follows in 4: 5–42 the story of Jesus and the woman of Samaria. And then in 4: 43f we read:

43 After two days he departed to Galilee.
44 For Jesus himself testified that a prophet has no honor in his own country.
45 So when he came to Galilee, the Galileans welcomed him, having seen all that he had done in Jerusalem at the feast, for they too had gone to the feast.

Before we deal with the interpretation of 4: 44, notice that 4: 1–3 and 4: 45 imply that Jesus and his disciples had had a successful ministry in Judaea, which cannot, at this time at least, have been a place of rejection.

[71] *Locality and Doctrine in the Gospels*, New York, 1937, p. 148.

Clearly the Pharisees were alarmed at Jesus' success in Judaea, and Jesus had to leave for that reason. The picture of Judaea as consistently the place of rejection breaks down. So, too, in 7: 3, Judaea is the centre of the disciples of Jesus; one of them is mentioned as an acquaintance of the High Priest (18: 15), and in 2: 17; 3: 22; 9: 2; 11: 7 we find them in Judaea, as indeed R. H. Lightfoot recognizes.

But to return to 4: 44: does the *patris* here refer to Judaea? As it stands, the *patris* here would logically refer to Samaria, which is impossible.[72] The saying in 4: 44 is like one found in all the Synoptics. Luke interprets the *patris* as the town of Nazareth, and Mark and Matthew have placed the rejection referred to in Galilee. The word *patris*, therefore, outside John 4: 44, suggests Galilee. Moreover John elsewhere emphasizes that Jesus is from Galilee (1: 46; 2: 1; 7: 42, 52; 19: 19) and never refers to a Judaean birth.

But the context seems to rule out Galilee as the *patris* rejecting Jesus, because in 4: 45 the Galileans welcomed (*edexanto*) Jesus. To this R. E. Brown[73] replies that it is possible to receive or welcome Jesus falsely, and that 4: 46–54 supplies an example in Galilee of a false welcome, that is, one resting on signs and wonders (4: 48). 4: 45 is an introduction to 4: 46–54 and refers to the unsatisfactory faith of the Galileans, just as in 2: 23–25 Jerusalem had been shallow in its response, when "many believed in his name, for they could see the signs he was performing."

There is a certain subtlety in Brown's argument which is disturbing: it demands that 4: 44 refer not to the preceding passage, which the use of *gar* naturally suggests, but to the following, and this is difficult.

Does the view of Lightfoot that the *patris* is Judaea fare better? It is only tenable if we regard 4: 4–4: 42 as an insertion into an itinerary which originally ran from 4: 3 to 4: 43. The repetition of the phrase "he departed to Galilee" in 4: 3 and 4: 43 suggests an overlapping of sources. Originally the contrast between Judaea and Galilee would have been clear. But, even if this be granted, the difficulty remains that 4: 1–3 refers to a successful ministry in Judaea, not to a rejection. The conclusion of Dodd, who takes *patris* in the Fourth Gospel to refer to Jerusalem, which is in Judaea, that John "received the saying in 4: 44 from tradition, in general connection with a move from Judaea to Galilee, and inserted it here without completely integrating it into his narrative" seems inevitable.[74]

But some have not been content to let the matter rest thus vaguely, and have urged that the transition from Judaea to Galilee is of great significance

[72] Contrast, 8: 48.   [73] *The Gospel*, pp. 186ff.   [74] *Historical Tradition*, p. 240.

for John, who elevates Galilee to the place where Jesus is received, as over against Judaea, where he is rejected. Along with Samaria, Galilee is the country of those who, having received Jesus, have become the children of God.[75] The following considerations are proposed in favour of this view.

1. The transition from Judaea to Galilee, so far from being an undigested outcrop from a pre-existing itinerary, is not loosely used, but five times repeated (4: 43, 45, 46, 47, 54). Repetition spells importance. Jerusalem had rejected Jesus on his first visit, as is made clear in 2: 13 to 3: 21 (the cleansing of the Temple, Nicodemus, who remained unconvinced); 4: 43 looks back to this section as showing that Judaea the *patris* of Jesus had rejected him.

2. In 4: 44 occurs the phrase "his own country (*en tê idia patridi*)." In none of the Synoptic parallels do the words "his own" to qualify the *patris* occur. The conclusion is then drawn that 4: 44 looks back to 1: 11: εἰς τὰ ἴδια ἦλθεν, καὶ οἱ ἴδια αὐτον οὐ παρέλαβον; and the still further conclusions, first, that τὰ ἴδια in 1: 11 refers to Judaea—his own land (not his native land), where he is not received, and, second that ὅσοι δὲ ἔλαβον αὐτον, ἔδωκεν αὐτοῖς ἐξουσίαν τέκνα θεοῦ γενέσθαι refer to Galileans who receive Jesus.

3. The Galilean Nathanael is the "real Israelite (1: 49)"; Nicodemus behaves like a Galilean when he sides with Jesus (7: 52). "The Jews" are taken to "symbolize the natural people of God, who, however, reject God's messenger."

4. The journeys of Jesus to Jerusalem symbolize the coming of the redeemer to "his own" and his rejection by them. So, too, the movement to Galilee and Samaria symbolizes his acceptance. In the story of the woman of Samaria—after Jesus had left Judaea for Galilee—a non-Judaean group "receives" Jesus as the true prophet. In 8: 48 Jesus himself is called a "Samaritan." While the accompanying taunt ". . . and you have a demon," is explicitly denied, the accusation that Jesus is a Samaritan is passed over in silence (8: 49).

5. The incidence of the verb *menein* is significant. This verb has a theological or spiritual connotation in John. The verb is used at 1: 39f; 2: 12; 4: 40; 7: 9; 10: 40–42; 11: 6; 11: 54—in connection, that is, with the first two disciples; the Samaritans; Capernaum of Galilee; Galilee; Transjordan; the place of John's first baptisms; and where Jesus was when

---

[75] See the highly rewarding article by W. A. Meeks, "Galilee and Judea in the Fourth Gospel," JBL, Vol. 85, 1966, pp. 159–169. I have sought to summarize his points.

he heard of the death of Lazarus; Ephraim. In no instance is the verb used of time spent by Jesus in Judaea or Jerusalem. This is not accidental. The "itinerary" of the Fourth Gospel thus seems to inform the reader only that Jesus was unable to "stay" in Judaea. While in Galilee, Transjordan, and Samaria he "stayed" because he was "received" by those who became his disciples.[76]

6. The process whereby "Galilee" and "Samaria" became positive symbols of the Christian movement is illumined by the assumption that the Johannine circle was, at some point, accused of being "Galilean" and "Samaritan" by its Jewish opponents. This assumption may be made more probable by the fact that it is precisely in the sections dealing with Galilee in chapter 6 and Samaria in chapter 4 that topographical details are most convincing and that there was probably much tradition localized around or at Cana in Galilee.

Let us examine these items in turn under five headings (item 6 above is partly included under item 4 below and need not be dealt with in view of our total treatment here).

1. The fivefold repetition of the departure from Judaea to Galilee is, at first encounter, striking. But is the transition from Judaea to Galilee precisely emphasized five times? The entry to Galilee in 4: 43 is *ekeithen*, which in the context refers to Samaria: had John desired to emphasize the departure from Judaea, he would surely have made this more explicit here. Similarly in 4: 45. The phrase *eis tên Kana tês Galilaias* in 4: 46 is not to be used in this connection: it is a standardized one to distinguish a particular *Kana*. There remain only two of the five references—4: 47 and 4: 54. The former *may* be designed to emphasize the transition discussed, but it makes good sense apart from this. We are left only with 4: 54 which is a natural closure to the section. All in all, any necessary emphasis on the fivefold repetition is less than convincing. Nor does 2: 13–3: 21 present a clear picture of opposition in Judaea. There is the awkward passage in 2: 23f which suggests, at least, a superficial acceptance of Jesus in Judaea. Nor can Nicodemus, in 3: 1ff, be taken as hostile, even though he remained unconvinced. If we go outside the section 2: 13–21, what of 3: 22? This reads: "After this Jesus and his disciples went into the land of Judaea; there he remained with them (*dietriben*) and baptized." This implies the acceptance of Jesus. And in 4: 1 Jesus "was making and baptizing more disciples than John."

2. Two main interpretations of 1: 11–12 are possible. One interprets

[76] Meeks, "Galilee and Judea."

the verses in terms of the coming of the Logos to the created world or of the Law to Israel. The other finds in them a reference to the actual ministry of Jesus. The two interpretations *may* not be mutually exclusive, but the second is the more convincing. In any case, a neuter plural *ta idia* is not likely to refer to the land (*gê*; fem.) of Judaea. Such a reference would demand *eis tên idian gên*. So, too, *hosoi de elabon* is too undefined in its range to connote a specific group or groups such as "the Galileans" and the "Samaritans": such a connotation would best be indicated by *hoi de elabon*. Moreover, if 4: 45 was designed to recall 1: 11, there was nothing to prevent John from there writing *elabon* or *parelabon auton hoi Galilaioi* rather than *edexanto auton hoi Galilaioi*: he does use *lambanein* in 5: 43. It is best to take *ta idia* in 1: 11 in a general sense of what belonged to Jesus as a person in the world, that is, the heritage of Israel, the Promised Land, Jerusalem, without tying the term to Judaea in particular; and to interpret *hoi idioi* of the Jewish people as a whole (see 1: 31). In 1: 11 the activity of the Logos is narrowed to Israel (cf. Matt. 15: 24). The *hosoi* of 1: 12a again breaks this confine and suggests a larger context, as do 1: 12b and 1: 13.[77]

3. Neither the figure of Nathanael nor of Nicodemus are as un-ambiguous as the third proposal above indicates. The former does not, as a Galilean, immediately receive Jesus, but is somewhat sceptical. The proposal also seems to demand—does it not?—that Jesus should have said of him, not *ide alêthôs Israêlitês, en hô dolos ouk estin*, but *ide Galilaios*. . . . As for Nicodemus, a dweller in Jerusalem, despite his sympathy with Jesus, he remains uncommitted, so that although called as from Galilee he was not a Galilean in the sense demanded in the proposed interpretation. In fact, the negative *mê* expects a negative answer, and it is explicitly stated that he is "of the Jews (*heis ôn ex autôn*)."

4. Several factors make it difficult to take the movement of Jesus to Judaea from Galilee to be one from acceptance to rejection. Clearly there is a reference to disciples, 7: 1ff, who have accepted Jesus in Judaea (7: 3); not all the crowds in Jerusalem reject Jesus; some think that he is good (7: 12), and some confess him to be the Prophet who was to come (7: 40), and the Christ (7: 41); even the Temple police were impressed by him (7: 45); many believed in him (8: 30, compare 11: 45ff; 12: 1) (here the reasons for belief are poor); and in 12: 42 many *archontes* (many among the Sanhedrin) believed.[78] On the other hand, Jesus' own Galilean

---

[77] The distinction between ὅι and ὅσοι cannot be pressed, but ὅσοι at least suggests a more generalized connotation. See Arndt and Gingrich, *A Greek–English Lexicon of the N.T.*, trans., 1957, p. 590b.　　[78] On *archontes*, Martyn, *History and Theology*, pp. 74ff.

brothers did not believe in him (7: 5). For them Judaea is the world stage: to go there would be for Jesus to show himself to the world. We have already quoted C. H. Dodd on the deeper symbolism of the ascent of Jesus to Jerusalem in chapter 7, to the effect that it signifies the manifestation of the Messiah to Israel and the Logos to the world of human kind.[79] It is this symbolism rather than any suggesting a distinction between Galilee, as such, and Judaea, as such, that we are to find here. Galilee had simply been a place of retirement: Judaea or Jerusalem is the world stage. Similarly the response of the Samaritans to Jesus in 4: 39–42, following the meeting of Jesus with the Samaritan woman, immediately breaks through any geographical provincialism such as might suggest that Jesus is particularly accepted by Samaritans. Rather the conclusion turns us to the large world of which Jesus is the Saviour.

In this connection the larger context of chapter 4 must be recognized. In the course of the conversation with the Samaritan woman, Jesus makes it clear that geographic loyalties are to be transcended in the interests of the prompting of the Spirit. It is exceedingly difficult to believe that, after the views expressed in 4: 20–25, John reintroduced geographic symbolism of the kind that we are discussing immediately after this, in 4: 43ff.

The remaining point is that Jesus himself is called a Samaritan by his opponents and that this charge is not rebutted.[80] The use of the term Samaritan in 8: 49 may be simply tautologous: this would explain the absence of any specific rebuttal to it. That the charge of being a Samaritan was equivalent to the charge of possession is made likely by the fact that Dositheus and Simon Magus, Samaritans who claimed to be sons of God, "were regarded as mad (possessed)." Or again to call Jesus a Samaritan may simply have been a way of designating him a heretic;[81] or others have urged that since the Samaritans were born of "irregular unions between Israelite women and the Gentile immigrants" their inexact Judaism is a product of their origin, and it is implied here that Jesus is of irregular birth and therefore of inexact Judaism.[82] In this view, 8: 49 looks back to 8: 41. But such a subtle nuance is not likely. What is clear is that 8: 49 provides very dubious support for any Johannine view, if such

[79] See above p. 291.
[80] Barrett, *The Gospel*, p. 80. Compare Brown, *The Gospel*, p. 358. See 7: 20.
[81] Bultmann, *Johannesevangelium*, p. 225, n. 6.
[82] The charges in 8: 41 of Jesus' illegitimacy should then be brought into view here also. Brown, *The Gospel*, p. 357. On p. 366, he writes: "In the charges against Jesus of being illegitimate...of being a Samaritan and of being demented we have forerunners of the personal attacks on Jesus that became part of Jewish apologetics against Christianity...." See also p. 358, n. 48.

existed, that the Samaritans are a symbol for the believers, although there is no evidence that the term "Samaritan" was a technical term for "heretic." (This has a bearing on item 6 above.)

5. We come, finally, to the use of *menein*. In many passages, in the second half of the gospel especially, it bears profound spiritual connotation. But our dilemma is this: even if John often uses terms with a double meaning, must we *always* interpret terms so used in a double sense. Of the instances cited, where what appears to be a simple statement of fact that Jesus stayed at a certain place for some time, either delimited or left vaguely open, is also ascribed a spiritual dimension, not all are convincing. In 1: 38f the question "Where do you stay?" can hardly have a spiritual connotation, because in 1: 39 they "see" that is, physically where Jesus was staying, and the chronological datum "that day," an accusative of the duration of time, also militates against a "spiritual" interpretation. In 2: 12 the company that Jesus keeps at Capernaum— his mother and his brothers, who did not believe, as well as his disciples— and the words "not many days" again suggest a simple meaning for *menô*, even if the singular reading of P⁶⁶ᶜ F G 565 1241 be accepted. In 3: 36 *menei* is used of the "wrath of God": the mere use of the term does not, therefore, connote a blessed spiritual indwelling. In 4: 40 the Samaritans—presumably those who had come to accept him—asked Jesus to "stay" with them. And, while here again the note of time, "two days," should warn us against over-enthusiasm, 4: 41f does suggest that the staying of Jesus here has a spiritual significance. On the contrary, in 7: 9 *menô* can have no such significance: here Jesus is obviously "killing time," before finally going up to Jerusalem. His stay in Galilee had failed to convince his brothers, and it is impossible to ascribe to *emeinen* a profound spiritual meaning here in the sense with which we are concerned, that is, the communal. In 9: 41 *menô* is connected with sin. It is unlikely that in 10: 40 anything more is intended than a period of time, and so in 11: 6. Doubtless in 11: 54 *emeinen meta tôn mathêtôn* can be given a spiritual connotation, but it is not necessary to do so. Geographically *meinô* is used of a stay of Jesus on Judaean soil; the precise location of Ephraim is disputed, but it is generally assumed that it was in Judaea. The use of *menô* is not pertinent to our purpose in 12: 34; it has a purely temporal meaning. In 12: 46 *menô* has an unmistakable moral or spiritual association, although, in itself, it is neutral. From 14 on the intensely spiritual connotation of *menô* needs no documentation: apart from 19: 31, which has a temporal reference, it is ubiquitous.

One passage is to be noted where *diatribô* is used of Jesus spending time in Judaea, that is, 3: 22. Is it not significant that here, in connection with Judaea, John avoids his preferred term *menô?* The verse 3: 22 is Johannine if we follow Fortna, who does not include it in SG. On the other hand, however, the time is spent "with the disciples" and it is hardly credible that *diatribô* in this connection can have even the suggestion of a pejorative connotation. Moreover, the *ebaptizen* suggests a spiritually profitable stay.[83]

What shall we say to all this? Only by a *tour de force* can Judaea be made a symbol of the rejection, and Galilee and Samaria a symbol of the acceptance of the gospel. This is the conclusion we should expect if we are correct in seeing in the Fourth Gospel the displacement of holy places by a Person. To ascribe to John a developed geographical symbolism would be to run counter to his concentration on the Word made flesh in a Person. But there are also other considerations which would make such a conclusion natural. To these we now, finally, turn.

Throughout the Gospel the word *pothen* "whence," is frequently used in connection with Jesus. Consider the following passages: 1: 48; 4: 1; 6: 5; 7: 27, 28; 8: 14; 9: 29, 30; 19: 9. These suggest that the true origin of Jesus and of his power is unknown except to himself. In 7: 27 his opponents assert that they know whence he comes. This disqualifies him as the Messiah, whose origins were to be unknown. Jesus, on the other hand, knows that he is from God (7: 29, compare 8: 14 and 13: 1). Jesus accuses his opponents, who fail to see that he is of divine origin, of judging him "after the flesh"—that is, in this context, geographically (8: 15). On the other hand, in 9: 29, they contrast the divine origin of Moses' words with that of Jesus', which come they know not whence: certainly not from God. Here they assert that they do *not* know the origin of Jesus. To the blind man healed, he is obviously from God (9: 30).

It would seem, then, that the Fourth Gospel is concerned to emphasize the transcendent origin of Jesus. This implies that a concern with his geographical origin is unlikely. There is, however, one place where the geographical origin of Jesus is discussed, in 7: 40–52. Here members of the Jerusalem crowd declare that Jesus cannot be the Messiah because he comes from Galilee, and the Messiah was expected to be of the seed of David, born in Bethlehem. So, too, the Pharisees assert that Jesus cannot be the Prophet to come, because, like the Messiah, he could not come

[83] I came across Jurgen Heise, *Bleiben, Menein in den Johanneischen Schriften*, Tübingen, 1967, after I had written the above. He does not deal with 3: 22: his treatment is not contradictory to our conclusion.

from Galilee, but by implication only from Judaea. Notice that it is the enemies of Jesus that deny his Galilean origin. The implication of all this may be then, it has been suggested, that for the Fourth Gospel, Jesus was of Galilean origin. This was a matter of interest to Galilean-Samaritan Christians, who formed part of the Johannine circle from which that Gospel emerged, and adds weight to the theory we examined above that Galilee for John was the land of acceptance and discipleship.[84]

But this is not the only interpretation of material in 10: 40–52 that is possible. It depends upon emphasizing the twofold denial of any possible Galilean origin for the Messiah in 7: 41 and 7: 52, and holding the structure of 7: 40–52 to be "broadly chiasmic." This is possible. But 7: 40–52 should not be sharply separated from 7: 25ff. There, as we saw above, certain of the Jerusalemites claim that they know whence Jesus comes. But they also hold to the view that the place of origin of the Messiah, when he should come, is unknown. It followed that Jesus, whose origin was known, could not be the Messiah. The Jerusalemites think that Jesus is from Galilee. But, ironically, they are wrong. He is actually from heaven, and this they do not know.

In 7: 40–52 a different objection to Jesus is offered by certain ones in the crowd at the Feast in Jerusalem. This time they assert that they know whence Jesus comes, that is, from Galilee. But the scriptures asserted that the Messiah should be born of the stock of David in Bethlehem. Here again, ironically, the Jerusalemites are wrong. They think that Jesus comes from Galilee, and not from Bethlehem, whereas actually he was born in the latter, so that Jesus can be the expected Messiah. The Bethlehem tradition was known to the evangelist. The whole of the material in 7: 27–53 is concerned not to emphasize the Galilean origin of Jesus, according to the interests of a Galilean community, but to drive home the truth about his true origin—a question which emerges later in 8: 23, where again John's irony is at work to make clear that not the question of his geographical origin is important but that of his origin "from above": is he from God or not? The climax of the discussion in 7 is not 7: 52, although the present chapter divisions suggest this. Rather the whole of chapter 7 should be closely connected with 8: 12ff. How far the discussion of the Galilean origin of Jesus in 7: 37–53 reflects the interests of a Galilean-Samaritan group must remain an open question. But whatever may have been the original impetus to, or setting for, that discussion, it

[84] See Meeks, "Galilee and Judea."

is taken up by John into a far larger context, that of the wider discussion of the ultimate origin of Jesus in God, in which all geographical considerations become secondary.[85]

5. LIFE AND THE VINE

There is one further angle from which the question of "geography" may be approached. In a book published as far back as 1949, Jacques Guillet examined some of the themes that govern the Bible.[86] Among them he discussed themes of hope: he pointed out a fact familiar to us from Part I above that the "life" to which Israel looked forward, while it had much in common with "life" as understood by its neighbours in the Middle East, had one peculiarity: it would be "life" in the promised land flowing with milk and honey, centred in Jerusalem. We need not here examine the question how far the concept of "life," as a symbol of salvation, remained inseverable from the land and how far the land became a secondary element, if at all, in the understanding of "life." What is noteworthy is that in the Fourth Gospel the concept of "life" or "eternal life" assumes a significant role.[87] At no point is it connected with the land in any way. Rather it is always centred in Jesus himself, who, in this sense, has become "the sphere" or "space" where life is to be found. True, there is one passage, 5: 25ff, when the life of the Age to Come is apparently conceived within the framework of the traditional eschatology of Judaism.[88]

25   Truly, truly, I say to you, the hour is coming, and now is, when the dead will hear the voice of the Son of God, and those who hear will live,

26   For as the Father has life in himself, so he has granted the Son also to have life in himself,

27   and has given him authority to execute judgment, because he is the Son of man.

28   Do not marvel at this; for the hour is coming when all who are in the tombs will hear his voice

29   and come forth, those who have done good, to the resurrection of life, and those who have done evil, to the resurrection of judgment.

Here John doubtless conceives, in verse 29, of resurrection in the land:

[85] I have here profited greatly from C. K. Barrett and R. E. Brown.

[86] *Thèmes Bibliques: Études sur L'Expression et le Développement de la Révélation*, Paris, 1951, pp. 160ff.

[87] See especially Dodd, *The Interpretation*, pp. 144ff, 318ff, *et passim*.

[88] Bultmann, *Johannesevangelium*, p. 196, finds this to be a redactorial addition to the text. He compares 2 Tim. 2: 18 etc. Contrast Dodd, *The Interpretation*, pp. 364ff.

compare with Dan. 12: 2 (LXX).[89] But the main emphasis in the gospel is that expressed in 11: 24ff where the traditional doctrine is quietly laid aside in favour of a new.

Jesus said to her [Martha], "Your brother will rise again." Martha said to him, "I know that he will rise again in the resurrection at the last day." Jesus said to her, "I am the resurrection and the life, he who believes in me, though he die, yet shall he live, and whoever lives and believes in me shall never die."

The point of reference for understanding life in this world, and in the world to come, is Jesus Christ. Any traditional concepts, geographical and other, governing the understanding of "life" are dwarfed by the centrality of Christ. For example, Christ has replaced the manna of the future life expected by Judaism in the land: it is he who gives life to the world and it is "he who eats my flesh and drinks my blood," who possesses eternal life, and will be raised on the last day (6: 22–50). Or again in 17: 3 we read: "this is eternal life [that is, the life of the Age to Come] that they know thee the only true God, and Jesus Christ whom thou hast sent." To reveal the full extent of the way in which the traditional symbols and expectations of Judaism are swallowed up "in Christ" in the Fourth Gospel is not necessary here. We shall only refer to one other Johannine theme in illustration of this. In the Old Testament the vine is the symbol of what attaches a man to the land, of God's hopes for the land. This is clearly expressed in Amos 9: 13–15.

> 13 "Behold, the days are coming"
> says the Lord,
> "when the plowman shall over-
> take the reaper
> and the treader of grapes him
> who sows the seed;
> the mountains shall drip sweet
> wine,
> and all the hills shall flow with
> it.
> 14 I will restore the fortunes of my
> people Israel,
> and they shall rebuild the
> ruined cities and inhabit them;
> they shall plant vineyards and
> drink their wine,

---

[89] Although the point that C. K. Barrett makes, *The Gospel*, p. 219, must not be overlooked, here it is the resurrection of unbelievers which is being thought of.

> and they shall make gardens
> and eat their fruit.
> 15 I will plant them upon their land,
> and they shall never again be
> plucked up
> out of the land which I have
> given them,"
> says the Lord your God.

Hosea 10: 1a ascribes to Israel itself the name "vine" for this reason: to call it a vine is, among other things, to suggest its rootedness in the land.

> Israel is a luxuriant vine
> that yields its fruit.

Isaiah and Jeremiah and Ezekiel have the same metaphor. Throughout the Old Testament the geographical rootedness and location of Israel, the vine, is always implicit and often explicit, unmistakably so in Psalm 80. John takes up the metaphor and equates the "vine" with Jesus (15: 1ff). He personalizes it completely. He is a "vine" coming from God and going to God: geographical considerations are simply otiose in connection with this "vine." The spatially conditioned life, bread, water, and vine have given place throughout the gospel to the living Person, who is himself life and bread and living water and vine; and he is these for the world (1: 1ff; 3: 16).[90]

Our discussion of the Fourth Gospel in this way drives us back to the beginning of the Gospel to 1: 14, where the flesh of Jesus of Nazareth is said to be the seat of the Logos: that Logos, whether as Wisdom or as Torah[91] is no longer attached to a land, as was the Torah, but to a Person who came to his own land, and was not received. To judge from our examination, the Fourth Gospel was not especially concerned with the particular relation of Jesus of Nazareth to his own geographical land. In some ways the nature of the Gospel, at least as it was traditionally understood, prepared us for this, as we indicated at the beginning of this chapter. But, in another way, it must occasion surprise. There is now a growing recognition that the Fourth Gospel is to be connected with circles where the relationship between Moses and Jesus was a matter of acute concern and debate.[92] It is inconceivable that the discussion of the

[90] E.g., Is. 3: 14; Jer. 2: 21; Ezek. 19: 10–11.
[91] See especially on all this, Dodd, *The Interpretation*, ad rem.
[92] See the various commentaries, and especially Martyn, *History and Theology*; W. A. Meeks, *The Prophet-King in the Fourth Gospel*, Leiden; H. M. Teeple, *The Mosaic Eschatological Prophet*, Philadelphia, 1957; Peter Borgen, *Bread from Heaven*, Leiden, 1965.

figure of Moses who led Israel on the way to the promised land should not have led to discussion of the land among the earliest Christians. There is evidence that some Jewish-Christians[93] were involved in millenarian speculations of a political kind in the first century, even though the body of Jerusalem Jewish-Christians who left for Pella seem to have foresworn such. Discussion of the land, we must conjecture, lies behind the lines the speculations followed. John has reached a position beyond Paul, where there is no longer even an emotional attachment to Jerusalem which according to some, as part of Judaea, had become the city of his rejection, and where, if we are correct in the above pages, there is a deliberate presentation of the replacement of "holy places" by the Person of Jesus. In certain Jewish-Christian and Samaritan-Christian circles such holy places in the land were cherished, and we know that—as we pointed out before[94]—after A.D. 70 the land was much in the mind of Jews and, we must assume, of Jewish-Christians. In view of this, the demotion of "holy places" in the land would have a certain pertinence in John's day, although the land itself, as a totality, except as the place where Jesus was rejected (1: 11) did not occupy John.[95]

This must not be taken to mean that all geographical data about Jesus are of no concern to John: he has preserved, although brokenly, much geographical detail about Jesus' movements.[96] The Jesus of the Fourth Gospel is not a disincarnate spirit, but a man of flesh and blood who hungered and thirsted and was weary with his journey. His flesh was real

[93] J. Daniélou, *A History of Early Christian Doctrine*, Vol. 1. *The Theology of Jewish Christianity*, trans., London, 1964, pp. 67ff. He finds political tendencies among the Ebionites, and most typically in Cerinthus. Eusebius, *H.E.*, 3: 28: 4. Compare Bo Reicke, *Diakonie, Festfreude und Zelos*, Uppsala, 1951, pp. 283–287.

[94] See above pp. 54ff.

[95] Perhaps this sentence conveys a more negative nuance than is present in 1: 11. If we could be certain that in 1: 11 the term τὰ ἴδια (his own) did specifically refer to the land, as Brown certainly thinks it to be included in the term, then John at the very outset of the Gospel forcefully dismisses the land as the sphere of any possible redemption because it has rejected the Word. But this is to be too clear about the meaning of τὰ ἴδια and we prefer to leave the text above as it stands. This means that it is not so much that John *rejects* any preoccupation with the land as that he ignores it apart from 1: 11.

[96] The evidence is surveyed by Dodd, *Historical Tradition*, pp. 233–247. He finds "small undigested scraps of different material" which come from a single body of tradition which supplies solid information. He refers to the poverty of Northern places named in John and the greater abundance of references to Southern places, and connects this with R. H. Lightfoot's recognition of a tension between the claims of Galilee and Jerusalem (p. 246), where there was a "group of witnesses" to Jesus (7: 1–9), not mentioned in the Synoptics, through whom John received the material concerned either directly or indirectly. On the basis of this material, Dodd presents a summary of Jesus' activity at certain periods. Not many have followed Dodd in this reconstruction (see e.g. F. W. Beare, NTS, Vol. 10, pp. 517ff). But he has at least made it impossible to ignore a certain geographic curiosity or interest in John.

flesh, and he was geographically conditioned as all men. But, although John presents us with itineraries of Jesus to some extent, and, although these were real, not the horizontal, geographical movements matter primarily to him. Rather what was significant to John was the descent of Jesus from above and his ascent thither.[97] The fundamental spatial symbolism of the Fourth Gospel was not horizontal but vertical. It does not lend itself easily to geographical concern so much as to the personal confrontation with the One from above, whose Spirit bloweth where it listeth and is not subject to geographical dimensions that had been dear to Judaism.[98]

[97] See John 8: 23; 3: 31; 19: 11; 3: 13; 6: 33; 6: 38; 6: 41, 42, 50, 51, 58; 6: 62; 20: 17. Note that ὁ ἐρχόμενος of the Synoptics (Matt. 11:3; 12:9 etc.) is ὁ ἄνωθεν ἐρχόμενος in John (3: 31). See Barrett, *The Gospel*, p. 282, on τὰ ἄνω and τὰ κάτω and on 3: 12–13, pp. 176–178 on the ascent and descent of the Son of Man. Important also is the notion of the elevation of Christ, John 3: 14f; 12: 32, and of the sending of Christ into the world 3: 16f, 28, 34; 5: 36ff; 9: 7; 10: 36; 11: 42; 17 passim; 20: 21.

[98] The displacement motif implicit in John 1: 14 is assumed in our treatment. I have deliberately avoided lengthy discussion of it because it has so often been treated. The use of ἐσκήνωσεν in John 1: 14 has long been connected with the conviction that the tabernacle and by extension the Temple through the Person of Jesus is among men. (See Brown, *The Gospel*, pp. 321ff. Appealing to Exod. 25: 8–9; Joel 3: 17; Zech. 2: 10; Ezek. 43: 7; he writes, "When the Prologue proclaims that the Word made his dwelling among men, we are being told that the flesh of Jesus Christ is the new localization of God's presence on earth, and that Jesus is the replacement of the ancient Tabernacle. The Gospel will present Jesus as the replacement of the Temple [2: 19–22], which is a variation of the same theme.") John 1: 14b also by the use of σκηνόω may recall the Hebrew verb שָׁכֵן, whence the term *Shekinah*. The Shekinah and the glory of God were connected with the Temple in Judaism, and John is concerned to connect them with the Person of Jesus.

For a different reason we have not examined at length John 19: 31–37. The incident in 19: 34 ("However, one of the soldiers stabbed at Jesus' side with a lance, and immediately blood and water flowed out") has been taken to replace the story of the rending of the veil in the Temple recorded in Mark 15: 38–39 (with parallels in Matthew and Luke). In this view the point of that incident (the flowing out of the blood and water) is that, since in John the body of Jesus is the Temple (2: 21), 19: 34 is designed to denote the superseding of that holy place. But the symbolism elsewhere in the Gospel points rather to the outpouring of the Spirit through the death, the blood (Brown, *The Gospel*, p. 949), although 19: 34 does emphasize also that Jesus died as a sacrificial victim (see Mishnah Pesaḥim 5: 3, 5; Tamid 4: 2). This is made clear in G. Stemberger, *La symbolique du bien et du mal selon Saint Jean*, Paris, 1970, pp. 185–191.

XI. JESUS AND THE LAND

Our examination of the major documents of the New Testament, with the deliberate limitation of avoiding discussion of the transcendentalizing of the land in the Heavenly Jerusalem mentioned on p. 162 above, is over. We have discovered in the New Testament, alongside the recognition of the historical role of the land as the scene of the life, death, and resurrection of Jesus, a growing recognition that the Christian faith is, in principle, cut loose from the land, that the Gospel demanded a breaking out of its territorial chrysalis. This is another way of saying that Christianity increasingly abandoned the geographic involvement of Judaism which was deeply cherished by many Jews, even though it was transformed, transcendentalized or spiritualized, and perhaps even challenged by others.

We have now to ask whether in doing so Christians departed from the intent of their Lord or were, in fact, inspired by that intent. Was there a gulf fixed between early Christians who took the road away from the land and Jesus of Nazareth?

To begin with the attitude of Jesus himself is to confront the notorious difficulties involved in any attempt at rediscovering what Jesus said, did, and thought. We can only offer a brief statement of what seems the most probable way in which the attitude of Jesus to the land is to be understood, in full recognition that such a statement is necessarily precarious.

At the outset, it is well to clear the ground of an old misconception recently again brought into sharp focus.[1] According to this, Jesus was virtually a Zealot.[2] He was not averse to a military campaign against Rome because he shared the Zealots'[3] view that Yahweh was to be the only Governor and Master and that he had chosen the nation of Israel to be his own peculiar people and had given it the land of Canaan as its peculiar possession.[4] The pacifist Jesus is the creation of the writers of the Gospels

[1] S. G. F. Brandon, *Jesus and the Zealots; a Study of the Political Factor in Primitive Christianity*, Manchester, 1967.

[2] Brandon follows R. Eisler, *The Messiah Jesus and John the Baptist*, trans., New York, 1931. Eisler had a long progeny in S. Reimarus, "Von dem Zwecke Jesu und seine Junge," *Noch ein Fragment des Wolfbüttelschen Ungennanten*, ed. Gotthold Ephraim Lessing (Braunschweig, 1778); K. Kautsky, *Der Ursprung des Christentums*, Stuttgart, 1919. See M. Hengel, JSS, Vol. XIV, No. 2, Autumn 1969, pp. 231–240.

[3] We shall use "Zealots" as a term for a politico-religious group existing in the time of Jesus, but only for the sake of setting forth Brandon's position. That "the Zealots" only emerged as a distinct party later in A.D. 66 has been shown long ago by Kirsopp Lake, *The Beginnings of Christianity*, Part I, Vol. 1, London, 1920, pp. 421ff. See M. Smith, HTR, Vol. 64, Jan. 1971, pp. 1–19, "Zealots and Sicarii, Their Origins and Relations."

[4] Jos. *Antiquities*, XVIII. 1. 6.

whose interests were served by presenting a Christ innocuous to Rome. Jesus differed from the Zealots only in that he was more immediately concerned to attack the Jewish sacerdotal aristocracy than to embroil himself with the Romans. Very different from what the Church claimed him to be, the Galilean was a man nationalistically concerned to rid the land of its Roman usurper and to return it to its rightful owner, God.[5]

To rebut this claim in detail would take us too far afield. A living awareness on the part of Jesus of extreme nationalists, who have often, probably wrongly, been referred to as the Zealots, as if they already constituted a party of that name in the time of Jesus, was inevitable: they were a dynamic force in his world, especially in Galilee.[6] Many nationalists must have heard Jesus preach. At least one of the disciples, Simon, may have been a Zealot and may have been so named,[7] others have been claimed to have been such—Judas Iscariot, Peter, the sons of Zebedee.[8] Certain verses have been taken to point to a Zealot concern, for example, Matt. 10: 34: "Do not think that I have come to bring peace on earth; I have not come to bring peace but a sword." The demand for a readiness to

[5] Brandon, *Jesus and the Zealots*, chapters 5, 6, and 7 especially: "a bond of common sympathy *surely* united Jesus and his followers with those who sought to maintain the ideals of Judas of Galilee (p. 358 our italics)."

[6] See now especially M. Hengel, *Die Zeloten: Untersuchungen zur jüdischen Freiheitsbewegung in der Zeit von Herodes I bis 70 n. Chr.*, Leiden, 1961, but see n. 3 above for Morton Smith's caution. The connection of Galilee with extreme nationalists has long been urged, but see an unpublished dissertation by Malinowski, *Galilee in Josephus*, Duke University, 1973. For different kinds of "Zealots," see G. Baumbach, "Zeloten und Sikarier" in *Theologische Literaturzeitung*, 1965, pp. 727ff, and further references in O. Cullmann, *Jesus and the Revolutionaries*, New York, 1970, p. 61, n. 3. For a critique of Baumbach and other bibliographical details, see M. Hengel, *Was Jesus a Revolutionist?*, trans., Facet Books, Philadelphia, 1971, pp. 10ff, illuminating.

[7] Luke 6: 15; Acts 1: 13. In Mark 3: 18; Matt. 10: 4 he is called Simon the Cananaean. This confirms his Zealot character, because "Cananaean" has nothing to do with Canaan, but is derived from the Aramaic word *qanna'i* (zealot): it is a loose transcription of the latter. So O. Cullmann, *The State in the New Testament*, New York, 1956, pp. 14ff.

[8] Cullmann, *The State in the New Testament*, pp. 15ff claims that Judas Iscariot stands for *Judas the Sicarius*—Iscariot being a transliteration of the Latin term *sicarius*, used for "Zealot." That Judas had the impatience of the Zealot to bring in the Kingdom helps to account for his betrayal of Jesus. So, too, Peter, in the light of Mark 8: 27ff, is Satanic (Zealotic) in his understanding of the Kingdom (compare Matt. 4: 8ff). His designation as *bar iona* is not to be taken to mean "Son of John," although he *is* so understood in John 1: 42; 21: 15. "Son of John" would be *bar iohannan*. *Bar iona* is derived from Accadian and has the meaning "terrorist." This is asserted without supporting evidence. Again, the description of the Sons of Zebedee as "sons of thunder" that is, Boanerges (Mark 3: 17), would be peculiarly appropriate were they Zealots, and in view of Mark 10: 3 and Luke 9: 54. For these reasons Cullmann, p. 17, thinks that: "One of the twelve—Simon the Zealot—*certainly* belonged to the Zealots; others probably did, like Judas Iscariot, Peter, and *possibly* the sons of Zebedee." Hengel, *Was Jesus a Revolutionist?*, does not touch on the proper names concerned (but see *Die Zeloten*, pp. 55ff). On the relationship of the *sicarii* to Zealots, see Hengel, *Was Jesus a Revolutionist?* p. 11, n. 39ff; *Die Zeloten*, pp. 47ff.

undergo crucifixion which is implied in the exhortations of Jesus to take up the cross (Mark 8: 34–9: 1; Matt. 16: 24–28; Luke 9: 23–27), has suggested that his followers were to be prepared to encounter the same hateful Roman punishment as was often meted out to Zealots. The obscure verse in Matt. 11: 12, "From the days of John the Baptist until now the kingdom of heaven has suffered violence, and men of violence take it by force," has been interpreted as containing a side-glance at the Zealots: compare Luke 16: 16.[9] So too Luke 24: 21, "But we had hoped that he was the one to redeem Israel...," as well as Acts 1: 6, "So when they had come together, they asked him, 'Lord, will you at this time restore the kingdom to Israel?'" have been taken to imply the presence of Zealot elements among the disciples. Moreover, there were charges that Jesus strove for political power. This is the implication of Mark 15: 2, 26, and parallels. Was he not the King of the Jews? Did he not incite people not to pay taxes (Luke 23: 2b)? Was he not seditious (Luke 23: 5)? And is it not clear that the entry of Jesus to Jerusalem and the events that followed are to be understood in Messianic and, therefore, political terms? Note especially the narrative in Mark, which underlies Matthew and Luke. In Mark 11: 1 reference is made to the Mount of Olives, which according to popular belief, was to be the place of the Messiah's appearance. The colt sent for in 11: 2 may have been a young horse, but even if this be rejected and "the colt" be taken to mean an ass, as is customary, the ass also had kingly and Messianic associations in the Ancient East. The references to garments spread in 11: 7 is a sign of kingly honour, and the cry "Hosanna" in 11: 9ff, recalling Ps. 11: 25–26, as well as the use of the term "He that cometh" in 11: 9, all point to the Messianic connotation of the events for Mark. And, finally, for that evangelist the cleansing of the Temple itself is a Messianic act, as the citation of Is. 56: 7 in 11: 17 indicates. In Is. 56: 1–8 Deutero-Isaiah looks forward to the time of the revelation of Yahweh's deliverance (56: 1). Mark connects the cleansing with this eschatological hope of Judaism that all nations should come to Jerusalem in the end of the days (Is. 2: 2–4; Micah 4: 1–4; Is. 25: 7; 66: 18–23; Zech. 14: 16–19; T. Levi 18: 9) and that there should be a purification of the Temple (Ezek. 40–48; Tobit 14: 5f; Jub. 1: 28f; 1 Enoch 90: 28f; Sib. Or. 5: 414–433; Pss. of Sol. 17: 33). In the mind of the earliest Evangelist at least, is not Jesus the King-Messiah with political, as well as religious, intent? And unless we

9 On this view the meaning of the verse is: from John's time until now, revolutionists or Zealots have sought to seize God's Kingdom, that is, have sought to establish it by their forceful methods. See Hengel, *Die Zeloten*, pp. 129–132.

are to accept the presentation of Jesus' ministry in Mark—a presentation which, it must be re-emphasized, underlies those of Matthew and Luke—as a radical falsification, must we not also ascribe to him a political concern? And, finally, was not Jesus crucified as a Zealot by the Romans? Does not the manner of his death make unmistakably clear his political intent?[10]

But even if one of the disciples were singled out, only in Luke-Acts, as a Zealot, this implies that the disciples, as a group, were not Zealots; in any case that Simon remained a Zealot after he had become a follower of Jesus is not clear.[11] The attempt to make Judas Iscariot, Peter, and the sons of Zebedee into Zealots is forced. All the verses to which reference has been made above need not be given a specifically Zealot reference.[12]

[10] On the points made in the above long paragraph note the following. On the Mt. of Olives as Messianic, see SB, I, p. 840; Jos., *Jewish Wars*, II. 13. 5; *Antiquities*, XX. 8. 6; Test. Zeb. 9: 8b; on the colt, see W. Bauer, "The 'Colt' of Palm Sunday," JBL, Vol. 72, 1953, pp. 220–229. He takes the "colt" to be a horse; see C. W. F. Smith, "The Horse and the Ass in the Bible," *The Anglican Theological Review*, Vol. 27, 1945, pp. 86–97. Zech. 9: 9b is a crucial text. See E. Lohmeyer, *Markus*, Göttingen, 1959, pp. 232f, and contrast S. B. Johnson, *Mark*, New York, 1960, p. 186, on the relations to Gen. 49: 11. On the kingly associations of the ass in the Ancient Near East, see J. B. Pritchard, ed. *Ancient Near Eastern Texts*, 3rd ed., Princeton, 1969, p. 482 (but is there here anything of real significance for Matt. 21: 5—at a remove of centuries from the patriarchal age, even though it is cited in the footnote?). Reference is also made to the *Archives Royales de Mari*, 15 vols., Paris, 1950ff, ed. G. Dossin, C-F. Jean, J. R. Kupper, 11. 37: 11; 1, 132: 19, 22 etc. With the references to the spreading of garments, Mark 11: 7, compare 2 Kings 9: 12; on Ps. 11: 25–26, see T. A. Burkill, *Mysterious Revelation*, Ithaca, N.Y., 1963, pp. 194f; Eric Werner, "Hosanna in the Gospels," JBL, Vol. 65, 1946, pp. 116–117: D. Daube, *The New Testament and Rabbinic Judaism*, London, 1956, finds the possibility that the crowd expected Elijah; on "He that cometh," see D. Daube, *He that Cometh*, London, 1966. Historically, the purification of the Temple had constantly signified the political restoration of the people: 2 Kings 18: 4ff; 22: 3–23; 25; 2 Chron. 29: 12ff; 34: 3ff; 1 Macc. 4: 36–60; 2 Macc. 10: 1–8. The cleansing of the Temple might, therefore, very easily have been taken to be a political gesture (see nn. 42, 43 below). On Messianic allusions in the Passion Narrative of Mark, see H. W. Kuhn, "Das Reittier Jesu in der Einzugsgeschichte des Markusevangeliums," ZNW, 50, 1959, pp. 82–91. The question of the role of the Jewish and Roman authorities in the trial of Jesus is too complex for documentation here (see pp. 343f).

[11] It is by no means certain that in Luke 6: 15 and Acts 1: 13 the term "Zealot" should be taken as a substantive. It may simply be adjectival, "the zealous one." A. R. C. Leaney makes the additional point, in connection with the reference to Simon the Zealot, that "If . . . we follow the evangelists in seeing Jesus as distinct from all parties in the Jewish State, to label *one* of his disciples as a Zealot begins to have point. In view of the outlook of Jesus, it seems probable that this disciple is so called because he is not like the others." *The Pelican Guide to Modern Theology*, Vol. 3, Middlesex, England, p. 339. Leaney also notes that perhaps the Evangelist meant to imply that Jesus called him when he *was* a Zealot, and not *to be* a Zealot.

[12] It is still more likely that Iscariot stands for the "man from Kerioth," and that *bar iona* is simply the "son of John" as in the Fourth Gospel. The parallel to Matt. 10: 34 in Luke 12: 49–51 points to a symbolic meaning for the sword in the former passage, and Luke 22: 38 at least to a limit to any possible armed activity, as also does Luke 22: 51. The interpretation of Matt. 11: 12 and Luke 16: 16 has not been uniformly in terms of the Zealots (nor that of John 10: 8, 18, which Cullmann, *The State in the New Testament*, pp. 21f, has brought into

The claim that the Christian community deliberately falsified the historical figure of Jesus must be rejected: it ignores the evidence in the Pauline epistles, the earliest documents in the New Testament, for a suffering Lord who died for all; it does wholesale violence to the texts of the Gospels and ignores much in the tradition that sets Jesus over against the Zealots.[13] The injunctions "to take up the cross" need not point to a readiness to die as Zealots at Roman hands; although especially associated with the Romans, crucifixion was also used by Jewish rulers. Alexander Jannaeus was claimed to have ordered eight hundred Pharisees to be crucified (Jos., *Antiquities*, XIII. 14. 23). It is best to understand the word cross as a metaphor or symbol for extreme sacrifice. Luke's addition of the word "daily" in 9: 23 supports this symbolic approach. It need not be erased from Jesus' lips in this sense as a later addition of the Church.

Again Matt. 5: 41, "and if any one forces you to go one mile, go with him two miles," which refers to the right of the Roman soldiers to require non-Roman subjects to carry their equipment one mile, is anti-Zealot in its intent: it would be impossible on the lips of a Zealot.[14] So would be Matt. 5: 43–44. When Jesus was told of the slaughter of Galileans by Pilate in the Temple, he did not respond with indignant denunciation of Roman brutality as an extreme nationalist might, but with a warning to his own people to repent (Luke 13: 1–2).[15] He had a tax-collector, a

connection with Matt. 11: 12). The following possible translations of *biazetai* in Matt. 11: 12 are given in Arndt and Gingrich.

1. *Translated as a passive:*
A. in a bad sense *be violently treated, be oppressed* (so the pass. e.g. Thu. 1, 77, 4; Paus. 2, 1, 5 *ta theia biasasthai*; POxy, 294, 16 [AD 22]; Sir 31: 21. —GSchrenk, TWZNT, Vol. I, pp. 608ff; RSV text: *the kingdom has suffered violence*: NEB: has been subjected to violence.
a. through hindrances raised against it (*biazomai* = hinder Jos., *Ant.* 1. 18. 2) It., Vulg., Syr. Sin. and Cur.; Dalman, *Worte*, pp. 113–16; ALoisy; A. Schlatter; MDibelius, *Joh. d. T.* 1911, pp. 26ff: hostile spirits:
b. through the efforts of unauthorized persons to compel its coming BWeiss; JWeiss, D. *Predigt Jesus vom R. Gottes*, 2nd ed., 1900, pp. 192ff; Wlh; HWindisch, *D. mess. krieg*, 1909, p. 35f; HScholander, ZNW, 13, 1912, pp. 172–5. RSV. NEB.
B. 1. in a good sense = *is sought with burning zeal*: HHoltzmann; FDibelius, Schniewind.

2. *Translated intransitively: makes its way with triumphant force:* FCBaur; ThZahn; AHarnack, WBrandt, ZNW, 11, 1910, pp. 247f; ROtto, *Reich Gottes u. Menschensohn*, 1934, pp. 84–8; RSV, NEB, mg. MM and suppl. Schweitzer's view should be noted, *The Quest of the Historical Jesus*, trans., p. 357. "It is the host of penitents which are wringing it from God, so that it may now come at any moment."
[13] I have not ventured a full-scale critique of Brandon's work, because it is not the individual data appealed to, in themselves, that come into question so much as his method of dealing with them. I find myself in agreement with M. Hengel's review in JSS, XIV, 2, 1969, and in his *Was Jesus a Revolutionist?* See also W. Wink, *Union Seminary Quarterly Review*, Vol. xxv, No. 1, Fall 1969, pp. 37–59. J. Jeremias, *New Testament Theology*, New York, 1971, p. 228 n. 2; G. R. Edwards, *Jesus and the Politics of Violence*, New York, 1972, chapter 2, *et passim*.   [14] K. Stendahl, *Peake, ad rem.*
[15] A. Schlatter, *Das Evangelium des Lukas*, Stuttgart, 1960, p. 322, took the Galileans here, possibly, to stand for Zealots. But this is to use the term Zealot as "a party name" prematurely. See n. 3 above.

Quisling, as well as a possible former Zealot, among his disciples, so that he transcended Zealot intolerance (Matt. 9: 9ff; 10: 3). The third temptation to pursue "the kingdoms of this world and the glory of them (Matt. 4: 8, with parallel in Luke 4: 5f)" is rejected by Jesus, a rejection that rules out Zealot activity.[16] Luke 23: 31, "For if they do this when the wood is green, what will happen when it is dry?" has been plausibly claimed to refer to the time when the Zealots would have made Jerusalem politically culpable in the eyes of Rome, a pejorative note against the Zealots being clear.[17] And if the Messianic presentation of Jesus in Mark is unmistakable, it is also true that the Markan Jesus is not so much a nationalist Messiah as a Messiah whose nature was hidden in suffering: he is not a triumphant and militant, but a despised and humiliated figure (Mark 8: 27–34; 9: 12; 10: 33). And, finally, the claim which is under discussion flaunts the fact that the Jerusalem Christians refused to take part in the war against Rome, but fled instead to Pella, and were persecuted by Bar Kochba in the second rebellion.[18]

At this point we must refer to an event that figures most prominently

[16] On the temptations, see T. W. Manson, *The Servant-Messiah*, Cambridge, 1953, pp. 56ff. He traced the story of the temptations of Jesus himself, and with F. C. Grant in *The Economic Background of the Gospels*, London, 1926, p. 126, found their substance to be that: "One after another he [Jesus] rejects the ways proposed by political Messianism; the use of supernatural powers to provide earthly sustenance; the imperialist dreams of world-empire, the sudden, historic appearance of the celestial Messiah in the Temple Court." Jeremias, *New Testament Theology*, pp. 68ff prefers to speak of the trials or ordeals of Jesus, but he also (not as directly as T. W. Manson, nor limiting them to "the allurement of gaining political power and external success," but giving them eschatological significance as "the vanquishing of Satan"), traces them to the experience of Jesus himself. J. Dupont, *Die Versuchung Jesu in der Wüste*, Stuttgart, 1969, after recognizing the redactional work of Matthew and Luke (strangely, he virtually omits Mark from serious discussion), traces the material in Q, which was, indeed, treated parainetically by the Church, to an experience of Jesus himself. These scholars, even Jeremias, who allows the motif of the second Moses to be operative in the temptation to turn stones into bread in the wilderness, do not do justice to the possibility mentioned by D. Daube, *Studies in Biblical Law*, Cambridge, 1947, pp. 24–39, that the sight of the kingdoms of this world has a legal connotation: in showing them to him Satan was virtually giving those kingdoms to Jesus—if he desired them. It is extremely precarious to relate the developed temptation narratives directly to Jesus, but that they reflect aspects of the struggle he faced against espousing a political movement seems to us probable. P. Hoffmann, "Die Versuchungsgeschichte in der Logienquelle: Zur Ausein-andersetzung der Judenchristen mit dem politischen Messianismus," *Biblische Zeitschrift*, N.F., Vol. 13, 1969, pp. 207–223, finds in the Temptation narratives the explanation of the community, which handed them down, why Jesus was not a "political" or "revolutionary" Messiah. The intention of the Zealots to erect a Messianic world empire was a demonic temptation: Christians like Jesus himself had to serve God alone.

[17] G. B. Caird, *Jesus and the Jewish Nation*, Ethel M. Wood Lecture, London, 1965, p. 11. See on this also Cullmann, *The State in the New Testament*, p. 48. He takes the dry wood to refer to the Zealots.

[18] Eusebius, HE, III. 5: 3; IV. 8: 4; Justin, *Apology*, 1. 31. 6. See my article "The Apostolic Age and the Life of Paul," *Peake*, p. 761d; H. J. Schoeps, *Theologie und Geschichte des Judenchristentums*, Tübingen, 1949, pp. 242–247.

in all the Gospels, when a crowd of about four or five thousand people followed Jesus to a solitary place where he had sought not only to rest, but almost certainly to escape from the embarrassment of a popularity which he knew rested on a false understanding of his intention. Out of his compassion and in solidarity with them, Jesus in the presence of the multitudes, by the breaking and blessing of bread, a foreshadowing of the last supper, symbolically enacted his relationship to them as the giver of life. But uncomprehending, the multitudes did not grasp the nature of the life to which he called them. Their intent was political. According to John, Jesus became "aware that they meant to come and seize him to proclaim him a king." A critical situation arose. The Galilean crowds, ever easily moved to rise against Rome, sought to push Jesus into the role of a nationalist, political leader. Jesus deliberately rejected such a role, and as a result many defected from his cause.[19]

And, finally, full weight must be given to certain broad considerations which militate against a Zealot emphasis in Jesus: his avoidance of the self-designations, Messiah and Son of David;[20] the absence of the terminology of holy war (found at Qumran); his emphasis on non-violence (Matt. 5: 38–42 and parallels); his openness to the Samaritans (Luke 10: 25–37; John 4) and to Gentiles (see p. 353); his harsh criticism of worldly authorities (Mark 10: 42, parallel Luke 22: 25; compare 13: 32); his judgment upon the Temple and his anticipation that it would be superseded, which certainly ran counter to the understanding of the Temple among Zealots. This last point, in view of what we wrote above about the relationship between the land and the Temple, requires attention. We find in the cleansing of the Temple Jesus' symbolic enactment of his judgment upon the people of God and his hope for them, a hope including the Gentiles. Despite Matthew's change of Mark 11: 17 in 21: 15, by which he omits: "to all the nations," we adhere to this view. The fact

[19] See especially John 6: 60–67; compare Mark 9: 42–50; Matt. 18: 23–35; Luke 11: 37–54. See Manson, *The Servant-Messiah*, pp. 69ff; C. H. Dodd, *The Founder of Christianity*, 1970, pp. 131ff; R. H. Fuller, *A Critical Introduction to the New Testament*, London, 1966, p. 80. On the nature of the feeding of the five thousand, see H. Montefiore, "Revolt in the Desert," NTS, Vol. 8, Pt. II, 1962, pp. 135–141. The Transfiguration also has been understood as a rejection of military Messianism, see H. Baltensweiler, *Die Verklärung Jesu*, Zurich, 1959, pp. 87ff, *AZTANT*, Vol. 33.

[20] Compare Jeremias, *New Testament Theology*, pp. 228, 258; G. Bornkamm, *Jesus of Nazareth*, trans. 1960, pp. 169ff. The omission of "to all the nations" in the cleansing of the Temple in Matthew and Luke has been explained as due to: (1) the use by both of a Markan text different from ours; (2) the tendency of both to reduce the Markan narrative; (3) in the case of Matthew reservation of the emphasis on the Gentiles till 28: 16–20. If the location of the cleansing in the court of the Gentiles be taken seriously, such theories are not needed. For the difference in the treatment of the Temple in Mark, Matthew, and Luke, see R. Dowda, *The Temple in the Synoptic Gospels*, unpublished dissertation, Duke University, 1972.

that Luke omits the phrase also should make us chary of pressing its omission in Matt. 21: 15. In our view the very location of the cleansing in the Court of the Gentiles indicates in Matthew, Luke, and Mark that it bears upon "all nations." Not the geographic Temple but the community of God's people mattered to Jesus.

Similarly, care is needed in assessing the implications of the form of Jesus' death by Roman crucifixion, and the evidence of the Gospels about his trial. The question of the respective roles of the Jewish and Roman authorities in the trial of Jesus is too complex for examination or documentation here. There is an increasing tendency to emphasize the role of the Romans and to question the historicity of the trial before the High Priest. That the Romans probably saw in Jesus a nationalist rebel is suggested by the nature of the questions to which his opponents, Jewish and Roman, subjected him: the former would naturally be concerned to ask questions which might lead him to compromise himself with the Romans. In Mark 14: 61, the High Priest's question is understandable if the Jewish authorities were seeking to establish grounds for a Jewish condemnation; Mark 15: 2, Pilate's question, needs to be compared to John 18: 33f; and Mark 12: 13ff, the question on tax-paying, with Luke 20: 19ff. Mark's collocation of Pharisees and Herodians is important here (see O. Cullmann, *The State in the New Testament*, p. 35). The coincidence of the crucifixion of Jesus with that of Barabbas, a rebel, points to the way in which the Romans looked at the former Mark 15: 7 (this is discussed by M. Hengel, in *Was Jesus a Revolutionist?*). For the Romans, Jesus, like Barabbas, seems to have been a Zealot; and, although doubts have been expressed as to the historicity of the episode concerning Barabbas, especially by P. Winter in *On the Trial of Jesus*, Ber'in, 1961, the *titulus* placed above the cross seems to prove this. But when all has been admitted that points to the Roman estimate of Jesus as a Zealot, the simple fact also remains that at no point according to the Gospels did Jesus admit the Roman accusation. Neither before the High Priest nor before Pilate did Jesus, according to the tradition, *unequivocally* accept such kingship as the Romans implied him to claim, and we have already indicated that, however conceived, his role was not to inflict, but to endure suffering.

To sum up: the value of the work of those who have emphasized the Zealots[21] is that it compels the recognition of burning nationalism in first-

---

[21] Especially W. R. Farmer, *Maccabees, Zealots and Josephus, An Inquiry into Jewish Nationalism in the Graeco-Roman Period*, 1956; and M. Hengel, *Die Zeloten*, Leiden, 1961. On the details concerning the role of Rome in the trial, the *titulus*, Barabbas etc., see P. Winter, *On the trial of Jesus*, Berlin, 1961.

century Judaism. Jesus' ministry was conducted in an atmosphere of great tensions. He was constantly in contact with nationalists and, we must assume, fully aware of the seduction of their appeal. He withstood that appeal. But, if he rejected the nationalist movement, how did he come to terms with the political realities of his day? That the Gospel tradition has undergone a process of depoliticization has to be recognized. Mark and Luke, especially, reveal a tendency to decrease any possible tension that may have existed between Jesus and Rome.[22] On the other hand, political factors which might have loomed large during the actual ministry of Jesus would soon have lost their interest for the churches within which the Gospels emerged, which were largely Hellenistic and removed in time and space from the Palestine of Jesus' day, so that there may have been political dimensions in the ministry of Jesus which were minimized or overlooked or misunderstood in our Gospels.[23] Nor should the fear of anachronism oppress us. It has been suggested that our twentieth-century political involvement and concern should not be allowed to mislead us to think that a first-century figure such as Jesus would necessarily share such concern and involvement: the peril of modernizing Jesus is real. But to this we can only reply that such a suggestion should be allowed only as a warning, not as a norm: we cannot completely anachronize Jesus either.

What do the texts themselves reveal about Jesus and politics? Two positions have to be noted which are almost diametrically opposed.

First, the view has recently been powerfully expressed by Bornkamm that, although he was intensely involved in the human condition, and despite the political passions of his times, "it is most astonishing and remarkable that political problems should take second place in Jesus' preaching."[24] And again, "Not a word does Jesus say either to confirm or renew the national hopes of his people."[25] The reason given for this is "without any doubt the expectation of the approaching reign of God."[26]

[22] See Winter, *On the Trial of Jesus*, on the gospel tradition and its tendentiousness in this connection.

[23] Jeremias, *New Testament Theology*, pp. 71f, rightly makes much of this in discussing the trials of Jesus. He writes: "Now we can say with absolute certainty that this temptation of a political messiahship simply did not exist for the early church. It never thought for a moment of being a movement with political aims. The question of a political Messiah has no 'Sitz im Leben' in the early church. On the other hand, it was a burning issue in the lifetime of Jesus, not only for the disciples, who came from Galilee, the home of the Zealot movement, and had at least one Zealot among their number, but also for Jesus himself. This political temptation, which brought with it the possibility of avoiding the way of suffering, accompanied Jesus like a shadow throughout his whole ministry. Thus the nucleus of the temptation story goes back to a *pre-Easter* tradition."   [24] Bornkamm, *Jesus of Nazareth*, p. 61.
[25] *Ibid.*, p. 66.   [26] *Ibid.*, p. 121.

"All the conceptions and pictures in Jesus' message are directed with concentrated force on one thing only, and are contained in that one thing —that God will reign."[27]

The obvious retort to this is that in one passage at least, "Render to Caesar the things that are Caesar's *and to God the things that are God's* (Mark 12: 17)," a directly political concern does come to the surface. Jeremias finds in this passage what we may call a negative political concern. Here Jesus, under pressure to take the Zealot line, that is, to repudiate taxes to Rome, rejects the Zealot view that by hostility to the Roman State and the furtherance of its collapse, by the refusal, among other things, to pay taxes, God's will would be furthered. He prefers to allow God himself, in his own time, to bring about that collapse, and so does not forbid the payment of taxes to the pagan State. This is also the import of Mark 4: 26–29, the parable of the seed growing by itself: men are to wait with patience. Jesus was a quietist.[28]

Bornkamm goes a little further and seems not to find even a negative political attitude here, but one of indifference. For him the second half of Mark 12: 17, italicized above, has all the weight, and just because of this the first half has its weight taken from it.

This means that the question concerning the Caesar tax, taken so seriously and put so provocatively by [Jesus'] opponents, is put in the margin. It is certainly not declared unimportant or to be left to the whim of the individual, but it is, nevertheless, dismissed as a question which has been long ago decided. Not decided, however, is the question of the meaning of "Render to God the things that are God's." This means: the coin belongs to Caesar but you to God. Probably it contains an even more specific thought: the coin which bears the image of Caesar, we owe to Caesar. We, however, as men who bear the image of God, owe ourselves to God. This is not meant as a timeless general proposition, but is to be considered, like all Jesus' teaching, in the light of the coming kingdom of God, which is already present in Jesus' words and deeds and has begun to realise itself. Through this interpretation of "Render unto God the things that are God's," the other part receives the meaning of a temporary, interim obligation, soon to end. For the reign of Caesar passes, but God's reign comes and does not pass away.[29]

For Bornkamm, therefore, the entire problem of the State is relegated by Jesus to the margin of things, indeed it is not allowed to come to the

[27] *Ibid.*, p. 67.
[28] *New Testament Theology*, pp. 228f and 122ff. By and large he agrees with Bornkamm here: "That man belongs to the reign of God also determines his political views."
[29] *Jesus of Nazareth*, pp. 122f.

surface. And this is "a very important word on the whole matter. For this means that because God reigns, the hearer is set free from a basic concern as to this *supposed* problem (our italics)." When we ask what Bornkamm understands Jesus to have meant by the reign of God, we are pointed to the ministry of Jesus himself, but not to any details about the future, national or otherwise.[30]

A Jewish scholar found the same a-political stance in the ministry of Jesus as do Bornkamm and Jeremias. To Joseph Klausner the attitude of Jesus to the Law, and *ipso facto* to the State, threatened the national existence; it was anarchistic.[31] The Law, it cannot be sufficiently emphasized, was inextricably bound up with the land and with the "culture" of Jews: it was the means of national as well as religious integration. Rightly or wrongly, the Pharisees and others sensed that Jesus' attitude to the Law involved the destruction of the Jewish people as a people. Klausner's words are noteworthy:

The Judaism of that time, however, had no other aim than to save the tiny nation, the guardian of great ideals, from sinking into the broad sea of heathen culture and enable it, slowly and gradually, to realize the moral teaching of the Prophets in civil life and in the present world of the Jewish state and nation. Hence the nation as a whole could only see in such public ideals as those of Jesus an abnormal and dangerous phantasy; the majority, who followed the Scribes and Pharisees (The Tannaim), the leaders of the popular party, could on no account accept Jesus's teaching. This teaching Jesus had absorbed from the breast of Prophetic, and, to a certain extent, Pharisaic Judaism; yet it became, on the one hand, the negation of everything that had vitalized Judaism, and, on the other hand, it brought Judaism to such an extreme that it became, in a sense, non-Judaism.[32]

Behind these words is the insistence that Jesus was extreme—extreme in his concern for the lost; in his refusal to be bound by traditional religious usages and forms such as tithing and the Sabbath; in his over-emphasis on the disposition behind an act; in his strictures on the weaknesses of the "religious"; in his refusal to emphasize the distinctions between the virtuous and the sinful.[33] This characteristic of the teaching of Jesus—its extremism—was connected with his conviction that a new order had dawned in which the traditional forms were no longer central.[34] Jesus

[30] *Ibid.*, p. 67.   [31] *Jesus of Nazareth*, trans. 1925.   [32] *Ibid.*, p. 29.
[33] These items are so familiar as to need no documentation. But it should not be overlooked that the so-called extremism of Jesus can itself be overemphasized. For a corrective, see SSM, p. 434.
[34] See the rich chapter in D. R. A. Hare, *The Theme of Jewish Persecution of Christians in the Gospel According to St. Matthew*, Cambridge, 1967, pp. 1–18.

inevitably offended the sobriety and realism of Judaism (*mutatis mutandis*, Baeck urged the same of Paul).[35] To follow the absolute demands and extreme emphases of Jesus would spell the end of the nation. He was beyond politics—the art of which is compromise—and, therefore, invited anarchy. Thus, although Klausner and Bornkamm draw different conclusions from this—the former finding in it a threat to the very existence of the nation and the latter the mark of being free to God—they both discover in Jesus an indifference to political considerations and realities.

Secondly, on the other hand, the ministry of Jesus has been understood as concerned throughout with presenting a political challenge to the nation of Israel. This has recently been urged by G. B. Caird.[36] At the risk of doing his position an injustice through excessive brevity, we may summarize it as follows. Beginning with the interpretation of John the Baptist's ministry as a summons to a national movement of repentance, Caird insists that Jesus was baptized by John because he "recognized the national character of John's summons to repentance and accepted his own involvement in the national life of his people."[37] He then asserts: "But this is to say that from the outset of his ministry Jesus was concerned with questions of national policy: What does it mean to be the Chosen *Nation* [our italics] of God? How can Israel preserve her character as the holy nation in a world overrun and controlled by pagans? What must Israel do if at God's winnowing she is to prove wheat and not chaff?"[38] The extreme urgency with which the disciples were sent out on their missionary tour (Matt. 10) arose from Jesus' belief that "Israel was at the cross-roads, that she must choose between two conceptions of her national destiny, and that the time for choice was horrifyingly short."[39] Jesus expected a mass, national response to this mission: he criticized his generation for not being able to read the signs of the times (Luke 12: 56): he regarded his generation, indeed, as being "in imminent danger of being the last in Israel's history."[40] It was the purpose of Jesus to bring

[35] See his *Judaism and Christianity*, Philadelphia, 1958, pp. 161ff, 177, and especially, pp. 196ff.

[36] *Jesus and the Jewish Nation*, London, 1965. The difference between the interpretations of Bornkamm and Caird goes back, ultimately, to radically different estimates of the degree to which the Gospels are historically oriented or historically illuminating. But Jeremias, who shares much of Caird's outlook, still offers an interpretation close to that of Bornkamm. Cullmann does more justice to the ambiguity of Jesus' position, but fails to do justice to the same ambiguity in Pharisaism, which he treats, too uncritically, as confusing the State and the Jewish congregation (*The State in the New Testament*, p. 10). It is not strictly true that "In view of their [the Pharisees'] theocratic ideal, they had to renounce the State unreservedly." The matter was not so simple. See n. 54 and text. Jesus was nearer the Pharisees than Cullmann allows.

[37] *Jesus and the Jewish Nation*, p. 7.

[38] *Ibid.*, p. 7.

[39] *Ibid.*, p. 8.

[40] *Ibid.*, pp. 9f.

into existence the restored nation of Israel promised in the Old Testament prophecies, a restoration that would be accompanied by the inclusion of the Gentiles in the Kingdom of God. The baptism at the hand of John, the choice of the Twelve, symbolizing the twelve tribes of Israel, constituting the little flock—a word used in the Old Testament to denote the Israel of the Messianic age (Micah 5: 4; Is. 40: 11; Ezek. 34: 12–24)—these point to the purpose indicated. Similarly the triumphal entry into Jerusalem and the cleansing of the Temple "are best interpreted as symbolic preaching, like the symbolic acts of the ancient prophets, by which Jesus was making his last appeal to the city not to sign the death warrant which would be both his and hers."[41] In the same light are we to understand Jesus' predictions of the fall of Jerusalem and the destruction of the Temple, which are both regarded as the direct consequence of the rejection of Jesus' preaching: Caird finds in the fall of Jerusalem in A.D. 70 the vindication of the cause of Jesus, "an open demonstration that Jesus was right and the nation was wrong."[42]

Bornkamm and Caird present clear conclusions: for the former, Jesus shelved the politics of his day: for the latter, Jesus issued a direct national, political challenge. But such clarity in dealing with the actualities of life is always suspect: it cloaks the perplexities. Bornkamm has too much separated the rule of God from the actualities of the communal life of the Jewish people and reduced it to an individual dimension, even though he does recognize that Jesus gathered a community around himself.[43] Caird too easily equates the Jewish community addressed by Jesus with a nation and the will of God with the slings and arrows of history, so that—over against Bornkamm—the eschatological language of Jesus becomes for him, as apparently for Jenni whom he quotes, a way of interpreting the national present and future. "'Eschatology' in the broader sense refers to a future in which the circumstances of history are changed to such an extent that one can speak of a new, entirely different, state of things, without in so doing, necessarily leaving the framework of history."[44] Bornkamm has sacrificed the communal dimension of the Kingdom of God to an exaggerated individualism; Caird has sacrificed the personal and transcendent dimensions of the Kingdom to an exaggerated politico-national concern. Is there a means of interpreting the data to which both Bornkamm and Caird point without endorsing either of their polarities?

---

[41] *Ibid.*, p. 16. [42] *Ibid.*, p. 20.

[43] *Jesus of Nazareth*, p. 186. Bornkamm, however, insists that the Church began not during the ministry, but at the Resurrection. See his rich chapter on "Discipleship," pp. 144ff.

[44] *Jesus and the Jewish Nation, ad rem.*

On one thing most interpreters are agreed: Jesus *was* concerned to gather a community of people to share in his ministry. It is in assessing the nature of this community that differences arise. Perhaps the chief difficulty arises from the use of the word "nation." It was not to the nation of Israel that Jesus sent his disciples, but "to *the lost sheep* of the house of Israel (Matt. 10: 6, our italics)," that is, of the *people* of Israel. It is impossible to rule out Jesus' concern with his own people, but it is a concern with his own people not as constituting a national entity—a Chosen Nation, as Caird designates it—over whose political destiny as such he agonized, but with his own people as intended to be the "Israel" of God and, therefore, as the matrix within which he could hope to reconstitute the Chosen People, "Israel," that is, to create the community of the People of God. This was the meaning of his call of the Twelve, of his friendship with the lost, his shunning of the title "Messiah," and his rejection of the "Kingship" of a political kind in John 6: such a political office was not for Jesus. On his entry into Jerusalem, it was the court of the Gentiles in the Temple that he cleansed.[45] His challenge was a religious

---

[45] In view of the ease with which Judaism passed from the land and the city to the Temple, the cleansing of the Temple assumes central importance for our purposes. It is difficult to think that there was no cleansing. The following interpretations of it have been given. 1. It was dictated by an anti-cultic attitude on the part of Jesus, such as has often been ascribed to the prophets of the Old Testament. E. C. Hoskyns, *The Fourth Gospel*, London, 1940, p. 194, who cites Is. 1: 11–17; Jer. 7: 22; Hos. 5: 6; 8: 13; Amos 4: 4–5; D. E. Nineham, *The Gospel of St. Mark*, Baltimore, 1963, pp. 300–301; A. Caldecott, "The Significance of the Cleansing of the Temple," JTS, Vol. 24, 1923, p. 384. But the attitude of Old Testament prophets to the cultus was not simply antagonistic, and Matt. 5: 23–24 and Acts 2: 46 become inexplicable on such a view of Jesus. 2. The cleansing simply points to the burning zeal for the honour of his Father of a rural puritan reformer, attacking the entrenched, Temple "establishment"—money-making, aristocratic, priestly (J. Schmid, *The Gospel According to Mark*, trans. K. Condon, New York, 1968, p. 209). 3. The cleansing was directed against the economic oppression of the Temple, which was a banking centre. Jesus was, in short, a first-century Robin Hood. (Victor Eppstein, "The Historicity of the Gospel Account of the Cleansing of the Temple," ZNW, Vol. 55, no. 1–2, 1964, pp. 42–58; Étienne Trocmé, "L'expulsion des marchands du Temple," NTS, Vol. 15, 1968, pp. 1–22; N. Q. Hamilton, "The Temple Cleansing and Temple Bank," JBL, Vol. 83, 1964, pp. 365–372. J. Jeremias shows that the Temple was also a business colony, see *Jerusalem in the Time of Jesus*, trans. T. H. and C. H. Cave, Philadelphia, 1969, pp. 33f., 49, 55ff. For the temple as a depository for money, see 1 Kings 7: 51; 2 Kings 18: 15; especially 2 Macc. 3: 6, 10, 11.) 4. The cleansing was a military action of a political revolutionary character. J. Carmichael, *The Death of Jesus*, New York, 1962, pp. 131–133, contends that Jesus entered Jerusalem with a group of armed men and forcibly seized the Temple. But there is no evidence for this (compare E. Trocmé, *Revue d'Histoire et de Philosophie Religieuses*, Vol. 44, 1964, pp. 245–251; S. E. Johnson, *Mark*, New York, 1960, p. 189). Brandon, *Jesus and the Zealots*, pp. 350ff, finds that the entry of Jesus into Jerusalem, the arming of the disciples, and the cleansing of the Temple point to "a carefully planned demonstration by Jesus of his assumption of Messiahship after the manner of Judas of Galilee." Compare pp. 8f, 237, 252, 324, 330ff, 342f. But Brandon is not consistent. He concedes, on p. 338, that the cleansing is an act of prophetic symbolism. 5. At the extreme opposite to Brandon stood Cecil Roth. He interpreted the cleansing in terms

one.[46] The prediction of the fall of the Temple points to the need to replace it, not by a new political policy, but by a new way of religion and a new community to embody it. Similarly Jesus went to Jerusalem not—

of Zech. 9–14. According to him the term "trader" in Zech. 14:21b is $K^ena^{'a}ni$, "Canaanite." This verse then, (And there shall no longer be a trafficer [Canaanite] in the house of the Lord of hosts on that day) may have been used to justify the exclusion of Gentiles from the inner court of the temple under pain of death (Jos. *Jewish Wars*, V: 5; *Antiquities*, XV: 11). There were nationalistically minded Jews who would exclude the Gentiles completely from the Temple and thought that in Messianic times there would be no Gentiles in it. This would ensure the permanence of the Temple. See 4Q Flor. 1: 3–6; J. M. Allegro, "Fragments of a Qumran Scroll of Eschatological Midrashim," JBL, Vol. 77, 1958, pp. 350–354. The term λῃστής in the phrase σπήλαιον λῃστῶν, Roth takes to mean either, in the light of the LXX and Apocrypha, "a den of brigands" or, in the light of Josephus and Strabo, "a cave of Zealots." The Temple had become a Zealot stronghold. Zealots, in Roth's view, had probably taken over the Temple and made it a nationalist centre. Jesus was opposed to this: he wanted a house of prayer for all nations (see Cecil Roth, "The Zealots in the War of 66–73," JSS, Vol. 4, 1959, pp. 332–355; G. W. Buchanan, "Mk. 1: 15–19; Brigands in the Temple," HUCA, Vol. 30, 1959, pp. 169–171; Vol. 31, 1960, pp. 103–105). 6. E. Schweizer, *The Good News According to Mark*, trans. Richmond, Va., 1970, p. 231, barely admits that "the story of the cleansing of the temple must be based upon some historical act of Jesus," but, as we shall see, offers what seems to us a satisfactory interpretation of its meaning. What that meaning was we seek to answer in the next note.

[46] (1) The importance of the event is seen in Matthew, Mark, and John. In Mark it was the decisive act which caused the chief priests and scribes to plot against Jesus (11: 18, compare 14: 1). In Matthew and Mark we can trace a progression in Jesus' ministry from Galilee to Jerusalem, to the Temple complex (*to hieron*), and then to the innermost shrine (*ho naos*). Reference to the Temple first occurs in Mark 11: 11. From there to 14: 39 Jesus acts in the Temple complex. After 14: 39 attention fixes on the shrine (*naos*) itself. In the Fourth Gospel the cleansing is the very second sign of Jesus. There is less emphasis on the cleansing in Luke. (For all this, see R. H. Lightfoot, *The Gospel Message of St. Mark*, Oxford, 1950, p. 60ff; on Luke, p. 69.) (2) In the Synoptics and John the centre of the action is the Court of the Gentiles, not the *naos* as such. On *to hieron* and *ho naos*, see Gottlob Schrenk, TDNT, trans. G. W. Bromiley, Grand Rapids, 1964, Vol. iii, pp. 222ff; on the distinction between them, G. Dalman, *Sacred Sites and Ways*, trans. P. P. Levertoff, New York, 1935, p. 285. He urged that: "The Jerusalem sanctuary is always *to hieron* in the Gospels as distinct from the actual temple within it, which was *ho naos*. ... It would be a good thing to restore the distinction. It is topographically indispensable." But Schrenk, TDNT, p. 235, and O. Michel, TDNT, Vol. IV, p. 882, do not find such a distinction between the two terms. See Matt. 27: 5; and possibly John 2: 20. Matt. 27: 5 certainly seems to contradict Dalman's view. But in forty-two other cases where *naos* occurs in the New Testament that view seems to be justified. Certain phenomena suggest that New Testament writers used *hieron* (temple) and *naos* (shrine) very consciously. Despite the widespread use of *hieron* for temple in Greek, and of the adjective *hieros* in much Jewish literature (1, 2, 4 Macc., Josephus, Philo), both noun and adjective are seldom used in the LXX, because, Schrenk suggests, their pagan cultic associations were undesirable to the translators, as the adjective was to New Testament writers also (Schrenk). Although the use of *hieron* by both Josephus and Philo would seem to militate against Schrenk's view, TDNT, 233–234, the New Testament frequently uses *hieron* to refer to the whole temple complex. Why were the New Testament writers free to use a word of which the LXX was chary? The answer may be that in the Church, which is always called *naos* (shrine) in contexts where the language of the cultus is used in the New Testament, they saw that the Jerusalem Temple (*hieron*) was superseded and could now be grouped with other pagan shrines as belonging to the old order. It is, indeed, possible that an intentional depreciation of the Temple (*hieron*) is involved in the use of that term.

A Jewish scholar, S. Zeitlin, "There was no Court of the Gentiles in the Temple Area," JQR, Vol. 56, 1965, p. 88, holds the view the title of his article indicates. But his view is not as Caird holds—to issue a challenge to a political decision—although this might, nay, would be ultimately implied—on the part of the nation (there

to be followed, and it is generally agreed that the cleansing took place in that court, although it is not named in the New Testament. See Jos., *Contra Apionem* 2: 8, "outer portico"; Philo, *Virtutibus et Legatione ad Caium*, 31 (Loeb, p. 111). For the stele bearing the prohibition against Gentiles entering the sanctuary, see A. M. Rabello, *Christian News From Israel*, Vol. XXI, Pt I, no. 3, 1970, pp. 28ff, on "The Lex de Templo Hierosolymitano"; it was set up according to Rabello during the *construction* of the Herodian Temple by Herod himself to avoid any compromising accidents during that period. Bickerman has shown that "A pagan visitor had no reason to be offended in finding himself excluded from the holy ground. In all ancient religions there were sancta inaccessible to the profane crowd and separated by a rail of wood or stone"; see E. Bickerman, "The Warning Inscriptions of Herod's Temple," JQR, Vol. 37, 1947, pp. 387–405. See further, Lloyd Gaston, *No Stone on Another*, Leiden, 1970, p. 87. To do full justice to this fact demands that the action of Jesus be understood as concerned with the right of, and the hopes of Judaism for, the Gentiles as with the Temple itself. Jesus acted both to judge the community that had slighted the rights of Gentiles in its supreme sanctuary (see especially S. E. Johnson, *Mark*) and to point forward to a better, larger community. (Compare B. Gärtner, *The Temple and the Community in Qumran and the New Testament*, Cambridge, 1965, pp. 107–108.)

This twofold dimension of the cleansing is traceable in two ways.

First, in the sayings attributed to Jesus. It is impossible to assert with any certainty what Jesus' words on the Temple were. But that he did utter a warning seems clear. This warning in Mark 14: 58 is placed on the lips of his opponents. "We heard him say, 'I will throw down this Temple made with hands' (NEB)." Compare with this John 2: 19: "Destroy this Temple . . .and in three days I will raise it again." John makes it clear that "the temple he was speaking of was his body (2: 21)," that is, probably "the Church." Here a lengthy quotation from Schweizer, *The Good News*, p. 329, on Mark 14: 58 is in order:

> Evidently Mark also interpreted the saying in this way. Whether we should attribute the same view to Jesus (since it seems likely that the promise to build a new temple originated with him) depends upon how we evaluate his other sayings. As early as the first century A.D., Ethiopian Enoch 90: 28–36 (cf. Jub. 1: 17, 27f) expected the destruction of the old temple and the building of a heavenly temple (in contrast to Rev. 21: 22). Accordingly, we may suspect that Jesus was referring to the Kingdom of God when he spoke of the new temple. However, since he emphasized time and again the great significance of God's offer and his demand in the present time (cf. 8: 38, et al.), it is more likely that he was thinking of his disciples as a new Israel called by God to obedience. In a way that is similar to Jesus' many sayings about the law (2: 1–3: 6, 7), the saying about the temple which is included here opposes that complacent security which presumes that possession of the temple and proper observation of the cult are a guarantee of salvation. Salvation can be anticipated only as a gift of grace which comes from God's new order. Since it includes the obedience of discipleship, salvation can be expected only within the fellowship of Jesus' disciples. When interpreted this way, the saying corresponds with Jesus' action in 11: 15–19, and especially with the Markan interpretation which regards that action as the opening of the door to the Gentile world. Another typical feature found in this saying is the fact that Jesus does away with complacent and secure temple religion but does not deny that the temple was God's good gift and must continue to exist as a spiritual temple along with the "cult" that must be practiced in it (Rom. 12: 1f).

This view seems to us justified. M. Hengel, *Was Jesus a Revolutionist?*, pp. 15ff is difficult to understand clearly. He rightly emphasizes that had the cleansing been a highly noticeable, violent act such as is implied in some of the views indicated above, the Roman cohort of five to six hundred men, stationed at the tower of Antonia in the N.W. corner of the Temple area with which it was connected by a staircase, would have intervened. He also rightly notes the "exaggeration" in the account of Mark and further in John, where alone the sellers of oxen and other large animals are mentioned. For him, the cleansing is not an act of rebellion but a prophetic protest against the traders in the Temple and the Temple aristocracy. But he then goes on to find the clue to the event in the quotation from Jer. 7: 11 in Mark 11: 17b, although he takes it to be a later interpretation by the Church (compare R. Bultmann,

would be a certain unreality in such a challenge when we recall that it was the Romans who had political control), but to offer to Jerusalem a chance to hear his challenge for the creation of a community of God. He did not address himself to Roman leaders: it is no accident that the Gospels nowhere mention the capital and residence of Herod, that is, Tiberias, called after the Roman Emperor Tiberius, and that Jesus' reference to Herod as that "fox (Luke 13: 32)" suggests distance from him, not anxiety to appeal to him. So, too, Jesus did not confront the religious leaders or the authorities among his own people. The aim of Jesus was neither non-political nor directly political: rather, it was focused on the creation of a community worthy of the name of the people of God within Israel. This community was to be governed by selfless service alone: it stands in sharp contrast to those existing political entities, national or imperial, in which the ignoble ambition to assume and exercise authority prevailed. "And Jesus called them to him and said to them, 'You know that those who are supposed to rule over the Gentiles lord it over them, and their great men exercise authority over them. But it shall not be so

Synoptic Tradition, trans. Oxford, 1968, pp. 36, 56), perhaps to be connected with the Hellenists (compare Acts 6: 13f). Finally, he concludes that "the symbolic action of Jesus and his word of warning declared the eschatological end of the temple altogether. In this case, the account which is more recent from the standpoint of tradition history, John 2: 13–19, best conveys the original theological intention [of Jesus]" (*Was Jesus a Revolutionist?*, p. 17, nn. 55, 56). The steps by which Hengel reaches this conclusion are tortuous, but his dismissal of the cleansing as an act of political rebellion (it may have involved—it seems to us—a very mild or minor act of civil disobedience which attracted no attention from the guardian soldiers) is valid, as is his refusal to see in references to the swords a revolutionary intent.

Secondly, the setting given to the cleansing in Mark and John confirms that it is a warning to the people of Israel, in symbolic action, such as was customary among the prophets (Jer. 13: 1ff; 19: 1ff; 27: 2; 1 Chron. 18: 10). For the setting in John enables us to take the cleansing to denote the passing of an old order and the advent of a new (see pp. 289ff). In Mark the Cleansing, 11: 15–18, is set within the framework of the cursing of the fig tree (11: 12–14 and 11: 19f) in typically Markan "sandwich" manner. The fig tree stands for the people of Israel: it is now under God's judgment. That the fig tree can represent Israel, although the vine is the more usual symbol for it (Is. 5: 7; Ps. 80: 8–14; see J. P. Brown, "The Mediterranean Vocabulary of the Vine," VT, Vol. 19, 1969, pp. 146–170), appears from Hosea 9: 10; Jer. 24; 29: 17, where the fig trees destroyed are associated with judgment. See also Micah 7: 16 (MT not LXX), and the use of this in Mishnah Sotah 9: 9, 15. (Bowman's attempt to find in the cursing of the fig tree the blasting of the Jewish messianic hopes of his time by Jesus is not convincing. He writes: "He is signifying to His disciples that the Jewish view of the New Exodus and the Messianic Age which was to see the fig tree putting forth its figs, in the light of Song of Songs Rabbah 11. 13 [compare Exod. Rabbah XV on Exod. 12: 1ff] is not to be"; John Bowman, *The Gospel of Mark: The New Christian Jewish Haggadah*, Leiden, 1965, pp. 221–222. Surely Jesus was expecting the fig tree to bear fruit according to the story.)

The undeniable concern of Jesus with the Gentiles is consonant with this judgmental aspect of the cleansing. See now David Daube, *Civil Disobedience in Antiquity*, Edinburgh, 1972, pp. 101ff. He regards the cleansing of the Temple as an act of civil disobedience, amounting to sedition, "emasculated" by scholars (p. 103). Unfortunately it arrived too late for discussion here.

among you; but whoever would be great among you must be your servant, and whoever would be first among you must be slave of all. For the Son of man also came not to be served but to serve, and to give his life as a ransom for many' (Mark 10: 42–45)."

The activity of Jesus, then, was not aimed directly at changing any national policy, but, by teaching, preaching, and healing, at creating a community—not a nation—"aware of the presence of God as an urgent reality" and at inducing "them to give the appropriate response, so that they might become effectively members of the new people of God which was coming into being."[47] This explains two other frequently discussed aspects of his ministry. First, his intense concern with individuals.[48] The disciples whom he called were challenged to a personal decision: insofar as they committed themselves personally to him and accepted his demands, the people of God was being formed. And, secondly, Jesus' assertions that, after the new people of God had emerged in Israel, there would also be an incursion of Gentiles into it. Jesus confined his mission to the people of Israel: his dealings with Gentiles were peripheral: even when he left the borders of "Israel" he only visited outposts of Israelite population.[49] But at the same time he rejected any idea of a divine vengeance on the enemies of Israel,[50] and included Gentiles in salvation and contemplated that the distinction between Jew and Gentile would finally disappear.[51] Not political organization and policy were his concern, but human community, loving and serving and ultimately inclusive.

In the complex scene of first-century Judaism it was easy even for Jesus' own followers to confuse such a concern with community as we have ascribed to Jesus, expressed in terms of the Kingdom of God, with that of the extreme nationalists. But, as we have seen, Jesus differed in

[47] C. H. Dodd, *The Founder of Christianity*, 1970, pp. 81ff.

[48] See T. W. Manson, *Jesus and the Non-Jews*, The Ethel M. Wood Lecture, Athlone Press, London, 1955, and compare R. Bultmann's emphasis on decision in his *Jesus and the Word*, New York, 1934, and *Theology*, New York, 1951, Vol. 11, pp. 9ff; Hengel, *Was Jesus a Revolutionist?*, p. 27, who points out again how Jesus' parabolic method of teaching, unlike methods designed to appeal to the masses, is "unemotional, . . . rational . . . scarcely usable by demagogues. Jesus seeks genuine agreement and appeals primarily to the conscience of the individual. . . ."

[49] See J. Jeremias, *Jesus' Promise to the Nations*, trans., London, 1958, p. 35, and references to the work of A. Alt.

[50] *Ibid.*, pp. 41ff, points out the many passages in which Jesus "detaches the nationalistic idea of revenge from the hope of redemption."

[51] Matt. 8: 11. Were it not for such a passage and the evidence provided by Jeremias concerning Jesus' concern with the Gentiles, it would be tempting to find Jesus sharing in the doctrine of the land which we traced. On the "duality" of Jesus' conduct and thought and its significance for our problem, see O. Cullmann, *Jesus and the Revolutionaries*, New York, 1970, pp. 1–15.

purpose and method from them. The Gospels record no direct confrontation between Jesus and nationalists. Clearly, even if the contemporaries of Jesus mistook him for a "nationalist," early Christians generally did not, and had no interest in preserving any traditions of encounters between Jesus and the Zealots: it is difficult to imagine that no such encounters took place.[52]

It is otherwise with the Pharisees, the encounters of Jesus with the Pharisees recorded in the Gospels are numerous. There were Pharisees who had a not wholly dissimilar aim to that of Jesus. Hillel,[53] for example, stands out over against the extreme nationalists and the contemporary rulers of Jerusalem. He rejected Herod's state and strove to build a community of people devoted to the Torah and to peace. This community of the Pharisees differed radically from that gathered by Jesus. The Pharisaic community was centred on the Torah and on the present, and lacked the eschatological dimension of that of Jesus; but, in its concentration on community rather than political organization, Pharisaism offers an illuminating parallel to the concern of Jesus. This parallel is not to be pressed to the end: the Law with which Pharisaism occupied itself was, as we saw, the Law of the land: the ideal community which it contemplated was ultimately, in principle, inseverable from the land. Probably—nay certainly—Jesus, too, knew the love of his native land, but his concentration on a loving, universal community suggests that the land itself played a minor part in his mind. What is the evidence? Only in four passages is it possible that the question of the land directly emerges.

[52] Perhaps encounters between nationalists and Jesus in Gospels written after A.D. 70 have been transformed into encounters between Jesus and others, such as the Pharisees. It should be noted that it is possible even to exaggerate the role of extreme nationalists in Jerusalem: anti-Zealots were very strong in Jerusalem. For a critique of Brandon at this point, see Hengel, JSS, vol. XIV, No. 2, p. 239.

[53] See N. Glatzer, *Hillel the Elder*, New York, 1966, pp. 63ff, on "Community vs. State." It is not to be overlooked that in the Gospels, especially in Matthew, the role of the Pharisees as such is emphasized: they have ascribed to them controversies which, probably, originally did not concern them. See SSM, p. 252, where I note that in Matthew what originally arose out of a confrontation of Jesus and the Essenes serves the purposes of a confrontation of Church and Synagogue in the Jamnian period and is designed to clarify the relationships between the Gospel and Pharisaic Judaism. On the emphasis on the Pharisees in Matthew, see also G. Strecker, *Der Weg der Gerechtigkeit*, 2nd ed., Göttingen, 1963; and R. Hummel, *Die Auseinandersetzung zwischen Kirche und Judentum im Matthäusevangelium*, 1963. How Jesus differed from the Essenes in Qumran, who contemplated a holy war by a closed community, will be apparent from the above. In view of Neusner's work the "pacifism" of Pharisaism is to be re-examined, although Daube, *Civil Disobedience*, pp. 84ff, finds all Apocalyptists quietest and passive, despite their (compensatory?) bloody visions. There were others who had emphasized nonviolence besides Jesus. See *The Assumption of Moses* (4 B.C.–30 A.D.) and 4 Macc. It should not be overlooked that it was precisely the Pharisaic ability to make the Law "a portable land" that enabled Judaism to survive.

1. *The Parable of the Fig Tree.* Luke 13: 6–9

This first passage is a parable that we can confidently regard as coming, with whatever modifications, from Jesus himself. It reads in the RSV as follows.

And he told this parable: "A man had a fig tree planted in his vineyard; and he came seeking fruit on it and found none. And he said to the vinedresser, 'Lord, these three years I have come seeking fruit on this fig tree, and I find none. *Cut it down; why should it use up the ground?* (ekkopson autên hinati kai tên gên katargei).' And he answered him, 'Let it alone, sir, this year also, till I dig about it and put on manure. And if it bears fruit next year, well and good; but if not, you can cut it down.'"

The words in italics particularly concern us. They are peculiar to Luke. It has been claimed that the cursing of the fig tree in Mark 11: 12–14, 20–21, with parallel in Matt. 21: 18–19, is a historization of this parable in Luke 13: 6–9. But the emphasis in both the Markan and the Matthaean passages differs from that in Luke. There the judgment on Israel is already accomplished, whereas in Luke 13: 6–9 the emphasis is on the forbearance or patience of the judge.[54]

Only in Luke is there a direct reference to the earth or the land on which the fig tree (Israel) grows. Matthew merely states that the fig tree withered immediately, but Mark notes later, in 11: 20, that it was withered from the roots. Did the land refuse to sustain it? This question cannot be pressed. But are we to ascribe any special significance to Luke's reference to the land? Did he here mean to claim that for Jesus the judgment on Israel included or would incur separation from the land?

Certain considerations favour an affirmative answer. An emphasis on "the land" or "the earth" may be apparent. The pertinent sentence is introduced suddenly: it is a typical Aramaic asyndeton. Its asyndetic and interrogative character lends it forcefulness. That the reference is to the land, not to the earth or soil, may be taken to be implied in the context: the land on which Israel grows, the vineyard, is the land of Israel about which Judaism had woven the dreams we have dealt with above. That the term the land *tên gên* occasioned difficulty appears from the substitution of "the place, *ton topon*" for it by the first corrector of B. "The earth" did

[54] A. R. C. Leaney, however, *The Gospel According to St. Luke*, New York, 1958, *ad rem*, finds an emphasis on the brevity of the time allowed for repentance. But see Jeremias, *Theology*, p. 140: "These sayings Luke 13: 6–9 are among the most powerful spoken by Jesus.... Judgment is due, but God's will is not unalterable." Schlatter, *Das Evangelium des Lukas*, p. 323 anticipates Jeremias and speaks of Jesus here as the Paraclete of Israel.

not make sense to the scribe: to speak of a fig tree affecting the earth in its totality would seem exaggerated. On the other hand, "the land," that is, the land of Israel, did not perhaps make sense to him either, and so he substituted *ton topon* (the place). Again, that Luke did intend to give prominence to "the land" in 13: 7 might be deduced from the presence of *kai* (and also) before (the land). The translation: "Why, in addition to doing no good, does it sterilize the land?" brings out the point. Luke is concerned, on this view, with Israel's pollution of the land.

But there are difficulties. It is tempting to emphasize the preposition *ek* (out of) in the verb *ekkopson* (*cut it down*, RSV and NEB) in Luke 13: 7 and to give it the force of "cut out of" or "cut out from" the land.[55] But there is no support for such a strong rendering: the verb simply means "to cut down." And, again, the verb *katargeō* (I use up) is not illuminating. It does not obviously recall terms used in the Old Testament and Judaism especially in connection with the land, and is not evocative of any theology of the land such as we traced in Part I. Certainly in Luke there is no suggestion, such as we found in the Old Testament, that the land itself is actively concerned to evict Israel.[56] The land is here passive. But the exact meaning of *katargeō* remains difficult to determine. To judge from the passages where *katargeō* is used in the LXX, Ezra 4: 21, 23; 5: 5; 6: 8, its meaning is simply "to hinder," or "to cause to cease" and has reference to a decree from Artaxerxes, the King, that the rebuilding of the city of Jerusalem should cease. *Bâtal* in these passages translates the *pa'el* form of *bâtal*. The verb is used by Aquila[57] in Lev. 26: 15, 44, of breaking or causing the covenant to cease, with very dire consequences for Israel, but with the consequence of giving the land rest—a rest which it had not enjoyed even in the Sabbaths Israel had kept, a rest born of its desolation and waste. In Paul and later Patristic sources,[58] *katargeō* has a wealth of meaning—"bring to nought," "render impotent," "do away with," "supersede," "mishandle," and, in the passive, "to be idle," "to be set free from." Most interesting is the use of *katargeō* to mean "to do nothing," "to be fruitless, ineffectual" and, by extension of the meaning "to do nothing," "to observe the Sabbath." Does the use of the very rare

---

[55] This was done by A. Jülicher, *Die Gleichnisreden Jesu*, 3rd ed., Freiburg, 1888, *ad rem.*

[56] That is unless we press the *ek* in *ekkopson* to mean "extract from the roots," as does Jülicher, a notion which finds a suggestion of support in Mark 11: 20. Perhaps we have allowed caution to govern us too much here, but see Moulton and Milligan.

[57] So Hatch and Redpath. But in Maclean's edition of the LXX the reading *katargēsai* is given as from M.

[58] Especially helpful here is G. W. H. Lampe, *A Patristic Greek Lexicon*, Vol. 3, Oxford, 1964, p. 716.

Biblical verb *katargeô* (*argein* is equally rare) signify a subtlety in Luke 13: 7? Is Jesus ironically saying that the conduct of Israel is to bring the land the rest of desolation such as Lev. 26: 27–39 had spoken of? Was the conduct of Israel to make the land "cease"? Such a possibility must be noted.

Moreover, the very term *tên gên* (the land) itself must always remain ambiguous: does it mean "the land," that is, the land of Israel ('*eretz*) or "the earth," "the soil ('*ªdâmâh*)"? We can never be sure. Here as in other places where we can be sure that we are in touch with Jesus's words (in a parable) we cannot be sure, from the Greek text, whether he meant the land, or simply, '*ªdâmâh*, the earth or the soil, and must be content with the mere possibility that he encouraged the separation of the people of God from its land.

On balance, it must be admitted that Luke 13: 6–9 affords little light on Jesus' attitude to the land.[59]

2. *The Parable of the Hidden Talent.* Matthew 25: 14–30

The parable of the talents (Matt. 25: 14–30) and its parallel in Luke (19: 11–27) have been taken by most scholars to be based on a common tradition.[60] The stages through which this common tradition passed before finally being variously formulated by the two Evangelists have been traced by Dodd and Jeremias,[61] and need not be disentangled here. It is not difficult to arrive at the original intent of the parable of Jesus and to gather that he was challenging his own people or their leaders, or possibly both, by mirroring their conduct in that of the servant with the one talent (Matt.) or the one pound (Luke). There is little doubt that it is

[59] It is significant that the passage is not dealt with by Sasse in TWZNT, nor do commentators on Luke find any difficulty here. Most do not even mention the possible connotation of the term *gê* (land, earth). The translations of the NEB ("Cut it down. Why should it go on using up the soil?") and of the JB ("Cut it down. Why should it be taking up the ground?") both probably err on the side of undertranslation. K. Rengstorf prefers "impoverish" for *katargein: Das Neue Testament Deutsch, Das Evangelium nach Lukas*, Göttingen, 1937, p. 152: "Wozu Saugt er das Land aus?": he retains "das Land." E. Klostermann, HZNT, *Das Lukasevangelium*, Tübingen, 1919, p. 143, however, finds the meaning: "er saugt auch noch *die Erde* aus" and rejects a reference not only to the land but to the bit of land on which the fig tree stood. A. Plummer, ICC, *St. Luke*, New York, 1902, p. 340, translates forcefully: "Why, in addition to doing no good, does it sterilize the ground." He points out that *argos* and *argia* "are used of land that yields no return." He refers to Xenophon, *Cyr.* 3. 2. 19; Theophrastus, *H. Phys.*, 5. 9. 8. We follow his translation in the text.

[60] J. Schniewind, however, takes the Lukan and Matthaean parables to be based on two different parables: he finds the differences, which Bultmann, Dodd, and Jeremias account for mainly in terms of differing allegorical enlargements, too great to be reconciled.

[61] C. H. Dodd, *The Parables of the Kingdom*, New York, 1961, pp. 114ff; J. Jeremias, *The Parables of Jesus*, 6th rev. ed., New York, trans. 1963, pp. 58ff.

this one-talent man who occupies the centre of the parable,[62] which would best be called "The parable of the hidden talent."

One item in the parable has not been adequately discussed: indeed, it is seldom recognized. Matt. 25: 24–25 describes the actual confrontation of the returned Lord and the slave entrusted with one talent as follows: "He also who had received the one talent came forward, saying, 'Master, I knew you to be a hard man, reaping where you did not sow, and gathering where you did not winnow; *so I was afraid, and I went and hid your talent in the ground.* Here you have what is yours.' (RSV)." The Greek for the italicized words in the above is: *kai phobêtheis apelthôn ekkrupsa to talanton sou en tê gê.* Like the RSV, both NEB and JB translate *en tê gê* by "in the ground." Luke has a different word at this point, a Latinism, which is found only here at 19: 20 in the New Testament, but which has crept as a loan-word into the Mishnah and the Talmud, so that it may have been domesticated in the language that Jesus used. The text of Luke 19: 20 reads: *kai ho heteros êlthen legôn Kurie, idou hê mna sou, hên eichon apokeimenên en soudariô* (*soudarion* from the Latin: *sudarium*). The NEB renders: "Here is your pound, sir, I kept it put away in a handkerchief." If Jeremias is right in detecting in Luke 19: 12–27 the fusion of two originally independent parables, one of which (it is suggested by the nobleman who goes on a journey to claim a kingdom, 19: 12) reflected an actual historical event (the journey of Archelaus to Rome to get his kingship over Judaea confirmed, while at the very same time a Jewish embassy of fifty went to the same city to oppose his appointment), the creeping in of a Latinism is perhaps more understandable. Certainly, at first sight, Matthew's *ên tê gê* (in the land or earth) appears more likely than *en soudariô* (in a handkerchief). And if Matthew's text be taken as the more authentic may it not best be rendered as "in the land"? Grammatically the translation "in the ground" would lead us to expect a text without the article, as in Jos. *Antiquities*, I. 21. 2 (*kai autous* [the gods of Laban] he [Jacob] *ekkrupsen en Sikimois eis gên hupo tina doun*). The translation "in the land" would fit the context admirably. Did Jesus originally mean to point out to the Jewish people and/or their leaders that they had too much confined their faith to their land? May Jesus have been concerned not only to point out that the pious Jews, who were seeking personal security in a meticulous observance of the Law, were denying the knowledge of God entrusted to them not only to simple people, publicans and

---

[62] From a literary point of view also, this is recognized by D. O. Via, *The Parables*, Philadelphia, 1967, p. 116: "the tragic shape of the plot derives from the experience of the one-talent man."

sinners within the land, but also to Gentiles and people "outside the land"? C. H. Dodd here recalls the words of Klausner which we have already quoted with telling force. Klausner wrote: "The Judaism of that time had no other aim than to save the tiny nation, the guardian of great ideals, from sinking into the broad sea of heathen culture." Put that way, writes Dodd,[63] "it seems a legitimate aim. But from another point of view, might it not be aptly described as hiding treasure in a napkin?" Yes: but is Matthew's "in the land" even more directly pointed at the doctrine with which we are concerned? There are difficulties. Should the detail be pressed in this way, are we not here dealing with an allegorical addition of Matthew's rather than with a word of Jesus? Or, again, as in Matt. 25:18, does not Pharisaic legal usage point to the translation "in the ground" rather than "in the land" as the most likely? As Jeremias[64] points out, burying money in the ground was regarded as the best security against theft. "Anyone who buried a pledge or a deposit immediately upon receipt of it, was free from liability (b. BM. 42a)." Odd as the notion of burying a talent in the ground might be to us, it reflects Palestinian conditions and customs, and the *en tê gê* of Matthew may have no such connotation as we have suggested. That suggestion also runs counter to what was, apparently, the actual practice of Jesus, who confined his ministry and that of his followers to Israel (Matt. 10). That the thought of Jesus turned to the question of the land in Matt. 25:14ff must remain questionable, even though the Syriac at Matt. 25:25 reads *'aro"*, which may mean "in the land," "in the country," or "in the earth." *'aro"* is the equivalent of *'eretz* and is the term employed also in Matt. 5:5.

3. *A Beatitude.* Matthew 5:5

"'Blessed are the meek, for they shall inherit the earth.'" The third passage to be dealt with is this beatitude in Matt. 5:5, usually translated as above. The Greek is: *makarioi hoi praeis hoti autoi klêronomêsousi tên gên*. There is no parallel to it in Luke. Let us ask two questions.

First, is it likely that Jesus himself uttered these words? There are difficulties in ascribing the verse to Jesus. 1. Matt. 5:5 is a direct quotation of Ps. 37:11 in its LXX form (Ps. 36:11). This in itself does not mean that it is not from Jesus, who could have used the Psalm and quoted it: but it would be precarious to use such a quotation for the detection of any

---

[63] *The Founder of Christianity*; the exact reference eludes me.
[64] *New Testament Theology*, p. 61, n. 51.

peculiarity in the teaching of Jesus.[65] 2. The beatitude is variously located in the manuscripts,[66] a sure sign, according to Wellhausen, of interpolation: in several manuscripts the beatitude is the second not the third (it is so in the Latin text published by Nestlé, 1927, and in the Jerusalem Bible). The significance of this, however, can be exaggerated, because the manuscript evidence favours the third place and, as we shall see in 4 below, it is easy to see why "the meek" of 5: 5 could easily have been drawn near to "the poor in spirit" of 5: 3 and later separated.[67] 3. Matthew elsewhere favours sevenfold groupings (he has seven petitions in the Lord's Prayer; seven parables in chapter 13; seven woes against the Pharisees in chapter 23). To remove the beatitudes in 5: 5 and in 5: 10 or 11, which have a different form from the others, would give the beatitudes a sevenfold character congenial to Matthew. 4. The terms for poor (*ptôchoi*) and meek (*praeis*) in 5: 3 and 5: 5 are translations of terms derived from a common verb '*nânâh-'anâwîm* and '*anîyyîm* respectively, and have been claimed to be identical in meaning. Assuming that 5: 3 comes from Jesus, is it likely that he should have uttered another beatitude (5: 5) dealing with the same group? 5. The same original identification of "the poor" and "the meek" in Hebrew helps to account for the variation in the location of 5: 5. If, originally, the third beatitude followed the first, when the connection between '*anâwîm* and '*anîyyîm*, *ptôchoi* (poor) and *praeis* (meek), was clear, later when the underlying Semitic was forgotten, the connection between the first and the third beatitude was overlooked and their separation became possible, since *praeis* (meek) seemed to have more in common with "those who hunger and thirst after righteousness" of 5: 6 than with the *ptôchoi* (poor) of 5: 3. But what was the original connection between 5: 3 and 5: 5? In the source on which Matthew and Luke drew in this section, 5: 5 was absent, because Luke does not have it. Whence, then, did Matthew get it? Spicq notes that in the very first beatitude Matthew's concern is evident. To interpret '*anâwîm* (the poor) properly he added *tô pneumati* (in the spirit) after *ptôchoi* (the poor). But even so this was not enough. To do justice to '*anâwîm* he needed

[65] The RSV renders the Hebrew of Ps. 37: 11 as: "But the meek shall possess the land. . . ." The LXX (36: 11) has: οἱ δὲ πραεῖς κληρονομήσουσιν γῆν; the M.T. וַעֲנָוִים יִירְשׁוּ־אָרֶץ (Lit: the meek shall possess land).

[66] The note on Matt. 5: 4 (in the order given by the RSV) in S. C. E. Legg, *Evangelium Secundum Matthaeum*, Oxford, 1940, reads as follows: Uers. in hoc ordine Uncs. pler. Minusc. pler. b.f. q.r² vg Sy^s pesh. hl. hier. Cop. sa.bo. Aeth. Arm. Geo. Tert. pat. 11: pon. uers. 4 post uers. 5 D 33 a c d ff¹ g¹·² h k l m aur Syr^c·. Aph.⁴¹ Eph⁶².

[67] See C. Spicq, RB, Vol. 54, 1947, pp. 321ff, on "Benignité, Mansuétude, Douceur, Clémence."

praeis (meek) as well as *ptôchoi to pneumati* (poor in spirit). And so, drawing on the LXX of Ps. 37: 11, he created the interpretative beatitude we now have in 5: 5. If Spicq be followed, there can, therefore, be no question of 5: 5 going back to Jesus. But here, again, it should be noted that the force of all this rests upon the identity of "the poor" and "the meek" in an exact sense. Older scholars have differentiated between them, although more recent work seems to confirm this identification.[68]

Almost all the considerations against taking 5: 5 to be from Jesus can be questioned, as we have seen, and yet cumulatively they are convincing. It is at least dubious whether Jesus uttered 5: 5.

But, secondly, even if he did, what did he mean? Is there any evidence that the verse had reference to the land of Israel? Here the work of J. P. Audet[69] is relevant. In dealing with Did. 3: 7 (*isthi de praus, epei hoi praeis klêronomêsousi tên gên,* that is, Be meek, since the meek will inherit the earth [the land]), Audet relates it naturally to Matt. 5: 5, emphasizing the Messianic overtones of this (only when God himself will intervene will the meek become "inheritors").[70] Audet holds that the Didache saw the light of day between A.D. 50–70 at Antioch,[71] and that Did. 3: 7 preserves the Christian version of what had circulated earlier with a more obviously Jewish Messianic connotation. He refers to a reading at Did. 3: 7 of "qui mansueti possedebunt *sanctam terram* (our italics)."[72] If this translates an original *tên hagian gên* (the holy land) (compare 1 Enoch 27: 1; 2 Baruch 29: 2) there are three possibilities. (1) Matthew may have been unaware of such a version in Greek; (2) he may have simply followed the LXX, bearing in mind that "the earth (*tên gên*)" meant "the land of Israel"; (3) he may have deliberately chosen to read "the earth (*tên gên*)" rather than *tên hagian gên,* "the holy land." If the last, he deliberately rejected the geographic connotation which the verse had in Judaism, and initiated what has become the main stream of the interpretation of Matt. 5: 5. Because it has become widely customary either to spiritualize the possession of the land, so that "to inherit the land" becomes a symbol for inheriting conditions under the Rule of God in a spiritual sense, in the light of Matthew's collocation of entering the Kingdom of God and inheriting the land in Matt. 5: 3 and 5 (compare Matt. 5: 10, 20; 6: 10, 33;

---

[68] A. H. McNeile, *The Gospel According to St. Matthew,* London, 1915, p. 51, distinguished *ᵃnîyyîm* and *ᵃnâwîm.* C. Spicq argues for their identity.

[69] *La Didachè: Instructions des Apôtres,* Paris, 1958.   [70] *Ibid.,* pp. 320ff.

[71] *Ibid.,* pp. 187–219: conclusion on p. 219.

[72] Audet quotes as his authority J. Schlecht, *Doctrina XII Apostolorum,* Fribourg-in-Br., 1900, which I have not been able to consult. The Douay translation of Matt. 5: 5 has the rendering: "Blessed are the meek: for they shall possess the land."

21: 31), or to universalize the land so as to refer it to all the earth. The NEB translates Matt. 5: 5: "How blest are those of a gentle spirit, they shall have the earth for their possession." The Jerusalem Bible is equally clear. And whether we ascribe the verse to Jesus (as is most unlikely) or to Matthew or to a source behind Matthew, it is difficult, not to disengage the verse, in its Matthaean context, from the territorial promise of the Old Testament and Judaism. It is the Kingdom of God that transcends geography as Jesus proclaimed it, not the geographically concentrated "promise" of the Old Testament that Matt. 5: 5 is concerned with.[73] To recognize this it is necessary to divorce Matt. 5: 5 from its meaning in Ps. 37: 11. Certainly the "inheritance" of Christians in other parts of the New Testament is supra-terrestrial.[74] True the term *tên gên* has an obstinately this-worldly connotation, and a recent commentator[75] still takes Matt. 5: 5 to refer to the inheritance of the promised land or perhaps the restored earth of the Messianic Age. In Ps. 37 itself, dwelling in the land is associated with security (v. 3, 9), with permanence (v. 10–11, 18, 29), and abundant prosperity (v. 11), with the Day of the Lord (v. 13), with Divine blessing (v. 22). There is an unmistakable eschatological dimension to the possession of the land in Matt. 5: 5 as to all the beatitudes.[76] The reference is not to a merely geographic earth, but to the "redeemed" earth of the Age to Come, "which eye hath not seen nor ear heard." There are two possibilities, either to combine the two alternatives referred to above and hold that Matt. 5: 5 refers to inheriting, not the earth, but the land of Israel in a transformed world, in the Messianic Age or the Age to Come, or to recognize that for Matthew "inheriting the land" is synonymous with entering the Kingdom and that this Kingdom transcends all geographic dimensions and is spiritualized. Despite the use of the term "earth," we need not be removed from such spiritualization in Matt. 5: 5, because we have previously recognized that in Judaism itself, as elsewhere in the New Testament, the notion of "entering the land" had been spiritualized. In any case, we are most probably not dealing here with Jesus but with Matthew and the church for which he wrote.

[73] So most recently G. Strecker, NTS, April 1971, p. 264, "Die Makarismen Der Bergpredigt."

[74] 1 Peter 1: 4–5, and comments by E. G. Selwyn, 1 *Peter*, London, 1947, pp. 71f, 124f. J. Dupont, *Les Béatitudes*, Bruges, 1958, pp. 293ff. "Ce que la troisième béatitude promet aux doux n'est donc qu'une autre expression de l'espérance eschatologique: 'posséder le Royaume,' 'être appelé fils de Dieu,' ou 'voir Dieu.'"

[75] S. B. Johnson, IB, Vol. 7, p. 282.

[76] See the striking statement of this in F. W. Beare, *The Earliest Records of Jesus*, Oxford, 1962, p. 55.

4. *The Palingenesia*

Matthew 19: 28	Luke 22: 30
Jesus said to them, "Truly, I say to you, in the new world, when the Son of man shall sit on his glorious throne, you who have followed me will also sit on twelve thrones, judging the twelve tribes of Israel."	that you may eat and drink at my table in my kingdom, and sit on thrones judging the twelve tribes of Israel.

In the Lukan passage quoted Jesus looks forward to a kingdom in which those who have remained with him in his trials, who in the context are "the twelve," on his authority, are to share his table and to judge the twelve tribes of Israel. The verses, Luke 22: 28–30, are a corrective comment. The disciples have argued (Luke 22: 24–27), as to who was greatest. They are told that the one criterion of greatness is service. They as servants are set over against the world's rulers. But they are to have their reward: they will sit judging the twelve tribes of Israel. The context makes it clear that the kingdom in which they are to do so cannot be compared with the kingdoms of this world. They are to rule in a new kind of kingdom—in another dimension of existence. For Luke the verse is symbolic: he does not even bother to note that there would be twelve thrones. The broad symbol alone suffices.

In Matthew the context is different. There the disciples ask what they, who had left all and followed Jesus, were to expect. Jesus replies that there is to be a *palingenesia*, a rebirth, possibly, not a wholly new order, but a renewing of the existing order. We may here have the view that there would be a restored Israel with twelve tribes and twelve thrones: on these the Twelve were to share his authority with the Son of Man. They would receive back more than they had abandoned and inherit "eternal life." In this view, the clear distinction drawn by Luke between This Age and The Age to Come is blurred by Matthew: his *palingenesia* ushers in this world in a renewed form, in which "eternal life" is to be enjoyed. These verses, then, point to a perspective which looked forward to a temporal restoration in which the Messiah or Son of Man should govern his people after the manner portrayed in the Psalms of Solomon, for example, in 17: 28. "And he shall gather together a holy people, whom he shall lead in righteousness, and he shall judge the tribes of the people that has been sanctified by the Lord his God."

But is the saying from Jesus? There is no reason to question that the Twelve existed before Easter and that they represent the eschatological Israel. But on the ground that the term *palingenesia* has no Aramaic equivalent and that the phrase *my Kingdom* is unlikely on the lips of Jesus, Bornkamm[77] ascribes both the Matthaean and Lukan verses to the Risen Christ: they reflect the expectation of the Early Church: such was the view even of Lagrange: the Lukan verse proves that such expectations were not confined to Jewish-Christians. McNeile[78] thinks that Matthew's verse is later, whereas, more plausibly, Schniewind sees in it the preservation of an old tradition reflecting strata which looked forward to the literal fulfilment of the Jewish hope for restoration, so too Käsemann.[79]

But not all have rejected Matt. 19: 28 and its parallel as deriving in substance from Jesus. Schlatter[80] has suggested that *palingenesia* is the Greek equivalent to *hiddush hā 'ôlām* (the renewal of the world). That there is no exact Aramaic equivalent for it does not demand that it should be referred to Hellenistic notions of rebirth and renewal: its connotation must be found in Jewish eschatology: compare Dan. 7: 9ff; 1 Enoch 62: 5 etc. The term *palingenesia* itself cannot be decisive. We must further ask whether it is likely that the Church of itself formulated such an embarrassing saying, because the role assigned to the disciples or apostles here is not that found to be theirs in the rest of the New Testament. In Acts they are "witnesses (1: 8, 22)." The passages usually cited in connection with and as parallel to Matt. 19: 28 are unsatisfactory. In 1 Cor. 6: 2f the reference is to the judgmental role of the saints as a whole, not of the twelve. In Rev. 21: 14, the apostles are not judges in The New Jerusalem so much as eyewitnesses and guarantors of the tradition of the revelation of God on which it is built: they are its foundations.[81] So, too,

---

[77] *Jesus of Nazareth*, p. 209, n. 13.

[78] McNeile, *The Gospel According to St. Matthew, ad rem*: M.-J. Lagrange, *Évangile selon Saint Matthieu*, Paris, 1948, *ad rem*.

[79] J. Schniewind, *Das Evangelium nach Matthäus, ad rem*. It should be emphasized that the literal interpretation of *palingenesia* is not the only possible one in Matt. 19: 28 no less than in Luke 22: 30. Varied and uncertain notions of "new creation" are here involved. On the whole we accept the literal interpretation; see especially A. Schlatter, *Der Evangelist Matthäus*, Stuttgart, 1948, p. 581, for the naturalness of this here. There is no need to introduce into the interpretation of *palingenesia* the Mystery Religions (S. F. Büchsel, TDNT, Vol. 1, pp. 686–689), nor even Stoicism, though a diffused Stoicism may well have infiltrated the circles for which Matthew wrote. Oddly enough Büchsel does not refer to such passages as Is. 54: 7; 66: 22 etc., but thinks of Stoic notions of the End invading Judaism. For such notions in first-century Hellenistic circles, see W. L. Knox, *St. Paul and the Church of the Gentiles*, Cambridge, 1939, chapter 1. See Käsemann's *Questions*, pp. 93f.

[80] *Der Evangelist Matthäus*, p. 582. There were previous attempts at discovering the Aramaic equivalent of *palingenesia*, but none convinced. See Büchsel, TDNT, p. 688, n. 9.

[81] G. B. Caird, *A Commentary on the Revelation of St. John the Divine*, London, 1966, p. 272.

in Rev. 3: 21 those who are to sit on the throne with the Conqueror are not the twelve only but those who have shared in the victory of Christ. Revelation 20: 6 belongs to the same tradition as Matt. 19: 28, but it does not refer specifically to the apostles but generally to the martyrs.

It cannot, then, be ruled out that Matt. 19: 28, with its parallel, does go back to Jesus, although on the whole this is unlikely, in view of Mark 10: 35ff. But even if it be regarded as stemming from Jesus himself, what it asserts of the future is bare. There is no specific reference to the land on which the restored Israel is to dwell, although such is assumed. Josephus[82] uses *palingenesia* of the restoration of the land of Israel, and the term may have a geographic connotation in 19: 28, but most frequently *palingenesia* evokes a cosmic renewal, so that in 19: 28 also probably the restoration of the twelve tribes is understood not so much in terms of a restored land of Israel as of a renewed cosmos. This lack of concentration on the land as such coincides with the evidence of those passages appealed to by Jeremias[83] to prove that Jesus looked forward to an eschatological pilgrimage of the Gentiles to the Mountain of God at Zion to celebrate the great feast at the redemption of Israel, when the Gentiles would be guaranteed a share in the revelation vouchsafed to Israel and inclusion in God's redeemed community at the time of the last judgment.[84] When Jeremias[85] speaks of the restoration of Israel as beginning at this point he lacks clarity, because the sources to which he appeals lack clarity.[86]

One thing only emerges from all the above. Jesus, as far as we can gather, paid little attention to the relationship between Yahweh, and Israel and the land. But we have seen indications that the Early Church was so concerned. This concern was part of the matrix which led to that process, often treated, whereby Jesus was increasingly draped in an apocalyptic mantle and specifically Jewish expectations developed in the Church in a form highly enhanced from that which they had assumed in Jesus' own teaching. Where were these expectations to be fulfilled? Judaism had given its answer in terms of the centrality of the land and the indestructible connection between it and Yahweh and Israel. The Church came both to reject and to transmute this answer in various ways. After struggles which we can now only glimpse with difficulty, she remained true to the intent of her Lord.

---

[82] *Antiquities*, 11 . 3. 9.   [83] *Jesus' Promise to the Nations*, London, 1958.
[84] See now also Jeremias, *New Testament Theology*, pp. 245ff. On Matt. 8: 11f, Luke 13: 28f, see p. 246.   [85] *Ibid.*, p. 247.
[86] Jeremias's words, *ibid.*, p. 248, command assent: "In the teachings of Jesus the conception of the *basileia* is stripped not only of all nationalistic features, but also of all materialistic features (his italics)."

XII. CONCLUSION

Our survey of the data is over. Can we draw any broad conclusions? The data fall into two groups although these cannot be regarded as watertight.

First, there are strata in the tradition where the understanding of the land, Jerusalem, and the Temple emerges in a critical or negative light. In one stratum (Acts 7) it was rejected outright. In other strata, which we could not examine here, the land, Jerusalem, and the Temple were taken up into a non-geographic, spiritual, transcendent dimension, even though in their transcendence they also impinged upon or invaded this world through the community of God and his Christ. They became symbols especially of eternal life, of the eschatological society in time and eternity, beyond space and sense. In such strata the physical entities as such—land, Jerusalem, Temple—cease to be significant, except as types of realities which are not in essence physical. It is justifiable to speak of the *realia* of Judaism as being "spiritualized" in the Christian dispensation.

But, secondly, there are other strata in which the land, the Temple, and Jerusalem, in their physical actuality, are regarded positively; that is, in a certain way they retain a significance in Christianity. This arises from two factors—History and Theology. The emergence of the Gospels— kerygmatic as they may be—witnesses to a historical and, therefore, geographic, concern in the tradition, which retains for the *realia* their full physical significance. The need to remember the Jesus of History entailed the need to remember the Jesus of a particular land. Jesus belonged not only to time, but to space; and the space and spaces which he occupied took on significance, so that the *realia* of Judaism continued as *realia* in Christianity. History in the tradition demanded geography.

But a theological factor also helped to ensure this. Especially in the Fourth Gospel, the doctrine that the Word became flesh, although it resulted in a critique of distinct, traditional holy spaces, demanded the recognition that where the Glory had appeared among men all physical forms became suffused with it. "We beheld His glory" had the corollary that *where* this had happened became significant.[1] If we allow a diffused

[1] An example of this appears in J. S. Whale, *Christian Reunion: Historic Divisions Reconsidered*, Grand Rapids, Mich., 1971, p. 60, where he quotes a letter from Bernard Manning. "The Son is dearer to me than the Father. *I love the flesh of Palestine infinitely* more than the very God who inhabited it...." Doubtless Manning reflects a Nonconformist tradition, but his emphasis recurs in Christian piety. The sentiment for the land finds expression in Shake-

Platonic as well as apocalyptic dimension to Hebrews and the Fourth Gospel,[2] then their authors believe in a sacramental process, that is, the process of reaching the truth by the frank acceptance of the actual conditions of life and making these a "gate to heaven." Physical phenomena for them are the means whereby the infinite God and spiritual realities are made imaginable and a present challenge. Such "sacramentalism" could find holy space everywhere, but especially where Jesus had been: this sacramentalism was later on to inform the devotion to the Holy Places among many Christians throughout the ages.[3]

The witness of the New Testament is, therefore, twofold: it transcends the land, Jerusalem, the Temple. Yes: but its History and Theology demand a concern with these realities also. Is there a reconciling principle between these apparently contradictory attitudes? There is. By implication, it has already been suggested, The New Testament finds holy space wherever Christ is or has been: it personalizes "holy space" in Christ, who, as a figure of History, is rooted in the land; he cleansed the Temple and died in Jerusalem, and lends his glory to these and to the places where he was, but, as Living Lord, he is also free to move wherever he wills. To do justice to the personalism of the New Testament, that is, to its Christo-centricity, is to find the clue to the various strata of tradition that we have traced and to the attitudes they reveal: to their freedom from space and their attachment to spaces.

It is these attitudes—negatively and positively—that have informed the history of Christianity. *Rejection, spiritualization, historical concern, sacramental concentration*—all have emerged in that history.[4] We illustrate

speare as elsewhere. The different note, to which we refer in the text, is, however, struck by a modern English poet, Francis Thompson, who finds Christ walking on the waters "not of Genessareth, but Thames (see his poem 'In no strange land')," and a modern English artist, Stanley Spencer, who depicted the Resurrection at Cookham in the Thames Valley. (See Sir John Rothenstein, *The Tate Gallery*, New York, 1958, pp. 103–105, and his illuminating comment.)

[2] That the Fourth Gospel and Hebrews are being more and more interpreted in terms of Judaism does not allow us to rule out their diffused Platonism. First-century Judaism itself was informed by such a Platonism.

[3] The history of the reasons that impelled the Eastern Emperors to build churches in the "Holy Land" is highly instructive at this point, but cannot be pursued here.

[4] Various emphases could appear in the same document, for example, the Fourth Gospel in different degrees illustrates the four attitudes indicated. Father Pierre Benoit in a private letter gives a succinct statement of what I have tried to state in this conclusion.

En somme, le lieu matériel peut être associé au salut de deux façons différentes. Premièrement il peut être une condition nécessaire du culte: ainsi le Temple de Jérusalem dans la religion juive et la Mecque dans la religion musulmane. Deuxièmement il peut être rattaché au cadre religieux du salut comme la coordonnée de l'histoire: les gestes de Dieu se sont produits en tel temps et en tel lieu. Le christianisme rejette la première façon de considérer le lieu. Pour lui le culte est spirituel et ne peut dépendre d'un lieu matériel comme d'une condition nécessaire. Mais la deuxième manière d'apprécier le lieu est riche-

with a brevity that is distorting. Much modern Theology, concentrating on demythologizing, tends to reject these *realia* of which we speak as anachronistic; Mediaeval and much Puritan thought witness to their spiritualization;[5] especially the archaeological intensity of much modern scholarship and much also of its literary criticism point to a historical concern centring in the quest of the historical Jesus; and, in Greek Orthodoxy and in Mediaeval Theology, expressed in the history of pilgrimages to Palestine and in the Crusades, connected as these are with the motif of the Imitation of Christ, the sacramentalism of which I spoke is a striking characteristic.[6] To illustrate all this in depth is beyond the range of this work. But one thing in the history of Christianity—I do not say Christendom—needs no illustration, so ubiquitous is it: its Christo-centricity. In the end, where Christianity has reacted seriously to the *realia* of Judaism, whether negatively or positively, it has done so in terms of Christ, to whom all places and all space, like all things else, are subordinated.

In sum, for the holiness of place, Christianity has fundamentally, though not consistently, substituted the holiness of the Person: it has Christified holy space. As we saw in *The Apostrophe to Zion*, recently discovered, Jerusalem is given a kind of divine status. Urbach has recently suggested that Jerusalem as "place (space) (*maqom*)" lent its name to God himself in Judaism: this is of penetrating significance for our purpose.[7]

---

ment préservée dans le christianisme: les lieux où se sont opérées la révélation et la rédemption bibliques sont précieux par le réalisme qu'ils donnent à l'histoire du salut.

A ce dilemme il faut ajouter un troisième terme. Si tel ou tel lieu n'a pour le christianisme d'importance que opportune (garantie d'historicité) et non nécessaire (s'il était une condition exigée du culte), en revanche, le "lieu" comme tel garde une importance capitale dans le message chrétien, parce que le salut Chrétien est physique et atteint le corps—comme l'âme. La spiritualité du salut chrétien ne doit pas être entendue d'une facon platonicienne, mais selon la conception biblique de pneuma divin qui pénètre et transforme la corporéité. Le Christ glorifié l'est dans son corps et occupe un lieu, assurément inimaginable. Ce caractère physique du salut chrétien donne au lieu une importance essentielle, toute différente celle de l'attachement à tel ou tel endroit particulier.

5 Mediaeval and Puritan hymns abundantly illustrate "the land of pure delight" and the golden city—*Urbs Sion aurea*—as a transcendent spiritual reality.

6 I once heard a lawyer expound the devotion of his fellow Eastern Orthodox Christians to the land. Veneration is due to places touched by the divine touch, that is, the Incarnation. To adapt a principle from Jewish Mysticism, "he who touches is touched." The believer is to seek God through traces of his tangible presence on earth. Those places where those traces appear are not idolized, but they are recognized as a means of living contact with Jesus himself. Moreover, their initial significance has grown across the ages because generations have there offered their prayers and devotion. They are not museums but scenes of and for worship where the spiritual unity of believers today with those of past centuries is affirmed. The classic statement is by Gregory of Nyssa (A.D. 335–394), M.P.G., Tome 46, Col. 1009–1016. περὶ τῶν ἀπιόντων εἰς Ἱεροσόλυμα.

7 Ephraim E. Urbach, *The Sages, Their Concepts and Beliefs (Hebrew)*, Jerusalem, 1969. In a review of it in *Christian News From Israel*, Summer 1970, Vol. xxi, No. 2, p. 47, Yehoshua Amir, summarizes Urbach's point as follows: "the name '*Hamaqom*,' literally, 'The Place,' or 'The Space,' has caused peculiar reactions. Bousset calls it 'the most abstract of all formulas'

Such a transference is unthinkable in Christianity where the Name that is above every other Name is that of a Person.

Finally, let us attempt to grasp more firmly the relationship between the two parts of this volume. The spiritualization of "holy space," we saw, is anticipated in Judaism; the historical centrality of the land *mutatis mutandis* remains in Judaism and Christianity. But it cannot but have forcefully impressed the reader that, whereas in Part I we had an embarrassment of materials with which to build our edifice of the doctrine of the land in the Old Testament and Judaism, in Part II we may have seemed, perhaps, to have had to comb the New Testament, assiduously even, for stray indications at least of a direct involvement with the theme that concerned us.

At first this must seem surprising. Daube pointed out, as we saw, that one of the temptations ascribed to Jesus by Matthew and Luke was to gain possession of the earth, and that Jesus was understood by both evangelists as a new and greater Moses, who, like the first Moses, surveyed the land to be possessed from afar. In other parts of these two Gospels, as elsewhere in the New Testament, the understanding of Jesus in terms of and over against Moses has been amply recognized. Is it not surprising, then, that the question of the land does not emerge more frequently and directly in the New Testament?

There are certain obvious reasons for this. One of the startling aspects of early Christianity is that, at a very early date, Gentiles, for whom the question of the land could not possess the interest that it had for Jewish Christians, soon became the majority.[8] By the time the New Testament documents came to be written, even by the time of Paul, the Gentile flood had already overtaken the Church. It is not necessary to connect the Gentile predominance specifically with the Fall of Jerusalem, although it was that event that may have dealt the final blow to Jewish-Christian dominance.[9] The rapid spread of Christianity into the Gentile world

and concludes that such an abstract appellative of God is a token of a kind of reverence that 'stifles the living faith,' till 'faith itself becomes anaemic'...." Closer investigation reveals that the name "*Hamaqom*" is used predominantly in contexts where God's mercy or nearness is stressed.... Urbach offers his own interpretation of "*Hamaqom*," as meaning "The God of the Place," namely, "the chosen place, which is Zion...." See further, H. Koester, TWZNT, on *topos*.

[8] The speed with which Christianity spread has its parallel in the Sabbatian movement: its amazing dimensions are too easily overlooked.

[9] See my article in *Peake*, p. 878, where I suggest that S. G. F. Brandon, *The Fall of Jerusalem*, S.P.C.K., London, 1951, has over-emphasized the significance of that event. Contrast now Lloyd Gaston, *No Stone on Another: Studies in the Significance of the Fall of Jerusalem in the Synoptic Gospels*, Leiden, 1970, who finds various attempts at coming to terms with it in the Gospels.

carried with it the demotion of the question of the land, even though that question did not die out entirely, but persisted to emerge in later periods.

Again, another item is pertinent, although it cannot be enlarged upon here. It is this: in all strata of the New Testament the context within which all that we have written above, about Galilee, Jerusalem, the Temple, the land, is that of a cosmic eschatology. This must be emphasized, because it sets our treatment in true perspective. The cosmic awareness of primitive Christianity—its doctrines of the new creation, the new age, the cosmic Christ, the cosmic Church, and the cosmic salvation through these, all expressed variously and with differing intensity, but all, to some degree at some point, informing the minds of Christians, could not but place all Christian speculation on geographic entities that were central to Judaism in a minor key. Judaism had this cosmic dimension also. To that extent it, too, depressed the doctrine of Jerusalem and the land. But that dimension is far more immediate and ubiquitous in its intensity in primitive Christianity, and the consequent depression greater.

The last two sentences, however, true as they are, are not adequate. In the sense indicated, it is legitimate to claim that the concern of Judaism for the land was demoted, to a certain degree, by the cosmic scope of its eschatology. But this apart, we saw that the doctrine of the land was very alive in first-century Judaism, whereas the land does not occupy writers of the New Testament to any comparable, serious degree. To return to the question with which this work began, "How did early Christianity deal with the 'dogma' of the land?" it is imperative to recognize that the Gospel created a crisis of tradition within Jewish Messianism. This Messianism, in which conceptions of an ideal world, of the restoration of the Davidic Kingdom, of the centrality of the land and of Jerusalem were combined with those of the Day of the Lord and the Last Judgment, was a recognized aspect of Jewish revelation and tradition. Belief in a future redemption had become domesticated within the tradition of Judaism with little discomfort to that tradition. Hopes for a redemption either by the restoration of Israel and the world to a primordial or primeval condition, that is, in a restorative sense, or by the advent of a kind of Utopia, which represents "the conception of redemption as a phenomenon in which something emerges which has never before existed, in which something totally new is unmistakably expressed," could co-exist.

"Of course," writes Scholem, "these restorative and utopian elements in the Messianic idea could exist side by side *as long as it was simply a hope that was projected into the distant future, an affirmation of faith that corresponded to no real experience.* As long as the Messianic hope remained abstract, not yet concretized in people's experience or demanding a concrete decision, it was possible for it to embody even what was contradictory without the latent contradiction being felt. . . . Messianism could take over even a conservative attitude and in this way become part of the tradition. Messianic *activity*, however, could hardly do this. The moment that Messianism moved from the realm of affirmation of faith, abstract doctrine, and synthesizing imagination into life and took on acute forms, it had to reach a point where the energies that lay dormant in these two elements would emerge into conflict with each other—the conflict of the tradition of the past versus the presence of redemption. (Our italics.)"[10]

It was precisely such a conflict that erupted when the Gospel confronted Judaism. A familiar realm can illustrate this. In its eschatology Judaism could and did *speculatively* or *theoretically* contemplate changes in the Torah and even a New Torah.[11] But let a movement arise within Judaism actually annulling parts of the Torah and the reaction was swift to reject it, and that with passion.

So was it with the "dogma" of the land. Early Jewish-Christians proclaiming the advent of the Messianic Age and a future coming of Jesus as Lord, seem to have found little difficulty in remaining within the ambience of Jewish revelation and tradition, even though they anticipated an imminent incursion of Gentiles to worship in Jerusalem. They could have continued in such a conviction indefinitely, without objection from Judaism. They were free *to speculate* about the restoration of the land as about other matters. What created a crisis both within Judaism and the contiguous Jewish-Christianity was no "speculation" or even "conviction": it was a brute historical fact. *Before* Jerusalem had become the centre of the New Israel on Mt. Zion, a community had emerged in response to Jesus, the Messiah, which dispensed with the Oral Law as unnecessary to salvation. Outside the land, outside the Law, there was a Messianic activity, transcending old distinctions, the fence of the Torah, an activity which could not be masked or made innocuous by speculation. What were Judaism and Jewish-Christianity to make of this fact?

There was no difficulty for traditional Judaism: it rejected the new movement as dangerous. What of Jewish-Christianity? It attempted to

---

[10] G. Scholem, *The Messianic Idea in Judaism And Other Essays on Jewish Spirituality*, New York, 1971, pp. 51f.

[11] See my *Torah in the Messianic Age* and/or the *Age to Come*, Philadelphia, 1952; SSM, pp. 109ff, in an expanded, revised form.

contain and to interpret the new community of the Messiah, Jesus, by insisting that, in accordance with traditional expectations, the Gospel was first to be preached to the Jews and in due and proper course to the Gentiles. But facts intervened upon the anticipated procedures. Under the sheer actuality of Gentile converts, who could not be denied to reveal the grace of God, the terms of the Messianic redemption expressed by Jewish tradition and accepted by Jewish-Christianity were disproved. As a matter of history, it had to be recognized, however reluctantly, that the redemption of the Gentiles was not bound up with the prior establishment of the House of David in Jerusalem, to which the Gentiles were later to flow. The pattern imposed on the Messianic redemption by Jewish tradition was shattered and had to be abandoned. In fact, the movement inaugurated through Jesus reversed the anticipated course of Messianic events; the concourse of Gentiles taking up the collection to Jerusalem was the symbol, the effective symbol, of that reversal.[12]

"There are three ways," Scholem writes further, "in which tradition evolves and develops in history. It can be carried forward with a retention of continuity; it can be transformed through natural process of metamorphosis and assume a new configuration; and, finally, it can be subjected to a break which is associated with the rejection of the tradition itself."[13] Gentile Christianity, in abandoning the acceptance of the Law as condition of membership in the People of God and in the Messianic redemption, challenged Judaism in its very being, that is, in its interpretation of (1) the Law, the ground and guide of its life; (2) its self-identity as a people; (3) its promised future in the land and otherwise. It was not, primarily at least, any impulse derived from Judaism itself that led Paul to remove the requirements of the Law from his Gentile churches: it was an impulse born of or dictated by the concrete situation, demanding concrete decisions, in those churches. (The significance of our statement can be appreciated only if the discussion of "The Crisis of Tradition in Jewish Messianism," pp. 49–77 in the great work by Scholem, *The Messianic Idea*, be taken with full seriousness.)

The word "impulse" might suggest a sudden, unreflective reaction. But the writings of the New Testament reveal that they emerged out of an eschatological crisis which demanded intellectual and ethical wrestling with the tradition on several fronts—the suffering of the Messiah, the Law, the People of God, and the Remnant. They also, implicitly if not

---

[12] Here the work of Johannes Munck, *Paulus und die Heilsgeschichte*, Aarhus, 1954, is important.

[13] *The Messianic Idea*, p. 49.

often explicitly, reveal the attempts made to come to terms with the land. The overwhelming actuality and significance of Gentile Christianity soon swept away for many, if not most Christians, those patterns that had governed Jewish thinking on the land. This is why the question of the land so little occupies the writers of the New Testament. In coming to grips with Gentile Christianity, early Christians had radically to assess the geographic *realia* of Judaism, and they either abandoned or transformed them or lent them a new perspective.[14]

It has become a near-dogma in modern New Testament scholarship—another example of over-conceptualization applied to Christian origins?—that it was the delay in the Parousia that initiated early Christian Theology. Disappointment with a speculative anticipation, it has been emphasized, spurred reinterpretation of the ground and content of the Faith. But, in the light of Scholem's work, would the delay of the Parousia in itself have stimulated such activity? There is an essential irrationality in eschatological types such as the early Christians must, in some measure, be taken to have been; they can live with antitheses—the earnest expectation of a near End and extreme activity. It is not unlikely that early Christians were not only moved by the question: "What shall we do now that the End is delayed?" but also by: "How are we to understand our Faith in the light of the emergence of these Gentile Christians, who are without the Law and outside the land, but yet share in the redemption?" The emergence of a community in which there was neither Jew nor Greek, in which Jews and Gentiles were called upon *not only to think together, but actually to eat together, and that consciously and on principle,* compelled the reassessment not only of the place of the Law and the land, but of eschatological hopes.[15] The Jewish tradition, within which the earliest Christianity arose, had dictated the understanding of the End. Consequently the earliest Christians looked to the Parousia to confirm their faith. And, at first, Paul himself shared this view. Later, as we saw, it was the grace of God in the Gentile churches that amazed him: *there* was the confirmation of his faith. So too the Book of Acts has been called "A Confirmation of the Gospel": Luke saw in the progress of Gentile Christianity the explication and validation

---

[14] Compare Max Warren, "Christianity in its foundation document, the New Testament, is not territorialized." Unpublished paper on "The Concept and Historic Experience with Land in Major Western Religious Traditions," p. 5.

[15] See M. Barth, *The Journal of Ecumenical Studies*, Vol. 5, No. 2, Spring, 1968, on Jews and Gentiles: "The Social Character of Justification in Paul," pp. 241–267 and the use made of this by L. Mudge, in a probing article "Jesus and the Struggle for the Real," *The Journal of Religion*, Vol. 51, No. 4, Oct. 1971, pp. 229ff; see p. 243. Loisy wrote with irony, if not contempt, that Jesus preached the Kingdom and the Church emerged. Paul would not have shared his contempt.

of the Gospel, and so did Matthew. And in the Fourth Gospel the hope of John (17) lies in the quality of the life of the redeemed community. Community realized or fulfilled with all the "brute actualities" that this implied in face of the deepest cleavage probably known to the first century—that between Jew and Gentile—played perhaps as great a part as hope deferred in the reinterpretation of the tradition to which we refer. This suggestion we cannot here pursue. For our purpose, we recall again that life "in Christ," abiding in him, taking the yoke of the kingdom— these signify in the New Testament the fulfilment of the hope for that fullness of life in the land that Judaism had cherished. There are those who have claimed that in abandoning the earthly, geographic national *realia* of Judaism, the Gospel has romanticized the Jewish tradition and en-nervated it. Doubtless there is at times a romanticism or false "spiritu-ality" in much later Christianity which, although it has other sources also, may not be wholly unconnected with its break with the doctrine of the land as much of Judaism understood it.[16] That that break in itself does not lead to an effete Christian romanticism appears from the following words, from the Epistle to Diognetus (*circa* A.D. 150), 5, which, lament-able as is their generally anti-Jewish setting, are sufficiently down to earth.

1. For Christians are distinguished from the rest of men neither by country nor by language nor by customs. 2. For nowhere do they dwell in cities of their own; they do not use any strange form of speech or practise a singular mode of life. 3. This lore of theirs has not been discovered by any design and thought of prying men, nor do they champion a mere human doctrine, as some men do. 4. But while they dwell in both Greek and barbarian cities, each as his lot was cast, and follow the customs of the land in dress and food and other matters of living, they show forth the remarkable and admittedly strange order of their own citizenship. 5. They live in fatherlands of their own, but as aliens. They share all things as citizens, and suffer all things as strangers. Every foreign land is their fatherland, and every fatherland a foreign land. 6. They marry, like all others; they breed children, but they do not cast out their offspring. 7. Free board they provide, but no carnal bed. 8. They are "in the flesh," but they do not live "after the flesh." 9. They pass their days on earth, but they have their citizenship in heaven. 10. They obey the appointed laws, yet in their own lives they excel the laws. 11. They love all men, and are persecuted by all. 12. They are unknown, yet they are condemned; they are put to death, yet they are made alive. 13. "They are poor, yet they make many rich." They suffer the lack

[16] See especially L. Baeck, *Judaism and Christianity*, trans., Philadelphia, 1958, on "Ro-mantic Religion." On the emphasis on the delay in the Parousia see C. H. Dodd, *The Apostolic Preaching and Its Developments*, London, 1936, p. 34. M. Werner, *Die Entstehung des christlichen Dogmas Problem dargestelt*, 2nd ed., Bern, 1953.

of all things, yet they abound in all things. 14. They are dishonoured, and yet are glorified in their dishonour. They are evil spoken of, yet are vindicated. 15. "They are reviled, and they bless"; insulted, they repay with honour. 16. When doing good they are punished as evil-doers; suffering punishment, they rejoice as if quickened into life. 17. By the Jews they are warred against as foreigners, and are hunted down by the Greeks. Yet those who hate them cannot state the cause of their hostility.[17]

The author of these words was not typical; his picture of Christians is idealized; but it cannot be wholly divorced from actualities. Such people as he describes, "aliens" by choice in this world, might be expected to understand and sympathize with Jews, those other "wanderers," who are not always such by choice, but have clung to the hope of their ancient "Fatherland." Alas, Diognetus himself did not live up to such an expectation. Was it because he failed to recognize the ultimate source of that very "wandering," which he ascribed to Christians, in the other "wandering" of the Jews? Because in the last resort this study drives us to one point: the person of a Jew, Jesus of Nazareth,[18] who proclaimed the acceptable year of the Lord only to die accursed on a cross and so to pollute the land, and by that act and its consequences to shatter the geographic dimension of the religion of his fathers. Like everything else, the land also in the New Testament drives us to ponder the mystery of Jesus, the Christ, who by his cross and resurrection broke not only the bonds of death for early Christians but also the bonds of the land. There were aspects of Judaism before his day, as we have seen, which anticipated that achievement, but, in the last resort, it was his impact that ensured that while the history of Judaism has generally, if intermittently and not universally, witnessed a continued, and for many an increasing, attachment to the land, that of Christianity, despite the Crusades, has largely been that of detachment from it. If it was the Hellenists and Paul who broke asunder the territorial chrysalis of Christianity, they did so in the name of Christ, to whom all space, like all time, was subordinated, and who has become in the Christian tradition—to adopt and adapt a metaphor from Rainer Maria Rilke—"for every ship a haven; for every land a ship."[19]

[17] Translation from H. G. Meecham, *The Epistle of Diognetus*, Manchester, 1935.

[18] On this it is important to emphasize what Scholem, *The Messianic Idea*, p. 62, recognizes: the significance of the "character" of Jesus. Contrasting Sabbatai Zevi with Jesus he writes: "[In Sabbatai Zevi] The figure of the Messiah himself takes on a sinister character which calls into question every traditional value. One cannot overlook the abyss which yawns between the figure of the Messiah who died for his cause upon the Cross and this figure who became an apostate and played his role in this disguise. . . ."

[19] From "Du bist die Zukunft"; *Poems from the Book of Hours*, Rainer Maria Rilke, New Directions, Norfolk, Conn., 1941, pp. 36f. Hans von Campenhausen's illuminating essay on

"Early Christian Asceticism," *Tradition and Life in the Church, Essays and Lectures in Church History*, trans., Philadelphia, 1968, pp. 90ff, suggests to us that the disenlandisement which was involved in the early Christian revolution was closely related to the development of asceticism and of the imitation of Christ. Two factors, a negative and a positive, have impinged upon our appreciation of this disenlandisement. Negatively, in modern times, nationalism (not pejorative here) in its extremist and passionate and absolutistic forms, has often blinded us to it. Positively, the precariousness of life in this atomic age, which has engendered the power to endanger the whole earth, together with a new sensitivity born of our experience in the space age to our common perilous existence on "the little, lonely, floating planet, that tiny raft in the enormous empty night" which we call earth, has made us more acutely conscious of the questionableness of overemphasizing territorial divisions, however desirable. As Archibald MacLeish expressed it, to see earth as it truly is, "small and blue and beautiful in that eternal silence where it floats" is "to see ourselves as riders on the earth together, brothers on that bright loveliness in the eternal cold—brothers who know now they are, truly brothers." *Brothers in the Eternal Cold*, New York Times Company, cited in *Phase Blue*, 1970, pp. 16–17.

APPENDIX I

REFLECTIONS ON JUDAISM AND CHRISTIANITY: THEIR MUTUAL DEPENDENCE[1]

In this essay we shall be concerned to answer the question: in what ways does Christianity depend upon and profit from its Jewish heritage?

Christianity as a phenomenon in history is so varied, complex and fluid that it is impossible to speak of it without generalization and consequent distortion. I shall understand Christianity here in terms of the New Testament itself, as the basic document of the Christian faith and the source whence we can best recover its genius and ethos. With Christianity as it developed in post-apostolic times I shall only be concerned at the end.

But what do we understand by the Jewish heritage of Christianity? The view has not infrequently been expressed that in the Christian Gospel there is a return to the great Prophets of Israel. The culmination of the Old Testament is enshrined in the work of the Prophets. After their day, Judaism developed into a religion of Law, Temple and Synagogue, in which the great prophetic notes were muted: there was a descent from the prophetic heights. What Jesus of Nazareth did was to appeal to the Prophets against Judaism—against the Law, the Scribe, the Pharisee, the Priest—to the submerged prophetic tradition. On this view, the Jewish heritage of Christianity can only mean its Old Testament heritage and particularly that of the Prophets. Christianity is a protest *against* Judaism in favour of the Old Testament. This point of view has been variously expressed. For example, the great R. H. Charles rooted Jesus in Apocalyptic, and Apocalyptic is the true heir of that Old Testament prophecy which stands over against the legalism of Judaism.[2] It is to this protest against Judaism that Christianity belongs.

A curious phenomenon consequently arose in the study of the origins of Christianity. It has a parallel in the study of the Classics. When I took an Honour's degree in Classical Greek, the authors whom I had to study reached down as far as Aristotle. After this there was a jump to Latin literature. The whole literature of the Hellenistic Age, including the slightly barbaric New Testament, was ignored. It was not until some years after, when I heard the classical scholar, Charlesworth, that I came to realize that the Hellenistic Age is, in a sense, the flowering of the Classical and that one cannot be rightly understood without the other.

[1] Republished from the *Festschrift* to Professor L. H. Leenhardt, *L'Évangile Hier et Aujourd'hui*, Editions Labor et Fides, Geneva, 1968, pp. 39-54.

[2] *Religious Development between the Old and the New Testament*, London, 1925, p. 14, n. 1. Compare B. H. Streeter: *Cambridge Ancient History*, II, Cambridge, 1936, p. 264.

So it was in much Christian treatment of Christian origins. Since Jesus was thought to be rooted in the Prophets, what came after them was largely overlooked. The whole complex development of Judaism in the post-exilic period tended to be treated very scantily by New Testament scholars, just as the Hellenistic Age was neglected by classical. When scholars referred to the Jewish heritage of Christianity, they meant primarily the prophetic heritage and secondarily the apocalyptic. The Pharisaic, Scribal or Rabbinic tradition was regarded as that which Christianity rejected.

This almost traditional approach to the Jewish heritage of Christianity we must abandon. I shall assume that not only the prophetic tradition but the whole complex of Judaism is meant by "the Jewish heritage." That is, Judaism as well as the Old Testament constitutes the heritage of Christianity. There are three main reasons for insisting on this.

First, the old distinction drawn between priestly, legalistic Judaism and prophetic Judaism has broken down.[3]

Secondly, there has been a rejection of any sharp distinction between Apocalyptic and Pharisaism.[4]

Thirdly, a deeper Jewish and Christian understanding of the first century, often informed by the agony of our time, has made it easier to do justice to the legal tradition in Judaism.[5]

By the Jewish heritage of Christianity, therefore, I shall signify the totality of Judaism.

THE RELATIONSHIP BETWEEN CHRISTIANITY AND JUDAISM IN THE LIGHT OF THE NEW TESTAMENT

The New Testament presents the relationships in at least three ways, the evidence for which is given below:[6] Christianity as the revision, not a radical one (as in Jewish-Christianity), or an antithesis (as in the Fourth Gospel), or the fulfilment (as in Matthew, Hebrews, and Paul) of Judaism. How are we to evaluate these three positions?

They can only be evaluated in the light of what we know of Judaism in the first century. Since the end of the last century, a new understanding and appreciation of first-century Judaism have emerged. The source is twofold.

In Christian scholarship, the impulse to the study of first-century Judaism came from the work of Johannes Weiss, who insisted on the eschatological or apocalyptic nature of the message of Jesus. The liberal approach to the historical Jesus was faced with the challenge of the eschatological Christ. It is from the

---

[3] See references in my essay on the *Pirqê Aboth* in the *Festschrift for John Knox*, Cambridge University Press, 1967.

[4] See my *Christian Origins and Judaism*, London, 1962, pp. 19–30.

[5] The new appreciation of the meaning of *Torah* in Judaism is especially important but is too familiar to need documentation here.

[6] Pp. 400ff below were originally also included at this point and are here omitted to avoid duplication: they should be consulted at this juncture.

end of the nineteenth century that the resultant Christian concentration on first-century Judaism dates. There followed, in the twentieth century, a stream of works dealing with that period, to our vast enrichment. I name especially those of Dalman, Schürer, Bousset, Jeremias, Moore, Bonsirven and Herford.

But alongside the work of Christian scholars there also appeared many works by Jews. In England there was a rich cooperation between the two, usually centring in New Testament seminars. From these came the works of Abrahams, Loewe and David Daube. Mention must also be made of the very important work of Schechter, Montefiore, Finkelstein and Lieberman.

The upshot was a far more realistic and sympathetic understanding of first-century Judaism. This, I venture to think, is particularly the case in British and American scholarship, where there has generally been a great readiness to deal justly by Judaism.

In the new assessment, there is a rough parallel to the three attitudes which we referred to in the New Testament.

In their first flush of enthusiasm, some scholars so emphasized the richness and depth of first-century Judaism that they failed to recognize any fundamental differences between it and Christianity. Their works are, as it were, long panegyrics: this is to some extent true of R. Travers Herford, the pioneer Englishman, who set the sympathetic stream flowing.[7] No one can deny the magnitude of his contribution, but few either will deny that his treatment of first-century Judaism tends to be as sentimentalized, let us say, as that of Claude Montefiore.[8] James Parkes—*quem honoris causa nomino*—may also be charged with such anxiety to do justice to Judaism that at times he falls into a "diluted" understanding of the Christian faith; for example, he finds the faith centred in Sinai to be a communal one and against it he sets the faith centred in Calvary, which is individual. His sympathy with Judaism has perhaps led him to neglect certain aspects of Christianity. The same zeal, I believe, governs my distinguished predecessor, F. C. Grant, in his *Ancient Judaism and the New Testament*. And I may be allowed to recall that my own work, wrongly in my opinion, has been described as "pro-Semitic." The swing of the pendulum in British and American scholarship has seemed radical at times. But it is wise to perceive that violent reactions are seldom acceptable in the long run. The cause of Jewish-Christian mutual respect must be founded on a sober recognition and assessment of facts, not on enthusiasms.

Second, there are scholars who have been little touched in their interpretation of New Testament Christianity by the emergent empathy with Judaism. For instance, Professor Bultmann's treatment of Judaism in his *Jesus*, Berlin, 1929, is moving and illuminating. But he uses it as a background *against* which Jesus

---

[7] See his *Pharisaism*, London, 1912: *Christianity in Talmud and Midrash*, London, 1903, and other works.

[8] See especially his *Judaism and St. Paul*, London, 1914; *Rabbinic Literature and Gospel Teachings*, London, 1930; *The Synoptic Gospels*, 2 vols., London, 1927.

is to be understood, and, in his later theology, the appraisal of the Judaic roots of Christianity lacks positivity.

Third, over a broad section of New Testament scholarship, there has increasingly developed the recognition that the Christian faith is not only rooted in Judaism but is also its fulfilment, and that it carries over into its own life the structure of Judaism. The growth of this awareness has been attractively set forth in an article by Markus Barth in the *Journal of Ecumenical Studies* entitled "The Challenge of the Apostle Paul," Vol. 1, No. 1, pp. 58–81. When all exaggerations have been reckoned with, it is more and more evident that the relation between Judaism and Christianity is far more positive and complementary than the mists of history and religious narrowness had allowed us to see. For the sake of convenience, we shall ask how the dependence of Christianity on Judaism manifests itself in three areas: the theological, the ethical, and the organizational.

We shall assume that the Christian faith is concerned from first to last with the reality and purpose of the Living God who governs and sustains the universe. This monotheism it shares with and derives from Judaism. The world into which early Christianity moved was one familiar with gods many and lords many: it was only able to assume monotheism because it had been born within Judaism. But the achievement of monotheism within Judaism to start with had not been easy; it was only after the fires of the Exile that it can be said that monotheism became the faith of most religious Jews. Down to the last of the canonical Prophets, the reality of other gods was by no means generally rejected: in the strictest sense, monotheism was a costly acquisition within Judaism, and it was at this point that Christianity entered into its riches. There is never a suggestion in the New Testament that the God whom Christians presuppose is not the very same God that Judaism worshipped. The God who speaks to Christians in Jesus Christ is the God of Abraham, Isaac and Jacob. The God who, Christians believe, wrought their redemption in Christ is also the God who brought the Jews out of the land of Egypt, led them through the wilderness, spoke to them at Sinai, gave them the Prophets and brought them safely out of Babylon. Christianity has never doubted that it is the God who spoke to Israel in diverse ways and manners who also speaks in His Son. It is true that there have arisen in the Church those who have tried to dispute this: in the second century the Marcionites, in the twentieth those who tried to oust the Hebrew Bible from the services of the Church as an outmoded volume which can only be read seriously as good literature, touched perhaps with good morality. But they have failed to move Christians from the conviction that the God of the Old Covenant is also the God of the New Covenant, that the voice heard at Sinai and at Calvary is the voice of the same God.

As a result, the Old Testament is still part of the Christian Canon of Scripture, and has thus become, we hope, bone of our bone. Through it, Christians, to some extent at least, breathe the same air as Jewry. As a recent Pope has expressed it, "spiritually we are all Semites."

This identity of origin then, the fact that both Judaism and Christianity purport to have their origin in a revelation of the same God, the One God, naturally gives them a peculiar intimacy. We may confidently claim that Christianity owes its belief in the One God to Judaism.

The Early Church not only assumed the God of Judaism; it also assumed the sacredness of the Scriptures of Judaism, that is, it took over from Judaism a body of tradition—the Old Testament. True, Judaism had not finally fixed its canon when Jesus appeared, but it did already have a written Torah—comprising Law, Prophets and Writings—which it accepted as authoritative. This the Church took over. The significance of this acceptance cannot be exaggerated, for the Church acted here in the conviction that its own faith was rooted in the Old Testament and fulfilled it. This is another way of saying that the Church understood itself in the light of the Old Testament. Among the myriad consequences which flow from this basic fact, two may be mentioned:

First, like its acceptance of the God of Abraham and Isaac and Jacob, acceptance of the Old Testament tied Christianity forever to the stream of tradition which we know as Judaism. As did Judaism itself, so also the Church understood itself in the light of a particular history; it placed itself in the same stream of revelation as Judaism did; it bound itself not only to the God of Abraham and Isaac and Jacob but to the concrete history of His dealings with Israel, to Moses, Elijah, the Prophets, the sweet singers of Israel and its priests. The history of Judaism became part of the history of the Church. This also meant that, in a Christian view, Judaism made the Christian faith an inseparable part of its own history. Christianity is in a specific stream of history; it can never be detached from it without ceasing to be itself.

But, in taking the Old Testament as its sacred Scripture, the Early Church did more than recognize its historical connection and even continuity with Judaism; it provided itself with the concepts, terminology and motifs through which it was both to comprehend itself and interpret its faith to the world. In short, Judaism provided what Professor C. H. Dodd has taught us to call the "Substructure of Christian Theology."[9] New Testament Christianity, even in its Johannine form, is articulated in the language of Judaism.

This is made most clear in an area which has attracted much attention in the scholarship of the last few decades, namely, the use of quotations from the Old Testament in the New. These are not merely strange bits of jigsaw puzzles wrenched from the Old Testament, but indications of the way in which the very structure of Jewish thought determines the Christian. The evidence for this statement is so copious that no attempt to present it can be made here; a few examples of a more general and a more particular kind must suffice.[10]

[9] *According to the Scriptures*, London, 1952.
[10] For detailed support of this claim, see PRJ and, for example, R. Le Déaut, *La Nuit Pascale*.

First, let us look at the *broad way* in which early Christians thought of the Christian era or dispensation. There are two figures or metaphors which are familiar in the New Testament. The first is that of a new creation, along with which there go certain concomitants, such as the concept of Jesus the Messiah as the second Adam.

Another broad category derived from Judaism is that of the new Exodus, with its concomitant of Jesus as the new Moses. The thought that there is a real parallel between the events at the Exodus and those which inaugurated the Christian era is frequent in the New Testament. The evidence for this in the Gospel of Matthew and to some extent in Mark was recently presented in my SSM. It re-emerges clearly in Paul and, by way of antithesis, in the Fourth Gospel and elsewhere. The Early Church understood itself as having undergone a new Exodus: it drew one of the basic categories for its self-understanding from Judaism. Other major categories which it employed are patently derived from the same source—the Kingdom of God, for example in the Synoptics, and Eternal Life in the Fourth Gospel.

But it is important to recognize that in the minutae of its theological activity, through and in which it reflected upon its own existence, the Early Church thought essentially in the categories of Judaism. In *Paul and Rabbinic Judaism* (1948), I sought to show how the main motifs in Paulinism—the Flesh, the Last Adam, the Old and the New Man, Christ as the Wisdom of God, Obedience, Resurrection—are all best understood against the background of Pharisaic Judaism. In other documents of the New Testament, including those that have most often been connected with the Hellenistic world, the same could be shown to be true. Here two examples will be instanced, both from Paul, where, it would appear, the thought of the Apostle cannot adequately be understood either apart from the Old Testament or apart from Judaism. They are chosen because the matter with which they deal has frequently been taken to point to Hellenistic sources, namely, the concept of being "in Christ" and that of the "Body of Christ."[11]

Even if these illustrations of the dependence of the Church on Judaism be rejected, there are others which could be adduced to attest it. Few would not now agree that primitive Christianity, both in its grand outlines or major categories and in its details, is dependent upon Judaism. In this sense, the very matrix of Christianity is Judaism: Christianity is of the very bone of Judaism. Professor Jean Daniélou in his *Théologie du Judéo-Christianisme* (Paris, 1957), endeavoured to show—with much success—that its Semitic substructure continued to inform Christian theology right down to Nicaea. His first sentence reads:

> La théologie chrétienne utilisera à partir des Apologistes les instruments intellectuels de la philosophie grecque. Mais auparavant il y a eu une première théologie de structure sémitique.

[11] For details, see PRJ, pp. 87ff, *et passim*.

We might go even further than Daniélou, who confines his attention chiefly to apocalyptic Judaism, in insisting that *after* Nicaea also—simply because of the perpetuation of the New Testament and Old Testament in the life of the Church (not to speak of other currents) as its foundation documents—this substructure continued to exert its influence. Unfortunately, the full extent of this influence has never been recognized, because of Christian ignorance of Judaism. There is little doubt that a deeper understanding of the governing concepts of first-century Judaism would throw a flood of light on early Christianity. This has come home with particular force to me in extended discussions with Professor Abraham Heschel.[12] Phenomena such as the Resurrection, the Ascension and, indeed, the whole range of early Christian concern can only be illumined for us by a profounder penetration of Pharisaic Judaism.

As in the realm of theology, so in the realm of Ethics the debt of Christianity to Judaism is profound, even if its precise nature be difficult to assess. In a broad sense, Judaism and Christianity have an identity of moral concern over a wide area. Just as the aim of Christianity is to give its adherents what the New Testament calls "eternal life," both in this world and in the age to come, so too the Torah has been given to Israel that men might live by its precepts. Life in conformity to the will of God is the aim of both Judaism and Christianity. Both Church and Synagogue pray that the rule or Kingdom of God may come and His will be done, so that the Lord may be one and His people one.

And we may claim that the ethical tradition of Judaism has passed over into Christianity. Jesus was, in a certain sense, a rabbi no less than a prophet. Both the method and very largely the substance and form of his ethical teaching were rabbinical. Nourished in the Synagogue, Jesus gave his followers much of the ethic of the Synagogue. The moral demands of Jesus as set forth in *The Sermon on the Mount* are introduced by the words: "Think not that I am come to destroy the law, or the prophets; I am not come to destroy, but to fulfil (Matt. 5: 17)." The teaching of Jesus is presented as the culmination—the full flowering —of the moral tradition of Judaism. This concept must be given its full weight. So also the motivation for the good life in Christianity and Judaism must be recognized as similar. For both, gratitude to God is the dynamic of the good life and obedience to the will of God its content. It is thus possible to speak of a Judaeo-Christian ethical tradition which Jews and Christians have in common.

The difficulty which presents itself at this point is brought to a sharp focus in Paul. Is it not true that Paul rejected the very essence of Judaism—salvation by the *mitzwoth*—in favour of salvation by faith and the spirit? Is it not also true that the New Testament generally forsakes the oral tradition of Judaism at least and concentrates on the strictly moral tradition of the Old Testament? Does it not so elevate the command of *agapé* that it depresses vast stretches of the ethical tradition of Judaism and ignores it? On this, one can only assert that, however

12 See his *Torah min ha-shamaim*, 2 vols., London, 1962, 1965.

far primitive Christianity departed from the *form* which moral concern assumed in Judaism, the reality of that concern remained. That the Gospel is nowhere set forth without a moral demand we owe to Judaism. I should go further. Christianity took over from Judaism a fundamentally *covenantal* structure within which morality is fundamental. Nowhere in the New Testament, because of its rooting in Judaism, does the moral demand cease to be endemic to Christianity. This is as true of Paul as of Matthew. However much it may be claimed that Christianity jettisoned the moral-legal tradition of Judaism, it retained the heart of the matter. The *new commandment* of John, the *Golden Rule* of Matthew, the *Law of the Messiah* of Paul, the *new Covenant* of Hebrews—they all presuppose that the *commandment* remains inseparable from the Gospel. This is part of Christianity's abiding debt to Judaism. It may be admitted that the *form* of morality in Christianity has come to differ from that of Judaism, but the concern with morality as the Divine Imperative has remained in the daughter-faith.

There is another area of indebtedness. Judaism and Christianity reveal an identity of conception as to the means whereby the purpose of God is to be achieved. For Judaism, as for the Old Testament, the community of God's people, the Israel of God, is the agent of God in the world. It was *a people* that God chose as the Exodus to be His messengers in the world, and, in a real sense, the Old Testament is the record of God's attempts to prepare for Himself a peculiar people that should make known His ways.

But what is true of Judaism is also true of New Testament Christianity. As in the Old Testament and for Judaism, God's purposes are now to be achieved through a community—the New Israel of God, the Church. For the New Testament, the Church is, in fact, Israel in a new manifestation of its history. This is so clear that, even in writing to bemused Corinthian converts, Paul can speak of the Jews of the Exodus as the "fathers" of Christians without having to explain what he meant. That God's purpose is to be fulfilled, not only and not chiefly by isolated individuals, but by the life of a witnessing community, is as true of Christianity as of Judaism. And the relation of the New Israel and the Old is one not just of antithesis but of fulfilment and continuity. The communal self-awareness of Christianity stems from Judaism.

Moreover, it is not only in the concept of the Church as constituting the true Israel that the New Israel is indebted to the Old. The very forms which the New Testament used to express the new life "in Christ" were borrowed from Judaism. In the early years of this century, under the influence of the school of comparative religion, the sacraments of Baptism and the Lord's Supper were traced to Hellenistic religions, the Mysteries. But more recent work has at least opened up the possibility that these two central moments of the Christian community are to be understood in terms of baptismal and Passover practices within Judaism.

When we turn to the disciplinary practice, spasmodically revealed in the New Testament, we find dependence on disciplinary forms already evolved in Judaism.

This is true, for example, of the "Manual of Discipline" in Matthew 18, where both Rabbinic and Qumran usages seem to be taken over by the Matthaean Church for its own purposes. A Jewish origin is suggested also by Paul's disciplinary activity.

In two other areas, the influence of the Synagogue emerges in the organizational aspects of the life of the Church. The forms of Christian worship can be shown to have been influenced by the Synagogue at various points and the structure of the ministries in the Church likewise reflects its impact.

We may now sum up wherein lies the debt of Christianity to Judaism. It owes to Judaism the awareness of the Living God, Who is no absentee landlord but actively engaged in the history of those whom He created. The sense of history as the sphere of divine activity and not the blind, meaningless outcome of a fortuitous conglomeration of atoms, or the ever-recurring expression of uncontrolled and uncontrollable cosmic force, of fate and death—this Christianity owes to Judaism. That is, it owes to Judaism the recognition of the meaningfulness of the stage on which the human drama is played and its awareness of the demand laid upon it—its moral seriousness, and its self-awareness as a community.

THE RELATIONSHIP BETWEEN CHRISTIANITY AND JUDAISM IN THE LIGHT OF HISTORY

How does the rooting of the Church in Judaism profit Christianity? This is, at first encounter, an ungracious question, as if a daughter asked how she profits from her mother. For Christians to ask it suggests such an insensitivity to the rock whence they were hewn that I feel hesitant in answering, apart from my lack of competence to discuss the many comparative issues involved. In the course of its history, Christianity has undergone Hellenization, Romanization and Westernization; in our day it is likely to undergo Asianization and Americanization. To reply to our question demands a comparative estimate of the value for Christianity of the influences it has absorbed and which have informed it. The problem already faces us in the New Testament, where Hellenistic and Roman factors are at work, even in Paul himself. In emphasizing the importance of its Jewish roots for Christianity, I shall, then, not attempt to evaluate it in comparison with other factors. Enough to say that I cannot accept the view that a rigid adherence to those roots alone would have sufficed for Christianity or imagine that the elimination of Roman and Greek and Western influences on, and from formulations of, Christianity would, in itself, be salutary. Christianity, no less than Judaism, cannot refuse to meet the challenge of new cultures and to some extent absorb their structures and thought-forms. And a return to the "simplest" Judaic expression of Christianity, in its neatness, would be as futile as it would be impossible. For example, there are those who would confine the meaning and significance of the Gospel to the eschatological categories of primitive Christianity and retain the Judaic understanding of history as an *essential* of the Gospel, while rejecting every Hellenization of the faith and every attempt to give another conceptual form to it. But the rejection of Hellenism in the understanding of Christianity is not a real possibility for us. Historically, even Judaism itself before the advent of Christianity was partially Hellenized and the New Testament itself, Judaic in its substructure as it is, is nevertheless Hellenistic in its dress. Moreover, I cannot concede that Christianity itself demands a resistance to all non-Judaic modes of interpreting our Christian experience.

Historically, nevertheless, Christianity has often been more prone to accommodate itself to new worlds than to remain true to its Judaic origin. So our question might, perhaps, be more pertinently phrased: "How could Christianity have profited from its rooting in Judaism?" Because, in fact, the history of Christendom, by revealing its neglect of Judaism, makes clear how it *could have* profited from it. So my best answer is to point out, using an indirect and negative method, how, historically, Christianity has suffered from its neglect of Judaism and the Church been impoverished; this may lead us to an appreciation of some of the positive values of the connection between Christianity and Judaism. In view of the intimacy between the two religions, it is not surprising that the Church of the first century continued a living dialogue between many Jews and Christians. Eminent rabbis were often in close contact with Christians. But as time went on, there was a severance and the recognition of a shared heritage was submerged by concentration on the points of difference.

The central such point has always been the evaluation of Jesus of Nazareth as the Messiah. But there were others—the evaluation and place of the Law, the significance of the Church as the New Israel. Is the Law superseded in the coming of Christ; has the Old Israel a *raison d'être* now that the New Israel has come? What difference would it make if synagogues and their endless reading of the Law ceased to exist?

Changes came as the Church spread more and more into the Latin world of the West, the Hellenistic and Slavonic world, and as it became the established Church of the Empire, West and East. With the growth of its social and political prestige, the religious emphases the Church had shared with Judaism became progressively weaker. In new climates of thought, what had once been in essence a Judaic religion became Hellenized. Gradually, as the minority Christian community became the dominant one and Judaism found itself subservient to its own daughter-faith, the dialogue became a war—a shameful war.

The price paid by Judaism has been relentless suffering. But the price paid by Christianity has been no less real, though less obvious. It has paid the price of shame and guilt for its bloody past. Its own life has been emaciated by the neglect of its own roots.

It might be argued that, for its abuse of its mother-Synagogue, for condemning and neglecting it, the Church ran the risk of forgetting the "democratic" note in Judaism. The birth of what seems, to many outsiders at least, an almost "militarily" hierarchical organization in the West, and a hierarchical system dominated by the State in the East, is connected with the Church's failure to understand itself as the "People of God," as had the Old Israel. By relinquishing the more humble Synagogue, the Church organism more easily developed into an organization, a community stratified like the surrounding society and organized in terms of a ministry separated from, though maintained by, a subservient laity.

The "imperialization" of the Church in the East and West was possible only because it refused to be true to the democratic genius of the Synagogue. A Jew in the Middle Ages expressed this point dramatically: "Through the establishment of the episcopate of the Church in Rome, the Christians may be considered Romans."[13] The Church preferred to imitate imperial forms rather than follow the more modest forms of the Synagogue. The results we know—in the papal pretensions of the Middle Ages, the clerical pomposities that still lay so much religious activity open to the charge of empty vanity.

It is significant that the changes being urged at Vatican II in favour of collegiality and decentralization have found their inspiration in the rediscovery of the Biblical understanding of the Church as the "People of God," which could not help but produce a revolt against any rigidly hierarchical organization. The Reformation moved in the direction of simplicity in religion, and away from authoritarianism, precisely because it deliberately returned to the Biblical roots of the faith.

Of course, the true democratization of religion still has a long distance to go. One way in which its progress can be helped is by the resumption of the dialogue with the Synagogue from which "democracy" in the sense here employed has never departed.

Linked with the democratic tradition of the Synagogue is its moral tradition. The Church has not been without its strong moral concerns. The Synagogue has often produced a most banal and barren moralism. But there can be little doubt that, when the Synagogue and the Church parted company, the Church was morally impoverished. The moral tradition of Judaism rooted in the Old Testament and interpreted by Scribe and Rabbi gave the Synagogue a depth of moral sensitivity and a communal awareness that were impressive. As the Church became more and more Hellenized and Romanized and Erastian, it largely lost these.

Two developments may be connected with the decline of living contact with the Synagogue, though they may not be directly caused by it.

First, the swiftly widening separation of the religious life from the common life of man. The monastic movement is the glaring example. The forces of moral seriousness were channelled to the cloister and the nunnery. A double morality

---

[13] Cited by H. J. Schoeps: *The Jewish-Christian Argument*, trans., New York, 1963.

arose: a higher morality for life out of the world and a lower one for life in it. The affirmation of all life as sacred, which has generally characterized the Synagogue, was ignored—and the Christian world became divided into clerical and lay people, secular and sacred institutions, holy persons and holy things being set over against unholy things. The wholeness of life that Judaism has stressed was lost. Nor has Protestantism escaped the sacred-secular dualism. The divorce of religion from life is part of the price paid for our neglect of the Synagogue. This is true despite the separation of things clean and unclean in Judaism, and the separation from the world involved in keeping the Law; throughout all this "separation" Judaism was attempting to take seriously the application of the Law, that is, God's will, to all life.

Second, and not unrelated, is the loss—more especially in Protestantism—of the communal awareness that the Synagogue has always fostered. Catholicism has always preserved a certain communal awareness. Within Protestantism, despite its biblicism,[14] an overdone individualism in piety and life has often reared its head. The strong communal sense of the Synagogue, within which each suffered for the other in the interest of the whole, often vanished and blatant forms of individualism (not seldom another name for callousness) found the benediction of religion. Reinhold Niebuhr has frequently said that what impressed him most in his fight for social justice was that most of those who were fighting beside him were Jews and Roman Catholics. His experience is not unique. There can be little question that the divorce of the Church from the Synagogue was accompanied by a lessening of its social awareness.

The divorce has meant a great loss *within* the Church: it has resulted in a dilution of that rugged "democratic" moral, prophetic tradition out of which the Gospel rose. But Christendom could not long deny its own origins without paying the price even more directly *from outside*. The Judaic thrust behind Christendom, suppressed across the centuries, reasserted itself in the last century, and in a strange quarter.

Within a Christendom in which the faith had more and more forfeited its Judaic flavour, there arose a mighty secular protest, that of international Marxism. Marx himself had little truck with Judaism, which he regarded with contempt. Nevertheless, that he was a Jew is symbolic—symbolic of the fact that a Christendom that denies its Judaic roots, does so at its peril. Marxism is largely the protest of the secular world against a Christianity that has sold its birthright and become so conformed to this world that it has failed to register its protest against the exploitation of men. Marxism is the nemesis of a de-Judaized Christianity.

In this sense, there is a connection between Moscow and what is going on now

---

[14] It should be recognized that Catholicism in the Middle Ages and later did not neglect the Old Testament, in a radical sense at least (see, for example, the work of Smalley), but it did cut itself off from the synagogal life.

in Rome. It is no accident that, when the vitality of communism is recognized, the Church should turn to its nexus with the Synagogue, heedlessness whereof led to this great outcry against pseudo-spirituality in so much of Christendom.[15]

Where its Jewish rootage is overlooked, Christianity tends to lose the living awareness of the Living God at work in history in favour of other worldliness, mysticism and "gnosis": it tends to lessen the astringent moral imperative of a call to live out its faith in the world; it tends to lose its sense of itself as, above all, a people and not a structured organization; and to forsake the world for the wrong reasons. Where the benefits of Judaism are consciously cherished, these aberrations can be avoided. But it is only now, beyond the great and terrible divide of Hitler and beyond the great and glorious divide of John XXIII, that we are at last speaking about these things openly. At long last we can confess our contribution to the murder of the Jews in Christian Europe; we can repent for the neglect of the Church's Jewish heritage. We are given in Romanism and Protestantism a unique opportunity to open the heart of the Church to the Synagogue, and to renew the dialogue that history has broken. The conditions are present for Church and Synagogue to coexist in mutual stimulus, respect and fruition. That the benefits to the Church would be enormous we have no doubt; that the Synagogue would also benefit we cannot but hope.

When Paul thought of what Israel could give the Church, he could only use the amazing expression: it would be "life from the dead" (Rom. 11: 15). There can be few more urgent tasks for the Church than to prepare for this dialogue, that it be really a dialogue and not a soliloquy, and marked by that radical frankness which alone makes genuine dialogue possible and profitable.

[15] It is an incredible, but significant, fact that the present Pope, Paul VI, is the first Roman Pontiff to have visited the land of Jesus.

APPENDIX II

THE DIFFERENCES BETWEEN JUDAISM AND CHRISTIANITY

TORAH AND DOGMA: A COMMENT[1]

The suggestion has often been made recently that the relationship between Judaism and Christianity can be adequately described in terms of a "schism." This suggestion is worthy of serious consideration. It has much to commend it. It promises new possibilities (badly needed in view of past history), because "schism" can be healed. But its mere attractiveness and beneficial potential should not blind us to the problems involved. Because the term "schism" presupposes an underlying unity, its use to describe the relation between the two faiths preserves an emphasis which, in our given situation, where the dependence of the Church on the Synagogue is not sufficiently recognized, is too easily lost. And yet, without very careful definition, the term "schism" may be misleading. Who are to be called schismatics? Is it Christians for leaving Judaism or Jews for rejecting the Christian Messiah and his people? As will become apparent in the following pages, there are two extreme positions to be avoided. On the one hand, that which regards the relationship between Judaism and Christianity at the present time as so close that that relationship is merely schismatic, and, on the other hand, that which regards that relationship as one of unrelieved antithesis.

I

The theme of one section of the Harvard Colloquium on Christianity and Judaism was entitled *Torah and Dogma*, and it was no doubt intended that the two terms in the title should stand for Judaism and Christianity respectively. Such a designation is understandable, but by no means unproblematic. It is important to recognize its implications and limitations. It implies that the characteristic mark of Judaism is *Halakah* or *Torah* and that of Christianity *Dogma*.[2] The one religion is primarily concerned with the "way to live"—*halak*, "to walk"—the other with the way to believe, with the proper creedal formulations.

Now, this distinction between the two faiths cannot be pressed to the last degree. In a limited sense it can be claimed that Judaism demands certain beliefs. Scholars have pointed out a kerygmatic[3] core in the Old Testament. Just as

[1] These reflections on Torah and Dogma were presented as a comment on a paper by Kornelius H. Miskotte, author of *Wenn die Götter schweigen*, and published in HTR, Vol. 61, No. 2, 1968, 87ff, reprinted in *Colloquium on Judaism and Christianity held at Harvard Divinity School, October 17–20, 1966. Introduction by K. Stendahl*, pp. 86–105.

[2] By dogma, I understand a truth necessary for Salvation propounded by an authoritative council or organ of the Church.

[3] The term *kerygma* (that which is preached) is Greek, but has now become domiciled in English to designate the content of the Christian proclamation or recital in the New Testament. See C. H. Dodd, *The Apostolic Preaching and its Developments*, London, 1936.

behind the New Testament there is a kerygma centred in an event—the life, death and resurrection of Jesus of Nazareth, so in the Old Testament the Exodus constitutes a kerygmatic core. This emerges clearly in passages where "creedal," confessional materials older than the texts in which they occur break through, as in Deut. 26: 5ff, which recapitulates the mighty deeds which gave birth to Israel (see also Deut. 6: 20–24; Joshua 24: 26–34; Deut. 4: 32–34, etc.). The kerygmatic core in the Old Testament is a kind of confession of faith. Again the *Shema* expresses the quintessence of a Faith—if you like a Dogma of Judaism. Occasionally in the *Mishnah* an anathema is uttered against those who deny certain cardinal tenets of Judaism. A famous passage in *M. Sanhedrin* 10: 1 reads as follows:

> All Israelites have a share in the world to come, for it is written, *Thy people also shall all be righteous, they shall inherit the land forever; the branch of my planting, the work of my hands that I may be glorified.* And these are they that have no share in the world to come: he that says that there is no resurrection of the dead prescribed in the Law, and [he that says] that the Law is not from Heaven, and an Epicurean. R. Akiba says: Also he that reads the heretical books, or that utters charms over a wound and says, *I will put none of the diseases upon thee which I have put upon the Egyptians: for I am the Lord that healeth thee.* Abba Saul says: Also he that pronounces the Name with its proper letters... (Danby's translation).

Later on Maimonides was to issue his understanding of Judaism as a creed, and nineteenth-century movements in Judaism, both Conservative and Reform, sought to clarify the tenets of Judaism.[4] A British author, in a volume entitled *Judaism as Creed of Life*, summarizes Judaism as Belief in God and Human Responsibility. The point is that there is a "dogma" or "creed" implicit, if not always explicit, in Judaism.[5]

But, when all this has been granted, the essential demand of Judaism is obedience to the Torah, the observance of the *Mitzwôth* (Commandments). The anathemas in *Mishnah Sanhedrin* 10 strike one as being haphazard: they are not the considered "dogmatic" pronouncement of an authorized body of leaders nor are they presented with the full-blasted force of a "dogma"; they do not stand out in any way from other materials in *Sanhedrin*; they are given no prominence, not to speak of preeminence.[6] Not dogmatic pronouncements, but legal directions are important. The musical "The Fiddler on the Roof" opens with a catching song on Tradition. Precariously balanced as Judaism has been on the whims of the Gentile world, what has kept it alive is Tradition—a way of doing things, a way of baking bread, sewing clothes, slaughtering animals, keeping the house clean. Judaism is a way. And the song asks: Whence

---

[4] This emerges clearly in Joseph L. Blau, *Modern Varieties of Judaism*, Columbia Univeristy Press, 1966.

[5] Morris Joseph, *Judaism as Creed and Life*, Macmillan, London, 1903.

[6] In the discussion at Harvard, Professor Judah Goldin drew a conclusion exactly opposite to mine from this fact. That the "anathemas" are inserted without special introduction or emphasis means, in his view, that their outstanding importance was assumed. I hesitate to differ from such a Rabbinist, but I fail in this instance to be convinced.

is this tradition? Who gave it? Nobody quite knows; but it is *here*, and Jews live by it. True, the composer of "The Fiddler on the Roof" may be an *am há-áretz*. But the song, nevertheless, illustrates the concern of Judaism. The primary concern is not the understanding of Tradition, not the formulating of it by doctrine and dogma, although there is a search for the grounds of Torah, that is, the reasons for the commandments. The heart of the matter is rather living it, observing it, albeit with love, joy and trust in God, the Father.

It agrees with this that within Judaism "belief" can range at will. There are certain implicit, and sometimes explicit, basic principles to which we have already referred. But these apart, it is rightly, if humorously, asserted that where there are three Jews, there can be four opinions. For example, there is no one doctrine of the Messiah. It is easily possible for a Jew to claim to be the Messiah without incurring censure, provided he observes the *Mitzwôth*. Herbert Danby is reported to have said, playfully no doubt, that he once lectured in Jerusalem when there were six Messiahs in his audience. To observe the Law confers freedom for almost anything else and, to parody Augustine, a Jew might urge: "Observe the Law and believe what you like." There was recently, for example, the extreme but interesting case of an American Rabbi who refused to believe in God and yet continued in the Rabbinate.[7]

Jewish scholars often affirm that what Judaism presents us with is a multiplicity of individual opinions, but no "theology." For example, a distinguished Jewish scholar on reading the chapter in my work SSM, which deals with the concept of a New Torah, courteously commented that, while all the data in the chapter were correct, he wondered whether one could deal thematically, as I had done, with any idea in the Rabbis. The Rabbis were individuals holding diverse opinions. Certainly they held certain ideas which were theological, but they were not systematic theologians in any sense; they never constructed a theology for Judaism nor any dogmatic system.[8] It is significant that Samuel Schechter wrote a book not on *Rabbinic Theology* as such, but on *Some Aspects of Rabbinic Theology*, a title which suggests the fragmentary, unsystematic character of its theme; and it is often hinted that he had great difficulty in writing even on aspects of it.

Related to this, and perhaps determinative of it, is the fundamental fact that, however much exaggerated by Christian scholars, Rabbinic piety is essentially

---

[7] *Time Magazine*. On all the above see Scholem, *The Messianic Idea*, pp. 282ff, especially pp. 289f. In Judaism "Truth is given once and for all, and it is laid down with precision. Fundamentally, truth merely needs to be transmitted...Not system but commentary is the legitimate form through which truth is approached" (p. 289). This remained true even though under the influence of Greek thought systems of "theology" were attempted (see below, n. 14).

[8] A Biblical student cannot but ask whether, if the same standards were applied to the Old Testament as are applied to the Rabbinic sources to deny the possibility of a Rabbinic Theology, Biblical Theology, as it has developed in our time, would ever have been possible. Does not it, too, often imply a system or connections between various documents and figures where none existed?

nomistic in that it was the Torah given on Mount Sinai in a past age that was regulative for all life. "The Rabbis," writes Cohen, "would have denied that they were originators of Jewish thought. All they would have admitted was that they were excavators in the inexhaustible mine of the divine Revelation contained in the Scriptures and brought to light treasures that lay hidden beneath the surface."[9]

In addition to all the above, another factor causes many modern Rabbinic scholars to hesitate to formulate a Theology of the Rabbis, and that is the unexamined and unsifted character of the Rabbinic texts on which such a formulation would have to be based. This can best be illustrated, for example, from the illuminating studies of Judah Goldin on various key texts. He shows how very fluid the Rabbinic tradition was and how precarious any theological construction built upon them must be.[10]

The upshot of all this is that there is what might almost be called a consensus that Judaism is essentially halakic, that is, concerned with the way to live according to the commandments, and not theological: it is not orthodoxy but orthopraxy that marks Judaism. Judaism—to use a term that has been used to express this point of view—is *pan-halakic*.[11]

There are Jewish scholars who hold a different view. Abraham Heschel has urged that *Haggadah* can be made to reveal distinct theological currents of thought within Judaism. He distinguishes a theological difference between the traditions emanating from the school of Rabbi Akiba and those from the school of Rabbi Ishmael, finding the one more mystical and the other more rational than the other.[12] Heschel's work is too recent to have been assimilated and assessed,[13] and it would be presumptuous on my part to enter into this debate, but we may point out certain factors that are pertinent in its evaluation. The implication of Heschel's position is that in the Tannaitic period theological speculation of a sophisticated kind prevailed in Rabbinic schools. One thing does suggest considerable speculation at least, even if it were not systematic, and that is the very great extent of the haggadic material extant in Rabbinic sources. It is far more extensive than strictly halakic material. Despite its formlessness, it is difficult to imagine that such extensive *Haggadah* has merely a kind of fanciful, homiletical significance, devoid of all serious theological value.

[9] A. Cohen, *Everyman's Talmud*, 1932, p. 122. See R. T. Herford, *Pharisaism*, 1912, chapters 1 and 2; J. Bonsirven, *Le Judaïsme Palestinien*, Vol. I, 1934, pp. 248f.

[10] See, for example, J. Goldin, "The End of Ecclesiastes: Literal Exegesis and its Transformation," *Studies and Texts*, Vol. III, *Biblical Motifs*, ed. Alexander Altmann, Harvard University Press, 1966, pp. 135–138.

[11] I owe this phrase to A. Heschel's work, *God in Search of Man: A Philosophy of Judaism*, 1955, pp. 323, 328.

[12] Two volumes of Heschel's work on this theme have already appeared (unfortunately only in Hebrew) and another is in preparation; *Torah min ha-shamaim*, Vol. 1, 1962, Vol. 2, 1965.

[13] There is a review of the second volume by Jacob Neusner in *Conservative Judaism*, Vol. 20, No. 3, 1966, pp. 66–73.

Would the haggadic materials have survived across the centuries, were merely this the case? Moreover, there are historical considerations which might have induced a diminution of theological interest in Judaism since Tannaitic times. Once Judaism came to occupy an inferior and despised position in a world where Christianity was dominant, particularly when it increasingly became confined to the Ghetto, it was natural that it should be overawed by the intellectual, no less than by the material and political, dominance of Christianity. The very magnificence of the theological achievement of medieval Christendom had an inhibiting effect on any Jewish theological speculation that might have arisen. And, later, in the period when Jewry was emancipated from the Ghetto, it was often understandably dazzled by the new world into which it entered. The lure and fascination of European culture often very naturally led to a neglect of Jewish theologizing. By and large, the intellectual energies of Jewry were consecrated to the newly opened, expansive, and insidious secular interests of nineteenth-century Europe, when assimilation became common. When Jewry did react "theologically" to Western culture, it was natural for it to do so either in a liberal fashion which, like Protestant Liberalism, did not foster theological profundity or in a conservative fashion, which led to renewed concentration on *Halakah*. The neglect of theology by secularized and religious Jews in modern times is historically understandable.

However all this may be, it is probably true to claim that the *dominant* position still among Jewish scholars is that in Judaism not opinion, doctrine, or dogma matter primarily, but practice, observance in trust and joy.[14] The peculiar genius of Judaism is expressed not in creeds, like the Nicene or the Chalcedonian in Christianity, but in a law book, *The Mishnah*. While in certain Kabbalistic and mystical circles, which have persisted throughout Jewish history, a speculative, even esoteric, interest constantly emerges, the main stream of Judaism appears not to have taken kindly to this and has preferred to retain a kind of massive halakic simplicity, suspicious of speculation and uninterested in dogma. The actuality of obedience to the Torah, not theological interpretation of it, has been

---

[14] Perhaps Heschel himself would agree with this statement. He has written eloquently of the "divinity of deeds" and the "wonder of doing" in Judaism. "A Jew is asked," he writes, "to take a *leap of action* rather than a *leap of thought* (*A Philosophy of Judaism*, p. 283)." Heschel is concerned, of course, not to deny or even minimize the significance of halakah for Judaism, but to hold it in proper balance with haggadah. He traces the pan-halakic emphasis back to Spinoza down through Moses Mendelssohn: "With Spinoza, [Mendelssohn] maintains that Judaism asks for obedience to a law but not acceptance of doctrines. 'Judaism is no revealed religion in the usual sense of the term, but only *revealed legislation*, laws, commandments, and regulations, which were supernaturally given to the Jews through Moses.' It demands no faith, no specific religious attitudes. 'The Spirit of Judaism is freedom in doctrine and conformity in action' [Heschel's text is here reproduced as it stands. Both quotations apparently are from Mendelssohn's *Jerusalem*, chapter 2. This is the only reference given by Heschel, who also refers to Hermann Cohen, *Die Religion der Vernunft*, pp. 415ff. See Heschel, *A Philosophy of Judaism*, pp. 321, 333]." How the question is exercising modern Jewry can be quickly gleaned from David Aronson, "Faith and Halakah," *Conservative Judaism*, Vol. 21, No. 1, 1966, pp. 34–48. (See n. 7.)

the hallmark of Judaism. The Torah is the peculiar property of Judaism: it is its
heart. The clean challenge of the commandments (*Mitzwôth*) cuts through all the
sentimentality, mysticism, Gnosticism, and irrelevance of which, according to
some Jews and many Christians, the Christian faith has been guilty. Leo Baeck
especially has forcefully set forth the cleanliness of the commandment in
Judaism over against the murky religiosity and the irrelevant piety of which
Christianity is so often capable.[15]

And it is at this point that Christianity is usually claimed especially to differ
from Judaism. "All the Christian objections to Judaism," writes Schoeps, "and
the corresponding Jewish replies pale into insignificance before the point of
dispute...which was decisive in the life of Saul of Tarsus: whether the Law has
not found its fulfilment and been abolished through belief in the Lord and
Savior, Jesus of Nazareth."[16]

Now, the Christianity that emerges in the New Testament is not as opposed
to Law as Baeck and other scholars, Christian no less than Jewish, have maintained. In Matthew, and even in Paul, there is room for Law, and for a new
commandment in John. The early Church often strikes one as a Bible class concerned with halakah. As Stendahl has suggested in his well-known book and
more recently in an as yet unpublished paper, there is in the New Testament a
halakic Christianity.[17] The earliest Christians among other things were called
those of "The Way"—of the Christian halakah. Probably this aspect of
primitive Christianity has been neglected for a simple reason. The kerygma has
so dominated recent scholarship that the didache, although recognized, has been
unconsciously and consciously relegated to a secondary status. This is not the
place to assess the role of the kerygma in the New Testament. Suffice that it has
too often been rigidly and even wholly separated from the total life of the
Church and presented as a phenomenon in a vacuum. In fact, the kerygma was
one aspect of the life of primitive Christianity embedded in and accompanied by
a rich communal life—a "way." This "way" has continued to inform the life
of the Church throughout the centuries. I am not competent to trace this fact
historically in its various forms—in the imitation of Christ and otherwise. But it
is safe to hazard the statement that it is witness to the "way" among Christians,
and not any kerygma proclaimed, that has most furthered the Christian faith.
In any case, it is well to recognize that a complete separation of Judaism as a
religion of Torah from Christianity as a religion of Dogma cannot be justified.
Christianity, too, is a halakah.[18]

[15] See Leo Baeck's chapters on "The Faith of Paul," "Mystery and Commandment,'
"Romantic Religion," in *Judaism and Christianity*, trans., Walter Kaufmann, 1959, pp. 139–
292.

[16] Hans Joachim Schoeps, *The Jewish–Christian Argument: A History of Theologies in
Conflict*, trans., D. E. Green, 1963, p. 40.

[17] *The School of St. Matthew* (1954; 2nd ed., 1968). Philadelphia.

[18] For the justification for most of the above paragraph, see SSM. Unfortunately I
have not seen Eero Repo, *Der Weg als Selbstbezeichnung des Urchristentums*, Helsinki,

But once this be admitted, it has further to be stated at once that, in fact, Christianity in the course of time did develop into a dogmatic system in a way which Judaism did not. I am not sufficiently versed in Jewish history to explain why this is so, that is, why Judaism did not pursue refined dogmatic speculation as did Christianity. In addition to the historical considerations suggested above, one may hazard the suggestion that the Jewish Halakah sufficiently safeguarded the uniqueness of Jewish faith. In the Torah Judaism possessed a wall of fire which needed no dogmatic justification to surround and safeguard it, so effective was it. And the most obvious reason why Christianity developed into a dogmatic system is that, as the Palestinian faith, without the benefit of a full and growing unmistakable fence, such as the Jewish Torah, spread throughout the Graeco-Roman world, it had to define itself over against the various forces that threatened it. The evolution of the New Testament Canon, the Episcopate and, especially, in this connection, Creed or Dogma is the response of Christianity to Gnostic and other well-known pressures. Gradually the Church became Hellenized, and with Hellenization came orthodoxy, which culminated in the great dogmatic statements of the Councils. *Belief*, not *Halakah*, became important. The increasing separation of the Church from its Hebraic root in the Synagogue meant increasingly the predominance of Dogma over Torah. I am tempted to think that, along with this separation, the threat of meaninglessness in the Church increased. Judaism has always managed to retain a massive awareness of the purpose of God, an awareness that made refined theological speculation unnecessary. Christianity, more exposed to the winds of the world, perhaps, has had to fight more the meaninglessness of things, and this fight is one of the sources of its dogmatic evolution. It had to impose a meaning, a creed, a dogma on meaninglessness in a way the more rooted Synagogue could afford to neglect.

Has not the time now come for the Church to recognize all this fully and by renewing its contact with the Synagogue to restore the balance between Kerygma and Didache, Dogma and Torah?

II

Let us turn to the next point. Broadly speaking only, I have suggested that it is justifiable to think of Christianity in terms of Dogma and of Judaism in terms of Torah. A concomitant of this is a point which, more than any other, I think, has always impressed me very forcibly. It is the absence in Judaism of a *crippling*

1964. Dr. Reinhold Niebuhr, however, warned me of the dangers that lurk in the sentence: "Christianity, too, is a *halakah*." He reminded me of the radical criticism of the Law implied and sometimes expressed in the ministry of Jesus and in the epistles of Paul. His point may be met, I think, by claiming that halakah in Christianity is not the means of salvation so much as its accompaniment. Christianity must always be antilegalistic even though it must never be antinomian. On the other hand, it should not be overlooked that for Judaism the Law is an expression of grace as well as a means to grace. The true emphasis in this matter is difficult of achievement.

sense of sin and guilt. One can hardly turn to any of the Christian classics, from the first century down through Augustine to Luther and thence to Barth and Niebuhr, without at times being overwhelmed by the profound sense of sin which everywhere apparently accompanies Christianity.

True, the sense of sin is not absent from the Old Testament, as in the familiar Psalm 139 and elsewhere. "Can the leopard change his spots?" is an Old Testament verse (Jer. 13: 23). The Day of Atonement is a central festival of Judaism. True also that the power of the unconscious in Freud has been traced to roots in Jewish thought about the *Yêṭzer hâ-râ'* (the Evil Impulse).[19] But by and large it is an invincible optimism that wells up in Rabbinic Judaism. The commandment was given to be obeyed, and the implication is that man *can* obey it. Jewish history presents the most incredible record of justification for utter despair and yet of the persistence of hope. The evil *yêṭzer* is recognized; the fall of Adam was momentous in its consequences; everything is determined. Yes: but free will is given (cf. *Aboth* 3: 19). I do not recall any Rabbinic passage where there is a pervading sense of the miasma of sin or anything like a doctrine of original sin. Sin is a sore to which the ointment of the Torah may be applied: significantly the evil *yêṭzer* is an impulse, not a condition or state, as, for example, is sin in Paul. There are, it is true, passages in the Dead Sea Scrolls which approach the Christian sense of the miasma of sin, but even here sin is essentially transgression.[20] The air that Judaism breathes is that of the commandment—direct, fresh, simple. There is in Judaism, as compared with Christianity, little introspection, little preoccupation with conscience, for which it has no word, comparatively little torturing of the soul.[21] Asceticism, for example, is largely alien to Judaism, and is condemned by the rabbis.

How different is the history of Christianity where Sin, with a capital S, has been recognized as "exceeding sinful" from the beginning, where "the bondage of the will" is a familiar doctrine. I suggest that where "optimism" of the kind that pervades Judaism, despite the tragedies of its history, is dominant, Dogma is likely to be secondary. It is the awareness of Sin that makes the theologian.[22]

---

[19] See N. P. Williams, *The Ideas of the Fall and of Original Sin*, 1927, ad rem.

[20] See, e.g., the closing psalm of the Manual of Discipline. The pertinent passage reads as follows in Millar Burrows's trans., *The Dead Sea Scrolls*, 1955, p. 388:

> But I belong to wicked mankind,
> to the company of erring flesh
> my iniquities, my transgression, my sin,
> with the iniquity of my heart
> belong to the company of worms and those
>   who walk in darkness.
> For the way of a man is not his own... (IQS xi. 9f).

[21] See my article on "Conscience" in IDB.

[22] In the Colloquium I said, "It is Sin that makes the theologian"—using a shorthand for: "It is the awareness of Sin that makes the theologian." The phrase "Sin makes the theologian (*Peccatum facit theologum*)" is an unconscious corruption on my part of a Latin scholastic tag which I learnt, long ago, at the feet of J. S. Whale; that is, "*Pectus facit theologum*." I did not recall that he gave the source of the tag, so I wrote to him, and he

Dogma develops where there is torture, moral and intellectual. The introspective conscience of the West, which is alien to Judaism, is surely one of the sources of the dogmatic concentration of Christianity. The robust, halakic character of Judaism has not been conducive to theological subtlety, of any systematic kind, at least. The commandment to be done, not the creedal conundrum to be unravelled, has been the central concern of Judaism. I should be prepared to say that the chief differences in ethos between Jewish and Christian life, worship and thought are all coloured by the difference in intensity with which the two religions have wrestled with sin.

III

I move now to the third point. In this discussion it has been agreed that Torah and Dogma are terms that can represent Judaism and Christianity. I assume also that the basic structure of Christianity in most of the New Testament documents is to a great extent parallel to that of Judaism. By and large the Christian dispensation or event was understood as a new Exodus from the realm of slavery to sin, the old Egypt, to the life of a new Canaan. Christianity, it may be argued, emerges as a specific kind of Judaism with a new Exodus and a new Moses and a new Sinai "in Christ." What, then, is the difference between the two faiths? This can be expressed somewhat as follows. Whereas in the complex often referred to as the Exodus, at which Israel's redemption was wrought, Judaism came to place more and more emphasis on the Torah, that is, the demand uttered on Sinai, which was itself a gift, the figure of Moses being a colossus because he mediated the Torah, the Church, as it looked back to the new Exodus wrought in Christ, first remembered the person of Jesus Christ, through whom the new Exodus was wrought, and who thus came to have for the Church the significance of Torah. This is why ultimately the tradition in Judaism culminates in *The Mishnah*, a code of *Halakot*, and in Christianity in the Gospels, in which all is subservient to Jesus as Lord.[23] What then is the essential dogma that has replaced the Torah

replied: "I don't know how we've managed to get this a bit muddled—as though the old tag said *Peccatum* rather than *Pectus*. And I don't know who first used [or, should I say, *coined*] this enduring phrase. I shouldn't be surprised to find it in Jas. Denney's Cunningham Lectures on Reconciliation—in the chapter on Augustine, where the great saint/sinner is described as 'an experiencing nature.' You must drop the actual phrase, of course—'Sin makes the theologian'; but it is a false reading which is nevertheless saying something true. Christian theology presupposes and begins with sin, and man's immemorial predicament. Hence the opening words of Milton's P. L....I can't plead guilty myself to having misquoted *pectus* as *peccatum* in any lecture I've ever given; but I remember how Wheeler Robinson used to remark with a chuckle about the inspired character of certain false readings in scripture (in a letter dated 3 February 1967)." The horror expressed at the idea that "Sin makes the theologian" by some of the Jewish participants was typical, as was the silent acceptance of it by the Christian significant. In any case the idea is not alien to the history of Christian thought, however infelicitously I expressed it. As J. S. Whale also writes: "Luther's *pecca fortiter*, like Thomas's 'O felix culpa!...' is a monstrously provocative statement of the truth that Christian Theology begins with *peccatum*!"

[23] Much of this formulation I owe to Professor David Daube.

of Judaism? As I argued in my work *Paul and Rabbinic Judaism*, it is the claim that the Torah now is Jesus of Nazareth, the Christ. There is a new ultimate in Jesus: the finality of Christ replaces the finality of Torah. To claim that the gulf between Judaism and Christianity is merely a schism is to imply that this new finality can be expressed in terms consonant with Judaism. Can this really be asserted?

The finality of Christ, to judge by the New Testament, can only be established even for Christians in terms of the Torah itself. It is a familiar fact that early Christians searched the Scriptures in order to show that the Torah and the Prophets pointed to Jesus. Christianity from the first involved the interpretation of the Scriptures, just as Judaism involved an understanding of them. The interpretation of the Old Testament variously given in the New Testament is governed by the assumption that Jesus is the Messiah. Throughout the New Testament appeal is made to the Old. The life, death, and resurrection of Jesus of Nazareth and the emergence of the Church are understood in terms of the Old Testament as its fulfilment. But although the New Testament writers draw upon the Old Testament to illumine what had happened in the Gospel, they do not draw on all the Old Testament indiscriminately. There are some prophecies which they ignore and others which they modify. Not all Old Testament expectations were suitable for the events which they were interpreting. The New Testament is not dominated by the Old. It is the Gospel itself that provides the pattern for the understanding of the Old: the New Testament interprets the Old in the light of Christ. It does not merely interpret Christ in the light of the Old Testament. To put the matter in another way, the New Testament does not paint a picture of its Lord out of all the colours found in the Old Testament. It used the Old Testament selectively, in a creative way; it rejected some colours and used others in the light of Jesus, the Christ.

And given the Christian presuppositions, this Christological principle of interpretation is convincing—but only given the Christian presuppositions. Recall Scholem's view that Christian exegesis of the Old Testament interprets it against its very grain.[24] That is, it is forced and, therefore, unacceptable exegesis: it imputes to the Old Testament a meaning it never intended. Jewish interpretation, on the other hand, springs naturally from the text itself: it is native, indigenous. The kind of schematization that is found, for example, in Romans 9–11, which Christians have always found illuminating and inspiring

[24] "Religious Authority and Mysticism," *Commentary*, New York, November 1964, pp. 31ff. Contrast with Scholem's view that of a Christian scholar, Gerhard von Rad: "The question should be put the other way around: how was it possible for the Old Testament traditions, and all the narratives, prayers, and predictions, to be taken over by the New Testament? This could not have happened if the Old Testament writings had not themselves contained pointers to Christ and been hermeneutically adapted to such a merger." *Old Testament Theology*, Vol. 2, 1965, p. 333. On Rom. 9–11 compare Buber's view with that of Scholem, see M. Diamond, *Martin Buber, Jewish Existentialist*, New York, 1960, pp. 180ff. Buber finds Rom. 9–11 highly Hellenistic. See further H. v. Campenhausen, *The Formation of the Christian Bible*, trans., Philadelphia, 1972, pp. 1–61.

in its vast historical and theological sweep, is a falsification of the intent of the Old Testament. The issue of the interpretation of Scripture, both in its wider sweep and in matters of minute detail, has cropped up again and again in Jewish-Christian Dialogue and it still does and always will. It will necessarily remain with us because the Christological principle of the interpretation of the Old Testament is implied in most forms of traditional and in all forms of essential Christianity.

And, despite its rejection by Jewry, this implies that Christian thought, Christological and other, can be expressed in categories derived from the root of Judaism, which is the Old Testament. And it is arguable that Jewish categories are, in themselves, sufficient to account for the essentials of later Christian Dogma, even that of the Trinity. Daniélou, for example, has sought to show how, right down to the Council of Nicaea, Semitic categories were influential in the formulation of Christian dogma.[25] On this view, Christianity can be regarded as essentially a schismatic branch of Judaism. But is it only this?

IV

This brings me, finally, to the term "schism." Although such a model is attractive and has influenced the creative thinking of men like Rosenzweig and Barth,[26] I would merely ask the question, in conclusion, whether the New Testament itself supports the notion that the relation between Christianity and Judaism is that of a "schism." The New Testament presents that relationship in at least three ways.

First, there are documents in which there is little awareness of any essential break between Judaism and Christianity. Jesus has come as the Messiah, but the essential structure of Judaism has remained virtually unaltered. Acceptance of Jesus does not mean any radical break with Jewish practice or belief. All that has happened in Christianity is that Judaism is now in possession of its long-awaited Messiah, but his advent has not demanded perceptible change. The earliest Christians, Judaizers and Jewish Christians who held this position have left few traces in the New Testament itself, although their presence can easily be discerned moving shadowily behind its pages, especially in the Pauline epistles. But they have left us noncanonical materials of fairly substantial extent. The Christianity which these reveal has been examined anew and given great prominence by Schoeps.[27] He finds Jewish Christianity to have been the chief bulwark in the primitive Church against Marcion and the threat of Gnosticism. That Jewish Christianity disappeared almost without vestige is no indication of its real significance in history. From its point of view, the Christian faith is a

[25] Jean Daniélou, *Théologie du Judéo-Christianisme: Histoire des doctrines Chrétiennes avant Nicée*, Vol. I, 1957, p. 1.

[26] Professor Miskotte's paper at the Harvard Colloquium did so interpret Barth with references to *Kirchliche Dogmatik*, Vols. III, pp. 3, 247; IV: 1, p. 749; IV: 3b, pp. 1005f.

[27] *Theologie und Geschichte des Judenchristentums*, Tübingen, 1949.

reformation or revision of Judaism, involving little radical newness, that is, it is a schism. It is, indeed, merely Judaism with an addendum—Jesus the Messiah. We may agree with Schoeps that the disappearance of Jewish Christianity may be no criterion for what it connoted in its heyday, but many have regarded the disappearance as almost inevitable because it provided no ultimate raison d'être for Christianity alongside Judaism.

At the opposite extreme, we find, in certain documents of the New Testament, the claim that the relation of Christianity to Judaism is one of sharp antithesis. This comes to clearest expression in the Fourth Gospel, where there is a sustained interpretation of the Christian faith which emphasizes that it replaced Judaism. On this view, Christianity is a revolution which so transforms Judaism that the latter can be regarded as superseded. It is true that the Fourth Gospel urges that salvation is from the Jews and uses categories that are derived from Judaism to expound Jesus' significance, but it does look away from Judaism also. The newness of the Gospel is such that the old order of the waterpots has given place to the new wine of the Gospel. The quintessence of the Fourth Gospel's attitude may perhaps be understood in the story of Mary and the beloved disciple at the cross (Jn. 19: 25–27). Near the cross where Jesus hung stood his mother, with her sister, Mary, wife of Cleopas, and Mary of Magdala. Jesus saw his mother, with the disciple whom he loved standing beside her. He said to her, "Mother, there is your son"; and to the disciple, "there is your mother"; and from that moment the disciple took her into his home. Mary is the mother of Jesus. She is now handed over to the respectful care of his disciple. Her function is over. If Mary here stands for Judaism, the implication is clear. Judaism is the aged mother. She is honoured and cherished, but a new order to which she has given birth replaces her. Such is the relation between Judaism and Christianity.[28]

To some, then, the Gospel is a revision, if not a radical one, of Judaism; to others it supersedes Judaism as its antithesis. The third attitude is best represented perhaps in Matthew and in Hebrews. It may be expressed in terms of Matthew 5 : 17: "I came not to destroy but to complete." The immediate context in Matthew concerns the Law, but the attitude can be extended to cover the whole of Judaism. The Christian Gospel has brought the intent of Judaism to full fruition. It has not only fulfilled the Jewish hope for a Messiah; it has brought with it a new Temple, a new Law, a new sacrifice, a new people. In all these cases the adjective "new" is meant to indicate not antithesis but fulfilment. What in Judaism was "shadowy," tentative, and preparatory is now fully realized in Christ. Readers of the Epistle to the Hebrews do not need to be reminded of the way in which the theology of that epistle is built upon the theology of Judaism as its "completion."

[28] I used this symbolic interpretation in my popular work *Invitation to the New Testament*, 1966, p. 492. The symbolism is suggested by A. Loisy, who is referred to, without specific annotation, by E. C. Hoskyns and F. N. Davey, *The Fourth Gospel*, 1947, p. 530.

There is one figure, possibly the major figure of the New Testament, apart of course from Jesus, whom it is difficult to place in any of the categories indicated. Paul has been regarded, particularly by Jewish scholars, but also by Protestants dominated by Luther, as having broken with Judaism in a radical fashion. In particular, Jewish scholars have accused Paul of breaking down the fence of the Torah, and Christian scholars have set his doctrine of "justification by faith" over against the emphasis in Judaism on "salvation by work." But there can be little question that Paul remained throughout his life, in his own mind, within the pale of Judaism. Christ was for him the end of Judaism in the sense not of its annulment but of its fulfilment. By and large, I should classify Paul with Hebrews and Matthew rather than with the Fourth Gospel. To him, also, Christianity is not the antithesis of Judaism but its culmination.

The New Testament, then, presents us with three main alternatives, only one of which, the first mentioned above, justifies the use of the term "schism." I think it must be clearly recognized that there came a point when the two faiths—conceptually as well as historically—had to part company, radically and not merely schismatically, that is, where Christian dogmatic developments made the gulf between the two religions so deep that the term "schism" becomes inapplicable. As long as Jesus was interpreted in strictly Messianic categories and, indeed, in terms of Torah, a merely schismatic relationship between Judaism and Christianity is conceivable. But once Jesus is claimed to be God incarnate, and this is already the case in parts of the New Testament itself,[29] then the Rubicon has been crossed and Christianity stands completely outside the conceivable confines of Judaism, the quintessence of which is expressed in the *Shema*. If Christianity be interpreted kerygmatically in terms of the Divinity of Jesus, the Christ, then we must speak of a new religion, not merely of a schismatic emergence. No Christian who has ever engaged in even the slightest discussion with Jews can doubt this. The doctrine of the Incarnation is the Rubicon between the two faiths.

The question then emerges whether essential Christianity can ever be expressed in non-incarnational terms which would lessen the gulf between it and Judaism. There are two possibilities to be considered.

The first possibility is to recognize frankly that there is a viable interpretation of the Gospel which does not require the affirmation of the historic creeds, couched as they are in mythological language which needs to be de-mythologized. It would seem that Bultmann, for example, if we are to follow one of his recent interpreters, has in fact given up the great dogmatic formulations of the Christian faith. Thus Ian Hendersen writes:

> More important is perhaps to ask whether Bultmann's position in the controversy about myths leaves open the kind of Christology we find in the statements of

[29] On this, see R. E. Brown, "Does the New Testament call Jesus God?" *Theological Studies*, Vol. 26, 1965, pp. 545–573.

Nicaea and Chalcedon. I do not think it does...Now this issue is quite vital. For all signs are that Christianity is going to split on the Christologies of Nicaea and Chalcedon...[30]

Because it seems to remove the offence of Christology, could Bultmann's understanding of Christianity, then, be acceptable to Judaism, and could it be described as merely a schismatic phenomenon? Apparently so. The Jesus of Bultmann stands within Judaism. But here we are faced with a paradox. While for him Jesus stands within Judaism, Bultmann's understanding of the Christian faith is so divorced from the Old Testament and Judaism that the Jesus he presents is divested of any serious significance for Judaism and is thus, from the Jewish point of view, rendered innocuous. A Jesus who is merely a bearer of the Word and not the Word himself, and especially as the bearer of a Word not fundamentally rooted in Judaism, such as he is for Bultmann, offers no challenge to Judaism as such. In such a view of Jesus the Rubicon between Judaism and Christianity is not so much confronted as by-passed. The theological barrier to a Jewish-Christian *rapprochement* in the dogmatic history of Christianity is thereby obviated, but it is also, from the Jewish point of view, trivialized. The possibility raised by Bultmann's view of Jesus not only raises in an acute form the question whether the dogmatic history of Christianity can or should be reversed, but also whether, if such were the case, it would really interest Judaism.

The other possibility, which is hesitatingly raised here, is that which would interpret Christianity, not in Kerygmatic, but in Halakic terms. Let us again raise the question how far Christianity can cease to affirm the historic creeds and yet remain itself. That is, would it be possible to conceive of Christianity adequately not primarily as a way of belief, a creed, but rather as a way of life, as *agapê*? It is certain that if Christianity finds the essence of its life in creeds such as those of Nicaea and Chalcedon, there can be no ultimate *rapprochement* with Judaism. On the other hand, could not a halakically oriented Christianity be at home with Judaism or, at least, remain as a merely schismatic aspect of it? The answer to this question also, to judge from the history[31] of the Church, would seem to be that even a halakically centred Christianity has had Christological implications that Judaism has not been able to accept. Even so conservatively halakic a figure as James, the brother of the Lord, was finally unacceptable

[30] *Rudolf Bultmann*, John Knox Press, Richmond, Va., 1966, *ad rem.*

[31] Since the above was written Krister Stendahl and D. N. Freedman have raised the question whether a more historical approach to the separation between Judaism and Christianity might not help in the process of reconciliation. As is clear from what I have written here and elsewhere, I would be the last to underestimate the degree to which the historical reexamination of Christian origins and first-century Judaism can be and has been salutary. But as the last paragraph but one in the above Comment makes clear, the appeal to history is ultimately not enough, because as a matter of historic fact Judaism and Christianity did go their separate ways. We need not only more knowledge of Judaism and early Christianity, but a new attitude or spirit towards the relationship called for between the two faiths.

to Judaism and died a martyr's death. How much less is any halakic Christianity conceivable in our time!

We seem to be driven to one conclusion. There is a Christological factor in Christianity, however expressed, which—to use a phrase borrowed from Reinhold Niebuhr—is non-negotiable even with its mother faith, just as there is a centrality of Torah in Judaism which is non-negotiable. The dogmatic development of Christianity, in short, remains as the barrier to reducing the relation between the two faiths to a mere schism. It is the part of wisdom to recognize this. But this, in itself, is not the tragedy of the history of the relations between the two faiths. Rather it is that the spirit of the Halakah demanded by both has not been more truly pursued by both, so as to make possible, within their dogmatic difference, mutual tolerance, respect, learning and even affection. At least, the time is long overdue for Christians to recognize that the attempt to overcome Torah by Dogma should be long past: its almost total ignominious failure is evident. This already points forward to the emergence of a new era or at least to new possibilities for Christian-Jewish relations.

APPENDIX III

R. Ardrey: The Territorial Imperative

At this point it is expedient to refer to a widely discussed work which has offered a territorial explanation of the evolution of the Jew, namely, Robert Ardrey's, *The Territorial Imperative, A personal inquiry into the animal origins of property and nations*, Dell Publishing Co., New York, 1966. Ardrey concentrates on territorial behaviour in animals and reveals that several species act by an instinctual command of the territory they occupy: there is among them an innate compulsion to defend their property (pp. 241, 244, 249). But "territory" is in essence a psychological expression (p. 169), and the possession of a territory serves the purposes of security, stimulation, and identity (p. 171).

Into the ramifications of Ardrey's argument we cannot enter, nor are we qualified to assess the evidence which he has collected for his theory. What makes it necessary to refer to his work is that he claims that man, too, obeys the laws of the territorial imperative and that the history of nations is illumined by his theory. In particular, he finds in the territorial principle the secret to the evolution of the Jew. According to him Jews do not constitute a race; they have less racial distinctiveness than the Southern Italian or Swede. They simply are descendants of a mixed bag of Middle Eastern tribes with no special genetic distinction. But they are different. Why? Because, writes Ardrey, "We have had territories, he [the Jew] has had none. Among modern civilized peoples he has been unique. And what we have described as a Jew has been nothing other than a de-territorialized man (p. 306)."

Ardrey then offers a résumé of Jewish history. And the separation of the Jews from their land, which Ardrey so emphasizes in his résumé, is a fact. The Dispersion—a population denied a social territory—did arise, and Antisemitism too. Ardrey expresses the matter thus: "The Jew faced a genetic problem confronting no other Western people: How, without the reproductive isolation of territory, could he maintain his genetic integrity? He owned nothing but memories. Anti-Semitism helped. He accepted the grim ghetto. He forbade marriage or intercourse with Gentiles. His rabbis and scholars maintained the memories. The Jewish family became the impregnable equivalent of a Greek phalanx. Spectacularly, the Jew refused to conform, cultivated outlandish costume, beard, headgear and outlandish dietary customs. He pursued the arts while we still reveled in illiteracy. He overlooked nothing, forgot nothing.... The Jew made memories from the dust of the years.... We regarded him as a race apart; it was to Jewish interest to agree. We derided the 'Jewish personality,' he exaggerated the personality. None of us guessed, of course, he or we,

that 'the Jewish personality' was nothing but a bundle of mannerisms preserving the identity of a de-territorialized man (p. 307)."

Ardrey finds confirmation for his theory in the transformation in the Jews
wrought by the creation of the State of Israel. Applying the criteria derived
from his studies of the territorial principle he notes the following:

1. The Arab League provided the Jews with hostile neighbours; this meant
stimulation and the opportunity to make legitimate their territory in the
strictest biological sense.

2. The slaughter of Jews by Arabs added to the respect held for Israel's title
to the land.

3. The Jews in Israel "fought"—they behaved just like anyone else. Contrast
the behaviour of European Jewry who did not oppose the Nazis.

4. The acquisition and defence of a territory brought an enhancement of
energy to Israelis just as in other nations and animals. The transformation of
much of the Promised Land, "an unpromising collection of rocks," to fertile
soil witnesses to this.

5. As a de-territorialized man, the Jew in his own territory ceased to exist:
the Israeli emerged and the gulf between the Dispersion and the land increased—
paradoxically and painfully to those who had supported the creation of Israel.
In the land itself, the "Jewish" personality is vanishing.

What shall we say to all this? Simply that Ardrey's understanding of the Jew
is not supported by the Jewish self-understanding as revealed in the sources of
Judaism. His résumé of Jewish history is often open to question. Did the
Egyptians cart the Jews away from Canaan to slavery (p. 306)? Was it the
querulousness, rebelliousness, and argumentativeness of the Jews that explain
their several disasters (p. 300)? But apart from such questions there are basic
difficulties in Ardrey's position.

In Gen. 12: 1 the call of Abraham, the father of Israel, to whom the promise
was given, is described as follows: "Now the Lord said to Abram, 'Go from
your country and your fathers' house to the land that I will show you.'"
Abram is urged to forsake his own territory. The pilgrim motif is primordial in
the Jewish consciousness not a late, compulsory result of its history. And we
have seen that the land which Israel entered was regarded as the land of the
Canaanites, the conquest of which was no part of "biological morality"—a
phrase used by Ardrey—but a recognized act of violence. The land was regarded
not as Israel's land, but as belonging to Yahweh. The relation of Israel to the
land, in short, was not regarded as a natural one, even after the conquest. There
was a religious dimension to the land which Ardrey insufficiently recognizes and
it was precisely this dimension—that of the promise and of the land's relation to
Yahweh—throughout Israel's history which cannot be accounted for in purely
territorial terms.

This is reinforced by the nature of the laws that Jews have observed. Are
they to be simply explained as mechanisms of defence against the encroachments

of the world in the Dispersion? Three factors militate against such a view. First, as we saw above on pp. 56ff, most of the laws are especially designed for and applicable to life in the land itself. Even though it must be admitted that life in the land was open to alien pressures, it is clear that the laws were not primarily understood as means of differentiation from the nations outside the land. Secondly, it was on the return to the land that life under the Law became especially obligatory, not in Babylon. This would suggest that neither the Dispersion in the Graeco-Roman world nor the later one in the Christian West (despite its hostility which, according to Ardrey, in line with his understanding of the evolutionary process as one in which amity within a group is fostered by enmity to those outside, the amity–enmity complex, was actually necessary to the development of the cohesion of the Christian West) called forth the development of Jewish observance of the Law. The Rabbis themselves did not advance such an understanding of the *mitzwôth*. These were to be obeyed, not for any utilitarian purposes, but simply because they were commanded (Num. Rabbah 19: 8 on 19: 2). Although the necessity of separation from the heathen *is* a dominant concern of Pharisaic Judaism, the *reason* for such a concern is not the preservation of genetic "purity," as such, nor is it inspired by territorial considerations, but essentially by loyalty to the Torah. Such a sociological-psychological interpretation of the commandments as is urged by Ardrey would be foreign to the Rabbis despite their concern for discovering the grounds of The Torah (see *The Jewish Quarterly Review*, New Series, 1951, pp. 217ff). In short, the commandments were not intended to be a fence around the Jew, as Ardrey holds, so much as around the Torah (M. Aboth 1: 1), although it is to be admitted that this distinction, valid as it is in theological analysis, was often blurred in the actualities of history.

And, finally, the emphasis placed by Ardrey on the distinction between Jews and Israelis, the quality of Jewishness as opposed to that of the Sabra, has to be scrutinized. The distinction is often made and is superficially obvious. But certain considerations are pertinent. The distinction between Palestinian and Diaspora Jews is not a recent phenomenon. Montefiore in his work *Judaism and St. Paul*, 1914, even made it the basis for his interpretation of Paul; compare J. Klausner, *From Jesus to Paul*, trans., by W. F. Stinespring, 1942; Schalom Ben Chorin, *Paulus*, 1970. And it is perfectly natural that, just as very often in times past the English tended to look down on "Colonials," the motherland taking a naturally senior and superior attitude to the daughter lands of the colonies, so a Palestinian Jew took the same attitude to those of the Diaspora. It would, however, be erroneous to elevate such an attitude to the status of a criterion for "Jewishness." We saw above that the term "Israel" has historically signified the Jewish people both without and within any existing State of Israel. "Israel" has not been finally conditioned by any territorial criteria. Judaism has subsisted and still does subsist without the land as well as within the land. Jewishness is not to be geographically defined or confined. We would urge over against Ardrey that: "Scratch an Israeli and find a Jew: scratch a Jew and find an Israeli."

This last sentence does point to the reality of that tradition about the connection between Israel and the land which we have discussed above. But despite the forcefulness of his treatment of Jews and Israel, Ardrey might perhaps be led to agree that it would be an error to elevate any one aspect of Judaism, in this instance the territorial, to a normative position for the understanding of Judaism and the State of Israel. On pp. vii–viii of *The Territorial Imperative* he does recognize the danger of isolating this principle and thus distorting its significance, even though he proceeds to ignore it.

APPENDIX IV

GALILEE—LAND OF SALVATION?

BY GÜNTER STEMBERGER

Although Galilee has been understood frequently since the beginning of this century as the place of the eschatological fulfilment of the hopes of Judaism, it has come to theological prominence only in the last thirty years. Characteristically enough, the Theological Dictionary of the New Testament by Kittel has not even an article on Galilee. When former exegetes had found a theological connotation in the geographical term "Galilee," they had been interested only in particular passages of the gospels, that is, Mark 14: 28: "But after I am raised up, I will go before you to Galilee," and 16: 7: "But go, tell his disciples and Peter that he is going before you to Galilee; there you will see him, as he told you." But E. Lohmeyer,[1] and shortly after him R. H. Lightfoot,[2] discovered in Galilee a major theological motif influencing the entire gospel of Mark, and—to a lesser extent—Matthew and John. Many New Testament scholars have criticized and rejected this theory ever since,[3] but usually without sufficient reasons or serious examination. On the other hand, Lohmeyer and Lightfoot have sometimes been favourably accepted, and in spite of the tenuous evidence to support their thesis, it seems to be gaining an ever wider acceptance, especially under the impact of the work of W. Marxsen on Mark.[4] Thus, a new examination of the theory seems to be necessary to serve as a background to the discussion in chapter VIII above. In the following pages, I shall first sketch the history of this interpretation and then go on to examine the alleged evidence for it.

[1] E. Lohmeyer, *Galiläa und Jerusalem*, Göttingen, 1936. Compare also his commentary: *Das Evangelium des Markus*, *Meyer Kommentar*, 15th ed., Göttingen, 1959.

[2] R. H. Lightfoot, *Locality and Doctrine in the Gospels*, New York–London, 1938.

[3] Besides the scholars mentioned in the following, compare W. G. Kümmel, *Verheissung und Erfüllung*, Zurich, 2nd ed., 1953, pp. 71f (in his review of Lohmeyer's *Galilee*, TLZ, 62, 1937, pp. 304–307, Kümmel was much more positive, although even then he criticized part of the theory); G. B. Caird, *The Apostolic Age*, London, 1955, pp. 87–89; C. E. B. Cranfield, *The Gospel According to St. Mark*, Cambridge, 1959, pp. 467–469; D. E. Nineham, *The Gospel of St. Mark*, Baltimore, 1963, p. 446 (Nineham thinks, however, that the view of J. Weiss—compare below—"should not be too lightly dismissed"); V. Taylor, *The Gospel According to St. Mark*, London–New York, 2nd ed., 1966, pp. 549, 575, 608; E. Schweizer, *Das Evangelium nach Markus*, Göttingen, 1967, pp. 212–214 (thinks of a lost ending of Mark).

[4] W. Marxsen, *Der Evangelist Markus. Studien zur Redaktionsgeschichte des Evangeliums*, Göttingen, 1956.

I. The Theory

BEFORE LOHMEYER

F. Spitta[5] thought that Mark 14: 28 originally was designed to promise that Jesus would place himself at the head of his disciples in Jerusalem. When Peter and his fellow-disciples had returned to Galilee without the Lord, however, the saying was transformed to mean what is stated in Mark 16: 7. J. Weiss in his *History of Primitive Christianity*[6] took up the suggestions of F. Spitta and regarded Mark 14: 28 as a prediction that the risen Christ would lead his disciples back to Galilee for the inauguration of God's Kingdom. He paraphrased the verse 14: 28 in this way: "After I have rejoined you here in Jerusalem, following my resurrection, I will lead you back home; there will come the fulfilment of our hopes—the Kingdom of God." This expectation was never realized. Luke and John, therefore, simply ignored this saying, whereas Mark 16: 7 misinterpreted it. The tradition of the Galilean resurrection appearances in Matthew and John 21 also arose from a misunderstanding of this verse, and "must be looked upon as a product of fantasy."[7]

A similar interpretation is given by W. Michaelis[8] who equates the resurrection and the parousia in the teaching of Jesus and holds that their separation came about only in the primitive community. If this be the case, Mark 14: 28 cannot originally have predicted the appearances, but was a prediction of the parousia. A. Schweitzer[9] follows J. Weiss more closely: "Jesus' disciples remain at Jerusalem because, in accordance with the last saying of Jesus at the Supper, they believe that after His resurrection He will celebrate such a meal anew with them, and then will journey with them into Galilee in order there to be manifested in His Messianic Glory." F. Hauck[10] is much more cautious: Mark 14: 28 and 16: 7 might point to resurrection appearances in Galilee; but the saying more probably means that the victorious Jesus will lead his disciples back to Galilee where they expected the establishment of the Kingdom of God. The verse would thus be a counterpart of Mark 10: 32: "And they were on the road, going up to Jerusalem, and Jesus was walking ahead of them" (the same verb as in 14: 28 and 16: 7). As Christ had led his disciples from Galilee to Jerusalem to his death, in the same way he would lead them back from Jerusalem to Galilee in triumph.

---

[5] F. Spitta, *Die synoptische Grundschrift*, Leipzig, 1912, p. 387.

[6] J. Weiss, *The History of Primitive Christianity*, completed by R. Knopf, ed. F. C. Grant, New York, 1937, p. 18 (German edition, 1917).

[7] Weiss, *The History of Primitive Christianity*.

[8] W. Michaelis, *Taufer, Jesus, Urgemeinde. Die Predigt vom Reiche Gottes vor und nach Pfingsten*, Gütersloh, 1928, p. 113.

[9] A. Schweitzer, *The Mysticism of Paul the Apostle*, New York, 1968 (reprint of 1931; first German edition 1930), p. 247.

[10] F. Hauck, *Das Evangelium des Markus*, Leipzig, 1931, pp. 171, 193f. W. Grundmann in his re-edition of Hauck's commentary, *Das Evangelium nach Markus*, Berlin, 1959, leaves the question open; he is even more cautious than F. Hauck.

Thus far, interest was limited to the interpretation of Mark 14. 28; 16: 7. The risen Christ would lead his disciples back to Galilee, and there the Kingdom would come; or, according to Michaelis, the disciples would return to Galilee to witness the parousia of the Lord. E. Lohmeyer starts with these presuppositions as to the meaning of Mark 14: 28 and 16: 7, but sees the problem within the context of the whole gospel. His starting point is the question: Did the resurrection appearances take place in Galilee or in Jerusalem? Lohmeyer thinks that it is impossible to combine these two traditions: one must not harmonize them; only one of them can be historically correct, although, as Lohmeyer himself ultimately concedes, we are no longer in a position to decide which.

For many the strongest evidence in favour of Galilean appearances is Mark 14: 28 *alla meta to engerthênai me proaxô humas eis tên Galilaian* and Mark 16: 7 *proagei humas eis tên Galilaian: ekei auton opsesthe, kathôs eipen humin.* But, objects Lohmeyer, although 1 Cor. 9: 1 and John 20: 18, 25 use the active voice of *horaô* of an appearance of the risen Lord, the active future tense (*opsesthe*) is "a fixed expression for the coming parousia (Mark 14: 62 par; cf. Mark 13: 26 par; John 16: 16; 1 John 3: 2; Apoc. 1: 7)."[11] The oldest tradition uses only the passive voice of *horaô* of resurrection appearances; the common use of the expression alone would in itself justify us in interpreting Mark 16: 7 "of the parousia." The journey of Jesus to Galilee, Mark 14: 28, is consequently to be the way from the resurrection to the parousia. "This will come about in Galilee; there is the Holy Land where he will dwell forever with those who belong to him."[12] Mark's meditation on the history of Jesus leads him to this view. The same is valid for Matthew: for him, too, Galilee is the Holy Land where Jesus appears to his disciples. The resurrection occurred in Jerusalem, true; but the most important miracle and truth of the Christian faith, the parousia, is finally revealed in Galilee. The command to the mission is given there; there is the birthplace of the eschatological community of God, of the Church.[13]

Lohmeyer concludes from Mark 3: 7 and 9: 30 that for Mark the term Galilee signifies more territory than that term is usually understood to include. Mark 3: 7 names several regions from which many people came to Jesus; but the Gaulanitis and Abilene where Jesus also was, are omitted, perhaps because Mark included these two regions in Galilee. Mark 9: 30 seems to indicate that Galilee reaches as far north as Hermon (when Mark 9: 30 is seen together with 9: 2 and 8: 27). Wherever non-Galilean names are mentioned in Mark 6: 30–8: 27, they connote for Mark the surroundings of Galilee, included in the Christian Galilee to which even Tyre, Sidon, and the Decapolis belong. For the common people and also for the gospel tradition, the Galileans are a *populus christianus*, Galilee is a *terra christiana* (cf. Mark 14: 70). Mark 1: 14–20, a kind of preamble

[11] E. Lohmeyer, *Galiläa und Jerusalem*, p. 11.   [12] *Ibid.*, p. 13.   [13] *Ibid.*, p. 17.

to the history of Jesus, emphasizes the beginning of the Gospel in Galilee. Only in the context of Galilee is the holy word *euangelion* used; there the apostles are called and there they work; the transfiguration also takes place in Galilee, and thus shows that it is the land of the eschatological fulfilment. Jerusalem, on the other hand, is the place of rejection. The theological idea that God had chosen the despised Galilee for his eschatological work, existed already in the tradition of the community (Mark 14: 28; 16: 7), but it was Mark who gave it fundamental importance. The same idea appears in Matthew: he also knows the same large geographic extension of Galilee (cf. Matt. 4: 12ff); but in Matthew the Galilean theory is no longer so strongly and thoroughly developed. John again regards the Galileans as *populus christianus* (cf. John 4: 45; 7: 41, 50–52), but for him the problem Jerusalem—Galilee no longer exists: for him, Jesus is "the Saviour of the world." Luke, on the other hand, concentrates his gospel totally on Jerusalem.[14]

The next step which Lohmeyer takes is to seek the background of the Galilean theory in the history of the primitive Church. The geographical names in Mark 3: 7f ("a great multitude from Galilee followed; also from Judea and Jerusalem and Idumea and from beyond the Jordan and from about Tyre and Sidon a great multitude, hearing all that he did, came to him"), according to him, do not tell us where Jesus worked (Jesus was never in Idumea; Samaria is not mentioned, although Jesus was there), but where it was that Christians lived in the time of Mark. Acts knows of a Christian Church in Galilee (9: 31 "So the church throughout all Judea and Galilee and Samaria had peace and was built up"), but seems to suppose that the Christians of Galilee had not been converted by Jerusalem: Galilee is already a *terra christiana*. It is for this reason, thinks Lohmeyer, that it is not mentioned in what is usually regarded as the programmatic statement in Acts 1: 8: "You shall be my witnesses in Jerusalem and in all Judea and Samaria and to the end of the earth." Luke seems to regard Galilee as the territory of the Lord's brothers; no Christian missionaries ever go there. Nor does Acts tell us of the origin of the Christians in Damascus, probably because they had been converted by the Galilean Church. When James the brother of the Lord, one of the leaders of the Galilean community, took over the government of the Church in Jerusalem, the holy city became attached to Galilee, the original home of Christianity. The transfer of James to Jerusalem signifies that Galilee recognizes the actual importance of the community in Jerusalem, but not that Galilee abandons its claim to be the Holy Land of the Gospel. When, some time after the death of James, the Judaean Christians went to Pella, this exodus is their return to the Galilee of the Gentiles which was not only the original, but also the final, home of Jewish Christianity (Pella was not in Galilee, but was within the wider territory which, Lohmeyer claims, was the Christian Galilee). The sects of the Nazoreans and of the Ebionites, with their

[14] *Ibid.*, pp. 36–44.

ideal of poverty, derive from this Galilean Christianity, which had a distinct theology of its own,[15] more strongly influenced by Hellenistic ideas than the theology of Jerusalem.

R. H. Lightfoot independently came to conclusions similar to those of Lohmeyer, but he could already make use of Lohmeyer's work when he formulated his ideas in *Locality and Doctrine in the Gospels*, 1938. Lightfoot was, however, much more cautious than Lohmeyer; he did not expound these ideas with the same conviction (and later he changed his opinion!),[16] and above all, he did not try to reconstruct the history of the primitive Church from these presuppositions, as Lohmeyer had done.

W. MARXSEN

W. Marxsen takes up the theory of Lohmeyer in his work *Der Evangelist Markus*, 1956. But Marxsen modifies it at several points and seeks to give it a stronger support by the methods of *Redaktionsgeschichte*. According to Marxsen, the strong interest of Mark in Galilee has to be explained by the fact that he writes for a Galilean Christianity. The Galilean Church, however, was not the primitive community prior to and then coexistent with the Church of Jerusalem. The early Christian community lived in Jerusalem. But in the years between A.D. 66 and 70 the Christians went to Pella for political reasons, but above all because of a heightened expectation of the parousia which was to take place in Galilee (Mark 14: 28; 16: 7). One could object that Pella is not in Galilee, but the frontiers of Galilee were very unstable; it is also possible that the Christian community gathered for some time at the lake of Galilee before they moved on to Pella.[17] In any case, at the time of Mark, the Christian community in Galilee already existed or at least was already growing and becoming organized. Galilee is a *terra christiana* (Mark 14: 70). It was for this community that Mark wrote his gospel and, therefore, he attributed theological prominence to Galilee, the land of the imminent parousia.

The main differences between Marxsen and Lohmeyer are to be found in their views of the history of the primitive Church. For Lohmeyer, the true origins of the Church are in Galilee, for Marxsen in Jerusalem. Marxsen regards the

[15] The main characteristics of this Galilean theology are, according to Lohmeyer: a Son of Man, and Servant, Christology. The final point of the earthly existence of Christ is not the resurrection, but the enthronization and elevation of the Son of Man as Lord and judge over the whole world. Typical for this theology is Matt. 28: 16–20. See Lohmeyer, "Mir ist gegeben alle Gewalt!" Eine Exegese von Matt. 28: 16–20: *In Memoriam E. Lohmeyer*, ed. W. Schmauch, Stuttgart, 1951, pp. 22–49. S. E. Johnson, "Jesus and First-Century Galilee," in the same memorial volume, pp. 73–88, tries to identify Galilean material in the gospels.

[16] R. H. Lightfoot, *The Gospel Message of St. Mark*, Oxford, 1950, p. 116.

[17] The evidence Marxsen gives for this opinion is the concentration of the gospel of Mark on the Sea of Galilee, Mark 14: 28; 16: 7, and the statement of Eusebius (HE, III: 5: 3) concerning the flight of the Christian community to Pella (cf. below, p. 60); *Der Evangelist Markus*, pp. 54f, 76. [On the historicity of that flight, see the defence by M. Simon, "La Migration à Pella: Légende ou realité," *Recherches de Science Religieuse*, Vol. 60, No. 1, 1972, pp. 37–54: convincing. Addition by W.D.D.]

Galilean Church as only emerging when Mark wrote his gospel: he, therefore, does not postulate a specific Galilean theology, nor does he try to connect the Galilean community with the brothers of the Lord. But Marxsen maintains the basic point of Lohmeyer that Mark wrote for a Galilean community which expected the parousia in Galilee, which it regarded as the chosen land of the eschatological fulfilment.

L. E. ELLIOTT-BINNS

Elliott-Binns in his *Galilean Christianity*[18] presents a somewhat different picture of the primitive Church although he goes along with Lohmeyer in all basic points. He, too, claims that the beginnings of the Church were in Galilee, and thinks that it is highly probable that the first name of the followers of Jesus was "Galileans." The Galilean Christians, whose special interests are to be found in Mark and Matthew, but above all in the epistle of James, were "proud of their spiritual past and jealous of the position of Jerusalem. They may well have included some of the Twelve, possibly St. Peter among them."[19] The Church of Jerusalem, on the other hand, was led by the brothers of the Lord: James took over the leadership after the death of Stephen, in "an abortive anticipation of the caliphate of Islam."[20] The derogatory references to the parents of Jesus in the gospels may have their origin in the Galilean resentment against the Jerusalemite Church and their leaders, who during the life of Jesus would not believe. Only in Pella, where fugitives from Jerusalem and Judaea assembled as well as those from Galilee, were the two communities drawn together and forgot their differences in their common misfortunes.

II. A RE-EXAMINATION OF THE GALILEAN THEORY

Our exposition of the Galilean theory has paid little attention to Lohmeyer's outline of a special Galilean theology (p. 413, n. 15 above). This point of Lohmeyer's thesis has been rejected almost unanimously. It was based on the theological differences of the resurrection accounts, elaborated with the aid of rather late and questionable sources. Without discussing here the claim that there was such a special Galilean theology, we shall now examine the following points of the Galilean theory apart from this:

1. Is there sufficient evidence for the idea of *a larger Galilee* than the geographical one? Did a special Christian notion of Galilee exist?

2. What do we know of *Galilean Christianity* at the time of Mark? If no significant Galilean community existed at that time, one cannot presuppose a

[18] L. E. Elliott-Binns, *Galilean Christianity*, London, 1956.

[19] *Ibid.*, p. 62. P. Carrington, *The Primitive Christian Calendar*, Vol. I, Cambridge, 1952, closely follows Lohmeyer, but—like L. E. Elliott-Binns—inverses the roles of the apostles and the desposynoi. According to him, in A.D. 44, "the Galilean leadership over the Jerusalem church came to an end; the leadership of James the brother of the Lord began (p. 84)."

[20] Elliott-Binns, *Galilean Christianity*, p. 60.

Galilean theology! What was the role of the relatives of Jesus in the primitive Church?

3. Are there any proofs of an expectation of the *parousia in Galilee*?

4. What are the origins of the *Galilean resurrection appearances*? Do they present a different theological outlook from those of Jerusalem?

5. How much of the importance attributed to Galilee in the gospels is due to the *redaction of Mark*? Can one maintain that for Mark, Galilee is the land of salvation, and Jerusalem the place of rejection and death? If the evidence for a Galilean Christianity and the expectation of the parousia in Galilee is too weak, is another theological interpretation of Galilee open to us?

It is on purpose that the question concerning redaction and tradition in Mark is left to the end. It is subject to too many uncertainties; the assumption of the Galilean theory is that the importance of Galilee in Mark is due to the redactor; on this assumption is the theory based. There is here a real danger of reasoning in a circle. Therefore, we examine first some historical data, although here, too, we have to rely heavily on the Marcan evidence.

1. *The extent of Galilee*

Only the assumption of a wider geographic notion of Galilee in Mark and Matthew than is usually entertained permits us to regard the first part of the Lord's ministry as a geographical unit. This assumption is a necessary part of the Galilean theory. The proponents of the theory insist that the boundaries of first-century Galilee fluctuated: it would therefore have been easy for the early community to make the name of Galilee include a larger territory than it "normally" does. The evidence adduced is usually that from Josephus, *Jewish Wars*, III. 3. 1, 4. But before we discuss this text, it will be useful to recall a few facts of Galilean history.

It is certain that the limits of Galilee were subject to frequent changes in the time between the Maccabees and A.D. 70. This was natural because Galilee was the northern outpost of the Jewish territory. King Solomon already is said to have given twenty Galilean towns to Hiram, king of Tyre (1 Kings 9: 11f). The political situation of Galilee[21] at the outbreak of the Maccabean revolt is not quite clear. It was not the name of an administrative unit under the Seleucids and was probably divided among the Phoenician cities Ptolemais, Tyre, and Sidon (cf. 1 Macc. 5: 15, 55). It was distinct from the Great Plain (that is, the plain of Jesreel or Esdraelon) (cf. 1 Macc. 12: 49) the political history of which is rather unknown. The plain may have been divided between the towns along its edge, but it may also be that it was a separate administrative entity, at least since the time of Herod the Great. When Herod died in 4 B.C., his son, Herod Antipas, received Galilee and founded Tiberias, which soon replaced Sepphoris as the

[21] For the following, compare F. M. Abel, *Géographie de la Palestine*, Vol. II, Paris, 1938, pp. 134ff; M. Avi-Yonah, *The Holy Land. From the Persian to the Arab Conquests (536 B.C. to A.D. 640), A Historical Geography*, Grand Rapids, 1966, pp. 36f, 66f, 135–142.

capital. Apparently, between the time of Herod the Great and that of Herod Agrippa I the whole lake of Gennesareth belonged to Galilee. After A.D. 44 the borderline of Galilee seems to have shifted to the western shore of the lake. In A.D. 55 another change of some importance took place: Nero gave Tiberias and Tarichea to Agrippa II, thus separating the two cities from the land of Galilee, which had been administered by procurators since A.D. 44. Since Tiberias now no longer belonged to Galilee, Sepphoris became again the capital of Galilee as it had been before the foundation of Tiberias.

Josephus[22] gives us a rather clear description of the Galilee of his time which had about the same borders as the territory of Herod the Great. Therefore, in spite of some changes, the boundaries of the region were stable enough to be known to the average man in Palestine. It will be useful to quote the pertinent text of Josephus:

"Galilee, with its two divisions known as Upper and Lower Galilee, is enveloped by Phoenicia and Syria. Its western frontiers are the outlying territory of Ptolemais and Carmel, a mountain once belonging to Galilee, and now to Tyre; adjacent to Carmel is Gaba....On the south the country is bounded by Samaria and the territory of Scythopolis up to the waters of Jordan; on the east by the territory of Hippos, Gadara and Gaulanitis, the frontier-line of Agrippa's kingdom; on the north Tyre and its dependent district mark its limits. Lower Galilee extends in length from Tiberias to Chabulon, which is not far from Ptolemais on the coast; in breadth, from a village in the Great Plain called Xaloth to Bersabe. At this point begins Upper Galilee, which extends in breadth to the village of Baca, the frontier of Tyrian territory; in length, it reaches from the village of Thella, near the Jordan, to Meroth.... The province of Samaria lies between Galilee and Judaea; beginning at the village of Ginaea situate in the Great Plain, it terminates at the toparchy of Acrabatene (*Jewish Wars*, III. 3. 1, 4)."

The claim that even Josephus did not exactly know the extent of Galilee because, in his description, the southern border of Galilee is the upper edge of the great plain whereas, on the other hand, Samaria reached only to the lower edge of the plain, ignores the possibility referred to above that the great plain was a separate political entity. Even W. Oehler,[23] who does not allow for this possibility, sees no contradiction in Josephus: according to him, the political frontier between Samaria and Galilee was probably in the middle of the plain. The opinion of G. A. Smith[24] that the southern edge of the plain was also the southern border of Galilee (he refers to Josephus, *Jewish Wars*, III. 3. 4, and a religious reason: the Samaritan schism would automatically have attached the

[22] Translation by H. St. J. Thackeray, Loeb Classical Library, *Josephus*, Vol. II, Cambridge, Mass., 1961 (reprint of 1927).

[23] W. Oehler, "Die Ortschaften und Grenzen Galiläas nach Josephus," ZDPV, Vol. 28, 1905, pp. 1–26, 49–74. Compare esp. p. 67.

[24] G. A. Smith, *The Historical Geography of the Holy Land*, New York/London, 25th ed., 1931, p. 417.

plain to Galilee) has little support in the sources: the text of Josephus does not prove anything at this point.

But Josephus sometimes also speaks of the Galilee as it had been in a glorious past, that is, in an ideal sense:[25] Galilee reached to Sidon (*Ant.* VIII. 2. 3), Upper Galilee to the Lebanon and to the sources of the Jordan (*Ant.* V. 1. 22). Also Kedasa, which in the time of Josephus was a Tyrian town (*Ant.* V. 1. 24), belonged to it. But he clearly indicates that Kedasa now belongs to Tyre (*Jewish Wars*, II. 18. 1; IV. 2. 3); the same is true of Carmel (*Jewish Wars*, III. 3. 1). There also seems to be some confusion about Ptolemais, which he once calls a city of Galilee (*Jewish Wars*, II. 10. 2), although Ptolemais belonged to Phoenicia. But the context shows that Josephus is aware of this fact: he says that the Galilean range is to the east of Ptolemais, at a distance of sixty furlongs (*Jewish Wars*, II. 10. 2), and continues in 10. 3 that Petronius left his troops at Ptolemais and advanced into Galilee. Thus, Josephus could not have regarded Ptolemais as a Galilean city. In *Jewish Wars*, II. 20. 4 Josephus tells us that he was appointed governor of the two Galilees and Gamala which was the strongest city in that region. Although his home is Gamala (*Ant.* XVIII: 1: 1)—and Gamala belonged to the Gaulanitis, east of the lake of Galilee—Judas, who led the revolt of the year A.D. 6, is called a Galilean. Is this to prove that for Josephus Gamala belonged to Galilee? And are the proponents of the Galilean theory right when they draw from this the conclusion that Pella also, which was not so far to the east as Gamala, could have been considered a part of Galilee (this would allow us to interpret the exodus of the Christian community at Jerusalem to Pella as the return to Galilee, commanded in Mark 16: 7)? The text of *Jewish Wars*, II. 20. 4 is not a very accurate statement, but *Jewish Wars*, II. 20. 6 expressly enumerates Gamala among the towns of the Gaulanitis. Our conclusion is that Josephus has no doubts about the borders of Galilee in his time although he may sometimes express himself in an imprecise way. That Judas is called a Galilean does not necessarily reflect the opinion that his hometown is in Galilee. It is different when Josephus speaks of the past of Galilee: he knows of a number of places which have once been Galilean—the territory north up to Sidon, the Lebanon and Carmel, and part of what was Tyrian in his time. This claim that the Phoenician coast belonged to Galilee has its basis in the fact that the coastland had been allotted to the Galilean tribes of Asher and Zebulon (Josh. 19); these tribes, however, could never subdue these territories.

When we ask whether a specifically Christian notion of Galilee could have existed, we have to base our answer on the above facts and on the evidence of the gospels: no other evidence is available for this period. The data in Josephus theoretically allow for the notion of an ideal Galilee which coincides with the desired territories of the Galilean tribes. On this basis, the primitive Christian community could have included the Phoenician territory in the "ecclesiastical

[25] Compare Oehler, *Die Ortschaften*, p. 65.

region of Galilee," that is, it could have extended the frontiers north to the Lebanon, west to the sea; it could also have included the whole lake of Gennesaret, because up to A.D. 44, that is, during the ministry of Jesus and the earliest years of the church, it actually belonged to Galilee. But it must be emphasized that this is only a possiblity. It is not certain whether the historical picture which Josephus gives of Galilee represented the ideal Galilee in the views of the people, or whether Josephus is merely displaying his scholarship. In any case, however, even the Old Testament evidence makes such a notion of an "ideal" Galilee possible. But it cannot be shown that this ideal Galilee (if such existed) included also some territory east of the Jordan. Pella would certainly never have been included in it: it is not only too far to the east, but also to the south. On the same evidence, Damascus must be excluded.

To judge from extracanonical evidence, then, the ideal Galilee is only a possibility. We have now to turn to the gospels to see whether such a concept finds support in the texts of the gospels and whether it helps to explain them.

Reading Mark, we can easily recognize that the evangelist (and certainly to some extent already in his tradition) has grouped together various stories about Jesus which were, in part, not yet localized. Mark did not have the intention to write a biography of Jesus; thus, it may be that pericopes are joined together without regard to the exact geographical and chronological order: some of the geographical implications which we deduce from Mark's outline, may, therefore, not represent Mark's ideas. This calls for caution. But there are passages where we clearly see the geographical ideas of Mark.

Mark 3:7f enumerates several regions: Galilee, Judaea, Jerusalem, Idumaea, and Transjordan, the regions of Tyre and Sidon. They are separate entities, and Galilee certainly is not regarded as including some of the territories here mentioned or parts of them. Mark's Galilee, therefore, does not reach into the land of Tyre and Sidon or across the Jordan. On the other hand, Mark 3:7 does give the impression that the sea to which Jesus withdraws lies outside Galilee. The sea is, as several passages reveal (for example, Mark 1:16; 2:13; 4:1; 5:13), charged with peculiar importance. The narrator seems concerned not so much with Galilee as with the sea: it is the significance of the latter, not the former that governs him.

In Mark 5, Jesus goes into the country of the Gerasenes, just across the lake. As always when Jesus crosses the lake, the evangelist does not emphasize that he left or returned to Galilee. The sea is, so to speak, his domain: on it he moves freely. Mark might have considered the region of the Gerasenes as part of Galilee. But in 5:20 the healed demoniac is said to have announced in the Decapolis what Christ had done to him. One might take this as an indication that Mark confused the Gerasa at the Lake which was Galilean, with the Gerasa of the Decapolis, and that he consequently included the Decapolis as part of Galilee. But 3:7f clearly distinguishes between the territory across the Jordan and Galilee.

Mark 7: 24 strongly marks the departure of Christ, when he leaves for the region of Tyre and Sidon. Mark does so also in 7: 31, when Jesus returns from there, going first even further to the north, to Sidon, whence he turns south again to the Galilean sea, into the very centre of the Decapolis. The travel-route is rather peculiar, but this problem does not concern us here (does the Decapolis, for Mark, begin directly on the eastern shore of the lake? cf. also 5: 20!); important for us is the fact that the region of Tyre and Sidon seems not to be regarded by Mark as a part of Galilee.

E. Lohmeyer[26] deduces from Mark 9: 30, seen together with 9: 2 and 8: 27, that the Markan Galilee reaches as far north as Hermon. But 8: 27 again clearly marks the departure of Jesus from Bethsaida (8: 22) to the villages belonging to Caesarea Philippi. There is no indication that they are thought to belong to Galilee. The context seems to place the mountain of the transfiguration of Christ outside Galilee. But, as we know, most of the pericopes are artificially connected with each other and thus do not necessarily indicate the proper location of a scene. Mark also seems to give much more weight to the theme of the mountain as such than to its geographical position,[27] and perhaps one should not even ask where this mountain was. In a certain sense, one could speak of an ideal mountain, as also the house which Jesus and his disciples enter afterwards (9: 28, apparently at the foot of the mountain) is more a literary-theological idea than a real house. This house is anywhere where Jesus wants to give some special instruction to his disciples.[28] Afterwards Jesus leaves the house and wanders through Galilee: the starting-point of this journey might be in Galilee or outside of it, the grammar admits both interpretations. The context (taken literally) leaves only the second possibility, and thus the text does not support Lohmeyer's opinion. In Mark 10: 1 Jesus leaves Capernaum: he goes into the region of Judaea and to the other side of the Jordan, and never sets foot again on Galilee.

Our conclusion is that one cannot prove from Mark the notion of a larger Galilee. He clearly distinguishes Galilee from the surrounding regions, the country across the Jordan, the lake, the Decapolis, the region of Caesarea Philippi and that of Tyre and Sidon. This leaves no room for a larger Galilee.

The same can be said for Matthew, who in 4: 23–25 tells us of Christ's ministry in all Galilee, which had the effect that Christ's fame spread throughout all Syria; then Matthew enumerates a series of regions from which the crowds followed Jesus: from Galilee, the Decapolis, Jerusalem, Judaea, and from beyond

---

[26] *Galiläa und Jerusalem*, p. 27.

[27] For the theme of the mountain in Mark, compare P. Carrington, *The Primitive Christian Calendar*, pp. 6–13.

[28] In Matthew, this house is always in Capernaum: compare G. Strecker, *Der Weg der Gerechtigkeit*, Göttingen, 1962, pp. 95f (for the "house" in the sense of "school" in Matthew compare W. D. Davies, SSM, p. 421, n. 2). It may be that already Mark thinks of the house especially (but inconsistently) at Capernaum (compare 9: 33). This might explain the wording of 9: 30, which may suppose that the house is in Galilee.

the Jordan. 16: 13 clearly indicates the departure of Jesus for Caesarea Philippi; 15: 21 that for Tyre and Sidon. This certainly does not define the borders of Galilee, but it narrows down the possible extension of this region and excludes, for example, the transfiguration or Peter's confession from Galilee, and distinguishes from it the territory beyond the Jordan. But it has been argued on the basis of Matt. 4: 13–15 that Matthew distinguishes between the geographical Galilee and "Galilee of the Gentiles."²⁹ According to M. Black,³⁰ this "Galilee of the Gentiles" extends beyond the geographical Galilee to the east and includes Peraea and the Decapolis, "possibly reaching as far as Damascus, and to the North as far as Hermon." It must be admitted that Matt. 4: 15 admits of such an interpretation: "Galilee of the Gentiles" could sum up the preceding terms and thus include the region "beyond the Jordan." But (1) this text is a quotation, and Matthew is not particularly interested in this clause "beyond the Jordan (4: 12–13 mention all the other geographical names of the quotation, but not this one!)." Knowing how Matthew uses his quotations, one could not insist on every detail of a citation as if it expressed Matthew's own view. (2) The clause "beyond the Jordan" is not quite clear. It usually designates the land east of the Jordan. But Matt. 19: 1 tells us that Jesus left Galilee and came into the territory of Judaea "beyond the Jordan (Mark 10: 1 'Judaea and³¹ beyond the Jordan' !)." This gives the impression that for Matthew "beyond the Jordan" is *west* of the Jordan. If this be correct, he probably also understood Is. 8: 23 in this sense: then the territory of Zebulun and Naphtali which is the "Galilee of the Gentiles" is the land *between* the Jordan and the sea (this corresponds to the older idea of Galilee mentioned above). We cannot insist upon this point. But no text in Matthew can be used as evidence for a larger Galilee. It might also be asked if the formula "Galilee of the Gentiles" in the quotation of 4: 15 really expresses Matthew's own thinking: for, in 10: 5, Matthew records Christ's saying to the disciples: "Go nowhere among the Gentiles, and enter no town of

²⁹ E. Grässer, *Das Problem der Parusieverzögerung in den synoptischen Evangelien und in der Apostelgeschichte*, Berlin, 1957, p. 30.

³⁰ M. Black, *The Scrolls and Christian Origins*, New York, 1961, p. 81. He accepts Lohmeyer's thesis of the double origin of primitive Christianity. "The origins of Christianity are to be sought in Northern Palestine (p. 88)." The reasons given by Black for his judgment are the use of Δύναμις (Power) as a name of God in Mark 14:62 and "Nazorenes" as the oldest name for the Christian Church. Δύναμις for God is, he writes, "a northern form of speech, certainly Samaritan, and possibly no less Galilean (p. 81)," a "North Palestinian idiom, attested especially in accounts of sectarian circles in this area." Therefore he sees in the use of this expression a link between the Galilean gospel tradition and North Palestinian forms of religion. But the expression is not certain to be Galilean, as Black himself notes, and if it were, this would not necessarily mean a Galilean Christian community, but could also be explained by the Galilean origin of the apostles and the first Christians. The use of the name Nazorenes is by no means clear. Even if there is a connection with the Nazirite vow, why should we locate these Nazirites exactly in Galilee? The same is true for the παρθενοί (unmarried maidens) in the Primitive Church: if their sexual asceticism is an inheritance of Jewish sectarianism, as Black maintains (p. 88), does this necessarily point to Galilee? The reasons given by M. Black are, therefore, inadequate to prove his point.

³¹ Marxsen, *Der Evangelist Markus*, p. 47, prefers to omit καὶ before πέραν τοῦ 'Ιορδάνου.

the Samaritans." This restriction of the mission of the disciples to Israel, and more especially to Galilee, seems to be in contradiction with Galilee's designation in 4: 15, as "Galilee of the Gentiles."

Thus we conclude that neither Matthew nor Mark thought of a larger Galilee, and consequently the first half of the ministry of Christ in these two gospels reveals no geographical unity: most important events like the transfiguration take place outside Galilee.

2. *A Galilean Christianity?*

The recognition of the prominence of Galilee in the gospel of Matthew, but especially in that of Mark, led to the assumption of a "primitive community" of Christians in Galilee (Lohmeyer), or of Galilee as the temporary home of Christianity after A.D. 66 (Marxsen). One has to assume that the author of Mark "wrote in or near Galilee because else one cannot explain such a marked emphasis on this region—does one write a 'Galilean gospel' without relation to this sphere?"[32] We have pointed out above what reconstruction of the history of the primitive Church these exegetes attempted on this basis. The first part of our examination of the Galilean theory has shown that the evidence of the gospels for a greater Galilee is not so strong as these scholars assumed; and we shall have occasion to test this evidence from another point of view. The question we have to ask here, now, is, whether there is some evidence for a flourishing Galilean Christianity either before the Jewish war or beginning with it, (*a*) in the New Testament, but independent of the theory; and (*b*) outside the New Testament.

In the New Testament, one usually refers to Mark 14: 70 parr. as evidence that Galilee was regarded as *terra christiana*, the Galileans as Christians: "Certainly you are one of them; for you are a Galilean." This remark which causes Peter to deny his Lord a second time, could be understood in this way, that is, as implying that "Galilean" means Christian, if other evidence supported the equation. But why should we draw such far-reaching conclusions from this verse? Peter is suspected to be one of Christ's disciples because of his Galilean pronunciation. This is quite natural: most of Christ's followers come from Galilee, and Jesus himself is referred to, in this same context of the Passion, as the Nazarene (Mark 14: 67) or the Galilean (Matt. 26: 19; Luke 23: 5f). Therefore, every Galilean, who in those days was in Jerusalem, was easily brought into connection with Christ.

Acts never mentions how Christians came to Galilee; but Acts 9: 31 implies the presence of Christians there: "So the church throughout all Judea and Galilee and Samaria had peace and was built up." This text, combined with Acts 1: 8, where Christ sends his disciples to be his witnesses "in Jerusalem and in all Judea and Samaria and to the end of the earth," is taken as proof that the Galilean Church had not begun in Jerusalem. But it might also be, as H. Grass[33]

---

[32] W. Marxsen, *Einleitung in das Neue Testament*, Gütersloh, 1963, p. 128.
[33] H. Grass, *Ostergeschehen und Osterberichte*, Göttingen, 2nd ed., 1962, p. 123.

has remarked, that the absence of Galilee in Acts 1:8 is of no importance: Luke does not want to enumerate all mission territories, but rather to point out that the Church expands in concentric circles: from Jewish to semi-pagan and pagan territories. And Acts 9:31 does not indicate whether there was an important community in Galilee or not. Luke's continuous silence about Galilean Christians rather points to the absence of such. One might even argue that Judaea, Galilee, and Samaria in Acts 9:31 serve only as a convenient formula to assert that the whole Jewish-Christian Church was at peace, without any implication that there was an organized community in Galilee or not. Anyway, it does not seem that the Galilean Christians can have played any real part in the life of the early Church.

Since Acts knows of a Christian community in Damascus, but does not tell us how Christians came to be there, Lohmeyer assumes that Damascus was converted by Galilean missionaries.[34] But would Acts have ignored a significant missionary activity of the supposed Galilean Christians? One could adduce as a reason for the silence of Acts in this regard that Luke writes from a Jerusalemite viewpoint. But is it not easier and more natural to assume that Damascene Jews who had come to Jerusalem for a feast, possibly the Pentecost of Acts 2, had been converted to the Christian faith? Acts also assumes the existence of a Roman community without telling us of its origin. If Paul had become a Christian in a strictly Jewish-Christian community (as Damascus on this hypothesis is regarded as having been), would there not have been some indication of this in his writings, and in his personal development?[35] Thus, the existence of the Damascene community is no evidence for a missionary activity based on a supposed Galilean Christian centre.

Do the Galilean resurrection appearances presuppose the existence of a larger Christian community in Galilee? H. Grass[36] considers the possibility that the appearance of Christ before the five hundred might have taken place in Galilee, a possibility made more probable if a Galilean community existed. But there is no way of telling where this appearance took place. We shall turn to this problem of the Galilean resurrection appearances later on, but one thing is clear: the tradition of an appearance to "five hundred" brethren (1 Cor. 15:6) does not necessarily presuppose a Galilean community.

Outside the New Testament, information about a Galilean community is very scanty and late.[37] It concerns the relatives of Jesus in Galilee and the exodus of the Christian community to Pella. Some valuable references can be found in

---

[34] Lohmeyer, *Galiläa und Jerusalem*, pp. 54f. Compare Carrington, *The Primitive Christian Calendar*, p. 82.

[35] Contrast Grass, *Ostergeschehen*, p. 125. R. Bultmann, *Theology of the New Testament*, trans., Vol. I, New York, 1951, pp. 187–189, strongly insists on the Hellenistic character of the Christian community in which Paul was converted.

[36] Grass, *Ostergeschehen*, pp. 123f.

[37] This information is gathered in H. J. Schoeps, *Theologie und Geschichte des Judenchristentums*, Tübingen, 1949, p. 235 (Schoeps accepts Lohmeyer's theory); L. E. Elliott-Binns, *Galilean Christianity*, London, 1956, pp. 12ff, and P. B. Bagatti, *L'Église de la Circoncision*, Jerusalem, 1965, pp. 16–19 (rather an uncritical presentation).

Rabbinic sources. As we have noted above, the proponents of the Galilean theory attribute great importance to the family of Jesus, although they see this importance in contradictory terms (the brothers of Jesus being leaders of the Galilean or of the Jerusalemite community, or being leaders first in Galilee and then in Jerusalem).

Hegesippus (about A.D. 250) tells us: "Now there still survived of the family of the Lord grandsons of Judas, who was said to have been his brother according to the flesh, and they were related as being of the family of David. These the officer brought to Domitian Caesar, for, like Herod, he was afraid of the coming of the Christ. He asked them if they were of the house of David and they admitted it. . . .They then showed him their hands, adducing as testimony of their labour the hardness of their bodies. . . . They were asked concerning the Christ and his kingdom. . . and explained that it was neither of the world nor earthly. . . . At this Domitian did not condemn them at all, but despised them as simple folk, released them, and decreed an end to the persecution against the church. But when they were released they were the leaders of the churches, both for their testimony and for their relation to the Lord (quoted by Eusebius, HE, III: 20, 1–6)."[38] Hegesippus also writes (Eusebius, HE, III: 32, 3) that "some. . . accused Simon the son of Clopas of being descended from David and a Christian and thus he suffered martyrdom, being a hundred and twenty years old, when Trajan was emperor and Atticus was Consular." Julius Africanus (Eusebius, HE, I: 7, 14) knows of men "called desposynoi, because of their relation to the family of the Saviour, and from the Jewish villages of Nazareth and Cochaba they traversed the rest of the land and expounded the preceding genealogy of their descent, and from the book of Chronicles so far as they went. Whether this be so or not no one could give a clearer account. . . ."

Only the last text quoted directly connects these desposynoi with Galilee; the first text, which introduces the relatives of the Lord as farmers, may imply this, but does not make it explicit. And, above all, these men are not connected with a Galilean community. Nevertheless, these few references are used, together with the not very favourable remarks about the relatives of Jesus in the gospels (Matt. 12: 46–50; 13: 54–58 and parallels; John 7: 1–10) and the statement of 1 Cor. 9: 5, that the brothers of the Lord are accompanied by their wives on their travels (missionary travels?), to reconstruct the history of the primitive Church and of the Galilean community. But (1) the patristic sources are late and not very reliable; (2) they do not refer to any missionary activity of the relatives of Jesus; (3) they also do not imply that they laid claim to the leadership of the Church because of their status as desposynoi (Eusebius, HE, III: 20, 6 indicates that their relation to the Lord was only one reason among others which made of the two desposynoi leaders of the churches). These references, therefore, cannot be taken to prove the existence of a Galilean Church. H. v. Campenhausen has shown

[38] We use the English translation of Eusebius by Kirsopp Lake, Loeb Classical Library, London, 1926.

how unfounded the conception of a Christian "caliphate," exercised by the family of the Lord, is.[39] The only point which the texts cited above prove, is that the family of Jesus had survived in Nazareth, that some had become Christians and that some of them had exercised a leadership in the Church (James, ?Symeon as his successor; the two who had testified before Domitian). But the earliest references connect the relatives of the Lord with the church of Jerusalem (or, in the case of Eusebius, HE, III: 20, 6, with no particular church at all) and not with that of Galilee, if such existed.

W. Marxsen seems to have recognized that there are no proofs for the existence of a Galilean Church before the Jewish war. But his theory that the community of Jerusalem was temporarily established around the Galilean Sea during the years of the war before moving on to Pella, is even less likely and has no support outside his interpretation of Mark 14: 28; 16: 7. Marxsen regards the patristic texts which tell of the flight of the community of Jerusalem to Pella as support for his Galilean theory. These texts will be dealt with when we discuss the question of the Galilean parousia. Here it is to be emphasized that these patristic texts are no evidence for the existence of a Galilean Church, because Pella was not in Galilee: we have shown above that it is unlikely and unprovable that the authors of the Gospels ever included the region of the Decapolis in Galilee. The settlement of the community of Jerusalem around the Galilean Sea is a pure hypothesis for which no evidence can be adduced.

The only real evidence concerning Christians in Galilee is to be found in Jewish sources dealing with the *Minim* in Galilee.[40] Rabbi Eliezer b. Hyrcanus, for example, is reported to have discussed halakah with Jacob of Kefar Sekanya, a Christian, in Sepphoris, shortly after A.D. 100.[41] Rabbi Ḥananiah, nephew of Rabbi Joshua b. Ḥananiah, who migrated to Babylonia before the war under Hadrian, reportedly was converted for a short time by one of the minim from Capernaum around 110.[42] The testimony of Justin Martyr may also be mentioned here that Bar Cocheba threatened those of his countrymen who refused to deny Jesus as Messiah:[43] this text also proves the presence of Christians in Galilee.

All in all there is no clear picture of a Galilean community in the first century. There were Christians in Galilee at the turn of the century, but whether they were of importance we cannot say. One can certainly suppose that the ministry

[39] H. v. Campenhausen, "The Authority of Jesus' Relatives in the Early Church," in H. Chadwick and H. v. Campenhausen, *Jerusalem and Rome*, Philadelphia, 1966, pp. 3–19. The idea of a caliphate has been applied to the history of the early Church by A. v. Harnack, M. Goguel and others (compare H. v. Campenhausen, pp. 3–4). L. E. Elliott-Binns also speaks of "an abortive anticipation of the caliphate of Islam" in the Church of Jerusalem (*Galilean Christianity*, p. 60).

[40] Compare W. D. Davies, SSM, pp. 273ff; H. L. Strack, *Jesus, die Haretiker und die Christen nach den ältesten jüdischen Angaben*, Leipzig, 1910; B. Bagatti, *L'Église de la Circoncision*, pp. 17f, 78.

[41] Compare G. F. Moore, *Judaism*, Vol. II, Cambridge, Mass., 1927, p. 250.

[42] Midr. Koheleth 1, 25; 7, 26; Schoeps, *Theologie*, p. 278.

[43] Justin, *Apol.*, 31. Compare G. F. Moore, *Judaism*, Vol. I, p. 91.

of Jesus in Galilee had not been without at least some lasting effect. Many of the Galileans who followed Jesus on his way to Jerusalem or had been converted there on later occasions, certainly, we may presume, returned to Galilee and spread the message. It may also be that the persecution following the death of Stephen drove some Christians as far as Galilee, or that some of the apostles occasionally exercised their ministry in Galilee. But it does not seem that the Galilean Christians ever exercised any real influence during the first century. The persecutor, Saul, did not feel it necessary to do anything against the new faith in Galilee, but went directly from Jerusalem to Damascus. And also in later texts we find no mention of a Galilean church, except for the remark of Acts 9: 31. This makes it difficult to believe in the existence of an organized Christian community in Galilee in the early years when Mark wrote his gospel.[44]

3. The Galilean Parousia

Before turning to the disputed passages Mark 14: 28 and 16: 7, we shall again first gather the evidence for connecting the End with Galilee outside the New Testament. There, naturally, it is not the parousia, but the final intervention of Yahweh, the coming of the Messiah, which is under view. Old Jewish sources never seem to connect the coming of the Messiah with Galilee. H. J. Schoeps[45] refers only to some late Rabbinical and cabbalistic texts which see in Galilee the place of Messianic events. But even if the old tradition did not expect the Messiah in Galilee, it found it possible to accept a Galilean Messiah. Thus Hezekiah, the "robber-chief" (Josephus, Antiquities, XIV. 9. 2), whom Herod suppressed when he was governor of Galilee, was accepted as the Messiah by Hillel (the famous Rabbi?).[46] Again his son, Judas the Galilean, made claims to be the Messiah, so that S. Mowinckel even speaks (following H. Gressmann) of a "dynasty" of Galilean Messiahs.[47] But to establish themselves firmly in the public opinion as Messiahs, they certainly would have had to proceed to Jerusalem. Also the Maccabees, whose achievements gave rise to the hope of a Messiah from their family, from the tribe of Levi,[48] achieved this fame not during their Galilean campaign, but only when they reigned over the country from Jerusalem. The Messiah, we may say, could initially appear in Galilee (or also at the Jordan, as did Theudas: Acts 5: 36; Josephus, Antiquities, XX. 97), but Jerusalem was the place of his complete manifestation.

[44] W. Bauer, "Jesus der Galilaer," Festgabe für A. Jülicher, Tübingen, 1927, pp. 16–34, who gives a good picture of Galilee in the first century, strongly denies the existence of early Christian communities in Galilee.

[45] Schoeps, Theologie, p. 272 refers to the texts quoted in Jellinek, Beth ha-Midrash III, Leipzig, 1855, XXIX, and SB, Vol. I, p. 161.

[46] The identity of both, Hezekiah and Hillel in T. B. Sanh. 98b, 99a is disputed. Mowinckel, He That Cometh, trans., New York, 1954, p. 284, identifies them with the Galilean would-be Messiah and the famous rabbi. G. F. Moore, Judaism, Vol. II, p. 347, n. 2, thinks of another rabbi and king Hezekiah. [47] S. Mowinckel, He That Cometh, p. 291.

[48] The question of a Hasmonean Messiah is discussed by D. S. Russell, The Method and Message of Jewish Apocalyptic, Philadelphia, 1964, pp. 310–315.

N. Wieder,[49] whose theories have been discussed above by W. D. Davies (pp. 221ff), claims that, at Qumran, Galilee was considered as the place of the eschatological events. We need not repeat here the arguments of Davies against this theory: some texts really connect the coming of the Messiah with the North, but is this Galilee? The identification of Galilee and the land of Damascus is very questionable. Davies has rightly emphasized that although the Messiah, according to these texts, appears first in the North, he does not remain there, but proceeds to Jerusalem. With regard to the Messianic expectations of Qumran, J. T. Milik[50] makes an interesting remark. Like the book of Enoch, Qumran also thought of paradise as located in the North, a fact which explains the South–North position of the tombs at Qumran: "Morts, en attendant le Jour de la Résurrection, ils gisent tête au sud, contemplant dans le rêve d'un sommeil passager leur future Patrie. Éveillés, ils se lèveront face au nord et marcheront tout droit vers le Paradis, la Montagne Sainte de la Jérusalem celeste."[51] Thus, the direction of the tombs would indicate Jerusalem as the place of the Messianic fulfilment, although it would also be compatible with the expectation of the Messiah farther north, in Galilee or in the land of Damascus. It is however always Jerusalem which is the centre of the eschatological hopes, even if other areas in some way are connected with the inauguration of the end (see p. 234 above).

One might ask why the Jews expected the events of the end to occur here or there. It was the land of Palestine where one expected the end (and the resurrection: recall the Rabbinic speculations how the Israelites who were not buried in Palestine would participate in the resurrection),[52] because God himself had chosen this country for his people, had consecrated it by his manifestations and by its history. If one wanted to be more precise in the localization of the eschatological events, then only Jerusalem, and more exactly Mount Sion, the Temple, could be the place of the final manifestation. God had revealed himself also in other places; there were many sacred locations. But sacredness thus conferred was alone not enough for the final revelation. This had to take place where heaven and earth were already connected, and where also was the entrance to Sheol, in short, the centre of the world. If we see the New Testament against this background, it is clear that the inauguration of the kingdom in Galilee is not enough to expect the parousia there. If the New Testament wanted to fix the parousia at a certain place, it seems that again only Jerusalem was qualified—

[49] N. Wieder, *The Judaean Scrolls and Karaism*, London, 1962.

[50] J. T. Milik, "Henoch au Pays des Aromates" (ch. XXVII à XXXII). "Fragments araméens de la grotte 4 de Qumran," RB, Vol. 65, 1958, pp. 70–77, 77, n. 1.

[51] For the idea of Paradise and God's mountain in the North in the Old Testament and in Judaism, compare P. Grelot, "Isaïe XIV, 12–15 et son arrière-plan mythologique," *Revue de l'histoire des religions*, Vol. 149, 1956, pp. 18–48, esp. p. 21; P. Grelot, "La Géographie Mythique d'Henoch et ses sources orientales," RB, Vol. 65, 1958, pp. 33–69, esp. pp. 35–37; J. T. Milik, "Henoch." See above, pp. 139f.

[52] Compare G. F. Moore, *Judaism*, Vol. II, pp. 379f; above pp. 62ff.

the place where Christ had been exalted on the cross (an event interpreted by the gospels, especially Matthew, as an eschatological event!), where he had poured out his Spirit (Luke, John), and from where, according to Luke, he ascended into heaven.

Thus the interpretation of Mark 14: 28; 16: 7 of the parousia seems *a priori* very unlikely. The linguistic reason given by Lohmeyer and Marxsen that the active future tense of *horaô* has to have this sense and cannot refer to the appearances of the risen Lord, loses all value since these authors themselves have to concede that the active form is used for resurrection appearances also (John 20: 18, 25; 1 Cor. 9: 1). We have seen at the beginning how this whole interpretation originated with F. Spitta and others: the verb *proagô hymas* is the starting point of the interpretation. N. Wieder has renewed the view that *proagein* here signifies to march at the head of the disciples, supposedly like the cloud or the fire-column in Exodus (see above pp. 228f). In general the word is now interpreted in the sense of being somewhere before the others, and this certainly is how Mark understood the sentence in 16: 7 (*ekei auton opsesthe*). But, one asks, why have the disciples to go to Galilee and cannot see the Lord at Jerusalem? This question applies to both understandings: resurrection appearance or parousia. We try to give an answer to this question later on. It seems to be clear, however, that the problems connected with the *wording* of the phrase remain the same whatever interpretation we choose.

But we also have to explain the abrupt ending of the gospel. It supplies the strongest reason for understanding these two verses of the parousia. Many exegetes still maintain that the ending of the gospel has been lost, whereas others have tried to explain that such an ending as Mark offers is perfectly possible. Since there are no signs whatsoever of this lost ending, a correct exegetical method has to cope with the text as it now stands. And we must agree that this keen expectation produced by the announcement of something which is not then related, better fits the parousia than the resurrection appearances, which for author and readers were already past. But why should the author connect the parousia with Galilee? And why does he not end his account with 16: 7? 16: 8 better fits the mood of the accounts of the resurrection appearances!

Before attempting an answer to these questions, let us examine more closely the theories of E. Lohmeyer and W. Marxsen. In the case of Lohmeyer, the Galilean Church is supposed to have been waiting for the parousia for decades: by the time when Mark wrote his gospel, would not the hope for an imminent parousia have faded away? By then, would not the Galilean Christians have reinterpreted this word of Jesus in the way of Matthew, that is, would they not have understood it of resurrection appearances? Mark certainly knew of resurrection appearances! By the time when Mark wrote, Peter, to whom this promise is especially addressed (16: 7 *eipate tois mathêtais autou kai tô Petrô*), had died, and Mark was probably in a position to know this (cf. Mark 10: 39);

Peter would no longer be there to expect the parousia.[53] The whole picture of the Galilean community, as drawn by E. Lohmeyer, is historically improbable.[54]

Theoretically more likely is the reconstruction of W. Marxsen. In his view, the eschatological hopes had been kindled anew by the Jewish war and by certain prophecies, one of which underlies Mark 16: 7 and 14: 28, and has been preserved in a transformed wording by Eusebius: "The people of the church in Jerusalem were commanded by an oracle given by revelation before the war to those in the city who were worthy of it to depart and dwell in one of the cities of Perea which they called Pella (Eusebius, HE, III. 5, 3)." According to this prophecy, Marxsen assumes, the Christians went out to the Galilean Sea to expect there the parousia, and after some waiting went further east to Pella where they settled down. This second stage is said to be reflected in the transformation of the saying which no longer speaks of Galilee but of Pella. The whole theory is a pure hypothesis![55] Although one cannot so easily dismiss the whole tradition about the Christian exodus to Pella, as R. Eisler and S. G. F. Brandon[56] did, this flight certainly was not the organized march of the whole community of Jerusalem and possibly all Judaea to the place of the anticipated parousia. The conditions during the Roman siege of the city made it absolutely impossible that large groups could leave the city. And Pella, which in an attack of reprisal had been laid waste by the Jews at that time (Jos., *Jewish Wars*, II. 18. 1), and which never had been a large town, would not have been in a position to receive so many refugees. The tradition about Pella may have arisen to explain the origins of the Christian community which existed there. It is not impossible that some Christian refugees from Jerusalem had settled there. More we cannot say. To connect this tradition with Mark 16: 7 has no support whatsoever. The whole gospel of Mark does not give the impression that it was written as a pamphlet to prepare for the imminent parousia. The apocalyptic discourse of Mark 13 sees

[53] E. Haenchen, *Der Weg Jesu, Eine Erklärung des Markusevangeliums und der kanonischen Parallelen*, Berlin, 1966, p. 546, interprets Mark 16: 7 of resurrection appearances and sees in the verse a listing of the witnesses of the resurrection appearances. He rightly remarks that the parousia is not a private experience of a few disciples, but a cosmic event.

[54] E. Trocmé, *La Formation de l'Évangile selon Marc*, Paris, 1963, pp. 186f, accepts Lohmeyer's interpretation of Mark 16: 7 of the parousia. Matthew has interpreted this verse as a prophecy of the Christophany on the mountain. The Markan redactor, however, intended at the end of his work to direct the attention of his readers towards the future. He changed the small ecclesiological tractate Mark 1–13 into a partial biography of Jesus and thus took away the original actuality of the references to Galilee; but he felt all the same that this region, from where the great News took its departure, was a holy place and would be the place of the parousia—a right which Jerusalem had lost. This justifies, according to Trocmé, the somewhat exaggerated space given to this obscure region in the gospel. The theory of Trocmé about the genesis of the gospel is questionable, but the abrupt ending of Mark's gospel is certainly well interpreted.

[55] Grass, *Ostergeschehen*, pp. 300–302 declares Marxsen's hypothesis as "highly phantastic," a purely hypothetical reconstruction of the history of the early Church without sufficient basis, and even more questionable than Lohmeyer's theory.

[56] Compare Elliott-Binns, *Galilean Christianity*, p. 67. To see a reference to Pella in Rev. 12, as has sometimes been suggested (compare Elliott-Binns, p. 68; H. J. Schoeps, *Judenchristentum*, p. 267f), is mere conjecture.

the events of the end still far away (in spite of 13: 30!) and does not expect them in Galilee, but as a cosmic occurrence: when the Son of Man comes on the clouds of heaven, it does not matter where everybody is; for "he will send out the angels, and gather his elect from the four winds, from the ends of the earth to the ends of heaven (13: 27)."

It is not possible to understand Mark 14: 28; 16: 7 (exclusively) of the parousia. But in addition there is something in these texts which points beyond the resurrection appearances: otherwise Mark would have given an account of such an appearance (especially if we suppose that originally each form of the Passion account ended with a resurrection appearance). We now turn, therefore, to the resurrection appearances.

4. *The Galilean resurrection appearances*

Only Matthew and John 21 speak of resurrection appearances in Galilee. We may suppose that Mark would have located the resurrection appearances in Galilee if he had continued his gospel (cf. Mark 14: 28; 16: 7). John 20 speaks of appearances in Jerusalem only, but does not exclude the possibility of other appearances (John 20: 30). Only Luke is in open contradiction with the Galilean tradition: his account leaves no room for appearances in Galilee.[57]

The evidence has frequently been discussed. We certainly do not pretend to solve the questions it raises here in a few lines. Only a few remarks will be made, as far as the Galilean theory is concerned. There will be few exegetes nowadays to dismiss the Galilean tradition so easily as F. Spitta had done. It is easier to assume that appearances which had taken place somewhere else, were later transferred to Jerusalem for theological reasons, than the opposite. The concentration of the post-Easter events in John 20 and Luke 24 on one day and at one place betrays a certain theological intention (in Acts, Luke himself feels free to change his scheme!). But must this insight lead us to reject the Jerusalem appearances? There is here no either-or. Both traditions are old and have to be accounted for. We must recognize that we no longer are in a position to reconstruct the sequence of the post-Easter events: Lohmeyer rightly warns us against a harmonizing historization of the accounts.[58]

[57] It seems, however, that Luke knew the Galilean tradition and in 24: 6 transformed Mark 16: 7. Compare A. George, "Les récits d'apparitions aux Onze, à partir de Luc 24: 36–53," in *La resurrection du Christ et l'exégèse moderne* (various contributors), Paris, 1969, pp. 75–104, 83f especially.

[58] Lohmeyer, *Galiläa und Jerusalem*, p. 8, writes that only one of the two traditions, Galilee or Jerusalem, can be historically correct. But then he adds (pp. 97–99) that both traditions are equally justified because they represent two different communities, two different theological outlooks. The necessity for historical harmonization was not felt. Only one tradition can be historically correct, but both are theologically justified. This approach too easily eludes the historical questions involved. W. Marxsen, *Die Auferstehung Jesu von Nazareth*, Gütersloh, 1968, also oversimplifies the realities when he tends to admit only one resurrection appearance, that is, the one before Peter (although he expressly affirms that he does not want to say that there was only one appearance—or whatever experience may have been behind Peter's faith; *de facto* he always assumes precisely this).

Does the Galilean tradition here suppose the flight of the apostles from Jerusalem to Galilee, embellished later on by a "command of Jesus (Mark 16: 7)?" This has been frequently assumed but there is no evidence for this flight (Mark 14: 27 gives no hint where the apostles will be dispersed; nor can John 16: 32 *eis ta idia* be pressed in this way); when Jesus was arrested, the disciples need not even have left Jerusalem (cf. the denial of Peter, Mark 14: 66ff!). The gospels do not tell us how the disciples returned to Galilee: Matt. 28: 16 gives the impression that they left Jerusalem for Galilee on Easter Sunday, immediately after having received Christ's message through the women, but this seems to be a "historical reconstruction" by Matthew. John 21 supposes a certain lapse of time between the crucifixion and the appearance at the lake of Tiberias, but this is due to the introduction of this story by the redactor.

Thus we do not know when these Galilean appearances occurred. To some extent we might also say that we do not know *how* they occurred. Matt. 28: 17–20 has no resemblance whatsoever to the appearances in Luke 24 and John 20 (except the motif of the doubting disciples in 28: 17 which is common to all the resurrection appearances). The mountain is said to be in Galilee, but is this not only because of 28: 7? This mountain could be anywhere (like the mountain of the transfiguration 17: 2, 9: "If you have faith as a grain of mustard seed, you will say to this mountain, 'Move hence to yonder place,' and it will move, 17: 20)." It was on a high mountain that the devil offered to Christ "all the kingdoms of the world and the glory of them (Matt. 4: 8)"; on a mountain Jesus revealed himself as the exalted Lord in his glory to whom all power over heaven and earth had been given. Christ's words have to be proclaimed on a mountain (theologically), but they are not limited to a certain place and to a determined time: they express the faith of the Church, her consciousness apart from time and space. Thus the scene can hardly be called historical. It is less a resurrection appearance than a "proleptic parousia,"[59] or better, the revelation of the pantokrator who is always present within his kingdom.

John 21 again is different. At some points this story recalls Luke 24: 36–43, but it is even more similar to some scenes which the gospels have placed in the earthly life of Jesus and which have sometimes been regarded as antedated resurrection appearances: for example, the miraculous catch of fish and Christ walking on the lake (Luke 5: 1–11; John 6: 16–21 par). May we suggest that there was a tradition that Christ had been seen in Galilee after his resurrection (cf. Mark 14: 28; 16: 7), but that details were no longer known? Matthew saw it fitting to combine this tradition with his idea of the Christos pantokrator (the mountain was then the necessary scene), whereas John 21 used other traditions of Christ's epiphany on the lake (again a theologically fitting localization), to give concrete form to this Galilean tradition.

Are the Galilean resurrection appearances more closely connected with the parousia than those of Jerusalem? (We must leave aside here the appearances

[59] W. D. Davies, SSM, p. 197.

before the women because their character and intention is too different.) The reference to the end of the world (Matt. 28: 20) and to the return of Christ (John 21: 22) is more explicit (Luke speaks of Christ's return only after the ascension, Acts 1: 11, because of his historization of the post-Easter events; in John the whole outlook is different because of his highly realized eschatology: the gift of the Spirit, 20: 22, inaugurates the world to come here and now). But this closer connection of the Galilean appearances with the parousia is not due to their localization in Galilee; it is the mountain or the lake (John 21 does not expressly mention Galilee!) which evoke the image of the eschatological Son of Man, not Galilee as such. These accounts of resurrection appearances therefore do not express the association of Galilee with the coming end.

5. *Tradition and redaction in Mark*

According to W. Marxsen[60] (and before him E. Lohmeyer),[61] most occurrences of Galilee in Mark are due to the redactor of the gospel. Our examination up to now has shown that many of the presuppositions of the Galilean theory (a large Galilee, a Galilean Christianity, the expectation of the parousia in Galilee, a special orientation of the Galilean resurrection appearances) are based on insufficient evidence. This calls for a closer examination of this last point. If it is (substantially at least) correct, we would have to look for some other explanation of the emphasis on Galilee than that offered by the proponents of the theory.

In Mark 1: 9 Jesus comes from Nazareth of Galilee (Matt. 3: 13 simply "from Galilee" because Nazareth has already been mentioned in 2: 23) to be baptized by John. Marxsen[62] thinks that the tradition said only that "Jesus the Nazarene (compare 1: 24; 10: 47; 14: 67; 16: 6)" came to John, and that Mark introduced "Galilee." This may be, but cannot be proved. Nazareth is frequently determined by the addition of "Galilee" (Matt. 2: 22f; Mark 1: 9; Luke 1: 26; 2: 4; 2: 39. Luke 2: 51 is the only synoptic text which does not explicitly connect Nazareth and Galilee), as also Cana is qualified as "Cana of Galilee (John 2: 1, 11)." This suggests that already the tradition may have included the name of Galilee; the other possibility would be that the tradition behind Mark 1: 9 did not indicate any place (compare John 1: 29) and that Mark gave this supplementary information from the common stock of traditional knowledge. If this be the case, nothing indicates that the Markan emphasis is on Galilee rather than on Nazareth.

In Mark 1: 14 (compare Matt. 4: 12; Luke 4: 14), after the arrest of John, Jesus comes to Galilee to announce the good news of God's kingdom. For Marxsen, "Galilee" here is certainly due to the redactor. But John 1: 43 (we are rather

[60] Marxsen, *Der Evangelist Markus*, pp. 35–59.
[61] Lohmeyer, *Galiläa und Jerusalem*, p. 26: except at 6: 21 (and perhaps 1: 9) Galilee is in Mark redaction (the verses 14: 28/16: 7 are not considered here).
[62] Marxsen, *Der Evangelist Markus*, p. 35.

sure that John did not know the Synoptics) indicates that this information may come from the tradition, although 1: 14a now serves as a transition formed by the evangelist. In Mark 1: 16 Jesus calls the disciples at the lake of Galilee. Marxsen hesitates as to whether only "Galilee"[63] or the whole localization comes from the redactor. The name "Sea of Galilee" occurs also in 7: 31; Matt. 4: 18; 15: 29; John 6: 1 ("Sea of Tiberias" John 6: 1; 21: 1; "lake of Gennesareth" Mark 6: 35; Matt. 14: 34; Luke 5: 1). The expression *paragôn para tên thalassan tês Galilaias* may be clumsy, but this is no proof that originally *para k.t.l.* was not there.[64] John again confirms (1: 43ff) that the tradition already placed the vocation of some disciples in Galilee. According to Mark 1: 28 "his fame spread everywhere throughout all the surrounding region of Galilee." According to Marxsen,[65] only *eis holên tên perichôron tês Galilaias* is an addition of the redactor to the original *pantachou*. This may be questioned. The whole verse is a first summary of the success of Jesus, and as such may be entirely due to Mark. One might suggest that in Mark 1: 14–23 the localization of 1: 16 (the vocation at the Sea of Galilee) was traditional and caused Mark to indicate in the transition of 1: 14 how Jesus came there; also 1: 28 could be explained from 1: 16: but this would not prove a special emphasis on Galilee. These indications serve only to make the account more concrete, more real. It is arbitrary to affirm[66] that Mark is not interested in the names of cities and that these all come from the tradition, but that it was always Mark himself who inserted Galilee!

Mark 1: 39 tells us of Jesus' preaching and exorcizing ministry in the synagogues in all Galilee: the verse summarizes the ministry of Jesus and as such it may be redactional. Marxsen is right that Mark is anxious to let Jesus work only in Galilee, but in the whole of Galilee. This, however, is true only of this chapter, of the beginnings!

Mark 3: 7 mentions a series of regions from which people come and follow Jesus. K. L. Schmidt[67] sees here a tradition concerning the territory of Christ's activity; to Marxsen, this seems impossible (because he overinterprets the earlier references to Galilee!): he prefers to think that in all these places Christians lived at the time of Mark.[68] We have found no evidence for an early Galilean Church; therefore, Schmidt's view still seems more likely.

Mark 6: 21 mentions the presence of noble men of Galilee at Herod's feast. Marxsen regards this as tradition.[69]

[63] K. L. Schmidt, *Der Rahmen der Geschichte Jesu*, Berlin, 1919, p. 43, thinks this is perhaps possible.

[64] Against Lohmeyer, *Das Evangelium des Markus*, p. 31.

[65] Marxsen, *Der Evangelist Markus*, p. 37.

[66] *Ibid.*, p. 38.   [67] Schmidt, *Der Rahmen*, p. 106.

[68] Thus already Lohmeyer, *Das Evangelium des Markus*, p. 72; Lightfoot, *Locality and Doctrine*, p. 119. Against this opinion Haenchen, *Der Weg Jesu*, pp. 130 n. 1, 226, 230. Trocmé, *La Formation de l'Évangile*, p. 147, n. 124, remarks that Mark 3: 7f constitutes not church statistics, but an allusion to the necessity of a mission among the Jews of these regions (not very probable).

[69] Marxsen, *Der Evangelist Markus*, p. 46; he gives no reasons for his opinion.

Mark 7: 31 gives the travel route of Jesus from Tyre by Sidon to the Sea of Galilee into the centre of the region of the Decapolis. This route is strange and has caused some changes in the manuscripts. We concede to Marxsen[70] that the "Sea of Galilee" is probably introduced by the redactor who wrote the verse as a transition between two miracle accounts which by tradition were fixed in the region of Tyre and in the Decapolis. Does this strange itinerary only indicate Mark's "ignorance of the geographical conditions"?[71] The construction of the sentence becomes clumsy because Mark wants to introduce too many geographical indications. Matt. 15: 29 simplified by omitting the Decapolis and Sidon. Mark seems to give some weight to the "Sea of Galilee": but is the important indication for him the Sea or Galilee? Marxsen[72] thinks the latter: Mark uses this indication to correct an "inconsistency" in his presentation of the Galilean ministry; although he speaks of a miracle outside of Galilee, he connects it with Galilee by this insertion. This argument is very tenuous since it cannot be shown that Mark wanted to restrict the first part of Christ's ministry to Galilee. If we have to see any special meaning in this indication (and not just an ill-placed geographical remark which intends to locate the following multiplication of the bread at the lake), the accent may well be on the "Sea," the scene of Christ's revelation and of his victorious fight against the demons (Mark frequently sees the healings as part of this fight!): Matt. 15: 29 places the healings on a "mountain" near the lake (which is also the scene of the multiplication of the bread), a similar theological theme.

Mark 9: 30 is again redaction.[73] Mark says that Jesus and his disciples "passed through Galilee and he would not have any one know it." Then follows the second prediction of the passion. Marxsen concludes that only this prediction of the passion was not localized: Mark uses this occasion to introduce Galilee: "thus the passion and resurrection of Jesus are announced in Galilee." This conclusion is exaggerated. It is not certain that it was not Mark who localized the third prediction: on the way to Jerusalem (10: 32). One might also ask whether here Jerusalem or Galilee are of first importance, or "the way" (an idea strongly elaborated in Luke).

In the passion account, Galilee occurs three times. 15: 41 speaks of the women who were with Jesus in Galilee and who followed him: probably a traditional element,[74] later elaborated by Luke. 14: 28 and 16: 7 (*proaxô hymas eis tên Galilaian*) are closely connected and may go back to a single traditional saying. Both verses are probably inserted at their present place by Mark himself (doubtful for 14: 28). We have already seen how the proponents of the Galilean theory explain these two passages: of the parousia in Galilee.

[70] *Ibid.*, p. 44.
[71] Thus Schmidt, *Der Rahmen*, p. 200.
[72] Marxsen, *Der Evangelist Markus*, p. 44.
[73] *Ibid.*, p. 46, following R. Bultmann and E. Lohmeyer.
[74] Compare R. Bultmann, *Die Geschichte der synoptischen Tradition*, Göttingen, 2nd ed., 1931; Marxsen, *Der Evangelist Markus*, p. 59, n. 4.

This short examination shows that some occurrences of Galilee in Mark may be due to the redactor, but certainly not as many as Marxsen claims. In several cases it is impossible to decide whether Mark himself introduced Galilee or whether the name existed already in his tradition. It is also questionable whether even redactional insertions of Galilee are always intended to emphasize Galilee or whether the evangelist used Galilee as a "stop-gap" where he had no special tradition, knowing that Christ's ministry, to a great extent, had taken place in Galilee. Certain answers will not always be possible; the texts, however, must not be forced and unified by a theory. There is no proof of a thoroughgoing Galilean redaction in Mark.

Lohmeyer and Lightfoot emphasize that Galilee is the land of salvation, Jerusalem the city of rejection.[75] But an unprejudiced reading of the gospel shows that not all miracles and exorcisms occur in Galilee (the argument as such is two-edged: one could also interpret it to mean that only Galilee is haunted by demons, full of disease as a consequence and symbol of sin!); the good news is announced not only there; and even in Galilee there are people hostile to Jesus.[76] Jerusalem gives him a triumphal entry; many people there are friendly to Jesus; on the cross, Christ is proclaimed King of the Jews and Son of God.[77] These scholars have rightly seen the changed character of Christ's ministry once he is on the way to Jerusalem and in the holy city itself: but is this due to a theological opposition between Galilee and Jerusalem? Is it not a more far-reaching difference between the first and the second part of Christ's ministry which,

[75] This statement (and other claims of the Galilean theory) is examined and rejected by T. A. Burkill, *Mysterious Revelation. An Examination of St. Mark's Gorpel*, Ithaca, New York, 1963, pp. 252–257, for the following reasons: (a) If Galilee is the land of revelation, why does John the Baptist give his witness in the wilderness, presumably near the southern fords of the Jordan (1: 4f)? The first testimony of the heavenly voice is located somewhere outside Galilee (1:11). (b) The absence of the term κηρύσσω in 10: 52 (conclusion of a healing story) is not surprising since it does not occur in 1: 31; 2: 12; 3: 6, etc. It cannot be inferred from St. Mark's use of the term that there is no present proclamation of the gospel elsewhere than in Galilee and its environs. (c) Galilee is to a considerable extent the scene of hostility (for example, 3: 20–35; 6: 1–6; 7: 1–23, etc.). (d) In a certain measure, is not Jesus well received in Jerusalem (11: 18; 12: 12; 12: 37; 14: 2)? One has to distinguish between the people and the hostile religious authorities. (e) That there are only two miracles in the Jerusalem period is probably due to the Evangelist's preoccupation with the passion. (f) The limits of the Messianic secrecy are overstepped not only in Galilee, but also (and most impressively) in 14: 62 in Jerusalem. (g) 14: 28; 16: 7 primarily refer to appearances of the Risen Lord and not to the parousia.

[76] Lohmeyer, *Galiläa und Jerusalem*, p. 32, sees that there is hostility against Jesus even in Galilee: but the dogma of the Evangelist (that is, Galilee as the land of salvation) cannot be refuted by single events. Who established the dogma, Mark or Lohmeyer? Lightfoot, *Locality and Doctrine*, p. 123, emphasizes that the last time Galilee is mentioned (Mark 9: 30) is also the last reference to the Messianic secret. As soon as Jesus leaves Galilee, there is no more proclamation of the Gospel: is it not the contrary conclusion we have to draw? The end of the secret is the beginning of the true proclamation.

[77] G. H. Boobyer, "Galilee and Galileans in St. Mark's Gospel," BJRL, Vol. 35, 1952, pp. 334–348, following M. Kiddle, sees in the Passion Christ's transfer from the unbelieving Jews to the responsive faith of the Gentiles; he is handed over to men and sinners (Mark 9: 31; 14: 41); the rejected king of the Jews becomes the Lord of the Gentiles (pp. 341–343).

among other things, is emphasized by a change in the locale? J. Schreiber may be right that Mark intended to represent Christ's life as the anabasis of the redeemer, and that it is for this reason that Jesus comes to Jerusalem only once.[78] However this may be, there is no clear-cut opposition between the Galilee of salvation and the Jerusalem of the rejection.

We must conclude that the Galilean theory in practically all its points is untenable, and goes back to the over-interpretation and undue unification of certain facts in the gospel. The whole theory, finally, has its origin in the resurrection accounts, and especially in Mark 16: 7. It is from there that we now try to give a tentative solution of the problem.

6. Conclusion

Although we had to reject the Galilean theory, we have seen a certain emphasis on Galilee in the gospels. But there is no uniform pattern behind this emphasis, no single ideology. Many factors contribute to this prominence of Galilee (which exists de facto although it is not so strong as the proponents of the theory thought). The strongest single influence is certainly the tradition of the life of Jesus, the knowledge that most of his ministry was dedicated to this region. Many of the followers of Jesus were Galileans, and they certainly constituted an important part of the earliest church in Jerusalem.[79] The Galileans were the official witnesses to Jesus because they had been with him from the beginning. This makes it understandable that a certain emphasis was laid upon Galilean traditions;[80] the first disciples were proud that it was in their own region, the despised Galilee that the Lord had proclaimed the good news. There were also traditions about resurrection appearances in Galilee. When Mark, on the basis of his traditions, began to work out a continuous narrative which had to cover

[78] J. Schreiber, "Die Christologie des Markusevangeliums," ZTK, Vol. 58, 1961, p. 171. But we need not see with Schreiber, pp. 158f, in Mark the gnostic myth of the redeemer, a Hellenistic Christology of the *salvator salvandus*.

[79] H. Conzelmann, *Die Mitte der Zeit, Studien zur Theologie des Lukas*, Tübingen, 3rd ed., 1960, insists that in Luke the Galileans remain such even in Jerusalem. "Galilean," in Luke, does not refer to a community in Galilee, but to the primitive community of Jerusalem. The central idea of the "Galilean ideology" is that the Galileans knew that they have been led by Jesus to Jerusalem where now their seat is. "Luke no longer knows of 'Galileans' in Galilee (p. 32, n. 1)." The future witnesses are gathered in Galilee. In the Jerusalemite tradition of Luke (esp. in Acts) the Galileans play an important, nearly dogmatic role (p. 64, n. 3).

[80] Trocmé, *La Formation de l'Évangile*, p. 43, rightly insists on the Galilean tradition about Christ's life. He, however, thinks more of traditions which developed in Galilee itself (but without supposing a separate Galilean Christianity; Jesus had a certain success with the people in Galilee, and it would not be astonishing if the memory of his prodigies had been handed on in wider circles which were not necessarily a Galilean community of fervent believers). The miracle-accounts give more the impression "d'un 'cycle galilée' (p. 42, n. 157)." This agrees with what we have already emphasized that frequently it is not so much Galilee but the Sea which is important for Mark. Trocmé is right that before one looks for a symbolical meaning of the localization of the miracle accounts, one should ask if the localization reflects, besides historical facts, the origin of the narrated material.

Christ's activity from the beginning, one of his main difficulties was to establish a sequence, to connect many separate small traditional units. It may well be that in his transitions and summaries he sometimes chose to mention Galilee because he knew of the Galilean ministry, but did not have sufficient geographical indications.

Having emphasized the traditional character of Galilee in the gospel, we may ask what Galilee meant for the Evangelist. The bad name which Galilee had among the Jews of Judaea, the common opinion that the Galileans did not know the Law and did not care to keep it, certainly influenced the Evangelists. That Christ had chosen to exercise his ministry in Galilee, this fact underlined the paradox of the incarnation, God's incredible love in his work of redemption. It is precisely to the despised and lowly people, that Christ comes, he who is not a doctor for the healthy but for the sick, and who did not come to save the just, but the sinners, Christ, who did not mind to eat with publicans and harlots. Galilee is part of this emphasis in Christ's activity. Only Matthew directly explains Christ's ministry in Galilee with an Old Testament quotation, but we may assume that Mark also knew the tradition of the Old Testament on Galilee, the "Galilee of the Gentiles." G. H. Boobyer[81] has rightly emphasized this tradition. It is however an oversimplification when C. F. Evans,[82] following E. Hoskyns, simply equates Galilee with the Gentile world in Mark 14: 28; 16: 7, and interprets these verses in the sense that Christ will lead his Church to the mission of the Gentiles. But one cannot deny that the Galilean tradition may have encouraged the young Church to take up this mission. The Church sees in Christ's life a paradigm for her own activity. In Christ's Galilean ministry she recognizes that her mission, too, is to the lowly, the despised, the sinners.

We have refused to see in Mark 14: 28; 16: 7 simply a reference to the parousia. On the other hand, to understand these verses only of resurrection appearances, one almost necessarily has to assume that the ending of Mark's gospel has been lost. But one should always try to explain a verse from the existing text. In order to do justice to the undeniable tension in Mark's abrupt

---

[81] Boobyer, "Galilee and Galileans"; Galilee is in the LXX frequently regarded as a Gentile country. Especially interesting is Boobyer's reference to Ezek. 47: 8: there the waters of the Temple-source at the end of the times are said to flow toward the eastern region and go down into the *Arabah*: הַגְּלִילָה. הַמַּיִם הָאֵלֶּה יוֹצְאִים אֶל הַגְּלִילָה הַקַּדְמוֹנָה וְיָרְדוּ עַל הָעֲרָבָה is any well-defined region; here it is the fields east of Jerusalem.) The LXX translate: *eis tēn Galilaian tēn pros anatolas*. Fishermen stand along this river, which according to Apoc. 22:2 is *eis therapeian tēn ethnōn*. Boobyer connects this with Mark 1: 17, the vocation of Simon and Andrew in Galilee to be fishers of men. The vocation of the two disciples would thus be a direct reference to the ideas connected with Ezek. 47. As to Mark 14: 28; 16: 7, Boobyer concludes that it is "likely that he thought that there they were not only to see the risen Lord, but were also under his guidance to begin the evangelisation of the gentiles (p. 340)." But the salvation, he rightly insists, does not go forth from Galilee, but proceeds there from Jerusalem (like the Temple-source).

[82] C. F. Evans, "I will go before you into Galilee," JTS, Vol. 5, 1954, pp. 3–18. Mark 16: 7 is for him "a prophecy of the mission of the flock of Israel to the Gentile world (p. 5)," and cannot point to resurrection appearances (p. 11f).

ending *and* to the Galilean tradition of resurrection appearances, the following interpretation may be suggested:

Every Passion account probably ended with a resurrection appearance. In Mark 16, verse 8 may still be a trace of this tradition (the verse is more fitting in the account of a resurrection appearance than as a preparation of the parousia).[83] Mark knows of resurrection appearances in Galilee (14: 28; 16: 7 point to this tradition), but he does not narrate them. This is his solution to the problem as to what the sacred past of Christ's history means for the time of the reader of the gospel, for the believer who had not the privilege of participating in these sacred events. He does not tell of the appearances, he does not close the circle, but points to something still ahead[84] (Matthew achieved this same purpose by Christ's words in 28: 18-20, Luke by the extension of his narrative in Acts, John by the whole transformation of the Christology). Reading the last verses of Mark, every reader expects the account of a resurrection appearance to follow. By omitting it, Mark teaches the reader that there is still something ahead, that Christ is still waiting for his believers, that the resurrection appearances are no privilege reserved to a few witnesses, but that the Risen Lord still appears. Before Easter the disciples could not have thought of Christ's resurrection in other terms than those of the parousia. The post-Easter experience has taught them not simply to equate the appearances of the Risen Lord with his last coming, but the appearances were still considered as an anticipated parousia. Mark keeps both together by the simple device of not relating a resurrection appearance.[85]

[83] Marxsen, *Einleitung in das Neue Testament*, p. 126, thinks that the pre-Markan Passion account probably contained no explicit Easter-kerygma (he sees a contradiction between 16: 1, 3 and 15: 46). The resurrection appearances have developed out of the ὤφθη (he appeared) (RSV; NEB) of 1 Cor. 15: 5 as an illustration of it. It is not certain if at the time of Mark accounts of resurrection appearances existed already, and, if this be the case (which seems more probable), one may still ask, adds Marxsen, whether Mark knew them. But is it not improbable that at the time when Mark was written, the Passion could be told without an explicit Easter-kerygma, or that Mark could ignore this tradition? It is by no means certain that the accounts of the resurrection appearances are just literary illustrations of the ὤφθη (he appeared). It seems more likely that such accounts have a tradition-history independent of that of the formulas. Since Mark does not give an account of a resurrection appearance, one must conclude that he omitted it voluntarily for theological reasons, as we shall show.

[84] Marxsen, *Einleitung in das Neue Testament*, p. 126f, says that Mark cannot tell of a resurrection appearance; for he announces the risen Christ already in his earthly life. Mark announces the Risen Lord with stories about the earthly life of Jesus. If Mark told of an event which would happen only after this early life of Jesus, he would have taken away from these stories their kerygmatic character. All these stories would then be relegated to the past to be distinguished from the time after Easter. Mark would have written a history—exactly what he tried to avoid. Mark does not want to tell a history of the past, but announces the risen Christ. The Gospel stands between Easter and the Parousia. In this we fully agree, but this must not lead us to underestimate the possible historical interest of the evangelist whose kerygma is the present value of past history. Thus one may also question Marxsen's revelars of Lohmeyer's statement that Galilee has special importance for Mark because it was the land of Christ's activity: "Galilee becomes the place of Jesus' activity because it (Galilee) is of *special* importance for Mark and plays a special role (*Der Evangelist Markus*, p. 37, Marxsen's italics)."

[85] A similar interpretation is given by H. W. Bartsch, "Parusieerwartung und Osterbotschaft," *Entmythologisierende Auslegung*, Hamburg–Bergstedt, 1962, pp. 61-69. The

Every resurrection appearance is two-sided: it connects with the past (normally the identification of the risen Lord with the earthly Jesus) and it points to the future (the command given by Christ). Both elements are contained in 16: 7: Galilee reminds of the past, of the beginnings of Christ's ministry; there is a continuity between the earthly work of Jesus and the ministry of the Church after Easter. The abrupt ending points to the future; the task of the past, begun in Galilee, has to be carried on until Christ's return. This idea is well expressed by R. H. Lightfoot, who thus discarded the interpretation of Mark 16: 7 of the parousia: "the disciples have a work awaiting them, and in it their Lord will still lead the way for them, as He did before...in the reference to Galilee in the Lord's last words to his disciples, 14: 28, which are taken up afresh in 16: 7, the reader's thought is turned back to the story of the ministry in the early chapters of the book, and he perceives that this is also the ministry to be fulfilled henceforth by the Lord...in and through his disciples.... The reader is thus enabled to discern both the task and the message of the church."[86]

---

account of a Galilean resurrection appearance is, says Bartsch (p. 67), an early form of the resurrection accounts which still sees the resurrection in the light of the parousia. The Galilean accounts are independent of the Jerusalem tradition. Bartsch's explanation for the missing end of Mark is that accounts which combine the expectation of the parousia with the hope of the resurrection were left out when it became clear that the parousia was still in the future. But were there ever such accounts? No longer development was needed to see that the parousia did not coincide with the resurrection! The existence of a Galilean community would be an explanation for the Galilean resurrection appearances, says Bartsch. A resurrection appearance was needed to constitute a church community in the same way as somebody had to have been a witness of the resurrection if he wanted to be recognized as an apostle. Does this mean that the Galilean tradition has been invented to justify the Galilean community? Bartsch does not make clear what kind of connection he sees between the resurrection appearance in Galilee and the Galilean community.

[86] R. H. Lightfoot, *The Gospel Message of St. Mark*, p. 116.

BIBLIOGRAPHY

A. DICTIONARIES AND ENCYCLOPAEDIAS AND SOURCE BOOKS

Aboth de Rabbi Nathan. Trans. and ed. J. Goldin. Yale Judaica Series, Vol. x. New Haven: Yale University Press.

American Daily Prayer Book. New York: Rabbinical Assembly of America, 1962.

Arndt, W. F., and Gingrich, F. W., trans. and eds. *A Greek-English Lexicon of the New Testament and Other Early Christian Literature.* 4th ed. Chicago: University of Chicago Press, 1957.

Baillet, M., Milik, J. T. and Vaux, R. de. *Les "Petites Grottes" de Qumran: Exploration de la Falaise, les Grottes* 2 Q, 3 Q, 5 Q, 6 Q, 7 Q à 10 Q, le *Rouleau de Cuivre.* Discoveries in the Judaean Desert, 3. Oxford: Clarendon Press, 1962.

Barthélemy, D. and Milik, J. T., eds. *Qumran Cave I.* Discoveries in the Judaean Desert, Vol. I. Oxford: Clarendon Press, 1955.

Black, M. and Rowley, H. H., eds. *Peake's Commentary on the Bible.* London and New York: Nelson, 1962.

Blackman, P. *Mishnayoth.* 7 vols. 2nd ed. New York: Judaica Press, 1964.

Brown, F., Driver, S. R. and Briggs, C. A., eds. *A Hebrew and English Lexicon of the Old Testament.* Oxford: Clarendon Press, 1907.

Brown, R. E., Fitzmyer, J. A. and Murphy, R. E., eds. *The Jerome Biblical Commentary.* Englewood Cliffs, N.J.: Prentice-Hall, 1968.

Buber, S., ed. *Midrash Tanchuma.* 3 (4) vols. Wilna, 1885.

Buttrick, G. A., ed. *The Interpreter's Bible.* 12 vols. New York and Nashville: Abingdon Press, 1952–1957.

——, ed. *The Interpreter's Dictionary of the Bible.* 4 vols. New York and Nashville: Abingdon Press, 1962.

The Century Bible. New ed., London: Nelson, 1967.

Charles, R. H. *Apocrypha and Pseudepigrapha of the Old Testament.* 2 vols. Oxford: Clarendon Press, 1913.

Cohen, A., ed. *Everyman's Talmud.* London: Dent, 1932.

Epstein, I., ed. *The Babylonian Talmud.* 35 vols. London: Soncino Press, 1935–1952.

Eusebius of Caesarea. *Das Onomastikon der biblischen Ortsnamen.* Ed. E. Klostermann. Hildesheim: Gg. Olms, 1966.

Friedmann, M., ed. *Siphre Deuteronomy.* Vienna: 1864.

Ginsburger, M., *Targum Pseudo-Jonathan* (Thargum Jonathan ben Usiël zum Pentateuch) nach der Londoner Handschrift Brit. Mus. Add. 2703: herausgegeben Berlin, 1903; reprint Jerusalem, 1966.

Gunkel, H. and Zscharnack, L., eds. *Die Religion in Geschichte und Gegenwart.* Zweite Auflage. 5 vols. Tübingen: Mohr, 1927–1932.

Hatch, E. and Redpath, H. A. *A Concordance to the Septuagint and other Greek Versions of the Old Testament including the Apocryphal Books.* Oxford: Clarendon Press, 1897.

Herodotus. *Herodotus.* Trans. A. D. Godley. The Loeb Classical Library. 4 vols. London: Heinemann, 1926– .

Jewish Authorized Daily Prayer Book. 13th ed. London: Eyre and Spottiswoode, 1925.

Josephus, F. *Josephus.* 8 vols. Trans. H. St. J. Thackeray. The Loeb Classical Library. London: Heinemann, 1926–1943.

Kautzsch, E., ed. *Die Apokryphen und Pseudepigrapha.* 1900.

Kittel, G., and Friedrich, G., eds. *Theological Dictionary of the New Testament.* Trans. G. W. Bromiley. Vols. I–VII. Grand Rapids, Mich.: Eerdmans, 1964–1971.

Koehler, L. H. and Baumgartner, W. *Hebräisches und aramäisches Lexikon zum Alten Testament.* 3 Aufl. Leiden: Brill, 1967.

———. *Lexicon in Veteris Testamenti Libros.* Grand Rapids, Mich.: Eerdmans, 1958.

Lampe, G. W. H., ed. *A Patristic Greek Lexicon.* Oxford: Clarendon Press, 1961–1968.

Léon-Dufour, X., comp. *Dictionary of Biblical Theology.* Trans. J. Cahill. New York: Desclée Co., 1967.

Migne, J.-P., ed. *Patrologiae Cursus Completus. Series Graeca.* Paris: 1857–1866.

Montefiore, C. J. G. and Loewe, H. M., eds. *A Rabbinic Anthology.* London: Macmillan, 1938.

Moulton, J. H. and Milligan, G. *The Vocabulary of the Greek New Testament: Illustrated from the Papyri and other Non-literary Sources.* London: Hodder and Stoughton, 1930.

Philostratus, F. *The Life of Apollonius of Tyana, the Epistles of Apollonius, and the Treatises of Eusebius.* 2 vols. Trans. F. C. Conybeare. The Loeb Classical Library. London: Heinemann, 1912.

Pritchard, J. B., ed. *Ancient Near Eastern Texts Relating to the Old Testament.* 3rd ed. Princeton: Princeton University Press, 1969.

Rahlfs, A., ed. *Septuagint.* 8th ed. Stuttgart: Württembergische Bibelanstalt, 1965.

Sanders, J. A., ed. *The Psalm Scroll of Qumran Cave 11 (11QPsa),* Discoveries in the Judaean Desert of Jordan, 4. Oxford: Clarendon Press, 1965.

Stenning, J. F., ed. and trans. *The Targum of Isaiah.* Oxford: Clarendon Press, 1949.

Strack, H. L. and Billerbeck, P. *Kommentar zum Neuen Testament aus Talmud und Midrasch.* 5 vols. München: Beck, 1922–1926.

Swete, H. B., ed. *The Old Testament in Greek, According to the Septuagint.* 3 vols. Cambridge: University Press, 1925–1930.

The Testament of Abraham: The Greek Recensions. Trans. M. E. Stone. Texts and Translations, 2; Pseudepigrapha Series, 2. Missoula, Montana: The Society of Biblical Literature, 1972.

Torrey, C. C. *The Lives of the Prophets*, JBL Monograph Series, Vol. 1. Philadelphia: Society of Biblical Literature, 1946.

B. BOOKS BY MODERN AUTHORS
REFERRED TO IN THE TEXT

Abel, F. M. *Géographie de la Palestine*, Vol. 11. Paris: Sabalda, 1938.

Abraham, Père des Croyants. *Cahiers Sioniens*, Ve Année, No. 2. Paris (June, 1951).

Allegro, J. M. *The Dead Sea Scrolls*. Middlesex, England: Penguin Books, 1956.

Allmen, J. J. von, ed. *A Companion to the Bible*. Trans. P. J. Allcock. New York: Oxford University Press, 1958.

Alt, A. "The God of the Fathers." *Essays on Old Testament History and Religion*. Trans. R. A. Wilson. Oxford: Blackwell, 1966.

Al-Tafahum, 'Abd. "Doctrine." *Religion in the Middle East*, Vol. 2. Ed. A. J. Arberry. Cambridge: University Press, 1969.

Altmann, A., ed. *Biblical Motifs: Origins and Transformations*. Cambridge, Mass.: Harvard University Press, 1966.

Amsler, S. *Osee, Joel, Amos, Abdias, Jonas*. Neuchâtel: Delachaux et Niestle, 1965.

Arberry, A. J. *Aspects of Islamic Civilization as Depicted in the Original Texts*. London: Allen and Unwin, 1964.

———, ed. *Religion in the Middle East: Three Religions in Concord and Conflict.* 2 vols. Cambridge: University Press, 1969.

Ardrey, R. *The Territorial Imperative: A Personal Inquiry into the Animal Origins of Property and Nations*. New York: Atheneum, 1966.

Avi-Yonah, M. *The Holy Land. From the Persian to the Arab Conquests (536 B.C. to A.D. 640), A Historical Geography.* Grand Rapids, Mich.: Baker Books, 1965.

Audet, J. P. *La Didachè: Instructions des Apôtres*. Paris: Gabalda, 1958.

Bacher, W. *Die Agada der Tannaiten und Amoräer. Bibelstellen-Register. Nebst einem Anhange: Namen-Register zur Agada der babylonischen Amoräer.* Strassburg: Trübner, 1902.

Baeck, L. *Judaism and Christianity*. Philadelphia: Jewish Publication Society of America, 1958.

Baer, J. F. *Galut*. Berlin: Shocken Verlag, 1936.

Bagatti, P. B. *L'Église de la Circoncision*. Trans., A. Storme. Publications du Studium Biblicum Franciscanum, Collection minor, n. 2. Jerusalem, 1965.

Baltensweiler, H. *Die Verklärung Jesu.* Zurich: Zwingli-verlag, 1959.

Baron, S. W. *A Social and Religious History of the Jews.* 2nd ed. 14 vols. Philadelphia: Jewish Publication Society of America, 1952–1969.

Barr, J. *Old and New in Interpretation: A Study of the Two Testaments.* London: SCM Press, 1966.

———. *The Semantics of Biblical Language.* London: Oxford University Press, 1961.

Barrett, C. K. *A Commentary on the Epistle to the Romans.* New York: Harper, 1957.

———. *A Commentary on the First Epistle to the Corinthians.* Vol. 9. New York: Harper and Row, 1968.

———. *From First Adam to Last: A Study in Pauline Theology.* New York: Scribner, 1962.

———. *The Gospel According to St. John.* London: S.P.C.K., 1955.

Bartsch, H. W. "Parusieerwartung und Osterbotschaft," *Entmythologisierende Auslegung.* Hamburg–Bergstedt, 1962.

Bauer, W. "Jesus der Galiläer." *Festgabe für Adolf Jülicher zum 70. Geburtstag 26. Januar 1927.* Tübingen: Mohr, 1927.

Beare, F. W. *The Earliest Records of Jesus.* Oxford: Blackwell, 1962.

Ben-Chorin, S. *Paulus: der Volkerapostel in jüdischer Sicht.* München: List, 1970.

Bennett, W. H. *The Post-Exilic Prophets.* Edinburgh: Clark, 1907.

Betz, H. D. "The Concept of Apocalyptic in the Theology of the Pannenberg Group." *Apocalypticism. Journal for Theology and the Church,* Vol. VI. Ed. R. W. Funk. New York: Herder and Herder, 1969.

———. "On the Problem of the Religio-Historical Understanding of Apocalypticism." *Apocalypticism. Journal for Theology and the Church,* Vol. 6. Ed. R. W. Funk. New York: Herder and Herder, 1969.

Bickerman, E. J. *Four Strange Books of the Bible: Jonah, Daniel, Koheleth, Esther.* New York: Schocken Books, 1967.

———. *From Ezra to the Last of the Maccabees: Foundations of Post-Biblical Judaism.* Part II. Trans. M. Hadas. New York: Schocken Books, 1962.

Black, M. *An Aramaic Approach to the Gospels and Acts.* Oxford: Clarendon Press, 1946.

———. *The Scrolls and Christian Origins.* New York: Scribner, 1961.

Blau, J. L. *Modern Varieties of Judaism.* New York: Columbia University Press, 1966.

Boer, P. A. H. de. *Second-Isaiah's Message.* Oudtestamentische Studiën, Deel xl. Leiden: Brill, 1956.

Bogaert, P. *Apocalypse de Baruch: trad. du Syriaque et Commentaire.* Vol. 1. Paris: Édition du Cerf, 1969.

Bokser, B. Z. *Pharisaic Judaism in Transition.* New York: Bloch, 1935.

Bonsirven, J. *Le Judaïsme Palestinien au temps de Jésus-Christ.* Paris: Beauchesne, 1934–1935.

Borgen, P. *Bread From Heaven: An Exegetical Study of the Concept of Manna in the Gospel of John and the Writings of Philo*. Supplements to Novum Testamentum, Vol. x. Leiden: Brill, 1965.

Bornkamm, G. *Jesus of Nazareth*. Trans. I. and F. McLuskey with J. M. Robinson. New York: Harper, 1960.

———. *Paul*. Trans. D. M. G. Stalker. New York: Harper and Row, 1971.

Bowman, J. *The Gospel of Mark: The New Christian Jewish Passover Haggadah*. Studia Post-Biblica, Vol. viii. Leiden: Brill, 1965.

Brandon, S. G. F. *The Fall of Jerusalem*. London: S.P.C.K., 1951.

———. *Jesus and the Zealots: a Study of the Political Factor in Primitive Christianity*. Manchester: Manchester University Press, 1967.

Braun, F. M. *Jean le Théologien*. 3 vols. Paris: Gabalda, 1964.

Bright, J. *A History of Israel*. Philadelphia: Westminster Press, 1959.

Brock, S. P., ed. *Testamentum Iobi*. Pseudepigrapha Veteris Testamenti Graece, Vol. ii. Leiden: Brill, 1967.

Brown, R. E. *The Gospel According to John*. Anchor Bible, Vols. 29 and 29a. Garden City, N.Y.: Doubleday, 1966–1970.

Bruce, F. F. *The Acts of the Apostles*. London: Tyndale Press, 1951.

Buber, M. *Israel and Palestine*. Trans. S. Godman. London: East and West Library, 1952.

———. *The Prophetic Faith*. Trans. C. Witton-Davies. New York: Macmillan, 1949.

Buchanan, G. W. *The Consequences of The Covenant*. Supplements to Novum Testamentum, Vol. xx. Leiden: Brill, 1970.

Büchler, A. *Types of Jewish-Palestinian Piety From 70 B.C.E. to 70 C.E.* New York: Ktav, 1968.

Bultmann, R. *Das Evangelium des Johannes*. Kritisch-exegetischer Kommentar über das Neue Testament, 2. Abt. Göttingen: Vandenhoeck und Ruprecht, 1941.

———. *Die Geschichte der synoptischen Tradition*. 2nd ed. Göttingen: Vandenhoeck und Ruprecht, 1931.

———. *Jesus and the Word*. Trans. L. P. Smith and E. Huntress. New York: Scribner, 1934.

———. *The Presence of Eternity: History and Eschatology*. New York: Harper, 1957.

———. *Theology of the New Testament*. Trans. K. Grobel. New York: Scribner, 1951.

Burkill, T. A. *Mysterious Revelation: An Examination of the Philosophy of St. Mark's Gospel*. Ithaca, New York: Cornell University Press, 1963.

Burrows, E. "Some Cosmological Patterns in Babylonian Religion." *The Labyrinth: Further Studies in the Relation Between Myth and Ritual in the Ancient World*. Ed. S. H. Hooke. London: S.P.C.K.; and New York: Macmillan, 1935.

Cadbury, H. J. *The Making of Luke-Acts.* New York: Macmillan, 1927.

———. "Overconversion in Paul's Churches." *The Joy of Study: Papers on New Testament and Related Subjects Presented to Honor Frederick Clifton Grant.* Ed. S. E. Johnson. New York: Macmillan, 1951.

Caird, G. B. *The Apostolic Age.* London: Allenson, 1955.

———. *A Commentary on the Revelation of St. John the Divine.* London: Black, 1966.

———. *Jesus and the Jewish Nation.* London: Athlone Press, 1965.

Campenhausen, H. von. *The Formation of the Christian Bible.* Trans., J. A. Baker. Philadelphia: Fortress Press, 1972.

———. *Tradition and Life in the Church: Essays and Lectures in Church History.* Trans., A. V. Littledale. Philadelphia: Fortress Press, 1968.

Carmichael, J. *The Death of Jesus.* New York: Macmillan, 1962.

Carrington, P. *The Primitive Christian Calendar.* Vol. 1. Cambridge: University Press, 1952.

Cerfaux, L. *The Christian in the Theology of St. Paul.* Trans. L. Soiron. London: Chapman, 1967.

———. *La Théologie de l'Église suivant Saint Paul.* 2nd ed. Unam Sanctum, Vol. x. Paris: Éditions du Cerf, 1948.

Chadwick, H. *The Circle and the Ellipse.* Oxford: Clarendon Press, 1959.

Chadwick, H. and Campenhausen, H. v. *Jerusalem and Rome.* Philadelphia: Westminster Press, 1966.

Charity, A. C. *Events and their Afterlife: The Dialectics of Christian Typology in the Bible and Dante.* Cambridge, England: University Press, 1966.

Charles, R. H. *A Critical History of the Doctrine of a Future Life in Israel, in Judaism and in Christianity.* London: Black, 1899.

———. *Religious Development between the Old and the New Testament.* London: Williams and Norgate, 1925.

Charlesworth, J. H. *John and Qumran.* London: Geoffrey Chapman, Publishers, 1972.

Chary, T. *Les Prophètes et le culte à partir de l'exil.* Tournai, Belgium: Desclée, 1955.

Childs, B. *Memory and Tradition in Israel.* Studies in Biblical Theology, No. 37. London: SCM Press, 1962.

Clements, R. E. *Abraham and David: Genesis XV and its Meaning for Israelite Tradition.* Studies in Biblical Theology, 2nd series, 5. London: SCM Press, 1967.

———. *God and Temple.* Oxford: Blackwell, 1965.

Coats, G. W. *Rebellion in the Wilderness: the Murmuring Motif in the Wilderness, Traditions of the Old Testament.* Nashville: Abingdon Press, 1968.

Cohen, G. "Zion in Rabbinic Literature." *Zion in Jewish Literature,* Ed. A. S. Halkin. New York: Herzl Press, 1961.

Cohen, H. *Die Religion der Vernunft.* Köln: Melzer, 1959.

Conzelmann, H. "Current Problems in Pauline Research." In *New Testament Issues,* ed. R. Batey. New York: Harper & Row, 1970.

———. *The Theology of St. Luke.* Trans. G. Buswell. London: Faber and Faber, 1960. (*Die Mitte der Zeit, Studien zur Theologie des Lukas.* Tübingen, 1960.)

Cook, S. A. *The "Truth" of the Bible.* Cambridge: Heffer, 1938.

Cooke, G. A. *A Critical and Exegetical Commentary on the Book of Ezekiel.* The International Critical Commentary. Edinburgh: Clark, 1936.

Cranfield, C. E. B. *The Gospel According to St. Mark.* Cambridge: University Press, 1959.

Creed, J. M. *The Gospel According to St. Luke.* London: Macmillan, 1930.

Cross, F. M. *The Ancient Library of Qumran and Modern Biblical Studies.* Garden City, N.Y.: Doubleday, 1958.

———. "New Directions in the Study of Apocalyptic." *Apocalypticism. Journal for Theology and the Church,* Vol. VI. Ed. R. W. Funk. New York: Herder and Herder, 1969.

Cullmann, O. *Early Christian Worship.* Trans. A. S. Todd and J. B. Torrance. Studies in Biblical Theology, No. X. London: SCM Press, 1953.

———. *Jesus and the Revolutionaries.* Trans. G. Putnam. New York: Harper and Row, 1970.

———. "Sabbat und Sonntag nach dem Johannesevangelium, Joh. 5, 17." *In Memoriam Ernst Lohmeyer.* Ed. W. Schmauch. Stuttgart: Evangelisches Verlagswerk, 1951.

———. *The State in the New Testament.* New York; Scribner, 1956.

Dalman, G. *Sacred Sites and Ways: Studies in the Topography of the Gospels.* Trans. P. P. Levertoff. New York: Macmillan, 1935.

Daniélou, J. *The Theology of Jewish Christianity.* Trans. and ed. J. A. Baker. London: Darton, Longman and Todd, 1964.

Daube, D. *Civil Disobedience in Antiquity.* Edinburgh: University Press, 1972.

———. *He that Cometh.* London: Council for Christian-Jewish Understanding, 1966.

———. *The New Testament and Rabbinic Judaism.* London: University of London, Athlone Press, 1956.

———. *Studies in Biblical Law.* Cambridge: University Press, 1947.

Davidson, R. and Leaney, A. R. C. *Biblical Criticism.* The Pelican Guide to Modern Theology, Vol. 3. Middlesex, England: Penguin Books, 1970.

Davies, W. D. *Christian Origins and Judaism.* Philadelphia: Westminster Press, 1962.

———. *Invitation to the New Testament.* Garden City, N.Y.: Doubleday, 1966.

———. "Paul and the Dead Sea Scrolls: Flesh and Spirit." *The Scrolls and the New Testament.* Ed. K. Stendahl. New York: Harper, 1957.

445

————. "Paul and Judaism." *The Bible in Modern Scholarship*. Ed. J. P. Hyatt. Nashville: Abingdon Press, 1965.

————. *Paul and Rabbinic Judaism*. London: S.P.C.K., 1948.

————. "Reflexions on Tradition: The Aboth Revisited." *Christian History and Interpretation: Studies Presented to John Knox*. Eds. W. R. Farmer, C. F. D. Moule, and R. R. Niebuhr. Cambridge: University Press, 1967.

————. *The Setting of the Sermon on the Mount*. Cambridge: University Press, 1966.

————. *Torah in the Messianic Age*. Philadelphia: Westminster Press, 1952.

Davies, W. D. and Daube, D., eds. *The Background of the New Testament and its Eschatology*. Studies in Honour of C. H. Dodd. Cambridge: University Press, 1956.

Dewailly, L.-M. and Rigaux, B. *Les Épitres de Saint Paul aux Thessaloniciens*. La Sainte Bible, traduite en français sous la direction de l'École biblique de Jérusalem. Paris: Éditions du Cerf, 1954.

Diamond, M. *Martin Buber, Jewish Existentialist*. New York: Gannon, 1970.

Dinkler, E., ed. *Zeit und Geschichte. Dankesgabe an Rudolf Bultmann*. Tübingen: Mohr, 1964.

Dodd, C. H. *The Apostolic Preaching and Its Developments*. New York: Harper, 1939.

————. *The Epistle of Paul to the Romans*. The Moffatt New Testament Commentary, Vol. VI. New York: Harper, 1932.

————. *The Founder of Christianity*. New York: Macmillan, 1970.

————. *Historical Tradition in the Fourth Gospel*. Cambridge: University Press, 1963.

————. *The Interpretation of the Fourth Gospel*. Cambridge: University Press, 1953.

————. *The Parables of the Kingdom*. Rev. ed. New York: Scribner, 1961.

Dossin, G. and Parrot, A., eds. *Archives Royales de Mari*. 15 vols. Paris: Imprimerie Nationale, 1950–1964.

Dostoievski, F. M. *The Possessed*. Trans. C. Garnett. New York: Heritage Press, 1959.

Dowda, R. *The Temple in the Synoptic Gospels*. Unpublished dissertation. Duke University, 1972.

Driver, S. R. *A Critical and Exegetical Commentary on Deuteronomy*. The International Critical Commentary, Vol. V. Edinburgh: Clark, 1895.

Dubnov, S. M. *History of the Jews*. Trans. M. Spiegel. 10 Vols. South Brunswick, N.J.: T. Yoseloff, 1967.

Dupont, J. *Les Béatitudes*. Bruges: Abbaye de Saint-André, 1958.

————. *Die Versuchung Jesu in der Wüste*. Trans. from French by A. van Dülmen. Stuttgart: Verlag Katholisches Bibelwerk, 1969.

Dupont-Sommer, A. *The Essene Writings from Qumran*. Trans. G. Vermes. Oxford: Blackwell, 1961.

————. *The Jewish Sect of Qumran and the Essenes*. Trans. R. D. Barnett. London: Vallentine, Mitchell, 1954.

Duprez, A. *Jesus et les Dieux Guérisseurs: à propos de Jean, V.* Cahiers de la Revue Biblique, Vol. 12. Paris: Gabalda, 1970.

Durkheim, E. *The Elementary Forms of Religious Life*. Trans. J. W. Swain. New York: Macmillan, 1915.

Easton, B. S. *The Gospel According to St. Luke*. New York: Scribner, 1926.

Edwards, G. R. *Jesus and the Politics of Violence*. New York: Harper and Row, 1972.

Eisler, R. *The Messiah Jesus and John the Baptist According to Flavius Josephus' Recently Rediscovered "Capture of Jerusalem" and the Other Jewish and Christian Sources*. New York: L. MacVeagh, the Dial Press, 1931.

Eissfeldt, O. *The Old Testament: An Introduction*. Trans. P. R. Ackroyd. Oxford: Blackwell, 1965.

Eliade, M. *Cosmos and History*. Trans. W. R. Trask. New York: Harper, 1959.

————. *Patterns in Comparative Religion*. Trans. R. Sheed. New York: Sheed and Ward, 1958.

————. *The Sacred and the Profane: The Nature of Religion*. Trans. W. R. Trask. New York: Harcourt, Brace and World, 1959.

Elliott-Binns, L. E. *Galilean Christianity*. Studies in Biblical Theology, No. 16. London: SCM Press, 1956.

Ellis, E. E. *The Gospel of Luke*. London: Nelson, 1966.

Ellis, P. *The Yahwist*. Notre Dame, Ind.: Fides Publishers, 1968.

Euripides. *Iphigenia in Tauris*. Ed. M. Platnauer. Oxford: Clarendon Press, 1938.

Farmer, W. R. *Maccabees, Zealots and Josephus*. New York: Columbia University Press, 1956.

Farrer, A. *A Study in St. Mark*. London: Dacre Press, 1951.

Feuillet, A. "Le sens du mot Parousie dans l'Evangile de Matthieu. Comparaison entre Matth. xxiv et Jac. v. 1–11." *The Background of the New Testament and its Eschatology*. Eds. W. D. Davies and D. Daube. Cambridge: University Press, 1956.

Finkelstein, L., ed. *The Jews: Their History, Culture, and Religion*. 3rd ed. New York: Harper, 1960.

————. *New Light From the Prophets*. London: Vallentine, Mitchell, 1969.

————. "The State of Israel as a Spiritual Force." *Israel: Its Role in Civilization*. Ed. M. Davis. New York: Seminary Israel Institute of the Jewish Theological Seminary of America; distributed by Harper, 1956.

Fitzmyer, J. A. *Essays on the Semitic Background of the New Testament*. London: Chapman, 1971.

————. *Pauline Theology: A Brief Sketch*. Englewood Cliffs, N.J.: Prentice-Hall, 1967.

Flender, H. *St. Luke Theologian of Redemptive History.* Philadelphia: Fortress Press, 1967.

Flew, R. N. *Jesus and His Church: A Study of the Idea of the Ecclesia in the New Testament.* London: The Epworth Press, 1938.

Foakes-Jackson, F. J. and Lake, K., eds. *The Beginnings of Christianity.* 5 vols. London: Macmillan, 1920.

Fortna, R. T. *The Gospel of Signs: A Reconstruction of the Narrative Source Underlying the Fourth Gospel.* Society for New Testament Studies. Monograph Series, 11. Cambridge: University Press, 1970.

Frazer, J. *The Worship of Nature.* New York: Macmillan, 1926.

Freedman, D. N. and Greenfield, J. C., eds. *New Directions in Biblical Archaeology.* Garden City, N.Y.: Doubleday, 1969.

Fuller, R. H. *A Critical Introduction to the New Testament.* Studies in Theology, No. 55. London: Duckworth, 1966.

Gärtner, B. *The Temple and the Community in Qumran and the New Testament: A Comparative Study in the Temple Symbolism of the Qumran Texts and the New Testament.* Society for New Testament Studies. Monograph Series, 1. Cambridge: University Press, 1965.

Gaster, T. H. *The Dead Sea Scriptures.* Garden City, N.Y.: Doubleday, 1956.

Gaston, L. *No Stone on Another: Studies in the Significance of the Fall of Jerusalem in the Synoptic Gospels.* Supplements to Novum Testamentum, Vol. 23. Leiden: Brill, 1970.

George, A. "Les récits d'apparitions aux Onze, à partir de Luc 24: 36–53." *La Resurrection du Christ et l'exégèse moderne.* Paris: Éditions du Cerf, 1969.

Georgi, D. *Die Gegner des Paulus im 2 Korintherbrief: Studien zur Religiösen Propaganda in der Spät-antike.* Wissenschaftliche Monographien zum Alten und Neuen Testament, Bd. XI. Neukirchen-Vluyn: Neukirchener Verlag des Erziehungsvereins, 1964.

———. *Die Geschichte der Kollekte des Paulus für Jerusalem.* Theologische Forschung: wissenschaftliche Beiträge zur Kirchlich-evangelischen Lehre, 38. Hamburg–Bergstedt: Reich, 1965.

Gerhardsson, B. *Memory and Manuscript: Oral Tradition and Written Transmission in Rabbinic Judaism and Early Christianity.* Trans. E. J. Sharpe. Acta Seminarii Neotestamentici Upsaliensis, 22. Uppsala: C. W. K. Gleerup, 1961.

Ginzberg, L. *Eine unbekannte jüdische Sekte.* New York: 1922.

Glatzer, N. N. *Hillel the Elder: The Emergence of Classical Judaism.* Rev. ed. New York: Schocken Books, 1966.

Glover, T. R. *Paul of Tarsus.* New York: George H. Doran Company, 1925.

Goldin, J. "The End of Ecclesiastes: Literal Exegesis and its Transformation," *Studies and Texts,* Vol. III: *Biblical Motifs.* Ed. A. Altmann. Cambridge, Mass.: Harvard University Press, 1966.

————. "The Period of the Talmud (135 B.C.E.–1035 C.E.)." *The Jews: Their History, Culture, and Religion.* Ed. L. Finkelstein. 2 vols. New York: Harper, 1960.

Goppelt, L. *Jesus, Paul and Judaism: An Introduction to New Testament Theology.* Trans. and ed. E. Schroeder. London: Nelson, 1964.

Goulder, M. D. *Type and History in Acts.* London: Allenson, 1964.

Grant, F. C. *The Economic Background of the Gospels.* London: Oxford University Press, 1926.

Grass, H. *Ostergeschehen und Osterberichte.* Göttingen: Vandenhoeck und Ruprecht, 1962.

Grässer, E. *Das Problem der Parusieverzögerung in den synoptischen Evangelien und in der Apostelgeschichte.* Beihefte zur Zeitschrift für die neutestamentliche Wissenschaft und die Kunde der älteren Kirche, Beiheft 22. Berlin: Töpelmann, 1957.

Gray, G. B. *A Critical and Exegetical Commentary on the Book of Isaiah.* The International Critical Commentary. Edinburgh: Clark, 1912.

Gray, J. *The Legacy of Canaan.* New York: Humanities Press, 1967.

Griffiths, D. R. *The New Testament and the Roman State.* Swansea: John Penry Press, 1970.

Guillet, J. *Thèmes Bibliques: Études sur l'Expression et le Développement de la Révélation.* Théologie, études publiées sous la direction de la Faculté de théologie S. J. de Lyon-Fourvière, 18. Paris: Aubier, 1951.

Gutmann, J. "Eres Israel ba-Midrash u-ba-Talmud." *Festschrift zum 75 jährigen Bestehen des jüdisch-theologischen Seminars Fränkelscher Stiftung.* 2 vols. Breslau: M. and H. Marcus, 1929.

Haenchen, E. *The Acts of the Apostles: A Commentary.* Trans. B. Noble and G. Shinn. Philadelphia: The Westminster Press, 1971.

————. *Die Apostelgeschichte.* Kritisch-exegetischer Kommentar über das Neue Testament. Abt. 3, 10 Aufl. Göttingen: Vandenhoeck und Ruprecht, 1957.

————. *Der Weg Jesu, Eine Erklärung des Markusevangeliums und der kanonischen Parallelen.* Berlin: Töpelmann, 1966.

Halkin, A. S., ed. *Zion in Jewish Literature.* New York: Herzl Press, 1961.

Hare, D. R. A. *The Theme of Jewish Persecution of Christians in the Gospel According to St. Matthew.* Society for New Testament Studies. Monograph Series, 6. Cambridge: University Press, 1967.

Harner, P. *The "I Am" of the Fourth Gospel.* Philadelphia: Fortress Press, 1971.

Harper, W. R. *A Critical and Exegetical Commentary on Amos and Hosea.* The International Critical Commentary. New York: Scribner, 1915.

Hauck, F. *Das Evangelium des Markus.* Leipzig: Scholl, 1931.

Heaton, E. W. *The Hebrew Kingdoms.* The New Clarendon Bible. Old Testament, Vol. 3. London: Oxford University Press, 1968.

Heise, J. *Bleiben, Menein in den Johanneischen Schriften.* Hermeneutische Untersuchungen zur Theologie, 8. Tübingen: Mohr, 1967.

Henderson, I. *Rudolf Bultmann.* Richmond, Va.: John Knox Press, 1966.

Hengel, M. *Judentum und Hellenismus: Studien zu ihrer Begegnung unter besonderer Berücksichtigung Palästinas bis zur Mitte des 2. Jh. v. Chr.* Wissenschaftliche Untersuchungen zum Neuen Testament, 10. Tübingen: Mohr, 1969.

———. *Was Jesus a Revolutionist?* Trans. W. Klassen. Philadelphia: Fortress Press, 1971.

———. *Die Zeloten: Untersuchungen zur jüdischen Freiheitsbewegung in der Zeit von Herodes I bis 70 n. Chr.* Arbeiten zur Geschichte des Spätjudentums und Urchristentums, 1. Leiden: Brill, 1961.

Herford, R. T. *Pharisaism.* New York: Putnam, 1912.

Heschel, A. J. *God in Search of Man: A Philosophy of Judaism.* Philadelphia: The Jewish Publication Society of America, 1956.

———. *Israel: Echo of Eternity.* New York: Farrar, Straus and Giroux, 1969.

Hester, J. D. *Paul's Concept of Inheritance: A Contribution to the Understanding of Heilsgeschichte.* Scottish Journal of Theology Occasional Papers, No. 14. Edinburgh: Oliver and Boyd, 1968.

Hicks, F. C. N. *The Fullness of Sacrifice: An Essay in Reconciliation.* London: Macmillan, 1930.

Hoftijzer, J. *Die Verheissungen an die drei Erzväter.* Leiden: Brill, 1956.

Hill, D. *The New Temple in the Messianic Age.* Unpublished STM thesis. New York: Union Theological Seminary, n.d.

Horst, F. "Zwei Begriffe für Eigentum." *Verbannung und Heimkehr: Beiträge zur Geschichte und Theologie Israels im 6. und 5. Jahrhundert v. Chr.* Wilhelm Rudolph zum 70. Geburtstage dargebracht von Kollegen, Freunden und Schülern. Ed. A. Kuschke. Tübingen: Mohr, 1961.

Hoskyns, E. C. and Davey, F. N. *The Fourth Gospel.* London: Faber and Faber, 1940.

Hummel, R. *Die Auseinandersetzung zwischen Kirche und Judentum im Matthäusevangelium.* Munich: Kaiser, 1963.

Huxley, A. *Collected Essays.* New York: Harper, 1959.

James, M. R. *The Testament of Abraham.* Texts and Studies: Contributions to Biblical and Patristic Literature, Vol. II, No. 1. Cambridge, England: University Press, 1891.

Jaubert, A. *La date et la Cène: Calendrier biblique et liturgie chrétienne.* Paris: Gabalda, 1957.

———, ed. *Hommages à André Dupont-Sommer.* Paris: Gabalda, 1971.

Jeremias, J. *Jerusalem in the Time of Jesus: An Investigation into Economic and Social Conditions during the New Testament Period.* Trans. T. H. and C. H. Cave. Philadelphia: Fortress Press, 1969.

——. *Jesus' Promise to the Nations.* Trans. S. H. Hooke. Studies in Biblical Theology, No. 24. London: SCM Press, 1958.

——. *New Testament Theology.* New York: Scribner, 1971.

——. *The Parables of Jesus.* Rev. ed. Trans. S. H. Hooke. New York: Scribner, 1963.

——. *Die Wiederentdeckung von Bethesda, Johannes 5, 2.* Forschungen zur Religion und Literatur des Alten und Neuen Testaments, n. F. 41, Heft; Der ganzen Reihe 59, Heft. Göttingen: Vandenhoeck und Ruprecht, 1949.

Johnson, S. E. *A Commentary on the Gospel according to St. Mark.* Harper's New Testament Commentaries. New York: Harper, 1960.

Joseph, M. *Judaism as Creed and Life.* London: Macmillan, 1903.

Jülicher, A. *Die Gleichnisreden Jesu.* Freiburg: Mohr, 1888.

Käsemann, E. *New Testament Questions Today.* Philadelphia: Fortress Press, 1969.

——. *Perspectives on Paul.* Trans. M. Kohl. London: SCM Press, 1971.

Kaufmann, Y. *The Religion of Israel, From its Beginnings to the Babylonian Exile.* Trans. M. Greenberg. Chicago: University of Chicago Press, 1960.

Kautsky, K. *Der Ursprung des Christentums: Eine historische Untersuchung.* Stuttgart: J. H. W. Dietz nachf., 1919.

Keck, L. E. and Martyn, J. L., eds. *Studies in Luke-Acts: Essays Presented in Honor of Paul Schubert.* Nashville: Abingdon Press, 1966.

Klausner, J. *From Jesus to Paul.* Trans. W. F. Stinespring. New York: Macmillan, 1943.

Klein, G. "Römer 4 und die Idee der Heilsgeschichte." *Rekonstruktion und Interpretation: gesammelte Aufsätze zum Neuen Testament.* Munich: C. Kaiser, 1969.

Klostermann, E. *Das Lukasevangelium.* Handbuch zum Neuen Testament, Bd. 2, 1. Tübingen: Mohr, 1919.

Knox, J. *Chapters in a Life of Paul.* Nashville: Abingdon Press, 1950.

Knox, W. L. *Some Hellenistic Elements in Primitive Christianity.* London: Published for the British Academy by H. Milford, 1944.

——. *St. Paul and the Church of the Gentiles.* Cambridge: University Press, 1939.

Koch, K. *The Rediscovery of Apocalyptic.* Studies in Biblical Theology. Second Series 22. London: SCM Press, 1970.

Kohler, K. "The Testament of Job: An Essene Midrash on the Book of Job: reedited and translated with Introductory and Exegetical Notes." *Semitic Studies in Memory of Rev. Dr. Alexander Kohut.* Ed. G. A. Kohut. Berlin: Calvary, 1897.

Krauss, S. *Synagogale Altertümer.* Berlin: Benjamin Harz, 1922.

Kümmel, W. G. *Verheissung und Erfüllung.* 2nd ed. Zurich: Zwingli-Verlag, 1953.

Lagrange, M. J. *Évangile selon Saint Matthieu*. 8th ed. Études Bibliques. Paris: Gabalda, 1948.

Lanternari, V. *The Religions of the Oppressed: A Study of Modern Messianic Cults*. Trans. L. Sergio. New York: Knopf, 1963.

Leaney, A. R. C. *A Commentary on the Gospel According to St. Luke*. Harper's New Testament Commentaries. New York: Harper, 1958.

Legg, S. C. E. *Evangelium Secundum Matthaeum*. Vol. 1 of *Novum Testamentum Graece*. Oxonii: E. Typographeo Clarendoniano, 1940.

Lessing, Gotthold Ephraim, ed. *Noch ein Fragment des Wolfbüttelschen Ungennanten*. Braunschweig, 1778.

Lévi-Strauss, C. *The Savage Mind*. The Nature of Human Society Series. Chicago: University of Chicago Press, 1966.

Lightfoot, R. H. *The Gospel Message of St. Mark*. Oxford: Clarendon Press, 1950.

———. *History and Interpretation in the Gospels*. London: Hodder and Stoughton, 1935.

———. *Locality and Doctrine in the Gospels*. New York: Harper, 1937.

———. *St. John's Gospel*. Rev. ed. Ed. C. F. Evans. Oxford: Clarendon Press, 1956.

Lindblom, J. *Prophecy in Ancient Israel*. Oxford: Blackwell, 1962.

Lohmeyer, E. *Das Evangelium des Markus*. Kritisch-exegetischer Kommentar über das Neue Testament, 1. Abt., 2. Bd. 15, Aufl. Göttingen: Vandenhoeck und Ruprecht, 1959.

———. "Σὺν χριστῷ." *Festgabe für Deissmann zum 60. Geburtstag, 7. November 1926*. Tübingen: Mohr, 1927.

———. *Galiläa und Jerusalem*. Göttingen: Vandenhoeck und Ruprecht, 1936.

———. "Mir ist gegeben alle Gewalt! Eine Exegese von Matt. 28: 16–20." In *In Memoriam E. Lohmeyer*, ed. W. Schmauch. Stuttgart: Evangelisches Verlagswerk, 1951.

Lutz, H. M. *Jahwe, Jerusalem und die Völker: zur Vorgeschichte von Sach. 12, 1–8, und 14, 1–5*. Wissenschaftliche Monographien zum Alten und Neuen Testament, 27. Bd. Neukirchen-Vluyn: Neukirchener Verlag des Erziehungsvereins, 1968.

Luz, U. *Das Geschichtsverständnis des Paulus*. Beiträge zur evangelischen Theologie: theologische Abhandlungen, Bd. 49. Munich: Kaiser, 1968.

Maag, V. "Malkût Yahweh." *Congress Volume*. Oxford, 1959. Supplements to VT. Vol. VII. Leiden: Brill, 1959.

———. *Text, Wortschatz und Begriffswelt des Buches Amos*. Leiden: Brill, 1951.

McKelvey, R. J. *The New Temple: The Church in the New Testament*. Oxford Theological Monographs. London: Oxford University Press, 1969.

McNeile, A. H. *The Gospel According to St. Matthew*. London: Macmillan, 1915.

Malinowski, B. *Magic, Science and Religion, and Other Essays*. Boston: Beacon Press, 1948.

Malinowski, F. X. *Galilee in Josephus*. Unpublished Ph.D. dissertation, Duke University, 1973.

Manson, T. W. *Jesus and the Non-Jews*. London: Athlone Press, 1955.

———. *The Servant-Messiah: A Study in the Public Ministry of Jesus*. Cambridge: University Press, 1953.

———. *The Teaching of Jesus: Studies of Its Form and Content*. 2nd ed. Cambridge: University Press, 1945.

Manson, W. *The Epistle to the Hebrews: An Historical and Theological Reconsideration*. London: Hodder and Stoughton, 1951.

Marcus, R. *Law in the Apocrypha*. New York: Columbia University Press, 1927.

Martin-Achard, R. *Israël et les nations: la perspective missionaire de l'Ancien Testament*. Cahiers théologiques, 42. Paris: Delachaux et Niestlé, 1959.

Martyn, J. L. *History and Theology in the Fourth Gospel*. New York: Harper and Row, 1968.

Mauser, U. W. *Christ in the Wilderness: The Wilderness Theme in the Second Gospel and its Basis in the Biblical Tradition*. Studies in Biblical Theology, No. 39. London: SCM Press, 1963.

Marxsen, W. *Die Auferstehung Jesu von Nazareth*. Gütersloh: Gütersloher Verlagshaus Gerd Mohn, 1968.

———. *Einleitung in das Neue Testament*. Gütersloh: Gütersloher Verlagshaus Gerd Mohn, 1963.

———. *Der Evangelist Markus. Studien zur Redaktionsgeschichte des Evangeliums*. Göttingen: Vandenhoeck und Ruprecht, 1956.

Maybaum, I. *Creation and Guilt: A Theological Assessment of Freud's Father–Son Conflict*. London: Vallentine, Mitchell, 1969.

Meecham, H. G. *The Epistle of Diognetus*. Manchester: Manchester University Press, 1949.

Meeks, W. A. *The Prophet-King, Moses Traditions, and the Johannine Christology*. Leiden: Brill, 1967.

Messel, N. *Die Einheitlichkeit der jüdischen Eschatologie*. Giessen: Töpelmann, 1915.

Meyer, R. *Der Prophet aus Galiläa*. Darmstadt: Wissenschaftliche Buchges, 1970.

Meyers, E. M. *Jewish Ossuaries: Reburial and Rebirth. Biblica et Orientalia*. Rome: Institute Press, 1971.

Michaelis, W. *Taufer, Jesus, Urgemeinde. Die Predigt vom Reiche Gottes vor und nach Pfingsten*. Gütersloh: Bertelsmann, 1928.

Miller, S. H. and Wright, G. Ernest, eds. *Ecumenical Dialogue at Harvard: The Roman Catholic–Protestant Colloquium*. Cambridge, Mass.: Belknap Press of Harvard University Press, 1964.

Minear, P. *Images of the Church in the New Testament*. Philadelphia: Westminster Press, 1960.

Miskotte, K. H. *Über Karl Barths kirkliche dogmatik*. Theologische Existenz Heute, n. F., Nr. 89. Munich: Kaiser, 1961.

Moltmann, J. *Theology of Hope on the Ground and the Implications of a Christian Eschatology*. New York: Harper and Row, 1967.

Montefiore, C. J. G. *Judaism and St. Paul*. London: Goshen, 1914.

———. *Rabbinic Literature and Gospel Teachings*. London: Macmillan, 1930.

———. *The Synoptic Gospels*. London: Macmillan, 1927.

Moore, A. L. *The Parousia in the New Testament*. Supplements to Novum Testamentum, Vol. 13. Leiden: Brill, 1966.

Moore, G. F. *Judaism in the First Centuries of the Christian Era, The Age of the Tannaim*. Cambridge, Mass.: Harvard University Press, 1927–1930.

Moule, C. F. D. *The Phenomenon of the New Testament: An Inquiry into the Implications of Certain Features of the New Testament*. Studies in Biblical Theology, 2nd series, 1. London: SCM Press, 1967.

Mowinckel, S. *He That Cometh*. Trans. G. W. Anderson. Oxford: Blackwell, 1956.

Munck, J. *Christ and Israel: An Interpretation of Romans 9–11*. Trans. I. Nixon. Philadelphia: Fortress Press, 1967.

———. *Paul and the Salvation of Mankind*. Trans. F. Clarke. Richmond: John Knox Press, 1959.

———. *Paulus und die Heilsgeschichte*. Acta Jutlandica. Aarskrift for Aarhus Universitet, xxvi, 1. Teologisk serie, 6. Aarhus: Universitetsforlaget, 1954.

Neusner, J. *Development of a Legend*. Leiden: Brill, 1970.

———. *A Life of Rabbi Johannan ben Zakkai, 1–80 C.E.* Studia post-Biblica, Vol. 6. Leiden: Brill, 1962.

———. *The Rabbinic Traditions about the Pharisees Before 70*. 3 parts. Leiden: Brill, 1971.

Nickle, K. F. *The Collection: A Study in Paul's Strategy*. London: Allenson, 1966.

Nineham, D. E. *The Gospel of St. Mark*. The Pelican Gospel Commentaries. Baltimore: Penguin Books, 1963.

Noth, M. *The History of Israel*. New York: Harper and Row, 1960.

———. "Jerusalem und die israelitische Tradition." *Gesammelte Studien zum Alten Testament*. Munich: Kaiser, 1957.

Odeberg, H. *The Fourth Gospel Interpreted in its Relation to Contemporaneous Religious Currents in Palestine and the Hellenistic-Oriental World*. Uppsala: Almqvist and Wiksells, 1929.

Olmstead, A. T. E. *History of Assyria*. London: Scribner, 1923.

———. *The History of the Persian Empire, Achaemenid Period*. Chicago: University of Chicago Press, 1948.

O'Neill, J. C. *The Theology of Acts in its Historical Setting*. London: Allenson, 1970.

Orlinsky, H. M. "The So-Called Servant of the Lord and 'Suffering Servant' in Second Isaiah." *Studies on the Second Part of the Book of Isaiah.* Supplements to Vetus Testamentum, Vol. XIV. Leiden: Brill, 1967.

Otto, R. *The Kingdom of God and the Son of Man: A Study in the History of Religion.* Trans. F. V. Filson and B. L. Woolf. London: Lutterworth Press, 1938.

Parke, H. W. and Wormell, D. E. W. *The Delphic Oracle.* 2 vols. Oxford: Blackwell, 1956.

Patai, R. *Man and Temple in Ancient Jewish Myth and Ritual.* London: Nelson, 1947.

Pedersen, J. *Israel: Its Life and Culture.* 4 vols. London: Milford, 1926–1947.

Plöger, O. *Theokratie und Eschatologie.* Wissenschaftliche Monographien zum Alten und Neuen Testament, Bd. 2. Neukirchen Kreis Moers: Neukirchener Verlag, 1959.

Plummer, A. *A Critical and Exegetical Commentary on the Gospel According to St. Luke.* 5th ed. The International Critical Commentary. New York: Scribner, 1902.

Porteous, N. W. *Daniel: A Commentary.* The Old Testament Library. Philadelphia: Westminster Press, 1965.

———. "Jerusalem-Zion: The Growth of a Symbol." *Verbannung und Heimkehr: Beiträge zur Geschichte und Theologie Israels im 6. und 5. Jahrhundert v. Chr. Wilhelm Rudolph zum 70. Geburtstage dargebracht von Kollegen, Freunden und Schülern.* Ed. A. Kuschke. Tübingen: Mohr, 1961.

Rabin, C. *The Zadokite Documents.* 2nd rev. ed. Oxford: Clarendon Press, 1958.

Rad, G. von. *Old Testament Theology.* Trans. D. M. G. Stalker. 2 vols. New York: Harper, 1962–1965.

———. *The Problem of the Hexateuch and Other Essays.* Trans. E. W. T. Dicken. New York: McGraw-Hill, 1966.

———. *Studies in Deuteronomy.* Trans. D. Stalker. Studies in Biblical Theology, No. 9. London: SCM Press, 1953.

Ramsay, Sir W. M. *St. Paul the Traveller and Roman Citizen.* 3rd ed. London: Hodder and Stoughton, 1898.

Reicke, B. I. *Diakonie, Festfreude und Zelos, in Verbindung mit der altchristlichen Agapenfeier.* Uppsala Universitets Årsskrift 1951: 5. Uppsala: Lundequistska bokhandeln, 1951.

Reimarus, H. S. *Von dem Zwecke Jesu und seiner Junger: Noch ein Fragment des Wolfbüttelschen Ungennanten.* Ed. G. E. Lessing. Braunschweig, 1778.

Rengstorf, K. H. *Das Evangelium nach Lukas.* 5 Aufl. Das Neue Testament Deutsch, T. 3. Göttingen: Vandenhoeck und Ruprecht, 1949.

Repo, E. *Der Weg als Selbstbezeichnung des Urchristentums.* Helsinki: Suomalainen Tiedeakatumia, 1964.

Richardson, P. *Israel in the Apostolic Church*. Society for New Testament Studies. Monograph series, 10. London: Cambridge University Press, 1969.

Robertson, A. and Plummer, A. *A Critical and Exegetical Commentary on the First Epistle of St. Paul to the Corinthians*. 2nd ed. The International Critical Commentary. Edinburgh: Clark, 1914.

Robinson, J. A., ed. *Texts and Studies: Contributions to Biblical and Patristic Studies*. Cambridge: University Press, 1893.

Rosenzweig, F. *The Star of Redemption*. Trans., W. W. Hallo. New York: Holt, Rinehart and Winston, 1971.

Rössler, D. *Geset₂ und Geschichte: Untersuchungen ₂ur Theologie der jüdischen Apokalyptik und der pharisäischen Orthodoxie*. Wissenschaftliche Monographien zum Alten und Neuen Testament, Bd. 3. Neukirchen Kreis Moers: Neukirchener Verlag, 1960.

Rost, L. *Das kleine Credo und andere Studien ₂um Alten Testament*. Heidelberg: Quelle und Meyer, 1965.

Rostovtzeff, M. *The Social and Economic History of The Hellenistic World*. 3 vols. Oxford: Clarendon Press, 1941.

Rowley, H. H. *The Faith of Israel: Aspects of Old Testament Thought*. London: SCM Press, 1956.

———. *Israel's Mission to the World*. London: SCM Press, 1939.

———. *The Relevance of Apocalyptic: A Study of Jewish and Christian Apocalypses from Daniel to the Revelation*. Rev. ed. New York: Association Press, 1963.

———. *Worship in Ancient Israel: Its Forms and Meaning*. Philadelphia: Fortress Press, 1967.

Russell, D. S. *The Method and Message of Jewish Apocalyptic, 200 B.C.– A.D. 100*. The Old Testament Library. Philadelphia: Westminster Press, 1964.

Safrai, S. "Pilgrimage to Jerusalem at the End of the Second Temple Period." *Studies in the Jewish Background of the New Testament*. Assen: Van Gorcum und Comp. N.V., 1969.

Sanday, W. and Headlam, A. C. *A Critical and Exegetical Commentary on the Epistle to the Romans*. 13th ed. International Critical Commentary. New York: Scribner, 1911.

Sanders, J. A. *Suffering as Divine Discipline in the Old Testament and post-Biblical Judaism*. Rochester, N.Y.: Colgate Rochester Divinity School, 1955.

———. *Torah and Canon*. Philadelphia: Fortress Press, 1972.

Sandmel, S. *The First Christian Century in Judaism and Christianity*. New York: Oxford University Press, 1969.

———. *Philo's Place in Judaism: A Study of Conceptions of Abraham in Jewish Literature*. Cincinnati: Hebrew Union College Press, 1956.

Schechter, S. *Fragments of a Zadokite Work*. Vol. 1 of *Documents of Jewish Sectaries*. Cambridge: University Press, 1910.

———. *Some Aspects of Rabbinic Theology*. London: Black, 1909.

Schlatter, A. *Die Evangelien nach Markus und Lukas*. Erläuterungen zum Neuen Testament, 2. Teil. Stuttgart: Calwer Verlag, 1954.

———. *Der Evangelist Matthäus: seine Sprache, sein Ziel, seine Selbständigkeit*. 3 Aufl. Stuttgart: Calwer Verlag, 1948.

Schlecht, J. *Doctrina XII Apostolorum*. Fribourg-in-Br.: 1900.

Schmid, J. *The Gospel According to Mark*. Eds. A. Wikenhauser and O. Kuss. Trans. K. Condon. The Regensburg New Testament. Staten Island, N.Y.: Alba House, 1968.

Schmidt, J. M. *Die Jüdische Apokalyptik*. Neukirchen-Vluyn: Neukirchener Verlag, 1969.

Schmidt, K. L. *Der Rahmen der Geschichte Jesu*. Berlin: Trowitzsch, 1919.

Schniewind, J. *Das Evangelium nach Matthäus*. 5. Aufl. Das Neue Testament Deutsch, Teil Bd. 2. Göttingen: Vandenhoeck und Ruprecht, 1950.

Schoeps, H. J. *Aus frühchristlicher Zeit: Religionsgeschichtliche Untersuchungen*. Tübingen: Mohr, 1950.

———. *The Jewish-Christian Argument: A History of Theologies in Conflict*. Trans. D. E. Green. New York: Holt, Rinehart and Winston, 1963.

———. *Theologie und Geschichte des Judenchristentums*. Tübingen: Mohr, 1949.

Scholem, G. *The Messianic Idea in Judaism and Other Essays on Jewish Spirituality*. New York: Schocken, 1971.

Schonfield, H. J. *Secrets of the Dead Sea Scrolls: Studies Towards their Solution*. London: Vallentine, Mitchell, 1956.

Schubert, P. "The Structure and Significance of Luke 24." In *Neutestamentliche Studien für Rudolf Bultmann: zu seinem siebzigsten Geburtstag am 20. August 1954*. Beihefte zur Zeitschrift für die Neutestamentliche Wissenschaft und die Kunde der älteren Kirche, XXI, ed. W. Eltester. Berlin: Alfred Töpelmann, 1954.

Schweitzer, A. *The Mysticism of St. Paul the Apostle*. Trans. W. Montgomery. New York: Seabury Press, 1968.

Schweizer, E. *Egô Eimi. Die religionsgeschichtliche Herkunft und theologische Bedeutung der Johanneischen Bildreden, zugleich ein Beitrag zur Quellenfrage des vierten Evangeliums*. 2. Aufl. Forschungen zur Religion und Literatur des Alten und Neuen Testaments, n.F., 38 Heft. Göttingen: Vandenhoeck und Ruprecht, 1965.

———. "Eschatology in Mark's Gospel." *Neotestamentica et Semitica: Studies in Honour of Matthew Black*. Eds. E. E. Ellis and M. Wilcox. Edinburgh: Clark, 1969.

———. *The Good News According to Mark*. Trans. D. H. Madriv. Richmond: John Knox Press, 1970.

Scott, R. B. Y. *The Relevance of the Prophets.* Rev. ed. New York: Macmillan, 1968.

———. *The Way of Wisdom in the Old Testament.* New York: Macmillan, 1971.

Selwyn, E. G. *The First Epistle of St. Peter.* 2nd ed. London: Macmillan, 1947.

Simon, M. and Benoit, A. *Le Judaisme et le Christianisme Antique d'Antiochus Epiphane à Constantin.* Nouvelle Clio, 10. Paris: Presses Universitaires de France, 1968.

Skinner, J. *Prophecy and Religion: Studies in the Life of Jeremiah.* Cambridge: University Press, 1922.

Smith, D. M. *The Composition and Order of the Fourth Gospel: Bultmann's Literary Theory.* Yale Publications in Religion, 10. New Haven: Yale University Press, 1965.

Smith, G. A. *The Historical Geography of the Holy Land, Especially in Relation to the History of Israel and of the Early Church.* 25th ed. London: Harper, 1931.

Smith, Morton. *Palestinian Parties and Politics that Shaped the Old Testament.* New York: Columbia University Press, 1971.

Smith, W. R. *Lectures on the Religion of the Semites: The Fundamental Institutions.* 3rd ed. The Library of Biblical Studies. New York: Ktav, 1969.

Snaith, N. H. "The Servant of the Lord in Deutero-Isaiah." *Studies in Old Testament Prophecy. Presented to Theodore H. Robinson by the Society for Old Testament Study on his sixty-fifth Birthday, August 9th, 1946.* Ed. H. H. Rowley. Edinburgh: Clark, 1950.

———. "A Study of the Teaching of the Second Isaiah and its Consequences." *Studies on the Second Part of the Book of Isaiah.* Supplements to Vetus Testamentum, Vol. XIV. Leiden: Brill, 1967.

Spitta, F. *Die synoptische Grundschrift.* Leipzig: Hinrich, 1912.

Stauffer, E. "Petrus und Jakobus in Jerusalem." *Begegnung der Christen: Studien evangelischer und Katholischer Theologen.* Festschrift für O. Karrer. Eds. M. Roesle and O. Cullmann. 2nd ed. Stuttgart: Evangelisches Verlagswerk, 1960.

Stemberger, G. *La Symbolique du bien et du mal selon Saint Jean.* Parole de Dieu. Paris: Éditions du Seuil, 1970.

Stendahl, K. *The School of St. Matthew.* 2nd ed. Philadelphia: Fortress Press, 1968.

———, ed. *The Scrolls and the New Testament.* New York: Harper, 1957.

Strack, H. L. *Jesus, die Haretiker und die Christen nach den ältesten jüdischen Angaben.* Leipzig: Hinrich, 1910.

Strecker, G. *Der Weg der Gerechtigkeit, Untersuchung zur Theologie des Matthäus.* Göttingen: Vandenhoeck und Ruprecht, 1962.

Streeter, B. H. "The Rise of Christianity." In *Cambridge Ancient History,* Vol. XI. Cambridge: University Press, 1936.

BIBLIOGRAPHY

Sukenik, E. L. *Ancient Synagogues in Palestine and Greece*. London: Oxford University Press, 1934.

Talmon, S. "The 'Desert Motif' in the Bible and in Qumran Literature." *Biblical Motifs: Origins and Transformations*. P. W. Lown Institute of Advanced Judaic Studies, Brandeis University. Studies and Texts, Vol. 3. Ed. A. Altmann. Cambridge, Mass.: Harvard University Press, 1966.

Tanenbaum, Marc H., and Werblovsky, R. J. Zwi, eds. *The Jerusalem Colloquium on Religion, Peoplehood, Nation and Land: Proceedings*. Publication 7. [Jerusalem]: Truman Research Institute, [1972].

Taylor, V. *The Gospel According to St. Mark*. 2nd ed. London: St. Martins, 1966.

Tcherikover, A. *Hellenistic Civilization and the Jews*. Trans. S. Applebaum. Philadelphia: Jewish Publication Society of America, 1959.

Teeple, H. M. *The Mosaic Eschatological Prophet*. Journal of Biblical Literature. Monograph Series, Vol. 10. Philadelphia: Society of Biblical Literature, 1957.

Thompson, R. J. *Penitence and Sacrifice in Early Israel Outside the Levitical Law: An Examination of the Fellowship Theory of Early Israelite Sacrifice*. Leiden: Brill, 1963.

Toynbee, A. J., ed. *The Crucible of Christianity: Judaism, Hellenism, and the Historical Background to the Christian Faith*. New York: World, 1969.

Travers, R. *Christianity in Talmud and Midrash*. London: Williams and Norgate, 1903.

Trocmé, E. *La Formation de l'Évangile selon Marc*. Paris: Presses Universitaires de France, 1963.

————. *Le "Livre des Actes" et l'histoire*. Paris: Presses Universitaires de France, 1957.

Unnik, W. C. van. "Der Ausdruck 'ΕΩΣ 'ΕΣΧΑΤΟΥ ΤΗΣ ΓΗΣ (Apostelgeschichte 1: 18) und sein alttestamentlicher Hintergrund." *Studia Biblica et Semitica: Theodoro Christiano Vriezen Qui Munere Professoris Theologiae per XXV Annos Functus est, ab Amicis, Collegis, Discipulis Dedicata*. Wageningen: Veenman, 1966.

————. *Tarsus or Jerusalem: The City of Paul's Youth*. Trans. G. Ogg. London: Epworth Press, 1962.

Urbach, E. E. "Heavenly and Earthly Jerusalem." *Jerusalem Through the Ages* (Hebrew). Jerusalem: The Israel Exploration Society, 1968.

————. *The Sages, Their Concepts and Beliefs* (Hebrew). Jerusalem: Magnes Press, 1969.

Van der Ploeg, J. *Le Rouleau de la Guerre*. Leiden: Brill, 1959.

Vaux, R. de. *Ancient Israel: Its Life and Institutions*. Trans. J. McHugh. New York: McGraw-Hill, 1961.

————. "Jerusalem and the Prophets." *Interpreting the Prophetic Tradition*. Ed. H. M. Orlinsky. Cincinnati: Hebrew Union College Press, 1969.

Via, D. O. *The Parables: Their Literary and Existential Dimension*. Philadelphia: Fortress Press, 1967.

Volz, P. *Die Eschatologie der jüdischen Gemeinde im neutestamentlichen Zeitalter*. Tübingen: Mohr, 1934.

Vriezen, T. C. *The Religion of Ancient Israel*. Philadelphia: Westminster Press, 1967.

Walbank, F. W. *A Historical Commentary on Polybius*. 2 vols. Oxford: Clarendon Press, 1957 and 1967.

Wanke, G. *Die Zionstheologie der Korachiten in ihrem traditionsgeschichtlichen Zusammenhang*. Beihefte zur Zeitschrift für alttestamentliche Wissenschaft, 97. Berlin: Töpelmann, 1966.

Weiss, J. *The History of Primitive Christianity*. Completed by R. Knopf. Ed. F. C. Grant. New York: Wilson-Erickson, 1937.

Wellhausen, J. *Skizzen und Vorarbeiten*. Berlin: Georg Reimer, 1892.

———. Vol. 5: *Die kleinen Propheten*. Berlin: Reimer, 1898.

Wensinck, A. J. "The Ideas of the Western Semites concerning the Navel of the Earth." *Verhandelingen der Koninklijke Akademie van Wetenschappen te Amsterdam*, 1916.

Werner, M. *Die Entstehung des christlichen Dogmas problemgeschtlich dargestelt*. 2nd. ed. Bern: Haupt, 1953.

Westcott, B. F. *The Gospel According to St. John*. London: Clarke, 1958.

Westermann, C. *Der Schöpfungsbericht vom Anfang der Bibel: vom rechten Umgang mit der Bibel*. Calwer Hefte, Hft. 30. Stuttgart: Calwer, 1960.

Whale, J. S. *Christian Reunion: Historic Divisions Reconsidered*. Grand Rapids, Mich.: Eerdmans, 1971.

Whibley, L., ed. *A Companion to Greek Studies*. 4th ed. Cambridge: University Press, 1931.

Widengren, G. "Quelques rapports entre Juifs et Iraniens à l'époque des Parthes." *Supplements to Vetus Testamentum*, Vol. IV. Leiden: Brill, 1957.

Wieder, N. *The Judean Scrolls and Karaism*. London: East and West Library, 1962.

Wikenhauser, A. *Pauline Mysticism: Christ in the Mystical Teaching of St. Paul*. Trans. J. Cunningham. New York: Herder and Herder, 1960.

Williams, N. P. *The Ideas of the Fall and of Original Sin*. London: Longmans, Green, 1938.

Wink, W. *John the Baptist in the Gospel Tradition*. Society for New Testament Studies. Monograph Series, 7. Cambridge: University Press, 1968.

Winter, P. *On the Trial of Jesus*. Studia Judaica: Forschungen zur Wissenschaft des Judentums, Bd. 1. Berlin: W. de Gruyter, 1961.

Wolff, H. W. *Amos' geistige Heimat*. Wissenschaftliche Monographien zur Alten und Neuen Testament, 18. Bd. Neukirchen-Vluyn: Neukirchener Verlag des Erziehungsvereins, 1964.

Wolfson, H. A. *Philo: Foundations of Religious Philosophy in Judaism, Christianity, and Islam.* 2 vols. Cambridge, Mass.: Harvard University Press, 1947.

Young, J. C. de. *Jerusalem in the New Testament: The Significance of the City in the History of Redemption and in Eschatology.* Kampen: J. H. Kok, 1960.

Zimmerli, W. *The Law and the Prophets: A Study of the Meaning of the Old Testament.* Trans. R. E. Clements. Oxford: Blackwell, 1965.

———. *Man and His Hope in the Old Testament, Studies in Biblical Theology.* Second Series. Naperville, Ill.: Allenson, 1968.

Zinz, J. L. *The Use of the Old Testament in the Apocrypha.* Unpublished Ph.D. dissertation, Duke University, 1966.

C. PERIODICALS REFERRED TO IN THE TEXT

American Academy of Religion Journal (1971). Vol. XXXIX. (J. M. Robinson, Review of D. M. Smith. *The Composition and Order of the Fourth Gospel,* pp. 339–348.)

American Journal of Semitic Languages and Literature (1936), Vol. LII. (H. G. May, "The Ark—A Miniature Temple," pp. 215–234.)

Angelos: Archiv für Neutestamentliche Zeitgeschichte und Kulturkunde (1926), Vol. II. (J. Jeremias, "Golgotha und der heilige Felsen: Eine Untersuchung zur Symbolsprache des Neuen Testamentes," pp. 74–128.)

(1932), Vol. IV. (F. Jeremias, "Das orientalische Heiligtum," pp. 56–69.)

The Anglican Theological Review (1945), Vol. XXVII. (C. W. F. Smith, "The Horse and the Ass in the Bible," pp. 86–97.)

Ariel: A Quarterly Review of the Arts and Sciences in Israel (1969), Vol. XXIII. (S. Safrai, "The Heavenly Jerusalem," pp. 11–16.)

Bible et Terre Sainte (1966), No. LXXXVI. (A. Duprez, "La Piscine Probatique," pp. 4–15.)

The Biblical Archaeologist (1970), Vol. XXXIII. (E. M. Meyers, "Secondary Burials in Palestine," pp. 1–29.)

Biblische Zeitschrift (1969), n. F., Vol. XIII. (P. Hoffmann, "Die Versuchungsgeschichte in der Logienquelle: Zur Auseinandersetzung der Judenchristen mit dem politischen Messianismus," pp. 207–223.)

Bulletin of the American Schools of Oriental Research
(1955), Vol. CXL. (W. F. Albright, "New Light on Early Recensions of the Hebrew Bible," pp. 27–33.)
(1957), Vol. CXLV. (D. N. Freedman, "The Prayer of Nabonidus," pp. 31–32.)

Bulletin of the John Rylands Library
(1934), Vol. XVIII. (C. H. Dodd, "The Mind of Paul: Change and Development," pp. 69–110.)
(1946), Vol. XXIX. (H. H. Rowley, "The Unity of the Old Testament," pp. 326–358.)

(1952). Vol. xxxv. (G. H. Boobyer, "Galilee and Galileans in St. Mark's Gospel," pp. 334–348.)

California Law Review (1971), Vol. LIX. (D. Daube, "Dissent in Bible and Talmud," pp. 784–794.)

The Canadian Journal of Religious Thought (1926), Vol. III. (R. B. Y. Scott, "The Expectation of Elijah," pp. 490–502.)

Catholic Biblical Quarterly

(1957), Vol. XIX. (A. Benson, "'... from the mouth of the lion' The Messianism of Amos," pp. 199–212.)

(1967), Vol. XXIX. (C. E. L'Heureux, "The Biblical Sources of the 'Apostrophe to Zion,'" pp. 60–74.)

Christian News From Israel

(1970), Vol. XXI, No. 2. (Y. Amir, review of E. Urbach, *The Sages, Their Concepts and Beliefs*, pp. 47ff.)

(1970), Vol. XXI, no. 3. (A. M. Rabello, "The 'Lex de Templo Hierosolymitano' Prohibiting Gentiles from entering Jerusalem's Sanctuary," pp. 28–32.)

Commentary

(1964), Vol. XXXVIII, No. 5. (G. Scholem, "Religious Authority and Mysticism," pp. 31–39.)

Conservative Judaism (1966), Vol. 20 (J. Neusner, review of Heschel, *Torah min ha-Shamaim*).

———. (1966), Vol. XXI. (D. Aronson, "Faith and Halakah").

Continuum (1968), Vol. VI. (R. L. Rubenstein, "The Cave, The Rock, and the Tent: The Meaning of Place," pp. 143–155.)

Eretz Israel: Archaeological, Historical and Geographical Studies (1956), Vol. IV. (B. Z. Lurie, "On the History of the Jewish Community of Damascus," pp. 111–118.)

Evidences, No. 60. (A. Dupont-Sommer "L'écrit de Damas," pp. 25–36.)

Expository Times

(1948), Vol. LIX. (W. D. Davies, "Unsolved New Testament Problems, The Jewish Background of the Teaching of Jesus: Apocalyptic and Pharisaism," pp. 233–237.)

(1958–1959), Vol. LXX. (C. F. D. Moule, "Once More, Who Were the Hellenists," pp. 100–102.)

(1969–1970), Vol. LXXXI. (G. B. Caird, "'My People' or 'Not My People,'" pp. 333–334.)

Harvard Theological Review

(1963), Vol. LVI. (K. Stendahl, "The Apostle Paul and the Introspective Conscience of the West," pp. 199–215.)

(1971), Vol. LXIV. (M. Smith, "Zealots and Sicarii, Their Origins and Relation," pp. 1–19.)

BIBLIOGRAPHY

Hebrew Union College Annual
   (1924), Vol. I. (J. Mann, "Rabbinic Studies in the Synoptic Gospels,"
   pp. 323–355.)
   (1957), Vol. XXVIII. (F. Landsberger, "The Sacred Direction in Synagogue
   and Church," pp. 181–203.)
   (1959), Vol. XXX. (G. W. Buchanan, "Mark 11: 15–19, Brigands in the
   Temple," pp. 169–177.)
   (1960), Vol. XXXI. (G. W. Buchanan, "Mark 11: 15–19, Brigands in the
   Temple," pp. 103–105.)
   (1969–1970), Vols. XL–XLI. (A. Guttmann, "Jerusalem in Tannaitic Law,"
   pp. 251–275.)
Jewish Quarterly Review
   (1929–1930), new series, Vol. XX. (H. Parzen, "The Ruaḥ Haḳodesh in
   Tannaitic Literature," pp. 51–76.)
   (1947), new series, Vol. XXXVII. (E. J. Bickerman, "The Warning Inscriptions of Herod's Temple," pp. 387–405.)
   (1951–1952), new series, Vol. XLII. (M. Waxman, "Heinemann's *Taame
   ha-mitzwot*," pp. 217–224.)
   (1965), new series, Vol. LVI. (S. Zeitlin, "There was no Court of Gentiles in
   the Temple Area," p. 88.)
Journal of Biblical Literature
   (1923), Vol. XLII. (J. W. Flight, "The Nomadic Idea and Ideal in the Old
   Testament," pp. 158–226.)
   (1946), Vol. LXV. (E. Werner, "'Hosanna' in the Gospels," pp. 97–122.)
   (1953), Vol. LXXII. (W. Bauer, "The 'Colt' of Palm Sunday [der Palmesel],"
   pp. 220–229.)
   (1957), Vol. LXXVI. (E. Arden, "How Moses Failed God," pp. 50–52.)
   (1958), Vol. LXXVII. (J. M. Allegro, "Fragments of a Qumran Scroll of
   Eschatological Midrāšîm," pp. 350–354.)
   (1960), Vol. LXXIX. (W. C. Robinson, Jr., "The Theological Context for
   Interpreting Luke's Travel Narrative (9: 51ff)," pp. 20–31.)
   (1963), Vol. LXXXII. (J. H. Hayes, "The Tradition of Zion's Inviolability,"
   pp. 419–426.)
   (1964), Vol. LXXXIII. (N. Q. Hamilton, "Temple Cleansing and Temple
   Bank," pp. 365–372.)
   (1966), Vol. LXXXV. (W. A. Meeks, "Galilee and Judea in the Fourth
   Gospel," pp. 159–169.)
   (1967), Vol. LXXXVI. (H. D. Betz, "The Logion of the Easy Yoke and of
   Rest (Matt 11: 28–30)," pp. 10–24.)
   (1970), Vol. LXXXIX. (D. M. Smith, review of R. T. Fortna, *The Gospel
   of Signs*, pp. 498–501.)
   (1971), Vol. XC. (F. S. Frick, "The Rechabites Reconsidered," pp. 279–287.)

Journal of Church and State
(1971), Vol. XIII. (R. T. Handy, "Studies in the Inter-relationships between America and the Holy Land," pp. 283–301.)
Journal of Ecclesiastical History (1951), Vol. II. (M. Simon, "Saint Stephen and the Jerusalem Temple," pp. 127–142.)
Journal of Ecumenical Studies
(1968), Vol. V. (M. Barth, "Jews and Gentiles: The Social Character of Justification in Paul," pp. 241–267.)
Journal of Religion
(1971), Vol. LI. (L. S. Mudge, "Jesus and the Struggle for the Real," pp. 229–246.)
Journal of Roman Studies (1961), Vol. LI. (A. Fuks, "Aspects of the Jewish Revolt in A.D. 115–117," pp. 98–104.)
Journal of Semitic Studies
(1959), Vol. IV. (C. Roth, "The Zealots in the War of 66–73," pp. 332–355.)
(1963), Vol. VIII. (L. R. Fisher, "The Temple Quarter," pp. 34–41.)
(1966), Vol. XI. (E. Wiesenberg, review of N. Wieder, *The Judean Scrolls and Karaism*, pp. 264–268.)
(1969), Vol. XIV. (M. Hengel, review of S. G. F. Brandon, *Jesus and the Zealots*, pp. 231–240.)
Journal of Theological Studies
(1923), Vol. XXIV. (A. Caldecott, "The Significance of 'the Cleansing of the Temple,'" pp. 382–386.)
(1952), new series, Vol. III. (E. W. Heaton, "The Root שאר and the Doctrine of the Remnant," pp. 27–39.)
(1954), new series, Vol. V. (C. F. Evans, "I will go before you into Galilee," pp. 3–18.)
(1971), new series, Vol. XXII. (C. K. Barrett, review of R. T. Fortna, *The Gospel of Signs*, pp. 571–574.)
Monatsschrift für Geschichte und Wissenschaft des Judentums (1932), n. F., Vol. XL. (J. Bergmann, "Schebua ha-ben," pp. 465–470.)
New Testament Studies
(1954–1955), Vol. I. (H. Chadwick, "'All things to all men' (1 Cor. IX. 22)," pp. 261–275.)
(1955–1956), Vol. II. (W. D. Davies, review of J. Munck, *Paulus und die Heilsgeschichte*, pp. 60–72.)
(1958–1959), Vol. V. (O. Cullmann, "L'opposition contre le Temple de Jerusalem, Motif Commun de la Theologie Johannique et du Monde Ambiant," pp. 157–173.)
(1962), Vol. VIII. (H. Montefiore, "Revolt in the Desert?" pp. 135–141.)
(1968), Vol. XIV. (J. M. Robinson, "The Coptic Gnostic Library Today," pp. 356–401.)

(1968), Vol. xv. (E. Trocmé, "L'expulsion des marchands du Temple," pp. 1–22.)

(1969), Vol. xvi. (E. Grässer, "Jesus in Nazareth (Mark vi. 1–6a)," pp. 1–23.

(1971), Vol. xvii. (G. Strecker, "Die Makarismen der Bergpredigt," pp. 255–275.)

(1971), Vol. xvii. (W. Baird, "Pauline Eschatology in Hermeneutical Perspective," pp. 314–327.)

Novum Testamentum

(1960), Vol. iv. (W. C. van Unnik, "The 'Book of Acts' the Confirmation of the Gospel," pp. 26–59.)

(1963), Vol. vi. (J. R. Díaz, "Palestinian Targum and New Testament," pp. 75–80.)

Proceedings of the Rabbinical Assembly of America (1949), Vol. xii. (S. Lieberman, "Response," pp. 272–289.)

Recherches de Science Religieuse

(1972), Vol. lx. (W. D. Davies, "Paul and Jewish Christianity in the Light of Cardinal Daniélou," pp. 69–80.)

Revue Biblique

(1934), Vol. xliii. (A. Robert, "Les attaches littéraires bibliques de Prov. I–IX," pp. 42–68, 172–204, 374–384.)

(1935), Vol. xliv. (A. Robert, "Les attaches littéraires bibliques de Prov. I–IX," pp. 344–365, 502–525.)

(1939), Vol. xlviii. (A. M. Dubarle, "Le signe du Temple," pp. 21–44.)

(1947), Vol. liv. (C. Spicq, "Benignité, Mansuétude, Douceur, Clémence," pp. 321 ff.)

(1948), Vol. lv. (A. Feuillet, "Le Discours de Jésus sur la Ruine de Temple," pp. 481–502.)

(1949), Vol. lvi. (A. Feuillet, "Le Discours de Jésus sur la Ruine de Temple," pp. 61–92.)

(1958), Vol. lxv. (P. Grelot, "La Géographie Mythique d'Hénoch et ses sources orientales," pp. 33–69.)

(1958), Vol. lxv. (A. Jaubert, "Le Pays de Damas," pp. 214–248.)

(1958), Vol. lxv. (J. T. Milik, "Hénoch au Pays des Aromates ch. xxvii à xxxii: Fragments araméens de la grotte 4 de Qumran," pp. 70–77.)

(1972), Vol. lxxix (J. Murphy–O'Connor, O. P., "The Critique of the Princes of Judah, c.d. viii. 3–19," pp. 200–216).

Revue de l'Histoire des Religions, (1956), Vol. cil. (P. Grelot, "Isaie xiv, 12–15 et son arrière plan mythologique," pp. 18–48.

Revue d'Histoire et de Philosophie Religieuses

(1947), Vol. xxvii. (A. Causse, "De la Jérusalem terrestre à la Jerusalem céleste," pp. 12–36.)

(1952), Vol. xxxii. (M. Simon, "La Prophétie de Nathan et le Temple," pp. 41–58.)

(1964), Vol. XLIV. (E. Trocmé, "Jésus-Christ et le Temple: éloge d'un naïf," pp. 245–251.)

Sciences Religieuses: Studies in Religion (1971), Vol. XIII. (D. O. Via, "Justification and Deliverance: Existential Dialectic," pp. 204–212.)

Scottish Journal of Theology (1955), Vol. VIII. (G. Ogg, review of W. C. van Unnik, *Tarsus of Jeruzalem,* pp. 94–97.)

Sitzungsberichte der Preussischen Akademie der Wissenschaften (1921), Vol. LIII. (K. Holl, "Der Kirchenbegriff des Paulus in seinem Verhältnis zu dem der Urgemeinde," pp. 920–947.)

Theological Studies (1965), Vol. XXVI. (R. E. Brown, "Does the New Testament Call Jesus God?" pp. 545–573.)

Theologische Literaturzeitung

(1937), Vol. LXII. (W. G. Kümmel, review of E. Lohmeyer, *Galiläa und Jerusalem,* cols. 304–307.)

(1960), Vol. LXXXV. (W. Michaelis, "Joh. 1: 51, Gen. 28: 12 und das Menschensohn-Problem," cols. 561–578.)

(1965), Vol. XC. (G. Baumbach, "Zeloten und Sikarier," cols. 727–740.)

Theologische Zeitschrift (1948), Vol. IV. (O. Cullmann, "Der johanneische Gebrauch doppeldeutiger Ausdrücke als Schlüssel zum Verständnis des vierten Evangeliums," pp. 360–372.)

Tradition (1958), Vol. I. (I. Jakobovits, "The Dissection of the Dead in Jewish Law," pp. 77–103.)

Union Seminary Quarterly Review (1969), Vol. XXV. (W. Wink, "Jesus and Revolution: Reflections on S. G. F. Brandon's *Jesus and the Zealots,*" pp. 37–59.)

Verbum Domini (1959), Vol. XXXVII. (P. I. Fritsch, "'...videbitis...angelos Dei ascendentes et descendentes super Filium hominis' (Io. 1, 51)," pp. 3–11.)

Vetus Testamentum

(1956), Vol. VI. (J. P. de Menasce, "Iranien Naxcir," pp. 213–214.)

(1969), Vol. XIX. (J. P. Brown, "The Mediterranean Vocabulary of the Vine," pp. 146–170.)

(1970), Vol. XX. (R. G. Hamerton-Kelly, "The Temple and the Origins of Jewish Apocalyptic," pp. 1–15.)

(1970), Vol. XX. (S. Terrien, "The Omphalos Myth and Hebrew Religion," pp. 315–338.)

The Way (1961), Vol. I. (J. L. Mckenzie, "Into the Desert," pp. 27–39.)

Zeitschrift für die Alttestamentliche Wissenschaft (1932), new series, Vol. IX. (H. H. Rowley, "The bilingual problem of Daniel," pp. 256–268.)

Zeitschrift des deutschen Palästina-Vereins

(1905), Vol. XXVIII. (W. Oehler, "Die Ortschaften und Grenzen Galiläas nach Josephus," pp. 1–26; 49–74.)

Zeitschrift für die Neutestamentliche Wissenschaft
(1925), Vol. XXIV. (H. H. Wendt, "Die Hauptquelle der Apostelgeschichte," pp. 293–305.)
(1937), Vol. XXXVI. (J. Jeremias, "Untersuchungen zum Quellenproblem der Apostelgeschichte," pp. 205–221.)
(1955), Vol. XLVI. (F. W. Young, "A Study of the Relation of Isaiah to the Fourth Gospel," pp. 215–233.)
(1959), Vol. L. (H.-W. Kuhn, "Das Reittier in der Einzugsgeschichte des Markusevangeliums," pp. 82–91.)
(1959), Vol. L. (H. Conzelmann, "Geschichte und Eschaton nach MK. 13," pp. 210–221.)
(1964), Vol. LV. (V. Eppstein, "The Historicity of the Gospel Account of the Cleansing of the Temple," pp. 42–58.)
Zeitschrift für Theologie und Kirche (1952), Vol. IL. (K. G. Kuhn, "Die Sektenschrift und die iranische Religion," pp. 296–316.)
(1961), Vol. LVIII. (J. Schreiber, "Die Christologie des Markusevangeliums," pp. 154–183.)
(1967), Vol. LXIV. (H. H. Schmid, "Das Verständnis des Geschichte im Deuteronomium," pp. 1–15.)

D. SUPPLEMENT

I. ADDITIONAL BOOKS BY MODERN AUTHORS
REFERRED TO IN THE TEXT

Barth, K. *Die kirchliche Dogmatik.* 5 vols. Zürich: Evangelischer Verlag, 1932–.
Ben-Chorin, S. *Paulus: Der Völkerapostel in jüdischer Sicht.* Munich: P. List, 1970.
Bietenhard, H. *Die himmlische Welt im Urchristentum und Spätjudentum.* Wissenschaftliche Untersuchungen zum Neuen Testament, 2. Tübingen: J. C. B. Mohr, 1951.
Bousset, W. *Die Offenbarung Johannis.* Kritisch-exegetischer Kommentar über das Neue Testament, begründet von H. A. W. Meyer, 16 Abt., 6 Aufl. Göttingen: Vandenhoeck & Ruprecht, 1906.
Braude, W. G., trans. *Pesikta Rabbati: Discourses for Feasts, Fasts, and Special Sabbaths.* Yale Judaica Series, Vol. XVIII. New Haven: Yale University Press, 1968.
Brütsch, C. *La Clarté de l'Apocalypse.* 5th ed. Geneva: Éditions Labor et Fides, 1966.
Burrows, M. *The Dead Sea Scrolls.* New York: Viking Press, 1955.
Charles, R. H. *A Critical and Exegetical Commentary on the Revelation of St. John.* The International Critical Commentary. New York: Scribner, 1920.

Comblin. J. *Le Christ dans l'Apocalypse.* Bibliothèque de Théologie. Théologie biblique. Paris: Desclée, 1965.

Dodd, C. H. *According to the Scriptures: The Sub-Structure of New Testament Theology.* London: Nisbet & Co., 1952.

Douglass, F. *The Life and Times of Frederick Douglass.* New York: Collier Books, 1962.

Downey, G. "Constantinople (Byzantium, Istanbul)." *New Catholic Encyclopedia,* Vol. IV, pp. 231–237. London: McGraw-Hill, 1967.

Dugmore, C. W. *The Influence of the Synagogue upon the Divine Office.* London: Oxford University Press, 1944.

Elbogen, I. *Der jüdische Gottesdienst in seiner geschichtlichen Entwicklung.* 3rd ed. Grundriss der Gesamtwissenschaft des Judentums. Frankfurt: J. Kauffmann Verlag, 1931.

Epps, A. ed. *The Speeches of Malcolm X at Harvard.* New York: W. Morrow, 1968.

Farrer, A. M. *The Revelation of St. John the Divine.* Oxford: Clarendon Press, 1964.

Ginzberg, L. *On Jewish Law and Lore.* Philadelphia: Jewish Publication Society of America, 1955.

Grant, F. C. *Ancient Judaism and the New Testament.* New York: Macmillan, 1959.

Halver, R. *Der Mythos im letzten Buch der Bibel: Eine Untersuchung der Bibelsprache der Johannes-Apokalypse.* Theologische Forschung; wissenschaftliche Beiträge zur kirchlich-evangelischen Lehre, 32. Veröffentlichung. Hamburg: Evangelischer Verlag, 1964.

Hamerton-Kelly, R. G. *Pre-Existence, Wisdom, and the Son of Man: A Study of the Idea of Pre-Existence in the New Testament.* Society for New Testament Studies. Monograph Series, 21. Cambridge: University Press, 1973.

Herford, R. T. *Christianity in Talmud and Midrash.* London: Williams & Norgate, 1903.

Heschel, A. *Torah min ha-Shamaim.* 2 vols. London: Soncino Press, 1962–1965.

Hogins, J. B., and Yarber, R. E. *Phase Blue: A Systems Approach to College English.* Chicago: Science Research Associates, 1970.

Johnson, S. E. "Jesus and First-Century Galilee." *In Memoriam Ernst Lohmeyer.* Ed. W. Schmauch. Stuttgart: Evangelisches Verlagswerk, 1951.

Le Déaut, R. *La Nuit Pascale: Essai sur la Signification de la Pâque Juive à partir du Targum d'Exode XII,* 42. Analecta Biblica, 22. Rome: Institut Biblique Pontifical, 1963.

Lohmeyer, E. *Die Offenbarung des Johannes.* Handbuch zum Neuen Testament, XVI. 2nd ed. Tübingen: J. C. B. Mohr, 1953.

Lohse, E. *Die Offenbarung des Johannes.* Das Neue Testament Deutsch; neues Göttinger Bibelwerk, Tbd. 11, 8 Aufl. Göttingen: Vandenhoeck & Ruprecht, 1960.

Malcolm, X. *Message to the Grass Roots: Malcolm X Speaks.* Merritt Publishers and Betty Shabaz, 1965.

Mendelssohn, M. *Jerusalem and Other Jewish Writings.* Trans. and ed. A. Jospe. New York: Schocken Books, 1969.

Miskotte, K. H. *Wenn die Götter Schweigen: Vom Sinn des Alten Testaments.* Trans. H. Stoevesandt. 2nd ed. Munich: C. Kaiser, 1964.

Neusner, J. *From Politics to Piety: The Emergence of Pharisaic Judaism.* Englewood Cliffs, N.J.: Prentice-Hall, 1973.

Nötscher, F. *Zur theologischen Terminologie der Qumran-Texte.* Bonner Biblische Beiträge, 10. Bonn: P. Hanstein, 1956.

Rhoads, D. *Some Jewish Revolutionaries in Palestine A.D. 6–73.* Unpublished dissertation, Duke University, 1973.

Rigaux, B. *Saint Paul: Les Épitres aux Thessaloniciens.* Études bibliques. Paris: Gabalda, 1956.

Rissi, M. *Time and History: A Study on the Revelation.* Trans. G. C. Winsor. Richmond: John Knox Press, 1966.

Rowley, H. H., ed. *Job.* The Century Bible, new series. London: Nelson, 1970.

Schlatter, A. *Die Theologie des Judentums nach dem Bericht des Josephus.* Beiträge zur Forschung christlicher Theologie, ed. A. Schlatter and W. Lutgert, Series 2, Vol. 26. Gütersloh: C. Gertelsmann, 1932.

Schlier, H. *Der Brief an die Galater.* Kritisch-exegetischer Kommentar über das Neue Testament, begründet von H. A. W. Meyer, 7 Abt., 10 Aufl. Göttingen: Vandenhoeck & Ruprecht, 1949.

Schürer, E. *A History of the Jewish People in the Time of Jesus Christ.* 5 vols. Edinburgh: T. & T. Clark, 1897–1901.

Scott, E. F. *The Book of Revelation.* London, SCM, 1939.

Stone, M. E., trans. *The Testament of Abraham.* Missoula, Montana: Society of Biblical Literature, 1972.

Trevor-Roper, H. R. *Men and Events: Historical Essays.* New York: Harper, 1957.

Trocmé, E. *Jesus as Seen by his Contemporaries.* Trans. R. A. Wilson. Philadelphia: Westminster Press, 1973.

Vermès, G. *Scripture and Tradition in Judaism: Haggadic Studies.* Studia Postbiblica, Vol. IV. Leiden: Brill, 1961.

Vogt, J. "Constantinus der Grosse." *Reallexikon für Antike und Christentum,* Bd. III, cols. 306–379. Lieferung 17–24. Stuttgart: Anton Hiersemann, 1957.

Zahn, T. *Die Offenbarung des Johannes.* 2 vols. Kommentar zum Neuen Testament, Vol. XVIII. Leipzig: Deichertsch, 1924–1926.

2. ADDITIONAL PERIODICALS REFERRED TO IN THE TEXT

American Academy of Religion Journal (1967), Vol. xxxv. (G. Strecker, "The Concept of History in Matthew," pp. 219–230).

The Biblical Archaeologist (1962), Vol. xxv. (G. E. Mendenhall, "The Hebrew Conquest of Palestine," pp. 66–87.)

Bulletin of the John Rylands Library (1972), Vol. LV. (J. Barr, "Man and Nature— The Ecological Controversy and the Old Testament," pp. 9–32).

Ephemerides Theologicae Lovanienses (1953). Vol. xxxix. (J. Comblin, "La Liturgie de la Nouvelle Jérusalem," pp. 15–40.)

Eranos-Jahrbuch (1950), Vol. xviii. (K. L. Schmidt, "Jerusalem als Urbild und Abbild," pp. 207–248.)

Expository Times (1962–1963), Vol. LXXIV. (G. B. Caird, "On Deciphering the Book of Revelation, III. The First and the Last," pp. 82–84.)

Harvard Theological Review
(1965), Vol. LVIII. (K. Baltzer, "The Meaning of the Temple in the Lukan Writings," pp. 263–277.)
(1971), Vol. LXIV. (B. A. Pearson, "I Thessalonians 2:13–16: A Deutero-Pauline Interpolation." pp. 79–94).

Jewish Quarterly Review
(1907–1908), old series, Vol. xx. (A. Büchler, "The Blessing בונה ירושלים in the Liturgy," pp. 798–811.)

Journal of Biblical Literature
(1954), Vol. LXXIII. (I. Rabinowitz, "A Reconsideration of 'Damascus' and '390 years' in the 'Damascus' ('Zadokite') Fragments," pp. 11–35.)
(1972), Vol. xci. (W. A. Meeks, "The Man From Heaven in Johannine Sectarianism," pp. 44–72.)

Journal of Ecumenical Studies (1964), Vol. i. (M. Barth, "The Challenge of the Apostle Paul," pp. 58–81.)

New Testament Studies
(1961), Vol. vii. (M. Smith, "The Dead Sea Sect in Relation to Ancient Judaism," pp. 347–361.)
(1964), Vol. x. (F. W. Beare, Review of C. H. Dodd, *Historical Tradition in the Fourth Gospel*, pp. 517–522.)
(1971), Vol. xvii. (R. Jewett, "The Agitators and the Galatian Congregation," pp. 198–212.)
(1971), Vol. xvii. (C. K. Barrett, "Paul's Opponents in II Corinthians," pp. 233–254.)
(1973), Vol. xix. (M. Borg, "A New Context for Romans XIII," pp. 205–218.)

Palestine Exploration Quarterly (Jan.–Apr. 1945). (S. Krauss, "Zion and Jerusalem: A Linguistic and Historical Study," pp. 15–33).

BIBLIOGRAPHY

Recherches de Science religieuse (1972), Vol. LX. (M. Simon, "La Migration à Pella: Légende ou Réalité," pp. 37–54.)

Revue Biblique

(1955), Vol. LXII. (M. Baillet, "Fragments Araméens de Qumran 2: Description de la Jérusalem nouvelle," pp. 222–245.)

(1970), Vol. LXXVIII. (J. Murphy-O'Connor, "An Essene Missionary Document? CD II, 14-VI, 1," pp. 201–229.)

Revue des Études Juives (1970), Vol. CXXX. (V. Nikiprowetzky, Review of R. J. McKelvey, *The New Temple*, pp. 5–30.)

Revue d'Histoire et de Philosophie Religieuses (1938). Vol. XVIII. (A. Causse, "Le Mythe de la nouvelle Jérusalem, du Deutéro-Esaie à la IIIe Sibylle." pp. 377–414.)

Science (1967), Vol. CLV. (L. White, Jr., "The Historical Roots of Our Ecologic Crisis," pp. 1203–1207).

Theology Today (1972), Vol. XXIX. (J. H. Cone, "Black Spirituals: A Theological Interpretation." pp. 54–69.)

Union Seminary Quarterly Review

(1956), Vol. XI. (J. Muilenburg, "The Significance of the Scrolls." pp. 3–12.)

(1965/66), Vol. XXI. (C. H. Dodd, Review of W. D. Davies, *Invitation to the New Testament*, pp. 474–476.)

La Vie Spirituelle (1963), Vol. CVIII. (R. Poelman, "Jérusalem d'en Haut," pp. 637–659.)

INDICES

I. INDEX OF QUOTATIONS

A. *The Old Testament*

473

INDEX OF QUOTATIONS

INDEX OF QUOTATIONS

B. The Apocrypha and Pseudepigrapha of the Old Testament

INDEX OF QUOTATIONS

C. The New Testament

INDEX OF QUOTATIONS

INDEX OF QUOTATIONS

INDEX OF QUOTATIONS

INDEX OF QUOTATIONS

INDEX OF QUOTATIONS

INDEX OF QUOTATIONS

INDEX OF QUOTATIONS

II. INDEX OF RABBIS

INDEX OF RABBIS

III. INDEX OF AUTHORS

INDEX OF AUTHORS